Copyright and neighbouring rights

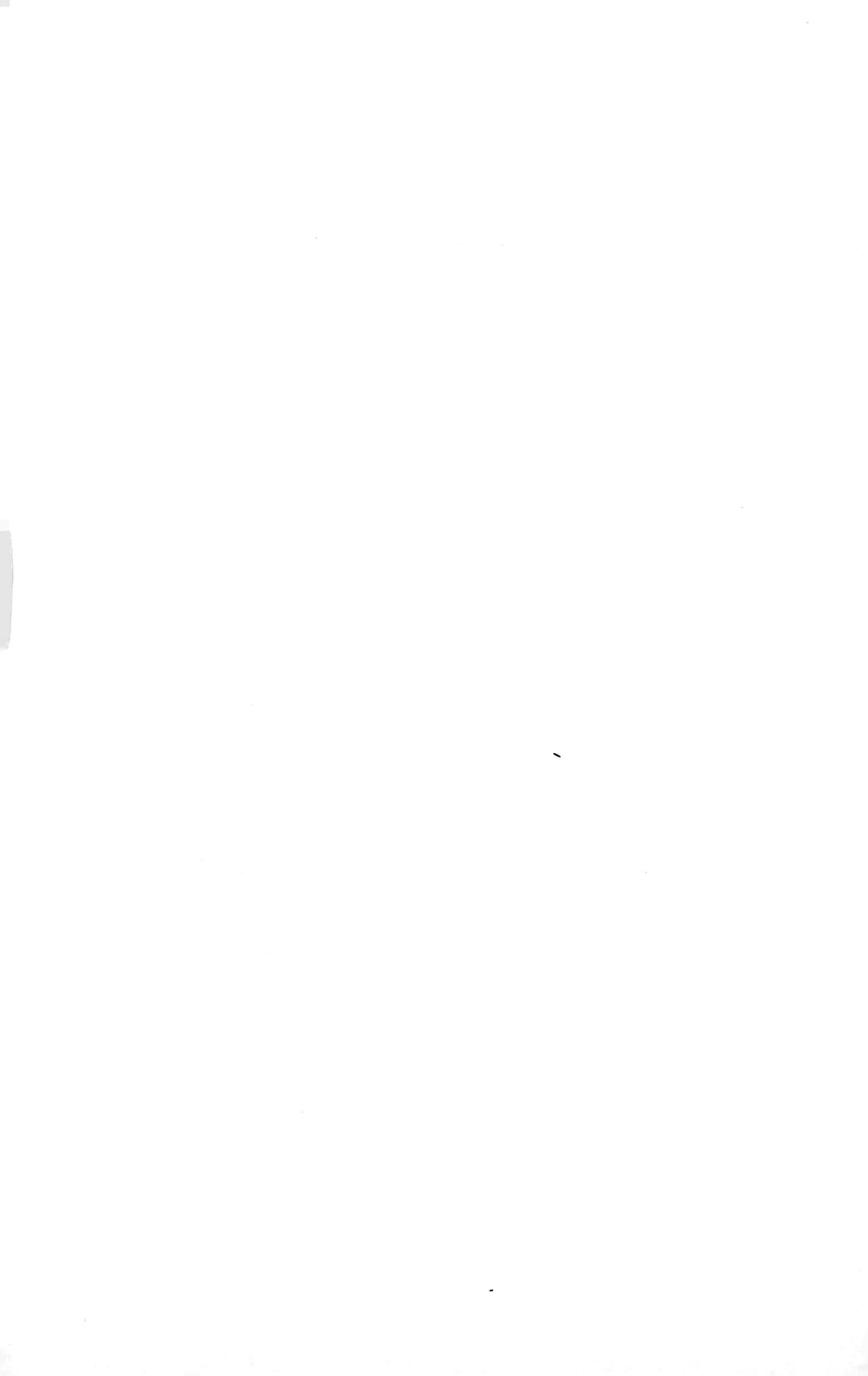

Copyright and neighbouring rights

Delia Lipszyc

UNESCO PUBLISHING

This work is the English translation, brought up to date, of *Derecho de autor y derechos conexos*, published in 1993 by the United Nations Educational, Scientific and Cultural Organization (UNESCO), the Regional Centre for Book Development in Latin America and the Caribbean (CERLALC, Bogotá) and Zavalía Editor (Buenos Aires).

The author is responsible for the choice and presentation of the facts contained in this book and for the opinions expressed therein, which are not necessarily those of UNESCO and do not commit the Organization.

The designations employed and the presentation of material throughout this publication do not imply the expression of any opinion whatsoever on the part of UNESCO concerning the legal status of any country, territory, city or area or of its authorities, or concerning the delimitation of its frontiers or boundaries.

Published in 1999 by the United Nations Educational,
Scientific and Cultural Organization,
7, place de Fontenoy,
75352 Paris 07 SP (France)
Composed by Asco Typesetters, Hong Kong
Printed by Imprimerie Darantière, 21800 Quetigny (France)

ISBN 92-3-102837-5

© UNESCO 1999
Printed in France

To Carlos Alberto Villalba

Preface

This work is not just another monograph on copyright and neighbouring rights. It represents a fundamental contribution to study of this discipline made, in response to UNESCO's request, by the eminent specialist on the subject, Professor Delia Lipszyc.

Since its creation, UNESCO has played an outstanding role in promoting the legal protection of copyright and neighbouring rights at the national level and in the context of international relations, having regard to the vital importance of this discipline in the cultural and economic development of nations.

From 1988 onwards, the Organization's efforts have, however, been concentrated in particular on the promotion of the teaching of this subject in the university context. Indeed, experience has shown that in the contemporary life of societies, the adoption of legislation in defence of copyright and neighbouring rights is not sufficient in itself. Accompanying measures are called for, which will ensure appropriate knowledge of this specific legislation in the cultural life, and more especially, the legal environment of the nation. Respect for the rights vested in authors and other holders of rights and their soundly based application means that lawyers, judges, magistrates and other legal authorities responsible for the application of the law must be familiar with every aspect of this discipline. It is through wide-ranging knowledge of the rules governing copyright and neighbouring rights that nations can most effectively provide a secure basis for the relationships between the different parties involved in cultural life and mobilize their efforts to create and produce works which will enrich the cultural heritage.

With a view to contributing to this important endeavour, UNESCO's programme for the promotion of teaching of copyright and neighbouring rights has sought to devise appropriate draft syllabuses, while encouraging the establishment of professorships for the study of this discipline in universities.

In collaboration with eminent experts in each region, the proposed syllabuses have already been brought into line with the legal contexts of Latin America, French-speaking Africa, the Arab States, the Asian and Pacific region, English-speaking Africa and the Commonwealth of Independent States.

The updated version of this work, the Spanish original of which was published in 1993, is an additional contribution to this endeavour. It responds to the deeply felt concern of universities to see the teaching programmes adopted by them supported by a work which covers the subject in its every aspect, its basis being statute law throughout the world and the experience of its application.

Professor Lipszyc's work represents a remarkable contribution in this respect. It gives the teaching of copyright and neighbouring rights a greater operational dimension in a universal context.

Set out as a university manual, it presents, with its clear and searching approach, the many and varied aspects of this important legal discipline as reflected in the different laws throughout the world, the relevant international conventions and current international thinking on the subject, in the light of technological progress in the methods of creation, production and dissemination of works of the mind. It offers appropriate clarification of legal concepts hitherto the province of specialists, and makes them more readily understood. This work is, in short, a precious resource with which students and specialists in copyright and neighbouring rights can be provided, and an invaluable tool in aiding the various parties involved in cultural activity to organize their professional relationships on a sound and equitable basis.

Because of the highly informative nature and clarity of the knowledge it transmits, serving the driving forces of the creation, production and dissemination of cultural values, it is destined to become a classic on the subject and is bound to win the well-merited approval of the public.

Milagros del Corral
Director of the Division of Creativity, Cultural Industries and Copyright, UNESCO

Contents

Chapter 1. Introduction   **21**

1.1. *Definition and content of copyright. Copyright's place among intellectual property rights: copyright and industrial property*   *21*
1.1.1. Concept and juridical nature   27
1.2. *History of copyright*   *37*
1.3. *The various legal conceptions of copyright: copyright and author's right*   *47*
1.3.1. Subject matter of the author's right   49
1.3.2. Concept of 'author'. Owners of the right   50
1.3.3. Moral rights   53
1.3.4. Economic rights and limitations   58
1.3.5. Formalities   60
1.4. *The economic importance of copyright in the present-day world: the production of cultural goods and the technological impact*   *62*
1.5. *The role of copyright in developing countries*   *66*

Chapter 2. The subject matter of copyright   **69**

2.1. *General criteria*   *69*
2.1.1. Copyright protects formal creations and not ideas   70
2.1.2. Originality, a necessary condition for protection   73

2.1.3. Criteria which are not relevant to recognition of protection: value, intended use, form of expression 74

2.1.4. The absence of formalities in copyright protection (with the exception of certain countries) 75

2.2. Protected works 76

2.2.1. Original works 77

    2.2.1.1. Literary works 78

    2.2.1.2. Musical works 81

    2.2.1.3. Theatrical works 82

    2.2.1.4. Artistic works 84

    2.2.1.5. Scientific works 94

    2.2.1.6. Audiovisual works 96

    2.2.1.7. Works of national folklore 99

    2.2.1.8. New categories of works: computer programs (arguments for and against copyright protection) 110

2.2.2. Derivative works 117

    2.2.2.1. Adaptations 118

    2.2.2.2. Translations 118

    2.2.2.3. Compilations and databases 119

    2.2.2.4. Anthologies 121

    2.2.2.5. Annotations and commentaries 121

    2.2.2.6. Arrangements and orchestrations 122

    2.2.2.7. Parodies 122

2.2.3. The title 124

Chapter 3. Owners of copyright 127

3.1. *Authorship and ownership. Natural persons and legal entities* 127

3.1.1. Original or first owners 130

3.1.2. Secondary owners 131

3.2.	***Joint authorship***	*133*
3.2.1.	Works of collaboration. Concept and legal system 134	
3.2.2.	Collective works. Concept and legal system 136	
3.3.	***Ownership in respect of anonymous and pseudonymous works. Unpublished works***	*137*
3.4.	***Ownership in respect of audiovisual works***	*141*
3.4.1.	Relationship between the creators of the work and the producer of audiovisual works 142	
3.4.2.	Protection of moral rights 144	
3.4.3.	Presumption of assignment of economic rights 147	
3.5.	***Ownership in respect of works produced on commission or by virtue of a contractual employment relationship***	*148*

Chapter 4. Substantive content of copyright — 155

4.1.	***Substantive content of copyright. The monistic theory and the dualist theory***	*155*
4.2.	***The moral right. Characteristics***	*158*
4.2.1.	The right of disclosure 164	
4.2.2.	The right of paternity 169	
4.2.3.	The right to respect for the work and for its integrity 172	
4.2.4.	The right to reconsider or the right of withdrawal 176	
4.3.	***Economic rights***	*179*
4.3.1.	The right of reproduction 184	
4.3.2.	The right of public communication 188	
	4.3.2.1. *Exhibition of works of art or reproductions thereof 190*	
	4.3.2.2. *Public performance 190*	
	4.3.2.3. *Projection or public showing of cinematographic works and other audiovisual works 191*	

        4.3.2.4. Broadcasting, public communication by satellite and distribution by cable 192
        4.3.2.5. Public communication of works with the use of information technology services 214
        4.3.2.6. The public nature of the communication 214
4.3.3. The right of transformation 216
4.3.4. The right of participation or *droit de suite* 216

4.4. Limitations on copyright   **223**

4.4.1. Free use without payment 226
4.4.2. Uses subject to remuneration: non-voluntary licences (compulsory licences and statutory licences) 242

Chapter 5. Duration of protection   253

5.1. Terms of protection   **253**

5.1.1. Origin 253
5.1.2. The aim 254
5.1.3. Terms of protection 255
5.1.4. Circulation of copies and the broadcasting of works in the public domain 264
5.1.5. The moral right after the author's death 265

5.2. Beneficiaries of rights after the author's death   **266**

5.2.1. Moral rights 266
5.2.2. Economic rights 268

5.3. Public domain   **269**

5.3.1. Legal nature 269
5.3.2. Paying public domain 270

Chapter 6. Transfer of copyright   273

6.1. General rules concerning the transfer of copyright   **273**

6.1.1. Transfer by *inter vivos* transaction 273
6.1.2. Transfer *mortis causa* 289

6.2.	***Publishing contracts: literary, musical and artistic works***	***290***
6.2.1.	Contracts for the publication of literary works 296	
	6.2.1.1. Rights and obligations of the parties 296	
	6.2.1.2. Termination of a publishing contract 304	
6.2.2.	Contracts for the publication of musical works 305	
6.2.3.	Contracts for the publication of artistic works 311	
6.2.4.	Publishers' rights concerning the typographical arrangement of their published editions 313	
6.2.5.	Entitlement of the publisher to institute proceedings in the case of infringement of exclusive rights which he possesses as transferee 316	
6.3.	***Public performance contracts: dramatic, musical and dramatico-musical works***	***317***
6.3.1.	Concept 317	
6.3.2.	Legal nature 320	
6.3.3.	Characteristics 320	
6.3.4.	Rights and obligations of the parties 322	
6.3.5.	Termination of public performance contracts 327	
6.4.	***Contracts for mechanical reproduction rights***	***328***
6.4.1.	Concept 329	
6.4.2.	Legal nature and characteristics 330	
6.4.3.	Rights and obligations of the parties 330	
6.5.	***Broadcasting contracts***	***336***
6.5.1.	Concept 336	
6.5.2.	Legal nature and characteristics 336	
6.5.3.	Rights and obligations of the parties 337	
6.5.4.	Sound broadcasting 338	
6.5.5.	Television 341	
6.6.	***Contracts for the production of audiovisual works***	***344***
6.6.1.	Concept 346	
6.6.2.	Legal nature and characteristics 347	
6.6.3.	Rights and obligations of the parties 347	

Chapter 7. Neighbouring rights   **351**

7.1.   *Rights of performers*   *364*
7.1.1.   Legal nature   366
- *7.1.1.1. Theories based on assimilation with authors' rights   366*
- *7.1.1.2. Criticism of theories based on assimilation with authors' rights   368*
- *7.1.1.3. The theory which considers that the performer's right is a personality right   371*
- *7.1.1.4. Criticism   371*
- *7.1.1.5. Labour law theories   371*
- *7.1.1.6. Criticism of labour law theories   373*
- *7.1.1.7. Independent theories   374*

7.1.2.   The subject of protection   376
7.1.3.   Holders of the rights   377
7.1.4.   Content   379
- *7.1.4.1. The performer's moral rights   379*
- *7.1.4.2. Economic rights of performers and their limitations   384*
- *7.1.4.3. Limitations   387*
- *7.1.4.4. Term of the economic rights of performers   391*

7.1.5.   Exercise of performers' economic rights in instances of collective performances   393

7.2.   *Rights of producers of phonograms*   *393*
7.2.1.   The subject of protection   394
7.2.2.   Owners of the rights   397
7.2.3.   Content: economic rights of producers of phonograms. Limitations   398
7.2.4.   Term of the rights of the producers of phonograms   400

7.3.   *Rights of broadcasting organizations*   *401*
7.3.1.   The subject of protection   401
7.3.2.   Owners of the rights   404

7.3.3. Content: economic rights of broadcasting organizations. Limitations 405
7.3.4. Term of the rights of broadcasting organizations 407

Chapter 8. Collective administration of copyright and neighbouring rights — 409

8.1. Societies of authors — *414*
8.1.1. History 414
8.1.2. Procedures for the collective administration of copyright 417
    8.1.2.1. Character and form of the organizations for the collective administration of copyright 418
    8.1.2.2. Legal nature of the representation provided by collective administration organizations 424
    8.1.2.3. Number of organizations entrusted with the collective administration of the various rights in each country 431
    8.1.2.4. One or more societies for each category of authors' rights administered? 432
8.1.3. Functions involved in the collective administration of authors' rights 442
    8.1.3.1. Authorization 444
    8.1.3.2. Remuneration 447
    8.1.3.3. Collection 451
    8.1.3.4. Distribution or sharing 453
8.1.4. Social welfare activities 462
8.1.5. Cultural activities 464
8.1.6. CISAC 466

8.2. Other societies responsible for the collection of royalties — *466*
8.2.1. Collective administration of royalties for reprographic reproduction 467

8.2.2.	Collective administration of rights in respect of private reproduction—home taping of sound recordings and audiovisual works for personal use 476	
8.2.3.	Collective administration of the *'droit de suite'* 479	
8.3.	***Collective administration of the rights of performers and producers of phonograms***	***480***
8.3.1.	Non-voluntary licences for secondary uses 481	
8.3.2.	Remuneration 482	
8.3.3.	Collection 484	
8.3.4.	Distribution or sharing of remuneration 484	

Chapter 9. Bodies set up to defend copyright and neighbouring rights   495

9.1.	***Bodies established under private law***	***495***
9.1.1.	International non-governmental organizations 495	
	9.1.1.1. Organizations set up to defend professional and sectoral interests 495	
	9.1.1.2. Organizations whose work lies in the academic field 505	
9.1.2.	National bodies established under private law 508	
9.2.	***Bodies established under public law***	***509***
9.2.1.	Intergovernmental organizations 509	
9.2.2.	National bodies established under public law. The supervisory function 519	

Chapter 10. Formalities   525

10.1.	***Legal deposit***	***527***
10.2.	***The National Copyright Registry***	***531***
10.2.1.	Classification of registration 532	
10.2.2.	Survival of registers for constituent purposes and application of the international conventions ('reverse inequality') 537	

10.2.3. Effects, subject of registration and procedures; entries in the register; publication of applications; opposition to registration 540
10.3. Registration of instruments and contracts *545*

Chapter 11. Infringements and other unlawful activities. Penalties **549**

11.1. Classification of infringements *549*
11.1.1. Legal protection (penal sanctions) 550
11.1.2. Criteria for the application of penal sanctions 551
11.1.3. Punitive measures. The 'open' approach to classification 552
11.1.4. Categories of offences 555
11.2. Penal sanctions *567*
11.3. Right to restrain the unlawful activity *570*
11.4. Compensation for prejudice suffered *571*
11.5. Procedural rules *576*
11.6. Preventive measures *578*

Chapter 12. International law on copyright and neighbouring rights **587**

12.1. Copyright relations between States. International protection systems *588*
12.2. Protection in the absence of international treaties *590*
12.2.1. Protection of foreign works under domestic law 590
12.2.2. Applicable law 593
12.2.3. Reciprocity 594
12.3. Bilateral agreements on reciprocity *598*
12.4. Multilateral copyright conventions (Berne Convention, Conventions of the Inter-American system, Universal Copyright Convention). General considerations *601*

12.4.1. Conventions of the Inter-American system   605

    12.4.1.1. The First Montevideo Treaty (11 January 1889)   605

    12.4.1.2. The Mexico City Copyright Convention (27 January 1902)   607

    12.4.1.3. The Rio de Janeiro Copyright Convention (23 August 1906)   608

    12.4.1.4. The Buenos Aires Copyright Convention (11 August 1910)   609

    12.4.1.5. The Caracas Copyright Agreement (17 July 1911)   610

    12.4.1.6. The Havana Copyright Convention (18 February 1928)   610

    12.4.1.7. The Second Montevideo Treaty (4 August 1939)   612

    12.4.1.8. The Washington Copyright Convention (22 June 1946)   612

12.4.2. World Copyright Conventions   615

    12.4.2.1. Berne Convention for the Protection of Literary and Artistic Works. Developments leading up to the current Paris Act (24 July 1971)   615

    12.4.2.2. Universal Copyright Convention. Developments leading up to the revised version adopted in Paris (24 July 1971)   748

    12.4.2.3. Multilateral Convention for the Avoidance of Double Taxation of Copyright Royalties (Madrid, 13 December 1979)   797

    12.4.2.4. Treaty on the International Registration of Audiovisual Works (Geneva, 18 April 1989)   803

12.5.   World Conventions on neighbouring rights   *815*

12.5.1. International Convention for the Protection of Performers, Producers of Phonograms and Broadcasting Organizations (Rome, 26 October 1961)   815

12.5.2. Convention for the Protection of Producers of Phonograms against Unauthorized Duplication of their Phonograms ('Phonograms' Convention, Geneva, 29 October 1971)   856

12.5.3. Convention relating to the Distribution of Programme-carrying Signals Transmitted by Satellite ('Satellites' Convention), Brussels, 21 May 1974   874

12.6.   International recommendations approved by the General Conference of UNESCO   *890*

12.6.1. Recommendation on the legal protection of translators and translations and the practical means to improve the status of translators (Nairobi, 22 November 1976)   890

12.6.2. Recommendation concerning the Status of the Artist (Belgrade, 27 October 1980)   893

12.6.3. Recommendation for the Safeguarding and Preservation of Moving Images (Belgrade, 27 October 1980)   896

12.6.4. Recommendation on the Safeguarding of Traditional Culture and Folklore (Paris, 15 November 1989)   899

Bibliography   **901**

Chapter 1

Introduction

Summary
1.1. Definition and content of copyright. Copyright's place among intellectual property rights: copyright and industrial property
   1.1.1. Concept and juridical nature
1.2. History of copyright
1.3. The various legal conceptions of copyright: copyright and author's right
   1.3.1. Subject matter of the author's right. 1.3.2. Concept of 'author'. Owners of the right. 1.3.3. Moral rights. 1.3.4. Economic rights and limitations. 1.3.5. Formalities
1.4. The economic importance of copyright in the present-day world: the production of cultural goods and the technological impact
1.5. The role of copyright in developing countries

1.1. Definition and content of copyright. Copyright's place among intellectual property rights: copyright and industrial property

A. DEFINITION AND CONTENT OF COPYRIGHT

It is the branch of law regulating the rights of the author in creative works, marked by individuality, produced by his intellectual activity and usually described as literary, musical, theatrical, artistic, scientific and audiovisual works.

Copyright recognizes the creator of such intellectual works as possessing exclusive rights, effective against all persons:
- those of a *personal character* concerning the protection of the personality of the author in relation to his work, which, since their purpose is to guarantee intellectual interests, form the so-called *moral right*; and
- those of an *economic character* concerning the exploitation of the work, which allow the author to obtain an economic reward; they constitute the so-called *economic right*.

The author's *moral right* consists of:

- the *right to disclose* his work or to keep it private;
- the *right to the recognition of his intellectual paternity* of work;
- the *right to respect for, and to the integrity* of the work, in other words, the possibility of ensuring that the work is disseminated in the form in which the author created it, without changes; and
- the *right of reconsideration or withdrawal* of the work from circulation by reason of the author's changed convictions.

The moral right is of an extra-economic character and, in principle, of unlimited duration.

The author's *economic right* consists of the right to the economic exploitation of the work, which the author may undertake himself or authorize others to do:
- the *reproduction* of the work in material form (publication, mechanical reproduction, etc.); and
- the *public communication* of the work in a non-tangible form by means of *public* performance, broadcasting,[1] cinematographic showing, exhibition, and so on; and
- the *transformation* of the work through its translation, adaptation, musical arrangement, etc.

The economic right is subject to a number of exceptions and is of limited duration.

B. COPYRIGHT'S PLACE AMONG INTELLECTUAL PROPERTY RIGHTS: COPYRIGHT AND INDUSTRIAL PROPERTY

a. Intellectual property rights

The traditional grouping of copyright with industrial property is firmly rooted[2] in theory and in teaching. Under this common

---

1. The term 'broadcasting' embraces both sound radio proper and television.
2. According to H. Baylos Corroza, dealing with rights which in some way involve or refer to intangible objects as a single group is a methodological postulate which does not conflict or prove incompatible with, first, the diversification of their study in different treatises, sectors or establishments in response to legislative or doctrinal requirements, or, secondly, with their linking up with other general principles and specific cases—concretely with a series of aspects involved in the discipline of economic competition, consideration of which is indispensable in view of the restrictive impact which both intellectual property

head—*intellectual property rights*—reference is made to a broad spectrum of rights of different kinds: while some find their origin in an act of intellectual creation and are recognized as a means of stimulating and rewarding intellectual creativity, others, whether they involve intellectual creation or not, are granted with the aim of regulating competition between producers.

As regards the international protection of copyright and industrial property, the grouping of these areas is apparent in the World Intellectual Property Organization (WIPO). In the Convention Establishing the World Intellectual Property Organization concluded in Stockholm on 14 July 1967 the disciplines included under this common head are set out in the provision (Article 2) which, for the purposes of the Convention, stipulates that *intellectual property* shall include the rights relating to:

- literary, artistic and scientific works,
- performances of performing artists, phonograms, and broadcasts,
- inventions in all fields of human endeavour,
- scientific discoveries,
- industrial designs,
- trademarks, service marks, and commercial names and designations,
- protection against unfair competition,
- and all other rights resulting from intellectual activity in the industrial, scientific, literary or artistic fields.

Literary, artistic and scientific works are the subject matter of *copyright*; performances by performing artists, phonographic fixations and broadcasts are the subject of *neighbouring rights*; inventions which result in a new product or a new procedure for industrial application, the subject of *patent rights*; scientific discoveries are covered by *the rights of scientists*—essentially the right to have their names publicly linked with their scientific discoveries

---

(the traditional term used in Spain in referring to copyright) and industrial property have in regard to industrial and commercial freedom—in short, in regard to the possibilities of competition in a market dealing with material goods. (*Tratado de derecho industrial. Propiedad industrial. Propiedad intelectual. Derecho de la competencia económica. Disciplina de la competencia desleal*, Madrid, Civitas, 1978, p. 50).

and to obtain rewards from the economic success resulting from the use of such discoveries (this area excludes those aspects of the activity of authors of scientific discoveries which are regulated by industrial property rights (when the discovery can be patented) and by copyright (in the literary, artistic or other work when the discovery is described in works of such kinds); industrial drawings and models are the subject of *industrial drawings and model* rights; trademarks, commercial designations, distinctive signs and denominations of origin are the subject of *trademark rights*; protection against acts of unfair competition which are contrary to fair practice in industrial and commercial matters are covered by the *discipline of unfair competition*.

All so-called intellectual property rights (author's rights and neighbouring rights, industrial property rights and rights in scientific discoveries) apply to intangible property, although these are not all rights recognized on the basis of acts of intellectual creation.

b. Copyright

Copyright protects the creations expressed in literary, musical, scientific and artistic works, in the broad sense, and originates with the work itself as a consequence of the act of creation and not because of recognition by an administrative authority, although formalities may be established for specific purposes (furnishing proof, forming and contributing to archives and public libraries, and so on). The 'constitutive' system of registration of copyright whereby the owner has exclusive rights effective against all persons in the work provided that the registration formalities established by law are complied with is, as we shall see further below (Chapter 10), a remnant of the institution of *privilege*, a view of the right to the economic exploitation of works which has been superseded by current doctrine and almost all existing legislation.

c. Industrial property

Patents, trademarks, industrial drawings and models and protection against unfair competition form so-called industrial property rights.

Among industrial property rights, only patent rights and industrial drawings and model rights are directed, in common with copyright, towards the protection of the external expression of an act of intellectual creation and are designed to ensure that an economic reward is obtained in respect of its utilization.

On the other hand, justification for trademark rights does not reside in the protection of an act of creation: the trademark is a distinguishing sign, a symbol intended to indicate the person responsible for the products and services being made available to the public. The same holds for commercial designations and names and for designations of origin. In the case of trademarks, legal protection is founded on the need to prevent the unauthorized use, for competitive ends, of the distinguishing signs of one company by another.

Designations of origin indicate the geographical source of a product or service, by means of the phrase 'made in ...', or else certain qualities of the product deriving from the natural raw materials used, such as, among many other examples, 'Sherry', 'Rioja', 'Champagne' wines, etc.; Dijon mustard; Limoges porcelain; Solingen steel. The basis of legal protection lies in the public's interest in the qualities inherent in the product relating to its origin in a specific country, region or place, and in the need to defend the producers in those geographical areas against unfair competition.

Plant strains are covered by a special system of protection, differing from the protection afforded by patent laws inasmuch as it concerns only the marketing of the materials for the production of new plant varieties (seeds, etc.), but not the cultivation and marketing of the plants themselves.

But even among the intellectual property rights protecting the results of creative activities—inventions, industrial drawings and models on the one hand, and literary, musical, scientific and artistic works on the other—there are important differences.

The right of patent protects the new product or the new industrial application procedure deriving from the invention. The exclusive right in the patented invention *is acquired by virtue of an official act: the patent*. This is granted when certain conditions are fulfilled: the product or procedure must be an invention with an element of novelty (in the objective sense) and it must result in a new industrial application.

Industrial drawing and model rights protect ornamental forms. Like the other industrial property rights (concerning patents and trade marks) and the right to the protection of plant strains, *they become effective upon registration with the administrative authority.*

d. Interconnections

The subject matter of intellectual rights is not always sharply delimited. Elements which are common to the creative activity of the human mind are interconnected (and, sometimes, overlap), as, for example, in the cases of artistic works, industrial drawings and models and advertising messages (or slogans).

A classic example is drawings. While in principle, copyright, on the one hand, protects them in themselves, as a non-applied art expression and, on the other, industrial drawing and design rights protect them as applied works of art in so far as they represent ornamental forms or aspects embodied in or applied to an industrial product, a number of laws allow them to be protected by both types of provision (the copyright law and the industrial drawing and model law), although with the proviso that they may not be invoked simultaneously in the legal defence of rights.[3]

The same holds for advertising messages which can be registered as trade marks without prejudice to the protection which copyright affords them, when they possess sufficient originality.[4]

The two major multilateral international copyright conventions (the Berne Convention and the Universal Copyright Con-

---

3. For example, Argentina, Decree-law 6673/63 (on industrial models and designs), Article 28: 'When an industrial model or design registered in accordance with this decree may have also been the subject of a deposit in compliance with Law 11.723 (on the legal system governing intellectual property), the author may not invoke both laws simultaneously in the judicial defence of his rights.'
4. For example, Argentina, Law 22.362 (on trademarks and commercial designations), statement of grounds, and Article 1; also, legal precedents concerning the protection of advertising messages under Law 11.723 on the legal system governing intellectual property.

vention) also provide for this double possibility in respect of artistic works (see below, Chapter 2, sect. 2.2.1.4, F *in fine*).

e. Autonomy of copyright

Copyright presents common connotations with the other areas which go to make up so-called intellectual property rights: exclusive nature, incorporeal character, effectiveness against all persons (*erga omnes*) and transmissibility of the right of exploitation. However, copyright enjoys legislative autonomy at the national level and in international conventions, and scientific autonomy in so far as it has specific principles and keys for the solution of various basic problems in this area. Accordingly:

- it concerns a result of intellectual creativity and *takes no account of its industrial applications*;
- following his decision to disclose the work, the author has the right *to have his name or pseudonym mentioned* each time that the work is reproduced or communicated to the public (or to remain anonymous), *to have the integrity of his creation respected* and *to reconsider* and withdraw the work from circulation. On the other hand, the moral right of the inventor, once he has decided to patent the invention, amounts to the right of recognition of his status as an inventor in the patent application or in any other similar official document, in accordance with the national legislation;
- the right *originates with the act of creation of the work* and not with recognition by the administrative authority.[5]

1.1.1. Concept and juridical nature

A. CONCEPT

Copyright, in the objective sense, is the term applied to the law; in the subjective sense, it alludes to the prerogatives which the

---

5. Baylos Corroza points out that the distinctive characteristics forming the basis of analytical study of intellectual rights reflect three clearly marked aspects: subject, content of the right and modes of acquisition; he describes these in detail (op. cit., pp. 75–92) but expresses the view that scientific study of these rights cannot produce satisfactory results if they are considered in isolation (p. 93).

author enjoys in relation to a work which has a sufficient degree of originality and individuality and which comes within the sphere of the legal protection afforded.

In countries with an Anglo-American (or common law) legal tradition the term used, copyright, literally means 'the right to copy', an expression which refers to the activity of exploiting the work by means of its reproduction.

In countries with a continental European legal tradition (or one based on Roman or Roman–Germanic law), the conception of the term is a markedly personalist one, as indicated by the expression *droit d'auteur* (author's right), which alludes to the subject of the law, the author, and to the whole set of legal prerogatives which the author is recognized as possessing.

These prerogatives are, on the one hand, of a *personal order*, extra-patrimonial and, in principle, of unlimited duration (moral right) as well as, on the other, of an *economic character* and with a limited duration (economic right). In countries with a Roman legal tradition, in addition to the expression *author's right*, the terms *literary and artistic property* and *intellectual property* are also used.

B. JURIDICAL NATURE

The different character of the prerogatives making up the content of copyright hindered the determination of its juridical nature, giving rise to lengthy debates—and to frequently contrary conclusions—which enriched and contributed in decisive form to the development of the subject matter.

Originally, the rights of printers and booksellers to print and sell books on an exclusive basis derived from a privilege—an exploitation monopoly which was granted by the governing authority. In England, the law of 10 April 1710, known as Queen Anne's Statute,[6] became the first legal norm which recognized the author's entitlement to copyright as an individual right, this being regarded as a property right.

---

6. *Queen Anne's Statute* (8 Anne, C.19).

From the last decade of the eighteenth century onwards, the assimilation of copyright to a property right became more clearly expressed.

a. Theory of property right

'There being no property more peculiarly a man's own than that which is produced by the labour of his mind' is stated in the Preamble to the law of the State of Massachusetts of 17 March 1789.

'The most sacred, the most personal of all properties'[7] were the famous words with which Le Chapelier qualified copyright in the report which was followed by the Decree of 13 and 19 January 1791. With this decree the Constituent Assembly of the French Revolution sanctioned the right of authors to the public performance of their works. The same concept was expressed by Lakanal in the report which preceded adoption of the Decree of 19 and 24 July 1793, whereby the Assembly extended protection to the right of reproduction.

Recognition of the author's property right in respect of his work, akin to the ownership rights concerning material things (movable and immovable property) sought—and this was its merit—to satisfy the just desires of authors, endowing them with a fundamental, clear and unequivocal right.

The influence of the revolutionary decrees referred to above, and of supporting theories which considered copyright to be a property right, was responsible for its widespread acceptance in the laws enacted during the nineteenth century and in many of those of the twentieth. The expressions *literary and artistic property* and *intellectual property* which designated them, reflect the widespread support for this process of assimilation.

However, when the subject was developed more fully through doctrine and legal precedents, and the specific characteristics of copyright became more clearly defined, its assimilation to an

---

7. 'La plus sacrée, la plus personnelle de toutes les propriétés', *Le Moniteur Universel*, 15 January 1791, quoted by M.-C. Dock, 'The Origin and Development of the Literary Property Concept', *RIDA* (Paris), Jan. 1974, p. 199, note 83.

ownership right in respect of tangible property (*jus in rem*) began to be vigorously challenged[8] by reason of the differences between the two rights:
- copyright is exercised in respect of an intellectual creation—the work—and not of a thing, since the ownership of the material object on which the work is fixed cannot be confused with the copyright in the work itself;
- copyright derives from the act of creation of the work and not from the forms provided in order to acquire ownership (appropriation, specification, tradition, receipt of benefits deriving from a property, etc.); in particular, it is not acquired by prescription;
- the term of protection of the author's economic right is limited (usually to the life of the author plus a number of years following his death); the duration of a property right is unlimited;
- the system of co-authorship is different from that of joint ownership;
- the *moral right*, characteristic of copyright, is inconsistent with ownership rights;
- there is no full transfer of copyright, since the work never completely leaves the context of the personality of its author, at least in so far as it is compulsory to mention the author's name each time that the work is utilized and to respect the integrity of his text.

Since a large number of the requirements that ownership of material property involved were lacking in the case of copyright, some opponents of its assimilation to a property right, especially in France and Italy, declared that it was a right *sui generis*, in order to underline its singular juridical nature.

In the nineteenth century, the evolution of copyright in the countries of continental Europe received a major contribution through studies carried out in Germany. There, the school of thought, for the large part, was that copyright should not be

---

8. This occurred even in France, although in isolated instances, in the first half of the nineteenth century (see Claude Colombet, *Propriété littéraire et artistique et droits voisins*, Paris, Dalloz, 1986, p. 18).

placed on the same footing as a property right and the term *Urheberrecht*—and also *Autorrecht* (author's right)—was adopted; however, the legal experts were divided as to where to place it: in the economic rights category—not as a common ownership right but as an intangible property right—or, on the contrary, in the category of personality rights. A middle-of-the-road school of thought considered that it could not be ascribed exclusively to either of the two categories because of its dual function of protecting economic rights and personality rights.[9]

The diversity of views on the legal nature of the copyright led to the division of theories into two major groups: the *dualist* theory which separated the whole set of prerogatives recognized as being vested in authors into two categories of rights (moral rights and economic rights) while considering that, although interrelated, these should not be confused with one another; and the *monistic* theory which viewed this separation as imaginary and untenable since all the recognized rights of the creator should be regarded as the duplication of a single, uniform author's right.[10]

b. *Theory of intangible property rights*

The theory of intangible property rights was developed by Josef Kohler for whom ownership, in its traditional construction, is legal possession which can refer only to tangible objects. The right of the creator does not, therefore, fall within this category; it is an exclusive right in the work which is regarded as intangible property of economic value, whose nature differs, therefore, from the property right applicable to tangible property.

A new category, hence, has to be introduced: a right in respect of intangible property (*Immaterialgüterrecht*) which, nevertheless, as Baylos points out, 'preserves a feature which is inseparable from the theory of ownership which is the interpretation of this legal possession as domain over autonomous property independent of the subject'. Baylos states that one of the aims of Kohler's

---

9. See E. Piola Caselli, *Trattato del Diritto di Autore*, Naples, Ed. Marghieri e Torino, Unione Tip.-Ed. Torinese, 1927, pp. 40–3.
10. See below, Section 4.1, Monistic theory and dualist theory.

thesis is, in fact, to construct a type of subject matter which will fit in with the special nature of the protection afforded to the author and the inventor.[11]

According to Kohler, copyright had an economic nature alone, both by reason of its historical origin—since it was created for the purpose of guaranteeing the economic interests of authors —and because the main provisions of the laws were directed towards the protection of the exclusive prerogatives of reproduction, performance, recitation, etc. of the work, by means of which the author was assured of obtaining an economic reward.

The author also had other rights in respect of his work which were not of an economic but a personal nature, Kohler terming these *Individualrechte*. But these rights, although contributing to the protection of the work, did not, in Kohler's argument, form part of copyright but of a different juridical area. He maintained that two different rights were involved (*Doppelrecht*): a right of an economic kind vested in the author for the economic exploitation of an intangible property (*Immaterialgüterrecht*)—his work— which lay outside the individual but was not corporeal, tangible or visible. Alongside the *Immaterialgüterrecht* the author had an *Individualrecht* which did not form part of copyright content but constituted a concrete expression of the general right of personality.

This exclusion was severely criticized. Some objected to it because it did not concord with positive law (Gierke, Stobbe, Allfeld). According to Piola Caselli, Kohler's theory broke, without reason, the unity and harmony of copyright, producing an unjustified split between the moment of the work's creation—in which the right was of a personal character—and the moment when the work was brought before the public, and economic rights became manifest. Piola Caselli declared that the author's rights of a personal character did not derive from the personality in general but from the personality of whoever created a work. For this reason they were an essential part of copyright, unlike other prerogatives of a personal character which might apply to

---

11. H. Baylos Corroza, op. cit., p. 417.

the work and belong to the author or to other persons, as in the case of correspondence (letters) and portraits (rights of the recipient of the letter and the subject of the portrait) and which were not bound up with the creation of the work but belonged, rather, to the general sphere of personality rights.[12]

According to Baylos, the proposal for a new and different legal category of property rights to describe the right of creators is not the true contribution of Kohler or his supporters. What really defines the theory of intangible property rights is, first and foremost, the consideration given to the characterization and definition of the subject matter to which these rights apply; the theory of intangible property is the doctrinal position in which, for the first time, consideration was given to the subject matter of the rights of creators, as a theme which merited separate examination.[13] Baylos points out that there is no doubt that Kohler's thinking represented one of the most important technical contributions to the construction and even the legal understanding of these rights; a common doctrinal heritage has been constituted on this basis, although not without certain modifications.[14]

In opposition to Kohler's doctrine, which was in line with the dualist school of thought, was the theory of the *right of the personality*, the monistic theory which considered that all the prerogatives enjoyed by the author derived from the protection of his personality which extended to the protection of his works.

c. Theory of the personality right

This theory finds a precedent in the thinking of Immanuel Kant as expressed in 1785; for Kant the author's right is, in actual fact, a right of the personality, a *jus personalissimum*. According to Kant the author's writings are a discourse which he addresses to

---

12. See E. Piola Caselli, op. cit., pp. 42 (note 1) and 58.
13. H. Baylos Corroza, op.cit., p. 420.
14. Ibid., p. 418. In note 112 the author quotes Ascarelli, who states that Kohler has been without any doubt, '*il Maestro che ha dato alla materia* [...] *una inquadratura logica e un architettura giuridica rimasta attuale, pur nel passare degli anni*'.

the public through the publisher. There is, in the copy of the book which represents a tangible artistic product, a real right. On the other hand, the book regarded simply as a discourse addressed by the author to his circle of readers, represents, for Kant, a personal right.[15]

The theory of the personality right was developed by Gierke (followed by, among others, Bluntschli and Gareis and, in France, Salleiles and Bérard). For Gierke, the subject of the author's right is an intellectual work emanating from the personality of its author, a reflection of the author's intelligence, which, through his creative activity, has given his work an individual stamp.

Although the historical development of copyright had its origin in the protection of the economic element, all the prerogatives guaranteed by the laws derive from the original right which the author has of keeping the work secret or of communicating it to the public: this is a personality right and, as such, its duration is unlimited and it is not subject to any form of action on the part of the creditors. Even the exclusive faculties of reproduction, performance, etc. do not necessarily have an economic character, since the author can exercise them without any economic interest. Not even the transferability of the right implies its total transfer, but only the faculties of multiplication, and so on, since the author always conserves rights in the work guaranteeing the protection of his personality. According to this theory, then, the author's right has its basis in the personality right and only assumes an economic character as an accessory element.[16]

According to Piola Caselli, to define the author's right as a right of the personality does not correspond to the reality of the situation; its own particular regulation is incompatible with the idea of its classification in the very broad, general category of personality rights. It has to be recognized, this author considers,

---

15. See G. Luf, 'Corrientes filosóficas de la época de la ilustración y su influjo en el derecho de autor', in *Filosofía del derecho de autor*, Bogotá, Dirección Nacional del Derecho de Autor, 1991, pp. 43–4.
16. See E. Piola Caselli, op. cit., pp. 42–3.

that the work of the mind is treated, from the legal standpoint, as something objective, external to the person of its creator and, with certain provisos, lying outside the sphere of his personality. Similarly, then, it has to be recognized that the exclusive rights are prerogatives of an economic character, existing not simply on an occasional or exceptional basis, but forming a normal part, on account of their particular nature, of the content of this category of right, deriving necessarily from the author's original prerogative of deciding on publication, or otherwise, of his work.[17]

The criticism levelled by Baylos at this theory also extends to the presumption of explaining copyright by means of an institution such as the personality right which has such extremely broad characteristics and features; what this theory did succeed in doing, on the other hand, was clearly to reveal the basis of the protection afforded to the author, the fundamental nature of the right which is manifestly 'ideal', the complementary character of any economic attribute which the right may generate or which may, in short, give rise to the monistic construction of the right.[18]

d. Theory of the personal economic right

The supporters of the middle-of-the-road theory, also of German origin[19] considered that copyright had a particular nature, since although it was rooted in the person, it included rights of an economic kind. Because of this double function of protecting personality interests and economic interests, it could not be assigned exclusively to one or other of the two categories of rights.

Piola Caselli, who at the outset was an advocate of the personality right theory, later subscribed to the middle-of-the-road doctrine of a right of a mixed character on the grounds that copyright represents a right of domain in respect of an intellectual

---

17. Ibid., pp. 57–8.
18. H. Baylos Corroza, op. cit., p. 468.
19. Stobbe Beseler, Derenburg in their manuals of German civil law and, among writers of treatises, Allfeld and Rietzler (see E. Piola Caselli, op. cit., p. 43, note 2).

property (*jus in re intellectuali*) the content of which, because of its special nature, covers prerogatives of both a personal and an economic order, for which reason it should be classified as a personal-economic right.[20]

e. Theory of intellectual rights

The theory of intellectual rights was first advanced by the Belgian jurist Picard; his initial postulate is the inadequacy of the traditional tripartite classification of rights (real rights, personal rights and rights of obligation).

Picard developed a general classification of juridical relations, placing copyright—along with inventions, industrial models and designs and trademarks—in a new category of a *sui generis* and autonomous nature: intellectual rights (*jura in re intellectuali*), setting this against the old category of tangible property rights (*jura in re materiali*).[21]

This classification concerns the subject matter of the right—the work—and is similar to Kohler's theory in that it opened a new juridical category in order to avoid assimilating tangible with non-tangible property; Picard considered, on the other hand, that intellectual rights were made up of two elements: the author's personal or moral rights and his economic rights.

Among his followers are Mouchet and Radaelli[22] and Satanowsky.[23]

f. Other theories

Many other theories have been formulated regarding the juridical nature of copyright (concerning natural rights, right to non-imitation, rights of clientele, monopoly rights, labour rights, per-

---

20. Ibid., pp. 43, 57, 60 and 61.
21. See Edmond Picard, *Le droit pur*, Paris, Flammarion, 1908, §45, 53 and 54.
22. See Carlos Mouchet, and Sigfrido A. Radaelli, *Los derechos del escritor y del artista*, Buenos Aires, Ed. Sudamericana, 1957, p. 22.
23. See Isidro Satanowsky, *Derecho Intelectual*, Buenos Aires, Ed. TEA, 1954, Vol. I., p. 52.

sonal rights and so on); the limitations of a work such as this mean that we must forgo their analysis.[24]

1.2. History of copyright

Regarding the evidence of copyright in the ancient world, Marie-Claude Dock[25] quotes examples from the periods of greatest development of the arts in Greece and Rome relating to the economic aspect of copyright. One example concerns Terence in regard to the play *The Eunuch*, which, according to Donatus, was performed with such success that it was sold a second time and staged as if it had not previously been played, for which reason the first sale would seem to have had as its object the right to stage the play once only.

Dock speaks of the existence of the recognition of the moral right, indicating that: 'Roman authors, moreover, were aware that publication and exploitation of a work involved intellectual and moral interests. The author was entitled to decide whether to divulge his work and plagiarists were exposed to public opinion.'[26]

Michaélidès-Nouaros points out that the right to the integrity of the work did not escape attention twenty-three centuries ago in the Athenian Republic. Copyists of the works of the great writers of tragedy and the actors who performed them showed scant respect for the text. To remedy this state of affairs, a law passed in 330 B.C. ordered that exact copies of the works of three great classical writers should be deposited in the State archives; actors should respect these official texts (see *Euripide*, text and translation by L. Meridier, Vol. I, Introduction, p. XIV, Collection Budé, Paris, 1925).[27]

Dock, after drawing our attention to Pouillet's notion of literary property, namely: 'Copyright has always existed, but it

---

24. Concerning the whole range of these theories, see H. Baylos Corroza, op. cit., pp. 385–473.
25. Marie-Claude Dock, op. cit., pp. 126–205.
26. Ibid., p. 144.
27. Georges Michaélidès-Nouaros, *Le droit moral de l'auteur*, Paris, Librairie Arthur Rousseau, 1935, pp. 11–12.

did not enter from the very start into positive legislation' (*Traité théorique et pratique de la propriété littéraire et artistique*, 1908, p. 2), concludes 'The right existed *in abstracto*, manifesting itself, assuming so to speak tangible form, in the relationship between authors and bibliopoles[28] and games organizers; social needs, however, had not yet imperatively introduced it in the realm of law.'[29]

Books were copied in manuscript form, slowly and laboriously. The resulting cost of the copies was extremely high and their total number very limited. This fact, plus the scarcity of literate people who could afford to purchase them, explains the absence of a specific juridical interest to be protected.

Intellectual creation was regulated by the common property right. When creating a literary or artistic work, the author produced a *thing*—the manuscript, the sculpture—of which he was the owner and which he could transfer in the same way as any other tangible property. The creators' main sources of income were teaching and patronage. Copying and circulating another author's book were considered to be praiseworthy activities.

In the middle of the fifteenth century, Gutenberg's tremendous technological invention, the movable type printing press, and the discovery of engraving, produced radical transformations in the world. They left the era of handwritten books behind them, an era which had lasted centuries (from the fifth century B.C. to the fifteenth century A.D.), making it possible to produce and reproduce books in large quantities and at a low cost.[30]

The possibility of utilizing the work now became independent of the person of its author. This accordingly gave rise to the need for regulating the right of reproduction of the works, although it

---

28. *Bibliopole*, from the Greek *biblion*, book, and *polein*, to sell: a bookseller, dealer in books.
29. See Marie-Claude Dock, op. cit., pp. 152–4.
30. The Canadian teacher and communication media specialist Herbert Marshall McLuhan pointed out that the movable type printing press constituted the first form of large-scale mechanical production. With the passing of time, this original assembly line process was extended to all industrially manufactured products (mass production).

would take several more centuries to define the characteristics that are now applicable. The first appearance of copyright was in the form of *privileges*.[31] The possibilities offered by the movable type printing press gave rise to the rapid development of a new industry. But printing equipment and materials were expensive and recovery of costs through book sales was a slow and uncertain process. Printers demanded some form of protection for their investments having regard to competition from other printers who reprinted the same books. This protection was established by means of privileges.[32]

The privileges were *exploitation monopolies* which the governing authorities granted to the printers and booksellers for a specific period of time on condition that the censor's approval had been obtained—a condition which was used as a political expedient for controlling the dissemination of views which were regarded as dangerous—and that the published work had been registered. They contained a great many of the characteristic features of copyright: they granted exclusive rights, for a limited period of time, to print copies of works and to sell them, as well as to take action against offenders by means of coercive measures (embargo and confiscation of the illicit copies) and afforded the posssibility of claiming compensation for the material injury suffered.

The most ancient privileges of which we have knowledge are those granted for a period of five years by the Republic of Venice in 1469 to Giovanni da Spira, who introduced the printing press into Venetian territory.

With the abolition of the privilege system, copyright was born as we currently know it and as modern legislation recognizes it.

---

31. Privilege, from the Latin *privus*, individual, and *lex*, law: individual law favouring one or a few individuals.
32. See G. Boytha ('The Justification of the Protection of Authors' Rights as Reflected in their Historical Development', *RIDA* (Paris), 1151, pp. 59–61) who points out that without the development of competition between publishers, no printer would have asked for an exclusive right to reproduce a given work, protecting him against reprints of the same work by others and securing him profit from the sale of its copies.

The end of this era began in England and was due to the enormous influence which, in the formation of liberal ideology, was exercised by both the theory and general philosophy of John Locke and his political doctrine and ethics.

From the end of the seventeenth century onwards, a strong movement began to gain ground in support of the freedom of printing and the rights of authors—who were considered to be protected by common law—and in opposition to the Stationers' Company[33] of London, the powerful guild which defended the interests of the printers and booksellers and which had been granted the privilege of censoring texts.

In spite of strong resistance on the part of printers and booksellers, the bill introduced in 1709 in the House of Commons became law in 1710. Known as Queen Anne's Statute, this law replaced the perpetual right to copyright instituted by a Royal Privilege in 1557 in favour of the Stationers' Company, which had thus obtained for itself the monopoly of book publication in England. To replace this feudal privilege, the Statute recognized the exclusive right of authors to print or distribute copies of any book (copyright).[34]

Any printer or bookseller, whether a member or not of the Stationers' Company, could acquire from the author, through a transfer under civil law procedure, the exclusive right to publish the book. But this transfer came to an end after a period of 14 years and, if at its termination the author was still living, this exclusive right could be renewed for another 14 years; after that, use was free. In the case of books already in print when the Statute was approved, a single period of 21 years was fixed in respect of protection.

The protection was conditional on compliance with a number

---

33. 'Stationer' was the term used in England for printers and booksellers.
34. *Statute of Anne*: 'I ... That from and after the tenth day of April, one thousand seven hundred and ten, the author of any book or books already printed, or other persons who had purchased or acquired the copy or copies of any books, in order to print or reprint the same, shall have the sole right and liberty of printing such books'.

of formalities: the entry of the title of the work in the Stationers' Company register (previously this had had to be done in the name of one of its members) and the deposit of nine copies of the work for a number of universities and libraries. The registration constituted a presumption of property. Unpublished works and possible author's rights of a personal order continued to be protected by common law.

In 1833 the *Dramatic Copyright Act* was enacted in the United Kingdom, recognizing the right of public performance. Later laws (1862 and 1882) regulated the protection of artistic and musical works, respectively.

In Spain, Charles III established by royal decree in 1763—a decree which remained in effect until 1834—that the exclusive privilege of printing a work could be granted only to its author and should be denied to all secular communities of ecclesiastical bodies. The privileges granted to such bodies—or what was termed mortmain—were to cease immediately. In 1764 Charles III rounded off this provision by ordaining that privileges granted to authors of books should not terminate on their death but should be handed down to their heirs (provided that these were not communities or that mortmain was not involved) who could expressly request their extension.

In France, the process of recognizing authors' rights had its origin in the lawsuits which, at the beginning of the eighteenth century, were brought by the 'privileged' Parisian printers and booksellers, who upheld the usefulness of renewing privileges on expiration, against the 'unprivileged' provincial booksellers (or those with few privileges) who challenged these renewals in the general public interest.

In a number of proceedings brought before the King's Council, the Parisian booksellers defended themselves against the attacks of their provincial counterparts, declaring that their rights were not only founded on royal privileges but also on the purchase of the manuscripts from the authors. They argued that creation was vested in the latter, who transmitted their property to the booksellers in integral form with all its attributes, chief of which was perpetuity. They claimed that privileges constituted nothing more than authentic approval of their transactions with the authors. The idea of replacing privileges by the notion of literary property was seized upon and defended by the authors and their heirs.

Finally, the Government of Louis XVI intervened in the matter; it enacted, on 30 August 1777, six decrees in which the author's right to publish and sell his works was recognized. Two different categories of privileges were established: the privileges of the publishers, which were for a limited period and proportional to the amount invested, and the privileges reserved to authors, which were based on creative activity and, hence, perpetual. But these decrees applied only to writers and not to authors of dramatic and musical works.

Recognition of the existence of the author's individual right to the protection of the work was strengthened at the end of the eighteenth century by means of laws enacted in the United States and France.

In the United States, several States enacted specific laws on the subject between 1783 and 1786. The Constitution of 1787 (Article 1, section 8, clause 8) gave Congress the power 'to promote the Progress of Science and useful Arts, by securing for Limited Times to Authors and Inventors the Exclusive right to their respective Writings and Discoveries ....'.

It was on this basis that the first federal law on copyright was promulgated in 1790, providing for the protection of books, maps and maritime charts. The term of copyright was fixed at 14 years, renewable for another equal period if, on its expiry, the author was still alive, and on condition that strict registration formalities were complied with.

The North American system followed the English model. The Federal Copyright Act established a uniform system of legal protection for published works throughout the country, leaving state systems intact. Unpublished works continued to be protected only by the American state common law systems.

In France the Constituent Assembly of the Revolution abolished, with effect from 4 August 1789, all privileges of individuals, cities, provinces and orders, including those granted to authors and publishers. When the dust settled, the Assembly adopted the Decree of 13 and 19 January 1791, which confirmed the performing rights of the authors of dramatic works as a property right, for the lifetime of the author and for a further five years in respect of his heirs and successors in title.[35] Subsequently, by the Decree of 19 and 24 July 1793, the Assembly extended protection to the authors of literary, musical and artistic works, guaranteeing them the exclusive prerogatives of distribution and sale thereof during their entire life and for a further period of ten years in favour of their heirs and successors.[36]

Valerio de Sanctis points out that

> ... although Queen Anne's Statute certainly led to the rapid decline of the system of booksellers' privileges in that it recognized the existence of an individual right to protection of a published work, it was nevertheless necessary to wait almost another century until the laws of the French Revolution in 1791–1793 recognized the right of an author to the protection of the work as a creation of the mind.
>
> In fact, Queen Anne's Statute and, in some respects, the United States Copyright, formally recognized by the United States Constitution of 1787, seem to be inspired above all by the necessity for controlling competition among publishers. The laws of the French Revolution established literary 'property' and thus placed the creator of the work at the centre of the protection and, among other things, linked the term of protection to the life of the author; under the Anglo-Saxon system, at this time at least, specific protection was based on

---

35. Art. 2: *'Les ouvrages des auteurs vivants ne pourront être représentés sur aucun théâtre public, dans toute l'étendue de la France, sans le consentement formel et par écrit des auteurs, sous peine de confiscation du produit total des représentations au profit de l'auteur.'* Art. 5: *'Les héritiers ou concessionaires des auteurs seront propriétaires des ouvrages durant l'espace de cinq années après la mort de l'auteur.'*

36. Art. 1: *'Les auteurs d'écrits en tout genre, les compositeurs, les peintres et les dessinateurs qui font graver des tableaux ou des dessins jouiront, leur vie entière, du droit exclusif de vendre, faire vendre, distribuer leurs ouvrages dans le territoire de la République et d'en céder la propriété en tout ou en partie'.* Art. 2: *'leurs héritiers ou cessionnaires jouiront du même droit pendant l'espace de dix ans après la mort des auteurs'.* The revolutionary decrees of 1791 and 1793, complemented by subsequent laws, constituted the legislation on rights of public performance and publication in France until the enactment of the current law of 11 March 1957, on literary and artistic property.

publication (the appearance of the work in writing) and legal protection began on that date; the protection of unpublished works and certain personal rights remained a matter for common law.[37]

The commercially oriented Anglo-American copyright stemming from Queen Anne's Statute, and the *droit d'auteur*, centred on the individual, and deriving from the decrees of the French Revolution, constituted the origin of modern legislation on copyright in, respectively, countries with a common law tradition and those with a continental European or Roman law tradition (see below, Section 1.3).

Boytha points out that the French revolutionary decrees represented a major step forward in developing the system of authors' rights for, in the first instance, they extended the protection of authors' interests from the field of reproducing books to the *realm of performing works*. Secondly, as a result of the enlarged scope of the protection of authors' rights, legislation abandoned the copy-oriented approach and *the expression of the work in material form ceased to be considered as a condition for its protection*. The French decrees focused more on the work and abandoned the copy-oriented philosophy of Queen Anne's Statute. A third consequence of this approach was that the *duration of the exclusive rights in the work was counted from the year of the author's death* rather than from the date of the work's first publication. However, no reversion of these rights to the author was provided for mandatorily within the term of their protection. A fourth important feature of the French philosophy of authors' rights was their designation as *literary and artistic property* as opposed to the Anglo-American term of copyright. A fifth notable consequence of the author-centred philosophy and the property type approach of the French decrees was, about a century later, the separate recognition by the French courts of the so-called moral right of

---

37. Valerio De Sanctis, 'The Development and the International Confirmation of Copyright', translation by Sheila Campitt, *RIDA*, LXXIX, pp. 206–8.

the author, in addition to the established concept of literary and artistic property rights.[38]

Recognition of the author's right as a property right was consolidated in the first half of the nineteenth century through general laws which were enacted in continental Europe. These laws confirmed the author as the owner of the rights of reproduction or public performance, although for a limited time and subject to the performance of formalities as a condition for the enjoyment and exercise of the right (a remnant of the system of privileges).

Studies in Germany based on the philosophical thought of Kant concerning copyright as a *personality right* of the creator made a decisive contribution to the development of the author's rights in continental Europe, especially in respect of the moral right.

In France, the moral right emerged as a judicial doctrine during the first half of the nineteenth century.

However, the protection of the right within the limits of the State itself was not enough to ensure its effective application. The ubiquitous nature of works of the mind and the internationalization of book and music markets made it imperative for copyright to be recognized in every place in which the work might be used.

International protection was gradually achieved through a variety of means: bilateral treaties, incorporation in national laws containing provisions for the protection of foreign works subject to reciprocal arrangements and, finally, the major multilateral conventions with, first, the Berne Convention concluded in 1886 and revised several times since (the last time in 1971), and then the Universal Copyright Convention adopted in Geneva in 1952 and revised in 1971. These two Conventions are landmarks of overwhelming importance in the history of copyright.

In the wake of the constitutive norms established during the eighteenth century, many countries included authors' rights in their national constitutions among the fundamental rights of the

---

38. G. Boytha, op. cit., pp. 77–81.

individual. This inclusion enabled courts of law, basing themselves on the concept of natural law or international law, which can and should be recognized without need of regulations, to apply copyright even before a specific law on the subject had been enacted.[39]

Finally, in the twentieth century, copyright became universally recognized as a *human right*. In the *Universal Declaration of Human Rights* proclaimed by the General Assembly of the United Nations in Paris on 10 December 1948, Article 27 includes the right to culture and copyright:

1. Everyone has the right freely to participate in the cultural life of the community, to enjoy the arts and to share in scientific advancement and its benefits.
2. Everyone has the right to the protection of the moral and material interests resulting from any scientific, literary or artistic production of which he is the author.

A similar text had been adopted some months previously in Article XIII of the *American Declaration of the Rights and Duties of Man* (Bogotá, 1948).

These provisions were subsequently included in the *International Covenant on Economic, Social and Cultural Rights* (New York, 19 December 1966). Its Article 15 states that:

1. The States Parties to the present Covenant recognize the right of everyone:
    (a) To take part in cultural life;
    (b) To enjoy the benefits of scientific progress and its applications;
    (c) To benefit from the protection of the moral and material interests resulting from any scientific, literary or artistic production of which he is the author ...

René Cassin, the principal author of the Universal Declaration of Human Rights, stated: 'The science of human rights is defined as

---

39. See Carlos Alberto Villalba, 'Los derechos intelectuales como parte de los derechos humanos', In *Libro-Memoria, XI Jornadas 'J.M. Domínguez Escovar' sobre Derechos Humanos*, Barquisimeto, Venezuela, 1986, p. 145.

a particular branch of the social sciences, the object of which is to study human relations in the light of human dignity while determining those rights and faculties which are necessary as a whole for the full development of each human being's personality'.[40]

The inclusion of copyright among fundamental rights in national constitutions, in the Universal Declaration of Human Rights and the International Covenant on Economic, Social and Cultural Rights, implies that it is recognized as an attribute of the human individual; as such, its appropriate and effective protection cannot be ignored.

As has been rightly pointed out,[41] the fundamental theory of copyright is based on mankind's need to have access to the fruits of knowledge and the corollary necessity to stimulate the search for knowledge by rewarding the searchers.

1.3. The various legal conceptions of copyright: copyright and author's right

Because of the differences between the Anglo-American legal conception of copyright and that of the continental European or Roman law tradition in respect of author's right, the two terms are not completely equivalent even though there has been a process of gradual *rapprochement* between the two standpoints as national legislations tend to be brought into line with one another as a result of the Berne Convention (in which the continental conception prevails), and the efforts which are being made within the European Union to achieve legal harmonization.

Stemming from the Queen Anne's Statute, the commercially oriented Anglo-American copyright system which prevails in countries with a common law legal tradition (United Kingdom, the Commonwealth countries and the United States, etc.), regulates the activity of exploitation of works.

---

40. Quoted by Karel Vasak, *The International Dimensions of Human Rights*, Paris, Serbal-UNESCO, 1984, Vol. 1, p. 16.
41. *The ABC of Copyright*, Paris, UNESCO, 1982, p. 22.

Therefore, in comparison with the 'author's right' according to the Roman law tradition, the scope of copyright is more limited from the standpoint of the personal rights which it recognizes, and more extensive both in relation to the subject matter of the protection (since it is not limited to works of creation, traditionally classified as literary, scientific, theatrical, musical, artistic and audiovisual works—or, more concisely: literary, musical and artistic works—having originality or individuality, but includes sound recordings (or phonograms), broadcast and cable programmes and the typographical arrangement of published editions) and in relation to the persons which it accepts as the original owners of the right. Consequently, copyright is used to protect rights originating in technical and organizational activities which are not acts of intellectual creation of an author-related nature, such as those performed by the producers of sound recording and cinematographic films, broadcasting organizations, cable programme distribution companies and the publishers of printed works.

The legal conception of author's right in the Roman law tradition is essentially individualistic. Having its origin in the decrees of the Constituent Assembly of the French Revolution and formed in the countries of continental Europe, it considers the author's right to be a personal and inalienable right of the physical person of the author to control the use of works of his creation. This interpretation was followed by the Ibero-American countries, and by numerous countries in Africa and Eastern Europe.

Recognition in French judicial practice of the author's rights of a personal character (*droit moral*), developed and expressed as a theory on the basis of a doctrine whose roots are philosophical —the work is an emanation or reflection of the author's personality—has had a decisive influence. The right originates in the act of creation and the author–work relationship is strengthened by the extension of the prerogatives of the creator and of his power of decision, preventing the work from completely moving out of the context of his personality. The attribution of the original author's right to persons other than the creator is admitted only in exceptional situations, since recognition of an author's right as being vested in the owners of neighbouring rights is rejected.

A more detailed comparison between the two systems will

help to bring out the differences between the two legal conceptions of author's rights.

1.3.1. Subject matter of the author's right

In the system reflecting the Roman law tradition, the subject matter of the author's right is, as we have said, the intellectual creation expressed in works which possess originality with the stamp of individuality, unlike the Anglo-American system where subject matter other than a work of creation can also be protected by copyright. In the United Kingdom *Copyright, Designs and Patents Act 1988* (in force as of 1 August 1989), the enumeration of the protected works includes sound recordings[42] (phonograms), broadcasts, cable programmes and the typographical arrangement of published editions—which the previous Act of 1956 had limited itself to considering as 'other subject matter'. They are, however, separated into three groups: (1) literary, dramatic, musical and artistic works; (2) sound recordings, films, broadcasts or cable transmissions; and (3) typographical arrangement of published editions (Section 1, (1)).[43] De Freitas considers that the rationale of the groupings is presumably that, as in the 1956 Act, the requirement of 'originality' applies only to works in group (1) thus necessitating a separate grouping for those in (2); while typographical arrangements (3) are put in a special group because of their special nature.[44]

In the legal conception that derives from the Roman law

---

42. 'Sound recordings' are also mentioned in the list of protected works under Sect. 102 (A)7 ('Subject matter of copyright: In general') of the 1976 United States law.
43. '1.(1) Copyright is a property right which subsists in accordance with this Part in the following descriptions of work: (a) original literary, dramatic, musical and artistic works; (b) sound recordings, films, broadcasts or cable programmes; and (c) the typographical arrangement of published editions.'
44. See Derig De Freitas, 'Letter from the United Kingdom', *Copyright*, 1990, p. 32.

tradition, the fixing of the work on a material support is not a prerequisite for its protection (barring certain exceptions).[45]

In the Anglo-American system, on the other hand, the fixation requirement continues to be decisive in ensuring that the work enjoys copyright protection.

In the United Kingdom, Subsection 3.2 of the 1988 Act establishes that in order to enjoy copyright protection, a literary, dramatic or musical work must be recorded, in writing or otherwise, and references in this part of the Act to the time at which such a work is made are to the time at which it is so recorded.

In the United States of America the fixation requirement is regarded as being directly related to the Copyright Clause of the Constitution (Art. I, para. 8) which restricts the guarantees of copyright to 'writings of authors', i.e. only works regarded as writings may enjoy legal copyright protection. The interpretation of the Supreme Court was that 'writings' should be understood to mean any material support of the fruits of intellectual activity (*Goldstein* v. *California*, 412, U.S. 546, 1973).[46]

1.3.2. Concept of 'author'. Owners of the right

According to the legal conception deriving from the Roman law tradition, authorship—and, hence, original ownership of the copyright—is recognized as belonging exclusively to the physical person who created the work; it is only exceptionally admitted that the original ownership can be vested in other persons, e.g. in collective works—unless otherwise agreed: Spain, Article 8, second part; France, Intellectual Property Code, legislative part, Art. L. 113-5, previously Art. 13. (In France legislation concerning

---

45. Choreographic works and pantomimes, for example, in France (Art. L. 112-2.4, former Art. 3); Italy (Art. 2(3)); Netherlands (Art. 10(4)); Brazil (Art 6.IV); see below, Chap. 2, Sect. 2.2.1.3. Note: when reference is made in this work to a national legislation by mentioning the country in question, the allusion is to the copyright law; in general such references are intended only to serve as examples and are not exhaustive.
46. See M. A. Leaffer, *Understanding Copyright Law*, New York, Matthew Bender, 1989, p. 31, para. 2.3.

intellectual property—literary and artistic property and industrial property—has been codified in Law 92-597 of 1 July 1992, no change being made in the text of the articles, but simply in the numerical order.)

Furthermore, in these countries rejection of the total transfer of author's rights *inter vivos* is becoming increasingly established with admission only of licences or authorizations for use or again, of the improperly termed partial 'transfers', instead of the 'granting', of certain exploitation rights. Delgado Porras points out that even in the case of 'exclusive transfer' under the Spanish law (Articles 48 and 49), where a transfer of rights takes place, the transmission is not, however, carried out by means of conveyance or alienation (to which the civil law concept of transfer applies), but by means of 'constitutive succession' in which the transmitter, on the basis of his right and without losing ownership thereof, 'constitutes' one or several new rights in favour of the transferee, which act as limitations.[47]

In isolated cases a presumption of transfer is established—unless otherwise agreed[48]—in respect of the exploitation rights of the works, although limited by the forms provided by the law (e.g. France, Article L. 132-24, previously Article 63-1, other than the authors of a musical composition, with or without words; Spain, Articles 88 (1) and 89 (1)).

In countries where the Anglo-American system prevails and in the case of authors who create works by virtue of a contractual labour relationship, or on commission or, again, create such works for cinematographic productions, the employer, commissioner or producer is considered to be the original owner of the copyright—although only in respect of the works created under such contracts—through the attribution of original ownership

---

47. Antonio Delgado Porras, *Panorámica de la protección civil y penal en materia de propiedad intelectual*, Madrid, Civitas, 1988, p. 58.
48. In general there are very few situations in which the author has sufficient negotiating strength to claim rights which, in principle, are not established by the law in his favour but to the advantage of the producer, impresario, employer, and so on.

established in law, transfer as a matter of right or a legal presumption of transfer, in all cases, unless otherwise stipulated.

According to Section 101 of the United States Act, works made for hire are considered to be: (1) a work prepared by an employee within the scope of his or her employment; or (2) a work specially ordered or commissioned for use as a contribution to a collective work, as a part of a motion picture or other audiovisual work, as a translation, as a supplementary work (defined and exemplified in the last part of the same paragraph), as a compilation, as an instructional text, as a test, as answer material for a test, or as an atlas, if the parties expressly agree in a written instrument signed by them that the work shall be considered as 'a work made for hire'.

According to paragraph 1(a) of section 201, copyright in a protected work is vested initially in the author or authors of the work; it is next established (b) that in the case of works made for hire, the employer or other person for whom the work was prepared is considered the author for the purposes of ownership and, unless the parties have expressly agreed otherwise in a written instrument signed by them, *owns all of the rights comprised in the copyright.*

The provisions of the United Kingdom Act of 1988 on original ownership of works, in comparison with those contained in the previous 1956 Act, benefit the individual author by establishing (Section 11) that the author of a work is the first owner of the copyright in it, with the exception—subject to any agreement to the contrary—of a work made by an employee in the course of his employment, in which case his employer is the first owner of the copyright. Paragraph 3 of the same section states that this provision does not apply to Crown copyright or Parliamentary copyright, which are regulated by sections 163 and 165, nor to the copyright of certain international organizations to which Section 168 applies.

A marked difference with the Roman law tradition system can be seen in the attribution of authorship to natural or juridical persons performing activities concerning the industrial exploitation of works (Section 9(2): producers of sound recordings and films, broadcasting organizations, cable programme distributors and publishers)[49] to which Cornish refers as contributions by entrepreneurial skills in an aesthetic field.[50]

1.3.3. Moral rights

The prerogatives of a personal nature (or rights of personality of the author) are protected in all countries to a greater or lesser extent, for the conditions in which the work is used and the need to ensure respect for its integrity, recognition of the author's intellectual paternity and observance of his wish to make use of a pseudonym or to remain anonymous are all matters of capital importance for the author; they are of similar importance to the community.

In countries where the Roman law tradition prevails, moral rights are regulated within the laws governing author's rights, at least in their basic aspects: right to paternity and to the integrity of the work. The extent to which the moral right of the creator is recognized depends on the importance attributed in the particular country to the author–work relationship (see below, Chapter 4, Section 4.1).

In the majority of countries where the Anglo-American legal

---

49. United Kingdom Act, Section 9:
    '(1) In this Part "author", in relation to a work, means the person who creates it.
    (2) That person shall be taken to be:
    (a) in the case of a sound recording or film, the person by whom the arrangements necessary for the making of the recording or film are undertaken;
    (b) in the case of a broadcast, the person making the broadcast (see section 6(3)) or, in the case of a broadcast which relays another broadcast by reception and immediate retransmission, the person making that other broadcast;
    (c) in the case of a cable programme, the person providing the cable programme service in which the programme is included;
    (d) in the case of the typographical arrangement of a published edition, the publisher.'
50. W. R. Cornish, *Intellectual Property*, London, 1981, p. 318, quoted by Herman Cohen Jehoram, 'Relationship between Copyright and Neighbouring Rights', *RIDA*, 144, p. 115.

system prevails, the protection of the author's rights of a personal nature has been traditionally referred to the courts, which recognize a substantial number of the prerogatives forming the moral right, regarding them as being protected by common law but not including their regulation (as a moral right) in copyright laws, except in the case of Canada, and subsequently, of Israel.

In Canada, explicit mention of moral rights had already been made in the previous law (R.S., c. 32, s. 12: 1931, c. 8, s. 5) by means of a provision worded along similar lines to that adopted in Article 6*bis* (1) of the Berne Convention. In Nabhan's opinion, the partial reform of the Canadian Act approved in 1988 clarifies its wording, but the right to claim authorship of a work is not established as absolute, since it is granted only 'where reasonable in the circumstances', for which reason some people think that this condition seriously weakens the moral right.[51] The Canadian provision recognizes that the moral right may not be transferred *inter vivos*, but permits it to be waived without any written proof being required. Nabhan points out that there is no doubt that a system which permits the waiver of moral rights on such a broad basis is likely to compromise the efficacy of these rights to a considerable extent.[52]

In the United Kingdom, the 1956 Act established non-economic rights providing for protection against the false attribution of authorship (Article 43); but this is a general personality right and not a specific personality right of the author (moral right). With a view to the ratification of the Paris Act (1971) of the Berne Convention,[53] United Kingdom legislation included, for the first time, specific provisions regarding the two basic prerogatives of moral right—paternity (Sect. 77) and integrity (Sect. 78)—in favour of the authors of works of creation (literary, dramatic, musical or artistic) and of the directors of films (Section 77), but with the proviso that any of these rights may be waived

---

51. See Victor Nabhan, 'A Glance over the Amendments to Canada's Copyright Law', *RIDA*, 142, p. 194.
52. Ibid., p. 196.
53. Cf. Robert J. Abrahams, *Copyright in the United Kingdom* (document).

by an instrument in writing signed by the person giving up the right (Sect. 87). These rights do not apply in the case of sound recordings, graphic editions, computer programs, the design of a typeface, any computer-generated work, works produced in the course of employment and in various other instances in respect of which analogous exceptions are established (Section 79).

In the United States of America—in the same way as in other countries with an Anglo-American legal tradition—the courts recognized many of the prerogatives making up the moral right: protection against acts of unfair competition (suppression of the author's name), right of obligations (requiring that contractual conditions should be honoured when the right to respect for the work is involved), protection against defamation (publication of a work in a substantially different version), the right to privacy (for publication of unauthorized versions of the author's work is regarded as intrusion in respect of his privacy).

Several states (California, New York, Massachusetts and Louisiana, among others) provided protection, through their laws, for moral rights although only in relation to specific artistic works (the most extensive list of artistic works to which moral rights apply is that of Massachusetts and includes audiovisual works).[54]

So that the United States of America might accede to the Berne Convention, Congress enacted the *Berne Convention Implementation Act* in October 1988, whereby United States federal legislation was brought into line with the provisions of the Convention.[55] The Implementation Act rejected the need to introduce specific regulations concerning protection of moral rights, affirming that the prerogatives recognized by United States law as a whole (the Copyright Act, other laws (federal and state) and legal precedents), satisfied the requirements of Article 6*bis* of the Berne Convention. Consequently, as regards the protection of moral

---

54. See M. A. Leaffer, op. cit., pp. 255–6.
55. Legislation concerning ratification of the Berne Convention by the United States of America was also enacted in October 1988; accession became effective on 1 March 1989.

rights and in spite of accession to the Berne Convention, the legislation of the United States has remained unaltered and the Berne Implementation Act (Sections 3, 4 and 6) prevents United States courts from making any reference to the Convention.

In order to understand this legal mechanism, it has to be borne in mind that the Berne Implementation Act was the result of unceasing efforts to reconcile the conflicting positions adopted by the various sectors of United States copyright industries, when faced by United States accession to the Berne Convention—and the consequent national legislation reforms which this required, particularly in regard to Article 6*bis* of the Convention which recognizes the author's moral rights—this was the most contested aspect. This explains why so many compromises were hammered out such as the decision that in the United States, the Berne Convention would not be self-executing, so that the Implementation Act would be the sole source of Berne Convention rights and rules under United States law.

Ginsburg and Kernochan state that this approach was essential to adoption by the United States of the Berne Convention[56] and a key element in the minimalist form of dealing with the Convention, since the Implementation Act sought to ensure that United States copyright was amended as little as possible and only to the extent that was strictly necessary in order to adapt it to Convention requirements. Only two substantial aspects were modified: (a) requirements in respect of formalities, especially the obligation to affix the copyright notice as a condition for maintaining copyright, which was deleted; and (b) the compulsory licence for public jukebox performances of non-dramatic music, incompatible with Article 11 of the Berne Convention (which establishes the author's exclusive right of authorizing public performance by any means or process and admits no limitations thereof).

---

56. See Jane C. Ginsburg and John M. Kernochan, 'One Hundred and Two Years Later: the U.S. Joins the Berne Convention', *RIDA*, 141, p. 71, in which the authors exhaustively describe and analyse the accession of the United States of America to the Berne Convention.

At the end of 1990, two provisions were introduced in the United States of America which made important additions to the federal copyright law (Title 17, United States Code) which, as Oman[57] points out, are a consequence of the country's accession to the Berne Convention, for one is designed to protect the author's moral rights in respect of works in the visual arts[58] (the first instance of recognition of the author's moral rights in United States federal legislation) and the other, architectural works.[59]

Works in the visual arts in respect of which the author's moral rights are recognized—rights which may not be transferred but which may be waived—include (a definition added to Sect. 101 of the federal copyright law): paintings, drawings, prints or sculpture existing in a single copy or in a limited edition of no more than 200 copies signed and consecutively numbered by the author and, under the same conditions, photographs produced for exhibition purposes only. Not included are posters, maps, globes, technical drawings, diagrams, models, applied art, motion pictures or other audiovisual works, books, newspapers and periodicals, databases, electronic information services, electronic publications or similar publications, merchandising products and works made under hiring-out or contract arrangements.

The provision introduced Section 106A in the federal copyright law which recognizes the *moral rights* of authors of visual works in their two basic aspects: authorship and integrity. As regards works made under arrangements for the hiring-out of services or a contractual relationship (in principle excluded from the new law), the right is conferred upon the author of a work of recognized stature of preventing any destruction of that work, any intentional or grossly negligent destruction being considered as a violation of the right of integrity. Similarly, the right is established of preventing the false attribution of authorship.

---

57. R. Oman, 'Letter from the United States of America', *Copyright*, May 1991, p. 117.
58. Title VI of Public Law 101-650 of 1 December 1990, effective as of 1 June 1991.
59. Title VII of Public Law 101-650 of 1 December 1990, effective as of that date.

The second provision is designed to protect *works of architecture* which are defined (text added to Section 101 of the federal copyright law) as the design of a building as embodied in any tangible medium of expression, including the building itself, architectural plans or drawings. The work includes the overall form, the arrangement and composition of spaces and elements in the design, but does not include individual standard features.

1.3.4. Economic rights and limitations

In both legal systems there is recognition of a principle which constitutes the characteristic of copyright: the author enjoys, on an exclusive basis, the right of undertaking himself—or authorizing third parties to undertake—the economic exploitation of the work. This allows him to determine the conditions governing use of the work and to obtain an economic reward.

In the concept reflecting the Roman legal tradition, the economic rights which the author possesses are not subject to *numerus clausus*.[60] They are as numerous as the possible forms of utilization of the work, not only at the moment of its creation but during the whole period in which it remains in the private domain, and there are no exceptions other than those provided under the law, for the *limitations* are specific, unlike the rights which are recognized generically; this contrasts with the copyright system in which exploitation rights are those typified in legislation. In this regard, Ascarelli shows us that the concept with its historical origins in the Anglo-American tradition of copyright as an exceptional monopoly for the exercise of a specific activity, accounts for the fact that allusion is made therein to the typical rights of use and that, on the other hand, no provision is made covering the author's exclusive right in respect of any type of utilization of the work of the mind which, in social terms, may be considered as such.[61]

---

60. See below, Chapter 4, Section 4.2.
61. Tullio Ascarelli, *Teoria de la concurrencia y de los bienes immateriales*, Spanish translation by E. Verdera and L. Suárez Llanos, Barcelona, Ed. Bosch, 1970, p. 670.

To satisfy the educational, cultural and information needs of the public and enable the community to have access to works, legislation authorizes certain public communication and reproduction to be made without requiring prior authorization from the author or the holder of the right, establishing various limitations of (or exceptions to) the author's exclusive right.

Such limitations permit the utilization of works freely and without charge (usually referred to as the free use of protected works) or else establish systems of non-voluntary licences—compulsory licences and legal (statutory) licences. In the latter instance, the work may also be used freely but use is subject to payment of a fee. The difference between the compulsory licence and the statutory licence resides in the fact that whereas in the first instance the amount of remuneration is not fixed, which enables it to be negotiated by the author (or, generally, the collective copyright administration society), in the case of the statutory licence, remuneration is fixed by law (or rather, by the competent authority) which, as regards the use involved, leaves no margin whatsoever for the exercise of the author's economic options. (In all cases of limitations of the author's right, the works concerned must have already been disclosed with the author's authorization.)

In the Anglo-American legal system, non-voluntary licences are more widespread than in the system reflecting the Roman legal tradition, which is reluctant to accept them. The Berne Convention (Art. 11*bis*(2) and Art. 13(1) provides that States forming part of the Union may establish compulsory licences in respect of the broadcasting and mechanical reproduction of non-dramatic musical works.[62] The Berne Convention's harmonizing effects on legislation have been demonstrated, as we have seen, by the modification of United States legislation with respect to the compulsory licence for the public playing of recordings of musical works

---

62. The United Kingdom Act of 1988 abolished the statutory licence for the mechanical reproduction of non-dramatic musical works set out in Article 8 of the 1956 law (see G. Dworkin in: *International Copyright and Neighbouring Rights*, Stephen M. Stewart, 2nd edition, London, Butterworth, 1989, p. 503, para. 18.50).

in jukeboxes. Section 116 of the 1976 Copyright Act was amended to the effect that jukebox operators and copyright holders should freely negotiate a licence contract concerning terms, rates and proportionate division of fees and the designation of agents; in case of disagreement, negotiations could be submitted to the Copyright Royalty Tribunal for arbitration.

The use of protected works freely and without charge is more widely admitted in copyright countries than in author's right countries, e.g. the reprographic (or photocopied) reproduction of copyrighted works by libraries and research bodies for the purpose of meeting their particular needs, and for personal use, is governed by the limitation of fair use (United States of America, Sections 107 and 108).

1.3.5. Formalities

In the legal conception stemming from the Roman law tradition, the author's right originates, as we have stated, in the act of creation of the work and its enjoyment and exercise are not dependent upon the fulfilment of formalities (in some Latin American countries, however—Argentina, Nicaragua, Paraguay, Uruguay—constitutive registration of the right is still maintained; in other words, a registration obligation as a condition governing exercise by the author of the economic rights which the law recognizes he possesses, with characteristics of exclusivity and effectiveness against all persons—see below, Chapter 10, Section 10.2).

In the United States, the 1976 Act maintained the obligation of affixing a formal copyright notice by means of the symbol ©, the word copyright or the abbreviation Copr., the year of first publication and the name of the copyright holder and, for phonograms, the symbol ℗ (Section 401 *et seq.*)

Since one of the basic criteria of the Berne Convention is automatic protection, i.e. protection is not subordinated to compliance with any formal requirement, the Berne Convention Implementation Act of 1988 introduced a modification in the United States law which we have already referred to as being of the greatest importance; this abolished the requirements concerning the performance of formalities (see below, Chapter 10, Section

10.2) with particular reference to the obligation to affix the notice of copyright as a condition for maintaining the author's right. In this way the domestic legislation of the United States was brought into line with the principle set out in the Berne Convention concerning the absence of formalities ('The enjoyment and the exercise of these rights shall not be subject to any formality ...'— Article 5, (2)).

Ginsburg and Kernochan point out, however, that although the affixing of the copyright notice is now optional, it is advisable to do so for although its omission does not deprive the work of copyright protection in the United States, the Berne Convention Implementation Act provides (Article 7, Sections 401(d) and 402(d)) that omission of the notice makes it impossible to defeat a defence of 'innocent infringement'. To avoid a risk of this kind, the copyright holder, whether from the United States or abroad, should therefore continue to affix the notice on all published copies.

The authors quoted explain how an innocent infringer may be successful in his defence in the absence of the copyright notice:

The 1988 legislation does not explicitly define 'innocent infringement'. The text does refer to the 1976 Act's provision on statutory damages.[63] This disposition permits a court to reduce the award 'in a case where the infringer sustains the burden of proving, and the court finds, that such infringer was not aware and had no reason to believe that his acts constituted an infringement of copyright' [...]. The Senate Report asserts that by incorporating an innocent infringer defence to absence of notice, the Berne Implementation Act was 'creating a limited incentive for notice which is compatible with Berne'. The stronger the incentive to affix notice, the greater the risk of conflict with Berne's no formalities rule, if that incentive is the prospect of insignificant recovery when notice is omitted. Were the actual damages awarded to notice-omitting copyright proprietors significantly reduced, it would be difficult to maintain that compliance with the notice formality is no longer a condition to enjoyment and exercise of copyright.[64]

---

63. Section 504, para (c).
64. J. C. Ginsburg and J. M. Kernochan, op. cit., pp. 79–83.

1.4. The economic importance of copyright in the present-day world: the production of cultural goods and the technological impact

The technological impact took copyright out of the secondary position which it had occupied by reason of the fact that it affected a small group—writers, playwrights, composers, artists in the visual arts—whose activities, although recognized as being vital, were carried out in economically restricted areas (culture, education, information and entertainment) without any repercussions on the creation of national wealth.

The arrival on the market, from 1950 onwards, of the new means for the reproduction, dissemination and exploitation of works, produced a substantial growth in the publishing business —in the broad sense of the term—, the entertainment and the computer industries and the mass media in the industrialized countries (and also, although to a lesser degree, in the developing countries), with a consequent increase in the international circulation of cultural goods and products.

The field of copyright was broadened in all aspects concerning the means involved in the use of works (transmission of programmes by satellite, cable, optical fibre and cellular telephony, video, commercial rental, reprographic reproduction and private copying, etc.); the material supports on which works are fixed and marketed (sound and audiovisual cassettes, compact discs, mass memories in data banks and CD-ROM,[65] etc.); and the means of fixation and reproduction (audio and video recording and reproduction equipment, photocopiers, digital computer signals, etc.).

The interests to be protected also broadened, leading to the recognition of so-called *neighbouring rights* (in favour of performing artists, producers of phonograms and broadcasting organizations).

---

65. CD-ROM: acronym for Compact Disc-Read Only Memory (compact disc which is used as a support for a read only memory, not capable of reproduction).

The extension of copyright protection to computer programs (or to software supports) contributed to the growing importance of cultural goods in the balance of trade. The economic importance of copyright came to the forefront as did its far-reaching political and social implications in stimulating creativity, producing investment and promoting the dissemination of cultural goods.

Research was carried out in several countries concerning the economic importance of copyright[66] which set out the findings of studies quantifying the impact of 'cultural' industries on national wealth. The general method of these studies was to assess the part of the gross national product (GNP) or the gross domestic product (GDP) created by the production of goods protected by copyright legislation.

The first study dates from 1959; it was carried out in the United States and, based on 1954 data, showed a figure of 2 per cent.

The study undertaken in Sweden by the Central Swedish Office of Statistics took account of the production of copyrighted material and 'revenue from copyright-related activities' (total payment of salaries, fees, bonuses, etc. to people carrying out intellectual activities which might result in a work or other result capable of being expressed in material form and protected outside the sphere of copyright laws). It used 1978 data established on the basis of the analysis of the national budget, and showed that the copyright share in the GNP, during that year, was 6.6 per cent. Given that the advent and use of video cassettes and satellite transmissions, and the growth of the computer industry dated from that time, it is safe to assume that this share would be even greater today.

---

66. Sources: Henry Olsson, 'La importancia económica del derecho de autor', DAT (Buenos Aires), October 1988, pp. 1–9; and Herman Cohen Jehoram, 'Critical Reflections on the Economic Importance of Copyright', *Rights*, Vol. 2, No. 4, Winter 1988–1989, pp. 4–6.

In 1984 a study was published in the United States by the Copyright Office on the basis of material relating to 1977, showing that the value added to the GNP by the copyright industries (in a more limited interpretation than the 'copyright activities' used in the Swedish study) was about 2.8 per cent.

In 1985 another United States study was published, made by Michael R. Rubin for the American Copyright Council. This analysis, based on 1982 material, reached 4.6 per cent of the total GNP and up to 5 per cent if semiconductors were included. Comparison with other studies is very difficult because Rubin used the 'final demand' concept instead of 'value added'.

In the United Kingdom, Jennifer Phillips' study published in 1985 by the Common Law Institute of Intellectual Property Ltd. (CLIP) dealt basically with the most important copyright industries such as literature (printing, publishing, retailing, libraries, remuneration of authors), music (printing and publishing, remuneration of composers and performing musicians, retailing, collective administration companies), sound recordings (phonographic records, tape recordings, retailing), films and video (production and dissemination of films, cinematography, video), broadcasting (radio and television) and theatre (actors), without covering the long list of industrial areas dealt with, for example, by studies such as the Swedish report. The United Kingdom study shows that, in 1982, the copyright share in the GDP (basically the GNP, but excluding the product originating outside the country) was 2.6 per cent, surpassing in importance the automobile and food industries and occupying a place practically on the same level as the chemical and synthetic textile industries. Over half a million people were then employed in these industries.

In the Netherlands, the Department of Economic Studies of the University of Amsterdam published a report in 1986 on the value added to the GNP by creative activities in which copyright was the main element. The creative activities covered were more limited than in the other studies; it was found that, in 1982, approximately 2.4 per cent corresponded to copyright-related activities.

In Australia, a report published towards the end of 1987 demonstrated that 3.1 per cent of the GNP came from the value added by copyright industries, which employed 3 per cent of the total national work force.

Reports were published in 1988 in the former Federal Republic of Germany and in Austria, but with a different focus. They did not concern the economic impact of the copyright industries as such but, rather, the economic impact of the arts and culture. This means that the reports do not include the computer program industry; on the other hand, the German study takes account of the protection of monuments and of cultural administration which up to then had not been considered. In the former Federal Republic of Germany the share in the GNP was 2.3 per cent and in Austria, 2.053 per cent. In the former country, 680,000 people were employed in the arts and culture, i.e. 2.7 per cent of the work force; in the latter, the figure was 77,000.

In Finland, the value added to the GNP by the copyright industries amounted to approximately 3.5 per cent in 1981 and 3.98 per cent in 1985. In 1981, 3.18 per cent of the national work force was employed in those industries, and in 1985, 3.36 per cent.

Since all these studies were based on different criteria in determining which activities were considered to be copyright industries, the author of the United Kingdom study made her own calculations of the estimates contained in four of them, applying the same criteria to all.[67] The percentages which resulted were as follows: United States, 2.38 per cent, United Kingdom, 3.2 per cent, Netherlands, 2.2 per cent, and Sweden, 3.16 per cent (instead of 6.6 per cent). An international value in respect of copyright was also calculated; an average was taken between these four countries which showed that the contribution of the copyright industries amounted to 2.7 per cent of national revenue; in current terms, this could be as high as 3 per cent.

The implication of these percentages becomes more meaningful when compared with the portion of the GDP created by agricultural production which, in 1987, was: United States and the

---

67. See *The Economic Importance of Copyright*, International Publishers Association, 1988, quoted by Herman Cohen Jehoram, op. cit., p. 5.

United Kingdom, 2 per cent, Netherlands, 4 per cent and Sweden, 3 per cent.[68]

The studies listed are eloquent as regards the economic importance which copyright has attained, and the unsatisfactory situation that exists when it continues to be considered as a little-known area outside the mainstream of government concerns.

The economic importance of copyright in the modern world, attained through the production of cultural goods, has also been demonstrated by the tremendous losses resulting from the unauthorized reproduction of works on a commercial scale (piracy) and the privately made reproduction of works (reprographic reproduction of printed works and private copying of recordings of musical and audiovisual works). 'Anti-piracy' legal proceedings have been filed, and demands made for the enactment of laws establishing compensatory remuneration for reprographic reproduction and private copying, in order to remedy the adverse effects of the technological impact (see below, Chapter 4, Section 4.3.2, A).

1.5. The role of copyright in developing countries

Copyright has proved its ability to stimulate creative activity by ensuring that creators have the possibility of obtaining an economic reward, respect for their work and recognition of their status of authors at the same time it benefits business interests by guaranteeing their investments and encouraging the expansion of cultural industries, with the consequent advantage for the community through promotion of the dissemination of works.

When legislation on the subject is absent or is not sufficiently developed to guarantee effective protection; when there are no authors' societies which can represent authors effectively; or when tolerance is shown towards offenders, all sectors concerned are deprived of the benefits which are to be reaped from copyright.

The developing countries need to promote the expansion of

---

68. Source: *World Development Report 1989*, World Bank, Washington, D.C., 1989, pp. 192–3.

national creativity and to accede to foreign production. In this sense copyright plays a preponderant role since it contributes decisively to the achievement of both objectives, which do not conflict with one another even when at first glance they may seem to do.

Failure to protect foreign works leads to the relegation of national works, it creates unfair competition since it is unlikely that producers will be inclined to pay for the use of the work of a local author when they can use foreign works freely, and it retards the process of increased awareness of the respect due to authors and to their rights, and of the economic and cultural benefits which they provide.

In many developing countries, national activities involving copyright are of importance in several areas such as education, music (especially folklore, indigenous rhythmic forms and popular music) and television; and even in the technological field, particularly as regards computer programs made to individual customer specifications, where there are considerable opportunities for individual creativity. The lack of suitable conditions for their development—including failure to protect authors' rights—results in the emigration of creators from their home countries to centres which offer them the chance of obtaining the economic rewards and the dissemination of their works which they merit. This situation also slows down the development of cultural industries, since it discourages the holders of rights in foreign works from authorizing their reproduction and dissemination in territories which do not offer legal guarantees, depriving the labour force of sources of work, and the taxation authorities of revenue. Fundamentally it restricts the community's possibilities of participating in the wealth created by the production and circulation of cultural products and from finding identity and fulfilment in the works of their creators.

Chapter 2

The subject matter of copyright

Summary

2.1. General criteria
    2.1.1. Copyright protects formal creations and not ideas. **2.1.2.** Originality, a necessary condition for protection. **2.1.3.** Criteria which are not relevant to recognition of protection: value, intended use, form of expression. **2.1.4.** The absence of formalities in copyright protection (with the exception of certain countries)

2.2. Protected works
    2.2.1. Original works. 2.2.1.1. Literary works. 2.2.1.2. Musical works. 2.2.1.3. Theatrical works. 2.2.1.4. Artistic works. 2.2.1.5. Scientific works. 2.2.1.6. Audiovisual works. 2.2.1.7. Works of national folklore. 2.2.1.8. New categories of works: computer programs (arguments for and against copyright protection). **2.2.2.** Derivative works. 2.2.2.1. Adaptations. 2.2.2.2. Translations. 2.2.2.3. Compilations and databases. 2.2.2.4. Anthologies. 2.2.2.5. Annotations and commentaries. 2.2.2.6. Arrangements and orchestrations. 2.2.2.7. Parodies. **2.2.3.** The title

The subject matter of copyright protection is the work. For copyright purposes, a *work* is the personal expression of the intellect in developing a thought which is manifested in a perceptible form, has sufficient originality or individuality and is suitable for public communication and transformation.

2.1. General criteria

The protection of the work is subject to the following general criteria:
- copyright protects formal creations and not ideas;
- originality (or individuality) is a necessary condition for protection;
- protection does not depend on the value or merit of the work, on its intended use or on its form of expression;
- protection is not subject to the performance of formalities.

2.1.1. Copyright protects formal creations and not ideas

Since the earliest studies on the subject, there has been widespread agreement that copyright protects only formal creations and not the ideas contained in works. Ideas are not works, and, hence, their use is free. It is not possible to acquire any form of protection or ownership over them, even when they possess novelty.

Copyright is designed to protect the form of representation, the externalization of its development in material works suitable for reproduction, performance, exhibition, broadcasting, and so on, according to the category to which they belong, and to regulate their use. Protection is given only to the *perceptible form* in which the idea is manifested and not the idea itself, whether expressed schematically or in a work. Copyright protects the form in which the development of thought is expressed, granting the creator exclusive rights of an economic character to the reproduction and public communication of the work, and rights of a personal character.

Copyright defends the creation of works. If exclusive rights were to be granted for ideas considered in themselves, their dissemination would be obstructed; this would prevent the development of intellectual creativity and, as Villalba states, would hamper the creation of an infinite quantity of different works. The same idea, the same research effort, the same subject are reworked over and over again in many ways. Each author, in developing it, imprints it with the special mark of his personality, his individuality. The result may sometimes be extremely enriching, and it may sometimes be trivial. But what enables each generation to contribute to the slow journey forward of civilization, is the possibility of working on what already exists, of continuing this journey without having to go back to the beginning.

The inadvisability of granting exclusive rights to ideas becomes clear if we consider, for example, that, as has been asserted by one author,[1] there are only 36 basic dramatic situations and it follows—a singular corollary—that there are only 36 emotions.

---

1. See Georges Polti, *Thirty-six Dramatic Situations*, N.Y. Writer, 1921.

For the sake of brevity we will reproduce only some of them. Situation number 1: *The entreaty* (indispensable dynamic features: a persecutor, a supplicant and an irresolute power); Situation 2: *The rescuer* (the unfortunate character, the threatening character and the rescuer); Situation 3: *Vengeance in pursuit of the criminal* (the avenger and the culprit); Situation 4: *Revenge taken by one relative on another* (Remembrance of the victimized relative, the avenging relative and the guilty relative); ... Situation 8: *Rebellion* (tyrant and conspirator); ... Situation 10: *Abduction* (abductor, victim of abduction and guardian); ... Situation 14: *Rivalry between relatives* (favourite relative, rejected relative and the subject of the rivalry); ... Situation 16: *Madness* (the madman and the victim); ... Situation 18: *Involuntary crime of love* (the lover, the loved one and the person who betrays them); ... Situation 22: *Sacrificing everything to passion* (the enamoured person, the object of the fatal passion and the sacrificed party); ... Situation 25: *Adultery* (the betrayed husband, the adulterous husband and the accomplice in adultery); ... Situation 27: *Learning of the dishonour of a loved one* (the person who makes the discovery and the culprit); Situation 28: *Thwarted love affairs* (first lover, second lover and the obstacle); ... Situation 30: *Ambition* (the ambitious character, his goal and the adversary); ... Situation 33: *Judicial error* (he who commits the error, he who is the victim, he who misleads, and the real culprit); ... and so forth.

How, then, would it be possible to recognize an author's exclusivity over the idea of structuring his work on the basis of a given human conflict? Not only is it possible to use the ideas pure and simple that are found in someone else's work, but also other elements taken in themselves, such as isolated events, concepts, the subject, the system, the method, the literary style, the literary form, the artistic manner, the vocabulary, etc. On the other hand, *it is illicit to take the whole set of elements which reflect the work's individuality.*

However, ideas may have great commercial and also artistic value. The appropriation of someone else's idea can cause injury which, if not repaired, could give rise to an unjust situation. In these cases it should be remembered that the fact that copyright does not protect ideas, for precise reasons, does not mean that such a situation should necessarily lack remedies. The obligation to make reparation can be found in other institutions of private law, such as unjust enrichment and unfair competition. The offence may even involve the criminal area if it can be qualified as violation of secrecy.

Practical application or industrial exploitation
Neither does copyright protect the creator in regard to the *practical application* or *industrial exploitation* of the idea or content of an intellectual work. These do not require his prior authorization. The author of a financial plan, for example, can prevent the reproduction of the literary work in which he describes and develops it, but not the application of the plan in commerce and industry, because practical use of it is free.

This criterion applies to every type of work, including those which refer to the organization of companies, educational syllabuses, advertising systems, games, and so on. The author of a book about chess moves or a collection of cookery recipes can prevent the work from being reproduced without his authorization but he cannot prevent chess players from applying his techniques, even in public competitions with cash prizes, or cooks from using his recipes in the home and even in commercial establishments. The author of a game or a recipe book has the monopoly of the disclosure of the text of the work in which he makes them known, explains them and develops them, but he does not have the exclusivity of the practice of the game or of cooking in accordance with his recipes.

With respect to the ideas contained in scientific works, the Inter-American Convention on the Rights of the Author in Literary, Scientific and Artistic Works, signed in Washington (1946), provides in its Article IV, paragraph 3, that 'The protection provided by the present Convention does not include protection of the industrial utilization of scientific ideas'. The protection which copyright affords covers the use of works by means of their publication, dissemination and reproduction. It is the function of industrial property laws—patents, industrial designs and models —to protect the *practical application* or the *industrial use* of the intellectual concepts, but not the publication, dissemination and reproduction of their description and illustration, which are the subject of copyright. These are two distinct and unconnected areas of protection.

2.1.2. Originality, a necessary condition for protection

In the area of copyright, originality resides in the creative and individualized expression—or representative form—of the work, however minimal such creativity and individuality may be. No work may be protected unless this minimum exists. The work is not required to possess novelty, unlike the situation in the case of inventions where novelty is a requirement for acceding to the protection afforded by patent rights. The invention must be new in the objective sense, which means that the applicant must be the first to present the invention for patenting.

Works may also possess novelty, but copyright does not require novelty as a necessary condition for protection. It is sufficient for the work to have originality or individuality: in other words, for it *to express something of the author's own character, for it to bear the mark of his personality*. Originality is a subjective notion; some authors prefer to use the term *individuality* instead of originality, considering that it expresses more accurately the condition imposed by the right in order for the work to enjoy protection: that it should have something of the author's own individuality and character about it.

The assessment of originality should not be the same in a case of unauthorized reproduction on a commercial scale (piracy) as in a charge of plagiarism. If it is claimed that the work is not protected because it lacks originality, in the first instance this should be assessed on the basis of a very broad criterion; account should be taken of the fact that although the expression of individuality may be minimum, the requirement is met. In the second instance a restrictive criterion must be used, since it will be necessary to determine if there is a recognizable identity of expression between the two works, if both are, substantially, the same formal representation.[2]

---

2. See E. Piola Caselli, op. cit., p. 628, who warns against the danger of legislation giving in to the pressure of writers, scientists and artists, with their *genus*

Determining whether a work is original is a question of fact. Originality cannot be appraised in the same way for scientific or technical works as for works of literary fiction, for items of popular music as for symphonic works, for original works as for derivative works.

In copyright, the term *creation* does not have the usual meaning of pulling something out of the void and the originality of a work does not have to be absolute. The author's inspiration does not have to be free of all external influences. The ideas used in the work can be old ones and the work nevertheless be original, since, we repeat, copyright allows intellectual creation to be based on pre-existing elements. All that is required is that the work should be distinct from its predecessors and not a copy or imitation of another.

Even in the case of derivative works, given that they are the result of the transformation of pre-existing works (adaptations, translations, revisions, updatings, annotations, compilations, summaries, extracts, musical arrangements, anthologies, and so on), they should express some degree of creativity and be the fruit of the author's personal effort.

2.1.3. Criteria which are not relevant to recognition of protection: value, intended use, form of expression

The cultural or artistic *value* of the work—its merit—does not count in order for it to benefit from the protection which is afforded by copyright.

It is a question of taste and, hence, a matter for the public and critics, not the law. Otherwise the result might be a host of arbitrary decisions, especially in an area in which examples abound of great works which, when first performed or shown were booed but which, with the passing of time, gained considerable recognition and prestige. This was the case of Verdi's *La Traviata*, Pirandello's

---

irritabile, and consenting to bring its heavy guns to bear in an attempt to hit the target of small-scale partial imitations, appropriations of the simple ideas of other people and hidden copies of inorganic scraps of other people's intellectual works.

Six Characters in Search of an Author, Stravinsky's *The Rite of Spring*, among others.

It should be borne in mind here that value or merit on the one hand and originality on the other are two different concepts. In the case of legal controversy, the judge must make sure that the work contains the mark of the author's personality so that the requirement of originality may be satisfied, without protection hingeing in any way on the value which may be attributed to the work.

The work is protected whether it is *intended* for a cultural or a utilitarian purpose. This point is especially pertinent in regard to works of art or science applied to commerce or industry. The fact that a drawing or any other artistic work has been produced for commercial or industrial activity does not deprive such works of the protection of copyright against reproduction and, in general, against unauthorized use.

The question has also been raised in respect of guides, catalogues, almanacs, year books, directories, advertising messages and slogans, collections of cookery recipes, advertisements, prospectuses, commercial circulars, and charts and diagrams, which may have cultural, scientific, commercial or financial purposes. The same holds for computer programs and for software as well which almost always have a utilitarian purpose.

Neither does the *form of expression* of the work have any bearing. For the purposes of copyright protection, the fact that the work is expressed in written or oral form, has been performed, or fixed on a sound or video tape is irrelevant. Neither does the form in which the work is disseminated or communicated to the public have any bearing.

2.1.4. The absence of formalities in copyright protection (with the exception of certain countries)

Protection is not subject to the compliance with formalities. Creation is the original entitlement to copyright. Unlike industrial property rights, copyright stems from the act of creation and not from recognition by an administrative authority. The main purpose of copyright is the protection of authors, while in industrial property rights, it is the rights of the community that are put first.

The *compulsory registration* of the work as a condition governing enjoyment of the right—or registration to establish the right—was something left over from the days of privileges; it was maintained in certain countries because of the erroneous assimilation with industrial property rights (especially patent and trademark rights). As the differences between copyright and industrial property rights grew gradually clearer, constitutive registration of works was abandoned under the law. Mention should be made here of the beneficial influence of the Berne Convention; in its first revision (Berlin, 1908), all conditions concerning the performance of formalities were abolished ('the enjoyment and the exercise of these rights shall not be subject to the performance of any formality').

The registration obligation as a necessary prior condition for the establishment and existence of copyright or a requirement for its exercise survives currently in a few countries only.[3]

2.2. Protected works

Copyright protects all types of intellectual works. Traditionally, protection is reserved for so-called intellectual creations of form: *original* works, in the sense of original or primogenial creations (literary, musical, theatrical or dramatic, artistic, scientific and audiovisual and also, for some time now, computer programs) and *derivative* works (adaptations, translations, compilations, annotations and commentaries, summaries and extracts, musical arrangements and other transformations) regardless of their mode or form of expression, although to claim protection they must be original, i.e. reflect originality or individuality.

Legislation on the subject usually includes, for illustrative purposes, a non-restrictive *list of examples* of protected works. To make clear that such lists are not subject to *numerus clausus*, they usually begin with the expressions 'such as' or 'particularly' or other similar phrases and they often conclude by stating 'and all

---

3. See below, Chapter 10, Section 10.2.

literary, scientific and artistic production, regardless of the procedure of publication and reproduction' or a comparable expression. Sometimes these lists are very detailed, as in the case of Brazil (Articles 6 and 7).

2.2.1. Original works

The term *original works* is habitually used to designate works of original creation or primogenial *works* and to distinguish them from works *derived* from them (translations, adaptations and other transformations). But this term may become confused with the attribute of originality which all works should reflect—both pre-existing works and those derived from them—in order to enjoy copyright protection, for which reason it makes for greater clarity to term the former *works of original creation*—or primogenial, pre-existing, initial or first-hand works.

In the creative process of a literary work three basic stages may be distinguished: first, the author conceives the *idea* of the work, then he draws up the plan of its development and its *composition*, and finally, he *expresses* it. Given that the originality of the idea does not count, since it does not enjoy legal protection, considered in itself, a work can be original in its *composition* or content or in its *expression* or form. In copyright works are deemed to be *absolutely* original when they are original both in their composition and their expression.

In the production of a literary work, the form in which the author carries it out is immaterial; he may write it by hand, type it on a typewriter or a word processor, or dictate it for subsequent transcription by another person. The same holds for the composition of a musical work.

On the other hand, artistic works, or works in the category of the visual arts, are characterized by a particular condition in regard to their originality: in their case, the personal execution of the work by the artist is of decisive importance.

Derivative works are considered to possess *relative* originality. They may be original only in their composition, as in the case of anthologies, in which protection is given to the selection of works or parts of work of other authors; they may be original only in their expression, as in the case of translations.

2.2.1.1. *Literary works*

Literary works are expressed in writing. They can also be expressed in oral form.

A. WRITTEN WORKS

a. Protected

Protection is granted on the basis of a broad criterion. As well as traditional literary works (poems, novels, short stories, scientific, instructional and technical works, and so on), protection is granted to advertising slogans, directories, almanacs, yearbooks, forms, charts and diagrams, pamphlets, catalogues, albums, compilations of cookery recipes, and so on, which, because of the selection and arrangement of the material contained in them, represent an intellectual effort meriting copyright protection inasmuch as it possesses some degree of originality or individuality distinguishing it from that which already exists.

Protection is also granted to letters. The following distinction has to be made between the copyright belonging to the author of the text of the letter whose authorization is necessary for its publication and the rights of the addressee in respect of both the document which belongs to him as a physical object and the secrecy of the correspondence. The latter factor constitutes a barrier for the free exercise by the author of the right of disclosure. The rights of the addressee are not of a copyright nature.

The breadth of criteria in the definition of literary works has made it possible to include computer programs among them, as has occurred in the United States.[4]

---

4. The United States Copyright Act enacted in 1976 defines, in Section 101, literary works as 'works, other than audio-visual works, expressed in words, numbers, or other verbal or numerical symbols or indicia, regardless of the nature of the material objects, such as books, periodicals, manuscripts, phonorecords, film, tapes, discs, or cards, in which they are embodied'. Law No. 96-517 of 2 December 1980 modified Section 101, adding, at the end, the definition of a computer program.

European Union Directive 91/250/CEE lays down that Member States shall protect computer programs, by copyright, as literary works within the meaning of the Berne Convention. For the purposes of the Directive, the term 'computer programs' shall include their preparatory design material (Article 1).

For its part, the TRIPS Agreement (on Trade-Related Aspects of Intellectual Property Rights) of the World Trade Organization (WTO) provides (Art. 10(1)) that computer programs, whether in source or object code, shall be protected as literary works under the Berne Convention (1971 Act).

b. Non-protected

In general, official texts, news of the day and press information are excluded from copyright protection. *Official texts* are considered to be all compulsory legal provisions: laws, decrees, regulations, bylaws, resolutions, etc. They may be original works but what is important is the need to encourage their free dissemination and reproduction so that there can be no pretext for non-compliance with them by claiming ignorance of the law.

The Berne Convention authorizes legislations to provide for the total or partial exclusion from protection of official texts of a legislative, administrative and legal nature and of official translations of such texts (Art. 2(4), Paris Act). In the Convention the non-protection of these texts is defined as a *copyright limitation* whose adoption in domestic law is left to the discretion of the national legislators.

There are, for the same reasons, free dissemination and reproduction of official studies in the preparation of legal provisions, reports and so on carried out by the State (at national, provincial or municipal level), parliamentary debates, and decisions of the judicial and administrative authorities. Official translations of these texts are also excluded from protection. If the translation concerned is not official, then it enjoys protection. Protection is also granted to summaries of rulings and their compilations which possess originality in terms of the selection and arrangement of the contents.

The *news of the day* and *press information* excluded from protection concern brief news items. As a rule they lack originality in their composition and expression. The main concern of the journalist is to transmit news of events as quickly as possible. Although the production of news entails huge costs, the protection of the public's right of access to information is a prime factor in their free dissemination; this does not, however, imply that there are no other available means of defence against abuses, i.e. legislation against unfair competition.

On the other hand, articles of substance, whether they concern current affairs or not, newspaper reports, editorials and commentaries are protected by copyright on condition that they are original, in the same way as other works. They represent an effort of analysis and opinion which reflects the author's personality.

Under the Berne Convention, the news of the day and miscellaneous facts having the character of mere items of press information are expressly excluded from protection (Paris Act, 1971, Article 2 (8)). News items are also excluded under the Inter-American Convention on the Rights of the Author, 1946 (Article 6, 3) in which it is stated that: 'The present Convention shall not give protection to the factual content of news published in newspapers.'

B. ORAL WORKS

Works communicated to the public in oral form are protected by copyright. The creative process and the effort of expression which they require are similar to those of written works. They reflect the personality of their author and originality appears both in the composition and the expression. For these reasons, examples of oral works are habitually cited in the list of protected works contained in national legislation.

Protection is also given to lessons which are given in the context of educational activities. Accordingly, the notes which students take during lessons cannot be reproduced without the teacher's express authorization, regardless of the means used (copying, printing, etc.). This includes the tape recording of the lesson while it takes place because, as a consequence of technological progress, the fixation by means of equipment for recording sound, images, or images and sound is considered to be an entitlement forming part of the author's exclusive right of reproduction.

Oral works are also mentioned in the Berne Convention, where examples of protected works include lectures, addresses, sermons and other works of the same nature (Paris Act, 1971, Article 2, para. (1)).

2.2.1.2. Musical works

Music is the art of combining the sounds of the human voice or of instruments, or of one and the other at the same time, stirring the emotions. Musical works include every type of original combination of sounds, with or without words. The elements constituting musical works are *melody*, *harmony* and *rhythm*.

Melody is the very general notion which refers, broadly speaking, to all the possible relationships of sounds in successive order. It is a coherent series of notes. It is the theme forming the basis for the development of the musical work, simple or compound, independently of the accompaniment.

Harmony is the combination of notes sounded *simultaneously* in agreement or consonance.

Rhythm is the sensation produced by the relations of relative duration of different consecutive sounds or of the repercussion or repetition of the same tone or sound.

The originality of musical works stems from the combination of their constitutive elements. However, it may reside either in the melody, in the harmony or, again, in the rhythm.

Notwithstanding this, for copyright purposes exclusive rights can only be obtained over the melody. It is equivalent to the *composition* or the *development* of the idea in literary works, and not to the idea itself. The melody is a formal creation. Exclusive rights cannot be obtained in respect of harmony because it is made up of chords, the number of which is limited. Neither can they apply to rhythm, because it would not be logical to grant exclusive rights in respect of the bolero, the mazurka, the samba, the bossa nova or the gavotte, any more than it would be in the case of literary genres—poetry, the novel, the short story, drama or comedy—for which such rights cannot be obtained.

The same melody can be harmonized in different ways and its rhythm changed. To be able to recognize it, when changes have been made to the harmony or rhythm (or both) of a musical composition, an understanding of music is required; the work will sound very different, even though the melody is still the same. Accordingly, unless he or she is a musician, the judge will have to seek expert advice to establish plagiarism of the melody when other elements of the musical work have been changed. In turn, plagiarism of a musical work exists only if there has been appropriation of its melody, its specifically original element.

In spite of the enormous influence of musical works, their omnipresence, the economic importance of their exploitation and the fact that all national and international laws expressly cite musical compositions, with or without words, in the list of protected works, they nevertheless fail to appear among the expressions whereby legal provisions indicate the subject matter of protection. The various legal provisions habitually refer to 'literary and artistic works', to 'literary, scientific and artistic works', and so on, but without mentioning their musical counterparts.

In seeking an explanation for such a striking omission, Uchtenhagen quite rightly pointed out that in the last century—and above all during the period when the Berne Union was founded (1886)—it was the protection of literary works which was the focus of interest. But later years brought the invention of the gramophone record, radio, television, 'talking' films, audiovisual recording, cable networks and satellite transmissions. Although literature retained its predominant cultural importance, it was gradually forced to give way to music as the overwhelming driving force in the development of copyright.[5]

2.2.1.3. *Theatrical works*

Theatrical works are works which are intended to be performed. The meaning of the word *theatre* is somewhat ambiguous. The Greeks used it first not only for the semi-circular tiers of seats

---

5. Ulrich Uchtenhagen, *La protección de las obras musicales,* Libro Memoria, *4th International Congress on the Protection of Intellectual Property*, Guatemala, 1989, pp. 97–106.

from which the audience watched (*theaomai*: I see) the dramatic performance but also for the audience itself. Then it was extended to the entire building used for the performance, as, in Athens, 'the theatre of Dionysius'. Later it came to mean the literary or musical work which was performed, as in 'the theatre of Alfieri', in other words, his tragedies, 'the theatre of Verdi', or his operas. Lastly it was adopted to indicate any form of performance or show (from *spectare*, to watch). Broadly speaking, the theatre could be defined as the communion of an audience with a *living performance*.[6]

Dramatic works, dramatico-musical works, choreographic works and entertainment in dumb shows are theatrical works. The expression 'dramatic work' includes both tragedy and comedy, reviews, comic sketches, vaudeville shows and any other variety of dramatic form. The word drama comes from the Greek '*dran*' which means to do, to act, and continues to be employed, as in antiquity, *to designate any literary form intended for stage performance*. The stage performance of a dramatic work constitutes a *theatrical show*.

Some laws (Brazil, Art. 6(IV); France, Art. L. 112. 2–4, previously Art. 3; Italy, Art. 2(3); Netherlands, Art. 10(4)) make the protection of choreographic works and entertainment in dumb show conditional on the *fixation* of their performance in writing or some other form.[7] This is because these dramatic forms are not habitually expressed by any system of notation.

This requirement is noteworthy in the context of laws which recognize that copyright exists by virtue of the sole act of creation, without being subject to the performance of formalities. The reason for this exception is founded on practical requirements: if the choreographic work or entertainment in dumb show are not fixed

---

6. See Silvio D'Amico, *Historia del teatro universal*, Buenos Aires, Losada, 1954, pp. 9–17.
7. The French law of 3 July 1985 imposes the same requirement on circus numbers and shows.

in any form, the author would find it impossible to prove what the work consists of. But the same can be said of oral works and these are not subject to the fixation requirement (neither would this be desirable). Fixation always facilitates proof of the work, but its omission does not constitute sufficient reason to validate uses made without the author's authorization.

It is not consistent for copyright protection to be granted on the basis of the fixation when protection is founded on the act of creation and recognized by virtue of that act.

2.2.1.4. Artistic works

Works of art affect the aesthetic sense of those who regard them. They include paintings, drawings, engravings, sculpture, photographs and architecture.

Some laws also mention original graphic characteristics (Mexico, Article 26) or the typographical arrangement of published editions (United Kingdom, Section 1(1)(c)). No enumeration of these works may be regarded as restrictive. In addition to copyright, some of the works mentioned enjoy protection under other laws, as we shall see when dealing with works of applied art.

Artistic works are protected irrespective of the materials and techniques employed. Originality, in regard to this subject matter, has particular connotations. The sketches and preliminary models which precede the work and by means of which the artist prepares his *composition,* constitute, in themselves, protected works.

In the *expression* of the work, the artist uses lines, colours, forms and materials. *Personal execution is of decisive importance*, unlike the case of literary and musical works, where the fact that the author may write out by hand, type or prepare a musical score on his own is immaterial.

In portraits, landscapes, still lifes, several artists may faithfully reproduce the same model and, despite this, all these works will be original and will be equally protected. In spite of their similarity, in each one each artist, through his handiwork, will leave the mark of his personality.

The proprietary right in the physical object (the painting, the carving, etc.), although it may constitute a single example, does not imply ownership of the copyright in the artistic work. These are two distinct and independent rights.[8]

Consequently, the alienation of a picture, sculpture, photograph or work included in the visual arts in general, does not, unless expressly stipulated otherwise, implicitly include the right of reproduction, which remains vested in the author or his successors in title; any reproduction of an artistic work—including its embodiment in an object in current use—must be authorized by its author or by the person who is the owner of this right, whoever may be the owner of the material object. Exception is made of *incidental* reproductions (a person is photographed in the place where the work of art is located); reproductions for the purpose of information regarding events of public interest (photographs are taken of the place at which a ceremony or an exhibition of works of art is held); and reproductions of works which are the property of the public authorities and are exhibited in public places.[9]

Neither can the owner of the physical object which contains the work—in the absence of a contractual stipulation or legal authorization—make it available for public exhibition (this is authorized, for example, in Germany, under Article 44(2) and Spain, Article 56(2), unless the author has expressly excluded this right in transferring the original).

In the case of artistic works again, even though they may exist as single examples, neither the alienation of the physical support nor the total transfer of the copyright in the work signify, for the creator, the transfer or loss of his *moral right*. In these cases, the artist retains both the right to claim paternity of the work—being entitled to demand that his name appears on it and on all its reproductions—and the right to its integrity—being entitled to oppose any deformation, mutilation or act which he deems

---

8. Principle of the independence of copyright vis-à-vis ownership of the material object: for example, France, Art. L. III-3, previously Art. 29; Spain, Art. 56; Brazil, Art. 38; Ecuador, Art. 3; Portugal, Art 10.1; Peru, Art. 5; Venezuela, Art. 1.2; etc.
9. See below, Chapter 4.

prejudicial to his honour or his reputation. After the death of the author, these rights can be exercised in the same way as those relating to other classes of works.

A. ARCHITECTURE

Works of architecture protected by copyright consist of both buildings and similar constructions, and the projects, designs, sketches, plans and preliminary models serving as the basis for the construction work. Copyright protects them as original formal creations. On the other hand, it does not protect the architectural methods or the purely technical procedures. Originality may be found in the form of the construction, in the design or in the ornaments.

The authors of works of architecture enjoy moral and economic rights. In relation to moral rights, they can demand that their name be placed on the façade of the building and on related constructions (right of *paternity*). The right to the *integrity* of the work is an extremely delicate matter. On the one hand, it is reasonable that the owner of the building should be able to carry out certain modifications *of a practical or technical order* which are necessary for its use. On the other hand, it is also reasonable that the author of the work should have the right to prohibit any distortion, mutilation, modification or other derogatory action in respect of the said work which might prove prejudicial to his honour or reputation. If, despite the author's prohibition or without his consent, the modification or derogatory action takes place, it is likewise reasonable that the person responsible should be obliged to restore the work to its former state, or to pay damages, according to the circumstances of the case. In the latter instance, the author has the right to demand that his name be dissociated from the work. The crux of the matter resides in the relation which exists between the character and substance of the modifications and the author's right to the integrity of the work.

As regards economic rights, the author of a work of architecture has the exclusive right of authorizing its reproduction in any form and medium. The reproduction of these works includes both the construction of another work of architecture which is similar to it in some or all of its original features, and the preparation of plans, preliminary models, etc., on their basis. In turn, the reproduction of such plans and models includes the making of copies thereof, as well as their use for the construction of buildings.

B. SCULPTURE

Sculpture is expressed in three-dimensional forms. It can be undertaken by carving, moulding, casting or using any other type of procedure, irrespective of the material employed (stone, metal, wood, clay, cement, synthetic materials, etc.). Sculptures are also those structures formed with pre-existing three-dimensional objects, as well as statues and high and low reliefs which form part of an architectural work.

Sculptures present special problems because of the possibility of obtaining copies of them by means of a plaster or terra-cotta mould which is then handed over by the artist for casting using the *cire-perdue* process (earth or sand may also be used). The caster reproduces the work in wax and this is touched up by the artist. The wax is then covered with refractory materials and liquid metal (bronze, aluminium, tin, copper, etc.) is poured into the cavity. Once the metal has cooled and the outer material has been removed, the metal sculpture remains. This technique makes it possible to obtain one or a number of copies or sculptures.

The problem is: which is the original sculpture, the mould or the copies which are obtained from it? It is considered that the mould is not the sculpture, even though it is protected in itself as an original work and is the subject of much interest among collectors—possessing, as it does, commercial value—because it was created for the specific function of making other copies.

The techniques which make it possible to obtain several sculptures from the same mould give rise to a special problem: can all the copies which are obtained from this mould be considered original works, or only some of them; in this case, which ones, and up to what number? The solution is not to be found in copyright laws.

In France, the matter was solved by means of a tax provision[10] which considers as originals the castings of sculptures limited to a series of eight pieces and marked by the artist or his successors in title. As well as these eight pieces there are the '*exemplaires dits d'artiste*' (artist's copies) of which there are usually three or four. They should bear the mention EA (*épreuve d'artiste* or artist's proof) or HC (*hors commerce* or not for general sale).

This text is applicable when the artist has not limited the series himself, since artists usually do this by marking the copies with a fraction, the numerator indicating the particular piece and the denominator the total number of copies of the work (e.g. 4/7 designates the fourth work in a total of seven). According to Dumas, a tax administration concession permits, exceptionally, an increase in the limited series to 12 copies, such limited series being considered as originals benefiting from a special tax regime.

How should we consider sculptures obtained by successors in title from a mould created by an artist whose death prevented him from completing the work himself? As an original work? This matter gives rise to conflicting positions.

For those who consider that the artist's personal participation in the retouching of the wax copy is decisive in order for the sculptures to be considered original, then they are not originals. On the other hand, according to Dumas, the French Cour de Cassation (Supreme Court of Appeal) considered that since the heirs and successors in title were entitled to decide on posthumous publication (right of disclosure of posthumous works) why should they not, in the same way, put into effect the practical modalities for exercising this right?[11]

However, we understand that even in these particular cases it is necessary to record, on the copy, the fact that it was made after the author's death, with an indication of those who authorized it and took part in its execution.

---

10. Code général des Impôts (Decree of 10 June 1967), Article 71, Annex III, quoted by Roland Dumas, *La propriété littéraire et artistique*, Paris, Presses Universitaires de France, 1987, pp. 93–4.
11. *Champin* versus *SPADEM* case. See Roland Dumas, op. cit., pp. 94–6.

Similar questions may also arise in relation to *engravings* (etching, aquatint, halftone, dry-point, xylography, lithography, etc.). Some engravings are made by means of incisions, usually shallow, on a certain material (metal, wood, stone), generally on the basis of a sketch. Engravings may be coloured.

The plates are usually engraved for the purpose of printing copies of the work created by means of the incising process. Since the original work is the print which is obtained from the engraved plate there is a marked similarity, in connection with the problems arising in regard to sculpture, between the mould of the sculpture and the sculpture on the one hand and between the engraved plate and the engraving or print on the other.

C. DRAWINGS

A drawing is a delineation, figure or picture executed in chiaroscuro, usually taking the name of the material with which it is done (pencil, ink, charcoal, and so on). In general, the artist also uses the drawing technique in the composition of other artistic works (painting, sculpture, etc.); these sketches or preliminary essays are, in themselves, works of drawing protected as such.

D. PAINTINGS

A painting is an artistic work expressed in lines and/or colours by the application of coloured substances on a surface. It can be executed with the use of watercolours, oil, pastel, tempera, acrylic, enamel or fresco methods or by combining two or more procedures—mixed techniques. It can be made on textiles, on an outer or inner wall or on any other material which proves suitable.

Complex and controversial problems arise in connection with copies of pre-existing paintings (and of artistic works in general). In general terms, they are considered to be protected.

But, if the pre-existing painting has been disclosed (and while it has not fallen into the public domain), is it lawful for an artist, art student or art-lover to make a copy intended strictly for personal use (for example, for study or as a practical exercise)?

Put in these terms, it seems reasonable to answer affirmatively, provided that the copy is not used for purposes identical to those for which the pre-existing work was created.

When the personality of the copyist is manifested in the copy, it would not be fair to deny him copyright protection, although this, of course, does not authorize him to attribute it to the author of the pre-existing work (falsification).

It should always be made clear that it is a copy, with an indication of the name of the author, the title of the original work and the name of the author of the copy.

But should slavish copies also be protected? Desbois answers affirmatively, because he considers that the personality of the copyist is necessarily manifested and that this is sufficient to allow copyright protection.[12]

Inasmuch as the copy inevitably represents the pre-existing work, it should be considered as a derivative work. However, this does not apply when the artist has simply drawn inspiration from another work.[13]

E. PHOTOGRAPHS

A photograph is a still picture produced on a surface sensitive to light or other radiation, irrespective of the technical nature of the process (chemical, electronic or other) used to take it (see the definition contained in UNESCO/WIPO Principle PHW1,1).[14]

The status of the photograph has long been the subject of debate. Many felt that it was the result of a mechanical process performed by the camera, and they resisted its recognition as a work and its consequent protection by copyright. However, the final conclusion was that photography should be regarded as art.

---

12. See Henri Desbois, *Le droit d'auteur en France*, Paris, Dalloz, third edition, 1978, pp. 73–4.
13. The great painters provide obvious examples such as—among many others —Picasso's *Portrait of Góngora* after El Greco (1541–1614), *David and Bathsheba* and *Portrait of a Woman* after Lucas Cranach the Younger (1472–1553). These works by Picasso are originals even though the sources of inspiration, indicated by the artist himself, can be recognized.
14. Document UNESCO/WIPO/CGE/SYN/3-11 Add., 17 May 1988, Principle PHW1 (1).

The photographer chooses the sensitive material which he is going to use, he observes, he chooses the subject, he frames or composes the image, seeks the best angle, measures the light, prepares the camera and takes several shots, from the same angle or from various angles. He uses a number of techniques, such as multiple exposure of a single negative, by which means he constructs a story in a given framework, 'producing' the picture of those involved in the event which he seeks to portray. Sometimes he works on the basis of a sketch or drawing of the scene before beginning to take the photographs.

There are also many 'snapshots' taken both by professional and amateur photographers, in which the photographer has done nothing more than focus and press the shutter-release; in spite of this the picture may have as much—or even more—artistic value as a carefully prepared photograph.

In his laboratory the photographer uses chemical substances, obtains negatives, observes each shot, evaluates their expressive qualities and aesthetic value, analyses their quality under a magnifying glass and develops prints; he also retouches photographs, accentuates details and effects, or enlarges pictures in different forms. He can use special effects such as photomontage, superimposing techniques, the interruption of the development process with a flash of light, achieving a strange colour effect ('solarization'), and so on. There are a considerable number of stages before the final result is achieved.

Photographs which possess originality in regard to their setting or composition, or any other important pictorial element are, without any shadow of doubt, entitled to copyright protection in the same way as other works of art. However, the problem arises when trying to decide on the protection merited by the vast majority of photographs which are taken and developed every day in a virtually mechanical way, and which are totally lacking in originality.

A number of countries have chosen to make the application of copyright subject to conditions concerning, for example, the choice of subject matter or the way in which the photographs have been executed as deciding factors in considering them as artistic works (Brazil, Art. 6.VII) or requiring that they possess an artistic or documentary character (France, Art. 3 prior to the 1985 reform, Senegal, Art. 1.11 and Côte d'Ivoire, Art. 5.11).

However, in the light of these provisions it may well be asked if, when a certain photograph fails to qualify for protection under them, it is legitimate to allow its free use. If someone chooses to reproduce it, regardless of the medium and the purpose, a reason must exist, obviously linked to the interest which the work creates; it follows that the person who finds it attractive enough to make use of it is precisely the one who is least able to invoke its banal character.

In Germany (Art. 72.3), a photographic work is protected to the same extent as other works if it constitutes a document of contemporary historical value, but if it does not fall within this category, it enjoys a shorter term of protection. Spain provides that authors of 'ordinary photographs' (or other reproductions obtained by a comparable process), when neither the one nor the other has the character of a protected work, enjoy the exclusive right to authorize their reproduction, distribution and communication to the public, under the same conditions as are recognized to the authors of 'photographic works'. This right, however, has a term of 25 years from the making of the photograph (Art. 118; this period bears a relation to the provisions of Art. 7(4) of the Paris Act (1971) of the Berne Convention).

In other countries as well, separate regulations exist in the case of simple photographs, for which a *neighbouring right* is recognized (Austria, Italy).

Although these criteria may be criticized for making the scope of copyright dependent on a concept which is inconsistent with recognition of protection—whether or not the photograph has artistic value or merit—they have the advantage of preventing futile discussions when there is clear interest in its use by a third party.

In most copyright laws, photographs are included among protected works, without subjecting them to particular conditions.

One current of opinion, however, advocates their regulation by a specific law. This criterion has prevailed in the Nordic countries (Norway, Sweden, Finland and Denmark) which have chosen to establish special legislation concerning photographic pictures.

F. Applied arts — the possibility of double protection

A creation can be an artistic work and, at the same time, perform a useful or ornamental function in a material thing. Works of applied art are artistic creations with utilitarian functions or incorporated in utilitarian articles, whether handicrafted or produced on an industrial scale. Under which legal regime should they be given protection?

In the case of artistic works, they are protected by copyright. The author enjoys the right in such works as a result of the sole act of creation, without the performance of formalities, for a relatively long term (in general, as long as he lives plus 50 years in favour of his heirs and successors in title).

In the case of a work which performs utilitarian and ornamental functions, protection is afforded by the industrial model and design law; its owner is required to make a deposit or carry out a registration procedure with the administrative authority. The term of the right is, in general, considerably shorter than in the previous case (dating from the moment of deposit or registration).

The main purpose of this deposit or registration procedure is to create a presumption of property in favour of its owner. This is simple presumption—*juris tantum*—and admits proof to the contrary.

Can both types of protection be enjoyed simultaneously? The answer is yes. In accordance with the principle of the unity of art, works of applied art may enjoy both the protection of industrial model and design rights and of copyright. The intended use of the work is of no concern to copyright, that is to say, if it is intended for artistic and cultural purposes exclusively or if it can also be used to satisfy utilitarian purposes. However, those laws which admit such double protection usually impose—as we have seen—the limitation by which both legal provisions cannot be invoked simultaneously in the judicial defence of the rights.[15]

---

15. For example, Argentina, Decree-Law 6673/63, Art. 28.

The major multilateral international copyright conventions also refer to this double protection possibility in respect of works of applied art:
- the Berne Convention (Article 7(4)) provides that it shall be a matter for legislation in the countries of the Berne Union to determine the term of protection of works of applied art in so far as they are protected as artistic works, although it stipulates that this term shall last at least until the end of a period of 25 years from the making of such a work.
- the Universal Copyright Convention (Article IV, 3) refers to the Contracting States which protect ... works of applied art in so far as they are protected as artistic works, determining that the term of protection shall not be less than ten years for the said classes of works.

2.2.1.5. *Scientific works*

Scientific works are deemed to be those in which the themes are developed in a way appropriate to the requirements of scientific method. They include works of the exact, natural and medical sciences as well as literary works of a scientific character, instructional works, writings of a technical character, works for the popularization of science, practical guides, maps, graphs, drawings and graphic works relating to geography, topography and to science in general.

On the other hand, scientific inventions, discoveries, research work and scientifically oriented endeavours are not included among the scientific works protected by copyright, quite independently of the originality of the experiment or of the theory described therein.

With respect to the requirement of originality as a necessary condition for copyright protection, it should be pointed out that such originality cannot be evaluated in the same way in scientific or technical works as in literary works of fiction (see above, Section 2.1.2.). The reason is that in a scientific work the author finds himself governed to a large extent by the principles of the subject matter, by the time-sequence, by points of necessary similarity, by schemas which do not vary because they concern established facts or matters over which no controversy exists. In developing his theme, the author has a considerable body of literature before him —much of which can be considered as a compulsory bibliography —in which he finds material from which the essential contribution of his new work is derived.

Originality, the imprint of the author's personality, is found not so much in the composition, as occurs in works of fiction and drama where the author can, in general terms, combine facts according to his fancy, but rather in the selection of the elements or details and in the form of expression.[16] The example of maps is highly illustrative. Their quality is directly related to their ability to represent the earth or a part of it (an atlas), the heavens, and so on. They can be physical, political, economic, demographic, orographic, hydrographic, meteorological....

Where is the originality of maps to be found if they are confined to representing aspects of reality which are in the public domain? It resides in the personal effort involved in the work as a whole: the selection of the aspects of the particular elements which are to be represented; the method of representing a three-dimensional body on a flat surface and the scale; the aspects which it deals with (whether or not it shows political divisions, cities and if so, which ones, since their importance may depend on various factors: population, production or the fact that they are administrative centres; geographical accidents and, if so, which ones; agricultural and industrial production and their distribution; and so on); whether a text or illustrations are to be used, or both, and whether or not they are to be accompanied by figures; what colours and type are to be used to highlight each aspect; if the place names are to be reproduced in the language of the country to which they belong or in the author's and, if in this territory another alphabet is used, which form is to be used if there are

---

16. On the subject of scientifically oriented works, Henri Desbois states (op. cit., p. 52) '*Les manifestations de personnalité seront, au point de vue des droits d'auteur qui ne concernent que la forme, confinés en deux secteurs: tout d'abord, l'aménagement de détail, puis la rédaction.*'

several to choose from. Lastly, the map should be clear—in other words, the quantity of details it contains should not make it difficult to read. Having regard to these considerations and given the material impossibility of including all the data relative to the actual area covered, the map is considered original by reason of the selection and composition of this host of elements and of its expression in visual terms.

2.2.1.6. *Audiovisual works*

According to the definition set out in the Spanish law, audiovisual works are understood as being creations expressed by means of a series of associated images, with or without incorporated sound, that are intended essentially to be shown by means of projection apparatus or any other means of communication to the public of the images and of the sound, irrespective of the nature of the physical media in which the said works are embodied.[17]

A. CINEMATOGRAPHIC WORKS

Cinematographic works are complex works, protected in themselves as a particular class of work made in collaboration (for example, Argentine Law on Literary and Artistic Property, Article 20; French Intellectual Property Code, Legislative Part, Article L. 113-7, previously Article 14; Spanish Law on Intellectual Property, Article 87), irrespective of the creations and artistic contributions which have gone into their making.

The moral and economic interests which come into play are multiple, since cinematographic works involve a large number of creators (authors of the pre-existing literary, dramatic and musical works; authors of the script and the dialogues, of the musical compositions, with or without words, of the set designs and costumes), performers (actors and performing artists), technicians and assistants. Cinematographic production requires substantial financial investments; the admission of a large number of owners

---

17. See Spanish Law on Intellectual Property, Article 86(1).

of rights, exercising them on an equal footing, would involve a tangle of complications which could paralyse exploitation and it is therefore accepted that cinematographic works must be considered as a special class of work in collaboration governed by a special regime.

The need—and the problem—therefore arises of determining who among all those people making creative contributions should be considered as co-authors and what rights they should be granted in the overall work (these questions will be analysed in the next chapter, when dealing with the ownership of audiovisual works, Sect. 3.4).

The term *film* is currently used as a synonym for cinematographic work, although it also alludes to the material support of the work which does not exist as such until it is fixed on a sensitive film suitable for the purpose.

The cinematographic work fixed by a photomagnetic process which is subsequently reproduced by a process of electronic fixation (video) on another support (videotape, videodisc, etc.) or in a computerized system, is not transformed into a new work and does not lose its original character.

B. OTHER AUDIOVISUAL WORKS

The expression *audiovisual works* has become widely used to designate cinematographic works together with those which the Berne Convention (Article 2(1)) refers to as 'works expressed by a process analogous to cinematography'. In France, Article 3 of the 1957 law adopted this latter designation but the 1985 reform replaced it by the expression 'other works consisting of moving sequences of images, with or without sound, together referred to as audio-visual works' (Intellectual Property Code, Art. L. 112-2).

The term *audiovisual works* is increasingly used to designate all works which present certain decisive common elements, without taking into consideration the technical procedure used for fixation or the essential purpose for which they were created (projection or exhibition in auditoriums or broadcasting, etc.). As well as cinematographic works, it therefore includes videographic works (especially created for the purpose of videograms but not necessarily intended for broadcasting) and 'radiophonic works'.[18]

It is, then, immaterial if the audiovisual work is silent or incorporates sound, which dramatic genre it belongs to (drama, comedy, animated cartoon, documentary, current events, and so on), its length (full, medium or short), whether a photomagnetic (film) or electronic (video) process was used in the fixation, the material support used (impression on celluloid, electronic videotape, etc.) and, even if it is not fixed,[19] for, as we have pointed out, and as reflected in a number of laws, this characteristic also applies to radiophonic works which can be broadcast by means of

---

18. As regards the term 'radiophonic work' in reference to audiovisual works intended essentially for communication to the public by means of television, Claude Masouye, in commenting on Article 2(1) of the Berne Convention, points out that it 'does not specifically refer to "radiophonic works" since radiodiffusion is considered as a method of exploitation of works; the works which are broadcast may be dramatic, dramatico-musical, choreographic, musical, cinematographic, etc. [...] If the Tunis Model Law expressly mentions 'radiophonic and audio-visual works' side by side with cinematographic works, this is because its draftsmen preferred to avoid any ambiguity. They therefore included them in a non-exclusive list of protected works and did not use the formula of assimilation which the Convention contains' (*Guide to the Berne Convention*, WIPO, Geneva, 1978, p. 16).

On the other hand, in the Draft Model Provisions for Legislation in the Field of Copyright of WIPO (WIPO document CE/MPC/I/2-II, 11 August 1989) in the definitions (section 1(i)) and among the protected works (section 2(vi)) mention is made only of 'audio-visual works'. In the commentaries (WIPO document CE/MPC/I/2-III, also of 11 August 1989) it is explained (paragraph 19) that this expression is used irrespective of the technique (cinematography, television or videotechnique) used for their creation, and that televised creations should be considered as such (para. 63).

With these comments in mind, we will use the expression 'radiophonic works' in the sense of Article 18 of the French Law of 1957 on literary and artistic property, as amended in 1985 (Intellectual Property Code, Article L. 113-8) and of Article 94 of the Spanish Law on Intellectual Property.

19. See Antonio Delgado Porras, 'Utilización de obras audiovisuales por satélite y cable. La intervención de las sociedades de autores', Libro-Memoria, *Fifth International Congress on the Protection of Intellectual Property*, Buenos Aires, 1990, pp. 214–15.

a performance made before the television cameras ('live') or be given only ephemeral fixations.[20]

Use of the expression 'audiovisual works' in legislation as a term embracing cinematographic works and other creations expressed by means of a succession of associated images does not entail in itself the application to 'radiophonic works' of the legal regime governing the other audiovisual works, unless expressly provided for in the same legal text as, for example, in Art. L. 113-8.2 of the French Intellectual Property Code (previously Art. 18.2); this indicates which provisions concerning audiovisual works are applicable to the 'radiophonic' category. This is of special importance as regards the presumption of transfer of the exploitation right established in legislation in favour of the producer of audiovisual works.[21]

Colombet[22] points out in this respect that there has been no declaration to the effect that Art. 63-1 of the French law (now the French Intellectual Property Code, Article L. 132-24) concerning audiovisual works applies to 'radiophonic works': the producer of the work cannot, then, benefit from a presumption of transfer —it must be expressly stated. The question is of considerable importance, for authors of 'radiophonic works', especially in the developing countries, determine their remuneration on the basis of dissemination which is restricted as regards the period of time and the territory involved.

2.2.1.7. *Works of national folklore*

A. DEFINITION OF TRADITIONAL CULTURE AND FOLKLORE

In the *Recommendation on the Safeguarding of Traditional Culture and Folklore* approved by the General Conference of UNESCO at

---

20. *Ephemeral fixations* mean those fixations made by broadcasting organizations whose only purpose is to facilitate the programming of their transmissions and which must be destroyed as soon as they have been broadcast (see below, Chapter 4.
21. See below, Chapter 3, Section 3.4.1.
22. Claude Colombet, op. cit., p. 224, No. 216.

its twenty-fifth session (Paris, 15 November 1989),[23] the following definition of *traditional culture and folklore* was adopted:

Folklore (or traditional and popular culture) is the totality of tradition-based creations of a cultural community, expressed by a group or individuals and recognized as reflecting the expectations of a community insofar as they reflect its cultural and social identity; its standards and values are transmitted orally, by imitation or by other means. Its forms are, among others, language, literature, music, dance, games, mythology, rituals, customs, handicrafts, architecture and other arts.

B. PROTECTION OF FOLKLORE

The commercial exploitation of productions of national folklore is a subject of concern to the developing countries which possess a rich heritage of expressions of this type and where they are either insufficiently appreciated or, for a variety of reasons (in general, the lack of economic resources and of cultural industries able to disseminate them adequately) it is not possible to preserve them or to promote their dissemination as a source of creative expression without distorting them.

There have been demands, in these countries, for the legislative recognition of their rights in the folklore expressions of their indigenous communities in order to prevent them from being used in such a way as to result in their distortion and to ensure that payment is made for their exploitation.

Their claims are based on the fact that these countries suffer, on the one hand, from the overwhelming domination of foreign cultural forms, and on the other, from the use of their folklore out of its original context, which gives rise to all manner of improper uses (distortions, mutilations, pillaging, etc.).

This gives rise to several complex questions: how far is it possible to regulate authorization for exploiting folklore expressions and to what extent can the source community participate in the rewards which are obtained from this exploitation? The first

---

23. See *Copyright Bulletin*, UNESCO, No. 1, 1990, p. 9.

attempts to regulate the use of expressions of folklore were made in the context of a number of copyright laws.

In the *national context*, the forerunner was Tunisia, in 1967. Bolivia then followed in 1968 (in respect only of folk music), Chile and Morocco in 1970, Algeria and Senegal in 1973, Kenya in 1975, Cuba and Mali in 1977, Burundi and Côte d'Ivoire in 1978, Guinea in 1980, Barbados, Cameroon, Costa Rica and Congo in 1982, Rwanda in 1983, Benin and Burkina Faso in 1984, Central African Republic and Ghana in 1985, and former Zaire in 1986. Folklore expressions were also included in the Model Law of Tunisia on copyright for developing countries (1976).

In the *regional context*, the text of the Convention of the African Intellectual Property Organization (AIPO) (Bangui, 1977) considers, in the same manner as the national laws referred to above, that works of folklore are part of the cultural heritage of the nation. It mentions the creations made by communities and not by authors, thus distinguishing folklore creations from works protected by copyright.

In the *international context*, the Berne Convention, Paris Act, 1971, contains, in Article 15, paragraph 4, a provision introduced in the Stockholm revision (1967) which refers to *unpublished works where the author's identity is unknown*. It is essentially aimed at the protection of works of folklore although they are not explicitly mentioned in the text of the Convention, due to the difficulty of defining them accurately.

In order to define this special category of works as accurately as possible, paragraph 4 referred to above establishes three concomitant conditions:
- the work in question should be *unpublished* (Article 3, para. 3, provides a definition of the concept of *publication* for the purposes of the Convention);
- the work should be by an unknown author;
- there should be good grounds for presuming that the author, although unknown, is a national of a country of the Berne Union.

If these three conditions are met, the legislation of the country of the Berne Union can designate an authority whose role shall be identical to the role of publisher in the case of anonymous or pseudonymous works (para. 3 of Article 15); in other words, he shall represent the author and in that capacity be entitled to protect and enforce his rights in all the countries of the Union (both in the country of the presumed nationality of the author and in the others). It shall be for this authority, principally, to assemble as many elements and documents as possible to demonstrate, in case of litigation, that there is every ground to presume that the author is a national, effectively, of the country to which the authority itself belongs.

The country of the Union which has designated such authority shall give notice of its designation to the Director-General of WIPO (the organization which administers the Berne Convention) who, in turn, shall immediately communicate it to the other countries of the Union. As of 1 January 1995, the only country of the Union which had made this notification was India.[24]

The provisions referred to have not had the desired effect. This can be attributed to the fact that copyright does not prove to be the best framework for the protection of folklore whose expressions are the consequence of a long process of *community* creation. Again, the identity of the authors of the various components of these expressions is unknown, since they are identified with *traditional* values and are transmitted by *imitation* and it is frequent that communities inhabiting different countries use the same expressions. Copyright grants personal rights to the creator of a work by reason of the fact that it is the result of a personal effort which should have sufficient originality or individuality.

Furthermore, and having regard to its traditional character, expressions of folklore are usually very old or at least of undetermined age, much older than the copyright protection term (generally limited to the life of the author and a period of 50 years after his death).

In 1973, Bolivia requested UNESCO to study the possibility of adding a protocol to the Universal Copyright Convention to regulate 'folklore preservation, promotion and diffusion'. As from that time the Intergovernmental Committee of the Universal

---

24. See *Copyright*, Jan. 1995.

Copyright Convention and the Executive Committee of the Berne Union have held a series of meetings at which analysis was made of studies entrusted to working groups and to committees of governmental experts on the problem of the legal protection of expressions of folklore. It was observed that the issue was one of an essentially cultural character which extended beyond the field of copyright in the strict sense of the term.

C. UNESCO/WIPO Model Provisions for National Laws on the Protection of Expressions of Folklore against Illicit Exploitation and Other Prejudicial Actions[25]

In 1982, a Committee of Governmental Experts convened in Geneva by UNESCO and WIPO examined and approved these Model Provisions, the content of which, in general terms, is as follows:

a) expressions of folklore are defined (Section 2);

b) the terms 'expressions' and 'productions' of folklore are used instead of 'works'—although in the majority of cases they constitute formal creations of the same order as works—for the purpose of emphasizing that these are provisions *sui generis* and should be distinguished from copyright;

c) reference is made to 'artistic heritage' which means that, *inter alia*, beliefs (e.g. the traditional cosmogonies), the content of legends (e.g. the life and feats of heroes) or purely practical traditions as such are not considered to be expressions of folklore;

d) the illustrative list of expressions of folklore is divided into four groups according to the form of expression: words (verbal), sounds (musical), corporal expression and expression incorporated in material objects (tangible expressions);

e) two principal categories of acts are specified in respect of which expressions of folklore need to be protected: 'illicit exploitation' and 'other prejudicial actions';

---

25. See *Copyright Bulletin*, UNESCO, No. 4, 1982, p. 62 *et seq.*

f) *'illicit exploitation'* (Section 3) is considered to be any utilization made outside the traditional or customary context, with or without gainful intent, without the authorization of the competent authority or community concerned. In *contrario sensu*, utilization made within the traditional or customary context, even with a gainful intent, is not considered illicit. However, utilization by the members of the community in which the expression of folklore has been developed and maintained should be authorized if it is made *outside that context and with gainful intent*;

g) four *exceptions* or cases in which authorization is not necessary are specified (Section 4):

1) utilization for purposes of education;

2) utilization by way of illustrations (e.g. quotation in an original work of an author);

3) borrowing of expressions of folklore for creating an original work (e.g. an air for a musical composition). This exception is very important because it permits the development of original creativity, drawing its inspiration from folklore (influence of folklore);

4) incidental utilization (e.g. for information on current events);

h) *'other prejudicial acts'* (Section 6):

1) section 5 requires, as a general rule, that when expressions of folklore are utilized, their source should be indicated, whenever it is identifiable, by mentioning the community and geographical place from which they have been derived. Failure to comply with this requisite is punishable. This is without prejudice to the obligation to indicate the name of the author in the case of an original work of folklore, in compliance with the provisions of copyright legislation;

2) utilizations which exceed the limits of the authorization granted or are contrary to its conditions;

3) deceiving the public by creating the impression that expressions of folklore derive from a certain community, when this is not the case;

4) distortion of expressions of folklore; this includes any type of deformation or mutilation or other offence in respect of an expression of folklore, communicated to the public in any form by the offender.

In order to be punishable, the offences must have been intentional. However, the Model Provisions also admit the application of penal sanctions in the case of negligence. It is for each country to establish the sanctions and their degree of severity. Penal action is not an impediment to action for damages or other civil remedies authorized by legislation and which include, specifically, appropriate reparations.

Provision is made for the designation of a competent authority responsible for granting authorizations and fixing and collecting fees (Section 9). The community designates representatives to act on its behalf and exercise its rights. The need to determine the court to which appeals against refusals to grant authorization may be made is established (Section 11).

According to section 14, efforts at the national level should constitute the first step towards an international treaty which could be developed on the basis of subregional or regional agreements. Provision is accordingly made for the possible extension of the application of the Model Provisions to include expressions of folklore of foreign origin.

D. Subsequent activities. Recommendations on the Safeguarding of Traditional Culture and Folklore approved by the General Conference of UNESCO at its twenty-fifth session (Paris, 15 November 1989)

From 1985 onwards, various committees were convened by UNESCO for the purpose of carrying out a study on the possible scope of a general international instrument for the safeguarding of folklore. The Special Committee of Experts which met in 1987 at UNESCO Headquarters was unanimous in recognizing the urgent need for establishing such an international standard-setting instrument.

In 1989, the General Conference of UNESCO approved a Recommendation on the Safeguarding of Traditional Culture and Folklore which, reflecting considerable conceptual clarity, and utilizing altogether appropriate terms from the professional and academic standpoint, covered the whole spectrum of measures necessary for the protection of national folklore, without seeking first and foremost or exclusively legal regulation in the area of copyright.

In the definition *of folklore* (*or traditional and popular culture*) adopted in the Recommendation[26] the words *popular culture* appear for the first time, implying an extension of the scope of previous definitions. Similarly, the term *artistic*—with its more restricted connotation—used in these definitions, has given way to *cultural,* with its wider implications.

Six lines of action are proposed to Member States:

1) *Identification of folklore*, for which purpose appropriate survey research should be encouraged at national, regional and international levels in order to:

a) develop a national inventory of institutions involved;

b) create an identification and recording system;

c) stimulate the creation of a standard typology.

2) *Conservation of folklore.* To this end efforts should be made to:

a) establish national archive services;

b) establish a central national archive;

c) create museums or folklore sections at existing museums;

d) give precedence to ways of presenting traditional and popular culture that emphasize the living or past aspects of those cultures (surroundings, ways of life, works, skills and techniques produced);

e) harmonize collecting and archiving methods;

f) provide specialized training covering all aspects from preservation to analysis of documents;

g) provide means for making copies of all folklore materials, thus securing the cultural community access to them.

3) *Preservation of folklore.* To ensure the preservation of folklore it is suggested that Member States should:

a) design and introduce into curricula the teaching and study of folklore in an appropriate manner;

b) guarantee the right of access of cultural communities to their own folklore;

---

26. Set out at the beginning of this Section.

c) set up, on an interdisciplinary basis, a national folklore council;

d) provide moral and economic support to individuals and institutions studying, making known, cultivating or holding items of folklore;

e) promote scientific research relevant to the preservation of folklore.

4) *Dissemination of folklore.* To promote appropriate dissemination, Member States should:

a) encourage the organization of national, regional and international events and support the dissemination and publication of their materials, papers and other results;

b) encourage a broader coverage of folklore material in national and regional media;

c) encourage regions, municipalities, associations and other groups working in folklore to establish full-time posts for folklore specialists to stimulate and co-ordinate folklore activities in the region;

d) support existing units and create new units for the production of educational materials; encourage their use in schools and museums; and promote the holding of national and international folklore festivals and exhibitions;

e) provide adequate information on folklore through documentation centres;

f) facilitate meetings and exchanges between individuals, groups and institutions concerned with folklore;

g) encourage the international scientific community to adopt a code of ethics ensuring a proper approach to and respect for traditional cultures.

5) *Protection of folklore.* In so far as folklore constitutes manifestations of intellectual creativity whether it be individual or collective, it deserves to be protected in a manner similar to the protection provided for intellectual productions, and, leaving aside the 'intellectual property aspects' of the 'protection of expressions of folklore', there are various categories of rights which are already protected and should continue to enjoy protection in the future in folklore documentation centres and archives. To this end, Member States should:

a) *regarding the 'intellectual property' aspects*: call the attention of relevant authorities to the important work of UNESCO and WIPO in relation to intellectual property;

b) *regarding the other rights involved*:

(i) protect the informant as the transmitter of tradition (protection of privacy and confidentiality);

(ii) protect the interests of the collector by ensuring that the materials gathered are conserved in archives in good condition and in a methodical manner;

(iii) adopt the necessary measures to safeguard the materials gathered against misuse, whether intentional or otherwise;

(iv) recognize the responsibility of archive services to monitor the use made of the materials gathered.

6) *International co-operation*. In view of the need to intensify cultural co-operation and exchanges in order to carry out folklore development and revitalization programmes, as well as research made by specialists who are the nationals of one Member State on the territory of another Member State, Member States should:

a) co-operate with international and regional associations, institutions and organizations concerned with folklore;

b) co-operate in the field of knowledge, dissemination and protection of folklore, in particular through:

(i) exchanges of information of every kind, exchanges of scientific and technical publications;

(ii) training of specialists, awarding of travel grants, missions by scientific and technical personnel and the sending of equipment;

(iii) the promotion of bilateral or multilateral projects in the field of documentation concerning contemporary folklore;

(iv) the organization of meetings between specialists, of study courses and of working groups on particular subjects, especially on the classifying and cataloguing of folklore data and expressions and on modern methods and techniques in research;

c) co-operate closely so as to ensure internationally that the various interested parties (communities or natural or legal persons) enjoy the economic, moral and so-called neighbouring rights resulting from the investigation, creation, composition, performance, recording and/or dissemination of folklore;

d) guarantee Member States on whose territory research has

been carried out the right to obtain from the Member State concerned, copies of all research studies, documents, video-films, films and other material;

e) refrain from acts likely to damage folklore materials or to diminish their value or impede their dissemination or use, whether these materials are to be found on their own territory or on the territory of other States;

f) take necessary measures to safeguard folklore against all human and natural dangers to which it is exposed, including the risks deriving from armed conflicts, occupation of territories, or public disorders of other kinds.

E. DIFFICULTIES IN ADOPTING AN INTERNATIONAL CONVENTION

Acceptance of an international instrument for the safeguarding of folklore which would meet the aspirations of the developing countries within the basic guidelines of the 1982 Model Provisions runs into serious difficulties, given that:

a) many countries, including certain developing countries, consider that expressions of folklore belong to the public domain;

b) political borders and those of cultural areas frequently do not coincide;

c) the historical modifications of borders and the sometimes 'migratory' character of artistic expressions (stemming from cultural and not geopolitical factors) raise problems;

d) in many instances it is possible that the content of a folklore expression may not be absolutely unique. Several communities may utilize the same expression and, at least partially, may claim the same exclusive rights. Studies on folklore show that expressions with the same forms or common elements are frequently encountered even in regions which are distant from one another;

e) folklore expressions are constantly evolving, making it difficult for an authority to discuss the 'purity' of an expression which is going to be offered to the public;

f) it is considered that the explicit incorporation of folklore expressions in some form of *fee-paying public domain*, in favour of the State, communities, or author's societies, with the same rates and terms of payment as for copyright, would achieve the desired participation in the exploitation of folklore expressions. This would be without prejudice to the obligation to quote the source, whenever identifiable, indicating the community and the geographical location or, in fact, to inform the public concerning the lack of authenticity of the expression which it is being offered.

2.2.1.8. *New categories of works: computer programs (arguments for and against copyright protection)*

A 'computer program' is understood to mean a set of instructions expressed by means of words, codes, schemas or any other form, which is capable, when incorporated in a machine-readable medium and translated into electronic impulses, of causing a 'computer'—an electronic or similar device having information-processing abilities—to perform or achieve a particular task or result.[27]

In France, *logiciel*—according to an official definition quoted by Colombet[28]—covers all the programs, procedures and rules and, where necessary, documentation relating to the functioning of a whole data-processing sequence. Similarly, *software* is the English term commonly used to designate the central component, the *computer program* together with the respective supporting material. The content of software is, then, more extensive than that of the computer program since it includes technical literature and manuals for the use of the program.[29]

As Bertrand has pointed out, the computer program is the result of a sequence comprising six stages:
1) An idea for the solution of a given problem.
2) An algorithm, that is to say, a problem-solving method, generally expressed in mathematical formulas.

---

27. See definition in *Draft Model Provisions for Legislation in the Field of Copyright*, WIPO, document CE/MPC/I/2-II, 11 August 1989, Art. 1.
28. Claude Colombet, *Propriété littéraire et artistique et droits voisins*, Paris, Dalloz, 1994, p. 78, para. 100, note 1.
29. Spain, Art. 96(2): 'The technical literature and manuals for the use of the program shall enjoy the same protection as is afforded to computer programs themselves under this Title.'

3) An organigramme or plan for ensuring a solution or processing based on the algorithm.
4) A text in a high-level programming language, such as COBOL, FORTRAN, BASIC, etc., also termed 'source' program, which is directly based on organigramme elements.
5) A text in an intermediate, or 'assembler' language, which is simpler for the machine to assimilate.
6) A directly machine-readable text of a binary type, or the *'object' program*.[30]

The computer program in the form of a source program or source code, expressed in high-level language, can be perceived by the human individual, but the same is not true of the computer program in the form of an object program or object code, transcribed in machine language. Machine language, when printed, appears in the form of sequences of the digits 0 and 1 (binary system) or of numbers and letters according to the characteristics of the computer (the source program has been compared to a music score which is intelligible only to skilled persons, and the object program to a sound recording of the musical work on a disc or cassette).

The use of computers began to spread in 1964, with the advent of the IBM 360. At that time computers (hardware) were sold *jointly* with programs, manuals for use, etc. (software) created to satisfy the needs of the user. The problem of protection of the programs had not yet arisen, since they were considered to be an integral part of the computer, which was protected by industrial property rights. Shortly after, the practice of marketing programs 'attached' to the computers began to wane. Two independent markets were formed, giving rise to the need to cover programs with independent and sufficiently effective legal protection.

As early as 1964, a study was published in the United States by John F. Banzhaf advocating the copyright protection of computer programs. In 1966 the United States Copyright Office began to accept registration of such programs. In turn, in instructions which it drew up that same year, the Patent Office specified that

---

30. A. Bertrand, *Protection juridique du logiciel: Progiciels, video jeux, logiciels spécifiques, firmware*, Paris, Ed. des Parques, 1984, pp. 10 and 12, para. 16.

computer programs would not be patentable if they lacked 'utilitarian steps', as opposed to the concept of so-called 'mental steps'. Accordingly, for a program to be patented, it had to lead to the physical transformation of the computer which it would convert into a special-purpose machine. Numerous legal battles were waged in which patent applications for computer programs were rejected on the grounds that 'mental steps' were not patentable.

Over a number of years much thought and discussion have been devoted to the juridical nature of computer programs, and to whether the appropriate regulatory structure for their protection should be the industrial property right, copyright, or a new right.

What was involved was a new product of the human mind concerning which no previous notions existed and whose development required enormous investments. The protection of such valuable property was vital.

Opinions were divided. The copyright specialists insisted that computer programs had neither a literary nor an artistic character. They feared that their incorporation in copyright would eventually weaken a legal structure which had been built up so painstakingly.

Studies commissioned by UNESCO and WIPO and published during the first half of the 1970s by the German Professor Eugen Ulmer were highly influential. In them, Professor Ulmer analysed the equivalence between the entry of the program in the computer and the fixation of a work (which is included in the concept of reproduction as one of the author's exclusive prerogatives recognized by the relevant laws), and concluded that copyright protection was possible.

This opinion began to gain ground. It was recognized that computer programs constituted intellectual works resulting from a creative process similar to that required by a literary work or a film script, which, *when original in composition and expression, is protected by copyright.*

On the other hand, when the programmer is obliged, because of internal specifications (rules imposed by the program) or external stipulations (rules imposed by legislation, professional requirements, etc.) to develop the program in a certain way which allows no alternative, the program is not protected by copyright because the general principle in this domain is that the exclusive rights which it confers cannot be acquired in respect of ideas considered in themselves or of principles (see above, Section 2.1.1).

Exclusion from copyright protection should also be made when the program is exploited in such a way as to operate as an industrial product or process and, as such, comes within the context of something that can be patented.[31]

The Philippines was the first country to modify its copyright law to include, in 1972, the computer program.

In 1978, the United States Congress set up a Special Commission, the National Commission on New Technological Uses of Copyrighted Works (CONTU). In compliance with its recommendations a law was enacted in 1980 establishing the protection of computer programs by means of copyright.

Subsequently, several countries enacted laws along the same lines, such as Australia, France, Germany, Hungary, India, Japan and the United Kingdom. In other countries computer programs are considered to be protected without any need for legislative reform for the enumeration of protected works is not subject to *numerus clausus*.

The principle of protecting computer programs by copyright has drawn certain *criticism* which can be summed up as follows:
- the computer program cannot be directly discerned by the human being and is essentially utilitarian because it is used to make an electronic device execute a certain task and obtain a certain result; accordingly, it does not belong to the realm of the aesthetic but, rather, to that of utility;
- copyright does not protect ideas; in the area of computer programs these must be protected, as occurs in the case of patent law;
- it is also necessary to protect the content of the computer

---

31. Spain includes the computer program among the works protected by copyright, with the proviso (Article 96, para. 3) that 'Computer programs that form part of a patent or utility model shall, without prejudice to the provisions of this Law, enjoy whatever protection may accrue to them by operation of the legal regime governing industrial property.'

program and not its formal expression, which is the aspect protected by copyright;
- the general term of copyright is too long to be applied to the computer program;
- in the case of the computer program it would be inappropriate to accept an international order of protection as open as that which governs the area of copyright, especially for the developing countries, where it is necessary to establish—in the same manner as for hardware—a 'market reserve' in favour of locally developed programs which are 'functionally equivalent' to the computer programs which it is desired to import (Brazil);
- the computer program user must possess a back-up copy, a possibility which is not provided for by copyright in respect of works;
- it is not possible to incorporate the computer program in the list of works protected by copyright without forcing the structure of copyright protection which will ultimately result in distorting its nature.

The answers to these criticisms can be summed up as follows:
- the computer program is a work;
- the prerogatives of an economic order which copyright provides for the protection of works against unauthorized uses are compatible with the protection of computer programs, as shown by the evolution of jurisprudence which has accepted Professor Ulmer's theory that the incorporation of a work in a computer memory is equivalent to a reproduction and that the display on the screen is equivalent to an act of public communication of the work. Classical notions concerning the plagiarism of works are also compatible with the plagiarizing of computer programs;
- the fact that computer programs are not directly readable by human beings is not an impediment to considering them as works in the same way as others such as audiovisual and musical works fixed on electromagnetic tape, which can only be perceived by means of electronic devices;
- the merit, intended use and form of expression of the work are criteria which are not relevant to recognition of copyright protection (see above, Section 2.1.3). Accordingly, the fact that computer programs do not belong to the realm of the beautiful

or the aesthetic, that they have a utilitarian function (as do designs, models, architectural plans, and so on) and that they are expressed by means of codes or in any other form, does not constitute an obstacle to their protection by copyright.

As Villalba points out, some authors have called attention to the fact that computer programs, although works of the intellect, do not meet the requirement of being aesthetic works in so far as the term designates the science which deals with beauty and the philosophical theory of art. The word does not have its origin in classical antiquity as one might assume, since it was created in 1750 by the German, Baumgarten. For Baumgarten aesthetics is concerned with study of the objective forms of natural and artistic beauty, the beautiful, the sublime, the tragic, the comic, and so on. A large number of works protected by copyright lack any appeal to our sense of beauty. This points to the fact that the word has here been used in its original meaning, given that it comes from '*aisthêtikos*' which means *perceptible by the senses*, from '*aisthanesthai*', which means *perceive* or *comprehend* in the sense used by Kant when he applied the term *transcendental aesthetics* to the doctrine of our faculty of knowledge.[32]

Not all works come into the category of the beautiful, as, for example, trigonometry manuals and other instructional works; many more have a utilitarian function, such as models, designs and works of architecture.

In regard to the form of expression, numerous works are expressed in forms which, in order to be understood, require special knowledge, as, for example, for the reading of musical scores:
- the need to protect the ideas contained in computer programs is not met by placing them under the protection of patent rights, since (as in copyright), ideas are not protected under patent laws; if it were otherwise, excessive monopolies would be formed, preventing the continuation of intellectual development and making competition impossible;

---

32. See Carlos Alberto Villalba, 'La protección de los programas de computación y de los bancos de datos', Libro-Memoria, *Third International Congress on the Protection of Intellectual Property*, Lima, 1988, p. 66.

- copyright not only protects the formal expression of works but also their content;
- the system of copyright protection by means of international conventions functions automatically and efficiently in protecting works, and it would take a very long time to create an equivalent international system for protecting computer programs;
- the absence of legal protection discourages creation; if foreign works alone were to be unprotected, this would lead to unfair competition with protected national works and would supplant them, since it would be very unlikely that users would utilize the latter if they were able to use the former freely or at a derisory cost.

Reference is also frequently made, in support of copyright protection of computer programs, to:
- the fact that protection originates with creation and is not subordinated to the performance of formalities, particularly as regards the description of the invention which is required for the granting of the patent;
- the applicability of known and habitually respected principles and standards.

By the beginning of 1988, it had been recognized in some 50 countries—by means of express legal provisions or judicial rulings—that computer programs would be protected by copyright.

In some laws the protection of computer programs (or software) is regulated in a special manner through the establishment of a series of presumptions (which admit stipulation to the contrary) such as: the proprietary right of the employer (French Intellectual Property Code, Art. L. 113-9, previously Article 45 of the 1985 Law); the author may not object to the licensed user making or authorizing the making of successive versions of the program or of programs derived therefrom (French Intellectual Property Code, Art. L. 121-7, previously Art. 46 of the 1985 Law; Article 98 of the Spanish Law on Intellectual Property); the author may not exercise his right to correct or to retract (French Intellectual Property Code, Art. L. 121-7, previously Art. 46 of the 1985 Law); the user has the right to make a back-up copy (French Intellectual Property Code, Art. L. 122-6, previously Art.

47 of the 1985 Law; Article 99(2) of the Spanish Law on Intellectual Property).

2.2.2. Derivative works

Derivative works are those which are based on a pre-existing work. They include adaptations, translations, updatings, anthologies, summaries, extracts and any transformation of a previous work which results in a different work. The originality of the derivative work may be found in the composition and the expression (as in adaptations), in the composition alone (as in compilations and anthologies) or in the expression alone (as in translations).

When the pre-existing work is in the private domain, its author must authorize the creation of the work derived from it. This is the *right of transformation.*

On the other hand, when the pre-existing work is in the public domain no authorization is necessary for making the derivative work, since the right of transformation constitutes an aspect of the author's economic right. However, as Delgado Porras points out, the right of transformation comes very close to the moral right, although it should not be confused with it,[33] for transformation may distort the thinking or intention of the author, and even constitute injury as regards the personality of the author of the original work.

Derivative works which are the fruit of their author's personal effort and possess some degree of creativity, are protected without prejudice to the rights of the author of the previous work.

Since the derivative work is the sum of creative elements taken from the previous work and those contributed to the new work, it may not be used without the authorization of its author and the author of the pre-existing work.

Derivative works are *composite works.* A composite work is the new work which incorporates a pre-existing work without the collaboration of the author thereof. Should the author of the original work collaborate in the creation of the derivative work,

---

33. Antonio Delgado Porras, *Panorámica* ..., op. cit., p. 38, para. 20.

the latter will accordingly be a composite work created in collaboration, just as if it had been produced by more than one author, even though none of them is the author of the pre-existing work.

2.2.2.1. Adaptations

Adaptations, together with translations, constitute the most widely found categories of derivative works. By means of an adaptation a work changes from one genre to the other (e.g. cinema or television versions of novels, short stories, stage plays, etc.) or the work may be altered without the genre being changed (e.g. when the number of parts in a television work is increased).

The adaptation should respect the original creation; in principle the author of the derivative work should adhere to the work he is adapting and produce a faithful adaptation; the extent to which he may deviate from the pre-existing work, by introducing extraneous elements, and make a free adaptation and even use it simply as the inspiration for a new work, depends on the express authorization for this granted by the author of the original work.

2.2.2.2. Translations

By means of translation a work is expressed in a language other than the language used in the original version. Translations should remain faithful to the content and the style of the original work. This obliges the translator to overcome the language difficulties, which are often of such importance that they may demand a real linguistic re-creation of the work (this happens frequently with poetry). But even when the obstacles which the translator must face are of a less challenging order, it remains that translation always requires the creative mastery of another language and a considerable effort in rendering the author's thoughts.

However, since the various translations of a work are always made from the same original text, it is often difficult to prove plagiarism or the improper use of the translator's effort. Pending solution of this problem and so as to have a means of pointing to the existence of plagiarism, many translators often resort to expedients such as slipping in inconspicuous but tell-tale errors which, when repeated in another translation, serve as conclusive evidence of copying.

2.2.2.3. Compilations and databases

Compilations or collections of literary or artistic works, or of selected passages which possess originality in the selection or arrangement of the items forming them, are protected by copyright.

In compilations, originality is shown in the element of composition. The selection of the works or the fragments of works which compose them and the methodology with which they are treated constitute intellectual efforts which result in a work which is different from those which form it.

Compilations, and especially those of laws, jurisprudence and doctrine, may contain full texts, summaries or abstracts[34] of them, or both. Summaries and abstracts constitute derivative works in themselves, are protected as such and come under the system of prior authorization on the part of the authors of the protected works to which they refer.

Database is a term given to an aggregate of information data, selected in accordance with certain constant principles, systematically arranged, and stored in the memory of a computer system to which a certain number of users have access.[35]

Databases are *electronic* deposits of data and information. They are composed of connected or related files designed to make the documentation which they contain available to the public.

Computers have substantially modified the importance and economic value of compilations and collections of data through the creation of databases which are able to process limitless masses of information and transmit them almost instantaneously to any part of the world. The possibilities of storage in videodiscs, microchips, etc., are constantly increasing.

---

34. An *abstract* seeks to reproduce, in a very condensed form, all the information in a document which is considered useful, drafted in such a way as to transmit the maximum of information with the minimum of words.
35. See document UNESCO/WIPO/CGE/SYN/3-II, 11 April 1988, Principle PW16(1); and Antonio Delgado Porras, 'El derecho de autor y las modernas tecnologías', Libro-Memoria, *Fourth International Congress on the Protection of Intellectual Property*, Guatemala, 1989, Section 2.14, p. 149.

Databases can be formed on the basis of their own documentary system. In these cases they are works which enjoy full copyright protection.

When the database is made up of the full texts of pre-existing documents, the question of recognition of the rights of its owner arises.

If the pre-existing texts are copyrighted works, they may not be incorporated in a computer memory without the author's consent. Such incorporation is equivalent to a reproduction and must, accordingly, be expressly authorized: it concerns a material fixation of the work on a magnetic record, a procedure which allows it to be communicated to the public.

If the owner of the database has not obtained the consent of the authors of the pre-existing works, he may not claim any right. If he has obtained such consent, his rights depend on the scope of the respective contracts.

The question may seem less clear-cut when the texts of copyrighted works are not reproduced in full but in the form of quotations. Laws admit the right of quotation as a limitation of copyright. The Berne Convention establishes a limitation *jure conventionis* in respect of quotations:

> It shall be permissible to make quotations from a work which has already been lawfully made available to the public, provided that their making is compatible with fair practice, and their extent does not exceed that justified by the purpose, including quotations from newspaper articles and periodicals in the form of press summaries (Article 10(1), Paris Act, 1971).[36]

If the texts are not protected by copyright they may be included freely in a database (as in the case of legal provisions, rulings of judicial and administrative courts, etc. as we saw when dealing with non-protected literary works—see above, Section 2.2.1.1).

---

36. The celebrated case 'Microfor vs. *Le Monde*' (see *Banques de données et droits d'auteur*, Paris, Librairies Techniques, 1987, Annex 1, p. 141 *et seq.*) touched off a debate in France over the interpretation of the scope of the right of quotation applied to the formation of data banks.

However, the setting up of a database requires substantial economic investments. It calls for the electronic organization of data and information, a system for handling databases, controls which allow users to enter the system in accordance with their access rights, the administration and handling of the data, the design of the database and its structure as well as the selection and start-up of the computer program used to operate it.

Even when the owner of the database is not required to request authorization or pay for entering texts in the computer memory, the system nevertheless demands an investment which warrants protection against its unauthorized use. However, the owner does not acquire any exclusivity over the reproduction of the texts forming the database. Anyone is entitled to use them for the setting up of another database, but without taking advantage of the investment and efforts of others.

2.2.2.4. Anthologies

Anthologies are collections of works or literary passages compiled for a specific purpose. They are protected by copyright for the same reasons as compilations. In this regard, the Berne Convention provides that:

Collections of literary or artistic works such as encyclopaedias and anthologies which, by reason of the selection and arrangement of their contents, constitute intellectual creations, shall be protected as such, without prejudice to the copyright in each of the works forming part of such collections (Article 2(5), Paris Act, 1971).

Some laws exempt collections and anthologies from the requirement of prior authorization provided that they have educational or scientific purposes and that fair payment is made to the authors.

2.2.2.5. Annotations and commentaries

Annotations and commentaries are derivative works whose originality resides in their composition and expression. In principle, the rules on adaptations apply to them. However, in the case of annotations and commentaries concerning works *not protected* by copyright or works which are in the *public domain*, the respective publications constitute absolutely original works. Notwithstanding this, authors of annotations and commentaries acquire exclusive rights in respect of them alone, for which reason they may not oppose others from also making their own notes and comments on the same pre-existing works.

2.2.2.6. *Arrangements and orchestrations*

An arrangement is the transcription of a musical work for other instruments. By means of orchestration a musical work is transcribed for the various instruments which make up an orchestra.

Since the right of transformation which the creator enjoys includes arrangements and orchestrations, while the work remains in the private domain, *prior authorization* by the author or his successors in title is required in such cases.

Arrangements and orchestrations are very common. They are protected by copyright when they make a creative contribution, as, for example, Ravel's famous orchestration for symphony orchestra of Mussorgsky's piano work *Paintings at an Exhibition*.

On the other hand, they are not protected when the contribution is merely technical, as in the case of simple transpositions and transcriptions, the omission or duplication of voices, the simple addition of voices in parallel or of ornaments. Arrangements and orchestrations are frequently the means of obtaining participation in the remuneration of the author or payment for the public utilization of a work which has fallen into the public domain (in colloquial language this is known as a way of 'withdrawing the work from the public domain', even though it is only partial); sometimes arrangements and orchestrations are essential for a work to be performed with modern instruments. Societies of authors dealing with musical works are very skilled in distinguishing between protected arrangements and those which are not.

2.2.2.7. *Parodies*

Parody is a humorous or satirical mimicry of a serious work. It is a derivative work, original in its composition and expression. However, the satirical nature of parody leads to the question of whether or not it should be governed by the same rules as those applicable to other works in equivalent circumstances, such as adaptations—in other words, if the right of transformation should be extended to it or not.

The ridicule which it naturally involves seldom fails to wound the feelings of the author of the pre-existing work. The view is, therefore, that it should be free (Pouillet, Stolfi, Piola Caselli). To subject the right of parody to the prior authorization of the author of the parodied work would be equivalent to condemning to death, unjustifiably, a large part of a literary genre and, with it, a form of the freedom of criticism, subject to the provision that the right of parody does not excuse offence, the harming of the original work or its author, or its use to create confusion with the parodied work.

The French Intellectual Property Code (Art. L. 122-5, previously Art. 41(4)) provides that when a work has been disclosed, the author shall not be entitled to prohibit ... parodies, pastiches and caricatures, with due consideration for the laws regarding this type of work (the same provision is found in the laws of Benin, Burundi, Cameroon, Côte d'Ivoire, Senegal). Brazil (Article 50) establishes that pastiches and parodies shall be lawful in so far as they are not real reproductions of the work on which they are based and do not discredit it.

On the other hand, for Satanowsky the solution provided under Argentine law (Article 25) is sounder; according to this the parody of a work which belongs to the private domain requires the author's authorization. In his understanding, parody is distinct from *criticism* because parody requires, logically, following almost all the episodes and the development of a work with humorous intent; for this reason, it is his view that there is clearly exploitation of the parodied work which cannot be made with impunity, if that work has not fallen in the public domain.[37]

---

37. Isidro Satanowsky, op. cit., Vol. I., Section 232, pp. 429–30.

2.2.3. The title

The title is an important element of the work which it designates. It individualizes the work and evokes or suggests its content, providing a means of identification which obviates confusion with other works and enables it to be related to the success it has achieved and to its author.

The author has the right in the title as an integral part of his work. Modification of the title without the author's authorization affects his *moral right* therein, linked to his right concerning the paternity and the integrity of the work. In the same way as the other components of the work, the title may be the subject of negotiation. The author may authorize its use separately from the work and, therefore, he also has the right to defend it against unauthorized utilization, imitation and, in general, against improper use.[38]

The question arises as to whether all titles are equally protected and covered by the same legal regime or if distinctions should be made.

A. CLASSIFICATION

The principal classification establishes the distinction between original and banal titles.

a) *Original titles.* On many occasions, titles constitute literary creations. Significant examples include *Les précieuses ridicules* by Molière, *A la recherche du temps perdu* by Marcel Proust, *La guerre de Troie n'aura pas lieu* by Jean Giraudoux, *A secreto agravio, secreta verganza* (Secret Vengeance for Secret Insult) by Calderón de la Barca.

---

38. It is inappropriate to make the right of defence of the title dependent on the fact that unauthorized utilization has been made in a work of the same genre. The author has the exclusive right to adapt his work to other genres and if, even indirectly, authorization has been given for use of the title in a work of a distinct genre by a third party before being used by the author, both rights would enter into open collision.

Arbitrary expressions or expressions of fantasy constituting creations are also considered as original titles.

b) *Banal titles* are those which lack any originality. They do not represent a creative effort although they are well suited to the work and finding them may have cost the author time and effort. *The Fire, The Legionnaire, The Ingot, Funeral March,* are examples of titles in this category. They serve *only* to identify the work.

The same classification is given to the so-called generic or necessary titles because they make reference to the genre of the work (encyclopaedia, guide, theatre, sonata, etc.) or to the usual designation of its content (the names of historical or legendary characters, place names, and so on, without any addition to distinguish them).

B. REGIME OF PROTECTION

The differences referred to have led to distinctions also being made with respect to the legal regime applicable to the protection of the title, when it is used separately from the work and without the author's authorization.

a) *Protection by copyright.* When the title is original and is, accordingly, a creation, copyright regulations are applicable.

b) *Protection against acts of unfair competition.* Even in the case of a banal title, use by a third party can cause prejudice which may call for reparations in favour of the author who is the injured party. In such cases it is appropriate to apply the regime of protection against acts of unfair competition. But in this case, the inapplicability of copyright protection is not related to the lack of artistic value or merit in the title, but to the absence of originality, an essential condition for copyright protection to become applicable.

The regime of protection against acts of unfair competition establishes, among other requirements, that the title must have (as in the case of trademarks) some distinctive meaning; that use must have been made in circumstances liable to cause confusion; that the party who considers himself injured must prove the prejudice which the imitation has caused him; that his work must have been disclosed or, at least, publicized, and that the intentional nature of the utilization must be identified.[39]

c) *Protection by trademark rights*. Trademarks identify the product, its provenance or quality. The title of a work is not a trademark, since it cannot be used to identify the product in which the work is fixed in relation to its manufacturer or its retailer, which is the function of trademarks. Accordingly, trademark rights are not applicable to the protection of titles.

This is not the case of the titles of newspapers, periodicals and magazines. They constitute trademarks because these publications, in themselves, are not 'works' within the meaning of copyright. This is without prejudice to the copyright protection of these publications and of the works included in them.

The same may be said with respect to publishing houses. The name of the publishing house, of its collections and its various series are trademarks because they identify the *provenance of the publication*. The titles of the works, in contrast, distinguish such works individually and their authors.

d) At the international level, the Inter-American Convention on the Rights of the Author (Washington, 1946) establishes that:

When a copyrighted work has become internationally famous and its title has thereby acquired such a distinctive character as to become identified with that work alone, that title cannot be attached to another work without the consent of the author (Article 14).

---

39. Highly reputable authors such as Pouillet, Piola Caselli, Mayer, Vanois and Darras maintain that use of the title is always governed by the regime of unfair competition; they consider that the right to protection of the title is independent of copyright in the work since, irrespective of how specific and original it is, it cannot be considered as a work or a part of an intellectual work.

Chapter 3

Owners of copyright

Summary
3.1. Authorship and ownership. Natural persons and legal entities
  3.1.1. Original or first owners. 3.1.2. Secondary owners
3.2. Joint authorship
  3.2.1. Works of collaboration. Concept and legal system. 3.2.2. Collective works. Concept and legal system
3.3. Ownership in respect of anonymous and pseudonymous works. Unpublished works
3.4. Ownership in respect of audiovisual works
  3.4.1. Relationship between the creators of the work and the producer of audiovisual works. 3.4.2. Protection of moral rights. 3.4.3. Presumption of assignment of economic rights
3.5. Ownership in respect of works produced on commission or by virtue of a contractual employment relationship

3.1. Authorship and ownership. Natural persons and legal entities

The term 'author' denotes the person who creates the work. The author is the person in whom copyright is originally vested.

Only natural persons are capable of acts of intellectual creation. Learning, thinking, feeling, composing and giving expression to literary, musical and artistic works are actions which can be performed only by human beings.

Copyright originates with the act of intellectual creation. Since the latter is the sole preserve of natural persons, the logical consequence is that original ownership rests with the natural person who creates the work.

This logical and pre-juridical consequence, as Dietz states, is consistent with the theoretical foundation of copyright which stems from the needs of mankind in the matter of access to knowledge and, more specifically, *from the need to promote the search for knowledge by rewarding those who engage in it* (see above, Chapter 1, Section 1.2, *in fine*).

Legal entities cannot create works. Only the natural persons who are members of them may do so. They may be the *secondary proprietors* of certain authors' rights, but a *legal fiction* must be used to ascribe authorship or original ownership in respect of works to a corporate body.

The *fictio juris* by virtue of which the capacity of author, or the original ownership in respect of works, are ascribed to persons —natural or legal—other than the natural person who creates the work, serves the interests of the third parties who exploit those works.

The *Copyright Charter*[1] contains the following provisions (Chapter 2, paras. 5 and 6):

5. The author's right is based upon the act of creation itself. It has its origin in the very nature of things. The law is concerned only with the protection and regulation of that right. Accordingly the existence of the right itself should not be subject to the completion of formalities.
6. Since entitlement to the author's right derives from the act of intellectual creation, it is solely in the physical person of the creator that this right can originate.

    A corporate entity can never be regarded as the original owner of the author's right in a work of the mind, and it is important to reject the unacceptable conception of such a work as a piece of merchandise, and the author as a mere employee of an industrial organization which owns his work.

In the countries in which the system of authors' rights is founded on the Roman legal tradition, either no exceptions whatever are admitted to the principle that copyright can only be vested in the natural person who created the work (as in Germany), or else exceptions are treated as an anomaly which is permitted only in respect of certain works such as collective works (France, Art. L. 113-2, previously Art. 9.3 and Art. L. 113-5, previously Article 13) or in the case of works created and published in the name, for the account of and at the expense of national, provincial and municipal public bodies (as in Italy, Article 11).

---

1. Adopted on 26 September 1956 in Hamburg by the Nineteenth Congress of the International Confederation of Societies of Authors and Composers (CISAC).

Original or first ownership is the corollary of the capacity of authorship and is accordingly vested in the natural persons who create the works concerned. It is a reflection of the real situation and of the legal and political aims in this area: to ensure that authors enjoy adequate protection of their creative output and to encourage creative activity.

In the countries with an Anglo-American legal tradition, there are many instances in which the capacity of authorship, for the purposes of original copyright ownership, or ownership itself are attributed (except where otherwise stipulated) to persons other than the individual who created the work; works which are commissioned or produced by virtue of a contractual employment relationship, and also film productions (see above, Chapter 1, Section 1.3.2).

The legal fiction which attributes original ownership—or the capacity of author or co-author—to persons other than the natural person who created the work, leads to confusion, as Antequera Parilli has pointed out, between authorship and ownership on the one hand and original ownership and secondary ownership on the other.

Situations of secondary ownership occur when some of the entitlements which were first held by the author are transferred to other persons (natural or legal) by *assignment* (either by specific agreement or automatically by virtue of statutory provisions), *by a presumption of assignment* or *by transmission of ownership after the author's death*.

Whereas in the secondary ownership system and that of first ownership there is a fair degree of similarity in the effects of the transfer of economic rights in favour of a person distinct from the creator of the work, there is a divergence between them as far as moral rights are concerned for these originate and remain vested in the true author.[2] The dichotomy between the Roman legal

---

2. See C. Colombet, *Major Principles of Copyright and Neighbouring Rights in the World. A Comparative Law Approach*, Paris, UNESCO, 1987, p. 24.

tradition and the Anglo-American is reflected in the Berne Convention in the fact that it refrains from defining the *author* and confines itself to stipulating in Article 15 who are the persons entitled to exercise the protected rights.

3.1.1. Original or first owners

The original owner is the person in whom copyright is first vested.

The author of a *derivative work* (adaptation, translation or any other transformation) is the *original owner* of the rights therein, without prejudice to the rights of the author of the work from which it is derived, that is to say, of the original work.

The use of the derivative work requires a twofold authorization: that of its author and that of the author of the original work. Since the original work is contained in the derivative work, any use of the latter in turn entails use of the former. Acceptance of the principle that the sole authorization by the author of the derivative work suffices for its exploitation would be tantamount to assent to an infringement of the rights of the author of the original work.

In the absence of proof to the contrary, it is assumed that the capacity of author is vested *in the person who appears as such in the work* through his name, signature (usually on works of art), sign or any other identifying mark. In this respect, Article 15(1) of the Berne Convention contains the following stipulation:

> In order that the author of a literary or artistic work protected by this Convention shall, in the absence of proof to the contrary, be regarded as such, and consequently be entitled to institute infringement proceedings in the countries of the Union, it shall be sufficient for his name to appear on the work in the usual manner. This paragraph shall be applicable even if this name is a pseudonym, where the pseudonym adopted by the author leaves no doubt as to his identity.

This is a presumption *juris tantum* (since proof to the contrary is admitted) which has been embodied in many domestic laws. A similar presumption is created by registration of the work in the name of the person who is cited as its author, whether under the legislation in question registration has a declaratory purpose or is a requirement for establishing rights.

3.1.2. Secondary owners

These are the natural persons or legal entities who have received *ownership* of some of the author's rights. *Secondary ownership can never include all the author's rights* (moral and economic).

The moral right is, in fact, inalienable and even in the case of transmission after death, the successors in title do not take over the essentially personal (*positive*) prerogatives which constitute the moral right of the author for, exceptions apart, these cannot be transmitted. The successors in title can only exercise the *negative* prerogatives (right to recognition of paternity and the right of respect for the integrity of the work) and the right of disclosure of posthumous works (see below, Chapter 4, Section 4.1.A and Chapter 5, Section 5.2.1). On the other hand, all *exploitation rights* (economic right) may be included. Secondary ownership may be acquired:

- by *assignment* (either by specific agreement or automatically by virtue of statutory dispositions—*cessio legis*);
- by *presumption of assignment* established by law, unless otherwise agreed;
- by *transmission after the death of the author*.

The habitual contracts for the exploitation of works by virtue of which the author, the owner of the rights, or the collective administration body authorize a person to use the work are either licences (or authorizations for use) which are not exclusive (as is normal, for example, in the case of public performance of non-dramatic musical works) or they establish exclusive rights in favour of the user; they are not, however, contracts of assignment under ordinary law since they do not transfer ownership of the exploitation rights.[3]

---

3. Such contracts habitually stipulate that the author 'transfers', although the conditions required under civil law for a transfer are not in fact met. The improper use of the term 'transfer' extends to legislative texts as, for example, in the Spanish law of 1987, whose Articles 48 to 50 refer to the 'transfer of exclusive rights' and 'non-exclusive transfer' instead of using the terms 'assignment' or 'licence' (see below, Chapter 6, Section 6.1.1, D(a)).

A. ASSIGNMENT

a. Contractual assignment

The assignees or secondary owners acquire, in respect of the work covered by the contract of assignment, the rights granted in it. The assignment may be total or partial, depending on whether it covers all or only some of the author's economic rights. To protect the author, some domestic laws place various limitations on total assignment. The statutes of societies of authors habitually impose the same limitation on their members.

b. Assignment by statutory provision—cessio legis

The assignees are, by virtue of the law, the secondary owners (original ownership being vested in the authors); the presumption of assignment is *juris et de jure* in respect of the rights of exploitation specifically laid down in the statutory provision. Italy establishes a *cessio legis* in respect of cinematographic works, exercise of the economic exploitation rights belonging to the producer who has the exclusive right to reproduce, bring into circulation, show and transmit such works (Articles 45, para. 1 and 46, para. 1); Austria also establishes this in favour of film companies producing films for commercial purposes (Art. 38, para. 1).

B. LEGAL PRESUMPTION OF ASSIGNMENT

Many domestic laws opt for the creation, in favour of the producer of cinematographic works, of a presumption—*juris tantum* —of assignment of the exclusive right of cinematographic exploitation; authors may enforce, vis-à-vis third parties who enter into contracts with the producer, the rights which they have reserved for themselves in their contracts with the latter (France, Art. L. 132-24, previously Art. 63.1; Spain, Art. 88.1).

Other legislations establish a presumption of legitimation in favour of the producer who is accordingly exonerated by law from the requirement to prove the entitlement by virtue of which he exercises the rights of exploitation expressly mentioned in the statutory provisions (Berne Convention system, Article 14*bis*(2)(b)). This is also a presumption *juris tantum*, which admits proof to the contrary as a consequence of the contract between the author and the producer.[4]

C. TRANSMISSION AFTER THE DEATH OF THE AUTHOR

The legatees receive the economic rights which the author has not transferred by an act *inter vivos*; they may exercise the *negative* or *defensive* prerogatives of the moral right and the right of disclosure of the posthumous works.

The secondary owners are habitually designated as the author's successors at law or successors in title.

3.2. Joint authorship

When several authors have taken part in the creation of a work, acting either jointly or separately, but making their own contributions of an identical or different kind in such a way that these works are exploited jointly and constitute a single entity, these are said to be works of joint authorship.

Works of this kind are very frequent. They comprise *works of collaboration* (including musical works with the accompanying lyrics, dramatico-musical, cinematographic and, more generally, audiovisual works) and *collective works* (such as dictionaries,

---

4. See Antonio Delgado Porras, 'Utilización de obras audiovisualés por satélite y cable. La intervención de las sociedades de autores', Libro-Memoria, *Fifth International Congress on the protection of intellectual rights (of authors, artists and producers)*, Buenos Aires, 1990, Section 10, p. 219. This author points out that the system of presumption of legitimation has been adopted by Argentina, Article 21: 'In the absence of special agreements, the producer of a cinematographic film shall have the right to show it, even without the consent of the author of the plot or of the composer, without prejudice to the rights which may flow from their collaboration ...'. (Article 20 of the same law stipulates that 'in the absence of special agreements, collaborators in a cinematographic work shall have equal rights. The author of the plot and the producer of the film shall be considered as collaborators. In the case of a musical cinematographic work in which a composer has collaborated, the latter shall have the same rights as the author of the plot and the producer of the film'.)

encyclopedias, newspapers, periodicals, compilations and collections of case law).

Works of collaboration and collective works constitute separate categories of works of joint authorship and the statutory provisions governing them also differ.

Audiovisual works or cinematographic works are governed by a special statute.

Composite works (adaptations, translations and other transformations; see above, Chapter 2, Section 2.2.2, *in fine*) are not treated as works of joint authorship because the new work incorporates the pre-existing work without the collaboration of its author. Likewise, joint authorship does not exist in cases where, without transformation of the pre-existing work, a new work is added to it, for example, the lyrics or choreography of a musical work or music to accompany the text of a poem.

For this reason, a distinction is made in copyright law between joint authorship and pluri-authorship—a situation in which there is simply a plurality of authors. These two terms have separate meanings as they refer to different situations.

3.2.1. Works of collaboration. Concept and legal system

A. CONCEPT

Works of collaboration are those created by two or more persons working together or, at least, taking mutual account of their contributions and drawing on a common inspiration.

In the *narrow* meaning, a work of collaboration exists only when the co-authors have co-operated closely in such a way that, once the work has been completed, it is impossible to determine which of its parts can be attributed to each of the authors: for example, two dramatists who together write a theatrical work.

In the *wider* meaning of the term, works of collaboration also include those in which, although the contributions of the different creators can be identified, agreement was reached between them on the manner in which they would individually contribute to the work as a whole and their respective shares appear to be linked by a common inspiration. Dramatico-musical works and, more generally, musical compositions with lyrics, may be cited as examples.

The collaboration is said to be *complete* when the work is indivisible and *incomplete* when the work is divisible because the contribution of each author can be readily identified individually and separated from the whole without changing the nature of the work.

The adoption of one or other of these notions of collaboration has a number of important practical implications:

- in respect of the duration of the rights in a work *after the death of the author*: if a work of collaboration is held to exist only when it is indivisible, should it not fall into this category the period is calculated from the death of each author in respect of his own creative contribution, since each such contribution is treated as an independent work. On the other hand, if a single work is deemed to exist even when the collaboration is divisible, the term of the copyright is calculated from the date of the decease of the last surviving collaborator;
- in respect of the entitlement of all the co-authors to a share of the remuneration which is obtained, even if use has not in fact been made of all the contributions to the work: for example, the entitlement of the author of the text when only the music of a song, opera or musical comedy is recorded or performed;
- in respect of the right of one of the authors to authorize, for any or all of the subsequent utilizations of the work, the replacement of the contribution of the other author: for example, the lyrics of a song, the *incidental* music composed specifically for a theatrical work, the choreography when the music has been specifically composed for a ballet and the choreographer has prepared his work at the request of, or by joint agreement with, the composer. The latter case differs from the frequent instance in which the choreographer works with pre-existing music which may or may not have been composed for the ballet; in this case, the work is said to be 'composite' and not one of collaboration.

B. Legal system

Rights in a work of collaboration accrue to all its co-authors. The consent of each one of them is required for the work to be *disclosed* and *modified*. The relevant laws provide for settlement of the dispute by legal means in the event of disagreement.

Once the work has been disclosed, by virtue of the fact that the rights are shared, they must be exercised by all the co-authors by joint agreement. Consequently, the uses must in principle be authorized by all the collaborators.[5] But it does not seem reasonable for a refusal by one of them to be sufficient to prevent publication and, in the event of disagreement, the matter may therefore be submitted for a decision by legal means. However, this solution inevitably involves a delay which will very probably result in a loss of interest on the part of the potential user of the work.[6]

When the collaboration is divisible, it is generally accepted that the creative contributions may be exploited separately (for example, printed edition of the lyrics on the one hand and performance or recording of the music on the other), provided that no prejudice is caused to the joint exploitation of the work.

3.2.2. Collective works. Concept and legal system

A. CONCEPT

A collective work is one created on the initiative and under the co-ordination of a natural person or legal entity who publishes and discloses the work under his own name using the personal contributions made for that purpose by the authors who participated in its elaboration, but whose identities merge into a single and autonomous creation.[7]

Traditionally, the commonest types of collective works are

---

5. Some laws (for example, that of Mexico, Art. 12) only require the consent of a majority of the collaborators.
6. Spain (Article 7(4)) stipulates that once a work has been disclosed, none of the joint authors may without justification withhold his consent to its exploitation in the manner in which it was disclosed. Argentine legislation has a similar provision (Article 19), although it refers only to dramatic or musical works in which case the authorization granted by one of the authors shall suffice for public performance of the work, without prejudice to any actions which the individual authors might institute.
7. Some domestic laws also include within the category of collective works those which incorporate *pre-existing* works or parts thereof by different authors (for example, Canada, Article 2).

dictionaries, encyclopedias, newspapers and reviews, compilations and collections of case law. Mention must also be made of a more recent phenomenon, namely the databases and highly complex computer programs developed by major undertakings with the joint or successive participation to varying degrees of many analysts.

A collective work differs from a work of collaboration through the importance accorded to the role of the individual who plans and co-ordinates the contributions and discloses and publishes the work; some domestic laws therefore grant original ownership to the natural person or legal entity concerned.

B. LEGAL SYSTEM

The attribution of original ownership in respect of the collective work to the natural person or legal entity who publishes and discloses it in his own name is based on the assumption that since production of the work involves a considerable number of authors whose individual contributions are hard to identify as they merge into a single creation, it would be impossible to grant each one of them separate rights in respect of the whole. Moreover, it may be difficult to establish which natural person is the author of the collective work, viewed as an autonomous work, so that full recognition of his rights would impede its exploitation.

However, the appropriateness of this exception to the principle that original ownership is vested in the natural person who creates the work has not gone unchallenged. It is deemed more appropriate to establish a presumption of assignment of the rights of exploitation by the authors in favour of the producer of the work, unless otherwise stipulated (as in France, Art. L. 113-5, previously Article 13 and in Spain, Article 8.2).

3.3. Ownership in respect of anonymous and pseudonymous works. Unpublished works

A. OWNERSHIP IN RESPECT OF ANONYMOUS AND PSEUDONYMOUS WORKS

An *anonymous* work is one which is disclosed without any indication of the name or pseudonym of its author. A *pseudonymous* work is one which is disclosed with the identification of its author under an artistic name which differs from his real name.

The pseudonym may serve to identify the author under a name differing from his real name (*false name*) or to maintain his anonymity (*no name*). In the first case, the pseudonym may leave no doubt as to the identity of the author (*transparent pseudonym*), in which case it may be considered equivalent to the real name (e.g. Molière, George Sand, Rubén Darío, Gabriela Mistral). In the second case, it may genuinely conceal the person; it is then a pseudonym equivalent to anonymity (e.g. Bruno Traven, author of the novel *The Treasure of the Sierra Madre*, among others).

The author may decide to remain anonymous or to adopt a pseudonym for the same reason. In such cases too, he is the owner of all the rights in his work but his prerogatives will be exercised by a third party, i.e. the natural person or legal entity who publishes the work[8] with his consent.

The person entrusted with the task of exercising the rights of the author is an *ex lege* representative of a special kind, since he must refrain from revealing the name of his principal to the persons with whom he has to deal in the course of his managerial activity. He is not the first or secondary owner of the author's rights since the latter may, simply by revealing his identity and providing evidence thereof, *ipso facto* exercise those rights without the need for any retrocession of the rights by the third party.

The author retains the possibility of revealing his identity at any time and thus of exercising his rights himself. But only the author has this option, since the rights to anonymity and to a pseudonym form an integral part of his moral right to authorship of the work.

As long as the work remains anonymous, the duration of the economic rights in it are calculated from the date on which it is disclosed. The same principle applies where the pseudonym is not generally known to be equivalent to the name.

If in his lifetime, or by testamentary disposition, the author

---

8. 'Who reveals it ...' is the portmanteau expression used in the Spanish law (Article 6(2)).

incontrovertibly reveals his identity, the period is calculated in the manner which is normal for the type of work concerned, without prejudice to the validity of the rights acquired while the work was still anonymous or pseudonymous.

Article 15(3) of the Berne Convention (Paris Act) stipulates that:

In the case of anonymous and pseudonymous works, other than those referred to in paragraph (1) above [*the pseudonym adopted by the author leaves no doubt as to his identity*], the publisher whose name appears on the work shall, in the absence of proof to the contrary, be deemed to represent the author, and in this capacity he shall be entitled to protect and enforce the author's rights. The provisions of this paragraph shall cease to apply when the author reveals his identity and establishes his claim to authorship of the work. (my italics).

B. UNPUBLISHED WORKS

An unpublished work is one that has not been made public. The term 'published work' denotes a work of which copies have been made available to the public *with the consent of the author, provided that the availability of such copies has been achieved so as to satisfy the reasonable needs of the public*, having regard to the nature of the work. The work is deemed to have been published if it is stored in a computer system *and is available to the public by any means of retrieval whatsoever.*[9]

A work remains unpublished as long as its author has not exercised his moral right of disclosure[10] in its regard, even though he may have made it known to a particular group of persons, e.g. by circulating to them copies obtained by photocopying or some other method of reproduction.

Antonio Chaves points out that *printing* is not synonymous with, and does not necessarily imply, publication or disclosure.[11]

---

9. See *Draft Model Provisions for Legislation in the Field of Copyright*, WIPO document CE/MPC/I/2-II of 20 October 1988, Definitions, (XV), p. 3.
10. See below: Chapter 4, Section 4.2.1.
11. See Antonio Chaves: 'El contrato de edición de obras escritas y musicales', Libro-Memoria, *II International Congress on the Protection of Intellectual Property*, Bogotá, 1987, Section 1, pp. 25–6.

Copyright limitations[12] *do not apply to unpublished works.* Works which have not been published, or made public, are protected both by domestic laws and by international conventions. In the case of the latter, the unpublished nature of the work determines, for the purpose of establishing whether it falls within the sphere of protection afforded by the Berne Convention, that only personal criteria of protection are adopted (nationality of the author or his habitual place of residence in a country which is party to the Convention).

Article 3(1)(a) of the Berne Convention (Paris Act, 1971), stipulates that: 'The protection of this Convention shall apply to: (a) authors who are nationals of one of the countries of the Union, for their works, *whether published or not* ...' (my italics).

Article 3(3), second sentence, provides that for the purposes of the Convention 'the performance of a dramatic, dramatico-musical, cinematographic or musical work, the public recitation of a literary work, the communication by wire or the broadcasting of literary or artistic works, the exhibition of a work of art and the construction of a work of architecture shall not constitute publication'.

Article II, 2 of the Universal Copyright Convention (1971 text) stipulates that: 'Unpublished works of nationals of each Contracting State shall enjoy in each other Contracting State the same protection as that other State accords to unpublished works of its own nationals, as well as the protection specially granted by this Convention.'

Works of folklore constitute a special category of unpublished works (Chapter 2, Section 2.2.1.7). *These are unpublished works by an anonymous author* which, because of their wide dissemination, come to the attention of third parties (in many countries, expressions of folklore are deemed to belong to the public domain).

In respect of such works, Article 15(4) of the Berne Convention (Paris Act), stipulates, although without mentioning them, that:

---

12. See below, Chapter 4, Section 4.3.

a) In the case of unpublished works where the identity of the author is unknown, but where there is every ground to presume that he is a national of a country of the Union, it shall be a matter for legislation in that country to designate the competent authority which shall represent the author and shall be entitled to protect and enforce his rights in the countries of the Union.
b) Countries of the Union which make such designation under the terms of this provision shall notify the Director-General by means of a written declaration giving full information concerning the authority thus designated. The Director-General shall at once communicate this declaration to all other countries of the Union.

3.4. Ownership in respect of audiovisual works

In the case of audiovisual works (cinematographic and video works[13]), the difficulties in determining the owner of the author's rights are greater than for other types of intellectual creation. Their production requires the involvement of a large number of creators, and artists and of ancillary activities: the author of the original screenplay created for the audiovisual work or the author of the adaptation if the latter is based on pre-existing works (novel, play, etc.); the author of the dialogues; the composer of the music; the director or the producer-director; the actors; the set designer; the director of photography; the cameraman; the sound recording expert; the wardrobe manager; the make-up expert; the hairdresser; the assistants of the director, of the director of photography, of the cameraman and of the set designer; the filming assistants; the producer (by which is understood the natural or legal person who takes the initiative and assumes the responsibility for producing the work); the executive producer; the associate producers and the head of production.

The following questions are hard to resolve: Can any single one of these persons be considered as the author because of his preponderant or exclusive activity? Or, given that the work is one of collaboration, are all or only some of the persons who contribute to its creation, co-authors of the audiovisual work? Must

---

13. See above, Chapter 2, Section 2.2.1. The Berne Convention mentions in its list of protected works (Art. 2(1)): 'cinematographic works to which are assimilated works expressed by a process analogous to cinematography'.

ownership of copyright, or at least its exercise, remain with the author or co-authors of the audiovisual work or is it to be vested in the producer to ensure that exploitation cannot be impeded by the right of prohibition enjoyed by each of the collaborators? What is the most suitable legal instrument: assignment of original ownership to the producer, *cessio legis* of economic rights or the presumption of such assignment which allows agreements to the contrary, with limitations on the moral rights of the authors?

We shall look at various solutions further below.

3.4.1. Relationship between the creators of the work and the producer of audiovisual works

Since the early days of film-making, producers have asked to be guaranteed the right to exploit their productions widely. They have sought to be recognized as the sole authors of the work. In some countries that title is granted to them; in others, original ownership.

However, in many countries this claim is held to be disproportionate. It is nevertheless generally conceded that a cinematographic work differs significantly from other types of works: in regard to its creation, since it is a work of collaboration of a special type differing from the habitual divisible collaboration; through the large number of creators who collaborate in the production; through the manner in which it is exploited and the scale of the economic investment which it requires. The need to safeguard the rights of the producer so as to guarantee satisfactory exploitation has been recognized.

Broadly speaking, the solutions adopted in existing laws to overcome *the problem of ownership in respect of audiovisual works* may be divided into two main categories.

The first concerns the countries which grant the producer the capacity of author or original ownership of copyright, without recognizing the authors who have made creative contributions to the audiovisual work as the authors thereof: these are the countries in which the copyright system applies, such as the United States, save where otherwise agreed (Section 201(b) and 101—'works made for hire'—(2)) and the United Kingdom (Section

9(2)(a)), although in the latter instance the moral right is granted to the director (Section 77). This is the system known as the producer's *film-copyright*.

The other category refers to the countries of the Roman or continental European legal tradition, or of the author's rights system—which consider that *only those natural persons* who have taken part in the creation of the audiovisual work may be authors and hence the original owners of the author's rights in the work in question.

Notwithstanding this, in the case of cinematographic (or audiovisual) works, special provisions are laid down to enable the producer to exploit the work without unnecessary interference. Consequently some domestic laws opt for the automatic assignment—*cessio legis*—of economic rights to the producer (for example Italy), although a majority establish a *legal presumption of assignment* or a *legal presumption of legitimation*, save where otherwise agreed, as well as certain limitations on the moral rights of the collaborators.

As we have stated, in line with Colombet's views, the fundamental difference between the two systems does not concern the aspect of the transfer of economic rights as much as the question of the moral right, which, in countries where the system of authors' rights prevails, is not transmitted to the producer, although it is affected by certain restrictions. It is possible that a relationship exists between this and the fact that the United Kingdom Act of 1988 establishes on the one hand—for the purposes of the original attribution of authorship—that in the case of films the author is the producer (Section 9(2)(a)) and, on the other—in regard to the moral right—that the right to be identified as the author of the film and the right not to have the work subjected to derogatory treatment are recognized as being vested in the director (Sections 77(1) and 80(1)).

In the countries with the Roman legal tradition, cinematographic works, and audiovisual works in general, are treated as works of collaboration and the persons to whom the capacity of co-authors or collaborators is attributed usually include the authors of the original scenario created for the work, or of the adaptation when it is based on a pre-existing work, of the dialogues and musical compositions, with or without lyrics, specially composed for the work concerned, and finally the director.

In some of these countries, the producer is also included among the co-authors of the audiovisual work, if he performs an act of intellectual creation in the same way as the other persons involved in the work (France, Art. L. 113-7.1, previously Article 14, first paragraph), or, under some general kind of arrangement if the person concerned is a *legal entity* (Argentina, Article 20, Brazil, Article 16, Costa Rica, Article 52(ch)); mention is also made of the author of the pre-existing work on which the audiovisual work is based, i.e. a novel, dramatic work, etc. (France, Art. L. 113-7, previously Article 14, last paragraph).

The aim of guaranteeing the producer's rights to exploit the cinematographic work lay at the basis of Article 14*bis*(2)(b) of the Berne Convention (Paris Act, 1971) (drawn up following the Stockholm Reform of 1967). This establishes the *presumption of legitimation* as a rule for the interpretation of contracts in countries in which neither the film copyright nor the *cessio legis* systems operate:

> However, in the countries of the Union which, by legislation, include among the owners of copyright in a cinematographic work authors who have brought contributions to the making of the work, such authors, if they have undertaken to bring such contributions, may not, in the absence of any contrary or special stipulation, object to the reproduction, distribution, public performance, communication to the public by wire, broadcasting or any other communication to the public, or to the subtitling or dubbing of texts, of the work.

The scope of application of this text is, nevertheless, very limited; unless domestic laws provide to the contrary, the presumption established in this provision of the Convention is not applicable to authors of scenarios, dialogues and musical works created for the making of the cinematographic work, or to the principal director thereof (Art. 14*bis*(3)).

3.4.2. Protection of moral rights

Protection of the substantial financial investment required in the making of audiovisual works often means that the moral rights in such works are subjected to limitations. These rights are applicable to the co-authors; some laws recognize the moral rights as belonging only to the director (Brazil, Art. 26, Costa Rica, Art. 56, Colombia, Art. 99, which adds: without prejudice to those that accrue to the various collaborators or artists in respect of their respective contributions). Recognition is given to its two basic prerogatives—paternity and integrity—excluding the right of withdrawal or reconsideration (exercise of this right by one of the collaborators could lead to extremely unfortunate situations and be highly detrimental to the others and to the producer), as German legislation expressly provides in its Article 90. It will also be seen from the provisions established that when an author fails to complete his contribution by reason of his unjustified refusal or of *force majeure*, the producer may use the section already completed, provided that the rights of its author are respected and without prejudice, according to the case in question, to his right to receive an indemnity (e.g. Spain, Article 91, France, Art. L. 121-6, previously Art. 15(1); Brazil, Art. 86, Colombia, Article 102). It must always be understood that the nature of the section which is used may not be altered.

The *right of authorship* requires mention to be made in the habitual manner, or in the form stipulated in the contract, of the names of all the collaborators; this requirement also applies to trailers and advertisements for the work.

The *right to integrity* is limited by the artistic and technical demands of film-making although changes may be made to the extent that is strictly necessary and always providing that the spirit of the work is not affected. It has been suggested that if, during the production of the audiovisual work, one of the co-authors should refuse to make the essential changes required, the producer may then entrust that task to another author provided that the original contribution is not distorted.

In such cases, the courts habitually take account of the needs of the collaboration. Such needs lead to the limitation of the moral right of each co-author which, for this type of work, is weaker than in the case of the work of a single author.

A co-author whose contribution has been modified or completed in the circumstances described above may demand that he should not be associated with it and that his name should not be mentioned in the audiovisual work. If he considers that the nature of his contribution has been altered, he may withhold his approval of the final version and protest against the use of his work under these conditions.

Infringement of the moral right is evident when cuts are made without the agreement of the joint authors; some laws include an explicit provision to the effect that any change made to the final version of the audiovisual work by adding, deleting or modifying any element thereof shall require the prior agreement of the persons whose common accord was necessary in order to establish that version (France, Art. L. 121-5.3, previously Art. 16, para. 3, Spain, Article 92, para. 2).

The insertion of commercial breaks, which is frequent during television broadcasts, has rightly given rise to strong protests; it is a major infringement of the integrity of the work. The situation is different when the audiovisual works are intended primarily for communication to the public by broadcasting (works for television). In such cases, it may be assumed that, unless otherwise agreed, the authors have taken account of this intention and given their authorization for the broadcast to be made with such modifications as are strictly necessitated by the manner of programming of the medium, provided that no prejudice is caused to their legitimate interests or damage to their reputation (Spain, Article 92(2), second paragraph).

More recently, the concept of infringement of moral rights has also been invoked to oppose the 'colouring' of cinematographic works produced in black and white, since this may be considered to be a betrayal of the original creation.[14]

---

14. In the much talked-of case of the *heirs of John Huston and Ben Maddow versus 5ème Chaîne and Turner Entertainment Inc.* as a result of the televising of the coloured version of the film *Asphalt Jungle* (*RIDA*, No. 139, 1989, pp. 205–10; *RIDA*, No. 143, pp. 329–43, with a note by André Françon; J. Ginsburg, and P. Sirinelli, 'Author, Creation and Adaptation in Private International Law and French Domestic Law. Reflections Based on the Huston Case', *RIDA*, No. 150, 1991, pp. 3–81).

3.4.3. Presumption of assignment of economic rights

To ensure that the producer does not encounter any unnecessary obstacles to the exploitation of the audiovisual work, legislation in countries with the Roman legal tradition of author's rights, establishes either a presumption of assignment of the economic rights of the collaborators in favour of the producer, which admits proof to the contrary (presumption *juris tantum* of assignment)—legal assignment, or presumption of legitimation in favour of the producer, unless otherwise agreed—covering the rights of *reproduction* (making copies necessary for communication to the public in the form provided for in the contract), of *distribution, public communication* (in the form set out in the contract or inherent in the specific purpose of the work) and of *translation* (by incorporating subtitles or dubbing), or a presumption of assignment of the rights mentioned in the relevant statutory provision, interpreted in a restrictive manner. (As regards the limited possibility granted by certain legislative provisions to apply the legal system governing audiovisual works to 'radiophonic'—televised—works, see above, Chapter 2, Section 2.2.1.6.B).

Audiovisual works have different specific purposes, depending on the category to which they belong. For example, the immediate objective of cinematographic works is their projection in commercial cinemas. Explicit authorization by the joint authors is thus required for the producer to exploit the work by any other means such as:
- total or partial reproduction of the work for a purpose other than that set out in the contract;
- reproducing and making copies available to the public in any

---

André Bertrand points out that as far back as the end of the nineteenth century, the French courts considered that the 'colouring' of photographs and postcards constituted a *contrefaçon* (any *contrefaçon* is an offence). The same conclusion was reached in 1959 in the case of a 'sepia' copy of Charlie Chaplin's film *The Kid* ('En la "jungla" del derecho de autor internacional: ¿el derecho moral francés resultará inmoral en Norteamérica?', translated by Antonio Millé, in the review *DAT* (Buenos Aires), April 1989, pp. 1–8.

system or format for use in the home (at present this mainly involves copies on videocassettes); and
- communication to the public by open television or by cable.

The remuneration of the authors of an audiovisual work must remain in an equitable ratio to the scope of the rights which are granted to the producer of the work, and to the conditions of exploitation stipulated in the relevant contracts.

The collaborators retain the right to make use of their personal contributions separately (for example, the right of the author of the original screenplay to authorize a printed edition or an adaptation for the theatre, etc.); this right is sometimes subject to the condition that they do not thereby prejudice the normal exploitation of the audiovisual work. They also retain the right to make a new contract for the inclusion of their personal contributions in another audiovisual work (a 'remake') once a reasonable period of time has elapsed. This period is generally defined as about five years from the date of the contract. Some laws fix such a period if none is stipulated in the contract (15 years is the period cited in Article 89(2) of the Spanish law). Failing any contractual stipulation or statutory provision, the author may ask for the period to be determined by the courts.

3.5. Ownership in respect of works produced on commission or by virtue of a contractual employment relationship

A contract commissioning a work does not constitute a contractual employment relationship. The situation of an author who creates a work on commission is different from that of a salaried author.

A. OWNERSHIP IN RESPECT OF WORKS PRODUCED ON COMMISSION

Commissioned works are those which are produced pursuant to an agreement by which the author creates, in return for payment, a specific work to be used in the manner and for the purposes stipulated.

The author who accepts the commission provides his services

of his own free will. He is the original owner of the rights in the work and enjoys to the full the prerogatives pertaining to both his moral and economic rights, even though isolated and specific exceptions may be encountered (for example in Article 16 of the Argentine law which covers the rights of anonymous contributors to a collective compilation in respect of the contributions commissioned from them).

The principal may only exploit the work for the purpose stipulated in the contract by virtue of which it is commissioned, even if the author is given guidance as to the subject matter, the main content and title, and even if these elements are themselves original since copyright protects formal creations.[15]

The provisions laid down in civil law for contracts for the hiring of services are applicable only secondarily and only in so far as they do not conflict with the author's rights, since, under such provisions, the work becomes the property of the hirer of the services or the principal.

B. OWNERSHIP IN RESPECT OF WORKS PRODUCED UNDER A CONTRACTUAL EMPLOYMENT RELATIONSHIP

Determination of ownership in respect of works produced under a contractual employment relationship poses problems arising from the conflict which exists here between the principles of labour law and those governing author's rights. In the context of employment, the product of the work of the employee accrues to the employer in return for the payment of a salary. In the area of author's rights, the prerogatives of the moral right are inalienable and both the assignment or the licensing of economic rights in a work are interpreted restrictively and confined to the forms of exploitation stipulated in the contract.

---

15. Such guidance does not have the effect of converting the principal into the author of the work, save in exceptional situations where the instructions given are so comprehensive and precise that the task of producing the work is purely material.

Works created by virtue of a contractual employment relationship are frequent in such areas as journalism, architecture, advertising, industrial arts, publishing activity (adapters, translators) and, more recently, in companies which produce complex computer programs. This situation presupposes that the salaried author creates the works in response to requests made by his employer.

The problems arising in connection with the ownership of the rights in such works are often compared with those encountered in the sphere of cinematography, since in both cases the exploitation of the work must not be unnecessarily hampered by the author's right to prohibit the use of his work.

In general, in the countries with the Roman legal tradition, respect for the principle that *the author is the natural person who creates the work* prevents the original ownership of the author's rights from being attributed to the employer although, save where stipulated otherwise, an immediate transfer of rights in favour of the employer may take place; however, the moral right continues to be vested in the author who is employed. There are occasional exceptions to this general rule, as, for example, in the case of computer programs (France, Art. L. 113-9, previously Art. 45 of the 1985 law which applies in all cases save where otherwise agreed; Chile, Art. 8(2); works produced by staff or civil servants in the discharge of their duties (Chile, Art. 88; Colombia, Art. 91, the second paragraph of which exempts lectures or courses given by professors).

In the countries with state-planned economies, recognition of the quality of author is also granted to salaried authors.

In the copyright countries, when authors create by virtue of a contractual employment relationship, the employer is regarded as the author for the purpose of the acquisition of the *first ownership* of copyright, save where otherwise agreed (for example in the United Kingdom, Section 11(2); United States, Section 201(b)— *works made for hire*) or the first ownership of copyright is attributed to the employer, including the moral right, save stipulation to the contrary (Barbados, Art. 15(b)).

The division between the two legal standpoints is reflected in the Draft Model Provisions for Legislation in the Field of Copyright (WIPO document CE/MPC/I/2-II of 20 October 1988) where, in Article 37, two alternatives are presented. *Alternative A* (intended for countries following the Roman legal tradition) attributes first ownership of economic rights to the *author*; *Alternative B* (for countries with an Anglo-American tradition) attributes first ownership of the economic rights to the *employer*.

a. Moral right

The capacity of author—whether independent or salaried— implies recognition of the moral right. However, the need to safeguard exploitation of the works means that, despite the inalienable nature of the prerogatives which constitute the moral right, some restrictions are permitted and the possibility of the salaried author exercising the right of withdrawal by reason of changed convictions is regarded as excluded, since it is not compatible with the contractual employment relationship in the light of the transfer of the right of exploitation to the employer which derives from that contractual relationship.

In regard to the *right of disclosure*, the employer may publish the work only when the salaried author delivers it to him for that purpose.

As regards the *right of authorship*, whereby the name of the author must appear or be mentioned in all copies of the work, or each time the work is communicated to the public, the validity of the waiving by the salaried author of such mention of his name is accepted even if, in principle, this is considered to be a precarious measure as he may change his mind.

In a study produced by the International Labour Organization,[16] it is reported that, in France, the waiving of the right of salaried authors to be named is termed 'abdicative' when authors agree to this procedure and 'translative' when they grant third parties the right to have authorship of the work attributed to them. The courts recognize the validity of both procedures, except

---

16. ILO, *The Protection of Salaried Authors and Inventors*, Geneva, 1987, pp. 67–70.

in cases of deceit or fraud by the employer. These agreements are, none the less, regarded as unreliable since the author-employee can at any moment disclose his authorship of the work, subject to recognition of liability for damages to the employer if the manner in which the disclosure is made is deemed abusive. Surrender of the right should normally be explicitly stipulated, interpretation of such a decision being restrictive. The Paris Court of Appeal, for example, ruled that the fact that a journalist was an employee could not invalidate his authorship rights (authorship being perpetual, inalienable and imprescriptible); a press enterprise could not claim, therefore, that a journalist had tacitly waived his or her right of authorship and certainly could not claim that the right had been waived once and for all (*Recueil Dalloz Sirey*, Paris, 1969, p. 702).

Interpretation of the extent of the right of salaried authors to withdraw the waiving of mention of their name in connection with their work depends on the particular circumstances in each case and, more especially, on the practice which is observed in certain sectors (e.g. advertising).

In Germany it is considered that employees do not have an unlimited right to claim authorship when this right does not conform to practice in the branch of activity in which they are employed or when it cannot be reconciled with the obligations arising out of the working relationship or with the nature of such relationship. The German Confederation of Trade Unions (DGB) noted that the employer could not, nevertheless, change the designation of the author once it had been approved.[17]

In regard to the right to the *integrity of the work* which would prevent the employer from modifying it, this is deemed to be governed both by the needs of the employer and the principles of labour law, whereby employers retain not only the product of their employees' work but also have the power to guide and direct that work, and by the degree of originality of the employees' contribution, for it would be pointless if this were insignificant or if the work in question had undergone a succession of transformations.

---

17. Ibid., p. 67.

Some domestic laws give explicit recognition to the right of modification of certain works: in France, for instance, Article L. 121-7, previously Art. 46 of the 1985 law, dealing with software, when the modification does not prejudice the author's honour or reputation (an addition introduced by law 94-361 of 10 May 1994 giving effect to European Directive 91/250/CEE), and the Italian law (Art. 4) dealing with press articles, which allows the newspaper or magazine editor, save where otherwise agreed, to make changes of form in the article for publication as may be required by the nature and purpose of the periodical.

In former Czechoslovakia, when changes are made without the consent of the employees, they may not prevent publication of their work but are entitled to withdraw their agreement to the use of their name even though this does not entail loss of their right to remuneration. Again, they may authorize other editors to use the original version of their work. Similar measures are to be found in Bulgaria, Hungary and the former Soviet Union.[18]

b. Economic rights

Save where otherwise agreed, *the right to exploit the work* is automatically transmitted to the employer in the manner established by the relevant law (granting of first ownership, assignment as a matter of right, presumption of assignment). However, a tendency can be seen towards a restriction of the scope of transfer of economic rights to the employer. Only those uses which fall within the normal scope of his activities are permitted (e.g. Spain, United Kingdom, India, etc.). The protective nature of copyright imposes a restrictive interpretation of the statutory or contractual provisions implying the transfer of the rights of creators.

The sphere of journalistic activity is the one in which this trend has become most apparent, and many domestic laws (e.g.

---

18. G. Palos, *General aspects of copyright ownership and its consequences for the relations between employers and employed or salaried authors in socialist countries* (roneod document ILO/UNESCO/WIPO/SA/CM/2, Geneva, 1982), quoted in *The Protection of Salaried Authors and Inventors*, ILO, 1987, pp. 70–1.

Argentina, Belgium, France, Italy, Spain, Portugal, etc.) contain provisions whereby, unless otherwise agreed, authors retain, to varying degrees, the right to publish their work in a collection or to exploit it in other forms, sometimes on condition that this does not compete with the publication in which it first appeared.

Chapter 4

Substantive content of copyright

Summary
- **4.1.** Substantive content of copyright. The monistic theory and the dualist theory
- **4.2.** The moral right. Characteristics
  - **4.2.1.** The right of disclosure. **4.2.2.** The right of paternity. **4.2.3.** The right to respect for the work and for its integrity. **4.2.4.** The right to reconsider or the right of withdrawal
- **4.3.** Economic rights
  - **4.3.1.** The right of reproduction. **4.3.2.** The right of public communication. 4.3.2.1. Exhibition of works of art or reproductions thereof. 4.3.2.2. Public performance 4.3.2.3. Projection or public showing of cinematographic works and other audio-visual works. 4.3.2.4. Broadcasting, public communication by satellite and distribution by cable. 4.3.2.5. Public communication of works with the use of information technology services. 4.3.2.6. The public nature of the communication. **4.3.3.** The right of transformation. **4.3.4.** The right of participation or *droit de suite*
- **4.4.** Limitations on copyright
  - **4.4.1.** Free use without payment. **4.4.2.** Uses subject to remuneration: non-voluntary licences (compulsory licences and statutory licences)

4.1. Substantive content of copyright. The monistic theory and the dualist theory

A. SUBSTANTIVE CONTENT OF COPYRIGHT

The work enjoying copyright protection is property of a special kind: it is a vivid and abiding expression of the personality of its creator. The author 'lives' in his work and projects his intellect through it. Copyright is therefore not confined to securing for the creator the possibility of obtaining economic benefits from exploitation of the work; it also protects his intellectual and personal relationship with the work and with the use which is made of it.

It is therefore generally accepted today at both national and international levels that the rights of the author have a twofold purpose and, hence, a dual structure.[1]

They comprise exclusive prerogatives corresponding to their essential substance: on the one hand the personal prerogatives constituting the *moral right* which protect the personality of the author in relation to his work, and, on the other, the pecuniary entitlement constituting the economic right which permits the author to undertake the economic exploitation of his work, or, as is usually the case, to authorize others to do so and to participate in this.

B. MONISTIC THEORY

The advocates of the monistic theory reject the notion that a clear distinction can be drawn between the two categories of prerogatives which make up the author's rights: they consider that all the prerogatives which belong to the creator, both personal and economic, are expressions of a unitary right which guarantees, as a whole, both the intellectual and economic interests of the author.

This is not to say that the monistic theory ignores this difference between the two categories of rights but that it gives a unitary interpretation of all the prerogatives and rights vested in the author, considering these to be simply derivations, expressions and modalities of a single right.

Ulmer, the celebrated representative of the modern German doctrine associated with monism (Rintelen, Dietz, etc.), states that the two categories of interests—personal and economic— that the work represents for the author, could be said to be the roots of a tree with a single trunk. From this trunk spring different branches and shoots representing the legal prerogatives which, like the branches on the trunk, at times derive their force from both roots—the personal and the economic—and at others, draw more heavily on one of them.[2]

---

1. See Adolf Dietz, *El derecho de autor en la comunidad europea*, Ministerio de Cultura, Madrid, 1983, p. 153.
2. E. Ulmer, *Urheber und Verlagsrecht*, p. 101 (quoted by H. Baylos Corroza, *Tratado de derecho industrial ...*, op. cit., p. 460, note 245).

Dietz explains that the monistic interpretation rejects the rigid delimitation of the two groups of prerogatives for it cannot be upheld in practice; the exclusive exploitation rights granted to the author also serve his intellectual interests while the prerogatives of the moral right also serve his economic interests. Thus, for example, the prerogative of opposing modifications or distortions of the work may serve both the personal interest of the author in keeping his work free from alteration, and his economic interest in ensuring that the economic value of his work is not marred by the introduction of changes or deformation. Conversely, the satisfactory economic exploitation of the work through reproductions and performances contributes to better knowledge of it and of its author, and also promotes his intellectual interests by helping to disseminate his ideas and ensure his personal fame.

From the monistic standpoint, all the individual rights granted by the legislator must be interpreted as facets of a sole, uniform author's right; it follows that different legal provisions governing individual rights give no grounds for prejudging on the nature of the author's right.[3]

C. DUALIST THEORY

The dualist theory, on the other hand, divides the whole set of prerogatives belonging to the author into two categories of rights; those of an intellectual kind and those of an economic character —the moral right and the economic right; they should not be confused although they are interrelated and interact. But the dualist interpretation is not confined to this distinction, to which, moreover, the advocates of the monistic theory also resort having regard to the twofold aim of the author's right (protection of intellectual and of economic interests).[4]

In the view of Desbois, a supporter of the dualist approach, protection of the intellectual interests and satisfaction of the economic interests represent two aims which can be separately

---

3. Adolf Dietz, op. cit., pp. 155–6.
4. See H. Baylos Corroza, op. cit., p. 393.

identified by logic and by observing the facts. Intellectual and economic interests have, moreover, different spheres of application; moral rights and economic rights do not have the same purpose, they do not come into being at the same time and do not terminate together. While economic rights simply remain a possibility after termination of the work pending the author's decision to benefit from them through publication, the moral right exists from the first strokes of the pen or the brush, from the first vision of an albeit rudimentary plan. It is in exercising the moral right of disclosure that the author brings his work into the sphere of economic values, deciding on the form that such disclosure will take and its extent. But let us look beyond the period of monopoly: once this has elapsed, the moral right, far from having terminated its validity, continues to exist and to serve until the work lies buried in final oblivion; anyone wishing to exhume it—no matter how many decades afterwards—has the imperious duty of doing so in exactly the same way as the author once produced and published it.[5]

In consequence, and since in the dualist interpretation two categories of rights are involved with distinct legal objectives, they are independent of one another and may be the subject of different legal regulations; while economic rights are governed by the basic norms of assignment and limitation in time, in the case of moral rights, on the other hand, the principles of unassignability, imprescriptibility and unlimited duration apply.[6]

It is the dualist approach that has prevailed in legislation.

4.2 The moral right. Characteristics

A. THE MORAL RIGHT

The moral right protects the personality of the author in relation to his work. It consists in essence of the right of the author to decide on the disclosure of his work—either making it known or reserving it for his own close circle—, to claim respect for his

---

5. See Henri Desbois, op. cit., Sect. 209, pp. 263–4.
6. See Adolf Dietz, op. cit., p. 156.

status as the creator and for the integrity of his creation, and to change his mind, in other words to withdraw the work from circulation by reason of changed convictions.

The substance of these rights differs and they may be classified in two categories: positive and negative.

The *positive* rights are those of disclosure and of change of conviction or withdrawal. They are termed positive because they require a decision or initiative on the part of the holder of the right: to disclose the work, modify it, withdraw it from sale, destroy it.

The *negative* or *defensive* rights are the right to recognition of authorship and the right to the integrity of the work; French authors designate these aspects under the generic term of *right to respect*, i.e. respect for the name of the author and his work. These prerogatives are termed negative because they generate a right to *prevent* or simply to ensure that a particular action is *not taken* by passive subjects. They are defensive in that, even after the death of the author and after his work has fallen within the public domain, they enable action to be taken in defence of a moral right in order to protect the individuality and integrity of the intellectual creation, action in which the general interest of the community also comes into play.

At the outset the author's right was approached almost exclusively from its economic aspect. However, as developments in this area progressed, acknowledgement of the importance of the moral right grew until today the pre-eminence of the intellectual and moral interests of the creator is recognized even in legislation.

Mention of this right is made in a number of laws in countries with the Roman legal tradition even when the dualist theory is adopted, and the moral aspect is regulated before the question of economic rights.[7] Acceptance is thus given to the right of the author to change his mind, or to withdraw his work, by virtue of which the intellectual or moral convictions of the creator take

---

7. Brazil, Articles 21 and 25 to 28; Costa Rica, Articles 13 to 15; France, Intellectual Property Code, Art. L. 121-1 to L. 121-9; Peru, Articles 2 and 32 to 34; Spain, Articles 2 and 14 to 16; etc.

precedence over the principle of the binding force of contracts and the rights acquired by third parties since, even after the publication of his work, the author is allowed to terminate the contract for the exploitation of his work and to withdraw it from circulation, provided that prior compensation is made for damage suffered by the other contracting party.

B. CHARACTERISTICS

a) The author's moral right is essential, exempt from economic considerations, inherent and absolute:[8]
- it is *essential* because it contains a minimum of rights that can be claimed on the basis of the act of creation of a work, in the absence of which the fact of being an author would be meaningless; but, unlike the rights of the personality, *it is not innate* for not all individuals possess it simply because they are persons, but only those who are authors;[9]

---

8. These are also characteristics of rights of the personality; see S. Cifuentes, *Los derechos personalísimos*, Buenos Aires–Córdoba, Ed. Lerner, 1974, pp. 138–51. For Cifuentes, the author's *moral right* does not belong to the legal category of the 'rights of the personality' which is very largely used (see pp. 152–5); he stresses, without omitting to point out that there are many points of contact between the former and the latter, that the moral right lacks a number of fundamental features of rights of the personality (among those quoted by Cifuentes we may mention: it is not innate, lifelong or necessary; its subject matter does not lie within the sphere of the personality and it may be transferred *mortis causa*; see pp. 164–9).

9. Diego Espín Cánovas points out that the connotation of *essentiality* in regard to rights of the personality—vested in all human beings—also characterizes them as innate rights. However, he states, this correspondence between innate rights and the essential rights of the person 'is not absolute, for there are some essential rights of the person which do not arise solely on account of the human personality but require some other accompanying factor; while they are still essential rights, they do not have the character of innate rights. This is exactly what happens in the case of the author's moral rights which, despite the fact that they are essential, cannot be applied to any person whatsoever, for not all are authors, but only to those who are.

'It is the factor of intellectual creation which determines the attribution of the status of author in legislation; although this is not innate, the fact that the creation of a work of the intellect is required means that it involves, nevertheless,

- it is *exempt from economic considerations* because it cannot be assessed in financial terms even if it generates indirect or secondary economic consequences—for example the possibility of obtaining greater revenue, as a result of the greater prestige for the author and his work through the circulation of the latter, accompanied by the name of its creator, both in the area of contracts and also when compensation comes to be fixed for infringements of the author's rights;
- it is *inherent* in the capacity of the author, that is to say *it is indivisible from the person of the creator*; the author retains it throughout his life even when the period of protection of the works in question has expired (calculated from the moment of their creation or publication). After the author's death some of these prerogatives (the *negative* rights and the right of disclosure of posthumous works) are exercised by the heirs or by persons designated for that purpose (see below, Chapter 5, Section 5.2.1);
- it is *absolute* because it is effective against all persons (*erga omnes*), enabling the holder to claim his rights *vis-à-vis* all other persons, including those who have received full economic rights in the work. Unlike relative rights, it is not confined to a right to make use of the asset which is effective only against the assignor of that right.

Given these characteristics, it follows that the moral right is *inalienable* and cannot be *waived*. By reason of the inalienability of the moral right, any transmission *inter vivos* of author's rights must of necessity be confined to the economic rights. It is:

- exempt from *attachment, legal execution* or *expropriation*;

---

a right of the personality which brings together its characteristics, as we shall describe below.'

'This division of rights of the personality into those that are innate and those that are not has been accepted and developed by theorists who have explored in depth the basis of the rights of the personality, assigning this characteristic of a personality right which is not innate to the author's moral right' (*Las facultades del derecho moral de los autores y artistas*, Madrid, Civitas, 1991, pp. 30–1).

- *imprescriptible* since it does not come within the commercial context;
- exempt from *subrogation* because it is inherent in the capacity of author. Its duration is, in principle, unlimited.

b) Some copyright laws *explicitly* recognize some of the characteristics of the moral right indicated (inherence, inalienability, imprescriptibility, impossibility of waiver and perpetuity) (e.g. Algeria, Article 22); Brazil, Articles 28 and 52 single paragraph; Colombia, Article 30; former Czechoslovakia, Articles 12(2) and 33(7); Ecuador, Article 18; France, Art. L. 121-1, previously Art. 6; Haiti, Article 5; Japan, Articles 59 and 60; Mexico, Article 3; Morocco, Article 2; Spain, Article 14; etc.).

Others do so *indirectly* by stipulating that the author retains the moral right, even if ownership of his work is alienated, and even after the term of protection has expired, infringements of the integrity of the work remain actionable (e.g. Argentina, Articles 52 and 83; Uruguay, Articles 12 and 16).

These rights may also be given *negative* recognition when it is stipulated that the transfer of moral rights is null and void and illegal (Libyan Arab Jamahiriya, Article 39).

c) However, the prerogatives which make up the author's moral right are—as are, in general, the rights of the personality—relatively unassignable by the original owner: the creator.[10] For example, in relation to the right to artistic paternity the author may ask—or simply agree—that no mention be made of his name, so that the work will be circulated anonymously or under a pseudonym. As regards the right to respect for the integrity of the work, in some sectors of creative activity it is commonplace for changes to be made, e.g. in the case of works created under a

---

10. Desbois makes the point that the 'inalienability of the moral right stems from the nature of the attributes of this right which are exempt from economic considerations; the author cannot relinquish the defence of his personality subject to the penalty of committing "moral suicide". But the extent of the prohibition should be assessed. The attributes of the moral right cannot have the same force in all circumstances [...]. It is for the judges, in observance of the spirit of the law, to find the right balance' (op. cit., p. 470, Sect. 382).

contractual employment relationship, audiovisual works, computer programs,[11] architectural works and the design of objects for everyday use.[12]

d) With respect to the moral right following the death of the author, see below, Chapter 5, Sections 5.1.5 and 5.2.1.

e) The moral right to respect for the integrity of the work differs from the right of transformation—adaptation, compilation, etc.—which forms part of the economic right and constitutes one of the normal ways of exploiting a work. If the work is in the private domain, the transformations may be authorized either by the author or by any secondary owner of his rights (heirs, assignees, etc.); once it falls within the public domain these changes are freely allowable, *provided that mention is made of the fact that the version has been modified.* The transformations leave the original individuality of the work unchanged and coexist both with the latter and among themselves; on the other hand, for the right to

---

11. In regard to audiovisual works and works produced under a contractual employment relationship, see above, Chapter 3, Sections 3.4.2 and 3.5(B)(a). In the case of works for broadcasting, Spanish law stipulates, in regard to television works, that contracts shall be presumed to include, unless otherwise agreed, authorization by the authors to make, *for the purpose of broadcasting the work*, such alterations as are strictly dictated by the manner of programming of the medium; in the case of computer programs, it provides that, unless otherwise agreed, the author may not object to the licensed user of the right of exploitation making or authorizing the making of successive versions of his programs or of programs derived therefrom (Articles 92(2) and 98).

12. Swedish and Finnish laws establish (Article 13 in both cases) that the proprietors of buildings and objects for everyday use may make changes without the consent of the author, but the Finnish provision adds: 'when this is necessitated by reasons of a technical or practical nature'. Venezuela (Article 20, second paragraph) makes a similar provision, even though it only mentions works of architecture and with the proviso that if the work has a special artistic character, the author is to be given preference in connection with the study and realization of these modifications; a third paragraph was added in the 1993 reform to the effect that 'in any case, if modifications are made to the architectural work without the author's consent, he may repudiate paternity of the modified work and the real owner will be prohibited from invoking in future the name of the author of the original project'.

respect safeguards the integrity of the work in its original expression which only the author himself may modify.

4.2.1. The right of disclosure

The right of disclosure resides in the prerogative of the author to decide whether his work is to be made known and if so in what form, or whether it is to be reserved for his close circle. It also comprises the right to make the essential content of the work publicly known or to publish a description of it.

This is a protestative prerogative of the author because he alone has the authority to decide when he considers his work to have been completed and wishes it to be made available to the public. Before disclosure, the author is at complete liberty to amend his work how and as often as he chooses or even to destroy it.

The author enjoys the right of disclosure and may exercise it in respect of all the possible forms of exploitation of his work; for example the author of a dramatic work who has decided to disclose it by means of a theatrical performance, still retains the full right of disclosure in a printed edition.

The right of disclosure is also referred to as the *right to make a work known, the right to communicate the work to the public, the right of publication or the right to withhold publication.*

It is recognized in every domestic law:
- some use the verb *disclose* or *divulge* (for example Spain, Article 14(i): 'The right to decide whether his work is to be disclosed, and if so in what form'; France, Art. L. 121-2, previously Art. 19: 'The author alone shall have the right to divulge his work');
- but the majority prefer an indirect provision, either through the right to *publish* the work (for example Uruguay, Article 11: 'The right to publish an unpublished work, to reproduce a work already published, or to deliver a work pursuant to a contract for the delivery, shall constitute a moral right not subject to compulsory alienation'); or
- more generally, by enumerating the various ways in which *a work may be made known* (for example Argentina, Article 2: 'Copyright in a scientific, literary or artistic work shall entitle

the author to dispose of, publish, publicly perform and exhibit
... as well as to reproduce it in any form'); or, again,
- as the *right to refrain from publication* (for example Brazil, Article 25(iii): 'the right to withhold publication of his work').

Although the different expressions used to designate the right of disclosure, and also the different legal formulations, are not strictly equivalent,[13] they are all concerned with protection of the same basic prerogative of the author, since any decision to exploit an unpublished work implies a decision to disclose it. The exclusive right of disclosure is therefore also protected in the countries with the Anglo-American legal tradition where it is granted as an *exclusive right of exploitation* (United Kingdom, Sections 16 to 27; Ireland, Sections 8(6) and 9(8) and the United States where the right of 'secrecy' or first disclosure, or more broadly the 'right of privacy', is recognized by virtue of the body of precedents which make up common law).

Since disclosure consists in making the work accessible to the *public*, the communication of the unpublished work in a *private form* to third parties, members of family or friends of the author or possible users with a view to concluding a contract for its exploitation, cannot be deemed to constitute disclosure and nor can the reading or recital of a work during rehearsals. Bringing the work to the attention of other persons does not in itself constitute disclosure; that requires the consent of the author and the presence of an audience, i.e. an indeterminate number of persons permitting the conclusion that the work has been divulged beyond the private circle of the author.

Considerable importance attaches to the disclosure of the work. The author's economic rights are generated by the creation

---

13. *Disclosure* has a broader meaning than *publication*. Disclosure comprises any expression of the work which, with the consent of the author, makes it accessible *for the first time* to the public in any form whatever, while the term 'publication', in its legal acceptation which is narrower than the usual meaning, means that it is disclosure with the consent of the author, copies of the work being made available to the public, regardless of the form of reproduction used.

of the work, but become effective only from the moment when he has made the decision to disclose it. The possibilities for making use of a work by virtue of limitations on the author's rights, whether this involves cases of free use or non-voluntary licences (see below, Section 4.3), are conditional on the work concerned having previously been disclosed with the consent of its author.

The question has been asked as to whether the sole and exclusive right of the author to arrange for the disclosure of his work is subject to any limits and whether it must take second place to the contractual right of the person who has commissioned its production or to the right of other creditors of the author to settle their claims. Let us examine situations of this kind:

A. RIGHT OF DISCLOSURE AND WORKS PRODUCED ON COMMISSION

When the author has entered into a contract to create a work and fails to discharge his obligation, can the forcible execution of the contract be entertained?

Contracts for the production of works on commission are extremely frequent (see above Chapter 3, Section 3.5 (A)). The author undertakes to create a work within a specified or unspecified period, and transfers all or only one or some of his rights to exploit that future work.

These are *obligations of performance* by virtue of which the creditor or person to whom an obligation is owed may demand performance of the work or of the service by various means other than the exercise of force against the person by whom the obligation is owed. In this particular instance, it is impossible to demand enforced performance but simply the payment of compensation. Even supposing that the exercise of coercive measures against the person who does not wish or is unable to perform the act could be effective, it would be irreconcilable with the necessary respect of human freedom and dignity.

Consequently the author, like any other person from whom works have been commissioned, may refuse to carry out the work. If he has already done so, he may invoke his moral right to withhold delivery, for example if he does not consider the work good enough to be made available to others.

But this failure to perform may have financial consequences for the author. The principal may seek reimbursement of the sums which have been advanced and, possibly, the payment of damages. However, both the claim and the subsequent ruling must take account of not only the damage effectively suffered by the party who has entered into a contract with the author but also the reason for the failure to perform, since intellectual creativity does not depend solely on the will of the author: subjective factors also come into play, such as the lack of inspiration or the desire to uphold prestige by refraining from bringing into circulation a work which does not satisfy the author. The failure to perform may also be due to a practical impossibility caused by a physical impediment or by a disparity between the scale of the work and the time allocated for its production, etc.

It may also be asked whether an author can be obliged to deliver the work by imposing pecuniary sanctions on him either as an injunction to perform or as a warning (penalty payments). The reply to this question must be negative because such a procedure would violate the author's creative freedom.

B. RIGHT OF DISCLOSURE AND CREDITORS OF THE AUTHOR

The moral right to decide on the disclosure of a work also precludes the possibility of other creditors of the author demanding the public communication of an unpublished work in order to recover moneys owing to them out of the proceeds of the exploitation of that work, for example, through the attachment of an unpublished manuscript for the purpose of publication.[14]

Having regard to the fact that the right of disclosure may be exercised by the author in respect of each of the possible forms of exploitation of the work, the creditors can only seize the profits generated by a right of exploitation which the author has already

---

14. The case of the purchaser of the manuscript of a work which *has already been disclosed* is different. In that instance, it is possible to demand performance of the service and to secure that performance through attachment of the asset which has been sold.

exercised.[15] It is possible to seek attachment of the remuneration accruing to the author of a novel in respect of the printed edition authorized by him. On the other hand, it would be inadmissible to attach the right of exploitation in general and, in consequence, to dispose of the use of the work in a form other than that authorized by the author, and without his consent.

C. RIGHT OF DISCLOSURE AND OWNERS OF THE MATERIAL SUPPORT

The habitual method of disclosing works of art is to exhibit them publicly in art galleries and other places designed for that purpose; they are commercialized by alienating the material support which contains them. The exploitation of such works by their reproduction on plates, posters, postcards, for publicity purposes, etc. is uncommon.

The acquisition of a work of art (a painting, engraving, sculpture, photograph, etc.) does not imply acquisition of the right to exploit the work, just as the purchaser of a manuscript, or of an original musical score, only acquires ownership of the physical object and may not undertake publication, representation, performance of the work, broadcasting or transformation thereof, etc. save where expressly agreed.

Alienation of the original material support constituting the work does not in itself signify any transfer of ownership of the rights accruing to the author. The latter retains both the moral right and the economic rights in his work.

However, as we have noted, some domestic laws recognize in favour of the owner of the original, unless otherwise agreed, the right to exhibit the work of art in public even if it has not been disclosed (Venezuela, Article 54(2); Spain, Article 56(2)). At all events, the author may always express his opposition to such dis-

---

15. This solution has been adopted in Spain, Article 53(2): 'The exploitation rights accruing to the author may not themselves be attached, but the profits or benefits therefrom may be attached, being regarded as salary for the purposes of both the order of priority for attachment and deductions or unattachable amounts'.

play if it is effected under conditions which are prejudicial to his honour or professional reputation (Spain, Art. 56(2), last para.).

It is probable that when the author of a work of art wishes to exercise his right of reproduction, he will require access to the material support which has passed into the possession of the person who acquired the work of art and it may happen that the latter, for a variety of reasons, does not wish to facilitate the taking of the photographs needed for the purpose of reproduction.

In such situations, protection of the moral right to the disclosure of the work means that the author may call upon the proprietor, if necessary through the appropriate legal channels, to grant him access to the work even when the law may not lay down specific provisions in this regard such as those, for example in France (Art. L. 111-3, previously Article 29, last paragraph: '... In case manifest abuse by the proprietor of the object prevents the exercise of the right of disclosure, the Tribunal Civil shall be empowered to take any measure that is appropriate ...'); Venezuela (Article 22: 'The author may require the proprietor of the material object to grant him access to it, in the manner most suitable to the interests of them both, provided such access is necessary for the exercise of his moral rights or of his rights of exploitation'); Spain (Article 14(vii): '... The aforesaid right shall not allow the author to demand to remove the work and access to it shall be had in the place and manner that cause the least inconvenience to the possessor, who shall be indemnified where appropriate for any damages and prejudice caused him').

In the case of works of architecture, the acquisition of plans, sketches and similar items is habitually made with a view to their use by the purchaser for the execution of the work concerned. He may not sell, reproduce or use them for other works since, unless otherwise agreed, these rights are vested in the author (Argentina, Article 55).

4.2.2. The right of paternity

The right of artistic authorship is the right of the author whose capacity as creator of the work is recognized. It protects the intimate bond which exists between the creator and the fruit of his intellectual activity which is unequivocally designated by the expressions 'paternity', or 'artistic authorship' which are commonly used in the relevant laws.[16]

Other expressions are also used in certain domestic laws such as the right to respect for the author's name (France, Art. L. 121-1, previously Art. 6 and other laws which have followed suit, e.g. Algeria, Art. 22; Senegal, Art. 3(a); etc.) or else a stipulation is made to the effect that, even if the author alienates the ownership of his work, he still retains the right to require the indication of his name or pseudonym on it (Argentina, Article 52; Uruguay, Article 12(1)).

This right is embodied in the Berne Convention as the right to claim authorship of the work, as follows: 'Independently of the author's economic rights, and even after the transfer of the said rights, the author shall have the right to claim authorship of the work ...' (Article 6*bis*(1)).

A similar wording will be found in the Inter-American Convention on the Rights of the Author (Washington, 1946): 'The author of any copyrighted work, in disposing of his copyright therein by sale, assignment or otherwise, retains the right to claim the paternity of the work ...' (Article 11).

In the countries of the Anglo-American legal tradition, where legislation does not embody a general rule on the moral right or on the right to recognition of authorship, certain provisions, however, enable the existence thereof to be inferred, such as the obligation to cite the source.

The mention of the author must be made in the manner chosen by him. It includes the pseudonym and also anonymity, since the prerogative of identifying the work with its author is granted as a right and not as an obligation on the author. This implies that the creator has the option of deciding whether he wishes this association to be made, and if so in what form (by his name,

---

16. Austria, Article 19; Belgium, Art. 1, para. 2, fifth sub-para; Brazil, Article 25(1); Bulgaria, Article 3; Chile, Article 14(1); Colombia, Article 30(A); Cuba, Article 4(a); El Salvador, Art. 6(e); Guatemala, Article 19; India, Article 57(1); Italy, Article 20; Peru, Article 32; Portugal, Article 27; etc.

a pseudonym, initials, etc.) or whether he wishes to remain anonymous.

The author who uses a pseudonym or opts for anonymity continues to be the owner of both the moral and economic rights in his work. As we have seen (see above Chapter 3, Section 3.3), the author may reveal his identity at any time but if he does not do so his prerogatives will be exercised by the natural person or legal entity who, with his consent, discloses the work. This person may not reveal the identity of the author. If he did so, he would be infringing the author's moral right.

By reason of the perpetual nature of the right of artistic authorship, the pseudonym and anonymity must be respected even after the death of the creator and neither his heirs nor any other persons are entitled to reveal the real name, unless the author has expressly authorized this in his testament or in any other manner which leaves no doubt as to his wishes. However, it must be understood that if *another* work, devoted in whole or in part to the author and to his creative work and published separately, does mention his true name, this could not be interpreted as a violation of the moral right since the right to freedom of research and criticism comes into play here.

The right to paternity comprises, on the one hand, the right to claim:
- the status of author when an indication of his name has been omitted, or another name or pseudonym has been shown;
- the special way of indicating his name—in an abbreviated form or with any addition;
- the pseudonym or anonymity when the author has opted for this solution and his true name is shown instead.

It comprises, on the other hand, the right to defend his authorship when it is infringed.

The right to defend his name or pseudonym when it is usurped and used in works which do not belong to him (wrongful attribution of authorship of a work) is closely linked with the right to paternity; however, it is not, properly speaking, included in the author's moral right, but forms part of the general right of the personality. In fact, this right is not the province of authors alone but of all individuals, for the false attribution of paternity includes the instance in which the purpose of the usurpation is to benefit from the prestige of an author—as frequently occurs with counterfeit works of art (for example, the signature of a famous artist may be imitated on a painting which is not by his hand)—and examples where the idea is to make use of the fame of other people (sports personalities, social celebrities such as those who fill the columns of the so-called 'press of the heart', etc.) and, again, cases where the same method may be used to cause prejudice to a person whose name is shown as author. Both persons involved have the right to take remedial action: the person whose name has been used without his being the real author and the real author whose name has been omitted, without prejudice to his own responsibility if he has caused the substitution to be made.

In the case of works of joint authorship, each of the authors enjoys these rights to the full so that they can be exercised by one or by several of the joint authors if the infringement has affected only one particular author or a number of them. These rights may be exercised at any time (imprescriptible character of the moral right).

4.2.3. The right to respect for the work and for its integrity

The right to respect for the work and its integrity makes it possible to prevent any alteration, deformation or interference with it. Its foundation lies in the respect which is due to the personality of the creator manifested in the work and also to the work itself. The author is entitled to protection against any alteration or misrepresentation of his own thinking, while the public at large has the right of access to the products of creative intellectual activity in their authentic expression.

This right, together with that of disclosure and recognition of paternity, constitute the corner-stone of the moral rights.

At international level, the right to respect for the work and for its integrity is recognized in the Berne Convention, as is the right of authorship set out in Article 6*bis* cited previously:

Independently of the author's economic rights, and even after the transfer of the said rights, the author shall have the right to claim authorship of the work and to object to any distortion, mutilation or other modifications of, or other derogatory action in relation to, the said work, which would be prejudicial to his honour or reputation.

In dealing with the right of authorship, Article 11 of the Inter-American Convention on the Rights of the Author (Washington, 1946) also recognizes this right, using a formula drawn from the Berne Convention: '... oppose any modification or use of it which is prejudicial to his reputation as an author ...'.

In the case of the domestic laws which establish this right, a distinction may be drawn between:
- those which follow the *objective conception* and protect the work against deformation, mutilation and other modifications which, *in an objectively demonstrable manner* may prejudice the author's lawful personal or intellectual interests[17] or else (this is more frequent and follows the text of Article 6*bis* of the Berne Convention) cause prejudice to his honour or reputation;[18] and
- those which follow the *subjective conception* and prohibit all modifications *without any qualifying conditions*.[19]

The right to respect for the work also extends to the technical conditions under which economic exploitation is effected whatever the medium chosen—publishing, public performance, mechanical reproduction, broadcasting, etc. For this reason the publisher,

---

17. Germany, Article 14.
18. For example, Brazil, Article 25(iv); Canada, Art. 28.2(1); Colombia, Article 30(B); Denmark, Finland, Norway, Sweden, Article 3(2); El Salvador, Article 5(j); Guatemala, Article 19; India, Article 57(1)(a) and (b); Italy, Article 20; Luxembourg, Article 9; Mexico, Article 2, II; Morocco, Article 2; Netherlands, Article 25(a), (b) and (c); Paraguay, Civil Code, Art. 2183, second para.; Portugal, Article 56; Russian Federation, Art. 15(1), last para.; Senegal, Article 3(a); Spain, Article 14(iv); United Kingdom, Section 80(2)(b); Venezuela, Article 20(1) and former Yugoslavia, Article 29.
19. For example, Algeria, Article 22; Argentina, Articles 51 and 52; Belgium, Article 1, para. 2, sixth sub-para; Burundi, Article 17; Costa Rica, Article 14(c); Cuba, Article 4(b); France, Art. L. 121-1, previously Art. 6; Hungary, Article 10; Japan, Article 20; Jordan, Article 28; Lebanon, Article 146; Libyan Arab Jamahiriya, Article 7; Peru, Article 32; Romania, Article 3(4); Senegal, Article 3(a); Switzerland, Article 11; Tunisia, Article 7(2); former USSR, Articles 98 and 480 of the Civil Code; Uruguay, Article 12(2).

impresario, producer or any other person who exploits the work is under an obligation to make sure that this is done in a manner which respects the moral right of the author.[20]

The obligation to respect the integrity of the work extends to all its users, regardless of whether the use is made by virtue of a contractual authorization[21] or within the framework of the limitations on the author's rights.[22]

The same obligation is incumbent upon the owner of the material support of the original work (work of art, manuscript, musical score, etc.).

A. RIGHT TO MODIFY THE WORK

Even if the work has already been disclosed, the author retains the right to modify it. This is a logical consequence of the right of creation: before a work is republished or a new edition issued, the author may feel the need to correct or clarify certain concepts, to improve the style and to make inclusions or deletions with a view to enhancing his work.

Mouchet and Radaelli[23] point out that the notion of a definitively completed work is hard for a writer or artist to accept. They quote Jorge Luis Borges:[24] 'The concept of a definitive text is mere superstition or lassitude.'

---

20. In relation to the protection of the moral right in audiovisual works, see above, Chapter 3, Section 3.4.2.
21. *In general* (Austria, Article 21) or as *a prohibition on the publisher* from amending or altering the text (Algeria, Article 45; Argentina, Article 39; Brazil, Article 67; Colombia, Article 126; Costa Rica, Article 27, second paragraph, etc.), as an obligation imposed on the theatrical producer to ensure the public performance of a work under technical conditions which will guarantee respect for the author's intellectual and moral rights (France, Art. L. 132-22, previously Art. 47; Venezuela, Art. 69) and also *as an obligation imposed on performers* (Brazil, Article 129).
22. Austria, Article 57(1).
23. See Carlos Mouchet and Sigfrido Radaelli, op. cit., pp. 39 and 40.
24. Jorge Luis Borges, 'Nota sobre el Ulises en español' in *Los anales de Buenos Aires*, No. 1, January 1946.

The laws which expressly recognize the author's right to modify his work do so to varying degrees:
- *Switzerland* (Code of Obligations, Article 385) and Colombia (Article 111) accord the greatest importance to it by laying down *an obligation incumbent upon the publisher*. Switzerland stipulates that the latter may not republish the work or issue a new edition without first having offered the author the possibility of making changes to his work. Colombia provides that the publisher may not make a new edition without having given [the author] the opportunity of making whatever changes and corrections may be appropriate. Nevertheless, if the additions or improvements are made when the work is already at the stage of corrected proofs the author shall allow the publisher the higher cost of printing. This rule applies also when the changes, corrections or additions are substantial and make the printing more costly, except in the case of works kept up to date by means of periodical supplements;
- *Sweden* (Article 36), in common with the other Nordic countries (*Denmark*, *Finland* and *Norway*), allows modification only in cases where production of the new edition is initiated more than one year after publication of the previous edition and on condition that the alterations can be made without unreasonable cost and without changing the character of the work;
- the two latter restrictions or one of them at least also appear in the laws of *Brazil* (Art. 71), *Costa Rica* (Article 27, last paragraph and 37), *El Salvador* (Art. 62), *Ecuador* (Art. 47), *Italy* (Article 129), and former *Yugoslavia* (Article 68). *Uruguay* (Article 12(3)) requires that the rights acquired in good faith by third parties shall remain unaffected. To this requirement for the rights acquired by third parties to be respected, *Spain* (Article 14(v)) adds the stipulation that 'goods of cultural interest' must be protected.
- the *Libyan Arab Jamahiriya* law (Art. 43) deals with essential modifications and the withdrawal of the work from circulation in the same way; the author may, for serious moral reasons, call upon the Court of first instance so as to obtain the corresponding authorization, subject to the obligation to pay fair compensation to the third party.

As we have already noted (see above, Section 4.2(B)(e), the right of modification which rests exclusively with the author, relates solely to the integrity of the work in its original form and must not be confused with the right of transformation which leaves the original individuality of the work unchanged so that it may be exercised by the successors in title of the author or by any other person once the work has fallen into the public domain.

B. Works of joint authorship

In the case of works of joint authorship, the right of modification and the right of change of mind or withdrawal may be exercised only by common agreement between all the joint authors.

4.2.4. The right to reconsider or the right of withdrawal

The right of change of mind or withdrawal denotes the author's prerogative to withdraw the work from circulation if it no longer reflects his intellectual or moral convictions, after having entered into a contract for its disclosure, and to suspend a particular form of utilization which had been authorized previously, subject to liability to compensate the holders of the rights of exploitation in respect of prejudice suffered by them.

The recognition of this prerogative reveals a high degree of respect for the intellectual scruples of the author and constitutes the natural complement to the right of the author to decide to disclose his work. Like the latter right, it is founded on the need to safeguard freedom of thought with the concomitant possibility of a change of opinion.

The expression 'the right to reconsider or the right of withdrawal' refers, as Colombet has pointed out,[25] to the two phases of the process: the 'right to reconsider' refers to the internal, mental phase of the process, and 'withdrawal' to the external phase, i.e. the practical manifestation of the act.

The laws which recognize this prerogative of the author use different expressions to designate it. Relatively few use the ex-

---

25. Claude Colombet, *Major Principles of Copyright* ..., op. cit., p. 38.

pression 'to correct or retract' (France, Art. L. 121-4, previously Art. 32 and other laws which have followed suit). Most use the term 'right to withdraw the work' from sale or circulation or control of the user.[26]

This is an exceptional prerogative which is in manifest opposition to the principle of the compulsory force of contracts, to a greater degree even than the possibility open to the author to refrain from delivering the commissioned work when exercising his moral right of disclosure. Therefore, the two apparently contradictory principles must be reconciled whenever possible: on the one hand the notion that *pacta sunt servanda* and on the other respect for freedom of thought which necessarily brings with it freedom for the author to change his opinions. In consequence, the withdrawal generally takes effect under certain specific conditions which always include a requirement to indemnify the party which has suffered prejudice.

Because of its personal and non-transferable nature, the right of reconsideration and of withdrawal is reserved exclusively for the author, and is not transmitted to his heirs.[27]

The conditions under which this right is exercised vary and are not always regulated in detail.

A. MOTIVES

Even if it goes without saying that the author will only be inclined to exercise his right if he has weighty reasons for doing so, few of the relevant laws include a liberal criterion and refrain from making reference to the determining reasons for withdrawal (Brazil, El Salvador, France, Portugal). Most follow a more

---

26. Brazil, Article 25(VI); Colombia, Article 30(E); Dominican Republic, Article 18(d); Ecuador, Article 17(f); Egypt, Article 42; Italy, Article 142; Libyan Arab Jamahiriya, Article 43; Portugal, Article 62; Spain, Article 14(vi); Uruguay, Article 13.
27. The German law provides (Article 42(1)) that the author's legal successor may exercise the right of revocation only if he proves that the author, prior to his death, would have been entitled to revoke and was prevented from so doing, or that he has done so by testamentary disposition.

restrictive criterion and establish what the nature of the author's reasons for taking such an extreme decision should be; if the work no longer reflects the author's point of view and personal convictions he cannot be expected to continue to agree to its exploitation (Germany, Article 42(1)), or if grave reasons of a moral nature come into play (Italy, Libyan Arab Jamahiriya, Uruguay), if serious causes arise (Egypt) or if there is a change in his intellectual and moral convictions (Spain).

The difference resides in the fact that when a liberal criterion is applied, this right is left entirely to the author's discretion, while the restrictive criterion leaves room for legal appraisal of the motives invoked when the right is exercised.

B. PUBLICITY

The withdrawal may affect the rights of exploitation of other persons in addition to the party with whom the author has entered into a contract. Italian law (Article 142, and Article 13 of the Regulation) establishes that the author must notify his intention to withdraw the work from sale not only to the parties who have entered into a contract with him, but also to all others who may be entitled to exploit the work; he must therefore make his intention known publicly through the channels made available by the authorities; the interested parties then have one year, calculating from the date of the notification or official publicity, to lodge legal proceedings in opposition to the decision by the author to exercise his right as he wishes or to claim equivalent compensation.

C. EXCLUSIONS

This right does not apply to audiovisual works (Germany, Article 90); computer programs (France, Art. L. 121-7, previously Art. 46 *in fine* (of the 1985 Law); works produced under a contractual employment arrangement (see above, Chapter 3, Section 3.5(B)(a)).

D. FURTHER CHANGE OF OPINION

It is possible that, after exercising his right of withdrawal, the author may change his opinion once again and decide to resume exploitation of the work. In that eventuality, it will be considered equitable for the party with whom he had previously entered into a contractual relationship to enjoy priority for the conclusion of a new contract to use the work under conditions reasonably similar to those which applied originally, so as to prevent the right of withdrawal or change of mind from being used to improve the economic conditions agreed in the first instance. This priority exists as a kind of counterpart to the author's right of withdrawal.

4.3. Economic rights

A. ECONOMIC RIGHTS ARE INDEPENDENT OF EACH OTHER[28]

This is the *principle of the independence of rights* expressly stipulated in the Charter of Author's Rights[29] (III, 9, second paragraph):

The various exclusive rights of the author over the exploitation of his works, such as the rights of graphic reproduction, or reproduction by any other means, mechanical recording, cinematographic adaptation, public representation, recitation and performance, broadcasting by radio or television, or adaptation to any other form of expression, are prerogatives independent one of the other, to be transferred to a third party only with the distinct and formal consent of the author.

B. THE ECONOMIC RIGHTS ARE NOT SUBJECT TO NUMERUS CLAUSUS[30]

The rights of exploitation available to the author apply to all the possible forms of utilization of the work, not only at the time of

---

28. Costa Rica, Article 19: 'The various forms of use shall be independent of each other inasmuch as authorization to fix the work or production shall not entail authorization to perform it or broadcast it, and vice versa'; Dominican Republic, Article 62: 'The different forms of use of the work shall be independent of each other and the author's authorization for one form of use shall not extend to other forms'; Spain, Article 23: 'The exploitation rights provided for in this Section shall be independent of each other'.
29. Adopted on 26 September 1956 in Hamburg by the Nineteenth Congress of the International Confederation of Societies of Authors and Composers (CISAC).
30. For example, France, Art. L. 123-1.1, previously Art. 21, para. 1. ('The author shall enjoy, during his lifetime, the exclusive right to exploit his work

its creation, but throughout the period for which it remains within the private domain.

However, for the purposes of information and so as to avoid problems of interpretation of a basic principle in a relatively new and little known area, the relevant laws mention in detail the various economic rights corresponding to the different ways in which the author may exercise them (for example, the right of reproduction is the right to reproduce a work by making copies of it in any material form; the right of performance is that of presenting a dramatic work in public; the right of broadcasting is that of transmitting or retransmitting the work by radio and television, etc.).

However, even where the law does not list such examples or if no specific right or method of using the work is mentioned, this is still not an obstacle since all the rights are at the author's disposal in equal measure. This is because *economic rights are recognized as having a generic character.*[31]

C. THE PRINCIPLE OF THE RESTRICTIVE INTERPRETATION OF EXPLOITATION CONTRACTS

Contracts involving author's rights should be interpreted in a restrictive manner, making it impossible to conclude in favour of the party with whom the author has entered into a contract more

---

under any form whatever and to take an economic profit therefrom'); Italy, Article 12 ('The author [...] shall have the exclusive right to the economic utilization of the work in any form or manner, whether original or derivative [...] and especially as regards the exercise of the exclusive rights indicated in the following Articles'); Dominican Republic, Article 20 ('The author [...] has the right to authorize or prohibit [...] (g) any other known or future form of use, utilization or exploitation').

31. Delgado Porras states that: 'since in the case of copyright the interest of the thing is protected "in the absolute entirety of its possibilities" (Pugliatti, quoted by Baylos), the monopoly in question extends to all the possibilities of exploiting the work, without the application to them of the legal principle of typification which appears to be required in the case of privilege and in those systems which preserve the remains of this (area of copyright) [...]' ('La propiedad intelectual y la explotación videográfica', *Revista de derecho privado*, Madrid, December 1983, p. 1125). See also Chapter 1, Section 1.3.4 above.

extensive rights than those explicitly agreed. Several laws make specific provision to this effect: Costa Rica (Art. 16); Colombia (Art. 78); Dominican Republic (Art. 63); others also embody this principle such as that of France (Art. 122-7, previously Art. 30, fourth para.); Germany (Art. 31(5)); Spain (Art. 43(1)); Venezuela (Art. 51(2)).

D. THE AUTHOR MAY DIVIDE THE GEOGRAPHICAL AND TEMPORAL EXTENT OF AUTHORIZATION TO USE HIS WORK

He may institute proceedings not only against uses made without his authorization, but also against those made by the other party to the contract in geographical areas not specifically included within the authorization or after the validity of the latter has expired.

E. THE RIGHTS OF EXPLOITATION KNOW NO LIMITS—OR EXCEPTIONS—OTHER THAN THOSE LAID DOWN IN THE LAW[32]

The limitations (or exceptions) to the rights of the author are subject to *numerus clausus*. They are specific, unlike the rights which are recognized as having a generic character. It follows that if the law fails to make express mention of any particular limitation, *the exclusive right of the author covers every possible form of utilization of the work* already existing at the time of approval of the norm or which may arise in future as a consequence of technological development or of new procedures for the marketing of works and cultural products.[33]

---

32. See below: Section 4.3.
33. In some laws, the enumeration of economic rights terminates, as a precaution, with expressions which leave them open, e.g. Article 2 in Argentina: 'Copyright in a [...] work shall entitle the author to dispose of, publish, publicly perform and exhibit [...] as well as to reproduce it in any form'. And Bolivia (Art. 16, *in fine*); Brazil (Art. 30); Costa Rica (Art. 16(d)); Cuba (Art. 4(c)); Guatemala (Art. 10(2)); Honduras (Art. 38); Mexico (Art. 4(1)); Peru (Art. 36, *in fine*); Venezuela (Art. 23); etc.

No restriction exists on the enjoyment of the rights in the works or in the forms and procedures for their exploitation.[34] The author's right confers on the creator a monopoly for the exploitation of his work as an exclusive and absolute right which is effective *erga omnes*.

Both the moral right and the economic rights are absolute. However, unlike the moral right, the economic rights are transmissible and their duration is limited. The author may exercise them himself or, as is frequently the case, may, either directly or through the intermediary of a society for the management of author's rights (or society of authors), assign by agreement the rights of exploitation to another person; however, for certain uses subsequent to the first, there has been a tendency to develop the systems of non-voluntary licences (statutory licences and compulsory licences, see Section 4.3.2 below).

F. THE AUTHORIZATION FOR THE USE OF A WORK BRINGS WITH IT THE ENTITLEMENT OF THE AUTHOR TO REMUNERATION

As Dietz points out,[35] the author must, in principle, have a share in any exploitation of his work.

All the other expressions which are sometimes also used to denote economic rights—*pecuniary rights, rights of exploitation, monopoly of exploitation*—make reference to a basic objective of authors' rights which, historically, was the one for which it was first intended: the author must be able to obtain an economic reward from the utilization of his work.

This substantive provision of copyright implies recognition of the fact that any utilization of a work must be paid for and lies at the origin of the right to receive remuneration (except in the

---

34. This essential concept of the author's right is clearly expressed in Art. L. 123-1.1, previously Article 21 of the French law which stipulates that *the author enjoys the exclusive right to exploit his work in any form whatsoever* and to obtain an economic profit from it.
35. Adolf Dietz, op. cit., p. 182.

cases defined in law where free and gratuitous use is permitted, see below: Section 4.3.1).

In so far as the pecuniary benefits—or profits or proceeds—received by the author for the use of his work constitute the remuneration for his intellectual activity, they must be considered to have the purpose of covering the cost of living and are equivalent to a salary.[36]

These benefits are derived essentially from the following forms of exploitation:
- *the reproduction* of all or part of the *work in a material, tangible form* which comprises publishing, mechanical reproduction, the reproduction of an audiovisual work, reprographic reproduction, etc.; and
- *public communication* of the work in a *non-material form* to spectators or listeners by means of exhibition, public performance, projection or showing of cinematographic works and other audiovisual works, broadcasting, distribution by cable networks, etc.

In some countries the authors of artistic works also enjoy the *droit de suite* in the revenue obtained from each new public sale of their works.

Under international law, the two main copyright conventions recognize that the creators of protected works should enjoy economic rights.

The Berne Convention establishes, *jure conventionis*, the economic rights of reproduction, including the right of sound or visual recording (Article 9), of translation (Article 8), of adaptation, arrangement and other alterations (Article 12), public performance and any communication to the public of the performance of their work (Article 11), public recitation (Article 11*ter*), broadcasting, distribution by cable and rebroadcasting of the broadcast work by an organization other than the original one (Article 11*bis*), rights relating to cinematographic works (Articles 14 and 14*bis*) and, subject to material reciprocity, *droit de suite* (Article 14*ter*).

---

36. See Article 53(2) of the Spanish law.

The Universal Copyright Convention as revised at Paris in 1971 recognizes the rights of reproduction by any means, of public performance and broadcasting (Article IV*bis*), in addition to the right of translation already granted in the 1952 text—(Article V).

4.3.1. The right of reproduction

A. CONCEPT

The *right of reproduction* is the prerogative of exploiting the work in its original or modified form by its material fixation on any medium whatsoever and by any procedure which permits its communication and the obtaining of one or more copies of all or part of it.[37]

The term *reproduction* is understood to mean the making of one or more copies of a work or parts thereof in any material form whatsoever, including sound and visual recording. 'Reproduction' also includes the making of one or more copies in three dimensions of a two-dimensional work and the making of one or more copies in two dimensions of a three-dimensional work, as well as the inclusion of the work or part thereof in a computer system (in either its internal storage unit or its external storage unit).[38]

B. SUBSTANCE

The substance of the right of reproduction is wide in scope, both in respect of the *reproduced object* and in regard to the *method of reproduction*:
- as to the *reproduced object*, this may involve manuscripts of literary, scientific, dramatic and musical works, computer programs, drawings, illustrations and photographs and also the interpretations of works, phonographic and magnetic recordings, audiovisual works, etc.;

---

37. See Spain, Article 18.
38. See *WIPO Draft Model Provisions for Legislation in the Field of Copyright*, WIPO document CE/MPC/I/2-II of 20 October 1988, Section 1 (xvi).

- the *method of reproduction* may also vary widely: printing, drawing, recording, photographing, moulding, photocopying, microfilming and any technique used in the graphic and plastic arts, mechanical, cinematographic and magnetic recording *which enables the work to be communicated indirectly*, that is to say *through a copy of the work* which embodies the reproduction.

Consequently the right of reproduction comprises:
- *publication* by printing, or by any other technique of the graphic or plastic arts (typography, linotype, offset, etc.); this is *graphic publication*, or publication in the narrow sense, since the term may also be used in a wider acceptance as an equivalent of the term *reproduction* to embrace any type of fixation of the work (not only by printing or by any other technique of the graphic or plastic arts but also sound and audiovisual fixation by electronic means, etc.) and also covers the tangible result of the act of reproduction (books, brochures, printed documents, musical scores, records, magnetic tapes, films, video copies, CD-ROM memories, etc.);
- *mechanical reproduction* of works in the form of sound recordings (phonograms) and audiovisual fixations produced by *mechanical* means in the widest sense of the term, including electro-acoustic and electronic procedures;[39]
- the *reprographic reproduction* by any system or technique by which visually perceptible, tangible facsimile reproductions may be made of copies of writings and graphic works in any size or form;[40]
- the *making of one or more copies in three dimensions of a two-dimensional work* (for example a building according to different plans) and the making of one or more copies in two dimensions of a three-dimensional work (for example the photograph of a sculpture). It follows that a reproduction exists even when the copy is made on a material other than that used for the original

---

39. See *WIPO Glossary of Terms of the Law of Copyright and Neighbouring Rights*, 1980, entry 154, p. 157. The *Glossary* is essentially the work of Dr György Boytha.
40. Ibid., entry 224, p. 229.

(reproduction of a drawing, an engraving or a painting on an earthenware or porcelain vessel, etc.) or by means of a different technique (photograph of a work of art).[41] In the case of *works of architecture*, and since the habitual method of reproducing them is by the *construction of the building* from a plan or by copying an existing building, some domestic laws specifically declare that this act likewise constitutes a reproduction;[42]

- the *entry of a work, or part thereof, into a computer system*, whether into its internal storage or external storage unit.

Given that the reproduction of a work in any manner or form, including sound and visual recording, constitutes reproduction, it follows that, as pointed out in the comments on the WIPO Draft Model Provisions, 'it is irrelevant whether the copy of the work can be enjoyed by human beings without equipment (for example a book or a copy of a drawing) or it cannot be enjoyed as it is not directly accessible to human beings without appropriate equipment (for example, a sound recording). A *work stored in a computer system* is not available directly to human beings without suitable retrieval equipment (such as screens, printers or facsimile terminals). Consequently, the storage of a work in such systems should also be considered as reproduction under Article 9(1) and (3) of the Berne Convention'.[43]

The right of reproduction covers not only the exploitation of the work in its original form, but also any transformations which it may undergo. Accordingly, any translation, arrangement,

---

41. See André Françon, *Cours de propriété littéraire, artistique et industrielle*, Paris, Ed. Les Cours de Droit, 1985–86, p. 301.

42. France, Article L. 122-3, previously Art. 28, third paragraph: 'In the case of architectural works, reproduction shall also consist in the repeated execution of a plan or standard draft'. Austria, Art. 42(4): 'For the execution of a work of architecture according to a plan or design, or for the imitative construction of such a work, the authorization of the person entitled thereto shall always be required.'

43. See *Comments on the Draft Model Provisions for Legislation in the Field of Copyright*, WIPO document CE/MPC/I/2-III of 20 October 1988, Section 39, p. 8. See Chapter 2 above, Section 2.2.1.8—Computer programs—(arguments for and against copyright protection).

adaptation, compilation, etc. and reproduction of the work, requires prior authorization from the author of the original work.

The author may authorize the performance of *one* or *all of these acts* of utilization. If the author of a dramatic work which is being performed in a theatre authorizes the television broadcasting of a performance and, in order to facilitate its deferred transmission, permits its fixing on a video recording, he thereby only authorizes the *fixation* for communication to the public on the stipulated occasion and by the stipulated medium (*ephemeral fixation*). No copies may be made (except in so far as these are required by the purpose of the contract, for example for retransmission on other television channels, provided that this is expressly authorized by the author), and still less may these copies be brought into circulation.[44] An art critic or an essayist authorized by an artist to take photographs of his works for the sole purpose of facilitating analysis, is in a similar position.

On the other hand, a publishing house or a producer of phonograms which enters into contracts for publication or phonographic production with the author, receives the right of reproduction in all its aspects: to fix the work, and to make and distribute copies. However, the bringing into circulation may be expressly or implicitly confined to the sale of copies, thus, for example, excluding their rental or loan.

The *right of distribution* is the author's exclusive prerogative to bring into circulation the original or copies of his work, to decide all questions relating to their circulation (by sale, rental, loan or any other procedure; territoriality, etc.) and to supervise their use.

It is considered that the right to authorize the bringing into circulation of the work or copies of it is the indissociable corollary of the right to authorize the making (reproduction) of these copies (see the memorandum of the International Bureau of WIPO for

---

44. Costa Rica, Article 51, expressly stipulates that: 'When the authors and performers have consented to the ephemeral fixation of their works and performances, broadcasting organizations may use them in their broadcasts for the number of times that has been stipulated and shall be obliged to destroy the fixation immediately after the last authorized transmission.'

the fourth session of a Committee of Experts on a possible Protocol to the Berne Convention, *Copyright*, WIPO, November 1994, para. 45, p. 219). Certain laws, moreover, give express recognition to a right of distribution independently of the right of reproduction (e.g. Costa Rica, Art. 4(n) and 16; El Salvador, Art. 7; Germany, Art. 15(1)(b), 17 and 85(1); Honduras, Art. 38(6); Italy, Art. 17 and 72; Panama, Art. 36(3) and 40; Spain, Art. 17 and 19; Trinidad and Tobago, Art. 8; United States of America, Section 106(3); Venezuela, Art. 41). Such recognition is not a requirement for the author to exercise the right of distribution as well.

Many laws which establish the right of distribution provide that this right should be considered to be exhausted after the first sale of copies. Exhaustion of the right of distribution relates only to verification of subsequent sales of the original or copies of the work but not to other forms of its utilization (rental, loan, public communication—performance, broadcasting—etc.).

4.3.2. The right of public communication

A. CONCEPT

The term 'public communication of a work' means any act by which a number of persons may be given access to all or part of it in its original or transformed form, by means other than the distribution of copies.

Whatever its purpose, communication is deemed to be public when it is effected in a context which is not confined to the family or domestic circle and even within that context when it is integrated into, or connected to, a distribution network of any kind (we shall return to the public character of communication further below).

Some domestic laws refer to the right of public communication generically as the *right of performance*,[45] as is traditional in

---

45. France, Article L. 122-2, previously Art. 27: 'Performance consists in the communication of the work to the public by any process whatsoever, particularly: [...]'; Venezuela, prior to the 1993 reform.

French legislation and in laws which have followed this example, even though the use of that expression is considered inappropriate to cover a whole range of acts which differ by their nature from the performance of a dramatic work. Here, Desbois points out that the expression *direct communication* might have been used more accurately to describe performance or interpretation properly speaking and *indirect communication* to cover the playing of a record or the projection of a film. Desbois is of the opinion that if the French Parliament failed to use the expressions in their proper sense, it conceivably did so because the notion of *performance* benefits from the authority of a long tradition.[46]

B. SUBSTANCE

The right of public communication covers all forms of *direct* ('*live*') communication or *indirect* communication (by *fixations* such as phonographic records, magnetic or other tapes, films, videocopies, etc., or through a *medium of transmission* such as broadcasting—including satellite communication—and cable distribution).

Enumeration of the different acts of public communication shows that the author's right also covers *every activity which permits the work to reach an audience different from that to which the original communication was directed*.

This happens in many cases, for example when a theatrical performance is televised. In that instance, the theatrical performance which is intended for a relatively small number of persons (physically present in the theatre) reaches an audience of an unspecified number within the area served by the broadcast. If this broadcast is then retransmitted by another broadcasting company or by satellite or distributed by a cable network, the audience for which this performance is intended will be progressively widened.

Each action by which the work reaches a 'new audience' differing from that stipulated in the original contract constitutes a new public communication and is subject to the requirement of

---

46. See Henri Desbois, op. cit., paras. 256–7, pp. 326–7.

prior authorization and payment of remuneration according to a varying scale. Such wider broadcasting, in fact, substantially changes the conditions of the initial contract since, in the economic implications of the legal contract, both for the organization concerned and for the author, the size of the audience to be reached by the performance is a decisive factor. In addition, as far as the author is concerned, this may deprive him of the possibility of further contracts since the work will already have been broadcast to these audiences.[47]

The most customary forms of public communication are as follows:

4.3.2.1. *Exhibition of works of art or reproductions thereof*

The communication of the exhibited works is made to an audience present on the premises. It comprises the display, in direct form, of the sole example of the work or of one of the original copies when there are a number (engravings, for example) or, in indirect form, by means of films, slides, television images or other methods of screen presentation or by means of any other device or process or, in the case of an audiovisual work, the showing of individual images non-sequentially (the presentation of images in sequence constitutes a public projection or showing of an audiovisual work).[48]

4.3.2.2. *Public performance*

A. DIRECT

This concerns:
- *stage performances* of dramatic, dramatico-musical, choreographic and pantomime works and of any other work intended for performance, together with adaptations for the theatre of works of various kinds (novels, short stories, etc.);
- *recitations and readings* of literary works;

---

47. See André Francon, op. cit., p. 314.
48. See Section I(ix) of the WIPO *Draft Model Provisions* ..., op. cit., p. 3.

- *dissertations, lectures, speeches, sermons, classes or instructional explanations*, etc.; and
- *performances* of non-dramatic musical works, with or without lyrics.

In the case of these forms of public performance as such, the communication of the work to the public is effected through the *live* performance of interpreters or performers. They are characterized by the presence of the performers before an audience which is physically present, and by the *uniqueness* of the communication.

Direct communication in these cases is always 'live' since it requires the presence of the performers before an audience.

B. INDIRECT

Indirect public perfomance consists of:
- *public performance by mechanical means* of non-dramatic musical works;
- *transmission or broadcasting in a place accessible to the public* (bars, cafeteria, etc.) of works which are broadcast or distributed by cable;
- *communication in a place accessible to the public* of the *fixation* of works which are broadcast or distributed by cable.

The communication to the public is *indirect* when it is effected by means of a *fixation* on a material support or through a *transmission agent* (broadcasting organization or cable distribution company). It is characterized by the existence of these features (a *material support* or a *transmission agent*); and by the *simultaneity* with which the public communication may be effected.

4.3.2.3. Projection or public showing of cinematographic works and other audiovisual works

This covers both the original, traditional form of communicating cinematographic works to the public, i.e. screening in a cinema or any other premises, and the showing of these works in a form other than that indicated, for example in a video bar. It includes the emission or transmission in a place accessible to the public (bar, cafeteria, restaurant) of broadcast works or those distributed by cable and the communication in a place accessible to the public of the fixation of such broadcast or cable-distributed works.

The communication is indirect (for it is effected by means of a copy of the work or through a transmission agent—broadcasting company or cable distribution enterprise—) and is made to a public which is physically present.

4.3.2.4. Broadcasting, public communication by satellite and distribution by cable

A. BROADCASTING

The term *broadcasting* denotes sound radio alone or radio and television. It means the long-range communication of sounds alone or of images and sounds for reception *by the general public by means of radio waves* (electromagnetic waves on frequencies lower than 3,000 gigahertz). Broadcasting is the transmission of sounds alone or of images and sounds by *any wireless means* (including laser beams, gamma rays, etc.) for public reception.[49]

The distinctive features of a broadcast[50] are:
- the transmission is made by radio waves (also known as Hertzian waves) which are electromagnetic waves propagated in space *without any artificial guide*;
- the purpose is to make reception *by the general public possible.*

The broadcasting of works protected by copyright may be made from *fixations* (sound recordings and audiovisual works) or *live performances* (when these take place at the time of transmission in front of the radio microphones or television cameras without previous fixation). In all cases, public communication by broadcasting is *indirect* since the public does not hear or see the performance directly, but *has access to it through a transmission medium.*

---

49. See *WIPO Glossary*, entry 26.
50. See 'Annotated Principles of Protection of Authors, Performers, Producers of Phonograms and Broadcasting Organizations in connection with Distribution of Programmes by Cable'. *Copyright*, WIPO, April 1984, paragraph 33, p. 141 and 50(i), p. 145.

The phrase 'live and direct' often used in broadcasting to show that the transmission of an event, a happening, a show, etc., is made from the place where and at the time when it occurs is liable to create an impression of simultaneity among the general public which is technically speaking incorrect. A communication made by broadcasting may be 'live' (in that it has not been previously fixed) but it is never 'direct', since, by definition, broadcasting is a form of *indirect* communication. The audience which is sometimes present in the broadcasting studio does not receive the show as a broadcast work but in direct form.

The right to broadcast protected works covers any medium used for the *wireless transmission* of signs, sounds or images, including public communication by satellite. In the case of broadcasting or public wireless communication, the public receives the programmes simply by tuning a radio or television receiver to the Hertzian wave frequency on which the broadcasting organization transmits.

On the other hand, in the case of *distribution by cable* the communication is transmitted by wire, cable, optic fibre, laser beam or other similar conductor and *is received only by the audience which has entered into a contract for the service with the distributor* by means of a subscription, or in some other way, but in all cases only after a specific relationship has been established with the distributor.[51]

In accordance with the *principle of the independence of the rights of exploitation*, the right of broadcasting comprises for the author not only the right to authorize the broadcast, but also the right to authorize *rebroadcasting,* by any means of the broadcast work (either by *wireless means*—radio waves or broadcasting by Hertzian waves—or by *cable distribution*—conductor devices— (the Berne Convention excludes retransmission carried out by the

---

51. See Mario Fabiani, 'Televisione via cavo e diritti de autore', in Rev. *Il diritto di autore*, 1981, p. 17, quoted by Antonio Delgado Porras, Utilización de obras audiovisuales por satélite y cable. La intervención de las sociedades de autores, op. cit., p. 223.

original organization) or by *loudspeaker* or any other similar instrument).[52]

B. PUBLIC COMMUNICATION BY SATELLITE

The development of satellite communications in combination with broadcasting and cable distribution has enabled programmes to be broadcast simultaneously—or with a time difference of only a few hours—to vast geographical areas taking in several different countries. As Marshall McLuhan[53] has pointed out, the world has become a *global village*, because an event which happens in one place is immediately reported throughout the world and takes place—as in a village—in full view of a universal public.

Prior to the development of satellite communications, broadcasting covered only the territory of the country in which the broadcast was made. The prejudice resulting from broadcasts made by transmitters in frontier regions and by short wave transmission was extremely limited.

Transmission by means of space satellites has brought not only unsuspected possibilities of access to information and enter-

---

52. Article 11*bis* (1) of the Berne Convention establishes these rights—as an exclusive preserve of the authors of literary and artistic works—in three sections.

In the first, the right of *broadcasting* including *public communication by satellite*, since reference is made to *wireless* broadcasting in general ('the broadcasting of their works or the communication thereof to the public by any other means of wireless diffusion of signs, sounds, or images').

In the second, the right of *retransmission by cable* ('by wire') or *by broadcasting* ('wireless') of the broadcast work when the retransmission is made by *an organization other than that responsible for the original transmission* ('any communication to the public by wire or by rebroadcasting of the broadcast of the work, when this communication is made by an organization other than the original one').

In the third, the public communication of the broadcast work by *loudspeaker* or by a similar instrument ('the public communication by loudspeaker or any other analogous instrument transmitting, by signs, sounds or images, the broadcast of the work').

53. See Herbert Marshall McLuhan, *War and Peace in the Global Village*, McGraw-Hill, New York, 1968.

tainment[54] but at the same time serious problems in regard to the protection of the interests of the owners of copyright and neighbouring rights involved in the broadcasting by this means of programme-carrying signals. These problems are linked more especially with the question of the legality of such transnational distribution, the conditions under which these acts of public communication are made (whether or not the moral right is respected), the payment of the remuneration generated by successive exploitation and the distribution of programme-carrying signals by a distributor for whom the signal is not intended ('piracy of signals').

a. Definitions

In Article 1 of the Convention relating to the distribution of programme-carrying signals transmitted by satellite (Brussels, 1974), usually termed the *Satellite Convention*,[55] it is established that, for the purposes of the Convention:
- *signal* is an electronically generated carrier capable of transmitting programmes (i);
- *programme* is a body of live or recorded material consisting of images, sounds, or both, embodied in signals for the purpose of ultimate distribution (ii);
- *satellite* is any device in extraterrestrial space and capable of transmitting signals (iii);
- *distributor* is the person or legal entity that decides that the transmission of the derived signals to the general public or any section thereof should take place (vii); and
- *distribution* is the operation by which a distributor transmits derived signals to the general public or any section thereof (viii).

---

54. The report of the International Conference of States (Brussels, 1974) which established the *Satellite Convention* pointed out that a 'geostationary satellite' might have a geographical coverage of one-third of the earth's surface and that its signals might be picked up and sent on to entirely new audiences (*Records of the Conference*, Ed. UNESCO-WIPO, 1974, p. 34).
55. See below, Chapter 12, Section 12.5.3.

The notion of *programme* is wider than that of a 'broadcast work' since it comprises not only the interpretations or performances of protected works but also news, sports events, current affairs, etc.

When the programmes carried by the signals include protected works, their transmission by satellite constitutes an act of public communication by *broadcasting* since it involves the *wireless* diffusion of signs, sounds or images (Berne Convention, Article 11*bis*(1)(i)).

b. Categories of broadcasting satellites

There are two categories:
- *direct broadcasting satellites* known by the acronym DBS (*direct broadcasting satellite*). The power of the transmitted signals is sufficient for them to be received directly by the public without the need for an intermediate ground relay station; and
- *fixed service satellites* (or telecommunications satellites) known by the acronym CS (*communication satellite*). In principle, the signals transmitted are not directed to the public but to ground stations which receive them ('receivers') from which they are then distributed by a broadcasting ('distributor') organization (by radio waves) or by cable (using a conductor—wire, cable, optic fibre, etc.).

In their turn, the CS are *distribution* satellites when their signals are received by *all* the ground stations situated within a particular geographical area and *point-to-point satellites* when their signals are received only by the ground station to which they are beamed.

Point-to-point satellites were the first to operate; the distribution of their signals required ground stations with extremely powerful and costly receiving equipment. In the past 20 years, technological progress has resulted in a constant increase in the power of satellites. This has made it possible for the *programmes carried by them to be received directly*, by means of parabolic antennas with signal decoding devices which are commercially available and can be connected to domestic receivers.

It thus became necessary to make a further distinction between the CS which require a ground station to distribute the programmes transmitted by them and those point-to-point CS whose signals *can be received directly by the public*, using the antennas which are commercially available, without the need for a distributing organization. Since the latter in effect function as DBS, it was held to be necessary[56] for them to be treated as such, and a functional classification for juridical purposes[57] going beyond the technical distinction between DBS and CS was called for.

This technological fact—the increase in the power of satellites—has legal consequences since the signals directed by the broadcasting organization to a CS for their subsequent transmission by a distributing organization in a specific territory can be directly received by the public in another territory.

This assimilation of CS with DBS when individuals have the possibility of receiving signals directly has already been reflected in the Directive of the Council of the European Communities dated 27 September 1993 (93/83/CEE) (*Official Journal of the European Communities*, 6 October 1993).

c. Operations

The transmission of signals by active satellites[58] is effected basically through the following operations:
- *the upleg stage* during which the transmission (or 'injection') of signals is made from a ground station towards the satellite. The natural person or legal entity who decides which programmes are to be carried by the transmitted signals is known as the 'organization of origin' or 'injector';
- *the processing of signals* in the satellite; the technical characteristics of the transmitted signals are modified by amplification and modulation to obtain 'derived signals' which may be stored; and
- *the downleg stage* during which the derived signals descend

---

56. See Antonio Delgado Porras, 'Utilización de obras audiovisuales por satélite y cable. La intervención de las sociedades de autores', op. cit., pp. 230–1.
57. Walter Dillenz, 'Legal system governing the protection of works transmitted by direct broadcasting satellites' in *Copyright*, 1986, quoted by Delgado Porras, op. cit.
58. Active satellites transmit or retransmit signals, while passive satellites are designed to retransmit signals by reflection.

from the satellite and are distributed by an organization known as the 'distributor' or, if the power of the satellite so permits, received directly by the public.

d. Nature of public communication by satellite

The public communication of programmes by satellite constitutes broadcasting.

As we have already seen, the Berne Convention makes no distinction between the various wireless systems used for public transmission so that transmission by satellite automatically falls within the concept of *broadcasting* (Article 11*bis*(1)(i) which includes: '... the broadcasting ... to the public by any other means of wireless diffusion of signs, sounds or images'.

The Rome Convention of 1961 gives us to understand that 'broadcasting' means the transmission by radio waves or *any other wireless means* for public reception of sounds alone or of images and sounds (Article 3: 'For the purposes of this Convention ... (f) "Broadcasting" means the transmission by wireless means for public reception of sounds or of images and sounds').

The Spanish law of 1987 provides, in its Article 20(2), that:

The following in particular, shall be considered acts of communication to the public ... (c) the transmission of any works by broadcasting or by any other means serving for the wireless dissemination of signs, sounds or images; the concept of transmission shall include the production of signals in a ground station for a broadcasting or telecommunication satellite.

In turn, in Section 1(iii) of the Draft Model Provisions for Legislation in the Field of Copyright drawn up by WIPO,[59] the definition of broadcasting (in accordance with Article 11*bis*(I)(i) of the Berne Convention) includes public transmission by satellite:

Broadcasting is the communication of a work to the public ... by wireless transmission ... "Broadcasting" includes broadcasting by a satellite ... from the injection of a work towards the satellite, including both the upleg and the

---

59. See WIPO document CE/MPC/I/2-II of 20 October 1988.

downleg stages of the transmission, until the work is communicated to (made available but not necessarily received by) the public.

e. The emission of signals

The emission (or injection) of programme-carrying signals which include copyrighted works to a DBS in itself constitutes an act of broadcasting.

The organization which performs such an act of broadcasting is responsible vis-à-vis the owners of the rights arising in connection with exploitation of the work.[60] It is not necessary for the work which is made available to the public to have actually been received, viewed or listened to by any individual; for the work to be deemed to have been transmitted, it is sufficient for it to have been effectively made available to the public.[61]

f. Situations of conflict

By virtue of the right of the author to delimit the scope of the validity of the contract in terms of space and time, the authorization to broadcast the work on a given territory is circumscribed to that territory.

The author of a dramatic work who has signed a contract for its broadcasting in one country, town, etc., is entitled to conclude similar contracts in respect of all the other places not included within previous contracts which are currently valid. Similarly, he has the right to decide that the work shall not be broadcast to particular territories not covered by the licence or that, in such territories, it shall first be performed in theatres and only be

---

60. It would be appropriate to include CS whose power is such that the signals can also be received directly by the public when such reception effectively takes place. This is one of the reasons for which calls are being made for a classification of satellites for legal purposes going beyond the technical distinction between DBS and CS (see Walter Dillenz, 'Legal System Governing the Protection of Works Transmitted by Direct Broadcasting Satellites', *Copyright*, 1986, quoted by Delgado Porras, op. cit., p. 230).
61. See Section 1(v) of the WIPO *Draft Model Provisions for Legislation in the Field of Copyright*.

broadcast thereafter (principle of the *independence of the rights of exploitation*).

Similarly, the producer of a cinematographic work is entitled to arrange for the progressive exploitation in *each country* which best corresponds to his interests and which generally begins with a showing in cinemas and later, when this has been completed and always provided that the respective rights have been granted, exploitation by means of reproduction on video copies for sale or hire, subsequently by cable distribution and finally by television broadcasting by Hertzian waves.

If a broadcasting organization which has received authorization for the television broadcasting of certain programmes in a particular territory transmits the programme-carrying signals to a satellite which covers territories not included within the authorization, it is performing an act of public communication which is contrary to the legitimate rights of the authors of the works included in those programmes, and also to the rights of the performers and producers of the audiovisual works and phonograms and those of the organization of origin and other organizations which may have been authorized to broadcast the programmes to these territories.

While the broadcasts had a range limited to the frontiers of the country within which the transmission was made, no problems arose in regard to the applicable law for the purpose of determining whether such emissions—or retransmissions—were legitimate; the process of transmission began (emission) and ended (reception) within the same country and the legality of the act of public communication was accordingly judged in the light of a single body of legislation—that of the country in which the broadcast was made (apart from those which were made in frontier zones and reached neighbouring countries, but, in general, these could not be considered significant).

1. Direct broadcasting satellites (DBS)
The development of satellite communications has brought with it the possibility of making *transnational broadcasts* on a large scale by transmitting signals to a DBS; these signals *are then directly received by the public in other countries* without the need for in-

tervention by a signal-distributing organization. In the countries covered by the 'footprint' of the satellite, these transmissions may affect the rights of the owners of copyright and neighbouring rights, since no organization responsible for distribution of the signals exists in the countries concerned.

Where the transmission is made in a country in which non-voluntary licences govern the broadcasting of protected works (see below, Section 4.3.2) and reception takes place in countries where such licences are not accepted or when, in the country from which the broadcast is made, protection is either non-existent or less than that applicable in the country of reception and such public communication affects the interests of the owners of copyright and neighbouring rights, the following problem of private international law arises: by which law is the legality of the act to be judged: only the legislation of the country from which the transmission is made, or that of all the countries covered by the 'footprint' of the satellite? For it is in the latter that the act of broadcasting is completed.[62]

The answers differ and have given rise to two different positions:

The emission (or injection) theory is based on the traditional interpretation of the definition of broadcasting contained in the Radio Regulations of the International Telecommunication Union (ITU) according to which the meaning of the following terms is provided by the accompanying definitions:

Broadcasting Service: a radiocommunication service in which the transmissions are intended for direct reception by the general public. This service may include sound transmissions, television transmissions or other types of transmission (Article III(3.17)).

---

62. The purpose here is not to determine from which point in time the injecting organization becomes responsible for the act of broadcasting (we have seen that for a transmission to exist there is no need for proof of effective reception by the public), but rather which body of law determines the legality of the act of broadcasting when differences apply in this respect between the laws of the countries of transmission and reception.

Radiocommunication: telecommunication by means of radio waves (Article I(1.5).

Telecommunication: any transmission, emission or reception of signs, signals, writing, images and sounds or intelligence of any nature by wire, radio, optical or other electromagnetic systems (Article I(1.2)).

The *theory of communication* or the *Bogsch Theory*, named after Dr Arpad Bogsch[63] who defined it in March 1985 at the meeting of the UNESCO/WIPO Group of Experts on the Copyright Aspects of Direct Broadcasting by Satellite in Paris and which, as Dr Ficsor states, was advanced on that occasion by its author as an expression of 'tentative views', is based on the updated interpretation given in Article 11*bis*(1)(i) of the Berne Convention in which broadcasting is defined as the *communication (of works) to the public by any ... means of wireless diffusion. ...*

At that meeting, Dr Bosch explained his theory as follows:

(i) Broadcasting through direct broadcasting satellites is broadcasting in the sense of Article 11 *bis* of the Berne Convention.
(ii) According to that Article, broadcasting is a means of communication to the public by wireless diffusion (namely by radio waves). The said Article uses the concepts 'communication to the public' and 'diffusion' and does not use the concept 'emission', a concept that is narrower than 'communication to the public' and 'diffusion'. Consequently, broadcasting takes place where the wireless diffusion takes place as a communication to the public. Where communication to the public by means of radio waves is effected through a direct broadcasting satellite, the communication takes place in all countries which are covered by the 'footprint' of the satellite.
(iii) Under the Berne Convention, which provides for national treatment, the national law of each country covered by the 'footprint' of the satellite is applicable. The national laws may grant an exclusive right (Article 11 *bis*(1)), or may provide for what may be called a non-voluntary licence (Article 11 *bis*(2)). Any broadcasting through direct broadcasting satellites, when the 'footprint' covers more than one country, must, therefore, comply with the copyright laws of each of the countries covered by such broadcasting. Otherwise, a communication to the public in one country would be governed by the national law of another country, a result contrary to the principle of national treatment.

---

63. Dr Bogsch has been Director-General of WIPO since 1973.

(iv) Where the 'footprint' covers only a part of a country, one might consider, according to the *'de minimis lex non regit'* principle, that the national copyright law of that country need not be taken into account.
(v) Compliance with the applicable national copyright laws is the responsibility of the person or organization that gives the order for the broadcasting through direct broadcasting satellite. No other entity has any responsibility. In particular, no person who receives the broadcast in any country has any responsibility, in particular needs no authorization from, and need not pay anything to, the owner of the copyright in the broadcast work, for such reception.
(vi) These views are based on the Berne Convention as it is today.

The Bogsch Theory takes as its starting point Article 11 *bis* of the Berne Convention; this latter provision is not taken into account by the supporters of the emission theory, for they base themselves solely on the Radio Regulations of the International Telecommunication Union in which the concept of 'emission' is used, a concept that is narrower than 'communication to the public' and 'diffusion' employed in the above Article. In this regard, Ficsor states that communication to the public by broadcasting via a direct broadcasting satellite begins with the emission of the programme-carrying signals towards the satellite, but is not completed at the point of emission. Communication to the public means that a programme has been made available to the public— without the further condition that it is actually received by the public—and it cannot be said that at the point of emission when the programme-carrying signals leave the earth station towards the satellite, the programme has already been made available— that is to say communicated—to the public. Communication to the public includes both phases, i.e. the upleg and the downleg. It is the whole process, consisting of a series of successive phases, that may be considered as communication to the public by wireless means—Hertzian waves—i.e. by broadcasting. Ficsor points out that to say that for the definition of broadcasting, not the Berne Convention but the ITU Radio Regulations should be taken into account and, therefore, direct broadcasting by satellite should be identified as the mere emission from the ground station, and then to be informed that according to those Regulations broadcasting is not only not completed by the emission from the earth station but does not even start there and is initiated only in the satellite, may be really very embarrassing for the advocates of the emission theory.[64]

Following its presentation in 1985, the Bogsch Theory was developed in greater detail in the memorandum prepared by the UNESCO/WIPO Committee of Governmental Experts on Audiovisual Works and Phonograms (Paris, May 1986). It assumed its final form in the Memorandum on the Evaluation and Synthesis of Principles on Various Categories of Works (document CGE/SYN/3-III, paras. 21–45) prepared for the UNESCO/WIPO Committee of Governmental Experts which met in Geneva in June–July 1988 and was accepted in the UNESCO/WIPO Principles (document CGE/SYN/3-II: Principles AW11 to AW14 (in respect of audiovisual works) and Principles PH14 to PH17 (in respect of rights in works and interpretations contained in phonograms, together with the rights of the producers of the latter); these principles are also applicable *mutatis mutandis* to other categories of works.

Ficsor points out that these principles contain only the most important elements of the Bogsch Theory. For example, although the principles do not state it explicitly, it necessarily follows from this theory that if the owner of rights is not the same person in the country of emission as in the 'footprint' country, it is not sufficient to take into account the rights of whoever is the owner in the emission country; the rights of the owner in the 'footprint' country, that is to say, where the work is actually communicated, should apply at least in equal measure.

Ficsor refutes the legal and practical difficulties raised in opposition to the principles based on the Bogsch Theory when these principles were set out in the memorandum for the Committee of

---

64. See M. Ficsor, *Direct Broadcasting by Satellite and the 'Bogsch Theory'*, study presented to the Section of Business Law Conference, Committee of Intellectual Property, Establishment and Communications of the International Bar Association, Strasbourg, 2–6 October 1989 (document) which contains a detailed presentation of this theory.

Governmental Experts on Audio-visual Works and Phonograms (Paris, May 1986).[65]

In the memorandum concerning the WIPO Model Provisions for Legislation in the field of Copyright (document CE/MPC/III/2 of 30 May 1990, prepared by the International Bureau of WIPO), reference is made to certain court cases in which the Bogsch Theory has been applied (para. 106):

> Those court cases concerned partly the question of applicable law (as in the case of the decision of December 19, 1989, of the Court of Appeal of Paris in which the court obliged *Télé Monte-Carlo* and the *Compagnie Luxembourgeoise de Télédiffusion*—that is, two broadcasters transmitting programmes from the territories of other States to the territory of France—to pay large amounts for the unauthorized broadcasting by them of commercial phonograms), and partly the exercise of the rights of owners of rights in the footprint country (as in the case of the decision of November 30, 1989, of the Court of Appeal of Vienna which stated that the permission of the rights owners of the country of footprint where the programme transmitted by a direct broadcasting satellite was made available to the public, was also needed for such broadcasting).

Application of the Bogsch Theory is also reflected in the provisions concerning direct broadcasting by satellite proposed in the memorandum prepared by the International Bureau of WIPO for the second session of a Committee of Experts on a Possible Protocol to the Berne Convention (Geneva, 10–17 February 1992) (see *Copyright*, March 1992, pp. 77–8).

It can easily be seen that in a few years' time, direct reception via broadcasting satellites (DBS) will have developed greatly and in many parts of the world every member of the population will be able to choose between the programmes offered by a number of different countries on the same and other continents, so that the viewing public will become increasingly multinational.

Despite the fact that no amicable solution has yet been found to the problem created by direct broadcasting satellites, what would be unacceptable, as Delgado Porras rightly points out, is the development of 'broadcasting havens' and 'legal colonialism',

---

65. Ibid.

as would happen if the users were permitted to choose the country with the least stringent protection system to organize their broadcasts and, by exporting their signals, to impose that system on the other 'footprint' countries.[66]

2. Communication satellites (CS)

A situation of conflict parallel to that described in connection with DBS also arises in the case of CS when the law of the country from which the emission is made differs from the law of the country where distribution takes place as regards the level of protection or when in one or other of these countries protection is non-existent or, again, is less effective than that applicable in the other; public communication adversely affects the interests of the owners of copyright and of neighbouring rights when authorization has not been granted to the organization responsible for emission or for distribution.

It has to be decided whether sole responsibility lies with the distributing organization or whether the transmitting organization is also responsible, in order to determine the organization against which action might be taken and which body of law is applicable. Opinions differ.

Some observers consider that, in the case of broadcasting by CS, the emission of signals to the satellite (or the injection of signals) is a purely *technical operation* and not an act of broadcasting, since the power of the transmission (in principle less than that of DBS) requires a ground station to distribute the programmes carried by these signals. They accordingly conclude that only the distributing organization performs an act of public communication and therefore bears sole responsibility vis-à-vis the owners of copyright and neighbouring rights who may have suffered prejudice, the law of the country in which the distribution is effected being applicable in this case.

Where the latter legislation does not make provision for legal

---

66. See Antonio Delgado Porras, op. cit., Section 32, p. 234.

action by the owners of rights who have suffered prejudice, they will not be able to direct their action against the injecting organization and the prejudice caused by the distribution of programmes via satellites in such countries will go unrepaired.

At the other extreme, starting out from the assumption that the 'injection' of signals in a satellite constitutes an act of broadcasting which, as such, is an act of exploitation which is the preserve of the author and must therefore be authorized by him, another body of opinion concludes that the emitting organization will be responsible to the author unless the latter has concluded a contract with the distributing organization to authorize the distribution of signals.

That argument has been accepted in France, where Article L. 132-20.3, previously Article 45(iii) of the Law of 1957, amended by the 1985 reform, rules that in the absence of a stipulation to the contrary:

> Authorization to telediffuse a work by electromagnetic waves shall not include its transmission towards a satellite enabling the work to be received by the intermediary of other organizations, unless the authors or their successors in title have contractually authorized the latter organizations to communicate the work to the public; in such case, the emitting organization shall be exempted from paying any remuneration.

In consequence, it follows that in the case of a DBS, the broadcasting organization which makes the emission must seek authorization from the author and pay the corresponding remuneration. If, on the other hand, the work is transmitted to the public via a distributing organization, it may happen that the latter has entered into a contract for diffusion with the authors or their successors in title and, in that case, will be responsible for payment of the remuneration; if not, the emitting organization is responsible for payment.

In his commentary on this provision, Colombet points out that the aim here was to avoid both double remuneration of authors and the absence of remuneration by placing an obligation on the emitting organization to seek authorization and make payment; however, if the distributing organization has received contractual authorization from the latter it will then be responsible for payment.[67]

Adopting a middle-of-the-road attitude, those who consider that public communication of programmes by CS must of necessity involve two organizations, one to emit the signal and the other to distribute it, conclude that these are not two separate acts of broadcasting (emission and retransmission) because an act of broadcasting is not repeated but merely *completed*. Save in cases where the signals are transmitted for the purpose of storage (and distribution depends on a subsequent decision by the transmitting organization or distributor), these are two phases of the same operation which requires one single authorization but, if no such authorization exists, both organizations are separately and jointly responsible to the owners of rights who have suffered prejudice.

That theory is accepted in the UNESCO/WIPO Principles (Principles AW15 to AW19 in respect of audiovisual works and Principles PH18 to PH22 in respect of rights in works and interpretations contained in phonograms, together with the rights of producers of phonograms).

In particular, Principle AW16 states that:

Both the broadcasting organization originating the programme and the broadcasting organization transmitting it from the receiving earth station further to the public are—separately and jointly—responsible towards the owners of copyright in audio-visual works and towards performers, phonogram producers and broadcasting organizations whose rights may be concerned as far as the final phase of broadcasting (from the earth station further to the public) is concerned. The originating organization alone is responsible towards the owners of rights for the phases preceding the final phase of broadcasting.

(The same concept is reproduced in Principle PH19 in respect of phonograms.)

---

67. See Claude Colombet, *Propriété littéraire et artistique et droits voisins*, op. cit., p. 210, para. 203.

C. Distribution by cable

Distribution by cable is the operation by which programme-carrying signals generated electronically are transmitted by a conducting device (wire, coaxial cable, optic fibre, laser beam and any other analogous medium) over a certain distance for reception by the general public or by any particular segment thereof.[68]

The distinctive features of the distribution of programmes by cable are:
- the transmission is made by electromagnetic waves which are conducted by means of an artificial guide; and
- it is received by the public.

This form of public communication of protected works has developed rapidly; today a number of cities and towns throughout the world are fully cabled.

The notion of cable ditribution comprises the transmission of sound signals only, and audiovisual transmissions, referred to as *cable television*.

The latter, widespread designation may lead to confusion in regard to the legal nature of distribution by cable since television is encompassed within the concept of broadcasting, while cable distribution does not constitute broadcasting as it is effected by means of a device which conducts the programme-carrying signals from a distributing installation to a receiving installation which then converts them into audible and visible oscillations. In the case of broadcasting on the other hand, the electromagnetic waves are transmitted by any kind of wireless system through Hertzian space without an artificial guide.

Television broadcasts are distributed by cable for various reasons, such as:
- the need to overcome topographic and building obstacles ('shadow zone'), because of which the quality of reception by radio waves of the broadcasts made by the broadcasting

---

68. See *Annotated Principles of Protection of Authors, Performers, Producers of Phonograms and Broadcasting Organizations in Connection with Distribution of Programs by Cable*, paragraph 33, p. 141 and paragraph 50(iii), p. 145.

organization leaves much to be desired, while any other solution would involve the installation of a great many costly antennas; or
- to extend the range of transmission to a zone in which reception is possible, but only through the use of individual antennas available on the market ('direct reception zone'), or to the territory to which the transmissions are directed in compliance with a legal provision ('compulsory zone') or for other reasons such as contractual clauses ('service zone').

The distribution of television broadcasts by cable may be effected by the originating organization or by another organization:
- the Berne Convention permits a provision in national legislation to the effect that the *organization of origin* may resort to cable distribution (i.e to devices which conduct radiomagnetic waves such as wire, coaxial cable, optical fibre, etc.) to overcome obstacles or to broaden the range of its *public broadcasting communications* within the territory of the country which grants it the licence to broadcast; it may also use wireless systems such as antennas, satellites, etc., for the same purpose;[69]
- but when the distribution of broadcast programmes is effected by an *organization other than the original one*, a new act of public communication occurs in every case and, as a consequence of the monopoly of exploitation enjoyed by the author, it must be specifically authorized by the author and remunerated accordingly.

---

69. Delgado Porras considers it wrong to define as an instance of free utilization in favour of the organizations of origin, the retransmission or public transmission by cable effected by broadcasting organizations, of works broadcast by them (as provided for in Section 21 of the Draft Model Provisions of WIPO); he is also of the opinion that Article 11*bis*(1)(ii) of the Berne Convention grants indirect protection to the author not only to determine by contract with the transmitter the conditions for distribution by cable of the broadcast work, but also expressly to exclude this form of exploitation (this is the reason for which he calls his theory the 'indirect protection of distribution by cable of programmes broadcast by the distributor himself'). See Utilización de obras audiovisuales por satélite y cable. La intervención de las sociedades de autores, op. cit., pp. 225–6.

In the latter instance, we are confronted with a secondary exploitation of the work distinct from its broadcasting since a new service—not provided by the originating organization—is now involved, consisting in the reception of the radio waves transmitted by the latter which are then amplified, modulated and distributed, thus enabling the works to be communicated clearly to new audiences which would otherwise not receive them or obtain only poor reception.

Hence, authorization by the author is required, as is payment of remuneration by the cable distributor not included in the payment made by the originating organization which covers only the activities performed by the latter which were *envisaged by the parties to the contract*.

That is why Article 11*bis*(1) of the Berne Convention, as a corollary to the right of broadcasting by any wireless means, expressly recognizes that the authors of literary and artistic works shall have the exclusive right to authorize: '... (ii) any communication to the public by wire or by rebroadcasting of the broadcast of the work, when this communication is made by an organization other than the original one ...'.[70]

There are *two types of distribution by cable*: distribution of broadcast programmes; and distribution of cable-originated programmes.

The original purpose of cable distribution was to retransmit broadcasts. A later development was the distribution of separate programmes produced by the cable distributor without using a broadcast transmission or using only parts thereof. These programmes are known as cable-originated programmes.

The *distribution by cable of broadcast programmes* means the simultaneous and complete retransmission by cable of a broadcast

---

70. This provision was applied in the rulings of the Swiss Federal Court of 20 January 1981 (RIDA, No. 111, p. 196) and 20 March 1984 (RIDA, No. 123, p. 206); idem, Court of Cassation of Belgium (ruling of 25 June 1982 (CISAC), document CJL/83/652. Report of the Legal and Legislation Committee, Washington, May 1983). Austria (Article 17) and United Kingdom (Section 73(3)(b)) differ despite the fact that these countries both belong to the Berne Union.

transmission. The retransmission may involve only part of the programme, but still be considered complete, if it is effected simultaneously and comprises an unmodified section of the broadcast programme (with a specific content and for an uninterrupted period of time).

The *distribution of cable-originated programmes* means both the distribution of programmes produced by the cable distributor (even when parts of programmes received by broadcasting are used); and
- the 'time-shifted' (non-simultaneous) distribution of programmes received by broadcasting with or without the addition of a musical background, or a text or commentary superimposed on the broadcast and specific to the cable distributor;
- the simultaneous distribution of broadcast programmes but with certain modifications, for example when the audience listens 'off' to a translation of the sound track of the original broadcast (direct dubbing); and
- any other distribution of broadcast programmes made on a 'time-shifted' basis or introducing changes to the original transmission (which is neither simultaneous nor complete).

The distribution of 'time-shifted' programmes or programmes with alterations (additions or deletions) affects the exclusive rights of the author. His simple authorization is not, therefore, sufficient for the cable distribution of broadcasts; he (or his representative) must grant a licence giving express authorization. For practical reasons, if he is to effect 'time-shifted' distribution, the cable distributor must fix the programmes at the time of reception of the broadcast in order to proceed later to their public communication which implies the exercise of the right of reproduction; in their turn, the alterations to the original broadcast involve the exercise of the right of transformation and encroach upon the moral right of the author.

D. SPECIAL SITUATIONS: TRANSMISSIONS TO HOTEL BEDROOMS AND GROUPS OF ACCOMMODATION UNITS

Transmissions to hotel bedrooms: when hotel bedrooms have television sets installed in them for the reception of programmes through an internal cable system controlled by the hotel management, then the latter is performing an act of *public communication.*

This transmission is an *intermediate* act in respect of the programmes which are received by traditional broadcasting—or by satellite broadcasting or distribution—for the public does not receive the programmes directly but only after *retransmission* within the meaning of Article 11*bis*(1) of the Berne Convention which provides that: 'Authors of literary and artistic works shall enjoy the exclusive right of authorizing: ... (ii) any communication to the public *by wire or by rebroadcasting of the broadcast of the work*, when this communication *is made by an organization other than the original one*; (iii) the public communication by *loudspeaker or any other analogous instrument* transmitting, by signs, sounds or images, *the broadcast of the work*' (our italics).

Hotel bedrooms are places intended for the public even though they are not public places. Neither are private houses for which the distribution of programmes by cable networks is intended. Communication is public not only when it is received in a public place, but when—as in the case of the guests in a hotel—the transmission is distributed by an intermediary—the hotelier—in a place to which the public has access and to persons who do not belong to his close family and private circle.

It has been stated that where each hotel room has a television set with its own antenna which captures from the air programmes transmitted by Hertzian waves, i.e. wireless, the communication is then termed 'broadcasting' as a variant of communication to the public (see document **WIPO BCP/CE/I/3** of 18 October 1991, para. 158, published in *Copyright*, March 1992, p. 80).

Groups of accommodation units: the distribution of programmes to the units forming part of a group of neighbouring accommodation units by their *own internal cable system* also constitutes an act of public communication by an organization other than the organization of origin. The same consideration applies when a powerful communal antenna is used to pick up programme-carrying signals broadcast directly or via a fixed service distribution or point to point satellite—i.e. intended for a ground station—, these transmissions then being distributed to the units of the residential complex or housing estate (urban development zone, locality, town) which would not otherwise receive them.

The fact that this distribution is made to private dwellings does not change the nature of the act (public communication), since the broadcasts by the organization of origin are also intended for private dwellings;[71] the observations made in respect of retransmissions to hotel bedrooms through internal cable systems controlled by the hotel management also apply here.

The fact that the service is provided without charge does not change the nature of the act, nor does it engender any limitations to the author's right since, as we shall see (see below, Section 4.3), exceptions are subject to *numerus clausus*; for that reason, they may only be invoked when they are expressly stipulated in the relevant law.

4.3.2.5. Public communication of works with the use of information technology services

Access by the public to computer databases by telecommunications also constitutes public communication. The Spanish law, for example, expressly mentions among acts of public communication 'public access to computer data bases by means of telecommunication where such data bases incorporate or constitute protected works' (Article 20(h)).

4.3.2.6. The public nature of the communication

The laws reserve to the author an exclusive right of public communication of his work. It is thus self-evident that when the communication is not directed to the public, it does not fall within the monopoly of exploitation recognized as being vested in the creator (unlike the right of reproduction which in principle is granted without any limitations other than those expressly established, whether private or public use is intended).

---

71. Ricardo Antequera Parilli, Intellectual Rights, Satellite Television and Cable Television, WIPO Regional Forum, Montevideo, 13–15 December 1989 (document).

The public nature of communication is extremely difficult to typify in all-embracing terms covering the various possible situations.

For that reason, some laws (and also the Berne Convention), avoid the distinction between public and private communication, while others, such as the French law (Article L. 122-5.1 previously Art. 41(1)), confine themselves to excluding from copyright 'free, private performances produced exclusively within the family circle' (idem, Venezuela (Article 43(1))); it is therefore to be understood that all communication not covered by this exclusion is public.

On the other hand, certain legislation, such as the German law (Article 15(3)) and the Mexican law (Art. 72) contain a clear provision, establishing in the first case, that 'the communication of a work shall be public if it is intended for a number of persons, unless such persons form a clearly defined group and are interconnected personally by mutual relations or by a relationship to the organizer'.

In other laws, such as those of Argentina and Peru (Supreme Decree 61 (1962), Art. 5), the definition of the term *public* is contained in a text implementing the law. Under the provisions of Article 33 of the Argentine Decree 41.233 (1934) 'the representation or performance is public when it takes place—irrespective of the purpose thereof—in any place which is not an exclusively private home, and even within such a home if the representation or performance is projected or propagated outside'.

The public nature of the communication may also be typified by a negative reference as in the Spanish law (Article 20(1), second paragraph) which provides that 'communication shall not be considered public where it takes place in a strictly domestic environment that is not an integral part of or connected to a dissemination network of any kind'.

In the memorandum of the International Bureau of WIPO for the second session of the Committee of Experts on a possible Protocol to the Berne Convention, it is stressed that 'it is increasingly accepted that every use should be considered "public" (rather than "private") that goes beyond the circle of family members and close social acquaintances of a family or an individual person' (*Copyright*, WIPO, March 1992, para. 153, p. 78).

4.3.3. The right of transformation

A. CONCEPT

The right of transformation constitutes the prerogative of the author to exploit his work by authorizing the creation of works deriving from it: adaptations, translations, revisions, updatings, summaries, extracts, musical arrangements, compilations, anthologies, and so on.

The work in its original form—or primogenial, pre-existing, initial, preceding, primary or original work as it is customarily termed (see above, Chapter 2, Section 2.2.1.) remains unchanged in its individuality. As a consequence of the transformation a new work is added to it—the derivative work—or subsequent or secondary work—a fact that should be clearly indicated so that there is no confusion with the work from which it is derived.

B. SUBSTANCE

See above, Chapter 2, Section 2.2.2.

4.3.4. The right of participation or *droit de suite*

The right of participation, which is commonly referred to by the French term *droit de suite*,[72] is the right of the authors of artistic works to receive a share of the proceeds of successive sales[73] of the originals of these works—to which may be assimilated the manuscripts of graphic works—sold by public auction or through the intervention of a dealer or commercial agent.

---

72. This right originated in France, where it was established by a law of 20 March 1920.
73. Successive sales by *public auction:* in France, for example; successive sales involving a *dealer* or *agent*: Germany, for example. Some countries such as Brazil, Portugal and Uruguay provide that *droit de suite* should apply to *all successive sales*, but it has to be said that this extension is not, in fact, realistic.

Reproduction and public communication, which are the traditional forms of exploiting works, only reward visual artists in exceptional cases since only famous works are the subject of reproduction on plates, slides, postcards or for advertising purposes. No payment is made to the authors of artistic works for their *public exhibition*.

The usual manner of exploiting these works commercially is by alienating the original copy of the work. Once the artist sells or even 'sacrifices' his work since he generally does so under the pressing necessity of earning his living, especially at the beginning of his career, he has no further share in later acts of exploitation which generally take place when the creation has achieved a resale value and has become a source of profit. Sometimes the profit is extremely high when the author acquires fame through his talent and because of his dedication to his work.

It is therefore appropriate that, by analogy with collectors and intermediaries (auctioneers, art dealers, art gallery managers, etc.), such artists should themselves have a share in the economic success of their work by receiving a percentage of the price obtained in subsequent sales by way of additional payment. The right of participation plays a compensatory role. It is equivalent to the benefits which the authors of literary and musical works receive for each communication of their works to a new audience.

Having regard to the time which has elapsed since it was embodied in the French law of 1920, the first to institute the *droit de suite*, and to its underlying equity, it has to be said that the countries which have since adopted the right of participation[74] are very few and still fewer those in which this right is *effectively*

---

74. Algeria, Belgium, Bolivia, Brazil, Bulgaria, Congo, Costa Rica, Côte d'Ivoire, Chile (only in favour of national authors, Art. 36), former Czechoslovakia, Denmark, Ecuador, El Salvador, Estonia, France, Germany, Greece, Guinea, Holy See, Honduras, Hungary, Iceland, India, Italy, Jordan, Luxembourg, Madagascar, Mali, Morocco, Panama, Peru, Philippines, Portugal, Russian Federation, Senegal, Spain, Tunisia, Turkey, Uruguay, Venezuela, former Yugoslavia, the Democratic Republic of the Congo, and, in the United States of America, the state of California.

applied,[75] despite the fact that in some cases its application has had *statutory*[76] force for half a century. One of the arguments which are frequently put forward against the *droit de suite* is the potential risk which it entails of transactions in artistic works being transferred to countries which do not establish this right so that those which do so may be prejudiced.

The Berne Convention recognizes the *droit de suite* as the right of the author to secure participation in the sale of original works of art and manuscripts which is subsequent to the first transfer by the author (Article 14*ter*(1), Paris text). This provision was introduced in the Brussels revision as Article 14*bis*. The Convention provides that this right is inalienable, although it can be transferred *mortis causa*, but the author does not enjoy this right *jure conventionis*: its recognition is not mandatory for the countries of the Union and it is subject to material reciprocity (Art. 14*ter*(2)). Article 14*ter* stipulates:

1. The author, or after his death the persons or institutions authorized by national legislation, shall, with respect to original works of art and original manuscripts of writers and composers, enjoy the inalienable right to an interest in any sale of the work subsequent to the first transfer by the author of the work.
2. The protection provided by the preceding paragraph may be claimed in a country of the Union only if legislation in the country to which the author belongs so permits, and to the extent permitted by the country where this protection is claimed.
3. The procedure for collection and the amounts shall be matters for determination by national legislation.

The overwhelming majority of national laws recognize the *inalienability* of the right of participation and the *impossibility of its waiver*, by reason of the social order on which it is based. If the

---

75. Belgium and France (sales by public auction), Hungary, Germany, Spain. In most of these countries, the rights of plastic artists are administered by the societies of authors: SPADEM and ADAGP (in France); HUNGART (Hungary); BILD-KUNST (Germany); and VISUAL (Spain).
76. For example, former Czechoslovakia (Law of 1926, maintained in the 1965 reform), Uruguay (1937).

right could be waived or transferred, this would be contrary to the protective purpose which justifies its existence.

On the other hand, there is no consensus as regards the *nature* of the right of participation—whether it constitutes an author's right or a *right of simple remuneration* (Germany, Article 26; Spain, Article 24) intended to compensate authors of artistic works in the case of unfair situations, the aim being to ensure that they obtain an equitable return from the proceeds resulting from the economic use of their work which lies outside the scope of their absolute exploitation right.

As regards the Spanish law, Delgado Porras considers that the criterion of regulating the right of participation within the section entitled 'other rights' is explained by the fact that 'it bears no direct relationship to the work but to the material thing (unique copy) in which it is embodied; the position of the passive subject of this right (whose relationship with respect to the author constitutes a case of obligation *propter ren*) has as its point of departure the acquisition of the copy whose circulation proceeds from its sale, and is not based on any right of exploitation of the work'.[77]

A. TRANSMISSION 'MORTIS CAUSA' OF THE 'DROIT DE SUITE'

Criteria vary:

Transmission *mortis causa* is not recognized in Chile, former Czechoslovakia, Germany, Hungary (in the event of the original being sold to a museum or public collection, Article 35-A of the decree concerning the application of the copyright law, and Italy.[78]

---

77. Antonio Delgado Porras, *Panorámica de la protección civil y penal en materia de propiedad intelectual*, op. cit., p. 26.
78. In Spain, the original text of Article 24 of Intellectual Property Law 22/1987 was modified in order to allow transmission *mortis causa* and protection for 60 years *post mortem auctoris*. The basis of the calculation was also increased to 300,000 pesetas in respect of each work sold.

In other countries, transmission *mortis causa* is permitted. However, there are differences as to the definition of the legatees:
- some laws mention only the heirs: Algeria (Article 70), Ecuador (Article 86), Philippines (Article 31), Senegal (Article 19), Tunisia (Art. 25 of Law 94-36 of 24 February 1994);
- in France, the legatees are expressly excluded (Article L. 123-7, previously Art. 42(2) *in fine*: '... but excluding all legatees and transferees'). Case law has ruled that the exclusion of legatees does not apply to the direct heirs and the heirs of the author until the term of protection expires, restricting the enjoyment of the right to members of the author's family;[79]
- in Italy, on the other hand, not only is it accepted that the legatees may benefit from the right of participation, but in the provision they even take precedence over the heirs (Article 150: '... shall belong to the author and, after his death, *and in the absence of testamentary provisions*, to his spouse and legitimate heirs to the third degree, according to the rules of the Civil Code').

In countries which do not accept transmission by succession *mortis causa* of the right of participation, this expires with the death of the author. In those which do accept it, the same duration as that applicable to the author's economic rights is adopted.

B. OPERATIONS TO WHICH THE PROVISION APPLIES

Systems vary:
- in general they apply to successive sales by public auction and to those effected through a dealer or commercial agent (e.g. Bolivia, Art. 50; France, Art. L. 122-8, previously Art. 42; Germany, Art. 26; Spain, Art. 24);
- in some countries, the provision applies to all types of sale or alienation (for example, Algeria, Article 69; Brazil, Article 39; Uruguay, Article 9).

---

79. See Claude Colombet, *Major Principles of Copyright and Neighbouring Rights in the World*, op. cit., p. 60.

C. Basis of application and amount

The amount is a percentage deducted from the sale price. It is laid down by law. As regards the basis of calculation, several systems exist:
- *a percentage of the price obtained on each new sale, without any deduction.* In Algeria, Bolivia, Costa Rica, Ecuador, Hungary, Morocco, Philippines, Senegal and Tunisia the percentage is 5 per cent of the total value of each new sale; in Portugal it is 6 per cent of the price of each transaction (provision is made for a deduction in respect of expenditure on advertising, hospitality and other similar items for the promotion and sale of the work and in respect of inflation rates). In Belgium the percentage follows a sliding scale (from 2 to 6 per cent) and depends on the price of the work (from 50,000 Belgian francs upwards it is 4 per cent);
- *a percentage of the price only if it exceeds a certain amount* (the fixing of an amount below which the right of participation does not apply constitutes a limitation based on the maxim of *de minimis lex non regit*. In France, the rate is 3 per cent of the resale price applicable only on the basis of a sale price fixed by regulations; in Germany it is 5 per cent of the sale price when it exceeds 100 German marks; in Spain it is 3 per cent of the price of alienation if this price exceeds 300,000 pesetas for the work sold);
- *a percentage of the value added,* i.e. the increase in the value of the work since its last sale. In Chile this is 5 per cent; in Italy (and the Holy See) the rate ranges from 2 to 10 per cent of the increase in value only if this increase exceeds a certain amount, which differs in the case of drawings, prints or engravings, pictorial works or sculptures. It also applies to sales which are not regarded as public, 10 per cent of the highest price of the work belonging to the author when the price reaches a certain minimum and exceeds the price of the first sale fivefold); in Turkey the percentage must not exceed 10 per cent of the increase in value over and above a minimum stipulated by decree; in Brazil it is 20 per cent of the increase in value; in Uruguay, 25 per cent.

In most countries, the *droit de suite* is borne by the vendor[80] and the percentage is deducted from the price obtained by him. This results in a reduction in the earnings of the auctioneer or intermediary since their remuneration habitually consists of a percentage of the net sale price. These circumstances (to a greater extent than the practical problems experienced in the exercise and application of the provision) must explain the lack of enforcement of the right of participation in general.

The procedure of applying the percentage to the value added might appear more equitable, but the difficulties which it presents are so great as to render it impracticable. It implies that the beneficiaries must know and *prove* the price of the first sale and subsequent sales and determine the difference *in constant value terms*. This in turn means that first the author and then his heirs must obtain and keep documentary evidence of the price obtained for each sale of each work and that, in addition to this documentation, they have the necessary expertise in calculating added value. The lack of feasibility of applying this system is apparent in the fact that it has never been successfully implemented in the countries which have adopted it (Brazil, Chile, former Czechoslovakia, Italy, Portugal, Uruguay). Hence, the procedure which appears to be the most equitable in fact becomes the most unjust. Only in the countries which accept the direct application of the percentage to the resale price and where this is administered by a collective administration body (see further below, Chapter 8, Section 8.2.3) (France, Germany, Hungary, Spain), has the right of participation been anything other than a dead letter.

In the WIPO *Draft Model Provisions* (document CE/MPC/1/2-II of 20 October 1988, the right of participation is covered in the following terms:

Section 9. Droit de Suite (1) In the case of the resale of original copies of a work of fine art at a public auction or through a professional art dealer, the author shall have the right to a share of [...] per cent of the resale price [where this price is higher than the amount that shall have been set by regulations mentioned in

---

80. Hungary is an exception: the right of participation is the responsibility of the purchaser.

Section 57] (hereinafter referred to as 'the *droit de suite*'). (2) The share mentioned in paragraph (1) shall be collected and distributed by a collective administration organization (see Section 51).

4.4. Limitations on copyright

The limitations—or exceptions—to protection of the author's right restrict the absolute right of the owner to the economic utilization of the work. Some have been motivated by reasons of social policy (the needs of society in the area of knowledge and information), others by the need to ensure access to works and their dissemination in order to satisfy the general public interest.

As Delgado Porras points out, the justification resides in most cases in an equitable, if not legitimate, reconciliation of the three different concurrent interests in intellectual productions, namely, the interests of the author, those of the undertakings which exploit the works and those of the public in general.[81]

The limitations are subject to *numerus clausus*. They do not affect the moral right of the author (they restrict his economic rights alone—his exclusive prerogatives to exploit the work—), and for this reason can be applied only *after the work has been published for the first time with the authorization of the author* (that is to say, after he has exercised his moral right of disclosure); *the name of the author and the source must be cited and no modifications are permissible.*[82]

Since the *generic nature* of the author's right is recognized, the limitations *must be interpreted and applied in a restrictive way.*

Limitations are basically of two types: those authorizing *free use without payment* and those subject to remuneration; the latter constitute *non-voluntary licences* (statutory licences and compulsory licences).

---

81. See Antonio Delgado Porras, *Panorámica de la protección civil y penal en materia de propiedad intelectual,* op. cit., pp. 39–40.
82. Germany (Article 62) permits modifications required by the ultimate use such as translations or alterations if they are limited to extracts or transpositions into another key or pitch (para. 2) and, in the case of artistic works and photographs, transpositions into a different scale and other modifications to the extent required by the method of reproduction (para. 3).

Limitations differ in regard to their scope, the reasons underlying them and the sphere of application in which the use authorized in the exception may take place.

A. THEIR SCOPE

The most broadly based are those which establish instances of free use without payment, since use of the work is not subject to the author's authorization and is free. On the other hand, non-voluntary licences are subject to payment: the author's exclusive right is limited to a right to remuneration.

Among non-voluntary licences, statutory licences are limitations with a broader basis than compulsory licences. In the case of statutory licences use is free and the remuneration due to the author for such use is stipulated in the legal provision or by the competent authority; as regards compulsory licences use is also free but the author retains the right to negotiate the economic conditions governing such use, generally through the collective administration body for the category of rights in question. Should the parties fail to reach agreement the amount of the remuneration is fixed by the competent authority (judicial or administrative).

B. MOTIVES

In regard to the underlying reasons: these may involve an *educational, cultural or informational interest*—as in the case of private copies, quotations and illustrations, retransmission of news, use for legal proceedings, etc.—or else the need to *satisfy the general public interest in the promotion of culture*, facilitating the activities of certain users in order to maintain the dissemination of works, as in instances where non-voluntary licences are established.[83]

Some laws also place limitations on the author's rights for humanitarian reasons—such as transcription into the Braille system for blind persons when this is done on a non-profit-making

---

83. Villalba points out that instances of general interest in support of which laws have established limitations on authors' rights have been: (a) of an educational kind with a view to promoting a literate community with a cultural level which will make it a suitable market for the consumption of cultural products;

basis—or else to preserve freedom of expression by allowing the rights of paraphrase and parody, and

C. SPHERE OF APPLICATION IN WHICH THE USE AUTHORIZED IN THE LIMITATION MAY TAKE PLACE

The works may be intended only for *private use* (private copy for personal use, for example) or for *public use* (use for information, quotations, non-voluntary licences for the recording of musical works, for broadcasting, etc.).

Although to a greater or lesser degree, limitations on the rights of the author are encountered in all domestic laws, generally grouped in special chapters (as in Brazil, 'Limitations on and exceptions to copyright', Articles 49 to 51 Costa Rica, 'Exceptions to protection', Articles 67 to 76; Peru, 'Limitations of copyright', Articles 62 to 77; Portugal, 'Unrestricted use', Art. 75 to 82; Spain, 'Limitations', Art. 31 to 40; Venezuela, 'Limitations of the rights of exploitation', Articles 43 to 49, etc.) although sometimes they are not listed in a systematic form (as in the case of Argentina). They are also accepted in international conventions.

There exists a relationship between the extent of the exception and the reasons underlying it. Free use without payment is permitted when it is justified by reasons of social policy linked with educational, cultural and information needs; statutory licences and compulsory licences are established in order to facilitate adequate access to the works.

Further below we shall refer to the different limitations which may be found in domestic laws, although each law embodies only certain of them: those which are either traditional (quotations, for example) or are regarded as absolutely essential in satisfying the public interest in the areas of education, information and culture.

(b) of a cultural kind, since it was necessary for the creators themselves to have access to that cultural background to which they belonged; (c) of an informational kind, in order to ensure that the communication needs of society are met (*Duración de la protección y excepciones*, study presented at the Regional Seminar on Copyright and Neighbouring Rights for Judges in Central America and Panama, held in Costa Rica, October 1992, pp. 7–8, document).

4.4.1. Free use without payment

The laws on copyright provide for the possibility that protected works may in some cases be used *freely and without payment* (with no special authorization and without paying fees to the owner of the rights). This is often referred to as the *free use of protected works*.

Free use without payment is always subject to compliance with certain conditions laid down in the law, especially in regard to the procedures for, and the extent of, the use and protection of the author's moral right. Consequently, use may be made only within the strict limits of the exception and the user must cite the name of the author, the title of the work and the source of publication, and must refrain from making changes to the work.

A. PRIVATE COPIES. PERSONAL USE

A *private copy* is a reproduction, *in a single copy*, of short excerpts or of specific single works protected by copyright included in a volume (magazines, newspapers, etc.) for the *personal use* of the person making the copy (e.g. for study purposes, teaching or amusement).

Personal use which, in addition to the making of a reproduction, may cover a transformation (translation, adaptation, arrangement, etc.)[84] of a protected work, implies that the copy produced is for the exclusive use of the copyist, that the latter is a *natural person*, and the copy will not leave his own personal sphere, that is to say, it will not be used in collective form or circulated, whether for profit-making purposes or not.

Despite the fact that the exclusive right of the author includes all forms of reproduction, including hard-copying[85] (any use of a

---

84. See *WIPO Glossary of Terms of the Law of Copyright and Neighbouring Rights*, p. 185, entry 181.
85. For example, Italy, Article 13: 'The exclusive right of reproduction has for its object the multiplication of copies of the work by any means, such as hand-copying, printing, lithography, engraving, photography, phonography, cinematography, and any other process of reproduction.'

work must, therefore, receive the author's prior authorization and be remunerated) it was traditionally accepted, as a limitation on copyright, that single works or portions of them might be copied for the exclusive use of the copyist, notwithstanding the fact that it manifestly constituted a loss for the owners of rights in the work.

The possibility of making copies was naturally restricted by the reproduction methods available; it was done in manuscript or in typewritten form, and required considerable time and effort. The loss to the author was therefore small; the principle that the law does not deal with minor matters, summarized in the maxim *de minimis lex non regit*, could therefore be applied here. Moreover, it was impossible to verify the manuscript copy of a work for the personal use of the person who made it, and a rigid prohibition strictly to safeguard the author's right of reproduction would inevitably have been infringed. Some laws, however, did not lay down any exception to the right of reproduction (e.g. the previous Spanish law, and those of Argentina, Bolivia, Chile, Guatemala, Haiti, Nicaragua and Uruguay. Other laws have admitted limitations, by fixing the procedures for private copying. The laws of Austria (1936) and Italy (1941) are very eloquent on this point, particularly the latter.[86]

Photography, as a means of copying, already existed but only wet processes were applied which were expensive, slow and far from being perfect. According to the account given in document UNESCO/WIPO/CGE/PW/3-I (1987), photocopying as practised today is a technique invented by an expert in intellectual property, the physicist Chester Carlson (1906–1968), a United States patent attorney who tried to get rid of the burden of

---

86. Italy, Article 68: 'The reproduction of single works or of portions of works for the personal use of readers, when *made by hand* or by a means of reproduction unsuitable for circulating or diffusing the work in public, shall be free. The *photo-copying* of works existing in libraries, when made for personal use or for the services of the library, shall be free. The circulating of such copies in public and, in general, any use thereof in competition with the rights of economic utilization belonging to the author shall be forbidden' (our italics).

retyping voluminous patent specifications and successfully devised a new process—which later became known as 'xerography'—and obtained a patent for it in 1940. 'The technical application of the invention was, however, delayed and it was only seven years later, after having signed a contract with Haloid Corporation (which later became Xerox Corporation) that a commercial machine was developed. The first Xerox machines were marketed at the beginning of the 1950s. From there, the success story of reprography is known to everybody.[87]

The rapid introduction of new means of 'private reproduction' (photocopiers, sound and video recorders, etc.), necessitated a review of the scope of the limitation of the right of reproduction in regard to private copies. The many new forms of use and reproduction of works brought about by technological development led to a more precise definition of the concept of *'personal use'* when it came to be recognized that this was not exactly the same as *'private use'*. Private use has a wider interpretation than personal use for the copies produced are not *exclusively for the individual use of one person*, but can also be made for shared use by a particular group of persons, as in the case of members of the family and close friends.

A further distinction is *internal use*, i.e. that made by organizations, institutions and industrial and commercial companies for their own professional need to distribute copies to employees, of firms, public bodies and educational establishments (a school or university). Internal use is considered to lie on the borderline between public and private use, so that the expressions *semi-public or semi-private use* are sometimes employed.

Most laws permit the making of a copy for personal use, although provisions vary. A distinction may be drawn between:
- laws which contain provisions expressly authorizing—under certain conditions—the free reproduction without charge of protected works for personal use in one single copy and with no profit-making aim (for example Brazil, Article 49, II; Colombia, Article 37; Peru, Article 70; Spain, Article 31(2); Vene-

---

87. UNESCO/WIPO/CGE/PW 3-I (1987), para 42, p. 13.

zuela, Article 44(1), etc.); while some laws permit only copies made manually—handwritten or typed (Costa Rica, Art. 74; Paraguay, Civil code (1985), Art. 2180); and
- those which follow the Anglo-American legal tradition and regulate the reproduction for private purposes by the limitations relating to *fair use* (or *equitable use*).

Fair use has developed as a legal doctrine and has been given statutory recognition in the United States (Section 107 of the Law of 1976). It constitutes an important general limitation of the exclusive right of the owner of copyright by authorizing the free and gratuitous use of a protected work for the purpose of criticism, comment, news reporting, teaching (including multiple copies intended for classroom use), scholarship or research. With a view to determining whether, in any given instance, fair use is being made of a work, certain circumstances will have to be taken into consideration, such as: whether or not it has a commercial nature or is for non-profit-making educational purposes, the nature of the copyrighted work, the size and importance of the portion used in relation to the copyrighted work as a whole and the effect of this use on the potential market for or value of the copyrighted work.

The degree of sophistication rapidly attained by the reproduction techniques and their utilization made it impossible for activities of reproduction for personal or private use by means of *reprographic reproduction* of printed works (or facsimile reproduction by photocopying books, reviews, etc.) and the domestic reproduction of recordings (sound and audiovisual) of published or broadcast works (specifically, *home taping*, which in some countries is referred to in general terms as *private copying*[88]) to continue to be considered as irrelevant from the standpoint of the interests of the authors, as was the case when only traditional personal copies existed (in handwritten and typewritten form). In those days, a *jus usus innocui* could still be invoked to include such

---

88. Use of the term 'private copy' has become general in some countries to designate home reproduction in a single copy of a sound or audiovisual recording of a copyrighted work which is made only to be heard or seen and not to be reproduced.

copies among the limitations on the right of reproduction vested in the author which result in use without charge.

The cumulative effect of all these individual copying activities was growing to such an extent that they were becoming a normal manner of exploiting works.[89] The need was thus felt for suitable means to remedy the adverse consequences of the impact of technological development on copyright.

Article 9(2) of the Stockholm Act, confirmed in the Paris Act, 1971, of the Berne Convention accepts the possibility of establishing limitations to the right of reproduction in the following terms:

It shall be a matter for legislation in the countries of the Union to permit the reproduction of such works in certain special cases, provided that such reproduction does not conflict with a normal exploitation of the work and does not unreasonably prejudice the legitimate interests of the author.

That provision reflects the level of development of technology in the second half of the 1960s when photocopying was the principal means of reproducing printed works for personal use and this process and home copying for the same purpose of sound and audiovisual recordings had not yet become, as was to happen later, a habitual form of exploitation of protected works which could be recognized as a limitation of the author's right.

But with the subsequent development of reproduction for private use by photocopying (or a similar technique) and the home copying of sound recording and audiovisual works, it became hard to admit that such reproduction could be regarded as being included in the category mentioned in Article 9(2) of the Berne Convention which does not conflict with a normal exploitation of the work and 'does not unreasonably prejudice the legitimate interests of the author'.

---

89. In 1993, experts estimated at more than 300,000 million the annual number of photocopies of pages of copyrighted works made throughout the world—or simply to give an idea of the significance of this figure, the equivalent of 1.5 thousand million 200-page books—while for each record or cassette acquired commercially, at least three home copies are made.

It was considered that when technical equipment of a non-typographical kind was used for reproduction—graphic, sound or audio-visual—exclusively intended for the personal use of the copyist, there should be remuneration for these activities in order to offset the huge losses suffered by authors, performers, publishers and producers in respect of the parallel exploitation by the public of works, performances and cultural products, and that the collection and distribution of this financial compensation for private copies for personal use could only be carried out by collective administration organizations.

Free reproduction for the personal use of the copyist, therefore, was maintained as a limitation of copyright giving rise to free use without charge. But provisions were introduced, varying according to the country in question (see below, Chapter 8, Sections 8.2.1 and 8.2.2), establishing an obligation to make fair payment for private copies made by reprographic reproduction of printed works and by recording in the home for personal use of musical and audiovisual works. 'Remuneration for private copying' is an institution designed to ensure that the third parties involved (who are not the members of the public for whom the personal copies are intended) contribute to the remuneration of those whose interests are prejudiced by reproduction (authors, performers, publishers, producers).

Private copies can be made provided that the works involved are those already published with the author's authorization. When the private copy concerns sound recordings and audiovisual works, it must be made by the user's own means—and not made to order, even if only on an 'individual' basis and the user provides the copy to be reproduced.

Private copies can only be made, it is generally considered, in respect of portions of works, excluding complete periodical publications, newspapers and whole books and also certain specific types of works because this impairs their 'normal exploitation' as occurs, for example, in the case of computer programs, databases scores (orchestrations, vocal works, etc.) and architectural plans.[90]

---

90. Concerning remuneration for private copies, see Section 4.3.2, A.

B. USE FOR EDUCATIONAL PURPOSES

A number of laws impose varying degrees of limitation on the author's right in relation to specific uses of works for educational purposes.

a. Illustrations

In the context of the limitations on copyright, an illustration for educational purposes is deemed to mean the use of works to a greater extent than quotations from them or in their entirety in the case of particularly short works, by way of illustration for teaching purposes in publications, broadcasts or sound or visual recordings, provided that the aim of this communication is educational. Illustrations are subject to the same conditions as quotations: the source and name of the author must be cited and their use must be compatible with 'fair practice' (i.e. the reproduction for the purpose of illustration must not enter into conflict with the normal exploitation of the work which is used and must not cause any unreasonable prejudice to the legitimate interests of the author) and there must be justification for the educational aim pursued.

The Berne Convention refers to the use of pre-existing works by way of illustration for teaching purposes in the following terms—Paris Act, 1971, Article 10(2):

> It shall be a matter for legislation in the countries of the Union, and for special agreements existing or to be concluded between them, to permit the utilization, to the extent justified by the purpose, of literary or artistic works by way of illustration in publications, broadcast or sound or visual recordings for teaching, provided such utilization is compatible with fair practice.

Similarly, the Convention states (Article 10(3)) that the source and the name of the author, if it appears in the source, must be mentioned.

b. Educational establishments

To enable these establishments to reproduce works, under certain conditions, in order to satisfy the needs of their students, some laws authorize the inclusion of extracts or short parts of works in anthologies, compilations or compendia intended exclusively for use in schools or for instructional purposes provided that mention is made of the title of the work, the name of the author and, in the case of translations, the name of the translator and that of the publisher if they appear on the reproduced work (for example, Italy, Article 70, third paragraph; Ireland, Article 12, paragraph (5)). These laws stipulate that the exception is applicable only to brief passages from literary and dramatic works which have not already been published for use in schools; the compilation must consist essentially of elements which are not protected by copyright and must not contain several extracts from works by the same author. In some countries, such as Germany, schools, teacher training institutions and other establishments mentioned in the provision are also allowed to make visual or sound recordings of individual works included in school broadcasts; such recordings may be used only for instructional purposes and must be destroyed not later than the end of the school year, unless an equitable remuneration has been paid to the author (Article 47).

Through a number of different formulations, the relevant laws draw attention to the fact that the reproduction effected by virtue of this exception must be compatible with fair practice, that is to say it must not come into conflict with the normal exploitation of the work used and must not unreasonably prejudice the legitimate interests of its author (principle laid down in Article 9(2) of the Berne Convention—Paris Act 1971). To that end, it is stipulated in some laws that the reproduction and the number of copies obtained in this way shall be intended solely for teaching use in the specific educational establishments and that the reproduction must not be made for a profit-making purpose (for example, Portugal, Article 75(e)).

However, the free reproduction of works for instructional purposes, even under the conditions summarized above, is always prejudicial to the interests of authors through the scale *per se* of the use of works in the context of educational establishments; accordingly, this limitation is not permitted under all laws, unlike other exceptions (such as quotations).

c. Libraries and archive services

Some laws authorize libraries and archive services to make reproductions, without the authorization of the author, of works included in their collections, for their own use (to preserve and, if necessary (in the event that it is lost, destroyed or rendered unusable), replace such a copy), for the use of other libraries or archive services (to replace, in the permanent collection of another library or archive, a copy which has been lost, destroyed or rendered unusable),[91] and for that of their users, provided that this is done without gainful intent and solely for research purposes.[92]

In addition to the conditions outlined above, Section 108 of the United States Copyright Statute also contains detailed regulations authorizing libraries and archive services to reproduce one single copy or one single phonogram of a published work, provided that they or their staff undertake not to engage in any *systematic* reproduction or distribution. The term systematic does not include agreements between libraries for the exchange of copies, on condition that they do not receive the copies for distribution in quantities which might replace subscriptions or the purchase of works.

d. Certain showings and performances in educational establishments

Another case in which free utilization without charge is permitted is that of certain showings and performances in educational establishments for instructional purposes and in the context of syllabuses and curricula, provided that the presentation or performance is not diffused outside the place where it is given and provided that the performers do not receive remuneration (Argentina, Article 36, second part; also Colombia, Art. 164; non-profit-making purpose: Brazil, Art. 49(vi); Costa Rica, Article 73; Chile, Article 47; Ecuador Art. 92(b), Peru, Article 77; etc.)

C. THE RIGHT OF QUOTATION

This is one of the traditional limitations of the author's right and is universally accepted.

---

91. See *Draft Model Provisions for Legislation in the Field of Copyright*, op. cit., Section 13.
92. Spain (Article 37) mentions museums, libraries, record libraries, film libraries and newspaper libraries, together with publicly owned archives or archives forming part of cultural or scientific institutions.

The term 'quotation' means the mention of a relatively short fragment of another written, sound or audiovisual work and of isolated artistic works, in order to support or render more intelligible the opinions of the writer or to make susbstantiated reference to the opinions of the other author.

Quotations may only be made from works which have already been disclosed with the authorization of their author. They must be correct and preserved as a quotation or for analysis, comment or critical judgement and may only be made for teaching or research purposes to the extent justified by the reason for their inclusion.

The source of the quotation and the author of the quoted work must be indicated in all cases so as to respect the moral right of the author and ensure that the opinion of the person who makes the quotation is not confused with that of the author quoted.

As regards the length of the quotation which is permitted if it is still to fall within the limits of the exception, there is a consensus that the quoted fragments must be short, but there is no consistency in the manner of defining that requirement.

Most laws merely stipulate either that the quotations must be short (for example, France, Article L. 122-5.3(a) previously Art. 41(3); Guatemala, Art. 17; Mexico, Art. 18(d)) or that they should be excerpts (for example, Chile, Art. 38; Colombia, Art. 31; Costa Rica, Art. 70; Dominican Republic, Art. 30; Spain, Art. 32), but this has the drawback of imprecision. Sometimes other conditions are added, for example that the quotation must consist of isolated passages and be used to the extent necessitated by its purpose (Germany, Article 51), that it must be made in accordance with the normal usage and custom and justified by the intended purpose (Denmark, Article 14) or cause no unfair competition to the author in regard to pecuniary benefits derived from the work (Peru, Article 69).

Some laws lay down precise figures for the permitted length (Argentina and Paraguay, Article 10 in the two laws: 'not more than one thousand words from literary or scientific works, or not more than eight bars from musical works' with the additional provision that 'in any case only such parts of the text as are indispensable for the aforesaid purpose' while the final paragraph of the Argentina law adds 'when inclusions from works of another person constitute the main part of a new work, the courts may, in a summary proceeding, equitably fix the proportionate amount to which the holders of copyright in the works included are entitled'. In former Yugoslavia, Article 49(b) of the law provides that 'the sum of the quotations should not exceed one quarter of the work from which the quotation is made'.

The Berne Convention makes provision for the right of quotation as a limitation *jure conventionis* in the following terms (Article 10(1) of the Paris Act, 1971):

It shall be permissible to make quotations from a work which has already been lawfully made available to the public, provided that their making is compatible with fair practice, and their extent does not exceed that justified by the purpose, including quotations from newspaper articles and periodicals in the form of press summaries.

D. Use for information purposes

Exceptions relating to use for information purposes are also traditional and are generally permitted by domestic legislation:

a. Press reports

Copyright is restricted in respect of articles published on topical economic, political or religious themes and circulated by the press, broadcasting or cable transmission; their reproduction, distribution and public communication are permitted provided that mention is made of the source and of the author's name—if the work appears under his signature—and that use of the article is not the subject of any special reservation made at the outset (for example, Colombia, Art. 33; Costa Rica, Art. 68; Ecuador, Art. 92.C; El Salvador, Art. 47(a); France, Art. L. 122-5.3(b), previously Art. 4.1.3; Guatemala, Art. 46; Peru, Art. 66, Venezuela, Art. 47.2).

b. Speeches

The reproduction by the press, with a view to providing information on current events, of speeches, lectures or addresses given in public is authorized. In some countries, this exception is confined to certain types of public speeches, i.e. those made in political, administrative, judicial or academic assemblies, public political meetings and official ceremonies (for example, France, Article L. 122-5.3, C, previously Art. 41(3); Venezuela, Article 47(1)). However, the publication of a *series* of speeches by a particular author must *always* have his authorization (for example, Argentina, Article 27; Brazil, Article 49(1)(c); Colombia, Article 35; Costa Rica, Article 69; Peru, Article 67; Uruguay, Article 45(2) and Venezuela, Article 47(1)).

c. Works involved in public events

The concept of free use extends to the communication to the public of a work which was not initially foreseen but became inevitable in the course of the reporting of public events in which the work was incidentally or accessorily involved (Berne Convention, Paris Act, 1971, Article 10*bis*(2)). Examples are the use of a musical work during a procession or sporting event, or, during the ceremony to unveil the bust of a famous composer, the performance of some well-known passages from his works. This type of utilization of a work on the occasion of the reporting of current events by broadcasting constitutes, by its very nature, free utilization with the additional feature that the name of the author of the work does not have to be indicated. On the other hand, if a particular piece of music is post-synchronized with a news film, the use of this music cannot be deemed to constitute an integral part of the report.[93]

The Berne Convention permits limitations concerning use for information: Article 10*bis* of the Paris Act, 1971, refers to the reproduction by the press, the broadcasting or the transmission by wire of certain articles and broadcast works (para. 1) and, in the course of reporting current events, works seen or heard during such events (para. 2):

---

93. See *Guide to the Berne Convention*, Geneva, WIPO, 1978, p. 59. The *Guide* was written by Dr Claude Masouyé.

1) It shall be a matter for legislation in the countries of the Union to permit the reproduction by the press, the broadcasting or the communication to the public by wire of articles published in newspapers or periodicals on current economic, political or religious topics, and of broadcast works of the same character, in cases in which the reproduction, broadcasting or such communication thereof is not expressly reserved. Nevertheless, the source must always be clearly indicated; the legal consequences of a breach of this obligation shall be determined by the legislation of the country where protection is claimed.
2) It shall also be a matter for legislation in the countries of the Union to determine the conditions under which, for the purpose of reporting current events by means of photography, cinematography, broadcasting or communication to the public by wire, literary or artistic work seen or heard in the course of the event may, to the extent justified by the informatory purpose, be reproduced and made available to the public.

d. Portraits

The free circulation of portraits is authorized when it is effected for scientific and educational purposes or related to facts or events of public interest which took place in public (for example, Argentina, Article 31; Colombia, Article 36; Costa Rica, Art. 76; Italy, Art. 97; Paraguay, Art. 29(3); Uruguay, Art. 21, last paragraph. However, care must be taken to ensure that use does not infringe the rights of the personality of the person photographed.

e. Official texts and news of the day

See Chapter 2, Section 2.2.1.1—non-protected works. However, some laws include among limitations of the author's right the free use of official texts (for example, El Salvador, Art. 39; Honduras, Art. 53; Mexico, Art. 21(1); Uruguay, Art. 45(5)) and news of the day (for example, Argentina, Article 28(2); Brazil, Art. 49.I(b); Colombia, Art. 34; Dominican Republic, Art. 33; Honduras, Art. 45(a); Paraguay, Art. 12(1); Uruguay, Art. 45(3); Venezuela, Art. 48). On the other hand, other laws indicate the non-protected nature of official texts (for example, Peru, Art. 64; Venezuela, Art. 4) and of news of the day (e.g. Costa Rica, Art. 67; Guatemala, Art. 16, *in fine*; Peru, Art. 65).

E. USE FOR LEGAL PROCEEDINGS

Some laws also classify the reproduction of works as a consequence of judicial and administrative proceedings or as a means of proof as free and gratuitous use, provided that mention is made of the source and name of the author (for example, Italy, Article 67; Peru, Article 71; Spain, Article 31(i)).

F. OTHER CASES OF FREE AND GRATUITOUS USE

Some laws also permit free and gratuitous use in other cases.

a. Ephemeral fixations

These are the fixations of literary, dramatic and musical works made by broadcasting organizations for the sole purpose of facilitating the programming of their broadcasts. They are permissible only for the purpose of broadcasts by the broadcasting organization concerned; they must be made by the latter with its own resources without calling upon the services of another undertaking and may be used only during the broadcasts authorized by the author. Given their ephemeral nature, they must be destroyed (erased) after the broadcast (for example, the law in Germany, Article 55(1) stipulates that this must be done within a period of one month after the first broadcast of the work).

The possibility of preserving the fixations is, however, envisaged when they have an exceptional documentary value, provided that they are transferred to an official archive for conservation, and notification is given without delay to the author of the fact that the recordings have been deposited in those archives (Germany, Article 55(2)).

Ephemeral fixations do raise the possibility of extremely awkward consequences from the standpoint of the author's interests, both through the potential risk implied and through their economic impact. The right of public communication is distinct and independent from the right of reproduction, so that each must be the subject of a special authorization and will give rise to different remuneration. Although it is clear that these fixations serve the sole purpose of broadcasting, they do in fact involve a form of utilization of the work (reproduction) which is different from that authorized by the author (public communication) for which reason, if they are permitted under domestic legislation, they must be subject to extremely vigilant control.

The Berne Convention provides for the possibility that national laws may lay down rules for the making of ephemeral recordings by broadcasting organizations. Article 11*bis*, paragraph (3), of the Paris Act, 1971, establishes that:

> In the absence of any contrary stipulation, permission granted in accordance with paragraph (1) of this Article[94] shall not imply permission to record, by means of instruments recording sounds or images, the work broadcast. It shall, however, be a matter for legislation in the countries of the Union to determine the regulations for ephemeral recordings made by a broadcasting organization by means of its own facilities and used for its own broadcasts. The preservation of these recordings in official archives may, on the grounds of their exceptional documentary character, be authorized by such legislation.

b. Reasons of a humanitarian nature

Reproduction by the Braille system, or by any other method intended for blind persons, provided that the works concerned have already been published with the authorization of their author and that the reproduction is made with no gainful intent (for example, Portugal, Art. 80; Spain, Art. 31(3).

c. Works of art situated in public places

The reproduction of works of art which belong to the public authorities and are on permanent display in public places—parks, streets, squares and public thoroughfares is free and gratuitous (for example, Brazil, Article 49(i)(e); Colombia, Article 39; Costa Rica, Article 71; Chile, Article 44; Spain, Article 35).

d. Performance of recorded music and reception of broadcast transmissions in specialized shops for demonstration purposes

The same applies to the performance of phonograms and reception of broadcast transmissions for demonstration purposes in the establishments which sell the corresponding sound and visual re-

---

94. Permission to broadcast and transmit by cable (broadcasting right).

production appliances for family use (for example, Brazil, Article 49(v); Costa Rica, Article 72; Peru, Article 75).

e. *Pastiche and parody*[95]

Some laws include under the heading of free utilization pastiches and parodies of other works (but not when these involve the personality of their author), provided that the result is not a real reproduction of the original work, permits no confusion with it and does not discredit it (Brazil, Article 50; France, Art. L. 122-5.4, previously Art. 41.4; Spain, Article 39—parodies). Under other laws, however, a parody must be authorized by the author of the parodied work, as long as it is in the private domain (for example, Argentina, Article 25).

f. *Illustrated catalogues*

Some legislations make express provision to the effect that photographs of artistic works which are exhibited to the public may be reproduced in the corresponding exhibition or sale catalogues published by the organizer with a view to the holding of the event (for example, Germany, Article 58; Switzerland, Art. 26).

g. *Private and gratuitous performances*

Some laws make express reference to the right of the public to hold private showings or performances without charge exclusively within the strict family circle (for example Brazil, Article 49(vi); Chile, Art. 47; Costa Rica, Art. 73; France, Article L. 122-5.1, previously Art. 41(1)).

h. *Performances by certain State agencies*

Some laws recognize the free use of the performance of musical works at concerts and public events by orchestras, bands, brass bands, choirs and other musical bodies belonging to the State, provided that the public is allowed to attend free of charge (Argentina, Article 36, last paragraph; Italy, Article 71; Spain, Art. 38; Uruguay, Art. 45(11)).

---

95. See above, Chapter 2, Section 2.2.2.7.

4.4.2. Uses subject to remuneration: non-voluntary licences (compulsory licences and statutory licences)

The so-called system of *non-voluntary licences* is exceptional. It constitutes a compromise solution which is accepted only when it is essential to preserve access to works and their appropriate dissemination. It is only permitted when the initial dissemination of the work has already been made with the authorization of the author and solely in respect of certain specific uses such as the *mechanical reproduction* of non-dramatic musical works and of the accompanying lyrics, *broadcasting* and *distribution by cable networks* in simultaneous and unaltered form of broadcast programmes and also in cases of *massive and uncontrollable use* (private copying).

Consequently, the difference between the cases of the free use of works which we have already analysed and the instances of non-voluntary—compulsory or statutory—licences to which we shall now be turning our attention, resides in the fact that, while the former are exempt from the requirement of any type of authorization and payment of remuneration, in the case of the latter the use of the work is also free (even though certain formalities are sometimes stipulated), *but is subject to remuneration.*

In these instances, it has been considered necessary in the legislations establishing them to facilitate the activities of users, without depriving authors—or the owners of rights—of the benefits accruing from such use.

The use of non-voluntary licences has been seen as a prelude to a substantial change in the traditional manner of using works and in the relationship between the author and the user, characterized by a decline in the exclusive rights of the creator (to control the diffusion of the work and ensure the respect due to his moral and economic rights), for under this system, once the author has exercised the moral right of disclosure, his control over the work disappears and instead he now only has the right to receive remuneration.

It is for this reason that the collective administration of copyright is considered the most appropriate alternative to avoid non-voluntary licences and when these are inevitable, the collective administration organizations may—and in many cases do—play an important role (even if it is not the collective administration organization which grants the licences, it may negotiate fees and, in general, it collects and when appropriate, distributes such fees).[96]

In actual fact, the use of musical works is based on contracts which the producers of sound recordings conclude with the collective copyright administration bodies, so that there is no need for recourse to non-voluntary licences, even in cases where legal provision for them exists.

Mention should be made in this connection, of the exclusion in the United Kingdom Act of 1988 of the statutory licence established in Section 8 of the 1956 Act to record musical works on phonograms, when these works had already been included in a phonogram produced with the authorization of the authors or of the owners of the rights in the works.

In the WIPO Memorandum (document BCP/CE/1/3 of 18 October 1991 published in *Copyright*, WIPO, March 1992) which was considered during the second session of the Committee of Experts to prepare a possible Protocol to the Berne Convention, the possible exclusion or restriction of the application of non-voluntary broadcasting licences was envisaged (see paras. 144 to 151) and it was proposed that the possible Protocol should stipulate that countries which did not provide for these should continue not to do so and that those which did provide for them should eliminate them within a certain period, e.g. five years (para. 148).

Statutory or legal licences are licences granted by the law for the use of a work protected by copyright in a specific manner and under certain conditions *in return for payment* to the owner of copyright. The remuneration is fixed by the legal norm, by the authority responsible for implementing the law or by the judicial authority, as the case may be.

Compulsory licences are those which the competent authority or society responsible for the management of authors' rights—

---

96. M. Ficsor, *Collective Administration of Copyright and Neighboring Rights*, Geneva, WIPO, 1990, p. 7.

depending on which body is entrusted with this matter—is obliged to grant, without prejudice to the obligation incumbent upon the user to pay the current charges (agreed between this management society and the chambers of users or, in the absence thereof, fixed by the competent authority).

These licences are granted in response to a formal application or are subject at least to previous notification of the owner of the copyright[97] or the collective management society which represents him.

A. REQUIREMENTS GOVERNING NON-VOLUNTARY LICENCES[98]

- Non-voluntary licences can only confer a non-exclusive right;
- they are non-assignable;
- they must not in any way prejudice the moral right of the author;
- they must safeguard the right of the author to receive an equitable remuneration by fixing payment scales or by establishing a judicial or arbitration body responsible for determining payments if the parties are unable to arrive at an amicable agreement.
- their effects are confined to the country which has established them.[99]

---

97. See WIPO *Glossary on Terms of the Law of Copyright and Neighbouring Rights*, p. 51, entry 50.
98. See Berne Convention, Articles 11*bis*(2) and 13(1).
99. It is important to note that this limitation prevents, for example, the transfrontier circulation of products carrying works protected by copyright and produced in a country under a non-voluntary licence to another country whose domestic legislation does not provide for such licences, or else the distribution by satellite of programmes which include works such as those mentioned from a country in which such licences are applicable to another whose national legislation does not provide for this. The same provision applies if in the first country (from which the exportation is made) the duration of copyright has expired, but in the country of importation such copyright has not expired and the work is still in the private domain (see below, Chapter 5, Section 5.1.4 *in fine*)

B. REMUNERATION FOR PRIVATE COPYING

Remuneration for private copying is frequently regarded as the result of a non-voluntary licence (more specifically, as an *indirect statutory licence*); this is how it is presented in the WIPO Draft Model Provisions (Section 22). It is not the copyists, i.e. the persons making a private copy for their personal use, who are obliged to make this payment; use of copies by them is not subject to such remuneration, but is the responsibility of the third parties involved: Those designated by the law as the manufacturers and importers of equipment and materials for reproduction purposes.

Many domestic laws have already established this remuneration. The first to do so was the former Federal Republic of Germany. On 29 May 1954, the Federal German Court of Justice handed down a ruling confirming the admissibility of an application for remuneration in respect of the private recording of protected works. That decision lay at the origin of Article 53(5) of the Law on Copyright adopted in 1965, which established the right of the author of the work to demand remuneration from the manufacturer of the equipment which enables visual or sound recordings to be made of broadcast transmissions or the transfer from one visual or sound recording to another. This payment, then, is not for the actual use but for the possibility that such equipment offers of making copies.

The other countries which stipulate remuneration for private copying did so at a later date, in particular after 1980.[100]

Even when the procedures for remuneration in respect of private copies differ in the various countries depending on

---

100. By the end of 1988 11 countries had adopted statutory provisions laying down remuneration for private copies: Austria, Congo, Denmark, Finland, France, Hungary, Iceland, Norway, Portugal, Spain and Sweden; since then, norms have been introduced in other countries, such as Belgium, Colombia, Greece, Venezuela. At the same date, societies responsible for collecting *reprographic rights* already existed in 17 countries: Australia, Austria, Canada, Denmark, Finland, France, Germany, Iceland, Japan, Netherlands, Norway, South Africa, Spain, Sweden, Switzerland, United Kingdom and the United States of America; since that time these societies have also been set up in Belgium, Brazil, Ireland, Italy, Kenya, Malta and New Zealand.

whether reprographic reproductions of printed works or home copying of sound and audiovisual recordings are involved, most of the characteristics are common to both:

a. Characteristics

This consists of remuneration[101] granted by way of compensation to the different categories of owners of rights prejudiced by the exploitation of the work by means of private copying through reprographic reproduction of printed works—authors and publishers—and home recording of sound and audiovisual works—authors, performing artists and producers.[102] The participation by industry in this remuneration is justified by the fact that it is not the work in itself but one particular edition, recording or fixation which is reproduced. In the countries which stipulate payment for the utilization of works in the public domain (see below, Chapter 5, Section 5.3.2 *in fine*—free use or otherwise of works which have fallen into the public domain), a proportion must still be made over to the agency which administers the sums collected by virtue of this concept.

b. Criterion for fixing remuneration

The mixed system is generally held to be the most appropriate. This consists of a royalty payment on equipment (photocopiers, recorders, video recorders) and a further charge—where appropriate—on the materials used for reproduction (audio- and videotapes suitable for making copies, etc.). If the royalty is applied only to the reproduction appliances, it can be seen that once a maximum quantity of equipment has been sold, the market for photocopiers and recorders will be saturated and sales will fall; the revenue from the royalty will then no longer reflect the constant increase in reprography and the home taping of sound recordings and audiovisual works.

---

101. This is often termed *equitable remuneration*.
102. This is not a tax, since it is not the state or the public at large, but authors, publishers, performers and producers that are being deprived of remuneration which is theirs by right.

c. Those required to pay

These are the persons designated in the legal provisions, such as the manufacturers and importers of the equipment and materials used in reproduction (e.g. Germany, Article 54(1); Spain, Article 25(2)) and the operators of photocopying equipment (e.g. Germany, Article 54(2)). But, as we have noted, the actual users, the members of the public who obtain copies for their personal use are not those who are required to pay, for collection and control in private homes is unthinkable, and in retail shops and similar outlets it would mean an absurd complication which would certainly be impracticable.

d. Collection and distribution

Each of the persons belonging to the categories concerned is entitled to a share of the funds collected. However, if each beneficiary were allowed to make a separate claim for payment against those who reproduce works for personal use, the system would not be viable. The relevant laws therefore opt for a provision to the effect that the collection and distribution of the remuneration shall be made through collective management bodies.

e. Exemptions

These apply in cases where it is self-evident that the reproduction appliances and recording means will not be used for private copying. This will be the case when:
- equipment is exported since it is not to be used in the territory where the legal regime covering the collection of remuneration applies; this is a counterpart provision to the application of the charge on those that are imported;
- the users are companies which produce phonograms and videograms, commercial copies of phonograms and videograms, and audiovisual communication companies;
- the equipment is intended for persons with impaired vision or hearing in which case the exemption is motivated by humanitarian considerations (e.g. in France, Article L. 311-8.3, previously Art. 37(iii) of the Law of 1985 stipulates that a right to reimbursement shall be granted to *legal persons and bodies*, of

which the list shall be established by the minister responsible for culture, that use recording mediums for the purpose of assisting the visually or aurally handicapped).

C. NON-VOLUNTARY LICENCES FOR MECHANICAL REPRODUCTION

Various domestic laws (for example, India, Ireland, Japan, Romania, Switzerland, United States) lay down systems of non-voluntary licences in favour of the producers of phonograms of non-dramatic musical works with or without lyrics, when they have been fixed on a phonogram with the permission of their authors and copies have been circulated for sale to the public. The compulsory licence for the production of phonograms laid down in Article 61 of the Law of Germany has no practical utility since it is not applicable when the corresponding right of exploitation is exercised by a collective management society, as is generally the case.

In consequence, once the author has concluded a contract for the mechanical reproduction of a non-dramatic musical work *and the recording has been made and circulated to the public*, non-voluntary licences may be used to facilitate access by other producers to the reproduced works.

Compulsory licences for mechanical reproduction are allowed by Article 13(1) of the Berne Convention—Paris Act, 1971—which reads as follows:

Each country of the Union may impose for itself reservations and conditions on the exclusive right granted to the author of a musical work and to the author of any words, the recording of which together with the musical work has already been authorized by the latter, to authorize the sound recording of that musical work, together with such words, if any; but all such reservations and conditions shall apply only in the countries which have imposed them and shall not, in any circumstances, be prejudicial to the rights of these authors to obtain equitable remuneration which, in the absence of agreement, shall be fixed by competent authority.

In consequence, the copies of a phonogram produced in one country under a non-voluntary licence may not be exported or circulated in a country whose domestic legislation does not provide for a similar licence. If the country into which importation is made establishes a similar licence, the producer of the phonogram used within the scope of that licence may not oppose such circulation since non-voluntary licences do not confer exclusive rights.

D. NON-VOLUNTARY LICENCES FOR BROADCASTING AND CABLE DISTRIBUTION OF BROADCAST PROGRAMMES

Some countries establish *non-voluntary licences* in favour of broadcasting organizations to transmit works protected by copyright, for example: United States, Section 110(5); Luxembourg, Article 24 (but only in respect of works whose total or partial exploitation belongs to the repertory of a collective management society for authors' rights); Netherlands, Article 17a, first paragraph; Italy, Articles 52 to 57 (confined, however, to broadcasting from theatres, concert halls and any other public place in which theatrical performances, concerts or other public performances are given and provided that the broadcast does not involve the first performance of the works performed or executed and that these are works which have already been published with the permission of the author. On the other hand, under Article 59 of the Italian law, transmissions of performances given in the studios of the broadcasting organization do not require licences for broadcasting, but only authorization from the author. Article 58 of the same law also establishes a compulsory licence for the public communication of radio transmissions).

Some countries have also instituted compulsory licences for the *cable distribution of broadcast programmes*, e.g. Austria, Denmark, the Netherlands and the United Kingdom. In these countries, distribution of this kind may be effected under a non-voluntary licence, provided that the cable distribution is simultaneous with the broadcast, that the content of the latter is not changed and that programmes transmitted in the country itself are involved; the United States (Section 111) has established a system of compulsory licences for the retransmissions of broadcast programmes intended for the subscribers of a cable television service (but only in the case of certain programmes) and for non-commercial broadcasting.

The Berne Convention allows the countries of the Union to establish such licences in their domestic legislation. After stipulating in its paragraph (1) the exclusive right of the author to permit broadcasting and communication of his works by cable, Article 11*bis* provides in paragraph (2) that:

It shall be a matter for legislation of the countries of the Union to determine the conditions under which the rights mentioned in the preceding paragraph may be exercised, but these conditions shall apply only in the countries where they have been prescribed. They shall not in any circumstances be prejudicial to the moral rights of the author, nor to his right to obtain equitable remuneration which, in the absence of agreement, shall be fixed by competent authority.

It should be noted that this provision of the Convention does not authorize national legislations to establish non-voluntary licences for the use of works *in programmes originated* by the cable distribution companies[103] but only for the *retransmission* in a simultaneous and unaltered form of broadcast programmes (as in the case of Austria, Denmark, the Netherlands and the United Kingdom). Paragraph (2) of Article 11*bis* of the Berne Convention permits non-voluntary licences in respect of the exclusive rights covered by paragraph (1)(ii) of this Article whereby: 'authors of literary and artistic works shall authorize any communication to the public by *wire* or by rebroadcasting *of the broadcast of the work, when this communication is made by an organization other than the original one.*

The condition that the rebroadcasting effected under a non-voluntary licence must be *simultaneous* and *unaltered* is explained by the fact that 'time-shifted' transmission constitutes much more than *public communication* (covered by the Berne Convention); it requires previous fixation which involves the exercise of an additional right—the right of reproduction (Article 9) which differs considerably from the right of public communication mentioned in Article 11*bis*.1(ii).

---

103. See above, Section 4.3.2.4. C—types of distribution by cable.

E. OTHER NON-VOLUNTARY LICENCES ESTABLISHED BY NATIONAL LEGISLATION

Other instances of non-voluntary licences can be found in national laws such as the case, following the death of the author, of *failure to act by the heirs or successors in title*; the law authorizes, in this instance, the reproduction of the work once the legal period established in this connection has elapsed (Argentina, Article 6; Peru, Article 63).

F. OTHER NON-VOLUNTARY LICENCES PERMITTED BY INTERNATIONAL CONVENTIONS

The Universal Copyright Convention provides for compulsory licences to effect translations of writings into a language in general use in the country making the request, once seven years have elapsed since the first publication of the work and provided that no translation into the language concerned has appeared during that period (Article V, 2).

In the texts of the Paris Acts—1971—of the Berne Convention and the Universal Convention (appendix to the Berne Convention and Article V*bis*, V*ter* and V*quater* of the Universal Convention), provision is made for special compulsory licences for the benefit of the developing countries for the translation of works published in printed or analogous form, for use in schools and universities and for research purposes and for the reproduction of works published in printed or any other analogous form of reproduction, in order to meet the needs of school or university teaching (see below, Chapter 12, Sections 12.4.2.1., L F and 12.4.2.2, G B, respectively).

Chapter 5

Duration of protection

Summary

5.1. Terms of protection
   5.1.1. Origin. **5.1.2.** The aim. **5.1.3.** Terms of protection. **5.1.4.** Circulation of copies and the broadcasting of works in the public domain. **5.1.5.** The moral right after the author's death
5.2. Beneficiaries of rights after the author's death
   5.2.1. Moral rights. **5.2.2.** Economic rights
5.3. Public domain
   5.3.1. Legal nature. **5.3.2.** Paying public domain

5.1. Terms of protection

5.1.1. Origin

The origin of the limitation in time of authors' economic rights is linked with the system of privileges which began to be granted following the invention of the printing press. These licences, which were awarded by the governing authorities, granted the exclusive right to exploit a work for a given period.[1]

The first laws which, in the eighteenth century, abolished these privileges and recognized that the right to exploit the work was an individual right of the author, continued to limit the duration of that right.

Queen Anne's Statute, which came into force in England in 1710, laid down that the author's exclusive right to publish a book (copyright) terminated after a period of 14 years from the date of first publication and, if at the end of that period the author was still alive, he could renew this exclusive right for a further 14 years;

---

1. See above, Chapter 1, Section 1.2.

subsequently publication was free. Protection was subject to the work being registered with the Stationers' Company.

The United States Federal Copyright Act enacted in 1790 adopted the English model.

In France, Decree 13-19 of January 1791 recognized the exclusive right of authors to authorize performance throughout their lifetime and that of their heirs and successors in title for a further five years after the death of the author. Decree 19-24 of July 1793 extended this protection to the right of reproduction of literary, musical and artistic works, guaranteeing authors the prerogatives of distribution and sale of such works throughout their lifetime and for a further ten years thereafter in respect of their heirs and successors in title. In 1866 the *post mortem auctoris* term was extended to 50 years.

With the emergence of these initial laws, which formed the basis for the development of the two main tendencies in this area—Anglo-American copyright and *droit d'auteur* in continental European countries with a Roman law tradition—several European States, with a few exceptions, such as the Netherlands and Portugal which at various times embraced the principle of perpetual protection, drew up similar legislation limiting the duration of authors' economic rights. In Latin America some countries also established the principle of perpetual rights (Mexico and Guatemala), but subsequently abandoned it and limited the term of protection.

5.1.2. The aim

The aim of limiting the term of protection in respect of economic rights is to foster access to works protected by copyright.

The main arguments *in favour* of limiting the term of protection take into account the following factors:
- authors draw upon the collective cultural heritage and take material from it to produce their works; it is proper, then, that these works should, in turn, form part of that common heritage;
- after a certain period has elapsed, it is practically impossible to locate all the heirs and reach a consensus to authorize the use of the work with the rapidity demanded by the high-powered nature of the publishing business;
- a perpetual right of protection increases costs to the public, a

factor which is particularly prejudicial in developing countries. As only the heirs benefit it does not stimulate creativity. Similarly, it hampers the circulation of works which runs counter to the needs imposed by access by all to culture.

Contrary arguments invoke:
- the injustice of depriving heirs of permanent enjoyment of this property when authors have devoted all their creative energy to producing these works which, in many cases, constitute their sole estate;
- the fact that once the term of protection has expired, use free of charge benefits only the industrial and business firms which exploit the works and not the public, for there are no price reductions for books, recordings of musical works, tickets to shows, and so on, when works in the public domain are used.

5.1.3. Terms of protection

A. Basically, the duration of protection of economic rights *spans the lifetime of the author and a certain number of years after his death (post mortem auctoris)*, calculated from the first of January of the year following the date of death, or from the date of death itself (Argentina, El Salvador).

Up to now, the general term adopted in most countries is 50[2] years *p.m.a.*, although a considerable number of countries have stipulated different periods, either shorter[3] or longer.[4]

---

2. Argentina, Australia, Bangladesh, Barbados, Bolivia, Bulgaria, Cameroon, Canada, Chile, China, Congo, Costa Rica, former Czechoslovakia, Denmark, Ecuador, Egypt, El Salvador, Finland, Gabon, Greece, Guatemala, Honduras, Hungary, Iceland, India, Ireland, Italy, Japan, Lebanon, Lesotho, Liechtenstein, Luxembourg, Malawi, Malaysia, Mali, Mauritius, Monaco, Morocco, Netherlands, New Zealand, Norway, Pakistan, Panama, Paraguay, Peru, Philippines, Portugal, Saudi Arabia, Senegal, Sri Lanka, Sweden, Thailand, Tunisia, Turkey, United Kingdom, United States of America, former Yugoslavia.
3. *Twenty-five years*: Algeria, Cuba, Haiti, Indonesia, Libyan Arab Jamahiriya, Kenya, Liberia, Malta, Poland, former USSR; *30 years*: Iran, Jordan, Nicaragua (dramatic works); *40 years*: Uruguay (but it is considered in this country that following ratification of the Berne Convention, the term of protection has been extended to the period of 50 years established by it).
4. *Sixty years*: Brazil, Spain, Venezuela; *70 years*: Austria, Belgium, France (in respect of musical compositions with or without words, in accordance

B. It was the Spanish law of 1847 (Art. 2) which originally adopted the term of 50 years *p.m.a.*, followed by the Belgian law of 22 March 1866 (Art. 2) and the French law of 14 July 1866. With this law, which was preceded by several extensions in favour of the widows and children of authors, France did away with the diversity of the previous system and, placing itself in the vanguard, prolonged protection *p.m.a.*

C. In recent decades the trend in favour of extending these periods in general and *post mortem* protection in particular[5] has become more marked, which is consistent with the enhancement of average life expectancy and also with the fact that copyright gains in value if the length of protection is prolonged. It is considered that the period should span the cycle of two generations after the death of the author; if the *post mortem* period is not extended, direct descendants of the author may be deprived of the economic benefits.

In order to prevent such situations arising some countries have decided to establish the principle that certain relatives shall enjoy these rights to the end of their lifetime if they outlive the generally established *p.m.a.* period. The relatives benefiting from this vary according to the legislation in question; for example, in Brazil (Art. 42(1)) and Peru (Art. 21) the spouse, children and parents

---

with Art. L. 123-1.2, previously Art. 8(1) of the Law of 3 July 1985; for other works the general term of protection *p.m.a.* of 50 years continues to be in force), Germany, Israel; *75 years*: Mexico; *80 years*: Colombia, Guinea; *99 years*: Côte d'Ivoire. In Nicaragua, Article 735 of the 1904 Civil Code provides that on the author's death the literary property right shall pass to his heirs in accordance with the law; this is also applicable to the reproduction of artistic works (Art. 790).

5. The Directive of the Council of the European Communities dated 29 October 1993 (93/98/EEC) on the harmonization of the term of protection of copyright and certain related rights adopted the *p.m.a.* term of 70 years. Accordingly, Member States of the European Union should adopt this term of protection, as well as the others stipulated in the Directive.

are the beneficiaries; in Chile (Art. 10), it is the author's spouse and his daughters who are unmarried or widowed or, if married, whose spouse is affected by a permanent disability preventing him from engaging in any form of work; in Romania (Art. 6(a)), the law designates the surviving spouse and the ascendants.

This exception in favour of certain of the author's relatives seems at first sight to be fair, but its disadvantage is that it makes the duration of copyright protection uncertain, and this is incompatible with the system covering the international exploitation of works. For an unspecified period of time following expiry of the general term of protection, to find out whether a work has fallen into the public domain a check has to be made first of all to see whether the relatives mentioned in the legal provision are still alive, and even, as in the case of Chile, to ascertain their personal circumstances.

The duration of protection covering the lifetime of the author and a certain number of years after his death is of a generic nature and it is applied under the laws to works made by a single author and published during his or her lifetime, either under the author's own name or a pseudonym, as long as the pseudonym leaves no doubt as to the identity of the author (transparent pseudonym).

In the case of works of collaboration, the *p.m.a.* term is usually calculated from the death of the last surviving co-author. A reduction of this term may be found when the rights belong to other heirs (Romania, Art. 6(c)), a transferee or his successors in title (Peru, Article 22, which lays down a period of 30 instead of 50 years *p.m.a.* which is contrary to the Berne Convention for this does not provide for such a possibility or any other similar reduction in the minimum *p.m.a.* term established by Article 7(1)).

D. Even in those countries where the general period of protection covers the life of the author and a given number of years after his death, periods differing from the *p.m.a.* established by law as the general norm are usually adopted for different situations and certain categories of works; *from the date of publication of the work or of its creation*, in the case of collective, anonymous and pseudonymous works (the pseudonym being equivalent to anonymity) and works where original ownership involves a legal entity,[6] photographic[7] and cinematographic[8] works, and computer programs.[9]

---

6. In general, protection covers the same number of years as that established for the *p.m.a.* term, but it is calculated from the date of publication of the work —or of its creation if it has not been published. The Directive of the European Union to which reference has been made, provides that in the case of anonymous or pseudonymous works, works belonging to legal entities and collective works, the term of protection should be 70 years from the time that they are lawfully made available to the public; if they have not been published, the term should be 70 years from the date of creation of the work.

7. *Fifty years post publicationem operis* (*p.p.o.*): Australia, Cyprus, India, Ireland, Pakistan, United Kingdom; *30 years p.p.o.*: Philippines; *30 years post creationem operis* (*p.c.o.*): Austria; *25 years p.p.o.*: Bulgaria, Finland, former Yugoslavia; *25 years p.c.o.*: Benin, Congo, Denmark, Sri Lanka; *20 years p.p.o.*: Argentina; *10 years p.p.o.*: Poland.

8. *Sixty years p.p.o.*: Venezuela; *50 years p.p.o.*: Argentina, Australia, Cyprus, Fiji, India, Ireland, Pakistan; *50 years p.c.o.*: New Zealand, Rwanda; *50 years p.p.o./p.c.o.*: Austria, Benin, South Africa, Thailand; *30 years p.p.o.*: Philippines; *25 years p.p.o.*: former Czechoslovakia; *10 years p.p.o.*: Poland. This refers to cinematographic productions as works independent of the literary, musical, artistic or other works that are reflected in them. The term of protection corresponding to the genre to which the work belongs is maintained with respect to the latter. On the other hand, having entered the public domain, cinematographic and other audiovisual works may be freely used with their original content (*reproduced*, e.g. by means of video cassettes, *communicated to the public* by screening in cinemas, *broadcast on television* and by cable networks, or translated). The Directive of the Council of the European Communities (93/98/EEC) provides (Art. 2), in the case of cinematographic or audiovisual works, for a general term of protection for the life of the author and for 70 years after his death (*Official Journal of the European Communities,* 24 November 1993).

9. *Fifty years after publication or creation* (if unpublished): Spain. The Council Directive of the European Communities of 14 May 1991 (91/250/EEC) on the legal protection of computer programs provides (Article 8) that protection shall be granted for the life of the author and for 50 years after his death, and allows Member States which already have a longer term of protection to maintain this until such time as the term of protection for copyright works is harmonized by Community law in a more general way (*Official Journal of the European Communities,* 17 May 1991).

E. *Posthumous works*[10] are, at times, the subject of special treatment. In principle, the general *p.m.a.* term is adopted, but some laws seek to motivate or accelerate the disclosure of these works in the interest of the community by granting additional periods.

a) Additional term in favour of the successors in title or the publisher of a posthumous work, as the case may be, e.g.:

France (Article L. 123-4.1, formerly Art. 23(1)) establishes an additional term of 50 years (70 for musical works with or without words) from the date of publication of the posthumous work. However, if disclosure takes place before expiry of the *p.m.a.* term (50 years and 70 years for musical compositions with or without words), the right to exploit the work shall belong to the successors (Article L. 123-4.2, formerly Art. 23(2)). On the other hand, if disclosure is made after expiry of the *p.m.a.* term, the exploitation right belongs to the publishers ('shall belong to the proprietors of the work, by succession or by other title, who effect publication or cause it to be effected') (Article L. 123-4.3, formerly Art. 23(3)).

As regards the German Law (Article 64(2)) this establishes an additional period of ten years *post publicationem operis* (*p.p.o.*). If the posthumous work is published during the last ten years of the *p.m.a.* term, the additional period is in favour of the author's successors in title. On the other hand, should the posthumous work be published after expiry of the *p.m.a.* term, Article 71 grants the publishers an exclusive right to exploit it during the ten-year period *p.p.o.* (this constitutes an exclusive right to exploit the posthumous work established in favour of the person publishing it when it has already fallen into the public domain).

---

10. A *posthumous work* is one which was not disclosed during the author's lifetime; it is also a work which, although disclosed, was modified by its author before his death to such an extent that it deserves to be treated as a new work.

b) Additional term in respect of posthumous works solely in favour of the successors in title, e.g.:

Italy (Article 31) fixes an additional period of 50 years *p.p.o.*, provided that publication of the posthumous work occurs within 20 years *p.m.a.* (the general term is 50 years *p.m.a*).

Spain (Article 27(1)) establishes, for its part, an additional term of 60 years provided that disclosure occurs within 60 years *p.m.a.* (while the posthumous work is in the private domain).

c) Additional term in favour of the publisher of a work that has fallen into the public domain

European Directive 93/98/CEE (Article 4) fixes an additional period of 25 years *p.p.o.* if the posthumous work is published after expiry of the author's exclusive rights.

F. Disparity in the periods of protection of economic rights adopted by each individual State in its domestic legislation adversely affects legal security in international transactions. For this reason the Berne Convention and the Universal Convention laid down *minimum terms* applicable among countries parties to these conventions.

G. THE BERNE CONVENTION

The original Act concluded in 1886 did not lay down a minimum term of protection. National legislations established widely differing terms and despite the fact that various countries had adopted the period of 50 years *p.m.a.*,[11] of the ten countries which were original signatories of the Berne Act only Belgium and France already applied that term at the date of their accession. The others laid down different periods, one a longer term (Spain), but the majority, shorter periods (Germany, Haiti, Italy,[12] Liberia, Swit-

---

11. Belgium, Bolivia, Denmark, France, Hungary, Norway, Portugal, Sweden (see S. Ricketson, 'Duration of term of protection under the Berne Convention', *Copyright*, Geneva, WIPO, April 1991, p. 85).
12. A particular system was in force in Italy until 1925. Under the Law of 1865-82, the exclusive right of reproduction was recognized as being vested in

zerland, Tunisia, United Kingdom).[13] So as to avoid any inequalities which might have resulted from such a range of terms of protection, Article II(2) *in fine* of the 1886 text established that '... enjoyment of these rights ... must not exceed in the other countries the term of protection granted in the said country of origin'. Hence, by applying the method of comparison of terms of protection, the principle of national treatment (or of assimilation of foreign treatment to national) was applicable as regards duration only to the extent that both legislations coincided (that of the country where protection was claimed and that of the country of origin of the work).

The adoption in the Berlin Act (1908) of the basic term of protection of the lifetime of authors and fifty years *p.m.a.* reflected trends in the countries where protection of authors' rights had attained a higher level of development; these countries had gradually extended the period of the monopoly of exploitation of works. But it was not imposed as a minimum term; if the domestic law stipulated a shorter period, then this was the term that should apply. Pending its uniform adoption by all countries in the Union, the term of protection would be regulated 'by the law of the country where protection is claimed, and must not exceed the term fixed in the country of origin of the work' (Article 7(2)).

---

the author during his lifetime; however should he die before forty years had elapsed from the date of publication, the right passed to his successors for the remainder of that period. Once the longer of these two periods had expired, a new 40-year period began, termed the 'paying public domain', during which use did not require permission, but was subject to the payment to the successors in title of 5 per cent of the gross sales price of each example or copy of the work. Under the 1875 law, the duration of public performance rights was fixed as a single period of 80 years (without 'paying public domain') from the date of the first performance or publication of the work.

13. In the United Kingdom different terms were in force until 1911, depending on the category of the work. Since 1842 the term of protection for literary works had been 42 years *p.p.o.* or the author's lifetime and seven years *p.m.a.* In 1911 the period of the author's lifetime and 50 years *p.m.a.* was adopted, but this was accompanied by a controversial system of compulsory licences, some of which could be invoked immediately following the author's death and others only 25 years after his death.

It was only in the Brussels revision of 1948 that the general principle of a minimum term of 50 years *p.m.a.* was adopted, allowing different terms of protection for certain categories of works. At that time, many countries in the Union had accepted the term of 50 years *p.m.a.* and the application of the method of comparing terms of protection was confined to instances of longer periods, that is to say, where the country in which protection was claimed had established a duration longer than the minimum provided in the Convention: '... where one or more countries of the Union grant a term of protection in excess of that provided by para. 1, the term shall be governed by the law of the country where protection is claimed, but shall not exceed the term fixed in the country of origin of the work' (Art. 7(2)).

In the Stockholm revision (1967), confirmed in the Paris Act (1971), the minimum of 50 years *post mortem* established under the Convention was maintained. During the Stockholm Conference the possibility of increasing the period was discussed, but the conclusion was that it was still not possible to do so, for in order to accede to the Brussels Act many countries had had to extend the minimum terms of protection in their domestic legislation and a further extension would make ratification of the new text difficult. However, in view of the fact that certain members of the Union had expressed a wish for the period to be extended, for some had already accepted a general term of protection in excess of 50 years *p.m.a.* and many others had extended the duration by means of wartime extensions and bilateral agreements,[14] the Conference recommended that negotiations leading to the conclusion of a multilateral arrangement on the prolongation of the term of protection should be pursued between the countries concerned.

---

14. Claude Masouyé recalls that the movement in favour of extending the term of protection *post mortem* 'started with the adoption, in some countries, of measures extending copyright to compensate for loss of the opportunity to exploit it during a period of hostilities (now known as 'wartime extension'). These differed from one country to another, and bilateral agreements were concluded between former enemies and countries which, although neutral, had felt the cold winds of the battlefields' (*Guide to the Berne Convention*, WIPO, p. 45).

In the 1967 text (confirmed in that of 1971), important changes were introduced concerning the duration of protection of cinematographic and photographic works and of works of applied art, compulsory minimum terms being established for them, whereas in the Brussels Act the fixing of these periods had been left to the discretion of the countries of the Union (see below, Chapter 12, Section 12.4.2.1., I).

H. THE UNIVERSAL COPYRIGHT CONVENTION

In Article IV.1, the Convention provides that 'the duration of protection of a work shall be governed ... by the law of the Contracting State in which protection is claimed'. It adds, in paragraph 4, that no Contracting State shall be obliged to grant protection to a work for a period longer than in the country of origin of the work. It fixes, as a compulsory provision, a general minimum period (para. 2), covering the life of the author and 25 years *post mortem*. The adoption of this term *p.m.a.*, noticeably inferior to that fixed in the Berne Convention, was designed to permit ratification of the Universal Convention by the many countries which, in 1952, had laid down terms of less than 50 years *p.m.a.*

The Convention admitted certain exceptions (Art. IV(2))[15] and different terms for cinematographic works and works of

---

15. These exceptions are as follows: (a) Any Contracting State which, on the effective date of the Convention in that State, has limited the term of protection for certain classes of works to a period computed from the first publication of the work, may calculate the period from the date of first publication, but must grant protection for a minimum period of 25 years from the date of first publication; (b) Any Contracting State which, on the effective date of the Convention in that State, does not compute the term of protection upon the basis of the life of the author, shall be entitled to compute it from the first publication of the work, if it is a published work, although it must be for a term of 25 years from the date of first publication or from its registration if it is an unpublished work. This provision should be seen in the light of the law in force in the United States at the time the Universal Convention was concluded, a law which granted protection for a term of 28 years after publication, renewable for a further period of equal length.

applied art (Art. IV(3))[16] (see below, Chapter 12, Section 12.4.2.2, C,d,3)).

5.1.4. Circulation of copies and the broadcasting of works in the public domain

If, in a particular country, advantage is taken of the fact that a work is in the public domain in order to make copies of it, it is not lawful to export them to a State where the work is still protected. For example, copies of a work whose country of origin is Brazil (60 years *p.m.a.*) and which have been produced in Argentina (50 years *p.m.a.*)—when the work was in the public domain in the latter country but not in the former—cannot be exported to the country of origin or to any other country where the work is still in the private domain (e.g. Colombia: 80 years *p.m.a.*). For this purpose the authorization of the holder of rights in the work is required (the three countries referred to are all members of the Berne Union; Argentina is bound by the Brussels Act while the other two have acceded to the current Paris Act of 1971).

The holder of rights in the countries where the work is protected can oppose both the export (in the country of manufacture) and the import and circulation of copies in the countries where the work has not yet fallen into the public domain.

This provision is also applicable to the broadcasting of programmes containing works which have fallen into the public domain in the country from which the programme-carrying signals are emitted. It is not lawful to direct these emissions (by satellite or any other means) towards countries where the work is protected, or to communicate them to the public in such countries, unless the express authorization of the holders of the rights involved has been obtained.

---

16. The Contracting States which protect photographic works and works of applied art as artistic works, may establish a shorter period, although it must not be less than ten years (the Convention does not go into details concerning the date from which this period should be calculated).

5.1.5. The moral right after the author's death

Three different legal positions may be noted here:
- the moral right is perpetual (Colombia, Art. 30; Costa Rica, Art. 13; Dominican Republic, Art. 18; Mexico, Art. 3; Peru, Art. 2(2); France, Article L. 121-1, previously Art. 6, and countries whose laws are modelled on this, e.g. Algeria, 1973, Art. 22; Benin, 1984, Art. 3.A; Central African Republic, 1985, Art. 2.A; Côte d'Ivoire, 1978, Art. 22; Senegal, 1973, Art. 3(a); and so on);
- the moral right has *the same duration as the economic right* (Germany, Art. 64(1); Guatemala, Art. 19, final paragraph; Luxembourg, Art. 9, second paragraph; Netherlands, Art. 25(c), second paragraph; Norway, Art. 48; and so on). It is considered in Germany and the Nordic countries that when the author's rights expire in the economic field, the moral right ceases to belong to the private sphere; from then onwards it is a question of safeguarding the cultural heritage in the public interest;
- author's rights of a personal character *terminate* on death (legal tradition based on 'common law').

These differences were reflected in the *Berne Convention*, protection of the moral right being introduced in the Rome revision (1928), Art. 6*bis*. The question of the length of protection was sidestepped since the so-called 'common law' countries expressed a number of objections (for in those countries the author's rights of a personal kind were not protected by copyright but, indirectly, by other means; for example in the United Kingdom, the right to the integrity of the work belonged to the sphere of 'common law', particularly the law on defamation, which did not authorize judicial proceedings after the death of the person attacked). In Brussels (1948) it was established in Article 6*bis*(1) that the author maintained these rights 'during his lifetime', with the addition, in paragraph 2, of the possibility ('in so far as the legislation of the countries of the Union permits') that they should be maintained after the author's death, at least until the expiry of the economic rights, and exercised by the persons or institutions authorized by the said legislation.

Finally, in the Stockholm revision (1967)—confirmed in the Paris revision (1971)—and despite the opposition of the countries whose legal tradition was based on 'common law', the phrase 'in so far as the legislation of the countries of the Union permits' was deleted and an obligation was introduced in the Convention by the member countries of the Union to protect the moral right at least until the expiry of the economic rights.

As a compromise solution, however, account was taken of the particular situation of countries in the copyright area by allowing an exception in favour of those countries whose legislation in force at the time of ratification of or accession to that Act did not contain any provisions ensuring protection after the author's death of the prerogatives of the moral right: those countries 'may provide that some of these rights may, after his death, cease to be maintained' (Art. 6*bis*, para. (2), last part)

5.2. Beneficiaries of rights after the author's death

5.2.1. Moral rights

Following the author's death the right to require recognition of his authorship and respect for the integrity of the work (*negative or defensive rights*) and the right to disclose posthumous works are exercised by the heirs for the whole period during which the work remains in the private domain, or during the lifetime of such heirs (e.g. Costa Rica, Italy, etc.).

On the other hand, the right to modify the work, to withdraw it from circulation or to destroy it (*positive rights*) can be exercised only by the author. The author may have expressed his wish to exercise the right of reconsideration or withdrawal in such a way as to leave no doubt as to his intention but died before being able to put this into effect. In this case the possibility of the heirs doing so should be considered.

Foreseeing that the author's heirs are not always interested in taking action to safeguard the right to respect for the author's name and the integrity of his works, or to authorize the disclosure of posthumous works, because they are not in sympathy with the works produced by the relative whose estate they have inherited, some laws allow the author to appoint an executor, whose wishes take precedence over those of the legal heirs (France, Article L. 121-1, previously Art. 6, final paragraph and Art. L. 121-2.2, previously Art. 19, second paragraph; Italy, Art. 24, first paragraph; Spain, Art. 15(1); and so on). Spain provides, moreover, in Article 40, that 'if, on the natural or declared death of the author, his successors in title exercise his right of non-disclosure of the work in a manner contrary to the provisions of Article 44 of the Constitution,[17] the court may order appropriate measures at the instigation of the State, the Autonomous Communities, local corporations, public institutions of a cultural character or any other person having a legitimate interest'.

Some laws lay down—in relation to moral rights—a special, more wide-ranging and autonomous system of succession, based on the assumption that certain people will be more willing than others to shoulder full responsibility for this matter in a disinterested fashion (e.g. Costa Rica, Art. 15; France, Article L. 121-2, previously Art. 19; Italy, Art. 23; Peru, Art. 33).

In view of the interest of society in safeguarding its cultural heritage, certain public or private bodies are also entitled to exercise the *negative* prerogatives of moral rights; such bodies may act automatically or in response to a complaint, either to supervise the heirs or to substitute for them (e.g. Italy, Art. 23, second paragraph; Portugal, Art. 57(3); Peru, Art. 33, second paragraph;[18] and so on) and to replace them once the legal term of protection of the economic rights has expired (e.g. Norway, Art. 48, second paragraph).[19] The reason behind this is that the bond between the work and the personality of its creator is an abiding one. This duty is incumbent not only upon authors' heirs but upon society

---

17. *Spanish Constitution, Art. 44*: '1. The public authorities shall promote and watch over access to culture, to which all have a right. 2. The public authorities shall promote science and scientific and technical research for the benefit of the general interest.'

18. *Peru, Art. 33, second paragraph*: 'Such action, when the merits of the work justify it, may likewise be exercised by the Minister of Public Education, or by the Professional Association to which the author belonged.'

19. *Norway, Art. 48, second paragraph*: 'Irrespective of whether the period of protection has lapsed, the Ministry concerned may, if the author is dead, forbid a scientific, literary, or artistic work being made available to the public in a manner or in a context as mentioned in the first paragraph of this section. [...]'

as a whole, for it is a matter of concern to the community that works should be attributed to their true authors and not to other persons and that they should reach the public in an integral form and not in a mutilated or distorted version. The public is interested in their preservation because they constitute a substantial part of humankind's common cultural heritage. For this reason, legislation includes various mechanisms whereby certain bodies can, once the private domain period has expired, take action in defence of the authorship and integrity of the work (e.g. Argentina, Art. 83; etc.).

5.2.2. Economic rights

After the death of the author, ownership of economic rights is transmitted in full to the author's successors in title for the term of protection laid down by law. They may exercise all the prerogatives relating to the exploitation of the work which were the author's, with the same characteristics as were applicable during his lifetime: exclusivity and effectiveness *erga omnes*.

Contracts entered into during the life of the author continue to be valid for the whole period stipulated by the parties to that contract, subject to the limitation on duration laid down by law, according to the category of work involved. If the author dies without heirs and the estate is declared in abeyance, then ownership of the economic rights falls to the State or to the body stipulated by law in the event of estate without claimants.

Having regard to the interest of the community in the question of access to expressions of creative talent, legal provision is usually made to ensure dissemination of works in the event of inaction on the part of the heirs or successors in title—through negligence or abuse of the right not to authorize publication—(e.g. Argentina, Art. 6, covering republication).[20]

---

20. *Argentina, Art. 6*: 'The heirs or successors in title shall not be entitled to oppose republication by a third party of the works of their predecessor [*de cujus*] if the heirs or successors in title have allowed more than ten years to elapse without themselves arranging for publication of the works. Furthermore, the heirs or successors in title shall not be entitled to oppose the translation by a

5.3. Public domain

The public domain, in the context of ordinary law, refers to ownership of material goods intended for the direct use of the community and liable to appropriation in the private context.

The public domain in the matter of authors' rights has different connotations. Once the term of protection of economic rights expires, the works do not become the property of the State. They may be used—reproduced, communicated to the public (performed, exhibited, broadcast, etc.) and transformed (adapted, translated, etc.) by any person but no one may acquire exclusive rights in the work; such rights may, on the other hand, be acquired in respect of the *creative input added to the work* (as in the case of translations) or *the new works that may result* (as in the case of adaptations).

These differences have given rise to objections concerning the use of the expression 'public domain' in relation to the legal status of works, once the term of economic protection has expired. Other designations have been suggested, such as 'free use of intellectual works', but the former expression has prevailed, consecrated as it is by universal use.

5.3.1. Legal nature

Opinions differ concerning the nature of the public domain in regard to intellectual works:
- for some it is the *normal situation* for the use of intellectual works which are communicated and made available to the community (although the author may previously have obtained a monopoly as regards economic exploitation for the period fixed by law);
- for others it is a *legislative restriction* on the individual's rights in the works, the aim of which is to ensure enjoyment of

---

third party of the works of the *de cujus* after the lapse of ten years from his death. In such cases, if there is no agreement between the third party publisher and the heirs or successors in title with regard to the conditions of printing or the pecuniary remuneration, these questions shall be decided by arbitration.'

intellectual creations by all. This kind of limitation is similar to the restrictions which, with social aims, are imposed on the ownership of material goods.

5.3.2. Paying public domain

A number of countries[21] have adopted the system of public domain subject to payment; following the French designation '*domaine public payant*' it is commonly called 'paying public domain'.

The *adversaries* of this system consider that the obligation to make payment for the use of works, once the term of protection of the author's economic rights has expired, obstructs, or at least hinders, the circulation of literary, musical and artistic works, since it increases costs.

They allege that the paying public domain may become a pretext for intellectual *dirigisme* and covert censorship if the State regards itself as the author's successor in title or heir and, in that capacity, attempts to act as the owner of the work demanding that authorization should be sought in each case. It might grant or refuse such authorization depending on whether it wished certain works or certain types of creation to be circulated, or otherwise. Intellectual *dirigisme* may also be practised through the end use for which the funds are earmarked.[22]

The adversaries of this system also maintain that payment for the use of works under these conditions may become simply another tax and the income derived from it may either be diluted in the sea of general revenue accruing to the State or be applied, in the widest and most imprecise sense, to foster literature and the arts. Moreover, the State may arbitrarily raise these fees thus

---

21. Algeria, Argentina, Benin, Bolivia, Burkina Faso, Cameroon, Congo, Côte d'Ivoire, former Czechoslovakia, Guinea, Hungary, Holy See, Italy, Mali, Rwanda, Senegal, Uruguay and Yugoslavia.
22. Some of the countries which have adopted the payment system have stipulated, even if incorrectly, that authorization must be obtained prior to the use of works which have fallen into the public domain (e.g. Congo, Art. 85, Côte d'Ivoire, Art. 59).

hindering the basic aim of the public domain institution, i.e. the dissemination of culture.

The *advocates* of the paying public domain system point out that use must always be unrestricted, whatever stance is adopted. There is no need to apply for State authorization because such a condition runs counter to the very nature of the institution of public domain, since the State does not replace the author's heirs as the owner of the economic rights in the work. In this matter public domain is not similar to other legal institutions, such as the domain of the State or the State as heir in the case of unclaimed estates or after a given period has elapsed. They agree, then, that the need for prior authorization from the State for the use of works under these circumstances fosters intellectual *dirigisme* and covert censorship, but point out that this circumstance bears no relation to the system of public domain whether free from, or subject to, payment. In the latter case the only obligation which exists is that of paying the required fee to exploit the works under such conditions. The obligation to pay for the use of works which have fallen into the public domain therefore constitutes a tax and not a compensatory payment since the author's economic rights have expired. The grounds for a State charge therefore reside in the power of the State to levy charges on certain economic activities which are freely carried on, as is the exploitation by users (publishers, impresarios, producers, etc.) of works which have fallen into the public domain.

They point out that, besides preventing works in these circumstances from competing unfairly with those in the private domain, the system of a paying public domain has the advantage of providing the State with funds for the promotion of creative activity or support of a social security system for authors.

Chapter 6

Transfer of copyright

Summary

6.1. General rules concerning the transfer of copyright
  6.1.1. Transfer by *inter vivos* transaction. **6.1.2.** Transfer *mortis causa*
6.2. Publishing contracts: literary, musical and artistic works
  6.2.1. Contracts for the publication of literary works. 6.2.1.1. Rights and obligations of the parties. 6.2.1.2. Termination of a publishing contract. **6.2.2.** Contracts for the publication of musical works. **6.2.3.** Contracts for the publication of artistic works. **6.2.4.** Publishers' rights concerning the typographical arrangement of their published editions. **6.2.5.** Entitlement of the publisher to institute proceedings in the case of infringement of exclusive rights which he possesses as transferee
6.3. Public performance contracts: dramatic, musical and dramatico-musical works
  6.3.1. Concept. **6.3.2.** Legal nature. **6.3.3.** Characteristics. **6.3.4.** Rights and obligations of the parties. **6.3.5.** Termination of public performance contracts
6.4. Contracts for mechanical reproduction rights
  6.4.1. Concept. **6.4.2.** Legal nature and characteristics. **6.4.3.** Rights and obligations of the parties
6.5. Broadcasting contracts
  6.5.1. Concept. **6.5.2.** Legal nature and characteristics. **6.5.3.** Rights and obligations of the parties. **6.5.4.** Sound broadcasting. **6.5.5.** Television
6.6. Contracts for the production of audiovisual works
  6.6.1. Concept. **6.6.2.** Legal nature and characteristics. **6.6.3.** Rights and obligations of the parties

6.1. General rules concerning the transfer of copyright

6.1.1. Transfer by *inter vivos* transaction

The use of works involves certain difficulties if the various interests involved—those of the author, the public and the user—are to be fairly balanced. Authors create works and will claim rights in them: the public is increasingly eager to be able to enjoy them without hindrance and the users (publishers, impresarios, producers, etc.), the essential link between the author and the public, wish to conduct their business as advantageously as possible and on the most efficient basis.

At first sight the interests of the author and those of society appear to present a certain degree of incompatibility and for some considerable time this was believed to be the case because, on the one hand, the author did not wish his work to be used without his authorization, he demanded respect for his authorship and the integrity of the work and he claimed remuneration, whereas the public needed to have unrestricted access to these works.[1]

With the passage of time it was observed that, in fact, this dichotomy or opposition between the interests of the author and those of the public was only seemingly so. Just as the public is interested in gaining access to works, so authors also wish their works to be disseminated as widely as possible, for, save in exceptional cases, they do not create them for themselves or an intimate circle. They need to see their works in circulation and, while anguished by the uncertainty surrounding the fate of their progeny, they also become anxious to see it living its own life. For these reasons, both authors and the public are interested in new works being created and circulated as widely as possible: lack of protection does not contribute to attaining this goal.

In the Charter of the Author's Right[2] this erroneous belief—and its consequences for authors—is tackled in the following terms:

The protection of the common interest by ensuring the unhampered diffusion of culture and information must not be confused with the concept of the protection of industrial and commercial interests which are concerned with the exploitation of works of the mind. It is in the author's interest that his works should be as widely distributed as possible; and it is through the protection of intellectual creation at source that the development and spread of culture can be most effectively fostered.

---

1. What had to be determined was whether author's rights did not represent an obstacle to the unhampered and prompt dissemination of information and culture among the different countries.
2. See above, Chapter 3, note 2.

Users, for their part, need to have works readily available in order to be able to choose the most propitious moment to publish, perform and record them and so on, and also to be in a position to launch new products on the market or replace one stage production by another at short notice. In their view, in order to do this they need to obtain exclusive authorization at the lowest possible cost, not to be subject to any time limits for use of the work and to continue to have the work available even though they may discontinue its use, because they consider that they shoulder the full economic risk of the enterprise and seek to diminish this so as to ensure the return on their investment.

The supply of works is always considerably greater than demand, for, while the number of companies using them (publishers, theatres, producers of films, phonograms and computer programs, broadcasting companies, etc.) increases very slowly—and sometimes declines, particularly in developing countries—the number of works available grows constantly with the substantial contribution of those falling into the public domain and of foreign works, whose probabilities of success have already been tested abroad.

Save natural exceptions, these particular factors usually place authors in a position of psychological submission in relation to users, preventing them from discussing contractual conditions freely and eventually causing them to suffer the full consequences of what they have consented to, and subsequent frustration. This happens even to established writers who find that at some point there is a sharp fall in demand for their works because their very success often turns against them, as the public reaches saturation point.[3]

As Dietz so rightly points out, if we consider the historical evolution of author's rights, we are forced to recognize that until relatively recently legislators did not trouble to establish rulings

---

3. The particular circumstances which surround contractual relations between authors and users have been set down and analysed in detail by Carlos Alberto Villalba, in 'Los contratos en derecho de autor', *Revista Mexicana de la Propiedad Industrial y Artistica*, No. 29–30, Mexico 1977, pp. 251–65.

for dealing with the conflict of interests between creators and users; with the passage of time this has led to considerable complaints and protests from authors who had no qualms about declaring in pithy terms that, in the last analysis, author's rights were publisher's rights, giving publishers or other exploiters[4] a means of taking advantage of authors or of expropriating them.

This has led to rejection of transfer *inter vivos* involving the transfer of ownership of exploitation rights. The trend has been to consider the author's economic right as a right to authorize the use of a work by means of specific licences, whether exclusive or not, and to recognize the need for legislation, through compulsory provisions, to incorporate a general part dealing with contracts for the exploitation of such works and the detailed typification and regulation of the rights and obligations of the parties to those contracts that are already an established feature of our socio-economic life (printed editions, public performance, mechanical reproduction, broadcasting and the production of audiovisual works).

The law which first incorporated an important schedule of general, compulsory regulations which were valid for all contracts was the French law of 1957 on literary and artistic property which is still in force (Articles L. 131-1 to L. 131-8, previously Arts. 31, 33, 35, 37 to 39 and 58). Although the French law does recognize total or partial transfer of exploitation rights and may be incomplete and imperfect in some respects, it does contain invaluable provisions which constitute a milestone in the contractual regulation of copyright and have provided an abundant source of solutions.

In Latin America, Venezuela followed in its copyright law adopted in 1962, the general lines of the French law, including a chapter of general provisions (Articles 50 to 58) which were expanded in the 1993 amendment. In the law of the Dominican Republic we also find a chapter on contracts in general containing extremely useful provisions (Articles 61 to 66).

---

4. Adolf Dietz, op. cit., Spanish version, Madrid, 1983, Vol. 2, p. 388.

Mention should also be made of the Spanish intellectual property law (1987) which contains an important chapter of general provisions (Articles 42 to 57); neither should we omit the German law (1965) which, because of the underlying monistic conception of author's rights, does not recognize either total or partial transfer of copyright but only the granting of utilization rights (whether exclusive or non-exclusive) in the chapter entitled *Copyright Licences* (Articles 31 to 44).

Although regulation of the transfer of copyright by *inter vivos* transaction is not specific to the law in this domain, such transfers may be made under contractual law (e.g. in Bolivia the Commercial Code, approved in 1977, regulates publishing contracts in its Articles 1216 to 1236 which, under an express provision in Article 32 *in fine* of the copyright law enacted in 1992, remain in force despite the fact that the new law also contains rules governing publishing contracts—Arts. 30–32) or by means of a specific law (e.g. in Germany publishing contracts are still regulated by the law of 19 June 1901, for this was not replaced by the law on copyright and related rights passed in 1965, which only introduced a number of amendments). However, regulation of authors' contracts within a specific law has the advantage of preventing the dispersal of fundamental rules which would impair the unity of regulation in a still little-known domain, a factor which might prejudice legal safeguards.[5]

A. LIMITATION OF THE PRINCIPLE OF THE AUTONOMY OF THE WILL

In general terms, Mosset Iturraspe points out that:

The role accorded to will in the making of legal transactions has undergone significant changes in the course of time [...] The declaration concerning the justice of what has been freely agreed—what has been consented to is fair said Fouillée—in a situation of full economic freedom, between individuals of

---

5. The same may be said of the inclusion in the copyright law of rules governing the activities of societies of authors, typifying and restricting illicit conduct, and laying down precautionary measures.

unequal negotiating power, is increasingly questionable [...] State interventionism in the life of the contract, when it is aimed at redressing the balance between the parties and their respective economic situations, replacing legal equality with equality in real terms, fulfils a beneficial, ethical role in dealing out justice.[6]

The principle that the will of the parties prevails—or contractual freedom—is prejudicial to the weaker party, usually the author, who has less economic leverage. Legal regulation of transfer by *inter vivos* transaction must help to achieve a balance between the positions of both parties to the contract, having regard to their legitimate interests. This does not mean that it fosters suppression of autonomy of the will because the number of atypical contracts, those that are still not recognized by law, is, inevitably, greater than the number of standard contracts, i.e. those specifically regulated by law. This is understandable because only a limited number of circumstances are covered by legislation whereas those which depend on private initiative are unspecified.[7] The parties are constantly creating new legal transactions or contractual terms, spurred on by the new methods of exploiting works afforded by technological developments. And in this respect contractual freedom is wide open. But laws must lay down minimum conditions, of a general and compulsory nature, which will allow works to be utilized without detracting from the essential political and legal aims involved in the domain.

B. NATURE OF THE REGULATIONS

The protective nature of regulations governing contracts leads to rejection of the unrestricted application of the principle of the autonomy of the will, for which reason the provisions regulating contractual relations should, as a general rule, be compulsory.

In this regard, the Spanish Intellectual Property Law (Article 55) stipulates that, except as provided in the Law itself, any bene-

---

6. Jorge Mosset Iturraspe, *Contratos*, Buenos Aires, Ed. Ediar, 1988, pp. 274–84.
7. See Juan Carlos Rezzónico, 'Contrato, concepto y tipo', Buenos Aires, *Rev. La Ley*, T. 1985-B, p. 935.

fits granted to authors and to their successors in title under this Title [Transfer of Rights] shall be unrenounceable.

C. FORM OF THE CONTRACT

Contracts must be evidenced in writing. Many national laws require the written form (e.g. Costa Rica, Articles 89 and 120; Ecuador, Art. 32(1); France, Article L. 131-2, previously Art. 31; Italy, Article 110; Spain, Article 45; Uruguay, Article 8; and so on).

However, non-compliance with this requirement should not automatically imply the invalidity of the contract, particularly as there are considerable areas of utilization of works in which the drawing up of a written contract is frequently evaded.

D. PURPOSE OF CONTRACTS

a. Authorization of use, or licences, excluding total or partial transfer of rights

As we have already said, this is the solution adopted by the German law in Article 31.

Although French legislation recognizes total or partial transfer of exploitation rights, it limits the prejudicial effects which this might have for the author by stipulating that such transfers shall necessarily confer to the author's benefit a proportionate participation in the receipts resulting from the sale or exploitation of the work (Article L. 131-4, previously Art. 35, first paragraph, second part)[8] and that the author may call for a revision of the price conditions of the contract when, as a result of loss under the contract or an insufficient advance estimate of the proceeds of a work, a disproportion between his contribution and his compensation is brought about (Article L. 131-5, previously Art. 37).

The Spanish law also recognizes '*the transfer of exclusive rights*' (*cesión en exclusiva*) (Articles 48 and 49)[9] but, as we have

---

8. Ibid., Venezuela, Article 55.
9. We have already mentioned the improper use of the term *cesión* in the Spanish law (see above, Chapter 3, Section 3.1.2, note 3).

already seen (Chapter 1, Section 1.3.2 above), Delgado Porras points out that this is not effected by conveyance or alienation (which is covered by the concept of transfer provided for in civil law) but by means of a 'constitutive succession'. Contrary to what occurs in the case of alienation which implies transfer of exploitation rights to the transferee, even in global terms, Delgado Porras points out that constitutive succession under the Spanish law means that the transferor is entitled, without forfeiting ownership of his right, to 'constitute' one or several new rights in favour of the transferee which act as restrictions on the right of the transferor. The author, then, despite this transfer, still retains ownership of the intellectual property, not only as regards his 'moral rights' but also in so far as he holds a monopoly over the utilization of his work, covering all possible means of its economic exploitation. This monopoly is limited by the rights of exploitation 'constituted' in favour of third parties by means of this inaptly named transfer (*cesión*).

The full transmission of exploitation rights in their entirety is not possible. All that can be done is to transfer 'exploitation rights' which are, as regards their origin, no more than prerogatives derived from that single right from which they have broken away, gaining relative independence as new personal rights to be attributed to third parties. But these rights (those covered by this supposed exclusive transfer) share in the 'real', claimable *erga omnes* nature of the basic right. The Spanish Intellectual Property Law establishes that transfer of exclusive rights grants the transferee the right, independent of that of the transferor, 'to institute proceedings for violations that affect the powers that have been assigned to him' (Article 48, first paragraph *in fine*). Hence the need to define the content and scope of the transfer (Article 43) and the requirement in respect of its written form (Article 45) [...].[10]

According to Delgado Porras, then, it must be concluded that the relevant regulations governing transfer in Spanish law belong to the system of concessions or licences and not transfer (*cesión*).[11]

In the practical use of works it may be seen that in those countries which have efficient societies of authors, such societies

---

10. See Delgado Porras, op. cit., Section 42, pp. 58–9.
11. Ibid., Section 49, p. 67.

play a decisive role in achieving a more equitable balance between the interests of authors and of users in the drawing up of contracts; even when the relevant laws allow transfer or alienation of the economic rights which are administered by such societies, only authorizations covering use or exclusive or non-exclusive licences are granted.

b. In accordance with the principles of restrictive interpretation of contracts for the exploitation of works and independence of economic rights, authorization of use is limited to the use or uses expressly mentioned in the contract and to the arrangements provided for therein

Provisions in this regard are to be found in the French law, Article L. 122-7, previously Art. 30, laying down this principle of the independence of exploitation rights and clarifying that transfer of performance rights does not imply transfer of reproduction rights, and vice versa, and that the scope of total transfer of any right is limited to the methods of exploitation provided for in the contract. In the Algerian law (Art. 37); the Brazilian law (Art. 35); in that of the Dominican Republic (Articles 62—principle of independence of rights—and 63—principle of restrictive interpretation of legal transactions) and in the Spanish law (Article 43(1)) which states that transfer by *inter vivos* transaction of the exploitation rights in a work is limited to the right or rights transferred and the means of exploitation expressly provided for, further stipulating, in Article 57, paragraph 2, that 'the licensing of rights for each of the various modes of exploitation shall be evidenced in independent documents'). In the opinion of Delgado Porras,[12] the aim of this regulation is not to multiply to infinity the number of documents corresponding to each and every mode of exploitation which the parties might have provided for; it is, rather, to try to prevent the regulations laid down by this law for the forms of exploitation included in particular contracts (publication, performance, audiovisual production)—whose structure reflects the

---

12. Ibid., Section 39, p. 54.

great pains taken to ensure their specific character—from being flouted by a transfer conceived in general terms.

Applying the same principle, some laws, such as the Argentine law (Article 38, second paragraph), specifically mention, notwithstanding the publication contract, that the copyright owner retains the right of transformation (adaptation, translation, arrangement, etc.).

c. As a consequence of the principles of restrictive interpretation of contracts for the exploitation of works and of independence of economic rights, global transfer of rights in future works is inadmissible

This is the case in France (Article L. 131-1, previously Art. 33: 'Total transfer of future works shall be void'). Invalidity does not involve management contracts signed with societies of authors whereby the latter are explicitly empowered to grant performance authorizations for future works, within the framework of their repertoire, since Article L. 132-18, previously Art. 43 specifically excludes the application of Article L. 131-1, previously Art. 33 under these circumstances. However, under certain conditions, the author is authorized to accord preferential rights to a publisher for the publication of his future works of a clearly specified kind and limited to five new works of each kind or the works which the author may produce within a term of five years (Article L. 132-4, previously Art. 34).

Spain (Article 43(3)) provides that 'Any global transfer of exploitation rights in all the works that the author may create in the future shall be null and void.' In some countries such transfers are recognized if the future works are specified individually, or on the basis of genre, but this provision is valid only for a maximum number of years from the date of the contract, even when the contract stipulates a longer period (e.g. five years in Brazil, Ecuador and Venezuela; ten years in Portugal).

d. Stipulations whereby the author undertakes not to create any work whatsoever in the future must also be considered null and void

Various laws contain a provision in this regard: Dominican Republic, Art. 66(b); Ecuador, Art. 39(c); Peru, Art. 3; Spain, Art. 43(4).

e. The contract cannot extend to methods of use or means of dissemination that do not exist or are unknown at the time the contract is drawn up

This is also a consequence of the principle of restrictive interpretation of contracts of exploitation. A distinction should be made here between the author's exploitation rights in the general sense (which comprise all means of exploitation possible both at the time the work was created and in the future) and the user's exploitation rights, which are limited to those means and methods provided for in the contract.

Remuneration is stipulated in the light of the existing exploitation context since the future is unforeseeable, particularly given the breakneck speed of technological development. If it is accepted, accordingly, that the contract covers means of exploitation which do not as yet exist, the bases of the agreement may alter substantially to the detriment of the author's interests.

Spanish legislation contains a provision in this regard (Article 43(5)). France recognizes the transfer of the right to exploit a work in a manner which is not foreseeable or is unforeseen, but such a transfer provision must be express and stipulate corresponding participation in the profits derived from such exploitation (Article L. 131-6, previously Art. 38).

f. The validity of the contract must also be conditional upon the requirement that it specifies the territorial extent and the period for which authorization is granted, as well as the intended use

France makes this stipulation (Article L. 131-3, first para., previously Art. 31, third para.), as does Spain (Article 43(1)), which adds that 'Failure to mention the time shall limit the transfer to five years and failure to mention the territorial scope shall limit it to the country in which the transfer is effected. Where the conditions governing the exploitation of the work are not mentioned specifically and categorically, the transfer shall be limited to such exploitation as is necessarily deduced from the contract itself and is essential to the fulfilment of the purpose of the contract' (Article 43(2)). Portugal stipulates much longer periods: ten years for photographic works and those of the applied arts and twenty-five years for all other works (Article 43(4)).

g. Although several works may be included in a single contract, it must be understood that there are as many contracts as independent works

h. The user shall be under the obligation to make all the necessary arrangements for the licensed exploitation to be effective, depending on the nature of the work and the practices prevailing in the professional, industrial or commercial field involved

This obligation is specifically stipulated in the Spanish law (Art. 48, second paragraph).

i. In accordance with the principle of independence between copyright and ownership of the material object, acquisition of the latter does not imply transfer of any of the rights recognized by law

Both the French and the Spanish laws (Article L. 111-3, previously Art. 29 and Article 56 respectively) contain provisions to this effect, as does legislation in Brazil, Art. 38; Ecuador, Art. 3; Peru, Art. 5; Portugal, Art. 10(1); and Venezuela, Art. 1(2), among others.

j. The user must be empowered to institute proceedings himself against those infringing the exclusive rights received from the author

The Spanish law recognizes this competency of the transferee holding exclusive rights, independently of that of the transferor (Article 48, first paragraph *in fine*).

k. 'Intuitu personae' nature of contracts

With regard to the author, contracts are always '*intuitu personae*' since, at the time of making a contract, the user takes into account the personality of the author. For the author, use of his work reveals it to the public and brings his prestige into play, involving all his moral rights in the work. However, in general terms, legislation does not usually embody the *intuitu personae* nature of contracts with regard to the user, so as not to weaken the contract too much. It is recognized nevertheless that the publisher may not transfer the publishing contract without first having obtained the authorization of the author (e.g. France, Article L. 132-16, previously Art. 62; Italy, Article 132 and Spain, Article 68.1 (d)). The Spanish provisions contain general rules in this regard, requiring the transferee holding exclusive rights to obtain the express consent of the transferor before proceeding to transfer his rights to a third party (Article 49, first paragraph), the right of the nonexclusive transferee being untransferable (Article 50(1) *in fine*).

On the other hand, isolated provisions can usually be found concerning cases of *change of ownership* of the company and the *collective procedure for settlement of liabilities* (*with meetings of the creditors*) or *bankruptcy of the user*. The principle is that cancellation of the contract need not necessarily follow since, with regard to the user, the contract may, as Delgado Porras[13] points out, be *intuitu firmae*, which points up the fact that in many instances the author's confidence is not based on the personal situation of the other contracting party but on that of his company. For this reason, in the event that exploitation should continue or that the business should be sold, the contract continues to be valid (Spain, Article 49, third paragraph, stipulates that the consent of the transferor shall not be necessary where transfer occurs as a result of the liquidation or a change of ownership of the corporate transferee).

However, French legislation recognizes that in the case of the alienation of the business, if it is of such a nature that the material or moral interests of the author will be seriously compromised, he shall be authorized to obtain reparation even by means of cancellation of the contract (Article L. 136-16, previously Art. 62, second para.).

Italian legislation (Article 132) stipulates that the publisher shall not transfer the rights he has acquired to other persons without the consent of the author unless there is an agreement to the contrary or a change of ownership of the business. However, in the latter event, the publisher may not transfer his rights if such transfer would be prejudicial to the reputation of the author or the dissemination of the work.

---

13. Ibid., Section 53, p. 71.

E. Respect for moral rights

The obligation to respect the author's moral rights is implicit in all contracts. Even if the contract contains no specific provisions in this regard, in the case of public communication, the user must indicate, in all copies of the work and in advertisements and presentations, the name of its author, the person who has translated or adapted it, and all other authors whose rights are involved, in the manner which is usually observed in similar instances of exploitation.

The manner in which the name of the author is displayed, the place, size of type, etc. are usually the subject of special discussions which are later reflected in the contract because, although moral rights cannot be assessed in economic terms, this does not mean that they do not have important financial repercussions such as, in the case of the displaying of the author's identity, the 'name' that he may make for himself.

The same may be said of the obligation of the user to respect the integrity of the text and to use it in a way appropriate to the type of work involved.

F. General guarantee obligation

The author is answerable to the user for the authorship and originality of the work and he must guarantee the user the peaceful exercise of the rights transferred. He shall be obliged to ensure respect for these rights and to defend them against third parties (with regard to publishing contracts: Costa Rica, Article 25; France, Article L. 132-8, previously Art. 54; Spain, Article 65(2)).

G. Author's remuneration

a. Remuneration proportionate to the revenue produced as a result of exploitation of the work

In principle, this is the fairest form of remuneration and it is considered as such in the *Charter of the Author's Right*[14] where, in

---

14. Idem, note 2.

Chapter III, Section 9, paragraph 3, the following is stated:

> The author must be associated with the fortune of his work, and the general principle of his participation in its economic success must be asserted in all and any relations between himself on the one hand, industry and the users on the other. Wherever possible, he should receive a percentage of the gross revenue accruing from the exploitation and utilization of his work, whatever the form and the manner of expression and reproduction of the work.

Remuneration as a percentage of the economic benefits is effective if the percentage is calculated on the basis of the gross revenue, as is indicated in the passage quoted above. When it is agreed that the percentage will be applied on the basis of net revenue, it is advisable to set out, in the contract itself, a detailed list of the costs which may be deducted from the gross revenue to arrive at the net figure and the maximum amount which will be accepted under this heading.

This form of remuneration is usual in some fields of use, such as the performance of dramatic works and the public performance of musical works (percentage of box-office receipts); the publication of books—except scientific and technical works, illustrations, dictionaries and encyclopedias, anthologies, reproductions of artistic works, translations, limited de luxe editions and low-cost popular editions—(percentage of the sales price); mechanical reproduction of musical works (percentage of the sales price).

This form of remuneration requires the author to have some means of verifying the declarations made by the user.

Some laws, such as the French (Article L. 131-4, previously Art. 35), the Venezuelan (Article 55) and the Spanish (Article 46), stipulate remuneration in proportion to the receipts from exploitation of the work as a general principle of a compulsory nature. However, they include a list of exceptions where lump sum remuneration is admissible.

b. Lump sum remuneration

The system of lump sum remuneration is designed as a countermeasure in order to offset the considerable risk that the author may find a disproportion between the remuneration agreed in the contract and the economic success achieved through utilization of the work. Measures to redress the balance therefore have to be provided for.

Laws which embody the principle of remuneration in proportion to the revenue resulting from exploitation of the work and provide for lump sum remuneration as an exception—although fairly widespread—reflect this need. We have already mentioned French legislation where Article L. 131-5, previously Art. 37 provides that when exploitation rights have been transferred for a lump sum and the author suffers a loss of more than seven-twelfths of the contractual amount as a result of undue hardship under the contract or an insufficient advance estimate of the proceeds of the work, the author may demand a revision of the price conditions of the contract.

The Spanish law also contains a provision in this regard (Article 47):

> Where in the case of a transfer for a lump sum the remuneration of the author is manifestly out of proportion to the profits obtained by the licensee, the former may apply for a review of the contract and, in the absence of agreement, may apply to the court for the award of equitable remuneration in the light of the circumstances of the case. That faculty may be exercised within the ten years following the transfer.

German law permits the parties freely to agree upon the form of remuneration but provides for the possibility of rectification of any contractual conditions which prove to be unfair, making the author's *right of participation* compulsory, in the following terms: (Article 36):

> (1) If the author has granted a licence to another party on conditions the effect of which is to cause the agreed consideration to be grossly disproportionate to the income from the use of the work, having regard to the whole of the relationship between the author and the other party, the latter shall, when so asked by the author, be required to assent to a variation of the agreement such as will secure for the author an equitable share of the income having regard to the circumstances. (2) Such claim shall be barred two years from the time when the author receives knowledge of the circumstances which give rise to the claim, and the author may not claim to have received such knowledge after more than ten years.

c. Mixed system

In some forms of exploitation it is common for remuneration to be stipulated partly as a lump sum and partly as a percentage of the receipts resulting from exploitation of the work (e.g. cinematographic works).

6.1.2. Transfer *mortis causa*

Unlike transfer of copyright by *inter vivos* transaction, which is generally regulated by copyright legislation, transmission *mortis causa* is governed by ordinary law,[15] except in the case of moral rights.

As we have already pointed out (see above Chapter 4, Section 4.1, A, and Chapter 5, Section 5.2.1), after the death of the author the *positive* prerogatives of his moral right, exceptions apart, are not transmitted. The successors in title—or the executor of the will—may exercise only the *negative* prerogatives (the right to claim recognition of the intellectual paternity of the deceased and respect for the integrity of his work) and the right of disclosure of posthumous works, but not with the same discretionary powers which enabled the author to do so (France, Articles L. 121-2 and L. 121-3, previously Art. 19 and 20; Spain, Articles 15(2) and 40).

Some laws permit transmission *mortis causa* of the *negative* prerogatives of the moral right (e.g. Brazil, Art. 25(1); France, Art. L. 121-1.4 and 121-1.5, previously Art. 6.4 and 6.5, in favour

---

15. In some laws we find specific complementary provisions, e.g. Italy, Article 115, where it is provided that, after the death of the author, the rights of utilization of the work, if not otherwise disposed of by the author himself, shall remain undivided between the heirs for a period of three years from the date of death, unless the judicial authority, at the instance of one or more of the coheirs, agrees, for serious reasons, that division shall be effected without delay; Germany, Article 28, 2: 'The author may by testamentary disposition assign the exercise of copyright to an executor. Article 2210 of the Civil Code shall not apply.'; France, Article L. 123-6, previously Art. 24: '... the surviving spouse ... shall benefit from the usufruct of the exploitation right of which the author has not disposed, under any matrimonial regime, and independent of the rights of usufruct held by virtue of Article 767 of the Civil Code ...'.

of the heirs and providing that exercise of this right may be conferred on a third party by testamentary provisions).

Other laws grant only entitlement—in respect of the heirs and other persons and institutions specified in the provision—to exercise these personal rights of the author (e.g. Belgium, Art. 7; Costa Rica, Article 15; Italy, Article 23; Portugal, Art. 57(1); Spain, Article 15(1). Delgado Porras maintains in this respect (*op. cit.*, p. 29) that '*Following the author's death*, we should not speak of a personal right but of situations of power created in favour of certain persons (under both private and public law), conferring on them the exercise (entitlement) of the prerogatives of asserting the paternity of the work and of ensuring respect for it, having regard to the general interest in preserving the identity of the national literary and artistic heritage.'

6.2. Publishing contracts: literary, musical and artistic works

In the wide sense, *publishing rights* are taken to mean the right of the author to authorize the material reproduction of his work by means of the manufacture in quantity of copies of the work. It is used as an equivalent of *reproduction rights* and consequently covers all methods of fixing a work (publication by printing, modelling, photography or any other process of the graphic or plastic arts, by electronic means, sound recording or audiovisual fixation). It also covers the tangible result of the act of reproduction (books and printed matter in general, photographs, three-dimensional copies, chips, discs, magnetic tapes, films, etc.).

Many laws define publishing contracts as reproduction contracts.[16] On the other hand, in Italian law (Article 118) a pub-

---

16. Argentina (Article 37): 'whatever the form or system of reproduction or publication'; France (Article L. 132-1, previously Art. 48) 'the right to manufacture or have manufactured in quantity copies of the work'; Venezuela (Article 71) 'the right to produce, or cause to be produced, a number of copies of the work'; Mexico (Chapter III: 'on the contract to publish or reproduce'); Brazil (Article 57) 'to reproduce by a mechanical process [...] the literary, artistic or scientific work'; Spain (Article 58) 'the right to reproduce his work'.

lishing contract refers to 'the right of publication ... by way of printing' ('*il diritto di pubblicare ... per le stampe*'). However, in the laws which adopt the broad concept of publication (as equivalent to reproduction), attention is usually drawn to the fact that the regulation was drawn up bearing in mind graphic publication.[17.]

In this discussion of publishing contracts, we shall refer to publishing rights in the restricted sense, i.e. graphic publication, consisting of the reproduction and multiplication in quantity of copies of a work whatever technical process is employed (typesetting, linotype, photocopying, offset, etc.) and including the tangible result of that publication (books, pamphlets, musical scores, calendars, posters, postcards, etc.).[18]

Contracts covering reproduction by means of sound recordings (Contracts for mechanical reproduction rights—see below, Section 6.4) and by audio-visual means (Contracts for the production of audiovisual works—see below, Section 6.6) will be discussed separately.

A. Concept

A publishing contract is a contract whereby the author of a literary, musical or artistic work—or his successors in title—authorizes a natural person or a legal entity (the publisher) to reproduce or cause to have reproduced in graphic form, in a uniform and direct manner, a given number of copies, to advertise, distribute and sell

---

17. Mexico (Article 60): 'The contract for the reproduction of any class of intellectual or artistic work, for which means other than printing are employed, shall be regulated in accordance with the provisions of this Chapter [on contracts to publish or reproduce] in so far as such provisions do not conflict with the nature of the particular means of reproduction'.; Costa Rica (Article 27): '[...] before the work goes to press ...'; (Article 29): 'The publisher shall decide on ... the typographical characteristics ...' and (Article 31): 'On expiry of five years following the date stated on the colophon.'

18. For example, Costa Rica, Article 27: '[...] before the work goes to press ...' Article 29: 'The publisher shall determine [...] its *typographical characteristics* ...'; Article 31: 'On expiry of five years following the date stated on the *colophon*.'

them to the public for his own account and risk, without legal subordination, and to pay the other party a remuneration proportionate to the receipts derived from the sale of the copies, or a lump sum.

B. LEGAL NATURE

The publishing contract is an autonomous contract, characteristic of copyright, which is usually regulated as such in national legislation on the subject. It shows points of similarity with the obligations typical of some contracts in civil law, such as the obligation of result inherent in *contracts for the hire of labour and services*, with the reciprocal obligations which arise in a *partnership agreement*, between the company and its partners, and also with *sales contracts* and *contracts of assignment*, if the hypothesis of the application of a warranty against dispossession is borne in mind (in the event that copyright should belong to another person because that person is the real author or the legitimate successor in title, or in the event that the author should authorize the publisher to publish a work which has already been contracted out to another publisher). But publishing contracts have their own particular features which set them apart from all these.

    a. It is not a contract for the *hire of labour or services*. 1. Although the publisher undertakes to produce a material result at his own risk—the obligation being to reproduce the work in a given number of copies and to advertise, distribute and sell them to the public—the author does not assume the role of the hirer of services since he does not pay the publisher a price.

    2. When the author pays the costs of publication, then this does constitute a contract to perform work, *but it is not a publishing contract*, although the parties may use this terminology, because *an essential element is missing*: the fact that the production, advertising, distribution and sale of the copies is to be carried out by the publisher *for his own account and risk*.[19]

---

19. France, Article L. 132-2, previously Art. 49: 'A contract for publication at the author's expense shall not be deemed a publishing contract in the sense of Article L. 132-1.

Such contracts are very common—and not only in developing countries. Many famous authors published their early works at their own expense. A large part of current poetry is also published by this contractual method since it is a well-known fact that 'poetry does not sell'. It is proper, then, that the law should include a regulation governing the basic aspects of contracts whereby the owner of copyright pays the publisher a sum to produce a given number of copies of a work and to ensure its reproduction, distribution and sale, whether or not the phrase 'author's edition' or some similar phrase appears in them. Examples of such aspects include:
- specified periods in which the publisher must fulfil the various obligations assigned to him, including the formalities of registration in countries where these exist and the inclusion of the symbol © as set out in Article III of the Universal Copyright Convention (see below, obligations of the publisher) and the return to the author of unsold copies;
- the schedule covering settlement by the publisher for the copies sold and the minimum percentage to be paid to the author based on the retail sales price of the copies—estimated at 40 per cent since the author paid for the edition;
- prohibition in respect of options giving the publisher the possibility of printing a greater number of copies than that agreed, or of printing new editions. When the author pays for the edition, the printed copies belong to him.

b. It is not a *partnership* even if the author receives a percentage of the revenue from the sale of the published copies. In this case the factor in common with a partnership agreement would reside in the distribution of the gross profits—since the

---

Such a contract is one whereby the author or his successors are to remit to the editor a sum agreed upon, on condition that the latter shall manufacture copies of the work in quantity, in the form and according to the modes of expression specified in the contract, and shall assure its publication and dissemination.

Such a contract shall constitute a contract for the making of a work, governed by custom, usage and the provisions of Articles 1787 *et seq.* of the Civil Code.'

percentage is calculated on the basis of gross income—but the element which is essential to a partnership relationship is missing: participation in losses. The whole cost of printing, advertising and distributing the work must be borne by the publisher since he undertakes to produce and sell the copies which constitute the edition *for his own account and risk*. This is the factor which distinguishes publishing contracts.

Since the losses which the publishing contract may cause the publisher must be borne exclusively by him, one cannot speak of a partnership agreement between the author and the publisher. On the other hand, a fortuitous association in the publishing contract does exist. In French legislation this is known as *de compte à demi*, or a 'shares' contract, but in this case there is no publishing contract.[20]

c. It is not a *contract of sale* for this involves the obligation to transfer ownership or co-ownership of a *thing* for a certain monetary price. Publishing contracts do not deal with *things*—material objects—but with an intellectual creation—intangible property—and furthermore, as we have already seen, there is no transfer of ownership, as full and perfect transfer of the intellectual right in the work never occurs.

d. It is not a *transfer*, even when rights and not material things are involved and although in contracts and laws this term is used, because such assignment also demands a fixed monetary price and the transfer of full ownership of the right conveyed. In

---

20. France, Article L. 132-3, previously Art. 50: 'A "shares" contract (*contrat dit: de compte à demi*) shall not constitute a publishing contract in the sense of Article 132-1.

Such a contract is one whereby the author or his successors commission a publisher to manufacture, at his expense and in quantity, copies of a work in the form and according to the modes of expression specified in the contract, and to assure their publication and dissemination dependent on an agreement reciprocally contracted to share the benefits and losses of exploitation in the proportion provided.

Such a contract shall constitute a partnership (*association en participation*) [...]. It shall be governed, subject to the provisions set out in Articles 1871 *et seq* of the Civil Code, by custom and usage.'

the majority of publishing contracts remuneration is agreed as a percentage of sales and no transfer of the author's economic rights occurs. Otherwise the author would never be able to make a contract for a new edition or the adaptation of the work to other genres (Article 38 of the Argentine law illustrates this point in providing that 'The owner shall retain his copyright unless he renounces it in the publication contract. He may translate, transform, recast, etc. his work and defend it against any infringement of his copyright, even against the publisher himself'.).

C. CHARACTERISTICS

a. It is *consensual* and not real, since the obligation to deliver the work to the publisher for printing, publicity, distribution and sale bears no relation to the stage of formalization of the contract but to that of performance.

It is not formal *ad solemnitatem* but only *ad probationem* since it is subject to a special regime of written proof and publicity by virtue of being registered with the administrative authority.

b. It is *bilateral or synallagmatic* since both parties assume reciprocal obligations: the author, the obligation to deliver the work to the publisher and the latter the obligation to print, publicize, distribute and sell it and to pay remuneration to the author.

c. It is *onerous* since otherwise it would not constitute a publishing contract.

The publisher must make the edition for his own account and risk, without legal subordination. Publication at the author's expense or 'shares' contracts do not constitute publishing contracts but contracts to do work in the first instance and on *association en participation* in the second case, as we have seen.

No publishing contract exists if the author refuses to accept remuneration.

d. It is *commutative* because the services to be provided by each party are fixed, since the author undertakes to deliver the work to the publisher and the publisher undertakes to print, publicize, distribute and sell it and to pay remuneration.

e. It is partially *intuitu personae* for the reasons set out above in the discussion of the purpose of contracts in general.

f. It is *exclusive* since, as de Sanctis shows, exclusivity appears as a natural element characteristic of graphic publishing contracts, while non-exclusive licences constitute an accidental characteristic which profoundly changes the economy of publishing contracts.[21]

g. It is *limited* to the exploitation rights that the author specifically authorizes the publisher to exercise within a given geographical area, during a given period and for the number of editions agreed upon.

6.2.1. Contracts for the publication of literary works

6.2.1.1. Rights and obligations of the parties

A. THE AUTHOR'S RIGHTS

a. Moral rights

The obligation to respect the moral rights of the author, as a basic right, is implicit in all contracts, although the parties may not have made any stipulations in this regard.[22]

1. *Right to authorship of the work*

The publisher is obliged to state, on every copy of the edition, the name of the author in the form chosen by the latter. This includes pseudonyms and anonymous attributions since, as we have already pointed out (see above, Chapter 4, Section 4.2.2), the prerogative of having the work identified with its author is considered a right and not an obligation on the author's part, which implies that the creator enjoys the right to decide whether he wishes such an as-

---

21. Valerio de Sanctis, *Contratto di edizione. Contratti di reppresentazione e di esecuzione*, Milan, Guiffré, 1965, section 22, p. 62.

22. Brazil (Articles 21 and 25–28); Costa Rica (Articles 13–15); France (Articles L. 121-1 and 121-4, previously Art. 6 and 32); Mexico (Article 2(I) and (II) and Articles 3 and 5); Peru (Articles 2 and 32–34); Spain (Articles 2 and 14–16); etc.

sociation to be made and in what way (using his name, a pseudonym, initials, etc.) or whether he prefers to remain anonymous.[23]

The name of the author or his pseudonym must be displayed on the cover, title page or half-title and on the spine of every copy,[24] in the usual manner and using type large enough to stand out. The publisher must also include it in all publicity or announcements concerning the work.

When the author has opted to remain anonymous, the publisher must avoid any reference, whether direct or indirect, to the author's identity.

2. *Right to respect and to the integrity of the work*

The publisher may not publish the work with any additions, deletions or other alterations of any kind, without the written consent of the author.[25] The author has the right to ensure that his thinking is not altered or misrepresented and the community is entitled to receive works of creative intellectual activity in their authentic form. Any person who publishes a derivative work (resulting from the transformation of an existing work), such as an adaptation, translation, alteration and amplification, abridged version or summary and compendium, must mention the fact that it is a transformation and display the name of the author of the original work.[26]

Before the work goes to press and during the period of correction of the proofs of the print-run of the first edition and of successive reprints, the author has the right to alter the work by making corrections, alterations, additions or any improvements which he may deem appropriate, as long as they do not alter the nature or purpose of the work or cause the cost of the edition to

---

23. Mexico, Article 56.
24. Spain, Article 64(1).
25. Argentina (Articles 51 and 52); Mexico (Article 43); Spain (Article 64(1)).
26. Mexico, Article 57, which adds that the publisher must mention the purpose of the transformation; Article 55 provides that 'In every translation, and immediately below the title of the work, the title in its original language shall be reproduced.'

rise substantially.²⁷ As we have already said, it is a logical consequence of the right to create: before the production of a new edition for a reprint, the author may feel the need to correct or clarify concepts, to improve the style, to include or eliminate material with the aim of perfecting his work, and a number of laws explicitly recognize this right although to varying degrees²⁸ (we refer back here to the discussion *in extenso* in Chapter 4, Section 4.2.3 on the right to alter a work).

3. *Respect for the work*
Respect for the work is, moreover, guaranteed by other rights enjoyed by the author, e.g.:
- the right to approve illustrations of the text;
- the right to revise and correct the proofs²⁹ and to demand modification of the print, or matrices, etc.;
- the right to consider that any alterations made by him have been approved if the publisher does not reject them within a reasonable period (normally estimated at thirty days);
- the right to approve the final presentation of the edition.

b. *Economic rights*

In accordance with the principle of the independence of economic rights and that of restrictive interpretation of contracts for the exploitation of works, authorization to use a work is limited to the uses explicitly mentioned in the contract and the methods provided for therein.³⁰

The author has the right:
- to have the contract formalized in writing. Even although there are still publishers who publish without a contract, on the basis

---

27. Mexico, Article 44; Colombia, Article 111; Dominican Republic, Article 78.
28. Switzerland (Code of Obligations, Article 385); Colombia (Article 111); Dominican Republic (Article 78); etc.
29. Spain (Article 65(3)) considers this an obligation of the author, except when there is an agreement to the contrary.
30. Colombia, Articles 130 and 131; Costa Rica, Article 39; Dominican Republic, Articles 62 and 63.

of mutual trust, a publishing contract should be formalized in writing and this is a requirement of many laws;[31]
- to have the edition—or each edition which is agreed upon—made and marketed only within the geographical area[32] and in the language or languages specified in the contract;
- to have the number of authorized copies produced;[33]
- to have the publisher fulfil each of the activities indicated within a specified period;[34]

---

31. Costa Rica, Article 89; France, Article L. 131-3, fourth para. previously Art. 31, fifth para.; Italy, Article 110; Mexico, Article 45; Spain, Article 45; Uruguay, Article 8, etc.

32. France, Art. L. 131-3, first para., previously Art. 31, third para.; Spain, Article 60(2).

33. Argentina, Article 40; Mexico, Article 45(I). In the event of lack of provision in the contract, Argentine legislation stipulates that the uses and customs of the place of the contract shall apply; in similar circumstances, Brazil considers that each edition shall consist of 2,000 copies (Article 61).

34. Mexico, Article 46: 'When no term is specified in the publication contract for the completion of the publication and the putting on sale of copies, it shall be understood that this term is one year. When this period has elapsed without the publisher having produced the edition, the author may choose between requiring fulfilment of the contract or termination of it, by means of notice in writing to the publisher, but in either event he shall be entitled to compensation in respect of loss or damage sustained which, in any case, shall not be less than any sums the author may have received by virtue of the contract.'

Spain, Article 60(6) stipulates that the time limit for the putting into circulation of the copies constituting the sole or first edition may not exceed two years from the time when the author delivers the work to the publisher in a form suitable for the reproduction thereof to be effected, and Article 63 clarifies that this limitation shall not apply to editions of anthologies of the works of others, dictionaries, encyclopedias and equivalent compilations, prologues, epilogues, presentations, introductions, annotations, commentaries and illustrations relating to the works of others.

Colombia (Article 109, second paragraph, second part) stipulates that, if no period is specified the edition shall be started within two months following the handling over of the originals, in the case of the first edition authorized, or within two months following the date on which the previous edition went out of print, where the contract authorizes more than one edition.

Formulas such as the Mexican or Spanish provisions are preferable, as it is in the author's interests that copies should be put on sale or, in general terms, in circulation, which is not ensured by merely starting the process of publication.

- to agree to the manner of distribution of the copies and the number of copies to be reserved for the author, for reviews and promotional purposes;[35]
- to receive remuneration; it has already been pointed out that one of the characteristics of publishing contracts is their onerous nature;[36]
- to verify print-runs[37] when the remuneration agreed upon is proportionate to the receipts from the sale of the copies. Verification of print-runs may be carried out by numbering all the copies of each edition,[38] by stamping the copies[39] or by any other effective method and includes the author's right to obtain supplementary information regarding the print-run;
- to verify, either personally or through third parties, and in all its aspects, the reliability of the settlement made when remuneration has been agreed as a percentage of sales. The author also has the right to check the number of copies that the publisher has in stock, as termination of the contract or the obligation of the publisher to reprint the work and the possibility of the author being free to contract a new edition are frequently related to the exhaustion of stock;[40]
- to obtain from the publisher, free of charge, a reasonable number of copies of the work;[41] should the author wish for more copies,[42] or if it is a joint work, these should be provided at the wholesale price.

---

35. Spain, Article 60(4).
36. Argentina, Article 40; Spain, Article 60(5); etc.
37. In Spain, Royal Decree 396/1988, dated 25 April, regulated the right to verify print-runs laid down in Article 72 of the Law on Intellectual Property.
38. Mexico, Article 45(I), *in fine*; Brazil, Article 64.
39. This is the method used in Italy, by means of an embossed stamp with which the Society of Authors and Publishers (SIAE) marks the sections which the publishers send it before binding.
40. Argentina, Article 44; Mexico, Article 51.
41. Colombia, Article 124(2); Dominican Republic, Article 85(2).
42. Costa Rica, Article 32.

B. Obligations of the author

- to deliver the work to the publisher within the agreed time-limit and in a form suitable for reproduction;[43]
- to correct the proofs of the print-run, unless agreed otherwise;[44]
- general guarantee obligation (see above, Section 6.1.1, F).

C. Rights of the publisher

- to fix the sales price of the copies which constitute the edition. If there is no agreement regarding the sales price of the copies, the publisher has the right to fix it; he may not, however, exercise this right in such an abusive manner that disparity between the quality of the edition and the price would make sales difficult;[45]
- to have a number of copies at his disposal for free distribution with a view to publicizing and promoting the work;
- to remainder an edition after a reasonable time has elapsed from the initial putting on sale of the copies,[46] after formally notifying the author who, within a reasonable period, shall have priority in acquiring them;
- to have the right of ownership of the copies of the work which constitute the edition;
- on expiration of the contract, unless otherwise provided, the publisher may dispose of any copies which he may still have in his possession and the author will have priority in acquiring them (Spain, Article 70, fixes this period at three years after expiry of the contract).

---

43. Colombia, Articles 107(c), 113 and 114; Dominican Republic, Articles 69(d) and 70; Spain, Articles 60(7) and 65(1).
44. Spain, Article 65(3).
45. Brazil, Article 63; Colombia, Article 118; Dominican Republic, Article 74; Mexico, Article 49.
46. Spain (Article 67) fixes this period at two years. Colombia (Article 135) stipulates five years, if during that period no more than 30 per cent of the copies have been sold; the Dominican Republic (Article 90) reduces the period to three years.

D. OBLIGATIONS OF THE PUBLISHER

Besides respecting the right to intellectual paternity of the author, translator, adapter, etc., the publisher must indicate his own name and address, those of the printer and the date on which printing was completed.[47] He must, furthermore:
- set out the text in accordance with the requirements arising from the content and the type of work, ensuring that the quality of the printing, the materials used and the style and size of type are appropriate to the kind of work in question and the edition provided for in the contract;[48]
- refrain from transmitting the manuscript to persons outside the publishing house without the express authorization of the author;
- submit proofs of the print-run to the author, unless otherwise agreed;[49]
- distribute the copies of the work within the period and under the conditions specified;[50]
- ensure that the work is exploited on an uninterrupted basis and distributed commercially in accordance with the usual practices in the professional publishing sector;[51]
- pay the author the remuneration stipulated and, when the latter is proportionate to receipts resulting from sales, to make appropriate settlement on the basis of accounts he will render to the author. In those countries where the currency is stable, it is considered that settlement should be made every six months[52]

---

47. Colombia (Article 125, E); Dominican Republic (Article 93(f) and (g)).
48. Mexico, Article 48, provides that 'When the contract does not stipulate the quality of the edition, the obligations of the publisher will be met by producing editions of average quality'.
49. Spain, Article 64(2).
50. Spain, Article 64(3).
51. Colombia (Article 124(1)); Costa Rica (Article 33); Dominican Republic (Article 85(1)); Spain, (Article 64(4)).
52. Colombia, Article 110, second part.

and, at the very least, once a year.[53] When such conditions of stability do not exist, settlement must be made more frequently;
- provide the author with an annual declaration containing all the data concerning the manufacture, distribution and stock of copies; should the author so request, the publisher shall furnish him with the relevant supporting documentation;[54]
- use the material received from the author only in the authorized edition and return the original (or manuscript) of the work to the author together with all other items received from him (photographs, illustrations, etc.), once the typesetting and printing operations have been completed;[55]
- compliance with formalities: the publisher must comply with the formalities (notice, legal deposit and registration in those countries where this still exists) stipulated by the law of the place where the work is published (not the law of the place where the work is printed if that is different) and display on all copies of the edition the formula laid down in Article III.1 of the Universal Convention (the symbol © accompanied by the name of the copyright proprietor and the year of first publication) placed in such manner and location as to give reasonable notice of claim of copyright.[56]

E. RESPONSIBILITIES OF THE PUBLISHER

If, after the work is printed, it is totally or partially destroyed while in the hands of the publisher, the latter must pay the author the agreed remuneration if this is a lump sum; if remuneration proportionate to the receipts resulting from sale of the copies had been agreed, the publisher must pay the author the anticipated amount for the sale of all the copies of the edition, when loss or destruction is, in whole or in part, due to the fault of or to negligence on the part of the publisher.[57]

---

53. Spain, Article 64(5).
54. Colombia (Article 124(3)); Spain (Article 64(5)).
55. Spain, Article 64(6).
56. Colombia (Article 125); Dominican Republic (Article 93(e)).
57. Colombia (Article 116); Dominican Republic (Article 83).

6.2.1.2. Termination of a publishing contract

A. NORMAL CAUSES

- On expiration of the agreed period;[58]
- when the edition is out of print.[59] It is considered to be out of print—unless an express agreement is made in this regard—when the publisher is unable to present a minimum number of copies in his stockroom, usually estimated at between 5 per cent and 10 per cent of the print-run;
- when the reprinting of the work has been agreed upon and this has not taken place within the period specified or, in the event that no provision was made in this regard and once the print-run is exhausted, reprinting has not been carried out within a reasonable period after the author has asked him to do so.

B. EXCEPTIONAL CAUSES

Termination of the contract in the event that one of the parties has not complied with his obligations, and, in particular:
- in the event of the liquidation or change of ownership of the publishing house, as long as reproduction of the work has not begun;[60]
- when remuneration has been agreed upon exclusively as a lump sum and a reasonable period has transpired since the making of the contract (Spain, Article 69(3) fixes this period at ten years);
- in all cases, once a reasonable period has transpired since the author has placed the publisher in a position to carry out reproduction of the work (Spain, Article 69(4) fixes this period at 15 years);
- when, due to the termination of the publisher's business or as a result of bankruptcy proceedings, exploitation of the work is suspended.

---

58. Spain, Article 69(1).
59. Argentina (Article 44); Mexico (Article 51); Spain (Article 69(2)).
60. Colombia (Article 134); Dominican Republic (Article 89).

C. OTHER GENERAL CAUSES FOR THE TERMINATION OF CONTRACTS

Once the contract has been terminated and unless otherwise agreed, the publisher may dispose of the copies which he may still have in his possession and the author will have priority in acquiring them (Spain, Article 70, sets this period at three years following expiration of the contract). It may be considered that cancellation of the contract because the publisher has not fulfilled his obligations is a different case.

6.2.2. Contracts for the publication of musical works[61]

Contracts for the graphic publication of musical works have specific features which clearly distinguish them from contracts for the publication of literary works. Rather than being the main object of such contracts, graphic publication of musical scores constitutes the beginning of a much wider and more complex contractual relationship between author and publisher.

Musical works are fundamentally designed to be performed. Therefore, publication in graphic form has never been their typical form of expression but the starting point so that the works might be performed by singers and instrumental musicians. However, the importance of the graphic publication of musical scores was originally comparable—to a certain degree—to that of the publication of literary works.

During the last century and part of the present century—the period in which the majority of laws concerning copyright were enacted and 'standard clauses' for contracts for the publication of musical works were drawn up—such works were played live before an audience and subsequently before the microphones of a broadcasting station.

But, over the last few decades, live public performance has ceased to be the main form of communicating musical works to

---

61. Whether or not these are accompanied by words.

the public. Live performance has fallen away considerably with the evolution of techniques in respect of the recording and dissemination of musical works and of broadcasting—discs, cassettes, films, video cassettes, radio and television emissions and cable broadcasts, etc.

The publication of scores as graphic editions has lost ground accordingly, although it still fulfils an important role in the dissemination of works among performers and in facilitating the transcription of works for other instruments and new orchestrations for the purposes of public performance and phonographic recording, and plays a considerable part in the domains of education and musical training.

The way in which musical works are initially disseminated has also changed. In general, dissemination begins with a recording and the work is later published as a graphic edition when it has achieved a degree of success which would suggest that other musicians will want to perform or record it. For these reasons, nowadays the majority of publishing houses are subsidiaries of phonographic recording companies.

The presence everywhere of music nowadays was made possible by the development of techniques for the recording and mechanical reproduction of sounds on phonograms, magnetic tapes, compact discs, etc., whose sale and different forms of performance, public use and reproduction for public and private uses (remuneration for private copying) generate the vast sums of money which keep the world market in musical works alive.

However, as Ulrich Uchtenhagen points out, music publishers have tried to maintain the same position which publishers in general—both publishers of literary and musical works—enjoyed in the period when they acted as the author's impresario, when it was they who managed the author's works and opened the doors to the public for him. Music publishers have continued to control all the forms of use of the works published by them and, for some time now, they only conclude contracts with authors who grant them, not only the right to produce, publicize, distribute and sell copies of the printed works, but *also the rights in public performance and broadcasting, dissemination by cable network and the public reception of broadcasts*; this is done through clauses ensuring them these '*additional rights*', which nowadays constitute the main object of contracts for the publication of musical works.[62]

By means of these additional rights[63] the publisher of musical works ensures for himself a proportionate participation in the receipts due to the author as a result of the exploitation of the work throughout the world (public performance 'live' and by means of phonographic recordings, phono-mechanical rights which are derived from the sale to the public of discs and tapes, inclusion in promotional material, in audiovisual works, etc.).[64] The procedures involved in the business of dissemination of musical works and the promotional efforts carried out by the publisher are invoked as an explanation for this participation.

Indeed, although the work is not always launched on the market by means of a graphic publication and nowadays it is customary for dissemination to begin by means of recordings on discs and cassettes, the promotional task carried out by the publisher is crucial to the success of the work and constitutes the justification for his share in the receipts from exploitation of the work in all the uses to which it may be put.

This task of dissemination which turns the publisher into the author's promoter or impresario is carried out by various means: distributing the copies which constitute the graphic edition of the work (the score) among well-known performers and orchestral conductors inviting them to perform the works and include them

---

62. Ulrich Uchtenhagen, 'El contrato de edición en el ámbito musical (Characteristics in comparison with contracts for the publication of literary works and their delimitation as regards contracts with the phonographic industry for the manufacture of discs, magnetic cassettes, etc.)' in the *Libro-memoria* of the *V International Congress on the Protection of Intellectual Property*, Buenos Aires, 1990, pp. 15–33.
63. However, as De Sanctis points out, it cannot be said that this constitutes plurality of contracts (op. cit., Section 132, p. 383).
64. Participation of the publisher in public performance and phono-mechanical rights is common in some countries: Argentina, 25 per cent when the works have not been recorded and 33 per cent when a recording exists; Brazil, 25 per cent in both cases; France, 33 per cent in public performance and 50 per cent in phono-mechanical rights.

in their repertoires; promoting phonographic recordings; making contracts at the publisher's expense for transcriptions of the work for other instruments, musical arrangements and versions of the accompanying words in different languages; making subcontracts with other publishers so that they will ensure the production of graphic editions and carry out the task of promoting the work in different geographical areas; attending music festivals and trade fairs regularly; verifying that publishing subcontractors fulfil their obligations; settling accounts with the author, at the prescribed intervals, for sales of the copies of the graphic edition, crediting amounts resulting from such sales and advances received from publishing subcontractors (when the work is successful). These activities require a considerable financial outlay and without them it would not be possible to ensure that works win public support.

Proceeds from the sale of the graphic edition cannot be compared with those derived from exploitation of the work in its other forms, but they are of great importance as evidence of the promotional activity carried out directly by the publisher and through the publishing subcontractors, since it is this activity which justifies their share of the amounts due to the author.

It is in practices such as these that the substantial differences between this type of contract and contracts for the publication of literary works reside.

In contracts for the publication of musical works it is customary:
- for the publisher to be granted exclusive subcontracting rights and the exclusive right to exploit the work in all its forms, including communication to the public;
- for the publisher to be granted a share of the receipts due to the author as a result of exploitation of the work;
- that not one, but an unspecified number of print-runs should be provided for in the contract although the publisher must maintain a certain level of stock available to the public.
- for the publisher to have the right: to make musical arrangements, translations of the accompanying words, orchestrations, transcriptions for other instruments or ensembles, and to publish and circulate these versions; to use the work in albums; to publish the words and music separately.

It is striking that despite the real situation which is so extensively reflected worldwide, legislation has not taken on board the considerable differences which exist between contracts for publication of literary works and those for the publication of musical works and, exceptions apart, has not included special regulations to ensure a balanced relationship between authors and publishers.

The explanation must be sought in the fact that this task has fallen to the societies of authors; through negotiations with publishers and by means of internal provisions which have gradually become unified and extended among them on the basis of the standards laid down by the International Confederation of Societies of Authors and Composers (CISAC), they have managed to change the 'standard provisions' of contracts for the publication of musical works which had been drawn up unilaterally by publishers.

They have also been very active in seeking regulation of the *publishing subcontracts* which the original publisher (i.e. the publisher who concludes the contract for publication with the author) signs with publishers in other countries, so as to ensure that the latter comply, within their respective geographic areas, with the obligations he has assumed. Traditionally, the subcontractor does not conclude a contract with the author, but with the publisher. Such subcontracts have been the means used by the original publisher to achieve the aim of disseminating the work in all geographical areas so as to attain worldwide use.

In 1938 CISAC adopted in Stockholm the *Confederated Statute for the subcontracted publication of musical works* (*with or without words*), which was completed and amended on various occasions, more especially at the London Congress (1947), the Paris Assembly (1949), Congresses at Amsterdam (1952), Hamburg (1956), Knokke-Le Zoute (1958) and Vienna (1968) and subsequently by the Management Committee of the International Bureau of the Societies Administering the Rights of Mechanical Recording and Reproduction (BIEM) in 1975, and by CISAC in 1976. This Statute regulates, through its common provisions, the distribution between the parties concerned—members of societies for public performance rights which are members of CISAC—of their respective share of receipts from public performance rights accruing from the subcontracted publication of a musical work with or without words.

The aim of this regulation was to unify and perfect the rules in force in societies of authors affiliated to CISAC, as regards the content of such subcontracts,[65] the distribution of the proceeds from utilization of works,[66] and the exchange of the information and documentation which serve as a support in the complex and arduous task of ensuring an equitable distribution of the receipts among the owners of rights in works.[67] The above-mentioned Statute distinguishes between assignee representatives—which the publishing subcontractors are considered to be—and publicity agents, according to whether or not they effectively publicize the works which they represent.

The subcontracted publication system is undergoing radical change at the present time in a number of important multinational publishers of musical works termed the 'major' publishing houses such as Sony Music Publishing, Emi Music Publishing, Warner Music, Peer Music and Poligram because of the international scale of their business interests. This change is due to the fact that these firms have subsidiary companies in many countries which have legal ties with the central establishment and

---

65. Publishing subcontracts must have a duration of at least three years and their territorial scope must correspond to that of the area managed by a society of authors.

66. By virtue of these rules adopted by the societies of authors affiliated to CISAC, following the general reform of 1975–1976 governing exploitation of works abroad, the percentage due to authors can under no circumstances be less than 50 per cent. The remaining 50 per cent is shared between the original publisher and the local publishing subcontractor in a proportion agreed between them.

67. Information is exchanged by means of a considerable quantity of documentation; the principal documentation available on an international basis comprises the international record cards, the CAP (Composer–Author–Publisher) lists of copyright-holders, the WWL (World Works List) list of works used most frequently and the GAF (General Agreement File) file of general agreements which are handled by the different societies of authors: SUISA in Switzerland, ASCAP in the United States and SABAM in Belgium, respectively (see below, Chapter 8, Section 8.1.3.4).

with one another. Accordingly they exploit their catalogues on a mutual basis by means of general representation contracts, or inter-company contracts which assign to the 'representative' firm between 20 and 50 per cent of the revenue accruing to the original publisher (see above, note 66).

It emerges from this commercial and legal practice that subcontracted publishing contracts in such companies are not necessary, except when relations with firms not belonging to the music publishing networks are involved.

In the laws of Colombia (Art. 138), El Salvador (Art. 67), Honduras (Art. 90 to 93), Panama (Art. 73) and Spain (Art. 71 to 73) we find provisions concerning contracts for the publication of musical works which take as their point of departure the actual situation of the music publishing business and tally with the practices current among authors and publishers, which are strongly influenced by the societies of authors.

6.2.3. Contracts for the publication of artistic works

The development of graphic printing techniques, particularly colour printing techniques, have made it much easier to reproduce a diversity of artistic works (drawings, sketches, vignettes, illustrations, paintings, engravings, sculptures, photographs, etc.) in books, magazines, newspapers, pamphlets, prospectuses, calendars, diaries, posters, postcards, greeting cards, etc., either on paper or on a textile support.

On the covers of nearly every book, scientific and technical works included, we find reproductions of artistic works. Reproductions of works of art in books or issued in instalment form for collection are also common. So, too, are works for instructional purposes and the popularization of knowledge produced in editions with profusely illustrated texts that make for easier understanding and enjoyment of the reading matter.

However, marked differences exist between contracts for the reproduction of works in the visual arts and contracts for the publication of literary works; in some laws we find rules which deal with these differences in detail:
- remuneration of the owner of the reproduction right is agreed as a lump sum and not as a proportion of the receipts resulting

from exploitation of the work. Laws which, as a general rule, fix this latter form of remuneration single out as an exception illustrations of the works of others (e.g. France, Article L. 132-6.4, previously Art. 36; Italy, Article 130; Spain, Article 46, 2(d); Venezuela, Article 56);
- reproduction is made from the original of the work; when this is a painting or a sculpture, often the owner of the reproduction right is not the owner of the material support, except when the latter is still the author—or his successors in title *'mortis causa'* —or a specific agreement has been made transferring exploitation rights in favour of the person acquiring the original of the work (concerning conflicts between the owner of the reproduction right and the owner of the single example of the work, and the legislative solutions see above, Chapter 4, Section 4.2.1: Right of disclosure and owners of the material support);
- the case of a publishing contract based upon a period of time which confers upon the publisher the right to make the number of editions which, within the said period, he deems appropriate, the limitations laid down by legislation concerning the maximum permitted duration and the minimum number of copies to constitute each edition are not applicable (Italy, Article 122, para. 5).[68]

As De Sanctis points out, application to works in the visual arts of regulations designed for contracts for the publication of literary works would not reflect the real situation. Publishing contracts properly speaking are found in domains such as art publications (when the works have not fallen into the public domain), works of collaboration, even when the contributions belong to different

---

68. Italy, Article 122, fifth paragraph: 'A publishing contract based upon a period of time shall be deemed to confer upon the publisher the right to produce the number of editions which he may consider necessary within the time specified, which period shall not exceed 20 years, and shall specify a minimum number of copies of each edition, to be produced: in the absence of such indication the contract shall be void. The maximum period of 20 years shall not apply to contracts concerning [...] sketches, drawings, vignettes, illustrations, photographs and similar works [...] cartographical works.'

genres (such as photo fiction) and collective works. Outside the context of these situations, the use of illustrative material in a scientific work or in a work of narrative literature, as in any other intellectual work, does not give rise to a publishing contract with the owner of the right of reproduction of the work of art. Use is authorized by the owner of the respective right in favour of the author of the text or directly in favour of the publisher by means of a simple licence which, unless otherwise agreed, entails only the payment of remuneration; use of the work is limited (save possible rights of a personal nature) to the use specified.

When it is a case of original illustrations—and even of manual copying of works in the public domain—contracts for the hire of labour or services (*contratti di commissione*) are often made with the artist, with exclusive clauses for given aspects of his activity when collaboration is continuous.[69] Such contracts are common in newspaper companies (publishers of daily newspapers, periodicals, magazines) with short story illustrators, comic strip artists, cartoonists, etc.

6.2.4. Publishers' rights concerning the typographical arrangement of their published editions

As a result of the development of electronic reproduction technology and the consequent increase in the parasitical activities of those enriching themselves at the expense of legitimate publishers through their abusive exploitation of printed texts, publishers have long been claiming recognition of specific rights—superseding the publishing contract and independently of the rights arising from such contracts which might apply to them—which would enable them to undertake the effective defence of their own production (publication of literary works and, in general, printed texts) against unauthorized reproduction of their published editions.

In the United Kingdom, the previous Act of 1956 had already established the right concerning the typographical arrangement of published editions (Section 15) as the right of the publisher to

---

69. Valerio De Sanctis, op. cit., Section 49, pp. 140–2.

claim protection against unauthorized facsimile reproduction (by photocopying or similar methods) of his published editions of literary, dramatic or musical works.[70] Similar provisions were adopted in a number of laws in the copyright area (Australia, Bangladesh, India, Ireland, New Zealand, Pakistan and Singapore).[71] The duration of the right was fixed as 25 years from the end of the year in which the edition was first published.

In the area where legislation is Roman in tradition, Mexico (Article 26) establishes that

> Publishers of intellectual or artistic works, newspapers or magazines, and producers of films or like media of publication, may secure the reservation of the right to the exclusive use of distinctive graphic characteristics which, in their case, are distinctive of the work or collection [...] The aforesaid protection shall continue for two years from the date of the certificate, and shall be renewable for like periods, if habitual use of the rights reserved is established. Original characteristics must be used in the form in which they were registered. Any modification of their constituent elements must be the object of a fresh registration.

Unlike the Mexican law, which requires the graphic characteristics to be original, the right concerning the typographical arrangement of published editions recognized by legislations reflecting Anglo-American tradition (even when stipulating that the edition should not be a reproduction of another) disregards the requirement of originality and protects the arrangement of the page as a whole—the 'image on the page'.[72]

Hence, the protection of the typographical arrangement of published editions also differs from the protection afforded by the Vienna Agreement for the Protection of Type Faces and their International Deposit, adopted on 12 June 1973 (although it has

---

70. The 1988 Act established this right in Part 1, (1)(c) and in Part 8.
71. See document UNESCO/WIPO/CGE/PW/3-II, 14 September 1987, paras. 327–8, pp. 79–80.
72. See C. Clark, *Summary of the Symposium* (International Copyright Symposium organized by the International Publishers Association in Heidelberg, April 1986), Ed. J. Schweitzer, Munich, 1986, Section 5—*Publisher's Rights*, p. 236.

still not entered into force because of the insufficient number of ratifications) in which the subject matter of protection consists of sets of designs of (a) letters and alphabets as such with their accessories such as accents and punctuation marks; (b) numerals and other figurative signs such as conventional signs, symbols and scientific signs; and (c) ornaments such as borders, fleurons and vignettes, which are intended to provide means for composing texts by any graphic technique. Protection does not include type faces of a form dictated by purely technical requirements (Article 2) and is subject to the condition that type faces should be novel or original, or both (Article 7(1)).

Protection of type faces is, therefore, designed to cover novel or original elements, or both, forming part of the typographical arrangement, but not the arrangement itself.[73] On the other hand, the right of the publisher in respect of the typographical arrangement of his published editions covers all those which do not constitute facsimile reproductions of others, whether or not the arrangement reflects originality or the published work is protected by copyright or not (work in the public domain, legal texts, etc.).

The requirement of originality cannot be applied when the publisher's rights are involved, unlike the case of author's rights which stem from the act of creation; the publisher's rights (in the same way as other neighbouring rights—producers of phonograms, broadcasting companies—) derive from the act of dissemination[74] (see below, Chapter 7). Such protection has nothing to do with the content of the publication; its purpose is to defend the publisher's efforts and investment and stimulate the activities of

---

73. See document UNESCO/WIPO/PW/3-II already referred to, para. 339, pp. 81–82.
74. 'Publication', states Desbois, 'serves literary, artistic or musical creation; it has no part in creative activity' (op. cit. p. 455, Section 363). On the other hand, in legislation that follows the Anglo-American legal tradition, it is possible to grant the publisher entrepreneurial copyright in respect of the typographical arrangement of his published editions (see above, Chapter 1, Sections 1.3.1. and 1.3.2.).

those who make the texts available to the public, constituting an irreplaceable link in the communication chain.

In Principle PW26[75] of the UNESCO/WIPO Principles on the protection of copyright and neighbouring rights in respect of various categories of works (document UNESCO/WIPO/CGE/SYN/3-II of 11 April 1988) it is maintained that States should consider granting appropriate protection in respect of the typographical arrangements of their published editions, irrespective of whether such editions contain works protected by copyright.[76]

6.2.5. Entitlement of the publisher to institute proceedings in the case of infringement of exclusive rights which he possesses as transferee

By virtue of the publishing contract, the publisher may carry out the acts of exploitation of the work authorized in it. Furthermore, he is owner of the rights which the law has specifically established in his favour.

If, then, there is no transfer of the author's right or, as in the case of collective works, the law does not recognize the original ownership of the right as being vested in the publisher (or a legal transfer or presumption of transfer in his favour), the publisher is not empowered to institute proceedings on his own account in respect of unauthorized uses of the works whose publication is the subject of the contract.

But publishers need to be empowered to defend their production themselves in the face of illegal reproduction, and this is recognized in a number of laws.

In the United Kingdom, the 1956 Act (Section 19) established in favour of the exclusive licensee the same rights of action and

---

75. PW: Printed word.
76. While these *principles* have no compulsory force, they reflect thinking on the subject and are designed to provide solutions to safeguard the rights of owners in literary and artistic works and other creative works protected by copyright and neighbouring rights and ensure that they enjoy equitable treatment, so as to promote the creative activity which is so necessary for the cultural development of every nation. There are, in all, 162 principles.

the same remedies in defence of his rights (except against the owner of copyright) as if the licence had been an assignment.

The United Kingdom Act of 1988 establishes (Part 17) that the copying or reproduction of the work is an act restricted by the copyright in every description of copyright work. In Chapter VI of this Act dealing with infringements and rights and remedies for them, the rights and remedies of the original copyright owner are set out (Sections 96–100) as well as those of the *exclusive licensee* (Sections 101 and 102).[77]

In Spain, Article 48(1) stipulates that the transfer of exclusive rights confers on the transferee 'the right, which shall be independent of that of the owner effecting the transfer, to institute proceedings for violations that affect the powers that have been assigned to him'.

6.3. Public performance contracts: dramatic, musical and dramatico-musical works

6.3.1. Concept

A contract for public performance is any contract whereby the author of a literary, dramatic, musical, dramatico-musical, pantomime or choreographic work—or his successors in title—authorizes a natural person or a legal entity (generally called the impresario) who undertakes to perform all or part of the work in public (by means of a 'live' performance or by using a fixation, a broadcast, or transmission by cable network) and also to pay the other party a remuneration proportionate to the box-office—or similar—receipts or a lump sum.

Such contracts encompass both the *live* performance of

---

77. Section 101 provides that the exclusive licensee: (1) has, except against the copyright owner, the same rights and remedies in respect of matters occurring after the grant of the licence as if the licence had been an assignment; (2) exercises his rights and remedies concurrently with those of the copyright owner, and (3) may avail himself, as a defendant, of any defence which would have been available to him if the action had been brought by the copyright owner. Section 102 regulates in detail exercise of the concurrent rights stipulated in Section 101.

dramatic, dramatico-musical and musical works (recitation of literary and dramatic works, stage performances of dramas, comedies, operas, operettas, musical comedies, concerts, etc.); and the *indirect* performance either by means of fixations (showing of audiovisual works, playing of discs, magnetic tapes, etc.) or the transmission of works by broadcasting or by cable network provided that such communications are effected in a place where the public is, or can be present or at a place not open to the public but where a substantial number of persons outside the normal circle of a family and its close social acquaintances is present.[78] In other words performances are considered to be public when they occur outside the strictly private or domestic circle and, even if occurring within the latter, when the performance is projected or communicated outside.

Public performance rights are generally administered by societies of authors (see below, Chapter 8, Section 8.1.3).

The contractual relationship between the author and a producer of phonograms, for instance, authorizes reproduction of the work but, because of the principle of the independence of exploitation rights, it does not authorize communication to the public by means of public performance. Furthermore, by virtue of the principle in civil law whereby no person may transmit to another a greater or more extensive right in an object than the one which he himself enjoyed, when a producer of phonograms puts copies of a phonogram on the market he cannot transmit to the purchaser of a disc or cassette the right to public performance using these devices, this right belonging to the author under the terms of the contract for mechanical reproduction he has concluded with the producer.

The author has the *right of distribution* by virtue of which he can control the use of his work when commercialization of copies in which it is fixed is carried out in forms he has not authorized

---

78. See memorandum prepared by the International Bureau of WIPO on questions concerning a possible Protocol to the Berne Convention, *Copyright*, WIPO, March 1992, para. 156 (b)(i) and (ii).

(see above, Chapter 4, Section 4.2.1, last paragraph); in French legal precedents this is termed *droit de destination*.

In turn, the broadcasting organization which simply receives the right to broadcast to domestic receivers cannot transmit to the latter the right to communicate the work to the public by means of its broadcast performance.

The right to *private communication*—i.e. use made within the family or private context or the circle of close social acquaintances of a family or individual—is, then, covered by the contract for mechanical reproduction which is made between the author and the phonogram producer (the aim of which is the fixation and reproduction of the work on copies for retail sale to the public), by the broadcasting contract drawn up between the author and the broadcasting organization (whose aim is wireless transmission of works for reception in family dwellings) and by the contract for the production of audiovisual works on video copies intended for sale or hire to the public (home video) made between the author and the producer, which we shall refer to separately (see below, Sections 6.4, 6.5 and 6.6, respectively).

On the other hand, *public communication* of discs, magnetic tapes, video copies, broadcasts, transmissions by cable network, and so on, must be specifically authorized by the author and constitute the subject matter of contracts generically known as public performance contracts.

When such fixations, broadcasts, etc., are used in shows or performances (in theatres, concert halls or any place equipped for this purpose), in places to which the public have access (such as dance halls, discothèques, restaurants, tea rooms, bars, cafeterias, hotels, fashion shows, etc.) or for providing background music (in shops, public transport, consulting rooms, professional offices, industrial establishments, commercial companies, offices, workshops, etc.), the work is being used for a purpose other than that provided for in the original contract between the author and the producer or broadcaster, substantially changing its economic dimension as it deprives the interested parties of the possibility of other contracts. It is accordingly necessary to secure the authorization of the author and to pay a remuneration for such public communication (see above, Chapter 4, Section 4.2.2—Content).

6.3.2. Legal nature

A public performance contract is an autonomous contract, typical of copyright contracts, and is regulated as such by domestic legislation[79] or, more commonly, as a performance contract.[80]

Like publishing contracts, public performance contracts reflect certain points of similarity in regard to obligations under some civil law contracts such as the obligation of result inherent in contracts for the *hire of labour or services* since the impresario undertakes to attain results: the show, i.e. the performance. But the impresario does not become the party hiring out his labour or services because the obligation of result is assumed at his own economic risk and the author does not become the hirer because he does not undertake to pay a price to the impresario.

Public performance contracts also share features which are inherent in *partnership contracts* since the author usually participates in the economic fortunes of the enterprise (his remuneration is a percentage of the box-office receipts or revenue from a similar source). But it is not a partnership, because the essential element of such contracts is missing since the author does not share in the losses.

6.3.3. Characteristics

A public performance contract is:
- *Consensual* and not real, even when the author must deliver a copy of the work to the impresario for public performance, since such an obligation is related to the stage of performance of the contract and not to that of its conclusion it is not formal although it is subject to a written proof regime

---

79. E.g. Spain: *Stage and Musical Performance Contracts* (Title V, Chapter III).
80. In some laws it is stipulated that the rules governing performance contracts are applicable to other contracts, e.g. Argentina. Article 50: 'For the purpose of this law, radio telephonic transmission, cinematographic exhibition, television transmission, or any other method of mechanical reproduction of any literary or artistic work, shall be considered a public performance.'

- *Bilateral or synallagmatic* since both parties assume reciprocal obligations: authorization on the one hand and the obligation to perform the work and to pay remuneration on the other
- *Onerous* because the impresario pays a remuneration, generally that agreed with the Society of Authors or fixed by the latter no public performance contract exists if the author refuses to accept remuneration
- *Commutative* because the services to be provided by each party are fixed: authorization on the author's part and on the part of the impresario the obligation to perform the work and to pay remuneration
- *Intuitu personae* as regards both the author (we have already said that the contracting of any work is made taking into account the author's personality) and the impresario when it is a case of 'live' public performances, the *intuitu personae* characteristic is even more marked than in publishing contracts where, once the author has approved the proofs of the edition, the work is reproduced in an unaltered form. Certain laws specifically embody this, e.g. Argentina, Article 47; Brazil, Article 77; Colombia, Article 148; France, Article L. 132-19.4, previously Art. 44, fourth paragraph, etc.
- *Non-exclusive*. This is explained by the fact that public performances are ephemeral. Laws also point out this characteristic, e.g. France, Article L. 132-19.2, previously Art. 44, second paragraph; Venezuela, Article 66, 1, etc.[81] However, it frequently happens that exclusivity is agreed in respect of the performance of stage works
- *Limited* to the use which the author has specifically authorized to be carried out in the place and within the period agreed

---

81. In Argentina, the non-exclusive nature arises *a contrario sensu* in Article 49, where it is stipulated that: 'In the absence of agreement to the contrary, the author of an unpublished work which has been accepted by a third party shall not be entitled, pending its performance by such third party, to have the work performed by any other person.' In Chile, Article 58, it is stated that: 'In the absence of any contractual stipulations, the impresario acquires the exclusive right of performance of the work for only a period of six months from the date of its first performance and, without exclusivity, for a further six months.'

6.3.4. Rights and obligations of the parties

Generally, it is clear from perusal of the legal regulations that they have been drawn up in the light of the particular characteristics of contracts for 'live' public performances, the purpose of which is direct communication in theatres or in concert halls (performances before an audience). However, it is the indirect communication of non-dramatic musical works which is constantly being carried out in a multiplicity of places, and this makes it practically impossible for each author and each user to maintain an effective direct relationship at a reasonable cost.

Here we realize the invaluable role played by the societies of authors acting as intermediaries between the author and the user, for which reason public performances are contracted through them by means of a special procedure: the authorization for the use of a whole set or *repertoire of works*, the fees fixed for such uses being received by them. Generally, the works performed are established by the user after utilization.[82]

This is the *contract for the public performance of a repertoire* where, in the time-honoured relationship of *author–work–user*,

---

82. In Argentina, Article 40 of Decree 41.233/34 which regulates Law No. 11.723 on Intellectual Property illustrates this *modus operandi*, providing that: 'Those who exploit premises where musical works of any kind, with or without words, are performed, or impresarios, organizers, conductors of orchestras, or the owners, or those responsible for the users, of reproductions of phonograms referred to in Article 33 of this decree, shall keep a daily record, in strict order of performance, of the titles of all the works performed and the names or pseudonyms of the authors of the words and the composers of the music, and, in addition, the names or pseudonyms of the principal performers and those of the producers of the phonograms or trademarks of the reproductions used as the case may be [...]. Anyone who, in these records, alters the titles and/or names of the authors of the words or the music of the works or those of the principal performers or the producers of the phonograms, or who omits a work which has been performed or communicated to the public or who inserts a work which was not performed or communicated to the public or who falsifies these records in any way whatsoever, shall be liable to the penalties referred to in Article 71 of the Law.' (The text transcribed includes successive amendments up to and including those introduced by Decree 1640/74.)

the author has been replaced by his representative—the society of authors—and the work has been replaced by a relatively established repertoire of works. Notwithstanding this, in the regulations governing public performance contracts included in legislation, even in those countries where such societies have been functioning effectively for a long time, regulation of repertoire contracts is still omitted, despite the fact that this is the usual procedure followed in a considerable number of such contractual arrangements.

In the following description of the rights and obligations of the parties, account is taken of the arrangements specific to contracts where societies of authors intervene as well as of those where authors negotiate their contracts directly with the impresario or through an agency, although at times they entrust the society of authors with the collection and settlement of the resulting receipts.

A. AUTHOR'S RIGHTS

a. Moral rights

1) Right to participate in the selection of the principal performers and, in the case of orchestras, choirs, dance ensembles and similar groups of performers, the conductor or director (Spain, Article 80(2)).

2) Right to agree with the impresario on the drafting of publicity concerning the acts of communication (Spain, Article 80(3)).

b. Economic rights

1) Right to have the contract formalized in writing.[83]

2) Right to receive remuneration.

In the case of the performance of dramatic, dramatico-musical and choreographic works, recitals and performance of musical

---

83. Chile, Article 56, last paragraph, states that: 'The performance contract can take the form of an attested deed or a private instrument signed before a notary.' In our view this constitutes excessive formalism which is also found in Article 48(2), and which may prejudice the interests of the author since it is not in line with common practice in this domain.

works in theatres, concert halls and public places, remuneration is usually a percentage of the box-office receipts at the place where the communication takes place. Current percentages are 10 per cent of gross box-office receipts[84] and for first night performances in theatres and public halls between 15 (e.g. Colombia, Article 143; Chile, Article 61) and 20 per cent (e.g. Argentina, by agreement with the users)—not applicable to concerts.

In the case of performances for which there is no admission charge, the percentage is fixed in proportion to the potential receipts or a lump sum is determined.[85]

Some laws specify that impresarios responsible for public performances shall be considered to be depositaries of the remuneration payable to authors for the communication of their works, when such remuneration consists of a proportionate share in the receipts (Spain, Article 79; Chile, Article 63(1) adds that the remuneration shall not be affected by any distraint imposed upon the property of the impresario).

3) Right to receive additional remuneration if the performance is also broadcast—*the principle of the independence of economic rights.*[86]

4) The right, once the authorized performances have begun, to ensure that the contract will have a limited duration regarding the period or the number of performances—the contract may be made for a specific period or for a given number of communica-

---

84. The only deduction permitted is deduction of the taxes payable on the entrance tickets (Chile, Article 61, *in fine*, establishes this explicitly).
85. With the exception of performances free of charge in respect of which copyright has been limited (see above, Chapter 4, Section 4.3.1: limitations on copyright in the case of certain performances in educational establishments and by certain state institutions).
86. Chile, Article 62: 'If the spectacle is also diffused by broadcasting or television, the author shall be entitled to receive a minimum of 5 per cent of the amount received for the emission by way of advertising effected during the programme or, if no advertising occurred, 10 per cent of the amount received by the impresario for the radio-diffusion of the performance. The remuneration shall be payable without prejudice to that paid to the person entitled in accordance with Article 61' (*the impresario*).

tions to the public—France, (Article L. 132-19.4, previously Art. 44, first paragraph); Spain (Article 75(1)); Venezuela (Article 65, second paragraph).

B. OBLIGATIONS OF THE AUTHOR

a. To deliver to the impresario a copy of the work and the fully orchestrated musical score when they have not yet been published in printed form (Spain, Article 77(1)).

b. To be answerable to the impresario for the authorship and originality of the work and for the peaceful exercise of the rights granted him—*general guarantee obligation*—(Spain, Article 77(2)).

C. RIGHTS OF THE IMPRESARIO

The right to fix the price of admission to the performance (or similar function, as in the case of a café-concert, that is to say, a place where food and drinks are sold and the price charged for the latter includes the right to enjoy the public performance).

D. OBLIGATIONS OF THE IMPRESARIO

a. It is incumbent upon the impresario to obtain the necessary copies for the public communication of the work. Such copies must be initialled by the author (Spain, Article 80(1)).

In the case of complex musical works (symphonies, concertos, operas, operettas, zarzuelas, musical comedies, etc.) the usual practice is for the impresario to make a contract with the publisher for the hire of the graphic material required for the performance.

b. To display the name of the author—or his pseudonym or the sign which identifies him—together with the title of the work and to include it in the individual programmes and in the direct or indirect publicity campaign. In the case of translations, adaptations or musical arrangements, in addition to the names of the respective authors, the nature of the adaptation or arrangement must be indicated (Argentina (Article 52); Chile (Article 60(1); Colombia (Article 142)).

c. To carry out the public performance without introducing any alterations, additions, abridgements or deletions in the work that have not been agreed to by the author (Argentina (Article 52); Chile (Article 60(1); Spain (Article 78(2)).

d. To present the public performance in the theatre or other place or the geographical area and in the language or languages specifically authorized by the author.

e. To present the first—or sole—public performance within the period agreed, which must be of a reasonable length (Spain (Article 75(2)) stipulates that it may not exceed two years from the date of the contract or, as appropriate, of the author having placed the producer in a position to effect the communication).

Should no provision have been made in this respect, the laws remedy the omission by establishing the period in a variety of ways: one year or the duration of the season corresponding to the time of the conclusion of the contract when the subject matter of the contract is the stage performance of the work (Spain (Article 75(2), second part)); within one year from the time that the work is delivered to the impresario (Argentina (Article 46, second part); Colombia (Article 141)); within six months from the date of the contract (Chile (Article 57); Mexico (Article 76)); authorization of the author to assign a period in accordance with local custom (Brazil (Article 74)).

f. To effect the communication under artistic and technical conditions which will not prejudice the moral rights of the author (Spain (Article 78(2); Venezuela (Article 69)).

g. To guarantee the author the right of attendance at rehearsals.

h. To guarantee the author or his representatives the right to inspect the public performance of the work (Chile (Article 60(2)) and to attend it free of charge (Spain (Article 78(3)).

i. Not to replace the principal performers of the work or the conductor of the orchestra or the choir without the prior consent of the author if they were selected with the common agreement of the impresario and the author, except in unforeseen circumstances where no delay can be permitted (Brazil (Article 78); Chile (Article 60(3); Colombia (Article 144)).

j. To remit punctually to the author or his representatives the agreed remuneration (Spain (Article 78(4)).

k. To submit to the author or to his representatives the exact programme of communications to the public, and, where remuneration is proportional, a statement of proceeds (*bordereau*). The impresario shall likewise allow them to verify the said programme and statements (Spain (Article 78(5)).

6.3.5. Termination of public performance contracts

A. TERMINATION AT THE AUTHOR'S DISCRETION

The author may terminate a contract in the following instances:

a. When, following an application by the author (except in the case of a cancellation clause), the impresario fails to pay the agreed remuneration (Chile, Article 63, second paragraph; Spain, Article 81(3)). If, despite this, the impresario continues to effect the communications, the author may request the competent authority to suspend performances of the work and to retain the sums which may be due to him without prejudice to any other legal actions that he may be entitled to bring (Colombia, Article 145, stipulates that the competent authority shall order the suspension of performances of the work and the withholding of receipts from ticket sales; similarly, Chile, Article 63, second paragraph).

b. When the impresario, following an application by the author, fails to submit the exact programme of communications; when remuneration is proportional and he fails to present a statement of receipts or does not comply with his obligation to allow the author or his representatives to verify such programmes and statements (Spain, Article 81(3)).

c. When the work fails to be performed for a reason imputable to the impresario. In this case the author may retain any advance payments which may have been made to him and may demand an indemnity for the prejudice caused (Chile, Article 59, second paragraph).

d. When the impresario who has acquired exclusive rights and who has started public performances of a work, suspends them for a prolonged period (Spain, Article 81(1), fixes this period at one year).

e. When the impresario fails to comply with the obligation to effect public communication of the work within the agreed period or the period laid down by law (Argentina, Article 46, second paragraph; Spain, Article 81(2)).

In this case the author has the right to receive an indemnity for the prejudice caused (Argentina, Article 46, second paragraph stipulates that '... the author may require as indemnity an amount equal to the copyright royalty corresponding to 20 performances of an analogous work').

f. When the impresario fails to comply with his obligations concerning respect for the moral rights of the author: the obligation to mention his name alongside the title of the work; to effect communication without subjecting the work to alterations, additions, abridgements or deletions which have not been previously agreed to by the author, and under artistic and technical conditions which do not prejudice the prestige of the author; to guarantee to the author or his representatives the right to inspect the public performance of the work and to attend it free of charge.

B. TERMINATION ON EXPIRY OF THE CONTRACT

a. When the work ceases to be performed for want of audiences (Colombia, Article 146(2)), the authorization given in the contract lapses.

b. When, in the case of the first performance of a work—stage performance being the sole form of communication contemplated in the contract—the work has been clearly rejected by the public, and when such an eventuality has been provided for in the contract (Spain, Article 82).

C. TERMINATION ON EXPIRY OF THE AGREED PERIOD

D. TERMINATION ON OTHER GENERAL GROUNDS FOR THE LAPSE OF CONTRACTS

6.4. Contracts for mechanical reproduction rights

Mechanical reproduction is a method of reproducing a work akin to publishing, for which reason the contract which we are about to study is strongly influenced by the specific features of contracts for graphic publication.[87]

In accordance with the WIPO glossary, *mechanical rights* are generally understood to mean the author's right to authorize the reproduction of his literary, dramatic or musical work by means of recordings (phonograms or audiovisual fixation) which are produced mechanically in the widest sense of the term, including electro-acoustic and electronic procedures.[88] But, what is termed a *contract for mechanical reproduction* is a contract whose subject matter is the fixation and reproduction, *in sound recordings, of musical works*, with or without accompanying words.[89]

6.4.1. Concept

The contract for mechanical rights properly speaking—of the greatest economic importance—is one whose purpose is the fixation of the sounds of a performance of non-dramatic musical works—and the words which accompany them—on a phonogram and its mechanical reproduction. By virtue of this contract the author of a work—or his successors in title—authorizes a natural person or a legal entity (the *producer*)[90] who undertakes to fix the sounds of the performance of the work and to reproduce them or have them reproduced mechanically on discs or magnetic tapes, in a direct and uniform manner, producing a given number

---

87. At the outset of our study of publishing contracts (see above, Section 6.2), it was pointed out that, in the broad sense, *the right to publish* is generally understood to include the author's right to authorize the material reproduction of his work by means of the manufacture in quantity of copies of the said work, including not only graphic publication (books and printed matter in general) but also sound recording (discs, cassettes, etc.), and audiovisual fixation (cinematographic and videographic works, etc.).
88. See: *WIPO Glossary of Terms of the Law of Copyright and Neighbouring Rights*, Geneva, 1980, entry 154, page 157.
89. Further below, in the section on contracts for the production of audiovisual works (Section 6.6), we shall deal with the mechanical reproduction of audiovisual fixations for the purpose of exploitation by means of copies of the work which are made available to the public (more especially video cassettes).
90. See below, Chapter 7, Section 7.2.

of copies, to publicize, distribute and sell them to the public for his own account and risk, without legal subordination, and to pay the other party a remuneration proportionate to the proceeds derived from the sale of the copies.

6.4.2. Legal nature and characteristics

In general, the same principles apply as for publishing contracts (see above, Section 6.2), although there are some important differences:
- Contracts for mechanical reproduction are not exclusive, whereas in publishing contracts exclusivity appears as a natural and characteristic element;
- the subject matter of publishing contracts is one or several specific works, whereas, under a contract for mechanical reproduction, the producer of phonograms receives an authorization covering all the works which comprise the repertoire of the Society of Authors when this is entrusted with administering the author's phonomechanical rights;
- the Society of Authors normally exercises *control of the pressing*;
- unlike publishing contracts, contracts for mechanical reproduction do not limit the possibility of making new pressings.

6.4.3. Rights and obligations of the parties

Mechanical reproduction rights are usually administered by societies of authors or other special organizations. Legislation fails to regulate the respective contracts.[91] In this regard certain laws, e.g. those of Colombia (Art. 151 to 157), Ecuador (Art. 57 to 64), El Salvador (Art. 73 to 76), the Dominican Republic (Art. 95 to 100), Honduras (Art. 94 to 98) and Panama (Art. 80 to 83), are exceptions to the rule since they each have a chapter dealing with the regulation of *contracts for phonographic fixation.*

In a number of countries, the societies administering mechanical reproduction rights are the same societies which are entrusted

---

91. For the same reasons as those set out in regard to publishing contracts for musical works; see Section 6.2.2.

with the collective management of the public performance rights of authors of non-dramatic musical works—with or without accompanying words—, e.g. in Argentina (SADAIC), Belgium (SABAM), Germany (GEMA), Israel (ACUM), Italy (SIAE), Spain (SGAE), etc.[92]

In other countries special organizations exist for this purpose, e.g. in Austria, Austro-Mechana, in France, SDRM (Société pour l'administration du droit de reproduction mécanique des auteurs, compositeurs et éditeurs), in the United Kingdom, MCPS (Mechanical Copyright Protection Society Ltd.), and so on. These bodies are affiliated to the BIEM—the International Bureau of the Societies administering the rights of mechanical recording and reproduction—a non-governmental international organization, with its headquarters in Paris, which was founded as a non-commercial undertaking in France in 1929.[93]

At the outset the BIEM acted as a central organization for all the organizations affiliated to it and was concerned with negotiations with phonographic companies and the collection of royalties directly from them. With the passage of time its role has changed and nowadays, although it is still the centralized negotiating organization, it is no longer the owner of rights; these are the concern of each affiliated organization which collects the royalties for which producers of phonograms in each individual country are liable. This is reflected on the labels on discs and cassettes and their respective packaging, which bear the name of the national society for collective management through which the respective contract for mechanical reproduction rights is made.

---

92. In those countries which establish non-voluntary licences for the mechanical reproduction of non-dramatic musical works and the accompanying words when a phonogram has already been produced and copies of it have been distributed for sale to the public with the authorization of the copyright holder (see above, Chapter 4, Section 4.3.2), the societies for the collective management of copyright usually also administer the royalties derived from uses made under such licences.

93. Until 1968 the initials BIEM indicated the title 'Bureau international de l'édition musico-mécanique' (see below, Chapter 9, Section 9.1.1.1).

BIEM carries out negotiations with the International Federation of Phonogram and Videogram Producers (IFPI), an international non-governmental organization founded in 1933 with its Secretariat in London, and bringing together companies or firms which produce phonograms or videograms and supply copies to the public in a reasonable quantity, or whose connection with the production of phonograms and videograms and their sale to the public is, in the view of the Council, sufficiently close to justify their admission as members of the Federation (IFPI statutes, Chapter 2, para. 2.1.).

Both bodies have formalized the standard BIEM–IFPI contract for the phonographic industry, the latest version of which, dating from 1975, was amended in 1980, 1985, 1988, 1989, 1990, 1992 and 1994 (this latest modification concerning Latin America). This contract regulates the authorization for use of the 'worldwide repertoire' which comprises the works administered by the member societies of the BIEM (Article I), royalty rates,[94] minimum royalties, and the method of calculating them (Articles V and VI), the accounting period (Article XII), export requirements, exceptions to the obligation to pay royalties (free copies for promotional purposes, returned copies, etc.) and control of the number of copies reproduced (Article XIII).

The standard BIEM–IFPI contract is put into effect, first of all through the standard contract which each national society for the collective management of reproduction rights concludes with each national IFPI group and then through the similar contract which the collective management society signs in turn with each national producer.

Those societies for the collective management of mechanical reproduction rights which are not members of the BIEM— because they have not been affiliated (e.g. the SCD in Chile) or

---

94. These are stipulated for continental Europe (including Turkey); it is provided that in Latin America they shall be the rates agreed between the Society or its representative and national producers (Annex IV, (1) and (3)). In 1994, the BIEM and the IFPI came to an agreement on a royalty rate for compact discs.

because they have withdrawn—make agreements directly with the national IFPI groups, or with each of the phonogram production companies when no such national group exists or the phonogram production companies do not belong to them.

The collective management societies also make contracts with producers of phonograms who do not belong to the national IFPI groups and who are, accordingly, usually known as 'independent producers'. The collective management societies usually have a 'system of recognition' of such producers. This system and the special contract which the society signs with each 'independent' producer reflect a certain difference as regards the procedure referred to above because a 'summary of sales' must be presented to the SADAIC with the monthly settlement.

As we have already said, contracts between the society for the collective management of mechanical reproduction rights and each phonogram producer who is a member of the national IFPI group or each independent producer basically include the clauses of the BIEM–IFPI contract.

We shall now describe the contractual arrangements for the mechanical reproduction of non-dramatic musical works between a society for the collective management of mechanical rights and a company producing phonograms, based on the model provided by one of the current standard contracts, the contract signed between SADAIC (la Sociedad Argentina de Autores y Compositores de Música which is a member of CISAC and the BIEM), and CAPIF (Cámara Argentina de Productores e Industriales de Fonogramas y Videogramas which is a member of IFPI), which is translated into practice by means of the contracts which the former signs with each producer.

a. The Society authorizes the producer to exercise three specific rights: to record works on phonograms made by him for his own account and risk; to make copies of the said phonograms; and to distribute them to the public 'for their individual use or that of a family circle' (private communication).

b. The authorization is non-exclusive (for which reason the Society may also make contracts for mechanical reproduction with other producers) and cannot be transferred (in accordance with the *intuitu personae* nature of the contract). Although authors enjoy the right to grant exclusive and non-exclusive licences, in the domain of mechanical rights it is felt more appropriate for creators to have their works exploited by all producers by means of different interpretations or performances, as long as such activities are subject to the control of the Society and comply with its obligations. All producers, then, have the same right of access to the whole repertoire and if an author decides that his work should not be recorded, the prohibition will be applicable to all producers, with one exception: if the prohibition is directed towards one particular producer and includes the whole SADAIC repertoire as a consequence of his failure to fulfil his obligations.

c. It does not imply total or partial transfer of author's rights and, consequently, all the prerogatives recognized by law continue to be vested in the holders of rights in the work. In accordance with the principle of the independence of economic rights, the Society accordingly retains, with regard to recorded works, the prerogative of authorizing or prohibiting their public performance, broadcasting, inclusion in audiovisual works, etc., irrespective of whether the said recording is used or not.

d. Payment of the economic consideration must be made exclusively to the Society, for which reason payments made directly to holders of rights, publishers or any other person are not valid.

e. In order to make copies of a phonogram (rerecording of an existing recording) third parties must also have the authorization of the producer of the phonogram.

f. The authorization granted to the producer is limited to recordings of the works as they were conceived by their respective authors, by means of a technical and artistic process which will not distort them or be prejudicial to the prestige of their creators.

The producer may not, hence, alter the works, their nature or their musical and literary texts without the express prior personal authorization of the author, who shall grant such authorization through the Society. The author may demand additional remuneration for the express authorization allowing the producer to make musical arrangements and translations of the work (transformation right).

g. A label on each side of the discs and cassettes shall provide the following information:

- the original title of each work, names of the composer, author of the words and of the adapter of the text and/or the music, if applicable, and the publisher;
- the acronym SADAIC–BIEM;
- the year for each production of copies; and
- the notice 'Reservados todos los derechos del productor, de los autores y de los intérpretes de las obras reproducidas en este ejemplar. Prohibida la reproducción, regrabación, alquiler, préstamo, canje, y su ejecución pública, radiodifusión y cualesquiera otros usos no autorizados de estas fonogramas' (derecho de distribución); ['All rights of the producer, authors and performers of the work reproduced in this copy reserved. Unauthorized copying, re-recording, hiring, lending, exchange, public performance, broadcasting and any other unauthorized use of these phonograms, prohibited' (right of distribution)].

h. Producers have other, complementary obligations concerning the need to verify production, sales prices, the place of manufacture, the existence of co-exploitation, the legal requirement of registration and legal deposit in the Dirección Nacional del Derecho de Autor—e National Copyright Directorate, the existence of new marks, the keeping of a clear and precise accounting system, and the obligation to facilitate access to the places of production and marketing.

i. Before manufacture, the producer must send the list of the works which he proposes to exploit to the Society. Although, in principle, global authorization has been granted to the producer, he must check to see whether any prohibition exists with regard to the recording of a particular work and that references to authorship and to the integrity of the work are correct.

j. Irrespective of the support, a royalty rate is stipulated which is equivalent to 10 per cent of the total amount invoiced by the producer to the dealer (before the allowances accepted in the contract are taken into account). The royalty rate is calculated on the basis of the total number of units leaving the warehouse or production depot, promotion copies excepted. However, a discount of 10 per cent is allowed (for packaging costs) and a reduction of 9 per cent (normally applied to invoices).

k. Should the producer fail to comply with even one of his contractual obligations, the Society shall request, by *registered letter*, that he remedy such omissions within a period of 30 working days, or a shorter period if stipulated in the contract. Should the producer fail to regularize the situation within this period, the Society shall repeat the request and propose a fresh 15-day period, on expiry of which it shall be empowered to terminate the contract. In the case of certain breaches of contract, special procedures are laid down.

l. This system of non-exclusive licences for the worldwide repertoire of the Society is applicable to the field of phono-mechanical reproduction, except when the end use is *advertising*; in this case a completely different regime is applicable.

6.5. Broadcasting contracts

6.5.1. Concept

A broadcasting contract is a contract whereby the author of a literary, dramatic, musical or audiovisual work—or his successors in title—authorizes a broadcasting organization (radio or television station) to communicate the work to the public by means of radio magnetic waves or any other wireless means and the organization undertakes to transmit the work and to pay the other party a remuneration proportionate to the proceeds from the sale of advertising space or other receipts, or a lump sum. The transmission may be made by means of a 'live' performance by performers, a sound recording or an audiovisual fixation.[95]

6.5.2. Legal nature and characteristics

These are similar to those of performance contracts (see above, Section 6.3).

---

95. The observations concerning broadcasting contracts are applicable, *mutatis mutandis*, to contracts for public transmission by cable (or any other analogous process—wire, optic fibre, laser beam, etc.) of programmes originated by the cable distributor.

6.5.3. Rights and obligations of the parties

In compliance with the principle of the independence of economic rights, each transmission made by a broadcasting organization (or by a cable distributor) other than the original organization—whether it is done simultaneously or is 'time-shifted'—must be expressly authorized and gives rise to the obligation to pay a remuneration. Similar requirements must be complied with in regard to an emission towards a direct broadcasting satellite (DBS) or a communications satellite (CS)—(in France, this does not apply in the case where the author, or his successors in title, have contractually authorized the organization which distributes the signals in the country of broadcast. In this instance the broadcasting organization is exonerated from the obligation to pay).[96]

Although the tendency is to use the designation 'audiovisual works' for all creative works expressed by means of a succession of associated images, this does not mean that the legal provisions for other audiovisual production (cinematographic and video works) apply to so-called 'radiophonic' (televised) works, particularly as regards the presumption of transfer of the exploitation rights (see above, Chapter 2, Section 2.2.1.6). It should be borne in mind, in connection with 'radiophonic' works, that their specific purpose is communication to the public by means of broadcasting and that the fixation of such works, including ephemeral fixations, must be specifically authorized.

Like authors of other types of work, the co-authors of the broadcast work retain the transformation rights. They may, then, unless otherwise agreed, freely dispose of their personal contribution for exploitation of a different kind. However, the case would justify special consideration if it were to cause serious and manifest prejudice to exploitation of the work of collaboration.

Broadcasting rights are generally administered by societies of authors. The laws do not contain specific regulations in this regard; some state that the provisions governing performance contracts are applicable (e.g. Argentina, Article 50). The societies

---

96. See France, Article L. 132-20.3, previously Art. 45(3).

which administer broadcasting rights are usually those which deal with the collective management of public performance rights in dramatic works or non-dramatic musical works—with or without accompanying words—e.g. in Argentina (for the former, the organization is ARGENTORES and for the latter, SADAIC); in Spain (SGAE); in Italy (SIAE); in Uruguay (AGADU); and so on.

As in the case of contracts for mechanical reproduction rights, we shall describe the rights and obligations of the parties to broadcasting contracts on the basis of current practices in a specific country (Argentina). Arrangements differ depending on whether a purely sound or television broadcast is involved and whether it is a broadcast of a non-dramatic musical work—with or without accompanying words—or of literary and dramatic works.[97]

6.5.4. Sound broadcasting

A. NON-DRAMATIC MUSICAL WORKS—WITH OR WITHOUT ACCOMPANYING WORDS[98]

a. SADAIC grants a *global* authorization to the broadcasting stations for transmissions—covering the full musical repertoire (national and foreign) which it administers—but only within the national territory (*repertoire contract*).

b. Such global authorization is *not exclusive* since all stations may broadcast the same works.

---

97. In some countries *non-voluntary licences* are established in favour of the broadcasting organization for the broadcasting of works protected by copyright, distribution by cable in a simultaneous and unaltered fashion of broadcast programmes and for communication to the public of the work broadcast (see above, Chapter 4, Section 4.3.2). Societies for the collective administration of copyright usually also administer the royalties derived from broadcasts made on the basis of such licences.

98. According to 'Copyright arrangements in respect of broadcasting' (Régimen Autoral para radiodifusión) mutually agreed by SADAIC and APRA (Asociación de Radiodifusoras Privadas Argentinas), APRA ensuring that all its members comply with these provisions.

c. The economic consideration is also *global* (covering the use of all works comprehensively) and is proportionate to the income of the station: it amounts to 3.75 per cent of 55 per cent[99] of total *gross income.*[100]

d. The sums paid by broadcasting companies are distributed among authors by the Society in accordance with the broadcasting transmission schedules which each broadcasting company is obliged to draw up and remit each month to the Society, together with payment of the remuneration.

e. Authorization is *non-exclusive*; it will be noted that it does not imply total or partial transfer of copyright, and that the act of broadcasting does not include any of the other acts of use of musical works. In particular *it does not include*: (1) the *recording* of musical works by the broadcasting company itself with a

---

99. The rate is less (3 per cent instead of 3.75 per cent) in the case of stations whose broadcasting licence was granted by the State under the 'low power' regime.

100. Gross income is understood to mean 'the total sum in currency, payment in kind or services, received on a monthly basis from the sale, exchange, payment in kind or any other method of invoicing, before any deduction is made, including the commercialization of programmes produced or acquired for that purpose, and any other income derived from exploitation of the broadcasting service (whether received by the broadcasting company in the form of cash or negotiable instruments). SADAIC shall not be affected by collection of payment by the broadcasting company from its users or clients, neither shall the statement of accounts which the broadcasting company maintains with the user or client be taken into consideration' (Article 3 of the amendment agreed on 9 November 1988); 'bearing in mind the broadcasting company's different operating methods, it is expressly established that, on any commission due to advertising agencies, direct advertisers and/or any natural person or legal entity carrying out such functions, the broadcasting company shall withhold the copyright percentage stipulated in Article 3. The said percentage must be withheld in all cases, even where the invoice is entered in the accounts excluding the usual agency commission' (Article 4 of the text approved by SADAIC on 27 May 1975). To this end the broadcasting company becomes, vis-à-vis SADAIC, a collecting agent, for which reason it is accepted that it should invoice separately 'the sum derived from the withholding of a percentage from the commission due to advertising agencies or similar organizations, destined for payment of copyright' (Article 5 of the same document).

view to time-shifted transmission (unless the recording is transmitted only once and then rendered useless—*ephemeral fixation*); (2) use (*inclusion*) in its own productions—serials, radio plays or programmes in which the music, although performing a merely complementary function, nevertheless forms a permanent characteristic or distinctive feature in such productions and in similar programmes.

f. When *recordings* are made for time-shifted use an additional fee is due.

g. For use (*inclusion*) in its own programmes, specific prior authorization is required; the fee and conditions are governed by a special arrangement.

h. When *recordings*—and/or *inclusions* are not made by the broadcasting company, but by a programme production company, different systems apply, i.e. the regulations for 'Producers of programmes for broadcasting containing musical works' (Productoras de programas destinados a la radiodifusión que contengan obras musicales) and 'Regulations concerning the rights of authors for the use of musical works in advertising' (Régimen autoral para el uso de obras musicales en actos de naturaleza publicitaria). It is the broadcasting company's responsibility to ensure that these regulations have been complied with by the programme producer.

i. Authorization to make *recordings* or *inclusions* cannot be transferred. Commercialization (assignment, transfer, sale, hire, etc.) of a recorded programme containing musical works made by the producer (whether the broadcasting company itself or a third party) must have the Society's prior authorization and remuneration and other conditions must be fixed in each case.

j. In accordance with the principle of the independence of rights, the author's rights are expressly reserved in the case of programme retransmission and public performance when the broadcast is made from premises or auditoriums other than the broadcasting station's own studios, whether for profit-making purposes or not.

k. It is incumbent upon the broadcasting station to announce in the programmes which it transmits the titles and names of all the authors (composers of music and authors of the accompanying words) of the works to be performed, before and after each performance. It must also respect the original content of the works so as not to prejudice the moral rights of authors.

B. LITERARY AND DRAMATIC WORKS

a. Very often they are works which the broadcasting company— or a programme producer—commissions directly from the author.

b. When an exclusive authorization is granted, it is usually limited to the duration of the contract.

c. The method of remuneration is a *lump sum*.

d. The broadcasting company must observe the legal obligations in regard to the author's moral rights (mention of the name and respect for the integrity of the work).

6.5.5. Television

A. NON-DRAMATIC MUSICAL WORKS—WITH OR WITHOUT ACCOMPANYING WORDS[101]

A number of the regulations governing the sound broadcasting of works apply.

a. Authorization for use is *global* (repertoire contract) and non-exclusive.

b. The economic consideration is *global* (a comprehensive form of payment covering use of all the works) and *proportionate* to the revenue of the station: it amounts to 1.5 per cent of 40 per cent of the potential monthly sales of the television station.[102]

---

101. The SADAIC General Regulations (notified to the Association of Argentine Broadcasting Companies—ATA—on 19 October 1973) which television companies must observe.

102. The potential monthly sales of each television station is understood to mean the sum derived from total sales of advertising spots repeated throughout the month. The factors taken into consideration to calculate this potential are the following: (a) number of minutes of advertising per hour permitted by law; (b) number of days (28, 30 and/or 31 as the case may be) involved so as to arrive at the authorized advertising time during the month; (c) number of six-second units obtained by dividing the number of minutes of authorized advertising each month; (d) number of hours of broadcasting per day carried out by each com-

c. The sums paid by the television companies are distributed among authors by the Society in accordance with a sworn statement which the companies are obliged to make and deliver monthly to the Society with their payment. This statement must include the current schedule of fees and the broadcasting timetable for the previous month.

d. Such remuneration is applicable exclusively 'to the specific nature of the act of television broadcasting' and does not include any of the other acts of use of musical works. Specifically it *does not include*: (1) *recording*, understood as the act of recording carried out by the television company itself with a view to televising the musical works on its own channel with or without an accompanying picture; (2) the use (*inclusion*) of musical works in its own productions: television series, televised plays or presentation of programmes in which the music, although performing a merely complementary function, nevertheless forms a *permanent characteristic* or *distinctive feature* in them or in similar productions, such productions being designed for transmission through the television station's own channel.

e. An additional fee is payable for recordings.[103]

f. Individual prior authorization is required for each use (*inclusion*) in the station's own programmes; the fee and conditions are governed by a special standard contract.

---

pany; and (e) the advertising rate charged by each television company for each second of advertising time. Successive multiplication of these five factors determines the potential monthly sales of each television company (Article 2 of the SADAIC General Regulations with which each television company must comply).

103. This is stipulated as 30 per cent of the fee fixed for each television station, proportionate to its use, in accordance with the regulation laid down by the BIEM (see above, Section 6.4.3 Rights and obligations of the parties). The figure of 30 per cent is not applicable to recordings received from other stations and transmitted by them. The formula to determine this additional fee is as follows: 30 per cent of the fee multiplied by the number of hours of the station's own recorded programmes divided by the total number of broadcasting hours in the month.

g. When *recordings* or *inclusions* are not made by the television station, the prior authorization and payment of fees is the responsibility of the natural person or legal entity producing the programmes and the regulations for 'Producers of programmes for television broadcasting containing musical works' and the 'Regulations concerning the rights of authors for the use of musical works in advertising' are applicable.

Recordings or inclusions made by the television station whose use is not limited to transmission by the station through its own channel are covered by the regulations referred to above, which govern the activities of programme production companies or advertising, whichever is applicable.

In the case of cable television, SADAIC receives 1 per cent of the total gross monthly revenue of each cable programme distributor (contract between SADAIC and ATVC (Asociación de televisión por cable—Cable Television Association).

B. LITERARY AND DRAMATIC WORKS

a. Contracts authorizing the television broadcasting by Hertzian means of literary or dramatic works are drawn up in respect of individual works. They must be made in writing and cannot be transferred.

b. Frequently the works have been commissioned by the station directly from the author.

c. Contract arrangements in respect of these works are commonly made directly by the author—or his successors in title—with a *programme production company* which is distinct from the television station which is to broadcast the programme for the first time (originating organization). In such cases the television station is considered to be jointly and severally responsible for payment of the remuneration agreed with the author in the contract.

d. Remuneration consists of a *lump sum payment* in the case of television broadcasting by Hertzian means and is *global* and *proportionate* to the revenue of the station when cable television is involved (ARGENTORES collects 0.65 per cent of the total amount of gross monthly revenue in respect of affiliation charges).

e. Fixation of the work must be specifically authorized. If ephemeral fixations are made, the author must be informed. He must also be informed of the place where these fixations are stored and the date on which they are rendered useless (erased). The television company is answerable, together with the production company, for any unauthorized use of such fixations.

f. Authorization is understood to be exclusive when the work is broadcast for the first time.

g. When any of the texts which make up a programme series is not broadcast for reasons which are not the responsibility of the author, the latter shall be paid the agreed price as if it had been broadcast.

h. In accordance with the principle of the independence of rights, authorization for the television broadcasting of a work covers that use only and the author reserves all other rights. Should the television station be concerned to ensure that the work is not used in certain ways while the agreed series of programmes is being televised, this shall be the subject of a specific agreement whereby the author receives remuneration in respect of each prospective use.

i. The broadcasting company must observe the legal obligations concerning the moral rights of the author (mention of his name and respect for the integrity of the work). For this reason alterations to the work (cuts, reworking, abridgement or alteration, even when imposed by adaptation of the work to the medium) must be specifically authorized by the author.

j. When cinematographic works are televised, the television station must take care that the copies used are in perfect technical condition as regards light and sound and that no cuts have been made which might alter continuity or distort the spirit in which such works were conceived and made.

6.6. Contracts for the production of audiovisual works

The term *audiovisual works* covers cinematographic productions and other works expressed through a medium similar to cinematography (such as videographic works—specifically created as videograms—and works specially created for television broadcasting).[104]

Television works (we use this term instead of 'radiophonic' works in order to avoid any confusion with works specially created for radio broadcasting, that is to say, by purely sound radio) have certain features which distinguish them from other audiovisual productions: they may be broadcast 'live' or ephemeral fixations may be made[105] and they are basically designed to be televised. For these reasons they have been dealt with along with broadcasting contracts and we shall not include them when discussing the type of contract which now concerns us, despite the fact that there are examples of works made for television which, due to their artistic qualities are also shown in cinemas (such as *Scenes from a Marriage* by Ingmar Bergman or *The Interview* by Federico Fellini) just as cinematographic works are constantly shown on television.

The 'basic end use' of the different types of audiovisual works must be taken into account for the laws contain different provisions concerning the scope of the rights and obligations of the parties depending on whether it is an audiovisual work basically intended to be communicated to the public by means of projection or exhibition (cinematographic works), by means of the sale or hire of copies in the form of video cassettes (videographic works), or by means of broadcasting (television works).

Here we shall deal with *contracts for cinematographic works*, basically intended to be communicated to the public by being projected or shown in cinemas or similar premises, and *videographic works*, produced on video cassettes, that is to say audiovisual works basically not intended to be shown on television (we have referred to those intended for television screening as television works—see our previous remarks in Section 6.5).

The aim of such contracts is the production of an audiovisual work (a film), either silent or with sound, irrespective of the

---

104. See above, Chapter 2, Section 2.2.1.6(B). Other audiovisual works.
105. However, cinematographic works exist only when they have been fixed.

type (dramas, comedies, animated cartoons, documentaries, news, etc.), length (feature-films, medium-length or short), the technical process (photomagnetic or electronic) and the material support used (celluloid, electronic videotape, etc.). The producer may be an individual, a commercial production company or a broadcasting organization. In some countries the latter are often the producers or co-producers of cinematographic works (e.g. Radiotelevisión Española S.A. in Spain; RAI in Italy; etc.), despite which neither the nature of the works nor the legal regulations applicable to the respective contract change.

6.6.1. Concept

In the broad sense, contracts for making audiovisual works encompass any contract whose purpose is a work or an artistic contribution for the production of such a work.

In the restricted sense used in the relevant laws (as in Colombia, the Dominican Republic, Ecuador, France, Spain), a contract for making or producing audiovisual works is any contract whereby the author of a literary, dramatic or artistic work[106]—or his successors in title—authorizes a natural person or a legal entity (the *producer*) to include it in an audio-visual work, which the latter undertakes to produce for his own account and risk, without legal subordination, publicize, distribute and communicate to the public (either directly or through a third party), basically by means of projection or exhibition if it is a cinematographic work and by means of the sale or hire of copies of the work if it is a videographic work not intended primarily for television. The producer also undertakes to pay the other party a remuneration proportionate to the proceeds derived from exploitation of the work, or a lump sum.

The inclusion of musical works—with or without accompanying words—in the soundtrack of an audiovisual work is

---

106. Our reference to the term 'artistic work' concerns mainly animated cartoons included in an audiovisual work.

termed *synchronization*[107] and does not form part of the contract we are analysing.[108] Societies for collective management which administer the rights of authors of musical works, which are generally responsible for granting the respective prior authorization for synchronization, have schedules of fees (known as 'synchronization rights'[109] drawn up specially for such uses.

6.6.2. Legal nature and characteristics

In general the remarks concerning publishing contracts are applicable (see above, Section 6.2).

6.6.3. Rights and obligations of the parties

Copyright laws contain regulations governing the producer's exploitation rights in cinematographic and audiovisual works in general. However, it is only recently that certain relevant laws have begun to regulate contracts for the production of audiovisual works as a standard contract (Ecuador—1976, Articles 70 to 80; Colombia—1982—Articles 100–104; France—1985 amendment —Chapter III, 'Audio-visual Production Contracts', Articles 63-1 to 63-7, now Intellectual Property Code, Art. L. 132-23 to 132-30;

---

107. By *synchronization* is meant the addition of words, sound effects and musical works to an audiovisual fixation, so that the correspondence between sound and image is perfect. Once the audiovisual work has been filmed, the dialogues and speech, either by the same or other actors (dubbing), sound effects (noises, etc.) and music are recorded and *synchronized* with the images (mouth movements, gestures, actions, etc.).
108. French law stresses this at the outset of the regulations governing contracts for the production of audiovisual works, since it stipulates (Article L. 132-24, previously Art. 63-1) that: 'Contracts binding the producer and the authors of an audio-visual work, *other than the authors of a musical composition with or without words*, shall imply, unless otherwise stipulated and notwithstanding the rights afforded to the author by Articles L. III-3, L. 121-4, L. 121-5, L. 122-1 to L. 122-7, L. 131-2 to L. 131-7, L. 132-4 and L. 132-7, assignment to the producer of the exclusive exploitation rights in the audio-visual work.' The laws of Colombia (Article 100) and the Dominican Republic (Article 115) exclude authors of musical works from the definition of contracts for cinematographic fixation.
109. In Argentina they are generally known as 'inclusion rights'.

the Dominican Republic—1986—Articles 115–120 (modelled on the Colombian law); Spain— 1987—Articles 88–94). Legislators have probably realized the need for such regulations in respect of audiovisual works in general due to the diversity of forms of exploitation to which such works may be subjected and to the economic importance they have attained following the tremendous expansion in their circulation as a result of the supremacy of the audiovisual media (television, cable, video) in relation to the other media (graphic, audio, stage, etc.).

a. The main characteristic of the legal regulations is 'the "legal" (not simply economic) protagonism of the producer in the exploitation of audio-visual works', as Delgado Porras has termed it.[110] We shall not dwell on this aspect since it has already been covered extensively when dealing with the question of ownership of rights in respect of audiovisual works (see above, Chapter 3, Section 3.4.1).

b. Although it is becoming increasingly frequent for cinematographic works to be exploited by the sale or hire of copies (for private showings—home video), television broadcasts and cable distribution, none the less public communication by such means is not included in the contract which concerns us here, unless expressly agreed or stipulated by law (as in Colombia, Article 103(B), first part). Each form of communication to the public must be expressly authorized by the authors (Spain, Article 88(1), second paragraph),[111] because the presumption of transfer of exploitation rights which the laws stipulate in favour of the producer of cinematographic works does not include the right to authorize the broadcasting of such works (including satellite broadcasts and cable distribution); this right belongs exclusively to the authors of the literary, dramatic, musical or artistic works included in them.

---

110. Porras Antonio Delgado, *Utilización de obras audiovisuales por satélite y cable—la intervención de las sociedades de autores*, op. cit., p. 219, No. 11.
111. Spain, Article 88(1), second paragraph: '... for cinematographic works the express authorization of the authors shall always be necessary for their exploitation by means of the furnishing to the public of copies in whatever mode or format for use within the family circle, or by means of communication to the public by broadcasting'.

c. Neither does it imply transfer to the producer of graphic rights and stage rights in the work (France, Article L. 132-24, second para., previously Art. 63-1; Spain, Article 89(2)).

d. Unless otherwise stipulated, the author of the pre-existing work may make use of his contribution separately, provided that exploitation of the audiovisual work is not thereby prejudiced (Colombia, Article 101, first part; Spain, Article 88(2)).

e. The contract must specify the periods within which the producer must complete production of the audiovisual work and commence its exploitation (Colombia, Article 101, second part, stipulates a maximum of three years from termination). It is incumbent upon the producer to exploit the work in conformity with the practice of the profession (France, Article L. 132-27, previously Art. 63-5).

f. After a given period has elapsed, the author may make use of his individual contribution in another audio-visual work (remakes). Should no contractual provision have been made, Spanish law (Art. 89(2)) fixes this period at fifteen years after the contribution has been made available to the producer.

g. Remuneration for the authors who contribute to an audio-visual work must be determined for each exploitation mode (France, Article L. 132-25, first para., previously Art. 63-2, first paragraph; Spain, Article 90(1)). Remuneration may be: (1) proportional to the proceeds received by the producer from exploitation of the audiovisual work; (2) proportional to the price paid by the public to receive public communication of it (France, Article L. 132-25, second para., previously Art. 63-2, second paragraph); or (3) a lump sum.

When remuneration is proportionate to the proceeds, the producer is obliged to furnish authors with a statement of revenue from exploitation of the work in respect of each exploitation mode and, at their request, all the documentary evidence necessary to establish the accuracy of the accounts, in particular copies of the contracts in which he assigns to third parties all or a part of the rights he enjoys (France, Article L. 132-28, previously Art. 63-3, which stipulates that settlement should be made at least once a year).

In some countries (such as Argentina, Mexico, Spain) and

irrespective of what may have been agreed in the contract, where the audiovisual work is shown in public places against payment of an admission charge, the authors shall be entitled to collect from those showing the work in public a percentage of the proceeds from such showing (Spain, Article 90(2), recognizes that the exhibitors may deduct the sums paid by way of such remuneration from those that have to be remitted to the licensors of the audiovisual work). In Argentina, where the parties concerned call this 'showing rights', the authors of literary and dramatic works embodied in a cinematographic work receive, for every day that the work is shown, a sum equivalent to a given number of times the fee charged for admission to the show (in proportion to the seating capacity of the hall and on the basis of a maximum of four admission fees). This right cannot be waived and cannot be transferred by *inter vivos* transaction (Spain, Article 90(2), second paragraph, first part).

But, as this method of remuneration—which is the responsibility of the exhibitors—is unknown in the majority of countries, in those countries where such payment is effected (e.g. Spain, Article 90(2), second paragraph, second part) provision must be made to ensure, should the audio-visual work be exported, that the authors may assign the said right for a lump sum in the event that it is impossible or extremely difficult to exercise that right effectively in the importing countries. The obligation to pay the sums corresponding to this 'showing right' is the responsibility of the impresarios of the public halls or premises where audiovisual works are projected or shown and payment must be made periodically (in Argentina, monthly).

If a duly authorized projection or showing of an audiovisual work is made and no admission fee is charged, the author still retains the right to receive remuneration for its use (Spain, Article 90(3)).

Authors of audiovisual works of a *promotional nature* are excluded from this 'showing right' (Spain, Article 90(5)).

h. Protection of moral rights: the reader is referred to Chapter 3, Section 3.4.2 above.

Chapter 7

Neighbouring rights

Summary

7.1. Rights of performers
  7.1.1. Legal nature. 7.1.1.1. Theories based on assimilation with authors' rights. 7.1.1.2. Criticism of theories based on assimilation with authors' rights. 7.1.1.3. The theory which considers that the performer's right is a personality right. 7.1.1.4. Criticism. 7.1.1.5. Labour law theories. 7.1.1.6. Criticism of labour law theories. 7.1.1.7. Independent theories. **7.1.2.** The subject of protection. **7.1.3.** Holders of the rights. **7.1.4.** Content. 7.1.4.1. The performer's moral rights. 7.1.4.2. Economic rights of performers and their limitations. 7.1.4.3. Limitations. 7.1.4.4. Term of the economic rights of performers. **7.1.5.** Exercise of performers' economic rights in instances of collective performances

7.2. Rights of producers of phonograms
  7.2.1. The subject of protection. **7.2.2.** Owners of the rights. **7.2.3.** Content: economic rights of producers of phonograms. Limitations. **7.2.4.** Term of the rights of the producers of phonograms

7.3. Rights of broadcasting organizations
  7.3.1. The subject of protection. **7.3.2.** Owners of the rights. **7.3.3.** Content: economic rights of broadcasting organizations. Limitations. **7.3.4.** Term of the rights of broadcasting organizations

The term *neighbouring rights* does not enjoy favour among theorists and writers on the subject and its content is imprecise, but it has become established through usage. The *WIPO Glossary* informs us that it is

usually understood as meaning rights granted in an increasing number of countries to protect the interests of performers, producers of phonograms and broadcasting organizations in relation to their activities in connection with the public use of authors' works, all kinds of artists' presentations or the communication to the public of events, information, and any sounds or images ...[1]

---

1. *WIPO Glossary of Terms of the Law of Copyright and Neighbouring Rights*, WIPO, Geneva, 1980, p. 167, entry 164.

Other terms are also used such as *related rights*. However, the rights vested in cable distribution companies in respect of their own programmes[2] and in publishers with regard to the typographical arrangement of their published editions also belong to the category of neighbouring rights.[3] Some laws also include under this head, furthermore, the protection of isolated photographs,[4] catalogues and compilations which do not fulfil the necessary requirements for protection as works, and also include a number of other productions.[5]

In spite of the fact that the expressions *neighbouring rights* and *related rights* suggest a degree of similarity with copyright, their use with respect to the protection of the rights of performers, producers of phonograms[6] and broadcasting organizations (the

---

2. See above, Chapter 4, Section 4.3.2.4, C—types of cable distribution.
3. See above, Chapter 6, Section 6.2.4.
4. See above, Chapter 2, Section 2.2.1.4, E.
5. The first copyright law to regulate neighbouring rights was the Austrian law of 1936. Part II of this law (Articles 66–80) established, in four chapters, the protection of recitals and performances of works of literature and music (performers); of photographs, sound recordings; of letters and portraits; of news, titles of works of literature and art.

The Italian law of 1941 adopted the expression *neighbouring rights*. Part II thereof contains '*Provisions concerning rights connected with the exercise of copyright*' (Articles 72–102) regulating, in separate chapters, not only matters concerning producers of phonograph records or like contrivances, broadcast emissions, and the activities of actors and performers, but also sketches of theatrical scenes, photographs, letters and portraits, engineering projects, the protection of the titles of works, the headings of sections used in periodical publications, the external appearance of works, articles and news items, and the prohibition of certain acts constituting unfair competition.

This criterion warrants criticism for lumping together rights of different categories under a common heading: *rights related to industrial activities* (of producers, broadcasting companies, publishers of periodical publications); *activities of performers*; *creative activities* (works protected by copyright, drawings, photographs, missives, etc.); *the rights of the personality in general* (concerning the content of letters, the image of the author, and so on).

6. The word *phonogram* comes from the Greek 'phone' (sound) and 'gramma' (writing). Henry Jessen points out that this is not, as it might seem, a newly coined legal term for it appeared on the labels of the first cylinders published

only categories that will be dealt with in this chapter) and those of other beneficiaries, should be attributed rather to the resistance which the recognition of new rights always creates—prompting a move to place them on the same footing as rights that are already established than to the real existence of similarities, since the protection concerns activities which—in the words of Dubois— are related to the dissemination rather than the creation of literary and artistic works.[7]

Thomas Edison's phonograph, the Lumière brothers' cinematograph and the radio pioneered by Heinrich Hertz and Marconi marked, between the end of the nineteenth century and the beginning of the twentieth, the starting point of the technological development which brought about recognition of neighbouring rights.

Viewed from this angle, the genesis of neighbouring rights reflects a marked similarity to the emergence of authors' rights which resulted from the invention by Gutenberg of printing by movable type in the middle of the fifteenth century, and the development of engraving. Just as these inventions made it possible to reproduce books in large quantities and enabled use of works to elude the author's control, so the phonograph, cinematography and broadcasting made the mechanical reproduction of musical, literary and dramatic works feasible, together with their public communication to virtually limitless audiences. Performances which could not previously have been imagined as being something separate from the person of the performer could, from that moment onwards, be preserved and disseminated independently of the artist involved.

---

by the inventor of the phonograph, Thomas Alva Edison, in the final decades of the nineteenth century (*La protección del fonograma*, study presented at the II Venezuelan Congress on the protection of intellectual rights, Barquisimeto, Venezuela, July, 1988).

7.   Henri Desbois, op. cit., p. 213: 'They play an auxiliary role in literary and artistic creation.' 'Activities under this head concern the dissemination and not the creation of literary and artistic works.'

A. THE MECHANICAL REPRODUCTION OF MUSICAL WORKS AND ITS HISTORY

Humankind's inveterate love of music and desire to enjoy it on every occasion led to the search for ways of preserving performances. The reproduction of music by mechanical means attracted the attention of inventors very early on; this enthusiastic quest over the centuries was finally crowned with success on 16 June 1888, thanks to the genius and efforts of Edison.

Walter Bruch,[8] in his excellent study on the subject, describes the history of this development, explaining how, through research, projects, inventions and devices, the possibilities of musical reproduction slowly but surely took shape, from the pin-studded revolving cylinder, the earliest music-storing device, to the invention of the phonographic record. This author tells us how, in the Middle Ages, songbirds were trained to repeat melodies, the particular piece being played to them several times each day on, for example, a flageolet, something like today's toy instrument, so transforming caged birds into veritable reproducers of popular airs and marches that were all the rage. Bruch goes on to relate how, at the beginning of the eighteenth century, miniature organs were produced for the purpose of training birds; these were soon enlarged and improved, leading to the creation of the mechanical domestic organ, and it became fashionable to combine pipe organs with a clock mechanism resulting in musical (flute-playing) clocks for which Haydn, Mozart and Beethoven composed small organ pieces. He describes how the pipe organs were enlarged in a number of places and transformed, at the beginning of the nineteenth century, into 'musical machines' (such as the 'Panharmonicon' and, later, the 'Orchestrion'). He tells us how, also at the beginning of the nineteenth century, the forerunner of 'canned' music appeared—the musical box, which played a certain programme of airs. Musical boxes were manufactured in appreciable quantities because they were inexpensive enough to find their way into peo-

---

8. Walter Bruch, 'From the Music Register to the Phonogram', in the publication marking the 50th anniversary of BIEM (1929–79), pp. 14–50.

ple's homes, becoming the first example of consumer goods in the history of the mechanical production of music. Great strides were achieved with the appearance, first of all, of the interchangeable round disc and the continuous cardboard loop, and, subsequently, the combination of the perforated paper roll with a pneumatic sound release system (these were mechanical musical instruments with interchangeable discs or perforated paper rolls, such as the 'Ariston', 'Herophon', 'Manopan' and 'Clariophon').[9] These early interchangeable discs, Bruch relates, were the forerunners of modern records, first of all because they made it possible for the listener to make a collection of pieces and build up his or her own repertoire, and, secondly, they could be purchased separately, like the cardboard loops of the 'Manopan'. Bruch recounts how another instrument was created which took the place of the musical box in middle-class homes—the mechanical piano, also called the pianola (player piano), phonola, etc., in which air pressure regulated a perforated paper roll. Music for the pianola was written by such famous composers as Igor Stravinsky who, in 1917, composed his *Etude for Pianola*. In 1905, the *Welte-Mignon* grand piano appeared, making it possible for a work to be performed with every detail and nuance of the pianist's interpretation which had been communicated to the master roll and presenting, in 1926, the first performances of works by Paul Hindemith, Ernst Toch and Gerhard Münch. These Welte pianos disappeared at the end of that decade, along with the other mechanical instruments (such as the pianola), supplanted by the phonographic record. Bruch describes how, on 7 December 1877, Edison presented his first model of the phonograph, in which, each time it was cranked, the words spoken into it were repeated, as if it were a 'talking machine'. On 16 June 1888, Edison put the finishing touches to his new phonograph, equipped with a battery-operated electric motor. Instead of wrapping a sheet of tinfoil around a cylinder (the procedure which he had used in his first phonograph), he

---

9. See Erich Schulze, 'Protection of Mechanical Reproduction Rights. Legal Development', in the publication marking the 50th anniversary of BIEM (1929–79), p. 7.

filled the inner grooves of the cylinder with wax; these cylinders could revolve repeatedly and be used for recordings over and over again. Bruch tells us how in Philadelphia, on 16 May 1888, the public witnessed the birth of the phonographic record—a small zinc disc which Emile Berliner played on his new gramophone—and how Edison succeeded in dominating the market thanks to his well-designed and well-built phonographs with their wax cylinders. Just as the phonographic record in its real form arrived on the market, Edison had also succeeded, through an ingenious moulding technique, in making as many copies as desired from a master cylinder; cylinder and disc coexisted until the cylinder was gradually supplanted by the disc. Bruch notes that in 1929 (shortly before the great world depression, which affected the phonographic industry very considerably) some 30 million discs were produced.[10] Next came long-playing records, hi-fi, magnetic tape in compact cassettes, compact discs and the digital recording process (DAT). The development of sound recording systems seems to know no limits either as regards the quality of reproduction, the miniaturization of the components or, again, the reduction of costs.

B. EFFECTS OF THE FIXATION AND MECHANICAL REPRODUCTION OF MUSICAL WORKS ON AUTHORS' RIGHTS; THE SITUATION OF PERFORMERS

a. Authors

Before the cylinder and the phonographic record became suitable for reproducing the performances of musical works, music reproducers (pinned cylinders, pipe organs, musical clocks, music machines, musical boxes, pianolas, phonolas, etc.) *affected no more than the rights of the composers whose works were fixed and reproduced by them.*

Until the musical boxes and mechanical music machines were perfected, composers willingly accepted the playing of their works

---

10. See Walter Bruch, op. cit.

in fashionable salons by means of musical (flute-playing) clocks since they regarded this as a form of publicity. But as Bruch points out, when musical boxes began to be manufactured on an industrial scale, mostly in Switzerland, and exported to many countries, operatic melodies, patriotic songs, folk songs and waltzes became widely disseminated.[11]

But the birth of the relationship between composers and the manufacturers of these music reproduction devices was not without its pangs.

According to Schulz-Köhn,[12] as long as the musical boxes were distributed in Switzerland, the composers (almost entirely French musicians) were not very much interested in them. When, however, they were imported into France, the situation changed. The musical boxes reproduced for the most part ballads which the composers themselves sang in the coffee houses on the boulevards. Rival establishments offered the same compositions played on musical boxes, and, partly because of the novelty of these instruments, they attracted a large public. Composers began to claim compensation for the use of their works; in spite of the fact that in France the principles of copyright had already been proclaimed in 1791 and 1793, and that these rights and obligations were already clearly established, the composers' claims were to no avail whatsoever. In 1864 France and Switzerland concluded a trade agreement in which the import of musical boxes into France was still the only bone of contention. The matter was settled in defiance of the rights of the composers for it was agreed that France should not regard the import of Swiss musical boxes as a violation of copyright, while Switzerland undertook to give preferential treatment to the import of French silk from Lyons.

Composers had no better luck at the international level. The original Act of the Berne Convention, signed on 9 September

---

11. Ibid., p. 23.
12. D. Schulz-Köhn, *Die Schallplatte auf dem Weltmarkt*, Berlin, 1940, quoted by Bruch, op. cit., p. 23.

1886, contained, in paragraph 3 of the Final Protocol, a provision which, as Schulze[13] observes, constituted a concession to the Swiss musical box industry, for it established that: 'It is understood that the manufacture and sale of instruments for the mechanical reproduction of musical airs in which copyright subsists shall not be considered as constituting an infringement of musical copyright'.[14]

Recognition of the rights of composers was particularly hampered by this provision. Mechanical reproduction techniques continued to progress; composers appealed to the courts claiming that interchangeable discs and perforated paper rolls were unknown at the time of the conclusion of the Berne Convention; there could be no comparison with what had existed previously for the new instruments had interchangeable components which opened up new exploitation possibilities. Composers should then share in the resulting economic benefits.

The situation of composers with respect to the reproduction of their musical works by mechanical instruments did not begin to turn to their advantage until 1908, when in the Berlin Act of the Berne Convention the above-mentioned paragraph of the Final Protocol of the original Act of 1886 was deleted, and it was established, in Article 13 (para. 1) that: 'The authors of musical works shall have the exclusive right of authorizing (1) the adaptation of those works to instruments which can reproduce them mechanically; (2) the public performance of the said works by means of these instruments.'

However, paragraph (2) allowed the countries of the Union to establish reservations and conditions relating to the application of Article 13, although the effects were strictly limited to the country which put them into force.

---

13. Erich Schulze, op. cit., p. 7.
14. '*Il est entendu que la fabrication et la vente des instruments servant à reproduire mécaniquement des airs de musique empruntés au domaine privé ne sont pas considérées comme constituant le fait de contrefaçon musicale*' (original Act of the Berne Convention, Final Protocol, para. 3).

Article 13 was included in the Rome Act (1928) and the Brussels Act (1948), until, in the Stockholm Act (1967), reproduced in the Paris Act (1971), explicit mention was made, in the list of protected economic rights, of the right of reproduction (Article 9(1)), set out in broadly based terms covering every form of reproduction of works: 'Authors of literary and artistic works protected by this Convention shall have the exclusive right of authorizing the reproduction of these works, in any manner or form'.

However, so as to avoid any ambiguity paragraph 3 of Article 9 stated clearly in addition, that: 'Any sound or visual recording shall be considered as a reproduction for the purposes of this Convention.'

b. Performers

The mechanical reproduction of musical works affected the situation of performing artists only when the techniques of the cylinder and the phonographic disc were perfected and their performances could be reproduced on a massive scale. The boom in the sale of gramophone records, produced and copied by mechanical means, and their diffusion with the use of loudspeakers and broadcasting, plus the advent of the 'talking picture', combined to supplant the performers who, in the cinema, had given dramatic effect to the plot which unfolded on the screen. The results were disastrous for them.

In a report published in 1939 by the International Labour Office, a number of statistics were given which reflect the gravity of the situation and the universal extent of the crisis. In France, where in 1932 there were about 10,000 theatrical artists, it was estimated that only 1,500 had employment. In the United States, in 1935, the list drawn up by the Administration of cases in which relief was urgently needed (a list far from registering all unemployment) contained the names of 15,000 unemployed musicians. An inquiry into unemployment among intellectual workers in Japan showed that the proportion of musicians unemployed in 1936 was 41 per cent, as against 16 per cent for technical employees in industry. Lastly, in 1937 a statistical survey of the music profession in Vienna showed that 90 per cent of its members were without employment.[15]

Technological development had made it possible for everyone to enjoy music in a permanent form. Performances had ceased to be ephemeral; they could be fixed and the public could enjoy them without leaving their homes. Furthermore, in theatres, concert halls, cafés, dance halls, family gatherings, the cinema, etc., performers were replaced by phonographic recordings, broadcasts and the soundtracks of films. The wider the access by the public to performances by musicians, the less work the players had. There was an inevitable reaction on the part of professional organizations.

At national and international meetings, *claims were voiced in respect of three rights*, corresponding to those recognized in the case of authors of literary, musical and artistic works:
- the *right to authorize* the reproduction, transmission and recording of their performances by mechanical, radioelectric or other means, as well as the public performance of such transmitted or recorded performances;
- the *moral right* to respect for the personality of the performer in its two basic aspects: the right to be identified or the right to be named and the right to oppose the alteration or distortion of the performance; and
- the *economic right* to receive special, equitable and compensatory remuneration for the use made of a performance each time that it was broadcast—provided that it had not been made for this purpose and specific payment made—or each time that a phonographic recording was performed in a public place, and to receive a percentage from the sale of records.

Economic compensation was sought in this instance:
- *in respect of the enlargement of the audience*. A performer engaged to appear in a theatre or concert hall should have the right to a special fee should the performance be disseminated beyond the physical limits of the place of performance (by

---

15. *The Rights of Performers in Broadcasting, Television and the Mechanical Reproduction of Sounds*, ILO, 1939, p. 6.

means of loudspeakers, broadcasting, etc.) in recognition of the enlargement of the audience by means of the new techniques. In regard to recordings, performers sought compensation for this incalculable enlargement of the audience by demanding a special form of payment when recordings were played in public places. They also demanded a percentage of the sale price of each record since, in this way, the sale of each copy would become equivalent to a live performance.
- *in respect of the combination of recording and broadcasting.* It began to be realized that rights were emerging which called for different categories of remuneration according to the various possible uses: a 'live' performance in a theatre or concert hall; the broadcast transmission of this performance; a recording of a 'live' performance; and the broadcasting of this recording.

Other questions were also raised concerning:
- the most appropriate method of collecting and accounting for the sums received in the exercise of these rights. It was realized that, as in the case of the composers of musical works, the efficient collection of payment could only be achieved through collective administration;
- whether the right existed independently of the artistic level or the quality of the performance;
- whether, in the case of an ensemble, each performer was the owner of a right or only the soloists and the conductor of the ensemble. It was observed that, even when rights were attributed to the group, it was necessary to delegate their representation to one person (the conductor, the impresario, etc.).

As a general rule, domestic legislation recognized the rights of performers in the framework of copyright laws, although in separate provisions. However, the French law of 3 July 1985, while recognizing them, did not incorporate them in the 1957 law which has continued to regulate the rights of authors alone.

At the international level, recognition of the rights of performers was also achieved in conjunction with the rights of the producers of phonograms and broadcasting organizations, but outside the context of copyright conventions. The respective convention was signed in Rome in 1961, under the aegis of three international organizations: the ILO (International Labour

Organization), the International Bureau of the Berne Union (subsequently WIPO) and UNESCO.

C. COPYRIGHT AND NEIGHBOURING RIGHTS. A CLASH

The claims of neighbouring rights, formulated along similar lines as copyright, means the possibility of a clash with authors' rights.

Authors, through their national societies and the international organizations which group them, have always refuted the possibility of placing the different categories of rights on the same footing, and, more especially, have considered that the protection afforded under neighbouring rights should not include prerogatives to authorize or prohibit the *secondary uses* of the fixations or broadcasts of the performances of works. Having regard to the fact that neither the interpretation of the performer nor the supporting medium of the producer, nor again, the broadcast transmission, can be dissociated from the work that is performed, fixed or broadcast, should a right to authorize or to prohibit the use of the work be recognized as being vested in performers, producers of phonograms and broadcasting organizations, then this would, implicitly, constitute the granting of rights in the work itself. Obviously, a right ceases to be exclusive in the presence of another exclusive right in respect of the same object—or the object which contains it.[16]

This is the reason for the efforts which have been made to define the legal nature of the subject matter of protection with regard to the different categories of the beneficiaries of neighbouring rights and the scope of their application.

For Desbois these are *auxiliary activities* in literary and artistic creation:

---

16. See Edoardo Piola Caselli, in *Il Diritto di Autore*, 1939, p. 18, in which he indicates that 'exclusivity' means belonging to a sole person; he stresses that 'coexistence' and 'conflict' are simply the two sides of a single legal situation, since the coexistence of rival desires and interests, both with respect to the right of authorization and to the reward that can be obtained, creates the potential conflict.

... They are linked by a common feature: they play an auxiliary role in literary and artistic creation, for performers fulfil the destiny of musical compositions and dramatic works, sound recording companies ensure the permanence of otherwise fleeting impressions, and broadcasting organizations abolish distances. But each of these activities calls for special comment because of their respective characteristics.[17]

He considers that they are rights neighbouring on authors' rights, for those who have an auxiliary role in literary and artistic creation move in the orbit of creators of works:

... the status of sound recording or broadcasting organizations is one neighbouring on that of authors, for those who have an auxiliary role in literary and artistic creation move in the orbit of creators of works; it is a neighbouring one also because it acquires, by osmosis, certain of their features. But 'neighbouring' implies relations which should be as harmonious as possible; the rights of those with an auxiliary role should not be built on the ruins of those of authors; creators will need to resign themselves to certain sacrifices, in their own economic interests, for the coexistence of rival rights brings with it, by force of circumstances, a reduction in the share of each of the parties.[18]

Jessen, the eminent Brazilian authority in the area of neighbouring rights, refutes this relationship and consequent subordination and claims that he has never succeeded in discerning such a link between these rights and the author's right in respect of his work:

What we can make out is an analogy, a parallelism between the two rights, but never a relationship—this would imply subordination which is non-existent in this case. They are independent and fully autonomous rights, which do not conflict but are, on the contrary, similar and convergent in a number of aspects.[19]

In the Rome Convention for the Protection of Performers, Producers of Phonograms, and Broadcasting Organizations,

---

17. Henri Desbois, op. cit., p. 213, Section 177.
18. Ibid., pp. 232–3, Section 189.
19. Henry Jessen, 'Los derechos conexos de artistas intérpretes y ejecutantes, productores de fonogramas y organismos de radiodifusión', in the Libro memoria of the *Ist International Congress on the Protection of Intellectual Property*, Caracas, 1986, p. 168.

consideration is given, in three articles, to the friction between copyright and neighbouring rights and the need to bring about their harmonious coexistence—the declaration in Article 1 and the condition established in Article 23 and Article 24, paragraph 2.

Article 1 of the Convention seeks to safeguard copyright by means of the following declaration: 'Protection granted under this Convention shall leave intact and shall in no way affect the protection of copyright in literary and artistic works. Consequently, no provision of this Convention may be interpreted as prejudicing such protection.'

In Article 23 and Article 24(2), signature and accession to the Rome Convention is conditional upon the State being a party to the Universal Copyright Convention or the Berne Union, or both.

We find similar provisions in, for example, Colombia, Articles 165 and 257; Dominican Republic, Article 125; Ecuador, Article 138; France, Article L. 211-1, previously Article 15 (Law of 1985); Mexico, Article 6; Portugal, Article 177; Spain, Article 121.

The provisions of the Rome Convention have had a great influence on national laws which frequently reproduce them.

7.1. Rights of performers

The term *rights of performers* alludes to the set of prerogatives of a personal (moral right) and economic character which are enjoyed by their owners in connection with their performances of literary, dramatic and musical works.[20]

A. LIVE PERFORMANCES

Artists who give performances of musical works in the presence of an audience (in a theatre or concert hall, etc.) or for broadcasting purposes establish a contractual relationship with the impresario

---

20. In some countries the expression 'rights of performers' is used in informal terms in referring to the artist's right to receive remuneration for the *secondary uses* of phonograms, i.e. for their communication to the public. This expression is also commonly used in referring to the amounts paid to performers in respect of such secondary uses.

or the broadcasting company giving rise to *exclusive rights*:
- *of a personal character* (publication of the artists' names in the usual manner—or in the manner agreed upon—at the entrance of the theatre or concert hall, etc., in the programmes distributed to the public and in the announcements and advertisements concerning the performance and, if the performance is broadcast, in the programme credits at the beginning and end of the programme); and
- *of an economic character* (authorization or prohibition of communication of the performance to a public which is different from that indicated in the contract with the impresario, the broadcasting company, etc.; authorization or prohibition of the fixation of the performance on a material support, or reproduction, when the fixation has been made without the performer's consent or for purposes other than those which have been authorized or are legally permitted as limitations of the performer's rights—e.g. when 'ephemeral fixations' are authorized and made by a broadcasting company using its own means and for its own emissions).

B. PERFORMANCES INTENDED FOR FIXATION

A similar process occurs when artists perform for the purpose of a fixation; they have rights similar to those just described:
- *of a personal character* (right to publication of their names on record labels and sleeves and cassette labels and containers, in the credit titles of the audiovisual work, on the containers of videocassettes, and so on, and the right to respect for the interpretation); and
- *of an economic character* (authorization or prohibition of the reproduction of the fixation for purposes other than those set out in the contract or those permitted by the law as limitations of their rights).

C. 'SECONDARY USES' OF PHONOGRAMS THROUGH PERFORMANCES IN PLACES TO WHICH THE PUBLIC HAS ACCESS

In the case of sound recordings, it should be noted that the sale to the public of records and cassettes (or copies of a phonogram)

constitutes their primary purpose. When these records and cassettes are communicated to the public (in dance halls, bars, restaurants, etc.—or are broadcast or transmitted by wire or cable, etc.), then *secondary uses* of phonograms are involved.

The *secondary use of sound recordings* was only made possible with the development of techniques for the fixation and reproduction of sounds, and of broadcasting. From that moment onwards, performances which had necessarily been ephemeral could be preserved; now that they had acquired permanence they could compete with the activity of the performers themselves and supplant it. This, then, gave rise to the *rights of performers* in regard to the mechanical reproduction of sounds and broadcasting which were intended to remedy the serious economic prejudice which secondary uses were causing to artists.

7.1.1. Legal nature[21]

7.1.1.1. *Theories based on assimilation with authors' rights*

These theories place the rights of performers on the same footing as the author's rights, although they differ as to the degree of equivalence.

A. THE RIGHTS OF PERFORMERS ARE SIMILAR TO THE AUTHOR'S RIGHTS AND SIMPLY CONSTITUTE ONE OF THEIR ASPECTS

For the advocates of this theory, the performance is equivalent to the creation of a 'new work', since the work performed constitutes an aesthetic act which is different from that of the work in itself. They consider that this new work bears the mark of the performer's personality, that the interpretation has originality in the same way as the work of the author and that the performer uses

---

21. See Carlos Alberto Villalba and Delia Lipszyc, *Derechos de los artistas intérpretes o ejecutantes, productores de fonogramas y organismos de radiodifusión. Relaciones con el derecho de autor*, Buenos Aires, Zavalía Editor, 1976, pp. 15–25.

the work as a writer may choose a subject or a painter may use a real-life model.

B. THE PERFORMER IS A COLLABORATOR OF THE AUTHOR OF THE WORK

Some works exist to which the public can accede directly, without the need for intermediaries, such as literary works (novels, poems, essays) and artistic works (paintings, sculptures, engravings). Others, on the other hand, such as musical compositions, require a performer in order to reach the public. Hence, in the view of the supporters of the theory in question, the reciprocal need which exists between the author and the performer makes them collaborators in a new work.

C. THE PERFORMER IS AN ADAPTER OF THE ORIGINAL WORK

The advocates of this theory consider that the performance or interpretation constitute works derived from the original work. The argument that the performer, although not a real author, can be regarded as an adapter of the work, was put forward by Josef Kohler in 1909; his influence was reflected in the German law of 22 May 1910, which modified the 1901 copyright law. The same provision was also adopted in other countries, such as Switzerland—copyright law of 1936—and Austria—law of the same year.

This argument was also supported at the Diplomatic Conference for the second revision of the Berne Convention held in Rome in 1928, when it was proposed to incorporate the following text in Article 2, paragraph 2, of the Convention: 'When a musical work is adapted for mechanical instruments with the collaboration of performers, the protection enjoyed by the adaptation also benefits such performers.' The proposal was rejected. The inclusion of performers' rights in the Berne Convention was also rejected at the following Revision Conference held in Brussels in 1948. These proposals gave rise to a clash with authors.

In the draft reform of the German copyright law published in 1932, the theory of the performer as adapter of the work was abandoned. This was on the grounds that the fiction of the re-elaboration by the performer contradicted the principle whereby what was protected under the author's rights could only be constituted by the product of the act of creating a work and never by the mere reproduction (performance or interpretation) of a pre-existing work and its fixation on a mechanical instrument (sound recording), even when the reproduction was artistically performed. It was indicated that at that time it was already universally recognized that the argument in support of this fiction should be rejected.

However, the theory of the performer-author of a derivative work is still upheld by certain recognized legal experts.[22]

7.1.1.2. Criticism of theories based on assimilation with authors' rights

According to Piola Casselli, the reasons which could be advanced to counter the legal argument which placed performers' rights on the same footing as authors' rights are simple and perfectly obvious for re-elaboration is something that is added to the work or is an adaptation of it (according to its various forms) and is not always absolutely necessary for the enjoyment of the original work on the part of the public. The author, in any case, can contractually require that the enjoyment of the work, in its original form, shall not be prejudiced. This is not the case of the performance and its reproduction or transmission by means of a record or broadcast. These are normal forms of communication and are almost always necessary. Sharing rights with the performer implies, undeniably, a substantial diminishment of the author's exclusive right, a diminishment which does not disappear simply because the German or Austrian legislator[23] affirms, without

---

22. Herman Cohen Jehoram and authors quoted by him in 'Relationship between Copyright and Neighbouring Rights', *RIDA*, 144, pp. 87–91.
23. This is a reference to the laws of 1910 (Germany) and 1936 (Austria) which have already been mentioned.

demonstrating it, that they are two independent rights which do not clash with one another.[24]

De Sanctis refers to several legal verdicts which criticize the theory of the performer as adapter of the original work: a ruling of the German Federal Court of Justice of 31 May 1960, which also qualified as fiction the provision of the 1910 law, deeming that the nature of the performer's interpretation was distinct from the creative act of the author; a ruling of the Swiss Federal Tribunal of 8 December 1959, in which a legal precedent of 1936 was overturned, the view being that the activity of the performer was never of a creative character and, therefore, did not constitute a work of the mind or an elaboration in the authors' rights sense, however fine the quality of the performance and however exceptional the talent of the performer might be. De Sanctis also refers to a decision of the Paris Court of Appeal of 24 December 1940, in which it was stated that the performer cannot be considered to have an elaborative role nor can his activity be interpreted in the sense of a copyright-related creation.[25]

Alphonse Tournier analyses the nature of the author's rights and the performer's rights by drawing a parallel between the work and the performance, and he stresses that the latter is not open to any form of interpretation whatsoever: 'It is specific to such a degree, according to the nature itself of the performance that is expressed, that for the same work, it varies from one performer to another, just as performances of the same work by the same artist may vary.' Tournier observes that, while the text of the work, immutably objective, gives rise to an infinite variety of interpretations, on the contrary, the text of the performance, identical with it, can only serve to repeat it, and it alone, invariably.[26]

Tournier's reasoning makes it clear that if, as the advocates of

---

24. Edoardo Piola Caselli, in: *Il Diritto di Autore*, 1937, p. 314.
25. Valerio De Sanctis, 'La convenzione internazionale per la protezione degli artisti interpreti o esecutori, dei produttori di fonogrammi e degli organismi di radiodiffusione', *Il Diritto di Autore*, 1962, No. 1, Section 6 *in fine*, pp. 28–9.
26. Alphonse Tournier, 'The Author and the Performer', in *RIDA*, XXVIII, July 1960, pp. 58 and 62.

the theories based on assimilation with authors' rights maintain, a new work emerges from the performance of the original work—as in the case of transformations (adaptation, translation, etc.) resulting in derivative works which, in turn, can undergo new transformations—then the performance should also be able to receive new interpretations. The fact that this is not feasible is because the performance does not result in a new work.

Together with Carlos Alberto Villalba, we considered that

> if we try to give it an author's right basis, the performer's right will be dealt a death blow. If there is one requirement that should not be imposed on a performance to ensure its protection, it is that it should be original or contribute some creative element distinguishing it from previous performances. [...] When a theatrical producer really adds something of his own creation which merits copyright protection, then this is not 'staging' but, rather, an adaptation of a pre-existing work, the result of which is a new work which contains the previous one and which can receive other interpretations. Everything that is non-protected in the author's rights is also non-protected in the performer's rights. However, in order to secure copyright protection under authors' rights, the condition of originality should exist, which is not required in order to obtain the protection granted by the performer's rights. The basic principles of both kinds of protection are distinct and not comparable; common elements may exist inasmuch as both reflect legal structures designed to protect expressions of the personality.[27]

We consider that

> protection of the author's right is basically founded on the creativity and originality of the work. However, a performance, in order to qualify for protection as the performer's right, is not required to be original or to contribute any creative element distinguishing it from previous interpretations. The contrary would be highly prejudicial for the performers and, more especially, for those forming an ensemble, which is why, in performers' rights, plagiarism or legally punishable imitation do not exist. The personality of the performer is revealed in his or her particular style and, as in the case of expressions of intellectual rights and especially in authors' rights, style does not confer exclusive rights. One can write 'in the manner of ...', one can paint 'in the style of ...' and one can perform 'in imitation of ...', but one cannot copy a work and attribute its authorship to oneself. However, one can imitate a performance without any prejudice to the

---

27. C. A. Villalba and D. Lipszyc, op. cit., p. 15.

right of the performer who is imitated or any legal sanction for the imitator—not even a restriction of his rights, irrespective of the reception given to the performance by the public and the critics.[28]

7.1.1.3. *The theory which considers that the performer's right is a personality right*

The advocates of this theory—which include Bruno Marwitz (due to whose influence, according to Piola Caselli, the criterion followed in the 1910 German law was abandoned in the 1932 bill)—consider that, since the artist's performance is made up of a series of elements of his physical person, such as his name, his voice, his image, over which each individual has a right which is identified as the right to one's own personality, this right constitutes the principal reason for rejecting the possibility of profiting from these elements without authorization from their 'owner'. Performers can, then, object to their work being used without their authorization, since use is being made of elements of their person, protected by a broader and more general right—a personality right—to which they are entitled as individuals and not simply as performers.

7.1.1.4. *Criticism*

The basis of the objections to this theory lies in inadequacies as regards personality rights, a legal category, regulating rights which are vested in all persons, but not dealing with those which relate specifically to performers, especially rights of an economic kind. The latter represent a normal aspect, whereas, in the case of personality rights in general, this is usually something exceptional.

7.1.1.5. *Labour law theories*

Labour law theories base the performer's rights on labour legislation. This argument was supported by the International Labour Office (ILO) throughout its active defence of performers' rights,

---

28. Ibid, pp. 28–9.

and was very well received by certain copyright specialists, particularly by Piola Caselli.[29]

According to this theory, consideration should be given to the fact that the performance represents, first, the product of the work of the artists, who are entitled to claim its full economic value. Before the advent of the new techniques of phonographic fixation and reproduction and of broadcasting, the legal issues which formed the context of their performances did not present great difficulty and had not given rise to major questions. Performers worked before the public and received the appropriate fee. If they dealt directly with the audience, it was they who fixed the price of admission to the performance. If an impresario was in charge of the hall, it was he who hired the artist with whom the form of payment and rights and obligations concerning the performance were agreed. Everything took place on familiar ground and the artist could agree to perform knowing what use was going to be made of his performance, since this was inexorably bound up with his person.

The new technologies broke this natural bond between the performer and his activity. From then on, the performance could be recorded directly or from a broadcast transmission which, in turn, could be retransmitted. These new uses no longer depended simply on the performer and the impresario but could be made by anyone. This went beyond the framework of the original contractual relationship.

Performers saw the adverse effects of these new uses because they supplanted their personal work. Impresarios saw how they removed the guarantees acquired in regard to their hold over the product involved in the contract (the performance of the artist).

After analysing the different arguments concerning the legal

---

29. Edoardo Piola Caselli, in *Il Diritto di Autore*, 1937, p. 315 *et seq*. This author's support for this theory meant a change in the position which he had defended in 1927 in his *Trattato*, where he advocated an author's right approach (the performer's right deriving from his status as adapter of the author's work. *Trattato del Diritto di Autore*, 1927, Sections 180–1).

nature of the performer's right, Piola Caselli[30] espouses the theory which sets this right in the context of the performer's prerogative of obtaining an equitable reward in respect of the latest ways of making use of his performance. In his opinion, the performer's right stems from the contract for the hiring of services between the performer and the author (or the interested party representing him: the impresario, the producer, etc.) whereby the author accepts that the work will be given the visual or sound form which will bring it before the public, but without any transfer of the author's rights in favour of the performer.

In pointing to the conflict between the rights of the author of the work and the claims of the performers, Piola Caselli says that the basis of such claims is a personal right in respect of their work; this cannot be transformed into a right of a distinct nature from which, indirectly, ownership over the work may be derived, for the work has belonged and continues to belong to the author, its inclusion in a record or broadcast being irrelevant. Only greater output by the performer as regards his activity can justify a personal right to a greater reward.

In a third and last article on this subject two years later, in 1939, Piola Caselli once more categorically states that the performer's right is, exclusively, an economic right in respect of the value-added corresponding to the service he has rendered, based on the modern principles of labour legislation which recognize that the worker has a right commensurate with the profit which the provider of the work obtains from the worker's services. These principles tend to give the rights of workers, in consideration of their public character, absolute effectiveness which, transcending the limits of the contract, can be made to prevail *erga omnes*.[31]

7.1.1.6. *Criticism of labour law theories*

While the notion of the workers' right provides a sufficient basis for building up a theory of the performer's right, this right can

---

30. Ibid., pp. 315–16.
31. Edoardo Piola Caselli, in: *Il Diritto di Autore*, 1939, p. 19.

only attain a sufficient dimension if recognition is given to the special character of the work that a performance demands. Only this special character can justify certain claims by the parties concerned, such as the moral right to respect for the performer's name (right to identification) and for the performance. Workers are not interested in becoming known to the public which consumes the products in whose manufacture they participate, products which can be altered without the economic value of their work being thereby reduced. Performers, on the contrary, see this value vary according to the degree of fame which they achieve and the public favour which they enjoy. They are, then, extremely interested in seeing their names attached to the product of their work and ensuring that this product does not suffer distortion or alteration which could damage their reputation in the eyes of the public.

Neither does labour legislation offer grounds for justifying the performer's right to additional payment for the public use of recordings made with his or her collaboration since there is no employment relationship between the performer and the owner of the premises or the broadcasting company which use these recordings.

7.1.1.7. Independent theories

These consider that the performer's right is a different right.

De Sanctis[32] considers that in the legal nature of the three categories of so-called neighbouring rights there is a certain analogy with authors' rights, even though these are completely distinct as regards both their justification (creation), the subject of protection (works of creation) and the content of the protection. He believes that in determining the legal nature of the rights of performers it would be simpler to refer to the principles of personality rights and of labour law, and to unjust enrichment.

In the case of the performers' activity, unjust enrichment would consist in the appropriation of profits derived from the

---

32. Valerio De Sanctis, op. cit., pp. 31 *et seq.*

artistic performance, while the corresponding reduction in the performer's earnings would be reflected in the loss of income resulting from the reduced possibility of undertaking performances personally. On the basis of these principles, De Sanctis considers that the right to equitable remuneration as provided for under Italian law (Article 80) can be seen as a personal right which, as such, can be transferred wholly or partially and, consequently, can be enjoyed by the principal, the employer or the transferee in general.

With the passing of time, the character of the rights of performers has become more clearly defined and there is at present a definite trend in doctrine which points to the presence of autonomous rights. We may quote here, among others, the opinions of Mouchet and Radaelli,[33] Desbois,[34] Chaves,[35] Moraes,[36] Millé,[37] Jessen,[38] and Obón León.[39]

We stated with Villalba that

it is our view, which coincides in large measure with that of De Sanctis, that performers' rights have their own specific and original characteristics. They stem from an artistic activity which should be protected as an act which is inseparable from personal activity. The performer's interpretation may never have been fixed or disseminated but this does not mean that its special nature is missing. It is a

---

33. Carlos Mouchet and Sigfrido A. Radaelli, *Los derechos del escritor y del artista*, Buenos Aires, Ed. Sudamericana, 1957, pp. 246–7.
34. Henri Desbois, *Le Droit d'Auteur en France*, Paris, Dalloz, 1978, p. 215, Section 180.
35. Antonio Chaves, *Proteção Internacional do Direito Autoral de Radiodifusão*, São Paulo, p. 239, quoted by Jessen, *Los derechos conexos de artistas intérpretes y ejecutores, productores de fonogramas y organismos de radiodifusión*, op. cit., p. 174.
36. Walter Moraes, *Artistas intérpretes e executantes*, São Paulo, Ed. Revista dos Tribunais, 1976.
37. Antonio Millé, 'Performers' Rights: a new, independent institution of intellectual property law' in *Copyright*, WIPO, Geneva, 1984, p. 289.
38. Henry Jessen, *Los derechos conexos...*, p. 175.
39. J. Ramón Obón León, *Derecho de los artistas intérpretes, actores, cantantes y músicos ejecutantes*, Mexico, D.F., Ed. Trillas, 1986, pp. 55–7.

professional activity which calls for special regulation which will define it independently of the employment relationship. Its definition must be worked out with special care so as to distinguish it from other areas of activity with which it is classified for lack of a professional status of its own.

Contracts for the hire of labour and services are, even today, supplementary regulations in the same way as those which protect one's name, image and the right to privacy. While remaining an artistic activity, the performance can become independent of the person by means of fixation and broadcasting or public dissemination.

As from that moment, it can be appropriated, affected adversely or distorted, requiring appropriate methods for its protection, with rights effective *erga omnes* in which connotations of social legislation will predominate with marked similarities to those of labour law, inasmuch as there is not only competition with the performer's own individual activity but *vis-à-vis* the professional sector as well.

Because of its nature, and in conformity with the requirements which its protection imposes, it is an individual right involving collective exercise and administration and is, therefore, necessarily bound up with professional bodies.[40]

7.1.2. The subject of protection

What is protected is the personal performance of the artist. This is something intangible which does not constitute a work; protection of the performer's interpretation is not, therefore, subject to the requirement that it should have originality or individuality (see above, Chapter 2, Section 2.1.2).

The performer carries out an *artistic activity*, an expression which, as De Sanctis points out, is not synonymous with literary and artistic creation any more than the latter is synonymous with *intellectual production*.[41] The artist's performance consists in making the author's work a *living reality*, a work whose constituent parts are already finalized and complete. De Sanctis makes it clear that performers are intermediaries between the creator and the public, since they transmit a thought which has already been completely and concretely expressed by the author of the work.

---

40. C. A. Villalba and D. Lipszyc, op. cit., pp. 24–5.
41. Valerio De Sanctis, '... *l'espressione "creazione letteraria e artistica" non è sinonimo di "produzione intellettuale" e neppure di un qualsiasi risultato di attivita artistica ...*', op. cit., *Il Diritto di Autore*, 1962, No. 1, pp. 25 *et seq.*

The performer is necessary in order to arouse appropriate aesthetic emotion among the audience, but he or she does not contribute anything new in respect of the elements which make up the work. The work, as such, is presented as something which is complete in its ideology, even when its purpose is, above all, fulfilled through its performance by the artist and even when it is the performance which makes it possible for the audience to enjoy the work.

De Sanctis points out that all this does not prevent performances from having a greater artistic value than the work performed and thus constituting the audience's main interest. He states, in this connection, that:

It may happen that an actor, or a performer in general, creates his mask, his unmistakable style; he even creates a character. But the content of such individual creation is not a complex of ideas, feelings, actions from which third parties can obtain elements for the creation of new works and does not constitute a link in the chain of the cultural evolution of humankind.

7.1.3. Holders of the rights

According to the definition contained in Article 3(a) of the Rome Convention of 1961, *performers* means 'actors, singers, musicians, dancers, and other persons who act, sing, deliver, declaim, play in, or otherwise perform literary or artistic works'.

With some variations, this definition has been adopted in the laws of several countries such as Brazil (Article 4(XII)); Colombia (Article 8, (K)); Costa Rica (Article 77(a)); Dominican Republic (Article 17(j)); France (Article L. 212-1, previously Art. 16 of the 1985 law); Spain (Article 101, the second part of which states expressly that stage directors and orchestral conductors shall have the rights conferred on performers).

The General Report of the 1961 Conference states that it was made clear in the debates that, in the Rome Convention, the expression 'literary or artistic work' was used in the same sense as in the Berne and the Universal Copyright Conventions and specifically included musical, dramatic and dramatico-musical works.

It was also agreed that conductors of musicians or singers should be considered as included in the definition of 'performers'.[42]

Excluded, on the other hand, are those who, although they do not perform literary and artistic works, nevertheless carry out work of an artistic kind, such as variety and circus artists (high wire performers, trapeze artists, acrobats, clowns, jugglers, magicians, etc.) and also ancillary personnel who do not perform an artistic activity (extras or those with 'bit' parts, etc.) as well as those who have technical duties (stagehands, prop-men, etc.).[43]

However, Article 9 of the Rome Convention[44] entitles Contracting States, through their domestic legislation, to extend protection also to artists who do not perform literary or artistic works. (The intention of this provision, which may seem superfluous, would seemingly be to mitigate the prejudice caused to those concerned by their exclusion from the field of application of Article 3). In this connection, Article 16 of the French law of 1985 (now Intellectual Property Code, Article L. 212-1), in conformity with the Rome Convention, expressly excludes 'ancillary performers' on the one hand and, on the other, includes those who perform '... variety, circus or puppet acts'.

Article 19 of the Convention is also extremely important for it establishes that once a performer has consented to the incorporation of his performance in a visual or audiovisual fixation he ceases to be protected against any use which may be made of the performance that has been so incorporated.[45] This means that the Rome Convention does not include protection of the performances of artists in audiovisual works. This provision is repro-

---

42. See *Records of the Diplomatic Conference on the international protection of performers, producers of phonograms and broadcasting organizations* (Rome, 10–26 October 1961), ILO–UNESCO–BIRPI, p. 40.
43. See *Guide to the Rome Convention and the Phonograms Convention*, Geneva, WIPO, 1982, pp. 26–7. The *Guide* was written by Dr Claude Masouyé.
44. Article 9 of the Rome Convention: 'Any Contracting State may, by its domestic laws and regulations, extend the protection provided for in this Convention to artists who do not perform literary or artistic works.'
45. Article 19 of the Rome Convention: 'Notwithstanding anything in this Convention, once a performer has consented to the incorporation of his performance in a visual or audio-visual fixation, Article 7 shall have no further application.'

duced in a number of domestic laws (e.g. Colombia, Art. 168; Dominican Republic, Art. 128).

The expression *'performers' rights'* implicitly provides a solution to one of the earliest conflicts which, as we have said, arose among the performers themselves, for it recognizes the status of performers as holders of rights, particularly as regards the *secondary uses* of recordings, and the rights of both those who take part in collective performances (members of orchestras and choirs) and those who perform as individual artists (orchestral conductors, soloists) and actors. It is maintained by some that only principal artists should be entitled to these rights for it is they alone who 'interpret' the work, giving their performance the stamp of their personality; on the other hand, the 'secondary' artists who take part in a collective performance follow the indications of the conductor and can display no more than their professional skill—'interpretation' of the work does not depend on them.[46]

7.1.4. Content

7.1.4.1. *The performer's moral rights*

A. PREROGATIVES

Performers carry out artistic activities of a personal order and for this reason laws establish prerogatives in their favour concerning the protection of their personality. These rights are not recognized as accruing to the other two categories of holders of neighbouring rights—producers of phonograms and broadcasting organizations—because of the technical and organizational nature of their activities.

---

46. In Argentina, for example, the Intellectual Property Law enacted in 1933 established in its Article 56, first paragraph, the right of *'interprètes'* to receive remuneration in respect of *secondary uses*. The inclusion in this provision of the term *'interprète'* without any qualification was used as a pretext for maintaining, until the 1970s, that the right was granted only to orchestral conductors and soloists, and that 'ejecutantes', i.e. orchestral players and members of choirs, did not benefit from it. The 'ejecutantes' had a long fight to reverse this situation (see, in this connection, C. A. Villalba and D. Lipszyc, op. cit., pp. 79 *et seq.*).

Performers' moral rights have been structured along the same lines as authors' rights, although with some particular features imposed by the differences between the two legal categories. Legislation usually recognizes the right to respect for the name of the performer and for the performance when it is reproduced. On the other hand, performers do not enjoy the right of disclosure or of withdrawal or reconsideration.

a. Right to respect for the performer's name

This is the right to have his or her name linked with the performance (also termed the right to identification of the artist). The obligation to display or mention the performer's name takes effect when the performance is announced or disseminated. Over and above the content of the legal provisions, this right is normally respected and is the subject of precise contractual stipulations as to the size of the print, the placing of the name, and the occasions on which it should be mentioned, and so on; the drawing power of the poster is of fundamental importance for the performer and has direct economic implications, for the greater the performer's popularity, the higher the fee he or she may command.

Generally speaking, the laws grant the right to respect for the name only to the principal performers (or to the 'artiste-interprète', according to Article L. 212-2, previously Article 17 of the 1985 French law[47]) or, as the Italian law states (Article 83) to artists who act, interpret or perform the leading parts in a dramatic, literary or musical work or composition.

On the other hand, Spain (Article 107) provides that: 'The performer shall enjoy the right to have his name mentioned in connection with his performances and to object, throughout his life, to any distortion, mutilation or any other act in relation to his performance that might adversely affect his standing or reputation....'

---

47. This provision also grants the performer the right to respect for his performance Article L. 212-2, first para.: '*L'artiste interprète a le droit au respect de son nom, de sa qualité et de son interprétation.*'

b. Right to respect for the performance

This right is intended to protect the artistic prestige of the performer. As Walter Moraes points out,[48] in national legislation this right is reflected in a number of different approaches, provisions sometimes concentrating on the interests of the performer and, at other times, on the integrity of the performance in itself.

1. *When the performer's interests are the focal point*, three general ways of protecting the performer's artistic personality can—according to Moraes—be identified:
- *by means of the prerogative whereby the performer opposes dissemination which prejudices his artistic interests*, as set out, for example, in the Argentine law (Article 56, second part: 'The performer of a literary or musical work can oppose the dissemination of his performance if the reproduction thereof has been made in such a form as to produce serious or unjust prejudice to his artistic interests'); Uruguay (Article 37); and Paraguay (Article 41);
- *by means of the prohibition to make available to the public a fixation of his performance in such a form or in such circumstances that the performer could suffer prejudice*. This is the formula adopted by the Scandinavian countries (Denmark, Article 45(c, 3); Finland, Article. 45(3); Sweden, Article 45(3));
- *by establishing the obligation to respect the moral right of performers*, as, for example, in the 1963 law of El Salvador, Article 59 (now replaced by the law of 15 July 1993).

2. *When it is the integrity of the performance that is the central issue*—according to Moraes—the laws envisage three other types of prerogative which can, in accordance with the recognized scope of the protection of the performer's personality, be set out as follows:
- the prerogative of preventing *distortion* of the performance. Germany provides (Article 83(1)) that 'The performer shall have the right to prohibit any distortion or other alteration of his performance of such nature as to injure his prestige or reputation

---

48. Walter Moraes, op. cit., pp. 193–7.

as a performer'; a formula of this kind has also been adopted in Article 81.2 of the law of El Salvador (15 July 1993); Hungary (Article 50) uses a broader formula, establishing that the performer (the leader and the principal participants of the ensemble) has a moral right to protection against distortion;
- the prerogative of preventing any *modification* of the performance. This formula is broader than the previous one; it not only covers distortion but also provides that any transformation of the structure of the performance is sufficient to authorize the performer's opposition. Once again the Scandinavian countries provide the best examples for the Danish law (Article 45(c, 3)), the Finnish law (Art. 45(3)) and the Swedish law (Art. 45(3)) state that Article 3, regulating the moral right of authors, shall apply to performers;
- the prerogative of preventing the *transposition* of the fixation of a performance to another supporting medium (e.g. reproducing a sound recording in an audio-visual work, or a part of an audiovisual work in another work of the same category or, again, a part of a sound recording in another, and so on). In Austria (Article 66(1)) this right belongs exclusively to the performer. In Denmark (Article 45(2)) and Finland (Article 45(2)) this performer's right is valid for 25 years and in Sweden (Art. 45(2)) 50 years, in all cases as from the year following that in which the first recording took place.

Laws do not usually recognize the entitlement of performers to the right of disclosure to the public and the right of withdrawal.[49] Omission of the *right of disclosure* is due to the fact that the participation of the artist in the performance of the work implies, *per se*, the authorization to disclose it. As to the *right of reconsideration and withdrawal*, its attribution to the performer would mean a direct clash with the author's rights, for its exercise by the per-

---

49. Colombia is an exception, for Article 171 establishes that performers shall have the moral rights specified in Article 30 of that law. The latter Article provides that authors shall enjoy, in addition to the rights of authorship and integrity, those of disclosure, alteration either before or after publication, and of withdrawal from circulation. *Idem*, Dominican Republic, Article 131.

former would have the effect of preventing exploitation of the work authorized by its author.

Isidro Satanowsky,[50] in analysing the prerogatives which make up the performer's moral rights, asks if the performer is entitled to object to the cutting of several scenes from a film, and, even, of all those in which he appears, and replies to the question in the negative. He comes to the same conclusion with respect to the actor's right to demand that the scenes in which he appears should be deleted because he is not satisfied with his performance of the role. We agree with Satanowsky, for if it were accepted that the performer had this right, its exercise would clash with the author's right to have the integrity of the work respected.

B. Characteristics

The performer's moral rights protect his or her personality in relation to the interpretation: they are essential, extra-economic, inherent and absolute (see above, Chapter 4, Section 4.1.B).

The French law expressly recognizes the inalienable, imprescriptible and inherent character of these rights.[51]

C. Term of the performer's moral rights

Some laws deal expressly with the duration of the performer's moral rights, providing for a different term than that recognized in respect of his economic rights, but without establishing perpetuity.

The French law provides that the right to respect for the performer's name, his authorship and his interpretation may be transmitted to his heirs *in order to protect the interpretation and the memory of the deceased* (Article L. 212-2.3, previously Article 17(3)).

Spain (Article 107) also establishes that the moral right to recognition of the performer's name and to the integrity of the

---

50. Isidro Satanowsky, *Derecho intelectual*, Buenos Aires, Ed. TEA, 1954, Section 374, T. II, p. 42.
51. Article L. 212-2, para. 2, previously Article 17, paragraph 2 of the 1985 law: '*Ce droit inaliénable et imprescriptible est attaché à sa personne.*'

performance shall be valid for his full lifetime, but that, after his death, exercise of these rights by his heirs shall be limited to the following 20 years.

We have already mentioned that in Denmark (Article 45(2)) and in Finland (Article 45, (3)) the performer's right of preventing the transposition of the fixation of a performance to another supporting medium is valid for a period of 25 years and in Sweden (Article 45(2)) for 50 years, as from the year following that in which the first recording took place.

7.1.4.2. Economic rights of performers and their limitations

a. The economic rights of performers (as well as those of other holders of 'neighbouring rights'), are subject to the system of *numerus clausus*.[52]

b. Rights are recognized as accruing to performers in the reproduction and public communication of their performances; these rights are frequently replaced by non-voluntary licences or by total limitation measures, many of which reflect a marked similarity to those established in respect of author's rights.

Laws establish these rights by means of different formulas. Some are broadly based and establish an exclusive right enabling performers to control the use of their performances, e.g.:
- 'The fixation of his performance, its reproduction and its communication to the public ... shall be subject to written authorization by the performer'. (France Article L. 212-3, previously Article 18, first paragraph of the 1985 law. This provision also makes the performer's authorization necessary for *any separate use of the sounds or the images of the performance* where the latter has been fixed as regards both the sounds and the images: it is, then, necessary to have the authorization of the performer of an audiovisual work in order to include the soundtrack in a record);
- 'the performer shall have the exclusive right to authorize

---

52. Unlike author's exploitation rights which are recognized as being of a general character.

the reproduction of his performances and the communication thereof to the public', an authorization which 'shall be granted in writing'. (Spain, Article 102, (1) and (2)).

Other laws, following the formula set out in Article 7.1 of the Rome Convention (1961), establish that the artist has the right 'to prevent'[53] certain acts carried out without his or her consent (e.g. Brazil, Article 95, Portugal, Article 178).

c. The purpose of the economic rights recognized as accruing to performers is to protect them against uses which fall outside the contractual system whereby their consent is given to the uses of their performance. However, these rights are often subject to limitations established for the purpose of preventing the effect of the protection granted to performers from hampering either exercise of the exclusive rights of authors to authorize exploitation of their works, or the public communication of the fixations.

For example, authors' rights recognize the exclusive and absolute right of the creator of the work to authorize the *secondary uses* of the musical works recorded. The fixation of the artist's performance contains, necessarily, the work performed. Should a right to authorize or prohibit such '*secondary uses*' be recognized as belonging to the performer, in a similar, or the same way as the right enjoyed by the author, it might happen that the public performance or broadcasting of a recorded work authorized by the author could be prohibited by the performer. In this hypothesis, since the performer would have a similarly exclusive and absolute right over the same object—the fixation of the work performed—the author's right would lose these attributes. The fact that such situations of conflict can only be regarded as exceptional does not change matters; it is hardly likely that performers would make use of such rights for systematically opposing the exploitation of their performances—it would not be in their interests to do so—unless it were to claim additional royalties.[54] It is for this reason that in

---

53. Concerning the scope of this formula, see below Chapter 12, Section 12.5.1, C,d,1.
54. See Claude Masouyé, op. cit., p. 35, Section 7.8.

the Rome Convention (Article 12) and most domestic laws, such further payment is recognized as the right of performers to receive a single equitable remuneration by means of non-voluntary licences.

The possibility of recognizing that performers possess unrestricted rights over the reproduction and communication to the public of their performances has aroused apprehension not only among authors but also among producers of phonograms and broadcasting organizations. Producers of phonograms fear that if artists were granted an exclusive right over the reproduction of their recorded performances, there would be a danger of their preventing the reproduction of phonograms, thus disrupting the record market. They point out that it is through recordings that artists achieve renown and that it is the record producer who is best able to defend the professional interests of the sector. The broadcasting companies, for their part, have similar fears in regard to original broadcasts and retransmissions.[55]

To sum up, it is generally recognized that performers possess the following economic rights:

- *in the case of direct or 'live' performances*, performers have the *exclusive right to authorize or prohibit* (Bolivia, Chile, Colombia, Dominican Republic, France, Panama, Spain, Venezuela) or, again, the right of preventing their fixation, reproduction, broadcasting and all forms of public communication which have not been included in the contract covering the performances (Brazil, Ecuador, Mexico, Portugal, Rome Convention).
- in the case of *performances which have been fixed*, no one may reproduce these without the authorization of the performer in any of the following instances: (1) if the original fixation has not been authorized by them; (2) if it is reproduced for purposes that differ from those authorized; (3) if the fixation was made originally in accordance with a legally established limitation and is reproduced for purposes that differ from those set out in the exception on account of which the fixation was made.

---

55. Ibid.

When, for example, a group of musicians presents a recital 'live' in a concert hall or stadium, etc., it has the exclusive right to authorize or prohibit the fixation of its performance for reproduction in records, cassettes or in an audiovisual work, or its transmission by radio or television (in conformity with the Rome Convention and legislation which employs the formula used in the Convention, performers have the right—or the prerogative—to prevent the fixation when it has not been authorized by the group). If the group authorized an ephemeral fixation of the recital for time-shifted television transmission, there is no question of its being an illicit fixation but the authorization of the group is necessary if the fixation is kept or reproduced for purposes other than those of the time-shifted emission.

Performers are entitled to receive remuneration for 'secondary uses' of phonograms produced for commercial purposes and with their authorization (see below, Section 7.1.4, 3D).

7.1.4.3. Limitations

Domestic laws establish limitations on the rights of public communication and reproduction. Laws enacted after the establishment of the Rome Convention (1961) generally follow its provisions in respect of the limitations it authorizes.

A. PRESUMPTION *JURIS ET DE JURE*

Generally speaking, it is considered that the performer's contract for the making of a *phonogram* or an audiovisual work implies the presumption *juris et de jure* in favour of the producer of phonogram or audiovisual work, to the effect that the *performer authorizes the fixation, reproduction and public communication of his performance* (e.g. Colombia, Articles 166(A)(1) and (C)(1), 168 and 172; France, Articles L. 212-4, L. 213-1 and L. 214-1, previously Articles 19, 21 and 22 of the 1985 law; Dominican Republic, Articles 126(a), 128 and 132; Spain, Article 102(3), etc.).

In the majority of cases (in conformity with the Rome Convention, Article 7, subparagraphs 1(c)(ii) and (iii), this presumption is not effective if the reproduction of the sound recording is made for purposes differing from those authorized in the contract signed by the performer and if the performance was initially fixed in accordance with a legal provision (Colombia, Article 166(C)(2) and (3); Dominican Republic, Article 126(c)(2) and (3)).

B. FREE AND GRATUITOUS USES

We find, in domestic laws, the limitations permitted under the terms of Article 15 of the Rome Convention; this article authorizes certain exceptions to be made under domestic legislation to the provisions covering protection guaranteed by the Convention. The exceptions that are admitted are the same in respect of the three categories of owners of protected rights (performers, producers of phonograms and broadcasting organizations);[56]

- *private copying for personal use*: e.g. Germany, Article 84 which refers back to Article 53; Hungary, Article 49(2) which refers back to Article 18(1); France, Article L. 211-3.2, previously Article 29(2) of the 1985 law;
- *use of short excerpts for the reporting of current events* (e.g. Austria, Articles 69(1) and 70(2); Germany, Article 84 which refers back to Articles 48(2) and 50; France, Art. L. 211-3.3, previously Article 29(3) of the 1985 law; Mexico, Article 91 (II);
- *ephemeral fixations made by a broadcasting organization by means of its own facilities and for its own broadcasts* e.g. Germany, Article 84 which refers back to Article 55; Mexico, Article 91(III) which refers back to Article 74 (c);
- *use solely for the purposes of teaching or scientific research* (e.g. France, Article L. 211-3.3, previously Article 29(3) of the 1985 law; Germany, Article 84 which refers back to Articles 46, 47 and 54; Hungary, Article 49(2) which refers back to Article 17(2).
- *Other free and gratuitous uses*: we find other limitations as well in domestic legislations such as that authorizing the free reproduction and public communication of the artist's performance where it is accessory to an event that constitutes the main sub-

---

56. See below, Chapter 12, Section 12.5.1, C,d,4,v.

ject of a sequence within a work or audiovisual document (France, Article L. 212-10, previously Article 29, last paragraph of the 1985 law).

C. Equivalence with copyright

Some laws establish that copyright limitations shall be applicable, where relevant, to neighbouring rights (Germany, Articles 84, 85(3) and 87(3); also Austria, Denmark, Finland, Hungary, Norway, etc.)

In this connection, the first part of Article 15(2) of the Rome Convention permits domestic legislation to make provision, in respect of the three categories of owners of rights protected by it, for limitations which are of the same kind as those established for copyright, the aim being to ensure that those owners of rights do not enjoy a more favourable situation than creators.

The purpose of this provision is to establish a uniform legal regime and to ensure that the owners of neighbouring rights do not receive preferential treatment in comparison with authors as a result of the limitations imposed on the rights of the latter. The Rome Convention does not make it obligatory for States to establish a strict parallel between the provisions of domestic laws on neighbouring rights and those on copyright; but the terms of Article 15(2) contain a clear indication that States should legislate in such a way that limitations—or exceptions—that are made in respect of the minimum protection of neighbouring rights should be compatible with the limitations admitted in respect of copyright.[57]

D. Uses subject to remuneration

a. Non-voluntary licences for 'secondary uses'

The right of performers and producers of phonograms to receive remuneration for secondary uses of phonograms produced for commercial purposes with their authorization, is established under

---

57. See Claude Masouyé, op. cit., Sect. 15.9.

national legislation which provides for *non-voluntary licences*[58] for the direct public communication of such phonograms, more especially by broadcasting (in France, Article L. 214-1.2; previously Article 22(2) of the 1985 law includes cable transmission when this is integral and simultaneous) and their playing in public places (the French law excludes in Article L. 214-1.2, previously Article 22(1) the use of these phonograms in an entertainment in which case the principle of the exclusive right takes precedence). Consequently, the public performance and the broadcasting of the phonogram are free, but entail the payment of remuneration to the performers, and to the producers of phonograms (Colombia, Article 173; Costa Rica, Article 83; Dominican Republic, Article 133(1); France, Art. L. 214-1, previously Article 22 of the 1985 law; Germany, Articles 76(2), 77 and 86; Spain, Article 103; and so on).

Generally speaking, national laws set out the way in which this joint remuneration is shared between performers and producers, either on a half-and-half basis (as in Colombia, Costa Rica, Dominican Republic, France, Spain) or by the assignment of a greater proportion to the performer (as in Argentina, Decree No. 1671, 1974, which establishes (Article 5) that performers shall receive 67 per cent and producers of phonograms, 33 per cent; in turn, the share assigned to leading performers is 67 per cent and secondary performers, 33 per cent..

The proportion due to the performers cannot be reduced by agreement between the parties, having regard to the labour-related nature of the payment, to its ultimate purpose—to compensate for the use of the work not paid for by the producer—and to the fewer opportunities available for personal participation in live performances as a result of the utilization of sound recordings. On the other hand, there is no impediment to agreement for an increase in the proportion due to the performers (Colombia (Article 174) expressly establishes that the producer and the performers may agree that the latter shall be paid a higher amount).

---

58. See above, Chapter 4, Section 4.3.2.

The amount of the remuneration is usually agreed with the users by the collective administration body dealing with the rights of performers and producers of phonograms. In the absence of an agreement between the parties, alternative arrangements are established, as, for example, in the French law (Articles L. 214-1, L. 214-3 and L. 214-4, previously Arts. 22 to 24) which lays down a special system: in principle, remuneration is fixed by agreements between the organizations representing the parties concerned (performers, producers and primary users); the term of such agreements is between one and five years and their provisions may be made compulsory by the Ministry of Culture. In the absence of an agreement, the amount of the remuneration is decided, on the basis of a type of arbitration procedure, by a Committee chaired by a magistrate of the judiciary and composed of representatives of official organizations, beneficiaries and users.

The right of performers and producers of phonograms to receive remuneration for the secondary uses of sound recordings is recognized in Article 12 of the Rome Convention, one of its key provisions.

b. Non-voluntary licences for private copying for personal purposes

Home reproduction of sound recordings for personal use not only prejudices authors[59] but also performers and producers of phonograms. It is, then, appropriate that they should receive *equitable remuneration for private copying* (e.g. France, Article L. 311-1, previously Article 31 of the 1985 law; Germany, Article 85(3) which refers back to Article 54; Spain, Article 25).[60]

7.1.4.4. *Term of the economic rights of performers*

Legislation differs as regards the choice of the act from which the term should be calculated. It may be calculated from the performance, the first circulation or the first publication of the fixation.

Under the Rome Convention provision is made, for the three

---

59. See above, Chapter 4, Section 4.3.1.
60. See Chapter 4, Section 4.3.2 A and Chapter 8, Section 8.2.2.

categories of beneficiaries of neighbouring rights, for a minimum (Article 14) period of 20 years calculated from the end of the year in which *the fixation was made or the performance took place (if it has not been fixed)* or, again, *the transmission took place*, in the case of broadcasts (the same period is established for the two other categories of beneficiaries of neighbouring rights).

Many countries have established a longer term, in general, 50 years (Austria, Costa Rica, former Czechoslovakia, Denmark, Finland, France, Germany, Greece, Norway, Portugal, Sweden, United Kingdom); or 60 years (Brazil, Venezuela).

Colombia (Article 29), adopting a singular system, establishes different terms according to the category of the respective owner: 80 years from the death of the owner of the rights, where such owner is a natural person (the same period as for the author's economic rights) and, where the owner is a legal entity, 50 years from the last day of the year in which the performance, or the first fixation of the phonogram, or the transmission of the broadcast, took place.

Argentina *makes no provision with respect of the duration of the performer's right.* This leaves room for various possibilities: that the right is perpetual, that it expires with the life of the performer or, again, that it has the same duration as the right of the author of the work performed. The latter solution seems to be the most reasonable since it avoids both the possibility of the performer receiving preferential treatment in comparison with the author, or of such treatment being arbitrarily changed and the term of protection shortened.

The Council Directive of the European Communities of 29 October 1993 (93/98/EEC) harmonizing the Term of Protection of Copyright and Certain Related Rights, provides (Article 3) that the period of protection in respect of the three categories of beneficiaries of such rights shall be 50 years. In the case of performers this period is calculated from the date of the performance or the first fixation, or the communication of this fixation. Member States of the European Union should, then, adopt this period together with the others set out in this Directive.

The Agreement on Trade-Related Aspects of Intellectual Property Rights (TRIPS) provides, in the case of performers, for a minimum term of 50 years computed from the end of the calendar year in which the fixation was made or the performance took place (Article 14(5)).

7.1.5. Exercise of performers' economic rights in instances of collective performances

These cases are the most frequent for the majority of performances require the participation of two or more performers. When the performance is a collective act involving a group of artists (groups of musicians, orchestras, choirs, etc.) it is essential that exercise of their rights should be carried out in a uniform and co-ordinated way in order to prevent any possible disagreement among them from adversely affecting their own interests.

Here, Spain (Article 105) provides that performers who collectively take part in one and the same performance, such as the members of a musical ensemble, choir, orchestra, ballet troupe or theatre company shall designate one of their number to be their representative for the grant of the authorizations. For such designation, which shall be set down in writing, the majority consent of the performers shall apply. This obligation shall not extend to soloists or to orchestra conductors or directors of stage performances.

In countries where performers have formed associations or other professional organizations, it is usually these bodies which are responsible for representing them in instances of collective performances (the Spanish provision referred to above would appear to take such situations into account).

7.2. Rights of producers of phonograms

The *producer of phonograms* is understood to be the natural person or legal entity on whose initiative and responsibility a fixation is made for the first time[61] of the sounds of a performance or other

---

61. This qualification does not refer, in absolute or exclusive terms, to the first fixation in time, but to the first initiative in the operation of fixing the sounds and covers, therefore, each first fixation that is made.

sounds.[62] The activities of producers of phonograms are technical and organizational, of an industrial order.[63]

7.2.1. The subject of protection

What is protected is the fixation of the performance of the work on a supporting medium which is termed a *phonogram* and which, in the Rome Convention (Article 3(b)), is defined as 'any exclusively aural fixation of sounds of a performance or of other sounds'.

Under the terms of the Convention protection is given only to *aural* fixations, whatever the source of the sounds. *Included*, then, are fixations in which sounds—such as birdsong and other sounds of nature—do not emanate from a performance, while those which incorporate images (audiovisual works) are *excluded*.

As regards the subject of protection, the continental European legal approach to author's rights is different from that of Anglo-American law.

a. In the continental European legal approach, it is not possible to attribute the character of a work to the phonogram. The activities of the producers of phonograms have a practical purpose—converting an ephemeral performance into a permanent one—and, independently of the calibre of the musical works that make up their phonographic catalogue and of the performers who interpret them, their entrepreneurial task is distinguished mainly (1) by the technical quality of the products they make (factors inter-

---

62. See Spain, Article 108(2) and definition set out in the Rome Convention, Article 3(c), adopted by several countries—Brazil, Article 4(X)(a); Colombia, Article 8(L); Costa Rica, Article 81(a); Dominican Republic, Article 17(k); etc.
63. See Henri Desbois, op. cit. p. 228, Section 187: '... Recording entrepreneurs carry out an activity of an industrial nature which is of immense benefit for the development of musical and literary culture but does not reflect the characteristics of intellectual creation. Their activity differs more fundamentally from such creativity than the contribution of performers for they, in fact, "create" their interpretation which bears the imprint of their personality and sensitivity....'

See also Claude Masouyé, op. cit., p. 12, para. XX.

vening here are the skills of the personnel hired—sound operators and engineers, recording directors, etc.—as well as the technique used in the fixation and reproduction of the work performed—recording equipment and materials) and (2) by the effectiveness of the marketing of these products. But these activities, although indispensable for the dissemination of the music, are not the source of any creative contribution to the author's work.[64]

In countries with a Roman legal tradition, author's rights reflect an essentially individualistic approach and are confined to the protection of formal expressions resulting from intellectual activity of a *creative*[65] nature; the attribution of the quality of author belongs to the natural person who creates the work and in whom certain rights of a personal and an economic character are recognized. In the Roman legal tradition, the legal concept of 'author' corresponds to its meaning outside the law.[66]

In both the Berne Convention and the Universal Convention, the term 'copyright' is used in the narrower sense attributed to it in Roman law tradition. This is why phonograms—or sound recordings—are considered not only as not belonging to the category of literary, scientific or artistic works which are protected by

---

64. See Valerio De Sanctis, op. cit. p. 29, Section 7; Carlos Mouchet, *Los derechos de los autores e intérpretes de obras literarias y artísticas*, Buenos Aires, Ed. Abeledo-Perrot, 1966, p. 86; Henri Desbois, op. cit. pp. 228–9, Section 187; Alphonse Tournier, op. cit. p. 54; Tullia Ascarelli, *Teoria de la concurrencia y de los bienes inmateriales*, Barcelona, Ed. Bosch, 1970, p. 773; Claude Colombet, *Major Principles . . .* op. cit., pp. 87, 93 and 98–9; Héctor Della Costa, *El derecho de autor y su novedad*, Buenos Aires, Ed. Cathedra, 1971, pp. 134–5.
65. In an earlier study, carried out in collaboration with Carlos Alberto Villalba, we indicated that the inapplicability of authors' rights benefits the producers, for if their activity were to be governed by the requirement of originality, as works are, scarcely any phonograms would be protected (*Reflexiones para un homenaje*, in *Il Diritto di Autore*, volume of studies in tribute to Valerio De Sanctis, commemoration of the fiftieth anniversary of the Review, 1979, p. 687, *in fine*).
66. See Adolf Dietz, *Copyright Law in the European Community*, Vol. 1, p. 110.

these conventions, but were expressly excluded from the protection provided under the Universal Convention.[67]

b. But the situation is different in countries with an Anglo-American legal tradition. Stewart points out that the basic philosophy of copyright, as opposed to authors' rights, is humbler; it simply involves the right to prevent material being copied in order to protect the copyright owner against reproduction of the material medium rather than the creation.[68] As a result, in the common law tradition it is considered possible to protect sound recordings as works, because copyright has a broader scope than the *'author's right'* with respect to the subject-matter of protection.

In countries in the copyright area the title of 'works' is given not only to works of creation which are the subject of protection under the continental European authors' rights, but to certain industrial products as well, such as sound recordings, inasmuch as they can be copied, in other words, reproduced by means of the multiplication of copies (see above, Chapter 1, Section 1.3.1).

However, in the copyright system a distinction is made between works of creation (literary, dramatic, artistic and musical works) and other 'works', which, as Cornish says, 'a more self-conscious system would denominate "neighbouring rights"'. Cornish points to 'the crucial difference' between copyright in works of creation, which recognizes the contribution of an original intellectual effort and the other copyright 'which recognizes entrepreneurial skills in an aesthetic field'.[69]

---

67. *Records of the Diplomatic Conference for the Adoption of the Universal Convention*, Geneva, 18 August–6 September 1952, published by UNESCO, 1955, pp. 173–6, quoted in document UNESCO/ WIPO/CGE/SYN/3-III, 11 April 1988, p. 18, Section 68. For the same reasons, protection has repeatedly been denied to producers of phonograms within the context of the Berne Convention (see below, Chapter 12, Section 12.5.1.A—Genesis of the Rome Convention, and Section 12.4.2.1, M, c)).
68. Stephen Stewart, *International Copyright and Neighbouring Rights*, 2nd ed., London, 1989, pp. 7 and 8, Section 1.15.
69. William R. Cornish, *Intellectual Property*, London, 1981, p. 318, quoted by Herman Cohen Jehoram, 'Relationship between Copyright and Neighbouring Rights', *RIDA*, 144, p. 115.

In the Anglo-American legal conception the holder of copyright is the copyright owner, (termed, indiscriminately, in the 1988 United Kingdom Act, *the author*). He is the legal owner of the right to protect the copy against unauthorized reproduction, both of works of creation and of industrial products. When what is protected is an industrial product, Cornish speaks, in reference to the 1956 United Kingdom Act, of 'entrepreneurial copyright' in sound recordings and broadcasts.[70]

In a memorandum containing comments on the draft Principles relating to different categories of works, prepared jointly by the Secretariats of UNESCO and WIPO, it is pointed out that there are several countries in which phonograms are protected under copyright acts, but the overwhelming majority of them are countries following Anglo-Saxon legal traditions in which this protection is called 'copyright' protection. But—as is pointed out in that memorandum—if the relevant provisions in those national laws are analysed, it will be realized that what is involved is not 'copyright' protection in the narrowest meaning of the word, that is, in the meaning in which the word 'copyright' is used in the international copyright conventions, but 'copyright' in a very different—wider—meaning. In nearly all countries where phonograms are protected under the copyright acts, it is made clear in the list of subjects protected by 'copyright' itself that phonograms are not literary and artistic works (but subjects other than works, or, although 'works', other than literary and artistic works).[71]

7.2.2. Owners of the rights

The owners of the rights are the producers of phonograms which fix the sounds for the first time, this qualification being applicable

---

70. Ibid., pp. 103 and 113–15.
71. Document UNESCO/WIPO/CGE/SYN/3-III of 11 April 1988, p. 20, Section 78.

both to natural persons and to legal entities. Industrial activity, and not personal activity, is protected.[72]

In this connection, in the Report of the Diplomatic Conference of Rome it is specified that when an employee of a legal entity fixes the sounds in the course of his employment, the employer legal entity, rather than the employee, is to be considered the producer.[73]

In Spain (Article 108(2) *in fine*) it is made clear that 'if the operation takes place within an enterprise, the owner thereof shall be considered the producer of the phonogram'.

The rights of the producer of phonograms do not arise by reason of the reproduction of a sound record produced by another enterprise (see Germany, Article 85(1), *in fine*).

7.2.3. Content: economic rights of producers of phonograms. Limitations

A. RIGHT OF REPRODUCTION, DISTRIBUTION, IMPORT AND EXPORT

Producers of phonograms have the exclusive right to reproduce the phonograms produced by them and to distribute (Germany, Art. 85(1))—or make available to the public by way of sale, exchange or rental—copies thereof (France, Art. L. 213-1.2, previously Article 21(2) of the 1985 law); in addition to the rights of reproduction and distribution, Article 184(1) of the Portuguese law gives express recognition to the right to authorize the import and export of copies of the phonogram and Article 109(2) of the Spanish law makes it clear that 'the right of distribution shall include especially the right to authorize the importation and exportation of copies of the phonogram for the purposes of marketing'.

The Rome Convention (Article 10) establishes the exclusive

---

72. Costa Rica (Article 81(a)) mentions only 'the recording enterprise'. Although this concept does not exclude unipersonal enterprises, the example serves to show that the ownership of the right of the producer of phonograms is assigned on the basis of the industrial activity which is performed.
73. See Claude Masouyé, op. cit., p. 23, Section 3.9.

right of producers to authorize or prohibit the direct or indirect reproduction of their phonograms. The Phonograms Convention—Geneva, 1971—covers, in addition to the right of reproduction, the rights of distribution and importation by establishing in Article 2 that

Each Contracting State shall protect producers of phonograms who are nationals of other Contracting States against the making of duplicates without the consent of the producer and against the importation of such duplicates, provided that any such making or importation is for the purpose of distribution to the public, and against the distribution of such duplicates to the public.

B. RIGHT OF PRODUCERS OF PHONOGRAMS TO RECEIVE REMUNERATION FOR THE SECONDARY USES OF THEIR PHONOGRAMS

Once a phonogram has been published for commercial purposes, it is admitted, generally speaking, that the producer may not oppose its public communication (France, Article L. 213-1, *in fine*, and Article L. 214-1, previously Article 21 *in fine* and Article 22 of the 1985 law).[74] As we have seen, neither can this be opposed by performers (Section 7.1.4.2, c) above).

Communication to the public is free but, in line with the terms of Article 12 of the Rome Convention, legislation establishes the right of producers—together with performers—to receive remuneration in this respect (Colombia, Article 173; France, Article L. 214-1, previously Article 22 of the 1985 law; Dominican Republic, Article 133(1); Germany, Articles 76(2), 77 and 86; and so on).

The limitation of the right of performers to authorize—or to prohibit—the *secondary uses* of the phonograms in which their performances have been fixed and which have been produced with

---

74. The French law of 1985 does not extend the limitation to the use of the phonogram in an entertainment: 'Article L. 214-1, previously Art. 22 of the 1985 law. Where a phonogram has been published for commercial purposes, neither the performer nor the producer may oppose: (1) its direct communication in a public place where it is not used in an entertainment; [...].'

their authorization, is imposed by the need to protect the marketing of the sound recordings and to safeguard the author's exclusive and absolute right to communicate the work to the public. If the limitation is justified in the case of performers, it is also justified in regard to the producers of phonograms, although in some legislation in Roman Law tradition countries, producers of phonograms (but not performers) are granted the right to authorize or to prohibit the public communication of their phonograms or copies of them (Bolivia (1992), Art. 54; Brazil, Article 98; Costa Rica, Article 83; Spain, Article 109(1)).

C. OTHER LIMITATIONS

When setting out performers' rights we referred to the other limitations which, both in Article 15 of the Rome Convention and in domestic legislation, are admitted with respect to the neighbouring rights protected under the Convention (see above, Section 7.1.4.3). The same can be said of the right of producers, together with authors and performers, to share in the *compensatory remuneration for private copying*, since in this case it is not only the work and the performance which are used, but also the fixation made by the producer.

7.2.4. Term of the rights of the producers of phonograms

The term of protection in respect of sound recordings is calculated from the moment of fixation or of its first publication.

Terms of protection vary according to the country: 75 years in the United States; 70 years in Brazil; in general, 50 years, as in Austria, Canada, Chile, Costa Rica, former Czechoslovakia, Denmark, Finland, France, Iceland, Norway, Portugal, Sweden, United Kingdom; 25 years in Iceland and Malta; 20 years in Cyprus and Hungary.

The TRIPS Agreement makes provision, in the case of producers of phonograms, for a minimum period of protection of 50 years computed from the end of the calendar year in which the fixation was made.

The European Directive 93/98/EEC of 29 October 1993 makes provision for a 50-year term of protection calculated from the date of first publication or fixation.

7.3. Rights of broadcasting organizations

Some laws define the broadcasting organization as *the radio or television enterprise that transmits programmes to the public* (Colombia, Article 8(N); Costa Rica, Article 85(a); Dominican Republic, Article 17(m)).

Others expressly include cable programme distribution enterprises, such as Brazil (Article 4(XI): *broadcasting organization* means the organization for radio or television, or for any other process which transmits programmes to the public *by wire or wireless*); and Portugal (Article. 176(9): *broadcasting organizations* ... mean the bodies which effect audio or visual broadcast programmes, broadcast programmes meaning the diffusion of sounds or images, separately or together, *by wire or not*, in particular by Hertzian waves, optical fibre, cable or satellite, and destined for public reception).

The Rome Convention does not define the broadcasting organization. During the Conference, several definitions were proposed, but the proposals were withdrawn.

The activities of broadcasting organizations, like those of producers of phonograms, are of a technical and organizational order.[75]

7.3.1. The subject of protection

In most laws what is protected is the *broadcast* (e.g. Colombia, Article 117; Costa Rica, Article 86; Dominican Republic, Article 135; Germany, Article 87; Italy, Article 79) or, again, the *broadcast or transmission* (Spain, Article 116).

---

75. Henri Desbois, op. cit., Section 189, pp. 232: 'the status derives from copyright and is developed along its lines but broadcasts are not regarded as artistic creations.... Sound recording companies contribute to the dissemination of literature and the arts by fixing what is ephemeral and arresting the passage of time; broadcasting companies make a symmetrical contribution by abolishing distance. Neither enterprise, however, develops a creative activity unlike writers, composers ...'.

In France, what is protected is the programme of the audio-visual communication enterprise (Article L. 216-1, previously Article 27 of the 1985 law).

It is understood that the *programme* is the sequence of sounds, images or sounds and images offered to the public by the broadcaster or the cable distributor through *broadcast or distribution by cable*, for hearing or viewing by the general public or a segment thereof, as the case may be.[76] The content of the term *programme* which also includes cable distribution, is, therefore, broader than *broadcast* which is understood as being the transmission of sounds or of images or, at one and the same time, of sounds and images, by electromagnetic waves propagated in space without artificial guide, for the purpose of enabling reception thereof by the public in general.[77]

However, the majority of national laws use, as we have said, the expressions 'broadcast' and 'broadcast or transmission' to designate the subject of the right of broadcasting organizations and in some of these laws broadcast (or broadcast or transmission) is defined as the dissemination by means of radio electric waves of sounds or sounds synchronized with images (Colombia, Article 8(Ñ); Costa Rica, Article 85(b); Dominican Republic, Article 17(n)).

When using the word 'broadcasting', laws follow the Rome Convention, in which Article 3(f) establishes that, for the purposes thereof: '"broadcasting" means the transmission by wireless means for public reception of sounds or of images and sounds'.

The term '*wireless means*' makes it clear that the Rome Convention refers only to transmission by Hertzian waves or by any other wireless means. During the Rome Conference it was proposed that transmission by wire should also be included in the definition, but it was not accepted because it was felt that only

---

76. 'Annotated principles of protection of authors, performers, producers of phonograms and broadcasting organizations in connection with distribution of programmes by cable', *Copyright*, WIPO, 1984, Section 50(vi), p. 145.
77. Ibid., Section 50(i).

transmission by Hertzian waves or other wireless means should constitute broadcasting.[78]

The fact that the Rome Convention does not protect distribution by cable does not prevent domestic legislation from protecting the rights of cable distribution companies and broadcasting organizations when they effect transmissions by any transmission by wire system: by wire, cable or optical fibre or by any other conducting device.[79]

In this sense, we have already pointed out that the Portuguese law expressly specifies (Article 176(9)) that *broadcasting organizations* mean the bodies which effect audio or visual broadcast programmes and that *broadcast programmes* mean the diffusion of sounds or images, separately or together, *whether by wire or not*, in particular, by Hertzian waves, optical fibre, cable or satellite, and destined for public reception. The reference to the diffusion by cable in the definition of the broadcast programme made by the Portuguese legislator is opportune since it enables protection to include, expressly, cable programme distribution enterprises; similarly, in France, the 1985 law has used (Article 27, now Intellectual Property Code, Art. L. 216-1) the expressions *audiovisual communication enterprise* and *programme*.[80]

The broadcasts which constitute the subject of the rights of broadcasting organizations include all those transmitted by them, whether or not they contain works protected by copyright, as in the case of sporting events, items of public interest, etc. (in the definitions of 'broadcast' and 'programme'[81] mention is made of

---

78. See *Records of the Diplomatic Conference for the Adoption of the Universal Convention*, Geneva, 18 August to 6 September 1952, op. cit., p. 40.
79. The expression *for public reception* used by the Convention in Article 3(f) should make it clear that broadcasts intended for reception by one person or by a well-defined group—such as ships at sea, planes in the air, taxis circulating in a city, etc.—are not to be considered as broadcasts (see Report of the Rome Conference, 1961, *Records*, p. 40).
80. See Claude Colombet, op. cit., pp. 92, *in fine* and 93, *in fine*.
81. See 'Annotated Principles', Section 50(i) and (vi), p. 145.

sounds, images, or sounds and images, without relating these exclusively to performances of works).

The subject of protection is then, the broadcast, irrespective of what it contains. Having regard to the nature of what is protected, broadcasts are not works, although in a number of countries—most of which follow the legal tradition based on common law (Australia, Ireland, Kenya, New Zealand, Nigeria, United Kingdom)—they are regarded as such, in the same way as programmes distributed by cable, although not of the same category as literary, dramatic, musical or artistic works (the same occurs in the case of sound recordings or phonograms). For the reasons already described concerning sound recordings,[82] this qualification would seem incongruous in the authors' rights system of Roman law tradition.

7.3.2. Owners of the rights

It is understood that the *broadcaster* is the natural person or legal entity which decides the broadcasts and determines the programme, including the day and time of the broadcast.[83]

As we have said, the Rome Convention does not define broadcasting organizations, in spite of the fact that, during the Conference, several proposed definitions were put forward, but subsequently withdrawn. Nevertheless, as is specified in the Report of the Rapporteur-General, the debate in question was useful in clarifying several matters. For example, if the technical equipment in a Contracting State is owned by the postal administration, but what is transmitted by this equipment is prepared and presented by organizations such as *Radiodiffusion-Télévision française* or the *British Broadcasting Corporation*, it is these organizations, and

---

82. Valerio De Sanctis (op. cit., Section 7, pp. 29–30): '... Phonograms and broadcasts seek to achieve technical perfection and ensure the best possible industrial product taking account of certain specific conditions. They seek to reproduce faithfully the selected work to that end, to fix it on material supports or carriers (even radio electric waves are material), bringing before a wider public in as many countries as possible a complete reality which would otherwise be highly ephemeral if perceptible to a limited audience (direct communication).'
83. See 'Annotated Principles ...', Section 50(iv), p. 145.

not the postal administration, that are to be considered as the broadcasting organization to which the Convention refers. Furthermore, if a given programme is sponsored by an advertiser or is pre-recorded by an independent producer of television films, and is transmitted by such organizations as the *Columbia Broadcasting System* of the United States, these organizations are to be considered as the broadcasting organization and not the advertiser or the independent producer.[84]

7.3.3. Content: economic rights of broadcasting organizations. Limitations

The broadcasting organizations enjoy, in respect of their broadcasts (or transmissions) or programmes, the exclusive right to authorize their reproduction, retransmission and public communication when such communication is carried out in places accessible to the public against payment of an entrance fee (e.g. Brazil, Article 99; Colombia, Article 177; Costa Rica, Article 86; Dominican Republic, Article 135; France, Article L. 216-1, first part, previously Article 27.1 of the 1985 law; Germany, Article 87(1); Portugal, Article 187; Spain, Article 116(1); Rome Convention, Article 13).

The rights conferred upon broadcasting organizations (to authorize the reproduction or the public communication of their broadcasts or programmes), does not exempt them or third parties from obtaining the authorizations of the authors, performers and producers (except when non-voluntary licences are in force).

A. RIGHT OF REPRODUCTION

Broadcasting organizations enjoy the exclusive right to make recordings of the whole or a part of their broadcasts or programmes on any sound or visual medium, including the obtaining of photographs (any isolated image) from them, but solely for their use within the limits of the contracts with the persons whose pictures

---

84. See *Records of the Diplomatic Conference*, Geneva, 18 August to 6 September 1952, op. cit., p. 41.

are reproduced (for example, in programme publicity in newspapers and magazines and in forthcoming programme announcements made by the broadcasting company itself), and the reproduction of such recordings (provided that they possess, in respect of the recording or fixation and of its reproduction, the authorization of the authors of the works, the performers, etc.).

In France, the Intellectual Property Code, Article L. 216-1, first part, expressly mentions the right of distribution by establishing that *making the reproduction of its programme available to the public by sale, rental or exchange* is subject to the authorization of the audiovisual communication enterprise (previously Article 27, first part, of the 1985 law).

The Rome Convention establishes in Article 13(b) and (c) that:

> Broadcasting organizations shall enjoy the right to authorize or prohibit ...
> b) the fixation of their broadcasts;
> c) the reproduction:
>   (i) of fixations, made without their consent, of their broadcasts;
>   (ii) of fixations, made in accordance with the provisions of Article 15, of their broadcasts, if the reproduction is made for purposes different from those referred to in those provisions.[85]

(Colombia (Article 177(B) and (C)) and the Dominican Republic (Article 135(b) and (c)) follow word for word the text of Article 13(b) and (c) of the Rome Convention).

B. RIGHT OF COMMUNICATION TO THE PUBLIC

a) by means of the rebroadcasting, by any technical procedure, of their broadcasts.

The Rome Convention (Art. 3(g)) defines rebroadcasting as 'the simultaneous broadcasting by one broadcasting organization of the broadcast of another broadcasting organization'. The requirement that it must be a simultaneous broadcast excludes deferred broadcasts since these require, for practical reasons, the

---

85. Limitations admitted by the Convention.

making of a fixation (reproduction) of the broadcast of the originating organization.

However, Brazil (Art. 4(III)) and Costa Rica (Art. 85(c)), for example, include deferred transmission in the concept of 'retransmission' (Costa Rica: ' "retransmission" means simultaneous or deferred transmission of a broadcasting organization's broadcast, effected by another broadcasting organization').

b) by means of the public reception of their broadcasts or programmes in places accessible to the public against payment of an entrance fee.

In commenting on Article 13(d) of the Rome Convention which grants broadcasting organizations the right to authorize or prohibit public communication in respect of television broadcasts, Masouyé[86] states that this right is justified on practical grounds for some users, such as proprietors of cafés, hotels and cinemas offer the showing of television programmes in order to attract clients, charging something for the privilege of watching. In doing so, they are, in a sense, using the programmes of the broadcasting companies for their own gain. But it is, more especially, when sporting events or special occasions are televised (although the problem remains the same in the case of sound broadcasts) that such activities can have an appreciable effect.

C. LIMITATIONS

The limitations established in Article 15 of the Rome Convention (see above, Section 7.1.4.3) may be applied to the economic rights of broadcasting organizations in the same way as those of performers and producers of phonograms.

7.3.4. Term of the rights of broadcasting organizations

The term of protection of the rights of broadcasting organizations is usually the same as that established in the case of performers and producers of phonograms.

---

86. Claude Masouyé, op. cit., Section 13.5, p. 54.

The Directive 93/98/EEC already referred to provides in respect of broadcasting companies, for a 50-year period of protection following the first transmission, whether by wire or otherwise, including cable and satellite transmission.

On the other hand, the TRIPS Agreement provides, in respect of broadcasting organizations, for the same minimum period as in Article 14(c) of the Rome Convention: 20 years from the end of the calendar year in which the broadcast took place (Article 14(5)).

Chapter 8

Collective administration of copyright and neighbouring rights

Summary

8.1. Societies of authors
    8.1.1. History. **8.1.2.** Procedures for the collective administration of copyright. 8.1.2.1. Character and form of the organizations for the collective administration of copyright. 8.1.2.2. Legal nature of the representation provided by collective administration organizations. 8.1.2.3. Number of organizations entrusted with the collective administration of the various rights in each country. 8.1.2.4. One or more societies for each category of authors' rights administered? **8.1.3.** Functions involved in the collective administration of authors' rights. 8.1.3.1. Authorization. 8.1.3.2. Remuneration. 8.1.3.3. Collection. 8.1.3.4. Distribution or sharing. **8.1.4.** Social welfare activities. **8.1.5.** Cultural activities. **8.1.6.** CISAC

8.2. Other societies responsible for the collection of royalties
    8.2.1. Collective administration of royalties for reprographic reproduction. **8.2.2.** Collective administration of rights in respect of private reproduction—home taping of sound recordings and audiovisual works for personal use. **8.2.3.** Collective administration of the '*droit de suite*'

8.3. Collective administration of the rights of performers and producers of phonograms.
    8.3.1. Non-voluntary licences for secondary uses. **8.3.2.** Remuneration. **8.3.3.** Collection. **8.3.4.** Distribution or sharing of remuneration

The term 'collective administration' denotes the system for the administration of copyright and neighbouring rights by virtue of which their owners delegate to organizations created for this specific purpose, authority to negotiate the conditions under which the utilization of their works, artistic performances or industrial productions, as the case may be, by distributors and other primary users is permitted; and for the granting of the respective authorizations, the monitoring of such use, the collection of the remuneration which falls due and its distribution to, or sharing among, the beneficiaries.

The scope of the functions performed by the collective administration bodies depends on the category and nature of the rights administered; however, even when systems of non-voluntary licences[1] are in force, the activity of collective administration includes at the very least two basic aspects: collection and distribution or sharing of royalties.

In most of their aspects, the exclusive rights which the relevant laws and international conventions grant to authors would be a dead letter if the authors were themselves obliged to administer and defend those rights.[2]

The world is a vast market for cultural works and products. Many of the uses take place through the public performance of musical works in dance halls, discothèques, restaurants, tea rooms, bars, cafes, hotels, as background music in stores and offices, transport vehicles, consulting rooms, professional offices, workshops, etc., either live or by means of sound recordings, broadcasting and cable distribution. The same applies to the projection or screening of cinematographic works and the video reproduction of those and other audiovisual works, the hiring of video cassettes, the reprographic reproduction of printed works and the home copying of sound recordings and audiovisual works for personal use.

It is impossible for the author to know where, when and how his works are being used. They are often used in many countries simultaneously. The same songs are played in Buenos Aires and Tokyo, Mexico City, Algiers, Melbourne, London, etc., in provincial capitals and in small localities all over the world. It is an acknowledged fact that music—and art in general—know no frontiers. It would be quite impossible for the distributors and other primary users to enter into direct contact with all the au-

---

1. See above, Chapter 4, Section 4.3.2.
2. In previous works, we have drawn attention to the fact that the author's right (in respect of many works and their uses) and the performer's right are *individual rights which are exercised collectively* (see Carlos A. Villalba and Delia Lipszyc, *Derechos de los artistas intérpretes o ejecutantes, productores de fonogramas y organismos de radiodifusión. Relaciones con el derecho de autor*, Buenos Aires, Ed. Zavalía, 1976, pp. 11 and 25; 'Reflexiones para un homenaje', *Il Diritto di Autore*, 1979, fiftieth anniversary issue, p. 521; and Delia Lipszyc and Héctor Della Costa, *Sistemas de administración de derechos de autor*, La Propiedad Intelectual, WIPO, 1978, No. 3, p. 131).

thors, composers and publishers of domestic and foreign musical works in order to secure the necessary authorization for their use and reach agreement on the prices and other conditions governing the utilization of the vast number of works which are used every day.[3]

In the case, for example, of musical works in which several different copyright owners are generally involved (the composer, the author of the words, the translator, the arranger of the music, the adapter, the publisher and the sub-publisher), the exploitation of, and responsibility for, those works covers a great many simultaneous, short-lived uses in many different places; *the effective exercise of the rights which the law grants to authors* can, then, only be achieved through collective administration—a system which is advantageous to both the creator and distributor. It is beneficial to authors who have no real possibility of administering their rights personally with even a *minimum* degree of efficacy; the cost of doing so would be disproportionately high and in any case they could still not monitor the uses which take place at such widely varying times and places with anything like the thoroughness achieved by the system of collective administration and the scheme of reciprocal representation contracts between societies of authors in different countries. It is beneficial to distributors in that it enables them to have lawful access to a vast repertoire of different national and foreign works which is constantly growing, to negotiate that use with a minimum number of persons on the basis of uniform scales of charges and to make payments with the certainty that they will thus be discharging their obligations.[4]

---

3. With reference to discothèques, for example, Thierry Desurmont points out that well-managed establishments, which are generally open for an average of five hours each night, use some 15 titles hourly, i.e. 75 titles each night; the disc jockey chooses the musical pieces on the basis of the taste of the audience, current musical successes (whose life span is short) and his own personal preferences, taking care to ensure that the audience never gets bored 'The SACEM and Competition Law', *RIDA*, No. 140, April 1989, p. 126).

4. During the WIPO International Forum on the Collective Administration of Copyright and Neighbouring Rights held in Geneva in 1986, Werner Rumphorst, the representative of the European Broadcasting Union (EBU) stressed

The collective administration of the rights in the public performance of non-dramatic musical works and of the rights accruing from the simultaneous and unaltered retransmission of broadcast programmes is thus the sole valid option if the author's right is not to be reduced to an altruistic, but innocuous set of rules or to a simple entitlement to receive remuneration, for the government authorities, confronted with the difficulties which stand in the way of the individual exercise of copyright in these cases, may conclude that the system of compulsory licences is the only way of ensuring that broadcasters are not placed in a situation of constantly infringing the law by using works without the permission of their authors.[5]

Collective administration is also a great help in respect of other forms of exploitation of works: mechanical reproduction, public communication of dramatic and dramatico-musical works, production of audiovisual works, publication of literary works and reproduction of artistic works, since it is very difficult for individual authors to be in a strong enough position to discuss the terms of their contracts, monitor their implementation and require

---

the importance of collective management organizations for the activities of broadcasters and stated that 'in fact, broadcasters would find it impossible to operate without collecting societies, particularly in the field of music. It is indispensable for the broadcaster, as a user of musical works and sound recordings, to know that a collecting society is in the position to clear any of the rights within both its national and foreign repertoires, thanks to contracts of mutual representation. In such cases, the individual clearance of rights by the broadcaster would be completely impracticable because of the sheer volume of work involved. On the other side, the role of collecting societies is to ensure that the right owner is fairly remunerated for the various uses of his material, which he would find impossible or impracticable to administer himself' (quoted by G. Davies, in *El Interés Público en la Administración Colectiva de los Derechos de Autor*, Buenos Aires, DAT, No. 15, November 1989, pp. 6–7.

5. And even where systems of *non-voluntary* (compulsory or statutory) *licences* exist in the cases allowed by the Berne Convention, that is to say, for the mechanical reproduction of non-dramatic musical works, the broadcasting and cable distribution of broadcast programmes and for massive and uncontrollable uses such as reprographic reproduction and private copying, the collection and distribution of the sums which have to be paid *can only be effected by collective management organizations*.

compliance with them; their moral and economic rights may be prejudiced as a result.

It has quite rightly been pointed out that

an exclusive right can be enjoyed, to the fullest extent, if it may be exercised individually by the owner of the right himself. In such a case, the owner maintains his control over the dissemination of his work, can personally take decisions on the economic conditions of its exploitation and can also closely monitor whether his moral and economic rights are duly respected. [...] It cannot be denied that, with such collective administration, the control by the owners of rights over certain elements of exercising their rights becomes more or less indirect, but, if the collective administration system functions appropriately, those rights will still preserve their exclusive nature and—although through collective channels—they can prevail in the fullest manner possible under the present circumstances.[6]

Collective administration is a regular and routine practice on all five continents in relation to a number of rights whose substantive content differs and in respect of works and other protected objects which are used in a variety of ways. The differences will be analysed separately by examining:
- in the first place, the collective administration by *societies of authors* of the rights in creative works when these are circulated in 'traditional' ways (public performance of musical works, mechanical reproduction, public performance of musical and dramatico-musical works, broadcasting, reproduction and resale of works in the visual arts, etc.);
- secondly, the collective administration by *other collection societies* (organizations responsible for collecting reprographic reproduction and home recording rights) of remuneration accruing to authors and owners of neighbouring rights when printed works and works performed and fixed on audio and audiovisual supports are the subject of massive and uncontrollable use through reprographic reproduction for personal or private

---

6. *Collective Administration of Copyright and Neighbouring Rights*, Geneva, WIPO, 1991, numbered paragraphs 3 and 9, pp. 5–6. This excellent study, whose main author is Dr Mihály Ficsor, writing in his capacity as Assistant Director-General of WIPO, is an invaluable contribution to our knowledge of this subject.

purposes and by home recording (for personal use or use within the family circle); and administration of the collection of remuneration in respect of the '*droit de suite*'; and
- lastly, the collective administration by *societies of performing artists and by organizations of phonogram producers* of the *secondary uses* of sound recordings (copies of phonograms).

8.1. Societies of authors

8.1.1. History

The societies which are responsible for the collective administration of authors' rights were first established in France. Their history began in 1777 with the foundation of the *Bureau de Législation Dramatique* (Dramatic Legislation Office) on the initiative of Pierre-Augustin Caron de Beaumarchais, the famous playwright and author of the *Barber of Seville* and the *Marriage of Figaro*. Adopting the slogan 'united and free', Beaumarchais, accompanied by a number of the leading dramatists of the day—Sedaine, Marmontel and Saurin, among others—fought with praiseworthy tenacity to secure recognition of author's rights. The *Bureau* lay at the origin of the first society of authors established to look after the collective administration of authors' rights, i.e. the *Société des auteurs et compositeurs dramatiques* (SACD) which was finally set up 50 years later (in 1829) and still exists today.[7]

'Glory is attractive', wrote Beaumarchais, 'but, to be able to enjoy that glory for just one year, nature condemns us to dine 365 times; and if soldiers and judges are not embarrassed to collect a worthy remuneration for their services, why should the lover of the muses, who after all has to pay his baker, blush at the idea of keeping accounts with actors'?[8]

---

7. The fervent struggle led by the persons directly concerned, who were convinced of the need to impose and defend their rights, marked the vigorous beginning of collective administration and, *mutatis mutandis*, preceded the birth of most of the societies of authors whose origins lay in a similar strength.
8. *Quoted* by J. B. Alpi, 'La Societá francese degli Autori, Compositori e Editori di Musica', *Il Diritto di Autore*, p. 479.

In 1791 (the year in which the Constituent Assembly of the French Revolution granted official status to the right of performance—the first authors' right to be given official recognition—through Decree No. 13-19 adopted in January) the *Bureau* was converted, due to the work of Framery, into a General Agency for the collection of authors' royalties. A considerable number of authors of dramatic and lyric works (some seventy) entrusted Framery—the first General Agent for authors of dramatic works—by means of a power of attorney, with the administration of their works, this arousing loud protestations and strong resistance on the part of theatre impresarios. Nevertheless, the first general contracts governing performances were concluded with a certain number of theatres;[9] the system of collection had now been introduced, and, in 1829, Eugène Scribe gave it definitive shape in the SACD, transforming in this way the first assembly of creative artists into a real society of authors.

Furthermore, on 31 December 1837, literary authors went on to hold the first general assembly of the *Société des Gens de Lettres* (SGDL) or Society of Men of Letters, the professional association which brought together such prominent French writers as Honoré de Balzac, Alexandre Dumas and Victor Hugo and whose primary aim was to campaign against the newspapers which reproduced works without permission or payment.

However, it was not until 1850 that *a fully developed collective administration of authors' rights*[10] saw the light of day in the area of the *public performance of non-dramatic musical works*. This was the outcome of an incident which was destined to become famous. In 1847, the composers Victor Parizot and Paul Henrion,

---

9. See J. Boncompain, 'Le droit d'être auteur', in: *La Révolution des Auteurs*, Paris, SACD, 1984, pp. 7–31; and the booklet *La Révolution des Auteurs (1777–1793)*, Paris, SACD, 1984.

10. See Mihály Ficsor, op. cit., paragraph 16, p. 9. Further below an explanation will be given of the differences between *fully developed* collective administration (effected by the bodies which administer the rights of the authors of non-dramatic musical works) and *partial* administration (practised by the societies which administer the rights of the authors of dramatic and dramatico-musical works for the theatre).

accompanied by the writer Ernest Bourget, went to a performance of one of their works *La Mère Michel à l'Opéra italien* at *Les Ambassadeurs*, a 'café-concert' on the Champs-Elysées in Paris, and declined to pay the price of their seats and drinks. Their refusal was based on the grounds that the owner sold music and songs to his customers but did not pay the authors (perfectly normal practice at the time). However, the protest went further: Parizot, Henrion and Bourget, with the support of their publisher, Colombier, cited *Les Ambassadeurs* before the Commercial Tribunal of the Seine which, in September 1847, prohibited *Les Ambassadeurs* from performing the works of the plaintiffs. The prohibition was flouted and they instituted new legal proceedings as a result of which a further ruling was handed down in August 1848 and confirmed by the Paris Appeal Court in April 1849, sentencing the defendants to pay damages and interest. In the following year, the same authors founded the 'Central Agency for the Collection of the Royalties of Authors and Musical Composers' which shortly afterwards, on 28 February 1851, was replaced by the collective administration society which is today one of the most important in the world: the *Société des Auteurs, Compositeurs et Editeurs de Musique—Society of Authors, Composers and Music Publishers* (SACEM). However, sustained efforts and many lawsuits were needed before SACEM managed to secure the acceptance of a system of fully developed collective administration.

The French example was followed in most European countries and elsewhere and, between the end of the nineteenth century and the early decades of the twentieth, various collective administration societies were set up.[11]

---

11. The organizations responsible for the administration of performing rights are sometimes referred to as 'grand rights societies' (dramatic and dramatico-musical works administered individually) or 'small rights societies' (non-dramatic musical works administered collectively). Today however, these designations are obsolete and have, to all intents and purposes, been abandoned. Their origin lay in the fact that the *right of performance of dramatic and dramatico-musical works* was already firmly established when the collection of *royalties for the performance of non-dramatic musical works* was organized; the fees collected for the

The new technologies which began to emerge at the end of the nineteenth century (first gramophone records, cinematography and radio and later television, cable networks and satellite broadcasting) were to create a universal music market and control over the transfrontier use of works became more imperative and complicated with each new development. Mutual representation contracts began to be concluded between societies of authors and, in 1926, the famous International Confederation of Societies of Authors and Composers (CISAC) was set up in Paris by 18 of these bodies to co-ordinate and strengthen their international relations. By 1990, the number of collective copyright administration organizations belonging to CISAC had reached 144, drawn from 72 countries on all five continents.

8.1.2. Procedures for the collective administration of copyright

The subject of the collective administration of copyright is closely bound up with that of contracts for the public use of works.[12]

The collective administration of copyright has developed and is effected by different procedures, in regard to both the character and juridical form of the organizations which look after it and in respect of the number of bodies which, in each country, are responsible for the joint administration of authors' rights, and of the capacity in which the society represents and administers those rights.

These specific features depend on national legislation, on political, economic and social circumstances, traditions and customs and on the existence and level of development reached in each country by the societies of authors, the length of time for which they have been established and the activities that they pursue. The situation regarding collective administration involves a vast range of specific local features and since exhaustive study would exceed

---

use of works in the second category were much lower than those charged for the performance of works in the first which were held to be of greater importance.
12. Chapter 6 makes frequent reference to the societies of authors and to their influence on the conclusion of contracts.

the limits of this work, our discussion will be confined to the commonest and most significant features. Relatively few copyright laws regulate the activities of societies of authors (for example, Brazil, Belgium, Colombia, France, Ecuador, El Salvador, Guatemala, Italy, Mexico, Switzerland, Venezuela). Specific legal provisions have been adopted in some countries (e.g. Argentina, Law 17.648 (1968) in respect of SADAIC and Law 20.115 (1973) covering ARGENTORES).

8.1.2.1. *Character and form of the organizations for the collective administration of copyright*

The collective administration of authors' rights first emerged and later developed through non-profit-making private bodies established by authors (with the participation of the publishers of musical works in many performing rights societies)[13] with a view to defending the personal interests (moral rights) and administering the economic rights of the authors of creative works.

These bodies also include other activities in their aims which are of vital importance to their members: *social welfare* (by the payment of pensions, assistance in the case of illness, maternity and circumstances of particular hardship, grants for funerals, collective insurance, contracts covering medical assistance and other services), *cultural activities, the amicable settlement of con-*

---

13. Analysis of the music publishing contract (see above, Chapter 6, Section 6.2.2) showed that, through the *additional rights* which authors grant to publishers, the latter secure for themselves a proportional share of the earnings accruing to composers and lyric writers for the exploitation of their works. Because of this practice, the membership of publishers in the organizations for the collective administration of the rights of authors of musical works has been usual in many of these bodies, from the outset in the case of SACEM, and continues today in all the societies existing in Europe and on other continents; it is justified by the advantages brought by joint administration of the interests of all the owners of similar rights in the works concerned. Other societies, especially in Latin America, do not admit publishers as full members because of the dominant position which they might enjoy in the event of conflicts of interests.

flicts between members (especially on matters relating to authorship), and so on.

The general opinion is that private organizations better suit the nature of the rights to be administered—normally the private rights of individuals—and the very purpose of the collective administration of such rights.[14] On the other hand, in a considerable number of countries there is a clear tendency, as we shall see further below, towards public and semi-public organizations.

The most appropriate legal form for groupings of authors in private societies is held to be that of a company established under *civil law*. That statute was adopted at the outset in France for the SACD and the SACEM (and was subsequently imposed as a general rule for collective administration societies by the French law of 3 July 1985, Article 38, first paragraph, now Intellectual Property Code, Article L. 321-1.1).[15]

In this regard, the model Statute for confederated societies adopted by CISAC at its XI Congress in Berlin (1936) made the following provision:

I. On no account shall a confederated society have a commercial or speculative nature, nor shall it pursue any directly and primarily lucrative purpose.
II. Every society of authors, in the broadest acceptance of the term, shall have and retain the physiognomy and juridical structure of a civil law company or of an association of the same kind, with or without a legal personality as the case may be, but in no case may it adopt the form and characteristics of a commercial company (limited liability, trust, etc.) as such.[16]

---

14. See Mihály Ficsor, op. cit., para. 248, p. 70.
15. Since the adoption in France of the law of 3 July 1985, the societies which collect and distribute authors' royalties and the royalties of performers and producers of phonograms and videograms must be established in the form of civil law companies (Article 38, first paragraph). In consequence, SDGL which was originally established as a *civil law association* had to be converted into the company form stipulated in Article 38, para. 1, of the 1985 law, now Article L. 321-1.1.
16. See CISAC, *Décisions, délibérations et voeux adoptés par les Congrès et Assemblées*, 1926–52, p. 328.

The civil law company model was also adopted in several countries of Latin America, such as Argentina (ARGENTORES and SADAIC), Brazil (UBC) and Mexico (SACM and SOGEM).[17]

However, not all societies of authors have adopted this legal form[18] (since not all domestic legislations make provision for civil law companies) and, as we have stated, by no means all organizations responsible for the administration of authors' rights are juridical persons established under private law.

In consequence, although the nature (private or public) of the bodies and the legal form in which they are constituted vary as a function of specific national features, the absence of profit-making purposes is a condition sine qua non (they shall not distribute profits and may only retain the sums which are essential for their own operation, etc.).[19]

In this regard, the first paragraph of Section 13 of the Charter of the Author's Right[20] makes it perfectly clear that:

> Authors' societies, however legally constituted, are trustee organizations administering the intellectual property of authors and of their heirs and assigns. They are not commercial organizations, nor are they actuated by motives of financial gain. They retain from what they collect only such sums as may be required to cover their expenses. For this reason they should enjoy a special legal standing, particularly in matters of taxation.

---

17. A list of the collective administration bodies referred to in this chapter is annexed.
18. Ulrich Uchtenhagen, who was the Director-General of SUISA for nearly three decades, recommended that new societies should adopt a legal form approximating as closely as possible to that of a *co-operative* (this is the form adopted by SUISA). In his view, experience has shown that this legal form gives the best assurance of participation of the authors themselves, and also of the publishers, in a collective administration society ('The Setting-up of New Copyright Societies—Experience and Reflections', *Copyright*, WIPO, June 1991, para. 39, p. 135).
19. In Spain, this condition has been expressly written into the law which stipulates that the bodies which administer rights 'may have no gainful intent' (Article 132, second paragraph).
20. See Chapter 3, note 1.

In Europe, most societies of authors have been organized as *private bodies, although they are generally subject to stringent control by the public authorities.* In some instances, the State participates directly in the societies, while in others they have a semi-official status. For example, in Italy the administration of the rights in the performance of dramatic and musical works of society members is, by law, the exclusive preserve of the SIAE (Italian Society of Authors and Publishers); this society was set up as a private society, subsequently becoming a public body, although it has, in substance, retained its original character which was further strengthened by the post-war statute which restored the society to its members. The SIAE was not established with the aid of public capital; it receives no contributions or subsidies from State bodies and society members are elected to its official organs at three-yearly intervals. The President of the society is nominated by a Decree of the Head of State, acting on the proposal of the Prime Minister; however, this appointment is only made after prior nomination by the Assembly of the Section Committees.[21] The budget and the annual accounts must be approved by the Office of the Council of Ministers (Article 57 of the Regulation implementing the Copyright Law).

In certain European countries, the collective administration organizations are public bodies (JUSAUTOR in Bulgaria, ARTISJUS in Hungary, VAAP in the former Soviet Union) although in some cases many of the members of the managing organs are themselves authors.

In Latin America, private bodies predominate (ARGENTORES and SADAIC in Argentina; SBAT, UBC, SICAM, SBACEM and SADEMBRA in Brazil—although, as we shall see later, the functions of the last four bodies are severely limited; SATCH and SCD in Chile; SAYCO in Colombia; SAYCE in Ecuador; SACM, SOGEM and DIRECTORES in Mexico; APA in Paraguay; APDAYC in Peru; AGADU in Uruguay; SACVEN in Venezuela, etc.).

---

21. See brochure entitled *What is SIAE?*, Rome, 1971, pp. 3 and 9.

In Africa, on the other hand, there is a general preference in the French-speaking countries to establish public or semi-public organizations (ONDA in Algeria; SOCADRA in Cameroon; BUMDA in Mali; BSDA in Senegal, etc.).

This preference is due to the fact that, as Salah Abada[22] has explained,

> for all developing countries with recent copyright provisions, experience seems to have shown that the public law entity is the most suitable formula. Under that system, authors do not have to face the initial expenses of installation which are always high and difficult to meet from individual contributions. Moreover, public entities, invested as they are with the authority and the consideration peculiar to public services, are demonstrably more efficient in their dealings with public users in relation to the respect and defence of the rights of authors.[23]

The preference of these countries for public organizations became apparent on the occasion of the meeting of the Committee of Experts held in Paris in 1980 under the auspices of UNESCO and WIPO to draft Model Statutes for Institutions administering Authors' Rights in Developing Countries and, in particular, to update the 'Draft Model Statute for Societies of Authors in African Countries' (adopted at Abidjan in 1969). After noting that the text of the Abidjan model statute referred essentially to private societies and signifying its own preference for the latter, the Committee of Experts pointed out that experience of recent years had shown that some developing countries felt it more appropriate to create public law agencies or offices.

---

22. Salah Abada, 'Objectives and Organization of an Author's Institution in a Developing Country', lecture delivered at a WIPO/SUISA training course in Zurich in June 1980 (quoted by Mihály Ficsor, 'Development and Objectives of Collective Administration of Author's Rights', *Copyright*, October 1985, p. 349.
23. In this regard, experience in Latin America differs completely (the case of DAIC—the Department of Copyright Law at the University of Chile—being a good example). In another work, Abada draws attention to the differences between Africa and Latin America in the area of collective administration (see 'Collective Administration of Author's Rights in the Developing Countries', *Copyright*, September 1985, pp. 314–22).

It was therefore necessary to make texts covering both approaches available to these countries. However, the Committee stressed that the texts resulting from its deliberations were in any case intended only as a guide and that it rested with the States themselves to decide on the nature of the organizations to be established by them on their territory, either in the form of private law societies or of public law agencies or offices; nor could co-operatives, societies of a mixed legal character or other legal forms be precluded.[24] (The societies in Belgium, Norway[25] and Switzerland have adopted the form of co-operatives; in Argentina, both ARGENTORES and SADAIC are at one and the same time civil law associations and mutual societies.)

In countries following the Anglo-American legal tradition, we find collective administration societies of a different type: for example, equivalent to a public limited company, such as ACUM in Israel, or to limited liability companies in the United Kingdom. In the United States, BMI (Broadcast Music Inc.), founded in 1939, is the sole body for the administration of performing rights whose capital belongs entirely to the broadcasters who are the main users of its musical repertoire.[26]

In an article written in 1969, Zavin,[27] the then Vice-President of BMI, pointed out that the capital in the corporation was offered

---

24. For details of the meeting of experts held in Paris in 1980, see the report and the texts of both model statutes—of a public agency and a private society for the administration of author's rights—in *Copyright Bulletin*, Vol. XIV, No. 3, UNESCO, 1980, pp. 4–19. The two alternatives are also set out in the Model Statutes for Institutions administering Authors' Rights in Developing Countries adopted by the UNESCO/WIPO Committee of Governmental Experts at Geneva in October 1983 (see *Copyright*, 1983, pp. 348–57).
25. See Léon Malaplate, *The Role of Societies or Associations of Authors and of CISAC*, Symposium on Practical Aspects of Copyright, BIRPI, Geneva, 1968, p. 19.
26. See John M. Kernochan, 'Music Performing Rights Organizations in the United States of America: Special Characteristics, Restraints and Public Attitudes', *Copyright*, November 1985, pp. 390–1.
27. Zavin, *BMI. The Complete Report of the First International Music Industry Conference*, 1969, pp. 131–132, quoted by Kernochan, ibid.

for subscription to the broadcasting stations at the price of $5 per share, on the understanding that the corporation would never distribute dividends and that the sale of its shares would be subject to restrictions so as to present them from ever falling into the hands of persons who might seek to acquire control of the organization in order to weaken its competitive position. The BMI has never paid dividends. According to Zavin, the BMI shares were still worth $5 in 1969 and its 500 or so shareholders enjoyed no special privileges of any kind; most of them were broadcasters (active or retired) or their successors-in-title and they had all left their shares on deposit.

8.1.2.2. Legal nature of the representation provided by collective administration organizations

Regardless of the particular nature and legal form of the organizations responsible for the collective administration of authors' rights, their main purpose is to defend the personal interests (moral rights) and to administer the economic rights owned by authors in their creative works.

Article 5 of the CISAC Statutes stipulates that the term 'society administering authors' rights' denotes any organization which:

(i) has as its aim, and effectively ensures, the advancement of the moral interests of authors and the defence of their material interests; and
(ii) has at its disposal effective machinery for the collection and distribution of copyright royalties and assumes full responsibility for the operations attaching to the administration of the rights entrusted to it; and
(iii) does not, except as an ancillary activity, administer also the rights of performers, phonograph producers, broadcasting organizations or other holders of rights.

An organization of authors which does not comply with either of the two first conditions, that is to say *does not administer* authors' rights or *does not have at its disposal suitable machinery* for the effective collection and distribution of copyright royalties and does not assume full responsibility for the operations corresponding to the administration of the rights entrusted to it, *is not a society for the collective administration of authors' rights* even if it may be *a society of authors*.[28] It therefore cannot be admitted to the status of ordinary membership of CISAC (although it may be accepted as an associate member). On the other hand, the public or semi-public agencies which comply with the two first conditions can be full members of CISAC even though they are not *societies of authors* (they do, however, tend to be referred to as such).

The *collection* of royalties for the authorized use of creative works and the *distribution* of the relevant amounts to the right owners (after deduction of the percentages required to cover running costs, but without the possibility of earning profits) are an integral part of the main purpose of a collective administration organization.[29] Sufficient authority to represent the rights whose administration is entrusted to it by the right owners, must therefore be vested in such an organization.

A. PRIVATE BODIES

The authority enjoyed by a collective administration body established under private law to represent authors' rights may be derived from one or more different sources: a mandate of representation granted to the society;[30] assignment to it of certain authors'

---

28. Example: certain professional bodies which are in reality literary and artistic circles.
29. When the organization effects full collective administration, the collection and distribution functions are also associated with a previous phase, i.e. the negotiation of authorizations for use or licences.
30. A distinction may be drawn between the *mandate, representation* and *power of attorney*, by virtue of the modern theory which differentiates between these legal concepts; however, the concepts are closely linked or, at the very least, coexist in a legal relationship. As Gastaldi points out, they have been, and still are, confused in legal theory to such an extent that most currently valid codes of civil law—probably under the influence of French law—do not deal with them in organic and separate provisions.

A distinction between these concepts is particularly useful in the area with which we are concerned here. The *mandate* arises from a contract (bilaterally negotiated) by virtue of which the parties agree that one shall perform one or more legal acts on behalf of the other. The mandate may be granted either with or without representation, as will be the case when the party who holds the rights by the owner of those rights; transfer—in the broad sense of the term—of such rights to the society (a civil law company, co-operative, etc.); statutory dispositions (*ex lege* right of representation), etc.

Often, the act of joining a society of authors (or the membership contract) involves by statute the conclusion of a *representative mandate* contract—see for example, the Statutes of SADAIC, Article 63:

> The admission of the member into the society [...] implies delegation by him to the society, with no limitation whatsoever, of the following rights and powers: (a) to grant or withhold authorization for the performance of his works both on national territory and abroad, to establish the conditions under which such authorization may be given and to fix, monitor and collect the corresponding royalties; (b) to grant authorization for the recording of his works [...] for composition and inclusion in cinematographic films [...].

Again, *authorization* for the society of authors to act in the name and on behalf of its members is set down in the act of member-

---

mandate enters into a contract in his own name as though the transaction whose performance is entrusted to him by the mandator were being concluded on his own behalf. *Representation*, on the other hand, as the authority to act in the name and for the account of a third party, is the result of a unilateral arrangement made by the *party who is so represented* (grant of authority to act) *or stipulated by law*. The mandate and right of representation may coexist and often in fact do: this is known as a *representative mandate* in which the mandate, the contract and the granting of a right of representation (this being a unilateral act) are combined for the benefit of the party holding the mandate, with the result that the self-same party may at one and the same time hold a mandate and be a representative. In his capacity as a representative, he may then act in the name and for the account of the mandator or the party represented by him, while, in his capacity as the holder of a mandate, he is required to work for the account and in the name of the party who has so appointed him. There may thus be a mandate without representation, in which case the holder of the mandate concludes the transaction whose implementation has been entrusted to him by the mandator, with the third party as though he were doing so on his own behalf; and there may also be representation without a mandate, or, lastly, the straightforward right of representation as such (José María Gastaldi, 'Representación, poder y mandato', *Enciclopedia Jurídica OMEBA*, Buenos Aires, 1967, Vol. XXIV, pp. 716–40).

ship, for example, in Article 7 of the Statute of ARGENTORES:

This condition implies, without the need for other legal formalities, the granting to the Association, for the duration of membership, of a special, irrevocable power to defend in the courts of law[31] or in such other bodies as may be appropriate, the rights of the member as an author, successor-in-title or simply as a represented party.

Some societies of authors are vested by law with the right to represent all the creators of works for the administration of which they are responsible, regardless of whether those creators are members, this right also being extended to the successors-in-title of those creators (for example SIAE in Italy,[32] SADAIC and ARGENTORES in Argentina).[33] In these cases, in relation to its members and to the members of collective administration organizations established in other countries with which representation agreements, generally of a reciprocal nature, have been concluded, the society acts as a mandatary-representative (by contract) and also as a representative *ministerio legis*. In regard to the other owners of authors' rights residing on national territory or elsewhere, the authority held by the society to represent them is derived solely from the provisions of the law.

---

31. Prior to the adoption of Law 20.115 of 1973, members granted to the society through a deed drawn up before a notary, a general authority to represent them for legal purposes, in conformity with Article 1184, paragraph 7, of the Argentine Civil Code: 'The following shall be drawn up in the form of notarial deeds [...] 7. The general or special authorities whose presentation is required for legal purposes [...].'
32. See Article 180 of the Italian copyright law.
33. *SADAIC*: Law 17.648 of 1968, Article 1: 'The Argentine Society of Authors and Music Composers (SADAIC) is hereby recognized as a civil and cultural association of a private character representing the creators of national, popular or classical music, with or without words, together with their heirs and successors-in-title and the foreign societies of authors brought into relationship with it by reciprocal assistance and representation agreements.'
    (Law 20.115 of 1973 establishes a similar provision with regard to ARGENTORES.)

In Spain, the law governing intellectual property establishes a *presumption of legitimization* in favour of authorized collective administration entities. Art. 135 stipulates: 'Once authorized, administrative entities shall be qualified, in such terms as are determined by their own statutes, to exercise the rights entrusted to their administration and to assert them in all manner of administrative or judicial proceedings.'

The Statutes of other collective administration bodies (for example SUISA and SACEM) stipulate that authors and publishers *assign* certain rights to them by the mere fact of becoming members.

The Statutes of SUISA provide (Article 7.2) that the authors and publishers of non-dramatic musical works assign to the society in particular the rights of public performance, broadcasting and distribution by cable networks, mechanical reproduction, etc.[34] This assignment includes future works and may be stipulated for a specific period, although it is generally made for an indefinite duration.

In France, the Statutes of SACEM stipulate that, by the mere fact of joining the society, authors transfer to it the exclusive right to administer their works and collect the corresponding royalties. In this connection, Carmet[35] quotes various rulings of French courts which define SACEM as the assignee of the economic rights in the works of its author-members. He points out that the transfer of rights is made by virtue of the provisions set out in the Statutes of the society and does not constitute a transfer in the strict sense but in the broad sense, that is to say on the basis of an assignment against payment; he goes on to state that beyond this case law, it will be observed that this assignment is indeed offset even though the amount is unspecified on admission to membership when the rights are transferred. He is of the opinion that in

---

34. See *Droit et musique, un guide pratique à l'intention des compositeurs, paroliers et arrangeurs d'œuvres musicales*, SUISA, p. 8.
35. Olivier Carmet, 'Statutes of SACEM', *RIDA*, No. 140, April 1989, pp. 28–54.

terms of common law, it is not necessary for a price to be specified on assignment if it can be determined, that is to say can be paid, notably by contractual methods agreed between the parties. Among these methods one can include the stipulations under SACEM's Statutes which provide for a distribution determined according to terms and conditions which vary depending on the nature of the right required by the user. Indeed, we know that, under Article 35 of the law of 11 March 1957 'the transfer by the author of the rights in his work may be total or partial. It must confer to the author's benefit participation in the receipts resulting from the sale or exploitation'.

According to this same author,

backed by this assignment, SACEM ... is in a position to exercise the prerogatives conferred on it and also enjoys the liens that are attached to them ... In other words, the combination of Article 65 of the law of 11 March 1957[36] and the transfers made to the authors' society confers on the latter the same rights and guarantees as those enjoyed by its members who have assigned them to it.

Having regard to the provisions of the Statutes of SACEM, Carmet is of the opinion that the rights to authorize or prohibit the public performance and mechanical reproduction of the musical works transferred to the society, manifestly constitute transfers in the broad sense and not in the narrow sense. Here, he cites Article 2*ter* of the Statutes which is categorical in this respect: the rights transferred to the society 'do not contribute towards the registered capital' adding that they are not remunerated by means of the allocation of assets. And he goes on to cite the ruling of the First Civil Chamber of the Court of Cassation handed down on 28 June 1988 which pointed out that 'the Court of Appeal had correctly noted the existence and the measure of the cash transfers which alone constitute SACEM's registered capital and are to be

---

36. Now Intellectual Property Code, Article L. 331-1: '[...] Regularly constituted professional protection bodies shall be entitled to appear before the courts of justice to defend the interests entrusted to them pursuant to their statutes.'

distinguished from the copyright assignments granted to the society by its members and thus vested in it'.[37]

In regard to the rights of foreign authors, Carmet points out that SACEM has concluded representation agreements—often reciprocal—with its foreign counterparts which entitle it to issue licences, against remuneration, under which 'users may exploit the works in its contractual partners' repertoires'. The legal instrument used for this purpose is the mandate—to which the reciprocal representation agreements between collective administration societies expressly refer—and the representative capacity of SACEM has been noted on many occasions by the Court of Cassation; the latter has additionally pointed out that 'this role was duly in keeping with the society's activities' (it had been claimed that SACEM had no authority to represent its foreign counterpart societies in France because its Statutes did not provide for and authorize such an activity). Carmet goes on to conclude that 'whether it be the assignee of its members' prerogatives or the representative of foreign authors' societies, SACEM is indeed responsible, under its Statutes, for interests which entitle it to take legal action pursuant to Article 65 of the law of 11 March 1957'.

The 'Model Statute for Private Societies administering Authors' Rights' adopted by the Committee of Experts (Paris, 1980), referred to previously, stipulates that, among their other obligations, all members shall (Article 6):

(ii) assign to the society the exclusive right, in respect of all countries and for the duration of [...] to act as their sole representative and to authorize or forbid all uses of those of their works in respect of which it exercises exclusive administration of rights or in respect of which they have requested its intervention.[38]

The assignment of rights made by members in favour of the society to enable the latter to perform its appointed task, is regarded as *fiduciary assignment* as it does not entail a transfer of owner-

---

37. See Carmet, op. cit., pp. 37–8.
38. See *Copyright Bulletin*, Paris, UNESCO, 1980, No. 3, p. 13.

ship of the rights in the works that the member has 'assigned', but simply means that it is the society that exercises such rights. Furthermore, its validity is either limited in time or conditional on the owner of the right remaining a member. Were that not the case, on the death of the author his successors-in-title would not inherit the assigned rights which might also be distrained to settle debts of the society, and the author or his successors-in-title could not transfer membership to an equivalent society in another country, etc.

B. PUBLIC ORGANIZATIONS

In the case of public organizations, the issues of interest to us here do not present the difficulties which arise with private bodies, since the representation of the owners of rights exercised by the public agency emanates from the legal norm which established it. There is no membership contract, no mandate, no assignment and no transfer of capital. The representation is strictly *ex lege*.

When the collective administration of authors' rights is entrusted to public bodies, we must suppose that the administration of certain prerogatives of local authors has been *brought under State control* and that foreign nationals or those whose habitual place of residence is outside the country, may only exercise their rights through these bodies. This government control over the exercise of authors' rights which has been adopted for pragmatic reasons[39] may be viewed as a transitional solution which has to be adjusted in each particular case to the political and legal system of the country concerned.

8.1.2.3. Number of organizations entrusted with the collective administration of the various rights in each country

In some countries, authors' rights are administered by societies which differ *according to the nature of the works and their uses*. Thus several civil law societies for the collective administration of

---

[39]. See explanation by S. Abada (Section 8.1.2.1 above) and that given by M. Ficsor in *Collective administration ...*, op. cit., paragraph 247, pp. 69–70.

authors' rights have been set up and coexist today in France: SACEM (rights in respect of the public performance of musical works); SDRM (mechanical reproduction rights); SACD (rights in the public performance and reproduction of dramatic works); SGDL (literary works); SPADEM (rights of reproduction of artistic works and '*droit de suite*') and ADAGP (essentially, the '*droit de suite*').

The system involving several different societies has also been adopted in other European countries, for example Austria (AKM, AUSTRO-MECHANA, LITERAR-MECHANA and LVG); the United Kingdom (PRS, MCPS, MCOS, DACS and ALCS); Switzerland (SUISA, PRO LITTERIS, SSA and SUISSIMAGE), Spain (SGAE, VEGAP) and also in some American republics, for example in Argentina (ARGENTORES and SADAIC); Chile (SATCH and SCD); Mexico (SACM, SOGEM and DIRECTORES), and so forth.

In other countries, on the other hand, a single general society is responsible for the collective administration of the various rights in works of different categories, for example in Belgium (SABAM), Israel (ACUM), Italy (SIAE), Uruguay (AGADU), Venezuela (SACVEN), and so on.

8.1.2.4. One or more societies for each category of authors' rights administered?

A. The organization of collective administration within a single general body responsible for administering all the different types of rights (such as AGADU, SGAE, SIAE) or in different societies which look after one or more categories of rights (as in Argentina, France, United Kingdom) depends on local circumstances. Either of the two systems may prove equally effective[40] with the proviso

---

40. The question as to which of these two structures for collective administration (a general society or a number of societies dealing with the different categories of administered rights) would prove more efficient was the subject of a detailed debate at the XXXI CISAC Congress, held in Toronto in 1978; opinions were divided.

that when more than one society exists, each category of rights in works of the same kind must be administered by one organization only, as in the examples cited above (Argentina, Austria, Mexico, Switzerland, United Kingdom, etc.).

Attention has rightly been drawn to the fact that 'in respect of determined categories of rights, many of the basic advantages of collective administration (easy and legally safe licensing of uses, possibility for the authorization of the use of the entire world repertoire in one single licence, substantial decrease of administrative costs, etc.) can be obtained only by means of one single organization. Therefore, it seems advisable to avoid parallelism and rather to establish only one organization for each category of rights'.[41]

The theory and reality of collective administration, confirmed by historical experience, coincide in demonstrating that competition between societies responsible for public performing rights in non-dramatic musical works, far from improving the conditions of their use, actually causes prejudice to the sectors concerned:

- prejudice to the distributors for, if—as is usually the case—they require access to the mass of works available on the market, the fact that the administration of works of the same category is shared between two or more bodies will give rise to demands for payment of duplicated royalties for use of the same work; this in turn may result in intervention by the government authorities in a manner which is not desired by the local authors (as happened, for example, in Brazil);
- competition is also prejudicial to authors because it tends to result in a 'tariff war'; this leads to a substantial reduction of the fees collected and creates conditions under which unscrupulous users may evade payment by resorting to various subterfuges: playing one society off against another, forcing societies to take legal action by maintaining that they have not used the repertoire of the claimant, requiring them to prove which works were actually used by the debtor, etc.

---

41. M. Ficsor, *Collective administration* ... op. cit, paragraph 243, p. 68.

A collective administration which is confronted with problems of this kind as a daily routine is not a viable proposition; its benefits are neutralized and at the same time it discredits societies of authors and weakens the entire copyright system.

This explains why very few examples can be found anywhere in the world of collective administration organizations which compete with each other in the administration of the right of public performance of musical works: United States of America (ASCAP, SESAC, BMI), Canada (CAPAC, PROCAN) and Brazil (UBC, SICAM, SBACEM, SADEMBRA).

B. Describing the situation in the United States, Kernochan points out that the system in that country has features which differ significantly from those found generally in other systems, precisely because at least three private licensing organizations exist and are in active competition with each other.[42] Vigorous anti-trust regu-

---

42. See John M. Kernochan, 'Music Performing Rights Organizations in the United States of America: Special Characteristics, Restraints and Public Attitudes', *Copyright*, November 1985, p. 389.

Kernochan points out that the American Society of Composers, Authors and Publishers (ASCAP), founded in 1914, was the first collective administration *organization* in the United States to handle performing rights in musical works. 'It is an unincorporated non-profit membership association established under the laws of the State of New York. Its members are composers, lyricists and music publishers.' In 1985, membership numbered some 25,800 writers and 9,600 publishers. In 1984, ASCAP's domestic and foreign receipts exceeded $208 million.

The Society of European Stage Authors and Composers Inc. (SESAC), is the second organization in chronological order and the third in importance. Its founder, Paul Heinecke, a former music publisher belonging to ASCAP, had previously set up Associated Music Publishers Inc., a performing rights organization which was later acquired by BMI. Originally, SESAC took its name from the fact that its repertoire was based on European music (including works controlled by the Society of Spanish Authors and Composers, the Society of German Stage Authors and the Polish Composers' Organization). Difficulties experienced during the Second World War over European rights, led SESAC to seek out North American music not hitherto represented and to specialize in popular and 'gospel' music. SESAC has retained its original name despite the fact that it now represents both European and American works of various kinds:

lation is pursued by the State on individual request; Congress and state legislatures impose restrictions on the collection and payment of fees and there is a marked tendency to resort to compulsory licensing and official fee-regulating machinery.[43]

In the United States, competition between collective administration societies is a consequence of the well-known fact that 'the basic policy of the United States economic system and the legal framework that supports it favour free competition'.[44] However, Kernochan wonders[45] whether it might not be 'easier and less expensive for users to deal with one organization for all music performing needs than it is to deal with three or more, or to embark in addition on direct licensing with multiple creators'. The existence of three organizations may well lead 'to higher costs for the consumer and user and to less return for the composers', as well as other serious disadvantages.[46]

---

variety music, rock, rhythm and blues, soul music, jazz and also 'classical' material. SESAC has always been a family-owned corporation. Originally, all its affiliates were publishers, but, beginning in the early 1970s, writers were admitted selectively and in 1985 there were roughly 1,800 writer and about 1,130 publisher affiliates. Neither writers nor publishers participate in the management of SESAC, which is conducted by an administrative staff. In this aspect, SESAC, like BMI, is unusual among the world's performing rights organizations. In the 1984–85 fiscal year, it collected just over $5.5 million. Through its subsidiary, Music Royalties Limited, SESAC offers, in respect of mechanical reproduction and synchronization rights, services similar to those provided by the Harry Fox Agency.

BMI was founded in 1939 and is entirely owned by broadcasters who are the main users of its musical repertoire. No author or publisher belongs to its governing board or has any voice in its management. In 1985, BMI had around 45,000 writer and 28,000 publisher 'affiliates' (they are not known as 'members'). For the fiscal year ending 30 June 1985, BMI reported domestic and international receipts of some $150 million (ibid., pp. 391–2).

43. Ibid., p. 389.
44. Ibid., p. 394.
45. Ibid., p. 395.
46. The highly prejudicial consequences of competition between collective administration societies include the 'tariff war' referred to earlier, disputes over the body entitled to collect royalties on the basis of the works used and the repertoire to which they belong (generally the user broadcasts a mixture of works

C. In Brazil, the coexistence of several societies for the collective administration of public performing rights in musical works created confusion, repeated claims by them for payment and other equally unfortunate situations which led to the disruption of activity and, ultimately, to the foundation in 1973 (Law 5.988) of the Conselho Nacional de Direito Autoral (CNDA) (National Copyright Council), a public agency which, pursuant to the provisions of Article 115 of that law, set up, by its Resolution No. 1 of 6 April 1976, the Escritorio Central de Arrecadação e Distribuição (ECAD) (Central Office for Collection and Distribution), which operated as a statutory body from January 1977 to 1988, the year when the country's new Constitution was promulgated.[47]

---

from the repertoires of the different societies), and a race between the societies to be the first to recover the entire fee, leaving the distributor exposed to claims by the other society or societies with the result that he may have to pay the same royalty more than once (as occurred in Peru, up to 1991, in regard to APDAYC and SPAC).

When several bodies collectively administer *different categories of rights* there may still be '*grey areas*', that is to say, situations in which doubts exist as to which of them is actually responsible for administration; that will be the case, for example, when ballets and other choreographic works are performed (administered by the performing rights society) in which pre-existing music is used, i.e. one or more non-dramatic musical works which were created with the original intention of being performed as such, unlike the music specially created for a ballet, (such as the 'Nutcracker' or 'Swan Lake' by Tchaikovsky). The situation is reversed when a dramatico-musical work (opera, operetta, *zarzuela*, etc.) or a fragment of it (the overture, an aria, etc.) is performed in a concert. In such cases, the best way of solving the problem is through an agreement between the societies on the procedure to be followed. For example, in Argentina, an agreement of this kind has been concluded between ARGENTORES (which, it will be recalled, administers the economic rights of all creators of literary, dramatic, dramatico-musical, choreographic and pantomime works when they are performed, broadcast or included in sound and audiovisual fixations) and SADAIC (which administers the economic rights of all creators of nondramatic musical works, regardless of the means and procedures governing their use).

47. See V. Santiago, 'Las entidades de gestión colectiva de los artistas intérpretes o ejecutantes en América Latina—Experiencias concretas', in *Libromemoria del I Congreso Iberoamericano de propiedad intelectual*, Madrid, 1991, p. 1041.

By virtue of its Statutes, ECAD has its headquarters in Rio de Janeiro (Article 2) and is a private, non-profit-making, civil law association, established for an unlimited period by the *copyright and neighbouring rights societies* (Article 1). It has the power to authorize or prohibit the public performance of musical works—with or without words—and of phonograms (it does not, however, administer mechanical reproduction rights), to determine royalties and arrange collection and distribution throughout the territory of Brazil in conformity with the provisions of Article 73 of the above-mentioned law (Article 3); it is mandated by its member societies and by the foreign bodies represented by them for the purpose of defending the authors' rights of their members (Article 3, para. 1); it is barred from receiving instructions directly from the owners of copyright (Article 4) and foreign bodies may only be represented through domestic associations in conformity with Article 105 of the aforementioned law of 1973 (Article 3, para. 2).

ECAD effects collection and calculates the distribution of the sums owed to each right owner; the corresponding amounts are remitted to its member societies which, in their turn, distribute the moneys to their members. The societies are responsible for all the tasks of documentation and identification of their repertoires of works or phonograms for the purpose of distribution. Collective administration in Brazil was thus unified by statutory provision and outside the framework of the Brazilian societies of authors of non-dramatic musical works, whose functions were severely curtailed.

Vanisa Santiago points out that in practice ECAD acts as a banking establishment and is not a substitute for the societies themselves which make direct payments to their members and are responsible for withholding all the taxes accruing to the State. The societies determine the working methods, rules of procedure and royalty tariff policy followed by ECAD.[48]

In the case of dramatic works on the other hand, collective administration of the right to perform them in Brazil has always

---

48. Ibid.

rested with the Sociedade Brasileira de Autores Teatrais (SBAT) (Brazilian Society of Stage Writers), the first collection society founded in the country in 1917 and recognized as a public service organization by Decree No. 4.092 of 1920.

D. Villalba is of the opinion that the essential value of collective administration derives precisely from the monopoly position, and points out that in this area the words 'competition' and 'monopoly' do not have the same meaning as in the area of commercial activities; in transactions involving the distribution of works, the competition takes place between the authors who fight to place their own creations, between publishers, impresarios, producers, etc. These are the persons involved in the process of competition and not the collective administration societies which simply administer a body of works.

Uchtenhagen highlights, with great aptness, clarity and conciseness, the main arguments against the monopoly position of societies for collective administration and the reasons for which such a monopoly is essential:

The monopoly situation of the copyright administration societies is often contested with the argument that it is incompatible with the constitutional freedom of forming associations. However, this objection is based on an error. Authors are free to set up as many associations as they may wish—although these associations are not permitted to concern themselves with the collective administration of authors' rights. This restriction in favour of a monopoly thus affects the freedom to trade but not the freedom to constitute associations. Practically every country has constitutional exceptions to the freedom of trade which may be classified together under the term of 'useful concentrations' such as transport, electricity, telephone or water utilities. Copyright societies are also to be included amongst these useful concentrations, and that should open for them the possibility of a monopoly.

'Why'—asks Uchtenhagen—'is it not possible to set up a satisfactory collective administration without a statutory or a *de facto* monopoly?' His answer is as follows:

The reason is that where a number of societies exist it is not possible to make any precise demarcation. Where are the rights to be found in a work that has been created by co-authorship if one author belongs to society A and the other to society B? Or in the case where the writer of the music for a song is a member of A and the writer of the words a member of B? Or again if an author belonging to A has his works published by a publisher belonging to B? But how do we inform the user of copyright of the scope of the powers of representation when he wishes to know what is represented by A, what is represented by B, particularly in those cases where authors daily change from A to B and from B to A? It is these dubious areas between the multiplicity of copyright societies that lead to uncertainty and to disputes which, as experience has shown, are a chronic source of infection from which the administration of copyright can never altogether recover.[49]

When account is taken of the characteristic features of the administration of intellectual works, the problem of monopoly versus competition is found to be merely superficial in respect of the administration of rights in vast repertoires of national and foreign works. The crux of the matter is the need to establish uniform procedures for the administration of rights in such a way as to ensure compatibility on the one hand with a multiplicity of complex international relations and the contractual use of repertoires of an indeterminate number of works and, on the other, with respect for the essentially individual rights of the author.

E. Some legislations, as in Italy and Switzerland, have reconciled these two apparently contradictory requirements through simple solutions: firstly, that of concentrating, in the hands of a single body, the collective administration of every identical category of rights, secondly, that of safeguarding the freedom of the author to decide whether to join the body concerned.

In Italy, the first paragraph of Article 180 of the copyright law grants a single body (SIAE) a legal monopoly to administer authors' rights in the following terms:

The right to act as an intermediary in any manner whether by direct or indirect intervention, mediation, agency or representation, or by assignment of the exercise of the rights of performance, recitation, broadcasting and mechanical and

---

49. Ulrich Uchtenhagen, 'The Setting-Up of New Copyright Societies. Experience and Reflections', in *Copyright*, WIPO, June 1991, No. 6, paragraphs 8 and 9, p. 126.

cinematographic reproduction of protected works, shall be reserved exclusively to the Società Italiana, degli Autori ed Editorí (SIAE).

However, the same Article 180 goes on to stipulate in its fourth paragraph that: 'The said exclusivity of powers shall not prejudice the right of the author or his successors-in-title to exercise directly the rights recognized in their favour by this law.'

Dietz points out that this latter provision is the justification for the ruling by the Italian Constitutional Court, on 17 April 1968, that the legal monopoly of SIAE was in the public interest and might therefore also be held to have been approved constitutionally in its favour.[50]

The Swiss Federal Law of 9 October 1992 on copyright and neighbouring rights contains provisions similar to those of the former Federal law of 25 September 1940 (Art. 1 and 2) concerning the collection of copyright royalties:

Article 40:
1. The following shall be subject to federal supervision:
    (a) the administration of exclusive rights for the performance and broadcasting of non-theatrical works of music and the production of phonograms and videograms of such works;
    (b) the assertion of the claims to remuneration provided for in this law under Articles 13, 20, 22 and 35.
2. The Federal council may subject further fields to federal supervision if the public interest so requires.
3. The personal administration of exclusive rights by the author or his heirs shall not be subject to federal supervision.

Article 42:
2. Authorization shall be granted as a rule to one society only for each category of works and to one society for neighbouring rights.

It follows that, in these two countries, the law delegates responsibility to a single legal person (in these particular instances, SIAE or SUISA respectively) for all legal procedures in respect of works which their author cannot, or does not wish to, exercise directly.

---

50. See Adolf Dietz, op. cit., Spanish version, Vol. II, p. 459, Section 613.

The law permits the existence of only one collective administration society but leaves the author or his successors the option of exercising their rights on their own behalf.

F. The WIPO Draft Model Provisions for legislation in the field of copyright envisaged guarantees against possible unlawful restrictions of authors' rights administered by collective administration organizations, many of which take into account the rules established by the International Confederation of Societies of Authors and Composers (CISAC). The Draft, in its Article 53, provides that:

1. The exclusive economic rights and the rights to equitable remuneration administered by collective administration organizations shall not be restricted as a result of such collective administration. To guarantee the elimination of such restrictions:
   (i) all decisions about the methods and rules of collection and distribution of fees and about other important aspects of collective administration shall be taken by all the authors whose rights are administered or by bodies representing them;
   (ii) the authors whose rights are administered by a collective administration organization shall receive regular, full and detailed information about all the activities of the collective administration organization that may concern the exercise of their rights;
   (iii) without the express authorization by all the authors whose rights are administered (given directly or by the bodies representing them), no fees collected by a collective administration organization shall be used for any purposes (for example, for cultural or social purposes, or for financing promotion activities) other than the purposes of covering the actual costs of administration of the rights involved and of distributing the amounts of fees that remain after the deduction of such costs;
   (iv) the amounts of fees collected by a collective administration organization shall—after the deduction of the actual costs of collective administration and other potential deductions that the authors may authorize in keeping with point (iii)—be distributed among the authors as much as possible in proportion to the actual use of their works.
2. Foreign authors whose rights are administered by a collective administration organization (either directly or on the basis of an agreement with foreign collective administration organizations by which such authors are directly represented) shall enjoy the same treatment as those authors—members of, or otherwise represented by, the collective administration organization—who are nationals of, or have habitual residence in, the country.

3. Foreign collective administration organizations shall receive regular, full and detailed information of all the activities of a collective administration organization of the country—with which they have concluded an agreement on the reciprocal representation of the rights administered by them—that may concern the exercise of the rights of, and the distribution of fees to, the authors whose rights are administered by such foreign collective administration organizations.[51]

8.1.3. Functions involved in the collective administration of authors' rights[52]

When the author administers his rights individually, that task comprises two aspects: negotiation with the user in regard to the terms governing the *authorization* which he is responsible for granting and undertaking *collection*. *Authorization* is the means by which the user secures permission to use the work; that permission is granted by the author through the contract which sets out the conditions governing exploitation of the work. The contract lays down provisions covering the personal rights of the author in matters which fall within his own discretion (characteristics and quality of the edition, form, position and size of the

---

51. WIPO document CD/MPC/1/2 II of 20 October 1988, pp. 21–22.

52. *We shall refer here to works in the private domain.* When works in the public domain are used and a charge is made (commonly known as the *paying public domain*), only the fixing of tariffs and collection are involved (collective administration bodies are usually responsible for collection). Authorization and distribution do not exist in these cases for the purpose of the public domain is to facilitate access to works protected by copyright and one of its main effects—regardless of whether a charge is made—is to permit the use of works without the need for any form of authorization; that is why, when this subject was discussed in Chapter 5, Section 5.3.2, we described as *inappropriate* the fact that some laws (for example, Congo, Côte d'Ivoire) stipulate a requirement for authorization.

The sums paid for the use of works which are in the public domain cannot be referred to as *remuneration* in that they do not constitute a counterpart consideration since the author's economic rights have expired. They are in the nature of a tax and the State fixes the respective tariffs.

Finally, there is no *distribution* or *sharing* of the collected sums since these are assigned to the organization established by the law which created the obligation to make payment for the public use of works in the public domain.

letters used to indicate the author's name, etc.), his economic rights (time-limits on use, number of copies or editions of the work, amount of the *remuneration,* manner, place and time at which the user is to make payments—or, similarly, where and when he is to collect or receive payment of the amounts accruing in respect of the use of his work, etc.), together with the other provisions found in any contract (grounds for cancellation, etc.).

In cases where a collective administration organization manages the author's rights, the activities indicated above (negotiation with the user of the terms governing exploitation of the work, the granting of *authorization*, agreement on the corresponding *remuneration,* and collecting of the *remuneration*) are supplemented by another function: that of *distributing* or *sharing* the amounts collected. As we shall see, this function tends to be extremely complex.

The bodies which effect fully developed administration are found—since the creation of SACEM as the first organization of this kind—in the area of the collective administration of authors' rights in *non-dramatic musical works.*[53] These societies of authors perform the four functions indicated above by virtue of the exclusive authority vested in them to exercise the rights of composers and authors of lyrics in their present and future works which constitute the repertoire of the organization.

The necessary authority may emanate from one or more separate sources (fiduciary assignment, transfer by members, representation mandate, compulsory *ex lege* representation) and is *entirely exclusive* since in general the authors are not allowed to continue to exercise for themselves the rights whose administration has been entrusted by them to the collective administration organization on the basis of the provisions set out *in its Statutes* (for example SACEM), *in law* (for example ONDA) *or in both* (for example SADAIC).

On the other hand, in the areas in which collective administration is a useful, but not the sole, way of ensuring reasonable

---

53. See Mihály Ficsor, op. cit., paragraph 16, p. 9.

management (for example, with regard to public performance and, in general, the communication to the public of dramatic works), the authors do not transfer to these organizations exclusive authority to exercise these rights. They confer sufficient powers on them to permit the performance of their appointed task and the bodies concerned effect partial administration: they grant permission for use after securing the agreement of the authors of the works concerned, i.e. they act in a manner similar to agencies holding a right of representation. The distribution of the sums collected by them presents few difficulties in comparison with those which arise from the public performance of musical works.

8.1.3.1. Authorization

The considerable role played by collective administration organizations in the conclusion of contracts[54] is discussed both in Chapter 6 and in the present chapter. It will therefore suffice to recall here that the societies which are responsible for the collective administration of the rights of public performance[55] grant authorizations for use without prior consultation of the authors (fully developed collective administration), and that *general licences* (or *global* or *blanket licences*) or *repertoire contracts* are the

---

54. See the opinion of Dietz on this question, op. cit., Spanish version, Vol. II, pp. 392–3.
55. Pursuant to Article 1 (III) of the 'Model Contract of Reciprocal Representation between Public Performance Rights Societies' (document CISAC/ 40.700 of July 1974), 'the expression "public performances" includes [...] all sounds and performances rendered audible to the public in any place whatever within the territories in which each of the contracting societies operates, by any means and in any way whatever, whether the said means be already known and put to use or whether hereafter discovered and put to use during the period when this contract is in force. "Public performance" includes in particular performances provided by live means, instrumental or vocal; by mechanical means such as phonographic records, wires, tapes and sound tracks (magnetic and otherwise); by processes of projection (sound film), of diffusion and transmission (such as radio and television broadcasts, whether made directly or relayed, retransmitted, etc.) as well as by any process of wireless reception (radio and television receiving apparatus, telephonic reception, etc. and similar means and devices, etc. ...) [...].'

main instrument used for this purpose. By this means, these societies authorize the distributors to use, in the manner, at the place and for the period agreed in the licence, *all* the works figuring in the repertoire administered by them—both national and foreign—(in respect of which the authors have already exercised their right of disclosure) generally referred to as the *world repertoire of works* or *of protected music*.

The conditions governing the global licences (or repertoire contracts or blanket licences) are negotiated between the collective administration organization and the associations or chambers of the user sector concerned. The latter conclude a general contract or collective agreement for the use of the repertoire which constitutes an *outline agreement*[56] setting out the conditions to which the authorization granted by the former shall be subject. It goes without saying that the stipulations set out in this general contract for use of the repertoire are binding only on the distributors who are members of the particular professional chamber with which the society of authors concludes the agreement; however, they generally also determine relations with users who are not members of the chamber, although the latter are frequently asked to produce more extensive guarantees of compliance with their obligations.

Global authorizations are a special feature of the system for the collective administration of the right of public performance; by this means, the society of authors grants the distributor the right to use one or more works from the repertoire administered by it (in French, this provision is habitually referred to as the '*clause forfaitaire*' or blanket clause).

The extent of the repertoire which the collective administration organization is able to place at the disposal of the distributors depends on the number of authors of national works who have entrusted it with the task of administering their rights and on the number of representation contracts concluded by it with counterpart societies in other countries. The societies which have had a

---

56. Ulrich Uchtenhagen, *Licence Agreements Made with Users*, Geneva, Symposium on practical aspects of copyright, BIRPI, 1968, p. 75.

long history and enjoy exceptional prestige because of their technical qualities and the rectitude of their working methods (for example SACEM, SGAE, SUISA, SIAE, GEMA, SABAM, PRS, JASRAC, ACUM, AGADU, SADAIC, etc.) represent practically the entire existing body of music. This involves a vast quantity of national and foreign works which, as we have indicated, are known collectively as the *world repertoire of protected music*. The distributors are entitled to use these works in accordance with their needs and under identical conditions, since one of the basic premises of the collective administration of foreign works resides in the fact that they are treated *on a basis of complete equality with national works* by virtue of the *principle of national treatment* established in the international copyright conventions (Berne Convention, Paris Act, 1971, Article 5.1 and Universal Convention, Article II.1).

In the Nordic countries—Denmark, Finland, Norway and Sweden (whose copyright laws date from the years 1960–61 and have similar structures and provisions), a special system is used—that of the 'extended collective licence' or the 'extended collective administration clause'. This is a specific *legal technique* by which, if a collective administration organization represents the rights of a large number or a substantial proportion of authors in the country of works of a particular kind and grants authorization for their use, the users may, without further specific authorization, make use of other works in the same category, provided that they pay the same remuneration and comply with the same conditions imposed by the organization for the use of the works whose utilization it authorizes.

A legal provision is required in order to extend the collective licence to authors who do not belong to the organizations concerned. These authors receive the same treatment as members of the organizations in regard, for example, to remuneration (it has therefore been pointed out that for non-member authors, this system contains an element of compulsory licensing).[57] Never-

---

57. Document UNESCO/WIPO/CGE/PW/3-I, Section 113.

theless, they retain the right to claim individual remuneration. There are also other guarantees to safeguard their rights, such as the possibility of notifying the organization in writing that they prohibit the use of their works. The areas of application of extended collective licences are, more especially, the following: terrestrial and satellite broadcasting; rebroadcasting of radio and television transmissions by cable or by Hertzian wave; recording of radio and television broadcasts; reprographic reproduction of printed material.

As regards the societies responsible for the collective administration of rights for the performance of dramatic and dramatico-musical works—which generally include other rights of communication to the public (broadcasting), production of audiovisual works and mechanical reproduction—they usually grant individualized authorizations, for each particular work and diffusion, after consultation of the owners (partial collective administration).[58]

8.1.3.2. Remuneration

The amount of the remuneration (scale of charges or minimum fees) is one of the main issues in negotiations between the collective administration organization and the bodies representing the users. Even where the society of authors has the prerogative to fix remuneration *per se*,[59] it is still preferable for this to be determined by agreement because of the obvious benefits which will

---

58. Mihály Ficsor, op. cit., Section 70, p. 24.
59. In Argentina, both SADAIC and ARGENTORES are legally empowered to determine fees (Decree No. 5146 of 1969, implementing Law 17.648, Article 3(b) and Decree No. 461 of 1973, implementing Law 20.115, Article 2(b) respectively).

In Venezuela the First Administrative Litigation Court (Corte Primera de lo Contercioso administrativo) has ruled that the fixing of charge scales by SACVEN in conformity with the law, constitutes an administrative act with all the characteristics of authority and obligatory force pertaining to such acts (cf. Ricardo Antequera Parilli, *La fijación de tarifas por las entidades autorales y el contencioso administrativo*, Barquisimeto, Instituto de Estudios Jurdicos del Estado Lara, Diario de Tribunales, 1986, which reproduces the pleas submitted during the proceedings and the ruling handed down).

accrue to all the interested parties if relations between the representative of the authors and the users are organized in a harmonious and concerted manner without recourse to the intervention of government agencies[60] or courts of law.

These agreements are generally reached only after long and complex discussions; in some countries they have to be approved by a State agency and/or published, or are subject to compliance with other requirements.

When the collective administration body and the professional chamber or association of the users are unable to reach agreement, in some countries an arbitration system is applied or alternatively a special mediation arrangement or similar procedure.

The schedules of charges are agreed (or fixed by the collective administration organization) on different bases,[61] depending on the category of use involved. They vary from one country to another—and also at different times within the same country—although some rules may be considered traditional (for they are respected internationally), e.g. in respect of the public performance of musical works, between 10 and 12 per cent for recitals and 6 and 12 per cent in general; between 10 and 15 per cent for the theatrical performance of dramatic, dramatico-musical and choreographic works; etc.

In general, the schedules of charges of societies of authors are broadly similar; it has been found that as these agencies consolidate their administration, they tend to abandon fixed rate remuneration and adopt instead proportional (or percentage) remuneration on the revenue obtained from use of the work. (A *mixed* system is frequently encountered: proportional, but subject to a

---

60. With the exception of those countries in which the fixing of charge scales is entrusted by law to an official authority.
61. In our study of the principles governing contracts in general, we referred to the different procedures for determining fees for the use of works: proportional to the revenue produced by the exploitation of the works, a flat-rate amount and mixed arrangements. The first system (a percentage) is in principle the most equitable because it is the only one which enables the author to enjoy a share in the economic success of his work (see above, Chapter 6, Section 6.1.1.G).

minimum which the user is required to pay when the application of the percentage would result in an amount below that minimum).

The fact that a performance is given without charge does not affect the right of the authors of the works used during it to receive remuneration, except in the specific cases where the law establishes limitations on the public performing rights which permit free use without charge[62] (just as, normally, the organizers cannot claim exemption from payment for the electricity consumed by them by invoking the absence of a profit-making purpose or the beneficial or cultural purpose of the event).

In the case of societies which administer *performing rights* for dramatic and dramatico-musical works (partial collective administration), the general royalties tend to be in the nature of *minimum* amounts (a notion which differs from that of the *minimum author's fee*).[63] The individual author may make the use of his work conditional on payment of a higher remuneration, but may not accept a lower figure. The 'minimum fees' are a safeguard (or 'floor', guaranteeing a minimum remuneration which cannot be reduced, by analogy with the provisions of labour law in respect of the wage rates fixed in collective employment agreements applicable to workers employed in a particular branch of activity). However, they are not 'ceilings' since the individual author—either in the advance negotiations which generally take place with the user or else when he is consulted by the society on the licence to use his work—may make that permission conditional on the payment of a remuneration exceeding the general fee; this often happens when the general fee is a flat-rate sum (but is exceptional

---

62. See above, Chapter 4, Section 4.3.1.
63. The *minimum author's fee* (for example, SADAIC Statutes, Article 3, VII) forms part of the *social and cultural* activities of societies of authors (see below, Section 8.1.4). It is paid in consideration of the person of the author and not of the actual use of the work, with a view to ensuring that the creator whose works were widely circulated in the past receives, on reaching a certain age, a monthly amount which in general is proportional to the payments received by him when he was fully active.

when the remuneration is paid as a percentage, especially if one of the traditional scales is used).[64]

A few examples of forms of remuneration agreed or fixed by societies of authors are given below.[65]

- Proportional remuneration, or percentage:
  - of revenue earned by the user from the sale of entrance tickets (for the performance of musical works in theatres and other public places; for the performance of dramatic, dramatico-musical and choreographic works; and for recitals);
  - of revenue earned by the user from the sale of advertising space (for the sound broadcasting of musical works);
  - by analogy, of the potential earnings which would have been obtained for the performance of musical and dramatic, dramatico-musical and choreographic works at *events to which no admission charge is made*;
  - of the earnings which could potentially be expected to accrue to the user from subsequent commercial use: from the potential monthly sale of advertising space on the television channel (in respect of the broadcasting of musical works); from the sale of copies to the dealer (sound recordings); and from the potential proceeds of the sale of cinema tickets (in respect of musical works included in films which are projected or shown);
  - of the price of sale or hire of copies (in respect of the musical works included in cinematographic works reproduced on video cassettes).
- Flat-rate remuneration:
  - for synchronization rights;
  - for the inclusion in films of original cinema scripts and adaptations;
  - for the broadcasting of radio and television scripts;

---

64. The scales of charges for the public performance of musical works—with or without lyrics—are also minimum amounts, but the collective administration organization does not consult the authors represented by it as is done for the communication of dramatic works to the public.
65. These examples mainly reflect the practice in Argentina.

- for the broadcasting of literary and dramatic works and adaptations thereof;
- for the television screening of cinematographic works, in respect of film scripts and adaptations for the cinema of literary and dramatic works included in films;
- for the projection or showing of films, in respect of the original film scripts and adaptations;
- for lectures;
- for the performance of musical works at social events (marriages, anniversary celebrations, birthdays, etc.), the amount being determined according to the size and/or the category of the premises;
- for the use of musical works by airlines;
- as a substitute for the percentage in some cases of recital and theatrical performance of dramatic, dramatico-musical and choreographic works to which admission is permitted *without payment.*

Flat-rate remuneration is also used when, as in the previous example, a percentage remuneration is the habitual practice but no basis is available for its calculation, for example in respect of the performance of musical works on *non-commercial* broadcasting stations.
- Mixed remuneration:
  - on a percentage basis, but subject to a fixed minimum (performance of musical works in premises with or without dancing, such as discothèques, cafés, restaurants, bars, fashion parades, etc.);
  - a fixed sum and a percentage of the producer's receipts or earnings including prizes and other rewards for production (inclusion in films of original film scripts and adaptations).

8.1.3.3. Collection

Every payment for the use of works must be accompanied by a detailed programme of the acts of communication which have taken place. The programme must indicate the place and date of performance, the titles of the works used, the names of their authors and all the other details required by the society of authors. When the remuneration is paid on a percentage or mixed basis, the distributor must also present a declaration of revenue (habitually referred to as a *bordereau* or schedule). This information is vital to enable the collective administration organization to verify the correctness of the payment and distribute the overall sums collected to the authors of the works which have effectively been used.[66]

Those persons wishing to make use of works assume certain basic obligations: they must obtain a licence from the right owners and comply with the conditions applicable to that authorization. Where a collective administration body is responsible for granting such licences, and does so in a global manner, authorization is conditional on users supplying detailed reports on the acts of communication made by them by submitting programmes of the works actually used. This is in general a contractual obligation, although some laws such as those of France (Article L. 132-21, previously Article 46) and Spain (Article 78(v)) expressly stipulate that the user is required to submit to the author or to his representatives a detailed programme of the acts of communication and, in cases where the remuneration is proportional, a declaration of revenue.

The principal difficulties which arise in connection with the collection of royalties originate, on the one hand, from the reluctance of some users to pay and, on the other, from the need to monitor use and check the veracity of the declarations made by the users in respect of the works used and the amounts stated in them.

The supervisory tasks performed by societies of authors are an essential part of collective administration and of their *raison d'être*. They are generally effected by inspectors although other methods are also used, such as 'cross-checking' information

---

66. The model contract of reciprocal representation between public performance rights societies referred to previously (document CISAC/40.700 of July 1974) stipulates (Article 7.1) that: 'Each society undertakes to do its utmost to obtain programmes of all public performances which take place in its territories and to use these programmes as the effective basis for the distribution of the total net royalties collected for these performances.'

against that held by a counterpart society in respect of a particular category of authors' rights or neighbouring rights or with certain official bodies and tax collection offices, etc.

The collective administration of authors' rights requires the activities of collection and monitoring to be supported by appropriate statutory and administrative provisions;[67] it implies that when disputes arise between societies of authors and users, the bodies responsible for settling them must pay adequate attention to the features of the legal basis for the use of works and the difficulties inherent in the administration of authors' rights.

8.1.3.4. Distribution or sharing

The distribution between the right owners of the royalties collected in respect of the public performance of each particular musical work is highly complex (it is often said that while collection is difficult, distribution is even more complex). The collective administration organization has to convert the total collected sum into individual payments.[68] For this purpose, it must know which works were effectively used, the names of the authors of the particular version used (when several such versions exist) and the owners of the rights—there may be between six and eight such right owners (the composer, the author of the lyric, the person responsible for the version, the arranger, the publisher and the sub-publisher). It must also determine the proportion of the royalty accruing to each of them and the names of the collective administration organizations which represent them before it can effect the necessary distribution.

---

67. For example, in Spain, Article 78(v), *in fine* stipulates that the assignee shall submit to the author or to his representatives the exact programme of communications to the public and ... a statement of proceeds; in Argentina, Decrees Nos. 5146 of 1969 and 461 of 1973 stipulate (Article 3(e)) that SADAIC and ARGENTORES, respectively, are authorized to verify the proceeds, tickets, takings, and other instruments and procedures necessary for the calculation of royalties.
68. Jean-Loup Tournier, *Collection and Distribution of Public Performance Fees for Musical Works*, Symposium on practical aspects of copyright, BIRPI, Geneva, 1968, p. 32.

As we have seen, declarations by the user are the main element enabling the society of authors to know the names of the works which were effectively performed; these declarations are essential to enable the society to verify the uses and effect distribution of the royalties. However, in order to perform its task, it must have, in addition to the programmes (or performance schedules), a substantial volume of technical documentation, an expression generally used in referring to all the data concerning authors, publishers and the works. These details are expressed in a schematic but nevertheless complete form and cover both the society's own repertoire and that which it administers by virtue of the representation contracts (generally reciprocal although they may also be unilateral) it concludes with its counterparts abroad; the declarations of the authors (and of the publishers or sub-publishers); an index of works (national and foreign) administered by the organization; the CAE (composer–author–publisher) list;[69] the World Works List (WWL);[70] the international index card;[71]

---

69. The CAE list contains the names of over 1,300,000 authors and 250,000 publishers worldwide, indicating if they are members of a society of authors or not (110 societies are included) and showing the territories covered if the mandate does not extend throughout the world. Each has a CAE list number; the list is published quarterly and is updated by SUISA, under the authority of CISAC and BIEM (over 100,000 modifications are made to the list each year).

70. The WWL is the list of non-dramatic musical works known internationally and in everyday use that the societies of authors have selected from their repertoires (the list contains the *active* world repertoire). It sets out the title and subtitle of each work, the names of the composers and publishers with their CAE list number and the proportion due to each in the sharing of royalties. The WWL contains over 1,300,000 works and is issued twice a year. It is updated by ASCAP, under the authority of CISAC and BIEM.

71. The international index cards represent the traditional means of exchanging documentation directly between societies. They consist of a standard form which each society completes in respect of the works of the right owners who are their members. The cards are sent to those societies with which they have concluded representation contracts. They contain details of a work or version of a work: title, subtitle, genre and instrumentation; length of performance; names of the rights owners, their title, CAE list number and society to which they belong; respective share of the right owners in the distribution of royalties for performing

the cue-sheet;[72] the inquiry lists or lists of unidentified works;[73] the GAF or General Agreement File;[74] and so on.

In the first phase of distribution, the organization assigns to each work that has been used its share of the total amount collected. Once that share has been established, it is distributed between the respective authors and the owners of the rights. In general, the total amount collected is not divided according to the number of works used, but on a pro rata basis, i.e. the length of each such work in relation to the total duration of the performance or communication (*pro rata temporis*). No allowance is made for factors of an aesthetic nature, commercial success or nationality of the work. The total duration is converted into a specific number of points (or shares) and the relevant points are then assigned to each work according to its own length.

In countries where the use of works in the public domain is permitted without charge and when they are used concurrently with works falling within the private domain, the overall fee paid

---

rights and mechanical reproduction; period of validity of the contract (in the case of publication and sub-publication); the society submitting the card and date of despatch.

72. The cue-sheet, also termed the 'music programme' or 'music declaration', is a document relating to an audio-visual work. It is a standard form for the direct exchange of information between societies which use it in distributing fees collected for musical works included in audio-visual works. It contains all the details concerning specially composed music contributions and pre-existing works synchronized with them; it therefore usually has much wider coverage than the international index card.

73. In proceeding with the distribution of royalties, the society lists unidentified works (also termed the inquiry list), those concerning which it has no documentation at the time the royalties are distributed and those to which the Warsaw ruling cannot be applied; i.e. when a work is identified only by the name of the composer who is a society member, the total amount of royalties due should be sent to that society. These lists are sent to all counterparts of the society so that they may identify the corresponding works.

74. GAF documentation consists of a compilation of all contracts concluded between music publishers covering complete publishing catalogues: GAF documentation is issued twice a year by SABAM, under the authority of CISAC and BIEM.

by the user diminishes in proportion to the time occupied by works in the first category. However, there are cases in which it is practically impossible for the collective administration organization to ascertain details of the works which have been performed. In that case, the only alternative open to the society of authors is to use additional methods of indirect distribution.

In the study already referred to[75] we pointed out, with Héctor Della Costa, that there were three basic systems for effecting distribution, as follows:
1. Complete information (direct distribution).
2. Selective or sample information.
3. Substitutive or presumed information.

A. THE SYSTEM OF COMPLETE INFORMATION (DIRECT DISTRIBUTION)

When this system is used, the items of information gathered to allocate the collected amounts enable each use of the work to be identified and the appropriate sum assigned directly to each author or right owner. This system is the only absolutely reliable and equitable arrangement and should be adopted whenever possible. It is feasible without difficulty in the area of the use of dramatic works, dramatico-musical and choreographic works and for some uses of non-dramatic musical works in concert performances, recitals, etc., for music performed 'live', broadcasting, and the showing or projection of films in cinemas. It should always be adopted when it is technically possible and economically viable, that is to say, for uses in respect of which reliable information is available and can be obtained without excessive cost.

However, although this system seems at first sight to be the only fair one, in many cases of the public performance of musical works it is not in fact altogether equitable, having regard to the fact that the necessary information is drawn from programmes

---

75. See Delia Lipszyc and Héctor Della Costa, op. cit., in note 2 above, pp. 137–8.

compiled by users and performers who, often through inattention, a lack of conscientiousness or, worse still, through malicious intent so as to favour themselves or third parties, do not note down the works which have been performed, but others. It necessitates *indirect distribution* based on sampling techniques (*muestreo* or *sondage*, *survey*, *amostragem*), constant verification of users by inspectors (often with the intervention of music experts), the making of recordings and the drafting of notarial acts to provide evidence.

In these cases and in others where it is practically impossible to obtain programmes or details of the works used (for example, musical performances by mechanical means, *juke boxes*, etc.), the *cost* factor is decisive and means that systems of selective information or sampling and of substitutive information or presumption have to be adopted.

B. THE SYSTEM OF SELECTIVE INFORMATION OR SAMPLING (INDIRECT DISTRIBUTION)

This system is based on the assumption that the information received for distribution purposes does not cover all the sums collected for the following reasons:
- lack of information on some proven uses;
- the information received is not reliable;
- processing of the information is uneconomical, because the sums calculated from the programmes or planning schedules bear no relation to the cost of the resulting settlement procedure, so much so that a significant proportion of the collected sum would have to be withheld from the authors to cover administrative costs.

This system is used when the total sum collected is distributed in accordance with the accepted partial information, e.g. when the settlement of the amount collected from *all* dance halls is made on the basis of the data obtained for *some* such halls.

The samples must be taken in such a way as to reflect the *true* situation (this depends on the extent to which the quantitative data obtained by the sample correspond to the information which would have been obtained if precise and complete individual listing of the works used were possible); they must also be *representative* of all the authors whose works have been used and *economical* in terms of the cost–benefit ratio.[76]

---

76. Máximo Perroti, an Argentine publisher of musical works and a leading expert in the procedures used by public performing rights societies considers that 'in order to avoid the disadvantages of uneconomical listings and their unjustified cancellation, it would be appropriate to adopt the modern system of statistical, zonal, stratified sampling which cuts costs, does not misrepresent performances and prevents fraud in a high percentage of cases' and 'is used at present by some societies of authors, prominent among them BMI and ASCAP'.

Perroti goes on to point out that 'our proposal for a mixed system of statistical, zonal, stratified sampling may be summarized as follows: in those countries where the performer and user are required by law to fill out their respective performance schedules, the submission of those schedules must be compulsory in every case with provision for regular, secret and unannounced inspections to check their veracity [...] At the next stage—when the schedules are received by the society—they will be the subject of a zonal and stratified classification, i.e. by zone, type of repertoire performed (dance, song, incidental music, etc.) and the level of the royalties collected. From each of the zones into which the country is divided, each type of repertoire performed and each level of collection, schedules will be extracted by statistical methods for further processing; these will constitute the sample as such. We are using the word "statistical" here to indicate the fact that this selection must involve no direct intervention by an agent or official of the society, but is to be effected by means of random sampling or programming in order to provide the necessary guarantees of objectivity and honesty since all the collected royalties will be settled on the basis of the statistically selected schedules and by random choice within each group' (*Creación y Derechos*, Mexico, Ed. Consejo Panamericano de la CISAC, 1978, pp. 111, 114, 115–16). In Annex 42 A (pp. 312–54) Perroti reproduces the ASCAP sampling system in which the sample is defined as 'a miniature of a larger whole (like the scale model of a locomotive). From this miniature (sample), quantitative data in respect of the whole (or *universe*) can be derived, when a complete survey (total census) would be excessively expensive or inaccurate. The touchstone by which a well-planned sample can be judged, is its greater accuracy in relation to its cost. The maximum return on the money spent by the members is the yardstick by which the ASCAP sampling plan is measured' (p. 324). Three features of the ASCAP sample are highlighted, i.e. the fact that it is a *random, stratified* and *asymmetrical* sample. 'Why random? So as to make sure that the sample resembles as closely as possible the universe which it represents, the sample must be random.' [...] 'Why stratified? The data extracted from the sample are used to obtain quantified results. But quantifications involve a margin of error. One way of increasing the accuracy of a sample is to stratify it, i.e. group together the users, the performances or the media and then to take samples from each one of

C. THE SYSTEM OF SUBSTITUTIVE INFORMATION OR PRESUMPTIONS (INDIRECT DISTRIBUTION)

This system is used for the same reasons as the that described previously. It consists in the concentration of data processing on a certain type of information which is sufficiently complete, reliable and verifiable and, in ideal statistical terms, can provide an adequate approximation to the reality of the repertoire utilized by the users—for example, settlement in respect of all types of public performance on the same basis as public performance by broadcasting.

These two latter systems are used in the area of the public performance of musical works by adopting procedures specific to the uses that may be made of these works, despite the fact that they often do not enjoy the favour of authors who distrust them because of the latitude which remains for arbitrary decisions.

D. THE RATING FACTORS SYSTEM

In addition to the three basic systems described above, a fourth, complementary system also exists: that of *rating factors*. It consists in enhancing the value, within the distribution process, of certain works whose length is significantly greater than the general, average length.

This system is habitually employed in the case of symphonic and chamber music, to allow for the relative importance of the

---

those strata.' [...] 'Why asymmetrical? The depth of the sample may be symmetrical or asymmetrical. If the ASCAP sample were symmetrical, each radio station would have to be sampled for an equal number of hours. The same number of samples would be taken for a broadcasting station which pays $1,000 as from a station which pays $30,000. It is far more meaningful to ascertain the performances by the station which pays $30,000 than those of the station which pays only $1,000. In consequence, a symmetrical sample would not provide the best justification for the distribution of royalty income in a cost-effective manner. This is one of the reasons for choosing an asymmetrical sample. As a general rule, the greater the importance of the user in terms of the fees paid by him to ASCAP, the larger will be the size of the sample of performances given by that user' (pp. 229–30).

different works concerned and in relation to popular works. In these cases, different values are assigned to the different types of musical works for the purpose of determining the apportionment of royalties, for example *one performance point* for tangos, sambas, cuecas, waltzes, foxtrots, twists, paso dobles, chacareras, etc.; *two performance points* for preludes, nocturnes, rhapsodies, serenades, minuets, suites, pot-pourris of more than 100 bars, etc.; *four performance points* for sonatas, overtures, trios, quartets, quintets, sextets, etc. and *eight performance points* for symphonies, masses, oratorios, major choral works, etc.

This points system is also applied when works of varying importance are used within a single public performance or broadcast.

E. THE MIXED COEFFICIENT SYSTEM

A *mixed system* may also be used in which simultaneous allowance is made for the *points* assigned to the work and its relative *length*.

The diversity of the distribution systems is due to the fact that in the complex area of musical performance two factors must be respected, although they are to some extent contradictory: *equity* and *economy*. However, equity does not consist solely in giving everyone his due (*cuique suum*) in the light of the information provided by the user (programmes or performance schedules); these items of information must also be a faithful reflection of reality so that they are *reliable*. 'Economy', as we concluded with Della Costa in the study that we have been following, 'demands, in turn, that the information gathered must be limited so as to reduce operating costs and the cost of internal and external control'.

Computer systems have become an invaluable aid for the tasks of collective administration and especially of distribution; they enable the information provided on the settlement statements forwarded to authors and owners of rights to be more complete and precise than in the past. However, the operations necessary for the distribution of the royalties in respect of public performance still take between three and six months.

As to the *rules for distribution* between the authors and their assignees, each collective administration society establishes rules which approximate most closely to the usage and habits in its respective country, while complying with the decisions adopted by the Confederal Assemblies of CISAC.

In the case of *published musical works* one of the most widely accepted criteria for distribution allocates one-third to the composers, one-third to the authors of the lyrics and one-third to the publisher. When musical arrangers or adapters of the text are involved, they receive 25 per cent of the share of the composer or of the author of the words or libretto, respectively (3/12 composers, 3/12 authors, 1/12 musical arranger, 1/12 adapter of the text and 4/12 publisher).

However, the publisher's share of the royalties collected on public performance and by way of phonomechanical rights, varies from one country to another: for example, in Argentina it is 25 per cent in the case of non-recorded works and 33.33 per cent when a recording is made; in Brazil it amounts to 25 per cent in both cases; in France it is 33.33 per cent for public performance and 50 per cent for phonomechanical rights; in Switzerland 35 per cent for public performance and 50 per cent for phonomechanical rights. At all events the publisher's individual share or the total share, *regardless of the number of publishers or sub-publishers of a work*, may in no case exceed one-half (50 per cent) of the total royalty collected for the work.[77]

In the case of unpublished works, the distribution is effected between the composers and authors of the lyrics in equal shares, regardless of the number of composers and authors involved.

Within CISAC, the societies of authors have codified the distribution procedures.

---

77. See Article 7(II)(d) of the Model Contract of Reciprocal Representation between Public Performance Rights Societies (document CISAC/40.700, July 1974) which followed a decision taken by the Federal Assembly in Knokke Le Zoute (1958): 'Distribution—Works by non-members—Maximum publisher's share. The publisher's share in the distribution of a work outside the repertoire controlled by the distributing society may not exceed 50 per cent of all the royalties accruing to the work' (*Décisions, délibérations et vœux adoptés par les Congrès*—1952–1962—CISAC, Vol. II, p. 307, No. 616).

The collective administration organization retains a percentage of the collected royalties to cover its own administrative costs. Acceptable percentages are held to be up to 30 per cent in the case of the administration of public performance and broadcasting rights, and up to 20 per cent in the case of mechanical reproduction and performance rights.

8.1.4. Social welfare activities

Authors who are in gainful employment, that is to say who pursue their creative activities within the framework of an employment contract (when the conditions for the existence of such a contract are met) enjoy the benefits of social protection by virtue of labour legislation and social security regulations applicable to employed persons in general, or to those who pursue their activities in a specific sector (journalism, cinematography, commerce, teaching, etc.).

On the other hand independent authors—who produce their works spontaneously or on a commission basis—are generally placed in a situation in which they are denied social protection. Domestic legislation rarely lays down provisions to make good that omission.[78]

---

78. In France, Law 75-1348 of 31 December 1975 which entered into force on 1 January 1977, laid down an original social security system for the authors of literary, dramatic, musical and artistic works which—as Annie Allain points out—reflects the notion of the unity of the literary and artistic profession in regard to social security in the case of the risks of illness, maternity, disability and death, family allowances and old-age pensions. Allain points out that this law associates two principles previously considered to be irreconcilable: the beneficiaries are assimilated with the scheme applicable to persons in gainful employment in industry and commerce without encroaching upon the independent nature of the creative activity. Its effect is to bring together the heterogeneous social security schemes in force hitherto within a single self-financing system, social protection now being extended to 'creators'.

At present in France, responsibility for the management of the social security regime established by the above-mentioned law of 1975 is vested in two associations which are under the administrative and financial control of the State on the terms set out in Decree 77-1195 of 25 October 1977 (Article 14). In two decisions by the Minister of Culture and the Minister of Social Security respon-

It is exceptional for copyright laws to embody measures to assist self-employed creators. That is, however, the case in Spain where the intellectual property law stipulates that:
- the remuneration received by authors for the exploitation of their works is regarded as *salary* for the purposes of both the order of priority for attachment and deductions or unattachable amounts (Article 53(2));
- the remuneration of authors shall be treated on the same footing as that earned by way of salary or other pay in bankruptcy proceedings brought by the licensees, subject to a limit of two annuities (Article 54);
- any benefits granted to authors and to their successors-in-title shall be unrenounceable (Article 55);
- the producers of public entertainments shall be considered *depositaries* of the remuneration payable to the authors for the communication of their works where that remuneration consists of a proportionate share in the proceeds. They shall make the said remuneration available to the authors or to their

---

sibility has been given to the *Maison des Artistes* to administer the social security regime for the authors of graphic and plastic works and to the *Association pour la Gestion de la Sécurité Sociale des Auteurs* (*AGESSA*) to administer the regime for the authors of literary, dramatic, musical, choreographic, cinematographic and audiovisual works in general, together with photographic works. Membership is subject to certain formal and substantive conditions (the beneficiaries must be domiciled in France, must 'habitually' exercise the activity of author and receive a 'sufficient income' from that activity; if the income is considered 'insufficient' the status of author may nevertheless be recognized by a professional commission). Any person who receives remuneration in the form of authors, royalties or similar fees makes a contribution to the unified system calculated on the basis of his declared income; users of works do likewise (in the absence of a declaration presented in the manner and within the time-limits stipulated in the Decree of 1977, the assessment is made automatically). The scheme institutes the rule of deduction of social security contributions by the employer or user, the State and public bodies. The independent author is treated as a person in gainful employment in respect of certain benefits only (Annie Allain, 'Droit social', in *Propriété littéraire et artistique* by Robert Plaisant, Paris, Delmas, 1985, pp. 211–36).

representatives every week (Article 79);[79] by virtue of this definition, a producer who withholds the sums accruing to the author renders himself liable for punishment under criminal law (as a *defaulting depositary*).

This latter provision also covers the sums accruing in respect of communication to the public by broadcasting (Article 84(1)), and of simple authorizations of communication to the public (Article 85).

The lack of social protection for independent authors is made good to a substantial degree by the bodies responsible for collective administration whose function is not confined to the administration of authors' rights as such. They provide extensive mutual services which are reflected in programmes for the social protection of their members. These activities are financed by a part of the sums accruing to the authors from the royalties collected in respect of the communication of their works to the public.

These schemes generally include the granting of ordinary and extraordinary pensions to authors: pensions for certain heirs of the author; assistance in the event of illness, maternity and circumstances of particular hardship; contracting of medical assistance services for members and their close family members; grants for funerals; collective insurance, etc.

8.1.5. Cultural activities

The societies of authors pursue cultural activities intended to advance the technical and aesthetic aptitudes of their members and to improve the quality of their production by organizing courses of musical, dramatico-musical, dramatic or literary training; to stimulate creative activity; to safeguard the cultural heritage ad-

---

79. Antonio Delgado Porras points out that a precedent for this provision is to be found in Article 96 of the Regulation of 3 September 1880 adopted for the purpose of implementation of the later Law of 1879 (*Panorámica de la protección civil y penal en materia de propiedad intelectual*, p. 77). It should be stated in this connection that although the latter was the source of many copyright laws in the Latin American countries, the regulation in question was unfortunately not also taken over.

ministered by them through the compilation and publication of works and the promotion and circulation of these works; to defend the national intellectual and artistic tradition; to advance the cause of copyright legislation and jurisprudence and to ensure its dissemination and defence at both national and international level; to establish or acquire libraries specializing in the artistic sector to which the works administered by them belong, record libraries, collections of musical and dramatic works, etc., catalogues of musical repertoires, treatises and publications concerning authors and other related creations, etc. (see, for example, Statutes of SADAIC, Article II, sections V, VI and IX).

The statutes of these societies may also embody limitations on activities for the promotion and circulation of works so as to prevent the organization from acquiring the character of a producer or investing its funds in the support or financing of activities for the distribution of the works of its members or from granting subsidies or loans to them (for example, Statutes of ARGENTORES, Article 2, *in fine*).

The twofold aim is to avoid arbitrary use of the society's assets for the benefit of individual members—generally its directors—and to ensure that the organization does not become a competitor with the users.

Societies of authors also withhold a percentage for the purpose of social protection and cultural activities. The Model Contract of Reciprocal Representation between Public Performance Rights Societies (document CISAC/40.700, July 1974), permits the allocation for this purpose of up to 10 per cent of the net proceeds—after deduction of operating costs—of collective administration.[80]

The bulk of the sums earmarked for social and cultural purposes are used to provide social protection.

---

80. Article 8(II) of that Model Contract reads as follows: 'When it does not make any supplementary collection for the purpose of supporting its members' pensions, benevolent or provident funds, or for the encouragement of the national arts, or in favour of any funds serving similar purposes, each of the societies shall be entitled to deduct from the sums collected by it on behalf of the co-contracting society 10 per cent at the maximum which shall be allocated to the said purposes.'

8.1.6. CISAC

The complexity arising from the transfrontier use of a vast quantity of works, the intangible nature of those assets and the multiplicity of relations necessary in this regard, all create the need for *uniform criteria for the collective administration of copyright.* That uniformity could not have been achieved without an organization such as the International Confederation of Societies of Authors and Composers (CISAC), which co-ordinates the enormous efforts necessary to integrate the national bodies into a wide-ranging international system of reciprocal representation and to unify the principles and methods of collective administration, without interfering in the internal organization of each society.

Founded in 1926–27 in Paris where it has its registered office, CISAC is a non-governmental, non-profit-making international organization which brings together bodies responsible for the administration of authors' rights.

The First International Congress of Societies of Authors and Composers was held on 13 June 1926 and was attended by representatives of 18 such societies from an identical number of countries; only five or six were major societies and only two or three were functioning perfectly.[81] In 1990, CISAC's membership consisted of 144 societies drawn from 72 countries, representing over 1 million authors of works of various kinds. It is in effect a world organization of authors and pursues its activities with no party-political or religious affiliations whatsoever (Statutes, Article 4, *in fine*).

Concerning CISAC's organization and functioning, see below, Chapter 9, Section 9.1.1.1.

8.2. Other societies responsible for the collection of royalties

Following the explosive growth of *reprographic reproduction techniques* (facsimile reproduction by photocopying or a similar technique) involving printed works and the *home reproduction* of sound recordings and audiovisual works, the scale reached by the

---

81. See Léon Malaplate, op. cit., p. 25.

phenomenon of private copying meant that the enormous prejudice caused by these activities—considered in their entirety—to authors, publishers, performing artists and producers became only too obvious. It was no longer possible to maintain, as had been the case in the past, that these activities were not prejudicial to their interests. Ways and means of remedying the situation were therefore sought. A ban on the use of the new technologies was bound to fail; that was particularly apparent in regard to the home taping of recordings of protected works because of the impossibility of verifying the activities of individuals in their own homes. A decision was therefore taken in favour of equitable remuneration.[82] However, if each beneficiary were to be authorized to make individual claims for payment against reproducers *the system would be totally unviable.*

Legislation which stipulates payment of remuneration for private or home copying therefore provides that recovery of the sums due *may only be effected through collective administrative bodies*. Likewise, in the countries where a fee is levied on reprographic reproduction, the collection and distribution of that income is also effected through organizations of this kind.

These bodies may be:
- an organization specifically created for this purpose; or
- the same organizations as are already responsible for collective administration; or
- a collecting agency of which the latter organizations form part.

8.2.1. Collective administration of royalties for reprographic reproduction[83]

A. GERMANY

The law on copyright and neighbouring rights of 9 September 1965 was the first to regulate the right of reproduction and the

---

82. See above, Chapter 4, Sections 4.3.1.A and 4.3.2.A.
83. Sources: Document UNESCO/WIPO/CGE/PW/3-I: *Memorandum on questions concerning the protection of copyright in respect of the printed word*; *Libro blanco sobre reprografía ilegal*, Federación de Gremios de Editores de España, 1986; M. Ficsor: IFRRO, 1994, op. cit., paragraphs 97–142, pp. 29–41; *Statistics and Information*, IFRRO, *EC Group of RROs*, March 1991.

limitations thereon in detail. As document UNESCO/WIPO/CGE/PW/3-I (para. 97) points out, although its provisions make no express mention of reprographic reproduction, they are designed to deal with this aspect. The antecedent for this statutory provision is a ruling on photocopying handed down by the Federal Court of Justice in 1955, in a case concerning the reproduction by an industrial company of articles published in scientific reviews for the use of its specialists. The Court held that this activity served the purposes of the company and was therefore not an instance of freely authorized private use, but an infringement of the author's exclusive right of reproduction.

This ruling led to the conclusion of a contract between the Federation of German Industry (BDI) and the Association of German Booksellers on the photocopying of periodical publications for internal use in companies which undertook to pay a remuneration in the case of journals published less than three years before the date on which the photocopy was made.

The 1965 law permitted the reproduction of one single copy of a work for personal use, although without any requirement to pay a fee. It also authorized the making or the causing to be made of a single copy of a work for personal scientific use, for its inclusion in internal archives and for other internal uses, and of brief extracts of printed works or individual articles published in newspapers or periodicals, including works which are out of print, when the owner of the right of use cannot be traced. If the owner of the right of use can be traced and the edition of the work has been out of print for more than three years, his consent to such reproduction may only be withheld for weighty reasons. If the reproduction is made for commercial purposes by the person authorized to reproduce the work, that person must pay equitable remuneration to the author (Article 54).

The law of 19 July 1985 amending and supplementing author's right and neighbouring rights established new regulations for private copying which introduced extremely important changes in the existing system:
- they permitted the making or the causing to be made of reproductions of small parts of published works or of individual contributions published in newspapers or periodicals for per-

sonal use or for teaching purposes in non-commercial establishments, in a quantity necessary for one school class or for the examinations held in schools, universities and non-commercial institutions of education (Art. 53, paras. 1–3);
- reprographic reproduction without the author's permission was strictly prohibited in three cases (Art. 53, para. 4): the scores of musical works, the complete text of a book or periodical and computer programs;
- it was established that authors had the right to receive equitable remuneration in all instances in which it was possible to effect reproduction by photocopying or any other similar process without the author's consent (Art. 54, para. 1). Account was taken of the fact that since 1965 technical progress had permitted the growth of private reproduction to such an extent that it was now causing unjustified prejudice to the legitimate interests of authors (Berne Convention, Paris, 1971, Article 9.2) and that this prejudice should be mitigated by equitable remuneration in respect of such use;
- however, the law made a distinction between reproduction effected in the homes of users themselves and that effected elsewhere; as document UNESCO/WIPO/CGE/PW/3-I (para. 103) points out, the law has taken account of the fact that, for the time being, photocopiers are less commonly encountered in private homes than in libraries, education establishments and other places where a great many protected works are available for photocopying. In such places the author is entitled to receive remuneration on the part of the operator of the equipment (Art. 54, para. 2).

In regard to the amount of remuneration, a mixed system was established:
- *a fee on the machines themselves to be paid by the manufacturer or importer*; the statutory amount of this remuneration ranging from 75 DM to 600 DM depending on the capacity of the machine. The fee is payable on every machine, regardless of whether it is intended for use in the private home of the user or elsewhere; it constitutes a single, flat-rate payment proportional to the volume of texts protected by copyright which are habitually photocopied by a machine of the type concerned; and

- *a fee to be paid by the operator* which is added to the fee payable on the machine itself. Per copied page in A4 format, the operating fee is 0.05 DM for school textbooks and 0.02 in other cases.

Recovery of the fee levied on the machines themselves presents no difficulties. The fee on use outside the private context (in schools, universities, public libraries, photocopying centres etc.) is determined by sampling; the percentage of photocopies of protected works is determined in relation to the total number of photocopies made in certain representative establishments of the sector and the fee payable by all similar establishments is calculated on this basis.

The law stipulates that the right to collect a fee in respect of reprographic reproduction *may only be exercised through the intermediary of a collective administration society* (Art. 54, para. 6). The society for the collective administration of literary rights, VG WORT, established in 1958, represents authors and publishers. It has concluded agreements with various organizations of photocopier users (industry, public administration, schools, public libraries, etc.) by virtue of which the payment of flat-rate sums has been decided, for although the method of sampling appears straightforward at first sight, in reality it is difficult to calculate the number of photocopies in respect of which the fee is payable. The flat-rate amounts agreed by VG WORT are based on statistical studies of the volume and structure of photocopying of works protected by copyright.

VG WORT collects fees in respect of the reprographic reproduction of all types of works, to the extent that photocopying is authorized by law. After deducting its operating costs, and even in cases where the parties have stipulated different percentages, VG WORT distributes the revenue in a proportion of half each to the authors and publishers in the case of scientific works and 70 per cent to the author/30 per cent to the publisher in the case of works of fiction.

B. THE NETHERLANDS

The first statutory provisions on reprography were adopted in 1972–74, but they did not alter the traditional criterion of permitting free reproduction without charge of a work in a few copies for private use; furthermore, the public authorities, libraries, education establishments and other institutions in the public service sector are authorized to make larger numbers of copies for their own internal use. Commercial organizations and establishments may also make a certain number of photocopies when a 'reasonable need' exists, but if they make a large number of photocopies, bodies in this and all other categories are required to pay equitable remuneration.

The remuneration due by the public authorities, libraries, education establishments and other institutions in the public service sector has been set at 0.025 florin per photocopied page of a scientific publication, and 0.10 florin per photocopied page of a non-scientific publication. In all cases, libraries are permitted to reproduce articles in a single copy for their users and for inter-library loans without being required to pay this fee.

Administration of this scheme rests with the REPRORECHT Foundation which serves both authors and publishers. It was founded in 1974 to collect photocopying remuneration and was authorized to operate in 1977. However, for nearly ten years, it faced many difficulties in the performance of its task since the users, except for the State itself, refused to deal with it. The law granted it no special facilities and it had few members until, on 23 August 1985, a Royal Decree was promulgated stipulating that reprography remuneration must be paid *solely* to the collecting society appointed by the Ministry of Justice which, on 19 February 1986, designated REPRORECHT for this purpose.

C. The Nordic countries

The copyright laws in Denmark, Finland, Norway and Sweden date from 1960–61 and their structure and provisions are almost identical. Matters relating to photocopying were dealt with in the 1970s and the bodies responsible for the collective administration of reprographic rights enjoy strong legislative backing.

The copyright laws in these countries recognize the exclusive rights of authors in regard to the photocopying of their works. They all contain the habitual limitation which authorizes reproduction for private use—provided that there is no profit-making purpose—of single copies of a work which has already been published, but these copies may not be used for any other purposes. The term 'private use' is interpreted, however, in its narrow sense and means personal, individual use; therefore, organizations and legal persons are not allowed to reproduce a work for their own account for 'private use' since in that case the term would mean 'internal use'. They may on the other hand entrust a third party, for example a library, with the task of making reproductions for private use by virtue of the authorization which the law grants to the latter. In these four countries, special provisions have been adopted in favour of public libraries and archives which authorize them to make reproductions for their own needs (conservation of their collections, reproduction for lending purposes of works or documents which are fragile or rare, etc.), and also to reproduce a single copy of an article or fragment of a published work for persons requesting loans for the purpose of scientific research, instead of lending them the original works.

As we have already seen (Section 8.1.3.1), the copyright laws of the Nordic countries establish a system of 'extended collective administration licences' whereby, in the area of photocopying, teaching staff of schools and universities which have received authorization from an association representing a large number of national authors in a particular sector (by virtue of the agreements concluded between societies for the collection of reprographic rights and State agencies and local authorities) are also entitled to reproduce works published in the same sector by authors who are not represented by the association concerned (in particular, foreign authors).

Under this system, authors who are not affiliated to the association receive the same treatment as members of the contracting organization in regard, for example, to remuneration and retain the right to claim individual remuneration for the reproduction of their works, even if the contracting organization decides to use its revenue for collective purposes. Document UNESCO/WIPO/CGE/PW/3-I (para. 113) points out, however, that certain guarantees exist for authors who are not affiliated to the organization; for example, a work may not be reproduced if the author has given written notice to any of the parties concerned that reproduction is prohibited.

Agreements between the users and the collecting organization impose many limitations on photocopying, beginning with the stipulation of a maximum number of copies which may be made and the length of the excerpts of different types of works which may be copied. The reproduction of certain publications is prohibited: music scores, manuals of school exercises which contain the solutions to these exercises and other similar publications for use on a single occasion.

In general, sampling methods are used in Finland, Iceland, Norway and Sweden for the purpose of calculating and collecting remuneration. The remuneration is remitted to the associations representing the authors and publishers, more or less on a pro rata basis to the effective number of copies made of the different categories of works. The sums collected are used for collective purposes (donations, subventions, etc.). The societies involved are KOPIOSTO R.Y. in Finland, founded in 1978; FJÖLIS in Iceland, founded in 1985; KOPINOR in Norway, founded in 1980, and BONUS in Sweden, founded in 1973.

In Denmark, on the other hand, a completely different system has been established: in all cases the users are required to make an additional photocopy indicating, on its first page, the total number of copies produced; this photocopy is then forwarded to COPY-DAN, the collecting organization, which commenced its activities in 1980, accompanied by a statement listing the title of the work, the name of the author and publisher and the year of publication. On the basis of that information, COPY-DAN distributes the collected sums between the authors and publishers.

D. UNITED STATES

The 1976 Federal Copyright Act laid down—by virtue of the concept of *fair use* limitation—various provisions relating to reprography which authorize free photocopying for teaching purposes (including multiple copies intended for classroom use), scholarship or research (Section 107), and for libraries and archives (Section 108) in respect of most protected works, either for their own use or for their users in the (extensive) cases stipulated. This authorization is subject to the provisos that the reproduction or distribution are not designed to secure a direct or indirect commercial advantage; that the library or archive collections are accessible to the public or placed at the disposal of specialized researchers; that the reproduction or distribution of the works includes an indication of the name of the author; and that the library or archives undertake not to effect concerted or systematic reproduction or distribution of multiple copies or of sound recordings of the same material, and further undertake not to engage in the systematic reproduction or distribution of single or multiple copies or sound recordings (Section 108(g), (1) and (2)).

Despite the considerable limitations on the author's right of reproduction embodied in the 1976 Act, that right prevails as a general rule and holds good in a number of important sectors (photocopies made by colleges and private universities, by corporations, etc.).

In these areas, the collective administration of the right of reprographic reproduction is vested, although not exclusively, in the Copyright Clearance Centre (CCC) which was set up in 1978, following a recommendation by Congress for the establishment of a mechanism for supervision and the granting of licences, to enable the publishers of scientific, technical and medical journals (STM publishers) to receive remuneration in respect of copies made by colleges, universities, libraries, documentation centres, corporations, etc. The CCC mainly serves the right holders of the publications indicated above and those of magazines, newsletters, books and newspapers.

Each publisher fixes his own conditions for the granting of licences to photocopy his publications. This is a system of collectively administered individual licences and not of general licences with a unified scale of charges. After deducting its own operating costs, the CCC distributes the sums collected to the publishers who share them with the authors in conformity with the contractual agreements reached between them (see Ficsor, para. 133).

E. UNITED KINGDOM

The 1988 Act contains a detailed list of cases in which the free use of protected works is permitted by libraries and archives (Sections 38–43) and by educational establishments in respect of passages from published works (Section 32). In regard to educational establishments, Section 36 lays down that (1) reprographic copies of passages from published literary, dramatic or musical works may, to the extent permitted by this section, be made by or on behalf of educational establishments for the purposes of instruction without infringing any copyright in the work, or in the typographical arrangement; (2) not more than 1 per cent of any work may be copied by, or on behalf of, an establishment in any quarter of a year; (3) copying is not authorized by this section if licences (in effect, a collective administration scheme for reprographic reproduction rights) are available authorizing the copying in question and the person making the copies knew or ought to have been aware of that fact.

The collective administration of reprographic reproduction rights is vested in the Copyright Licensing Agency Ltd (CLA), founded in 1982, which represents both authors and publishers.

In addition to the bodies already mentioned, organizations for the collective administration of reprographic rights were in existence in fifteen other countries at the beginning of 1995: Australia (Copyright Agency Limited—CAL); Austria (Literar-Mechana and Musikedition); Belgium (Reprobel); Brazil (Associação Brasileira de Direitos Reprográficos—ABDR); Canada (CanCopy and Union des écrivains québécois—UNEQ); France (Centre Français d'exploitation du droit de copie—CFC); Ireland (Irish Copyright Agency Ltd—ICLA); Italy (AIDROS); Japan (Japan Reprographic Rights Organization—JRRC); Kenya (KOPIKER); Malta (KOPJAMALT); New Zealand (Copyright Licensing Ltd—CLL); Republic of South Africa (Dramatic, Artistic and Literary Rights Organization—DALRO); Spain (CEDRO); and Switzerland (Pro Litteris).

However, the exercise of the right of reprographic reproduction is still in its infancy and the number of countries with collective administration bodies is relatively small. Some (for example Portugal) have legal provisions governing this right, but they have still not managed to develop means of recovering compensatory remuneration satisfactorily.

These bodies are grouped together within the International Federation of Reproduction Rights Organizations—IFRRO—created in 1980 as a working group of the Copyright Committee of the International Publishers Association (IPA) and of the International Group of Scientific, Technical and Medical Publishers (STM). In 1984 this working group became an informal consortium, the International Forum of organizations in defence of reproduction rights; in 1988, IFRRO became an official federation which in 1992 adopted new statutes.

8.2.2. Collective administration of rights in respect of private reproduction—home taping of sound recordings and audiovisual works for personal use[84]

A. GERMANY

The country which pioneered recognition of the right to remuneration in respect of the private copying of sound recordings, the Federal Court of Justice handed down a ruling on 29 May 1954 accepting the validity of claims for the payment of remuneration in respect of private recordings of protected works. This case lay at the origin of paragraph 5 of Article 53 of the 1965 law ('Where the nature of the work is such that it may be expected to be reproduced for personal use by the recording of broadcasts on video or audio recording media or by the transfer from one video or audio recording medium to another, the author of the work shall be entitled to demand from the manufacturers of the appliances intended for the making of such reproductions a remuneration in respect of the possibility provided by such appliances of making such reproductions ...').

By virtue of that provision a royalty was first imposed on *recording equipment* and later extended by the law of 1985 to the *recording media* (Art. 54, para. 1) so that a *mixed system* is in force today.

The remuneration in respect of *sound recordings* is distributed as follows:

---

84. *Sources*: IFPI, *Report by the Secretariat on Private Copying*, 1986 (document) and Mihály Ficsor, op. cit., Sections 175–95, pp. 49–53.

- authors 58%: GEMA 42%, VG WORT 16%;
- performers: GVL 27%;
- phonogram producers: GVL 15%.

Several other countries introduced remuneration for private copying did so after Germany, from 1980 onwards. They are: Austria, Congo, Denmark, Finland, France, Hungary, Iceland, Norway, Portugal, Spain and Sweden. We shall refer to some of these countries further below.

B. AUSTRIA

The royalty is applied to 'recording tapes or other media suitable for making copies and designed for that purpose' (Article 5 of the Copyright Amendment Law of 2 July 1980). A legal requirement has been imposed on the collective administration bodies to use over 50 per cent of the remuneration for social and cultural purposes.

In the case of *sound recordings*, the distribution is effected as follows:
- authors 56%: AUSTRO-MECHANA 49%, LITERAR-MECHANA 7%;
- performers 20%: LSG (recorded performance) 17%, OSTIG (live performance) 3%;
- phonogram producers: LSG 17%;
- radio broadcasters (only in their capacity as producers and not for broadcasting as such): 7%.

In the case of video fixations, distribution is effected by the same organizations as in the case of *authors and performing artists* and to:
- cinematographic producers: VAM 22.8%;
- broadcasting organizations: VG RUNDFUNK 25.8%.

C. FRANCE

The law of 3 July 1985 established remuneration in respect of private copying of phonograms and videograms in its Articles 31-37 (now Articles L. 311-1 and L. 311-3 to 311-8). The persons required to pay are the manufacturers or importers of recording media which are capable of being utilized for the reproduction, for private use, of works fixed on phonograms or videograms, at the time when these media enter into circulation. The remuneration is paid to the collective administration societies representing the right owners (Article L.311-6, previously Article 35), but these societies are required to allocate 25 per cent of their revenue for social and cultural purposes (Article L. 321-9, previously Article 38, fifth paragraph).

In the case of *sound recordings*, the distribution is made as follows:
- authors and music publishers: 50%;
- performers: 25%;
- phonogram producers: 25%.

As regards *video fixations*, the remuneration is shared equally between the authors, performing artists and producers of audio-visual works.

D. HUNGARY

The remuneration collected from the sale of *audiotapes* is distributed as follows:
- authors: ARTISJUS 50%;
- performers: 30%;
- phonogram producers: 20%.

In the case of *audiotapes*, distribution is as follows:
- authors and producers of audiovisual works: 70%;
- performers: 30%.

E. NORDIC COUNTRIES

In Finland, Sweden and Iceland, the government exercises close supervision over the fund into which the share of the collected remuneration reserved for social and cultural purposes must be paid.

In Finland, this share comprises two-thirds of the royalty on the sale of new, blank audio-tapes (investment in Finnish phonogram production and financial support for anti-piracy activities). The remaining one-third is distributed between:

- authors: 49%;
- performers: 25.5%;
- phonogram producers: 25.5%.

In Sweden (and similarly in Norway), the private copying levy charged on the sale of audiotapes and videotapes is regarded as a *tax*. The State uses two-thirds of the proceeds for unspecified purposes (as in the case of any other tax); 80 per cent of the remaining third is allocated to a cultural fund and 20 per cent (equivalent to 6.66 per cent of the total tax collected) to the right owners (although none of them receives an individual share), as follows:

- authors: STIM 40%;
- performers: SAMI 30%;
- phonogram producers: NIFF 30%.

Here again we find resistance to compliance with the principle of *national treatment*, as in the case of remuneration for the reprographic reproduction of printed works. In regard to the owners of neighbouring rights who are entitled to a share of the remuneration for private copying, it should be noted that this principle is also enshrined in the Rome Convention of 1961 (Articles 2, 4, 5 and 6), although it makes provision (Article 16) for a wide system of reservations concerning Article 12, which includes (Art. 16, 1(a)(iv)) material reciprocity, reservations which may be notified by States at any time.

8.2.3. Collective administration of the *'droit de suite'*

The effective implementation of the *'droit de suite'* is extremely difficult to achieve if there is no collective administration system, as can be seen in comparing the list of countries in which it has been given legal status[85] with that of countries in which the respective provisions are actually applied. It will be observed that in the latter countries this right is administered by societies of authors of works of art: BILD-KUNST in Germany, SPADEM and ADAGP in France, HUNGART in Hungary, VISUAL VEGAP in Spain.

---

85. See above, Chapter 4, Section 4.2.4.

This situation was taken into account in the WIPO Draft Model Provisions for legislation in the field of copyright, Article 9 of which, referring to *'droit de suite'*, provides (para. (2)) that 'the share mentioned in paragraph (1) shall be collected and distributed by a collective administration organization ...'.[86]

In addition, there are other collective administration organizations which deal with rights in works of art (as in the case of those already mentioned, they are members of CISAC), such as VBK in Austria, VIS-ART in Canada, DDG BEELDRECHT in the Netherlands, BONUS in Sweden, DACS in the United Kingdom, VAGA in the United States of America; other organizations administer the *'droit de suite'* along with rights in various other categories of works.[87]

8.3. Collective administration of the rights of performers and producers of phonograms

By analogy with certain authors' rights (public performance of musical works, broadcasting and cable distribution of such works) which can only be effectively administered through authors' societies, the right of performers and producers to receive remuneration in respect of *secondary uses* (direct use of phonograms for public performance, broadcasting and any form of communication to the public) can only be enforced through a system of collective administration.

The conclusion of contracts with performers for the purpose of live performances—concerts and entertainments in general, in dance halls and other places—or for the production of a phonogram, etc., that is to say, for *primary uses* (an expression which is used here only to establish a distinction from *secondary* uses), does not, on the other hand, require collective administration. An individual solution is habitually arrived at in these cases.

Nevertheless, and even when a contract of gainful employment does not exist, the interests and working conditions of per-

---

86. WIPO document CE/MPC/I/2-11, 20 October 1988.
87. See Mihály Ficsor, op. cit., p. 29.

formers are generally governed by collective employment agreements which, in most countries, are binding on all workers who exercise the activity covered by such agreements.

8.3.1. Non-voluntary licences for secondary uses

Pursuant to Article 12 of the Rome Convention and a large number of domestic laws, the secondary uses of phonograms *produced with the authorization of the performers* are subject to *non-voluntary licences*. The remuneration is agreed between the organization responsible for the collective administration of neighbouring rights and the users.

In regard to the performers themselves, it is habitually understood that the performance contract for the production of a phonogram or audiovisual work involves a presumption *juris et de jure* that the performer authorizes the communication of his performance to the public (Colombia, Articles 166(a) and (c)(1); Dominican Republic, Article 126(a); France, Article L. 124-1, previously Articles 19, 21 and 22; Spain, Article 102(3), etc.).

In regard to producers, it is also generally held that once a phonogram has been published for commercial purposes they cannot object to its direct use for communication to the public (particularly by means of *performance in a public place*—France, in Article L. 214-1, previously Article 22, first paragraph of the 1985 law, expressly excludes the inclusion of a phonogram in an entertainment—and by means of *broadcasting*—France, adds, in Article L. 214-1.2, that neither can the simultaneous distribution by cable of such a broadcast in its entirety be objected to).

In relation to both categories of beneficiaries (performers and producers of phonograms), the system of compulsory licences for secondary uses of phonograms is dictated by the need to safeguard the exclusive and *absolute right of authors to the public communication* of their works since a right ceases to be exclusive and absolute, if other rights with the same features are recognized in the same object—i.e. the fixation of the performed work.[88]

---

88. See above, Chapter 7, Sections 7.1.4.2 and 7.2.3.

8.3.2. Remuneration

A. Article 12 of the Rome Convention stipulates that: '... a single equitable remuneration shall be paid by the user to the performers, or to the producers of the phonograms, or to both [...]'.

By virtue of this norm, which grants the contracting States freedom to recognize the right to remuneration for secondary uses of phonograms in respect of both categories, or one single category, of beneficiaries covered by Article 12 of the convention, States have adopted diverse criteria and allocate remuneration to:
- *the performers only* (for example, Mexico); or
- *the producers of phonograms only* (e.g. Philippines, Ireland, United Kingdom); or
- *both categories of beneficiaries or to only one of them, but with the obligation to share with the other* (for example, Argentina, Austria, Barbados, Bolivia, Brazil, Chile, Colombia, Costa Rica, former Czechoslovakia, Denmark, Dominican Republic, Ecuador, Finland, France, Germany, Italy, Norway, Panama, Peru, Spain, Sweden, Switzerland, Uruguay, Venezuela).

B. In some countries, the remuneration is agreed between the organization responsible for the collective administration of neighbouring rights and the users (for example, Argentina, Brazil, Colombia, Uruguay).

C. Sometimes, alternative procedures are stipulated for fixing the scale of charges in cases where the parties concerned cannot reach agreement; such provisions exist in France for example. In that country, Articles L. 214-3 and L. 214-4, previously Articles 23 and 24 of the law of 1985 have established a special system by virtue of which the schedule of remuneration and conditions of payment are laid down by specific agreements for each branch of activity between the organizations representing the performers, the producers of phonograms and the persons using the phonograms for direct communication in a public place—where they are not used in an entertainment—and for the broadcasting and simultaneous distribution by cable of such broadcasts in their entirety (Article L. 214-1, previously Article 22). These agreements must stipulate the manner in which the users of phonograms are to discharge their obligation to submit to the societies responsible for the collection and distribution of royalties a detailed programme of the uses and all the documentation which is required for distribution purposes. By a decision of the Ministry of Culture, the provisions of these agreements, which remain valid for between one and five years, may be made compulsory for all of the parties concerned. But once the parties fail to reach an agreement, the schedule of remuneration and the conditions for its payment shall be fixed by an arbitration procedure, i.e. by a committee chaired by a magistrate and including as its members representatives of the official bodies of the different categories of beneficiaries and users (Article L. 214-4).

D. In some countries, agreements setting out schedules of remuneration must be approved by the authorities responsible. In others, these authorities and special tribunals intervene only in the event of a dispute, in particular when a situation of abuse is created as a result of the monopoly position enjoyed by the collective administration bodies concerned.[89]

E. In certain countries the remuneration schedules are fixed by statutory provisions (for example, Chile, Mexico).

F. Some examples of existing forms of remuneration are set out below:
- *in the case of the public performance of phonograms*, the scale may be proportional to the revenue received by the user (Argentina) or related to an indicator which objectively determines the potential income from such performance, e.g. the size of the dance floor in dance halls (Brazil), etc.;
- *in the case of the broadcasting of phonograms*, the royalties may be proportional to the revenue declared to the State for tax purposes (Mexico) or to the net proceeds accruing from the

---

89. See above, Section 8.1.2.4.

broadcasting of cinematographic works by television (Mexico); alternatively, the remuneration may consist of a royalty for each disc used which varies according to the category of the broadcasting organization (Argentina) or of a fixed monthly charge based on the power of the transmitter and the population of the area served by it (Brazil). In Mexico, remuneration is also collected for the *television broadcasting of cinematographic works* and consists of 0.15 per cent of the net revenue derived from such broadcasting;
- in some countries, remuneration is collected for the *projection or showing in cinemas of audiovisual works produced for that purpose*: it is either proportional to the overall gross receipts of the exhibitors (Mexico) or determined at a fixed rate based on the price of entrance tickets (Argentina, Chile).

8.3.3. Collection

In the area of the collective administration of neighbouring rights, collection is effected by means of various types of organization:
- *of performers only*, such as ANDI and ANDA in Mexico, etc.;
- *of phonogram producers only*, such as PPL in the United Kingdom, etc.;
- *joint organizations of performers and producers*, such as the collecting body AADI–CAPIF in Argentina, LSG in Austria, etc.;
- *joint organizations of authors, performers and producers*, such as the collecting organizations SAYCO–ACINPRO in Colombia, ECAD in Brazil, etc.
- *societies of authors* mandated by the organizations of performers and producers, such as AGADU in Uruguay which acts as the collecting agency representing SUDEI (Sociedad Uruguaya de Intérpretes) and CUD (Cámara Uruguaya del Disco).

8.3.4. Distribution or sharing of remuneration

A. The domestic laws which recognize the right to remuneration in respect of the secondary uses of phonograms for both categories of beneficiaries generally lay down the method of distribution: *in equal shares* between the performers and producers (Colombia,

Costa Rica, Dominican Republic, France, Spain, etc.)[90] or else *in a higher percentage for performers* (in Argentina, Decree 1671/74 of 1974—Article 5—stipulates 67 per cent for performers and 33 per cent for producers; the performers' share is distributed in a ratio of two-thirds to the main performers and one-third to the others).

B. Ficsor points out that in the European countries which allocate remuneration to one of these indicated categories only, an agreement reached between the International Federation of Musicians (FIM), the International Federation of Actors (FIA) and the International Federation of the Phonographic Industry (IFPI)[91] is applied, by virtue of which the entitled category makes over to the other one-third of the revenue received in respect of the broadcasting of phonograms. In some countries, this voluntary sharing is based on a national agreement between the organizations of performers and those of producers.[92]

C. When the collection is effected by a body which recovers the remuneration jointly for the performers and producers, the *first distribution* is made between the representative organizations of each category of beneficiaries at the agreed rates.

D. The *second distribution* is effected to the beneficiaries individually. Here a distinction must be drawn between the manner in which this second distribution is made between the producers on the one hand and between the performers on the other.

---

90. The ILO/UNESCO/WIPO Model Law concerning the Protection of Performers, Producers of Phonograms and Broadcasting Organizations adopted in 1974 (prepared by these three organizations in their capacity as joint administrators of the Rome Convention, with a view to facilitating the application or adoption of that convention) stipulates in its Section 5(2) that: 'Unless otherwise agreed between the performers and the producer, half of the amount received by the producer [...] shall be paid by the producer to the performers'.
91. See below, Chapter 9, Section 9.9.1.1.
92. See Mihály Ficsor, op. cit., paragraph 149, p. 43. See also Stewart, op. cit., Section 8.28, pp. 240–1.

a. The *national organizations of producers* distribute between their members (nationals or firms with their head office in the country) the totality of the sum collected in respect of the public performance of phonograms, including broadcasting.

b. On the other hand, the *national organizations of performers* act, for a variety of reasons, in different ways, some earmarking the sums collected for social and cultural purposes, while others habitually make over to their *individual members* only the fee collected in respect of the broadcasting of phonograms since, save for certain exceptions (such as Argentina), a varying proportion is always assigned for those purposes. This arrangement has been adopted, firstly, because of the difficulty of obtaining reliable information on the actual use of phonograms and, secondly, because the constant and uncontrolled use of sound recordings is highly prejudicial to the employment of performing artists; the remuneration accruing from 'secondary uses' can help to remedy that situation.

c. In regard to *foreign beneficiaries*, the bodies which represent the owners of neighbouring rights do not include them in the distribution of the remuneration pursuant to Article 12 of the Rome Convention (1961). Ficsor points out that this is due to the fact that 'certain jointly adopted principles[93] of FIM and IFPI accept —and in a way promote—the conclusion of bilateral agreements under which no payments are transferred between the contracting organizations'.[94] These agreements are termed type B agreements although the tendency is to replace them by type A. In the latter instance the fees identified as corresponding to the performances of artists of the other country are transferred globally and it is for the foreign organization to distribute, according to its own methods, the sum collected among those entitled to receive it.

d. Nevertheless, the national share with their foreign counterparts the sums received under this heading, since such distribution is one of the conditions included in the licence contracts for repro-

---

93. Known as the 'London Principles' or the FIM/IFPI 'London Principles', 1969 (see Stewart, op. cit., pp. 241–3).
94. Mihály Ficsor, op. cit., paragraph 159, p. 45.

duction of phonograms. In the Latin American countries where these sums are effectively collected (Argentina, Brazil, Colombia and Uruguay), they are generally used to meet the cost of 'anti-piracy campaigns' (action to combat the unauthorized reproduction on a commercial scale of sound recordings) and of institutional action by producers of phonograms (local associations and the Latin American Federation of Producers of Phonograms and Videograms (FLAPF)).

List of bodies responsible for the collective administration of authors' rights and neighbouring rights referred to in this chapter

AADI–CAPIF:	Collection organization AADI–CAPIF (Asociación Argentina de Intérpretes—Argentine Association of Performers—Cámara Argentina de Productores e Industriales de Fonogramas—Argentine Chamber of producers and manufacturers of phonograms)
ABDR	Associação Brasileira de Direito Reprográficos (Brazilian Reprographic Rights Association)
ACUM:	Society of Authors, Composers and Music Publishers in Israel
ADAGP:	Society of Authors in Graphic and Plastic Arts (France)
AGADU:	Asociación General de Autores de Uruguay (General Association of Authors of Uruguay)
AIDROS	Associazione Italiana per i Diritti di Riproduzione delle Opere a Stampa (Italian Association for the Reproduction Rights of printed works)
AKM:	Staatlich Gerehmigte Gesellschaft der Autoren, Komponisten und Musikverleger (State Authorized Society

	of Authors, Composers and Music Publishers) (Austria)
ALCS:	Authors' Licensing and Collecting Society (United Kingdom)
ANDA:	Asociación Nacional de Actores (National Actors' Association) (Mexico)
ANDI:	Asociación Nacional de Intérpretes (National Performers' Association) (Mexico)
APA:	Autores Paraguayos Asociados (Paraguayan Authors' Association)
APDAYC:	Asociación Peruana de Autores y Compositores (Peruvian Association of Authors and Composers)
ARGENTORES:	Sociedad General de Autores de la Argentina (General Society of Authors of Argentina)
ARTISJUS:	Hungarian Bureau for the Protection of Authors' Rights
ASCAP:	American Society of Composers, Authors and Publishers (United States of America)
AUSTRO-MECHANA:	Society for the Collection of Mechanical Rights for Musical Works (Austria)
BILD-KUNST:	Society for the Rights of Artists (Germany)
BMI:	Broadcast Music, Inc. (United States of America)
BONUS:	Pictures, words, printed music—joint Copyright Organization (Swedish Organization for Reproduction Rights)
BSDA:	Senegalese Copyright Office
BUMDA:	Malian Copyright Office
CAL:	Copyright Agency Ltd (Australia)
CANCOPY:	Canadian Reprography Collective
CAPAC:	Composers, Authors and Publishers Association of Canada Ltd

CCC:	Copyright Clearance Center (United States of America)
CEDRO:	Centro Español de Derechos Reprográficos (Spanish Centre for Reprographic Rights
CFC:	Centre Français d'exploitation du droit de Copie (French Copyright Centre)
DACS:	Design and Arts Copyright Society Ltd (United Kingdom)
DAIC:	Departamento de Derecho de Autor de la Universidad de Chile (University of Chile Copyright Department)
DALRO:	Dramatic, Artistic and Literary Rights Organization (Republic of South Africa)
DDG BEELDRECHT:	Authors' Society (Netherlands)
DIRECTORES:	Sociedad Mexicana de Directores-Realizadores de Cine, Radio y Televisión, S. de A. de I.P (Mexican Society of Film, Radio and Television Directors and Producers)
ECAD:	Escritório Central de Arrecadação e Distribuição (Central Collection and Distribution Bureau) (Brazil)
FJÖLIS:	Icelandic Reproduction Rights Organization
GEMA:	Musical Performing and Mechanical Reproduction Rights Society (Germany)
GVL:	Society for the Administration of Performing Rights (Germany)
HUNGART:	Art Fund (Hungary)
JRRC:	Japanese Centre for Reprographic Rights
JUSAUTOR:	Bulgarian Copyright Agency
KOPINOR:	Norwegian Reproduction Rights Organization

KOPIOSTO RY:	Finnish Reproduction Rights Organization
LITERAR-MECHANA:	Collective Administration Society for Copyright (Austria)
LSG:	Collective Administration Society for Performing Rights (Austria)
LVG:	Staatlich Gerehmigte Literarische Verwertungsgesellschaft (State Authorized Literary Rights Society) (Austria)
MCOS:	Music Copyright (Overseas) Services Ltd (United Kingdom)
MCPS:	Mechanical Copyright Protection Society Ltd (United Kingdom)
MUSIKEDITION:	Musikedition (Austria)
NIFF:	IFPI Group (Sweden)
ONDA:	National Office of Copyright (Algeria)
OSTIG:	Austrian Society of Performers
PPL:	Phonographic Performance Ltd (United Kingdom)
PROCAN:	Performing Rights Organization of Canada Ltd.
PRO LITTERIS:	Swiss Organization for Reproduction Rights
PRS:	The Performing Right Society Ltd (United Kingdom)
REPRORECHT:	Reprorecht Foundation (Netherlands Organization for Reproduction Rights)
SABAM:	Société Belge des Auteurs, Compositeurs et Editeurs (Belgian Society of Authors, Composers and Publishers)
SACD:	Société des auteurs et compositeurs dramatiques (Society of Authors and Composers of Dramatic Works) (France)
SACEM:	Société des auteurs, compositeurs et

	éditeurs de musique (Society of Authors, Composers and Music Publishers) (France)
SACM:	Sociedad de Autores y Compositores de Música, S. de A (Society of Authors and Music Composers) (Mexico)
SACVEN:	Sociedad de Autores y Compositores de Venezuela (Society of Venezuelan Authors and Composers)
SADAIC:	Sociedad Argentina de Autores y Compositores de Música (Argentine Society of Authors and Music Composers)
SADEMBRA:	Sociedade Administradora de Direitos de Execução Musical do Brasil (Brazilian Society for Performing Rights (Music) Administration)
SAMI:	Union of Swedish Artists and Musicians
SATCH:	Sociedad de Autores Teatrales de Chile (Society of Chilean Dramatic Authors)
SAYCE:	Sociedad de Autores y Compositores Ecuatorianos (Society of Ecuadorian Authors and Composers)
SAYCO:	Sociedad de Autores y Compositores de Colombia (Society of Colombian Authors and Composers)
SAYCO–ACINPRO:	Collection Organization SAYCO–ACINPRO (Sociedad de Autores y Compositores de Colombia—Asociación Colombiana de Intérpretes y Productores Fonográficos) (Society of Colombian Authors and Composers—Colombian Association of performers and producers of phonograms)

SBACEM:	Sociedade Brasileira de Autores, Compositores e Escritores de Musica (Brazilian Society of Authors and Music Composers)
SBAT:	Sociedade Brasileira de Autores Teatrais (Brazilian Society of Dramatic Authors)
SCD:	Sociedad Chilena del Derecho de Autor (Chilean Copyright Society)
SDRM:	Société pour l'administration du droit de reproduction mécanique des auteurs, compositeurs et éditeurs (Society for the Administration of the Mechanical Reproduction Rights of Authors, Composers and Music Publishers) (France)
SESAC:	Society of European Stage Authors and Composers Inc. (United States of America)
SGAE:	Sociedad General de Autores de España (General Society of Authors in Spain)
SGDL:	Société des gens de lettres (Society of Literary Authors) (France)
SIAE:	Società Italiana degli Autori ed Editori (Italian Society of Authors and Publishers)
SICAM:	Sociedade Independiente de Compositores e Autores Musicais (Society of Composers and Authors of Music) (Brazil)
SOCADRA:	Société Camerounaise du Droit d'Auteur (Cameroonian Copyright Society)
SOCINPRO:	Sociedade Brasileira de Interpretes e Productores Fonograficos (Brazilian Society of Performers and Producers of Phonograms)

SOGEM:	Sociedad General de Escritores de México (General Society of Mexican Writers)
SPAC:	Sociedad Peruana de Autores y Compositores (Peruvian Society of Authors and Composers)
SPADEM:	Société de la propriété artistique et des dessins et modèles (Society of Artistic Property and Designs and Models) (France)
SSA:	Société Suisse des Auteurs (Swiss Society of Authors)
SUDEI:	Sociedad Uruguaya de Intérpretes (Uruguayan Performers' Society)
SUISA:	Société suisse pour les droits des auteurs d'œuvres musicales (Swiss Society for the rights of authors of musical works)
SUISSIMAGE:	Société Suisse pour la gestion des droits d'auteurs d'œuvres visuelles et audiovisuelles (Swiss Society for the administration of the rights of authors of visual and audiovisual works)
UBC:	União Brasileira de Compositores (Brazilian Composers' Union)
UNEQ	Union des écrivains québécois (Canada) (Quebec Writers' Union)
VAAP:	Copyright Agency of the former Soviet Union
VAGA:	Visual Artists and Galleries Inc. (United States of America)
VAM:	Collecting Society of Audiovisual Media (Austria)
VBK:	Collecting Society for Performing Artists (Austria)
VG RUNDFUNK:	Collective Administration for Broadcasting (Austria)

VG WORT:	Collective Administration Society for Literary Works (Germany)
VIS-ART:	VIS-ART Inc. (Canada)
VISUAL (VEGAP):	Entidad de Gestión Colectiva de Artistas Plásticos (Spain) (Collective Administration body for plastic artists)

Chapter 9

Bodies set up to defend copyright and neighbouring rights

Summary
9.1. Bodies established under private law
   9.1.1. International non-governmental organizations. 9.1.1.1. Organizations set up to defend professional and sectoral interests. 9.1.1.2. Organizations whose work lies in the academic field. **9.1.2** National bodies established under private law
9.2. Bodies established under public law
   9.2.1. Intergovernmental organizations. **9.2.2.** National bodies established under public law. The supervisory function

This chapter deals with the bodies, other than collective administration agencies, whose purpose is to defend copyright and neighbouring rights.

9.1. Bodies established under private law

9.1.1. International non-governmental organizations

There are many international non-governmental organizations established under private law. Some represent and defend professional and sectoral interests: they include CISAC and BIEM (music composers and publishers), IFPI (phonogram producers), FIM (musicians), and FIA (actors), to name only a few. Others, such as ALAI, INTERGU, ICI, etc. are academic institutions whose object is the theoretical study and defence and promotion of the legal principles which are the foundation of copyright and neighbouring rights.

9.1.1.1. Organizations set up to defend professional and sectoral interests

A. CISAC

Founded in 1926/1927 in Paris where it has its headquarters, the International Confederation of Societies of Authors and

Composers (CISAC) is an international, non-governmental, non-profit-making organization which brings together the agencies responsible for the collective administration of authors' rights. The purpose of CISAC is to ensure that the moral and professional interests attaching to every kind of literary or artistic production are safeguarded, respected and protected; to watch over and contribute to the respecting of the economic and legal interests attaching to such productions both in the international sphere and in that of domestic legislation; to co-ordinate the technical activities of the societies of authors and composers and ensure their collaboration in this field[1] subject to the understanding, however, that each member society is master of its own internal organization; and, finally, to constitute an international centre of research and information.

In the previous chapter we noted that any society administering authors' rights may be admitted to CISAC in the capacity of an *ordinary member* on condition that it is an organization which

- has as its aim and effectively ensures the advancement of the moral interests of authors and the defence of their material interests;
- has at its disposal effective machinery for the collection and distribution of copyright royalties and assumes full responsibility for the operations attaching to administration of the rights entrusted to it; and
- does not, except as an ancillary activity, administer also the rights of performers, phonogram producers, broadcasting organizations or other right holders.

---

1. As we have already seen, the standardization of criteria for the collective administration of authors' rights is vital because of the complexities inherent in the international use of a vast quantity of works; that task would have been impossible without a body such as CISAC to co-ordinate the efforts necessary to integrate the national bodies into a vast world system of reciprocal representation and to unify the principles and methods of collective administration (see above Chap. 8, Sect. 8.1.6.).

Any authors' organization which does not fulfil one or other of the first two conditions may be admitted to CISAC as an *associate member*. We also stated that on 1 July 1994, 155 societies from 84 countries, representing over a million authors of works of various kinds, belonged to CISAC. It is an effective world organization of authors and pursues its activities in complete independence of any political or religious affiliation.

CISAC is headed by a President assisted by a Vice-President, one of whom is obligatorily an author and the other a composer, of different nationality. They are elected by the General Assembly.

The statutory bodies are:
- the General Assembly (World Congress of Authors and Composers);
- the Administrative Council;
- the Executive Bureau; and
- the Secretary-General.

The other statutory bodies of CISAC set up for the pursuit of its official purposes are:

a. Professional bodies

At the professional level, four International Councils of authors nominated by the societies to which they belong. These Councils meet at regular intervals to discuss matters relating to the profession.

The International Councils of Authors have a consultative character corresponding to the type of creative work engaged in by their members:
- the International Council of Dramatic and Literary Authors;
- the International Council of Authors and Composers of Music, to which publishers also belong;
- the International Council of Authors of Audio-Visual Works, and
- the International Council of Authors of the Graphic and Plastic Arts and of Photographers.

According to the specific artistic activity of their members, these Councils have particular responsibility for the study of all matters directly concerning the moral and professional interests of creators of works of the mind and of their representative bodies and also the examination of the draft resolutions laid before them by the Administrative Council or by the Executive Bureau. Their discussions cover technical and legal aspects and they bring the invaluable contribution of the creators themselves to the examination of practical matters pertaining to authors' rights. The opinions of the Professional Councils are taken into account by the executive bodies in reaching their decisions.

b. Technical bodies

At the technical level, the statutory bodies of CISAC are the Legal and Legislation Committee and the Technical Committees.

The Legal and Legislation Committee has a consultative character and is composed of 30 members who may not be members of the Administrative Council, but may be their substitutes. This Council nominates 18 members chosen among lawyers attached to the Collective Administration Organizations which are ordinary members of CISAC (one per organization) and 12 members chosen among experts, professors, advocates or magistrates who are specialists in the field of authors' rights belonging to the countries represented within the organization or who have the chief responsibility within national or international organizations more particularly concerned with the legal side of the copyright protection, these members being appointed on a proposal from the societies in the countries concerned.

The technical committees are composed of representatives of the member organizations of CISAC (not more than two representatives of each such organization).

Jean-Alexis Ziegler, who has been Secretary-General of CISAC for more than 20 years, points out that the Confederation provides the best framework for co-operation between authors' societies. This is reflected in a variety of different ways:
- *co-operation at the level of members of the profession*, i.e. between authors themselves within the International Councils;
- *technical co-operation*, which is the area in which the need for international co-operation between the societies is greatest. Ziegler points out that this co-operation takes place by various means:

- *standard contracts for reciprocal representation* between societies which administer rights of public showing, literary rights, performing rights and, more recently, between societies of authors of graphic, plastic and photographic works;
- *exchange of documentation* on works (nature, title, length, etc.) and on their authors (identity, date of birth, society to which they belong, pseudonyms used by them, etc.); the list of members of each society; the CAE list and AGP list covering authors in the graphic and plastic arts and photographers; the international registers; documentation on audiovisual works; documentation on general contracts for mutual representation concluded between publishers in different countries; international documentation and distribution rights in mechanical reproduction; the WWL list which is the 'active' world repertoire (see above, Chap. 8, Sect. 8.1.3.4);
- *general technical co-operation* in order to facilitate the sharing or distribution of the fees collected; this activity has for a long time given rise to exchanges of experience between the societies with a view to the establishment of the most accurate methods possible, while keeping the cost of the work necessary to achieve this at a reasonable level;
- *legal co-operation* through the work of the Legal and Legislation Committee;
- *regional co-operation* through the Committees established pursuant to Article 8 of the Statutes: the African, Asian-Pacific and European Committees and the Latin American Committee (which was the first to be created as the Pan-American Council), within which the societies from these different regions are able to establish more frequent contacts in order to analyse their specific professional, technical and legal problems;
- *international solidarity* which is expressed in particular through the provision referred to previously that up to 10 per cent of the net receipts of collective administration may be set aside for social and cultural purposes. This international solidarity is also reflected in other activities such as the promotion of training courses for officials from the less-developed societies by the technically more advanced organizations and contributions for

the establishment or development of national structures for collective administration in the developing countries.[2]

B. BIEM

BIEM was founded in Paris, where it has its headquarters, on 21 January 1929 as a civil law society known as the Bureau International de l'Edition Musico-Mécanique.

It changed its title in 1968 to become the International Bureau of Societies Administering the Rights of Mechanical Recording and Reproduction as part of a substantive reform of its statutes by virtue of which BIEM ceased to be the owner of mechanical reproduction rights. In consequence, these rights now accrue to each associated administration body which collects the royalties owed by the producers of phonograms in the country concerned.

Today, BIEM is a centralized negotiating body whose counterpart is the International Federation of the Phonographic Industry (IFPI) founded four years later. These two bodies have established a standard BIEM–IFPI contract for the phonographic industry which is periodically revised. The latest edition dates from 1975 with a number of amendments adopted since 1980. The BIEM–IFPI basic contract regulates authorization to use the 'world repertoire' consisting of the works administered by the organizations belonging to BIEM. This contract is put into effect through the standard contract which each national society for the collective administration of mechanical reproduction rights signs with each national group in IFPI, a subsidiary contract then being concluded between the collective administration society concerned and each local producer belonging to the relevant national group (for details of these contracts, see above, Chap. 6, Sect. 6.4.3).

The aim of BIEM is to contribute to the defence and furtherance of the protection of authors' rights in the area of mechanical reproduction; to prepare standard contracts for unilateral and bilateral representation between its members in order to

---

2. Jean-Alexis Ziegler, 'Sociedades de Autores. La Cooperación Internacional', in *Proceedings of the 5th International Congress on the Protection of Intellectual Property*, Buenos Aires, 1990, pp. 103–6.

ensure the administration by each associated society on its own territory of the repertoires of the others; to negotiate standard contracts with IFPI; to agree basic contracts or general conditions for use with interested parties; to take all the measures necessary to ensure that rights are also protected in countries where no societies exist for the collective administration of mechanical reproduction rights; to organize the provision of supporting documents and the international distribution of the fees collected by each member for the use of the foreign repertoires administered by associated societies and by the members and to contribute to the settlement by arbitration of any disputes which may arise between them.

In December 1994, 30 societies belonged to BIEM: ACUM (Israel), AEPI (Greece), AGADU (Uruguay), ARTISJUS (Hungary) AUSTRO-MECHANA (Austria), GEMA (Germany), HDS (Croatia), JASRAC (Japan), MCPS\ (United Kingdom), NCB (Denmark) OSA (Prague, Czech Republic), SABAM (Belgium), SACEM (France), SACERAU (Egypt), SADAIC (Argentina), SARRAL (South Africa), SDRM (France), SGAE (Spain), SIAE (Italy), SODRAC (Montreal, Canada), SOKOJ (Belgrade, former Yugoslavia), SOZA (Bratislava, Slovakia), SPA (Portugal), STEMRA (Netherlands), SUISA (Switzerland), ZAIKS (Poland), AMCOS (Australia), CMRRA (Toronto, Canada), SACM (Mexico) and The Harry Fox Agency Inc. (United States of America).

The statutory bodies of BIEM are the General Assembly, the Board and the Management.

C. IFPI

The International Federation of Phonogram and Videogram Producers (IFPI) was founded in 1933. It is the only international organization which represents the producers of phonograms.

The members of IFPI—which has its registered office in Zurich (Switzerland) and its Secretariat in London—are producers of phonograms or videograms, more especially, producers of video music recordings and video clips. Chapter 2, Section 2.1. of its Statutes states that: 'Membership of IFPI is open to legal entities which are producers of phonograms or videograms, or have a close connection with the production or manufacture of phonograms or videograms and/or their supply to the public. Admission to membership of IFPI is in the discretion of the Council....'

In 1988 IFPI had some 900 members drawn from 62 countries. A national group of IFPI may be formed in any country where there are two or more members.

The purpose of IFPI is to create and promote the rights of producers of phonograms and videograms nationally through statutes, case law or contract, and internationally through conventions and agreements and, where such rights already exist, to defend, preserve and develop them; to further the interests of producers of phonograms and producers of videograms vis-à-vis governments and international intergovernmental organizations or non-governmental organizations and other interested and representative bodies and, in general, to advance the present and future financial prospects of its members.

The statutory bodies of IFPI are the General Meeting, the Council and the Board.

IFPI has three regional organizations: FLAPF (Latin American Federation of Producers of Phonograms and Videograms), RIAA (The Recording Industry Association of America) and ARIA (The Australian Recording Industry Association).

The IFPI pursues its activities mainly in the following areas: action to prevent the unauthorized reproduction ('piracy') of sound recordings; the negotiation of standard BIEM–IFPI contracts on behalf of the phonographic industry; relations with international organizations of performing artists (FIM and FIA) for the purpose of collecting fees in respect of 'secondary uses' of phonograms, based in particular on a series of agreements concluded between 1954 and 1973; relations with broadcasting organizations on matters pertaining to contracts and negotiations; the creation and furtherance of the rights of producers of phonograms through the promotion of national and international statutory provisions and by encouraging governments to accede to the two Conventions (Rome, 1961 and Phonograms, 1971) of which the phonogram producers are beneficiaries; enhancement of the prestige of phonogram producers; recognition of the cultural value of records with a view to the abolition of customs tariffs and customs regulations and the attainment of a progressive reduction of national taxes levied on recordings.

IFPI represents the recording industry at Berne and Universal Copyright Convention meetings, in the Committees set up to look into aspects of copyright and neighbouring rights where matters directly or indirectly concerning the phonographic industry are discussed and recommendations adopted for the governments; it also represents it at the Review Conferences.

D. FIA AND FIM

The International Federation of Actors (FIA) and the International Federation of Musicians (FIM) are international trade union federations. The FIA (which incorporates the International Federation of Variety Artists (IFVA)) has its headquarters in Paris and its Secretariat in London; it is an international non-governmental organization which brings together unions of actors, singers and ballet dancers, variety and circus performers, choreographs, theatre, cinema and broadcasting producers, organized in affiliated unions or in others associated with the Federation for specific purposes. The FIM has its headquarters in Zurich and brings together union organizations of performing musicians.

These bodies are principally concerned with safeguarding the rights of the artists mentioned in connection with the dissemination and reproduction of their work by mechanical means, such as broadcasting, sound recordings, films, television, retransmissions, etc.; with the rights of performers in respect of the secondary uses of phonograms; the establishment of measures of protection on a national and international basis concerning the abusive use of recordings of their performances, irrespective of the recording process. They also further the international circulation of artists and the protection of their interests abroad; they seek employment openings for performers and support all the measures taken to combat unemployment; at the professional level, they protect and foster the artistic, economic, social and legal interests of performers, such as working conditions, salaries, social security systems, etc. They maintain ongoing contacts with various international organizations, in particular the IFPI, the International Labour Organization (ILO), WIPO, UNESCO, the Council of Europe and the Culture Sector of the Commission of the European Union.

E. OTHER ORGANIZATIONS

- Asia-Pacific Broadcasting Union (ABU);
- International Association of Art (IAA);
- International Association of Audio-Visual Writers and Directors (AIDAA);
- International Confederation of Music Publishers (ICMP);
- International Music Council (IMC);
- International Council for Film, Television and Audio-Visual Communication (IFTC);
- International Video Federation (IVF);
- International Federation of Library Associations and Institutions (IFLA);
- International Federation of Film Distributors Associations (FIAD);
- International Federation of Film Producers Associations (FIAPF);
- International Federation of Journalists (IFJ)
- International Federation of Translators (FIT);
- Information Industry Association (IIA);
- Intellectual Property Owners (IPO);
- International Federation of Reproduction Rights Organization (IFRRO);
- International Group of Scientific, Technical and Medical Publishers (STM);
- International Intellectual Property Alliance (IIPA);
- International Secretariat for Arts, Mass Media and Entertainment Trade Unions (ISETU);
- International Writers Guild (IWG);
- European Broadcasting Union (EBU);
- International Publishers Association (IPA).

9.1.1.2. Organizations whose work lies in the academic field

A. ALAI

By decision of the International Literary Congress convened by the Société des Gens de Lettres in Paris on 28 June 1878, the Association littéraire internationale was founded under the honorary presidency of Victor Hugo. In 1884, its membership was also laid open to artists and it adopted the title of International Literary and Artistic Association (ALAI).

The first objective of ALAI was to promote an International Convention for the Protection of Literary and Artistic Works. This aim was achieved on 9 September 1886 when the Berne Convention was adopted (see below, Chap. 12, Sect. 12.4.2.1.I).

ALAI, which has its headquarters in Paris, is an international non-governmental organization whose aim is to safeguard and promote the legal principles which ensure the international protection of copyright; to study and compare domestic legislation on copyright and on all related matters and to examine proposals designed to develop, enhance and unify such legislation together with measures intended to secure the recognition and legal protection of copyright in all countries; to improve and extend the area of application, more specifically through the revision of international conventions on the protection of copyright and in particular the Berne Convention and the Universal Copyright Convention and also to prepare new international conventions on the same subject; to examine all measures, in particular the adoption of international conventions, seeking to establish and amend related or neighbouring rights; to take part in the studies and activities of all national and international organizations which pursue the same aims.

ALAI brings together lawyers, legal experts, university professors, copyright experts, producers, creators and users, civil law or commercial associations, trade unions, syndical chambers, judges and government officials whose activities have a bearing on the issue of copyright. Its members are drawn from countries in Europe and on other continents. Natural or legal persons belonging to a 'national ALAI group' are also members. National ALAI groups have been set up in Belgium, Canada, Finland,

France, Germany, Greece, Italy, Netherlands, Spain, Switzerland and the United States.

ALAI carries out its work by means of bulletins, publications, reports, conferences, meetings, one-day seminars, congresses, resolutions and recommendations. ALAI's contributions to the international development of copyright played a particularly important role in the preparatory work leading up to the major national conventions, and, more especially, the Berne Convention and its subsequent revised versions (see below, Chap. 12, Sect. 12.4.2.1 onwards).

Since ALAI's foundation, its Presidents have been Victor Hugo, founder and Honorary President (1878); José da Silva Mendes Real (1879–80), L. M. Torres Caicedo (1880–85), Louis Ulbach (1885–88); Louis Ratisbonne (1888–90); Eugène Pouillet (1890–1905); Georges Maillard (1905–42); Marcel Boutet (1946–71); Henri Desbois (1972–80) and Georges Koumantos (since 1981).

B. INTERGU

INTERGU is the acronym for the *Internationale Gesellschaft für Urheberrecht* (International Copyright Society) founded in 1954 in Berlin where it has its headquarters.

It is a public service organization whose purpose is to engage in the theoretical study of copyright and its worldwide application, particularly with regard to legislation, with a view to contributing to the creation of a modern body of authors' rights which will serve the interests of authors and of the public alike.

Individuals and institutions, societies, associations and groupings based in all the countries of the world are eligible to become members of INTERGU. It has over 400 members drawn from more than 40 countries.

INTERGU organizes regular international congresses in different countries (Berlin 1955, Vienna 1960, Berlin 1962, Merano/Italy 1964, Sveti Stefan/former Yugoslavia 1969, Madrid 1974, Athens 1978, Toronto 1981, Santiago/Chile 1983, Munich 1985, Locarno/Switzerland 1988 and Prague 1991). It has published a series of some 70 studies, as well as a number of directories.

C. ICI

The Inter-American Copyright Institute (ICI) was set up in Brazil on 17 April 1974 pursuant to a resolution adopted by the XVIII Conference of the Inter-American Bar Association (IABA) held in Rio de Janeiro in August 1973.

It is a non-profit-making international association established under private law with its registered office in the city of São Paulo, Brazil. Its purpose is to promote the study and advancement of copyright and neighbouring rights, with particular reference to modern communication techniques, by engaging in a thorough and impartial examination of all relevant issues; to ensure that the American countries grant the broadest possible protection to authors' rights and to promote the development and implementation of existing international conventions; to provide its assistance as a consultative and planning organization of a technical kind; to carry out comparative law studies with a view to the harmonization of American legislation; to work towards the creation of copyright institutes in all the American countries and to act as a liaison body between them on the American continent; to promote and circulate specialized publications on copyright and neighbouring rights and to encourage the study of the subject in universities in American countries.

Active members of this Institute are attorneys specializing in this area and other individuals who pursue, on the American continent, the Institute's objectives or are interested in them, national copyright institutes and other bodies having similar aims on the American continent, and the participating representatives of the Intellectual and Industrial Property Committee of the Inter-American Bar Association (IABA). All individuals or corporate bodies who wish to co-operate with ICI may become sponsor members. The Institute has some 250 active members drawn from all the countries of the continent and also a number of sponsor members.

ICI pursues its objectives through continental conferences; by organizing courses and seminars; by the joint organization of international congresses (V International Congress, Buenos Aires 1990, and Ibero-American Congresses, the First in Madrid, 1991, and the second in Lisbon, 1994); by acting on a permanent basis as the joint sponsor of the international congresses which have been held annually since 1986 in different countries of the American continent; by providing technical assistance for the drafting of national laws on copyright and neighbouring rights; by organizing competitions for students of this discipline in universities of the Latin American countries, based on the submission of monographs.

ICI has promoted the creation of national centres or institutes for copyright and neighbouring rights in a number of Latin American countries such as Argentina, Brazil, Colombia, Mexico, Peru and Venezuela which belong to ICI. Their directors are also members of the Institute.

Since its creation, the Presidents of ICI have been: Antonio Chaves, founder and President from 1974 to 1990 and thereafter Honorary President, and Carlos Alberto Villalba who succeeded him in 1990.

D. OTHER BODIES

- International Association for the Advancement of Teaching and Research in Intellectual Property (ATRIP);
- Max Planck Institute (MPI) for foreign and international law in the area of patents, copyright and competition.

9.1.2. National bodies established under private law

A. *Organizations defending professional interests*: these are the authors' societies and organizations which do not collect royalties (for example in Argentina, the Argentine Authors' Society—SADE—which coexists with ARGENTORES and SADAIC but, unlike the latter, is not responsible for collective administration); the trade union organizations (such as those of journalists, photographic reporters, plastic artists, musicians, actors, etc.) which seek satisfaction of demands that are often related to the intellectual rights of their members; professional colleges (such as the colleges of architects, social communicators), etc.

B. *Study and research organizations*: these are the bodies whose work lies in the academic field (study and research) and which disseminate knowledge in the area of copyright (such as the Institut de Recherche en Propriété Intellectuelle Henri Desbois, IRPI, in France), the national groups of ALAI (such as the Asociación Literaria y Artistica para la Defensa del Derecho de Autor, ALADDA, in Spain), the national centres or institutes of ICI (such as the Argentine Centre of ICI), the Colombian Centre for Authors' Rights (CECOLDA); the Mexican Institute for Authors' Rights (IMDA), the Peruvian Institute for Authors' Rights (IPDA), the Venezuelan Institute for Authors' Rights (IVDA); the institutes of the Colleges of Advocates (such as the Institute of Communications and Authors' Rights of the Public College of Advocates of the Federal Capital in Argentina), etc.

9.2. Bodies established under public law

9.2.1. Intergovernmental organizations

A. UNESCO

Since the Preparatory Conference began work in London (November 1945), the fundamental objectives of UNESCO have included consideration of the subject of protection of literary, artistic and scientific property. That objective was reflected in the educational and cultural tasks entrusted to the Organization by its founder States and also in the capacity of UNESCO as the 'spiritual' heir of the International Institute on Intellectual Co-operation[3] which, together with the Belgian Government, the Secretariat of the Berne Union for the Protection of Literary, Artistic and Scientific Works and the Rome International Institute for the Unification of Private Law, made a major contribution and performed important work in the field of copyright.[4]

---

3. The International Institute on Intellectual Co-operation (IIIC) was set up in Paris in 1925 in response to a request made by the League of Nations. It began work in the following year and, after an interruption between 1940 and 1945, continued its activities until the end of 1946 when it entered into an agreement with UNESCO.
4. See below, Chap. 12, Sect. 12.4.2.2, Genesis of the Universal Copyright Convention.

The first session of the General Conference of UNESCO held in Paris in November/December 1946 reached the conclusion that one of the main factors preventing the free flow and exchange of intellectual works between countries was the incomplete and inappropriate system existing at the time for the international protection of authors' rights. The Organization proposed the convening, under its auspices, of an International Copyright Conference with a view to reaching an agreement whereby all countries might accede to a new international Convention regulating and facilitating the transfer of authors' rights and the circulation of their works through the organs of mass information. The General Conference adopted a resolution on the UNESCO Programme for 1947 in the area of copyright pursuant to which a Provisional Committee of Experts on Copyright was set up in order to carry out studies and formulate recommendations on UNESCO's role in the area of author's rights.

In conformity with the objectives laid down in the Programme for 1947, in February of that same year the UNESCO Secretariat carried out a survey among its Member States concerning their legislative and legal solutions to the problem of copyright and the means of disseminating culture (cinema, radio, television, rights of performing artists and rights of phonogram producers). In July of the same year, François Hepp was appointed as a consultant expert to supervise the survey and organize the convening of the Provisional Committee of Experts on copyright who were to advise the Secretariat on its action plan.

The first Committee of Experts met in Paris in September 1947. It was made up of leading specialists in authors' rights such as Jean Escarra (France), Eduardo F. Mendilaharzu (Argentina), Benigne Mentha (Director of the Secretariat of the Berne Union) and Valerio de Sanctis (Italy). The recommendations adopted by the Committee included the following: 'That UNESCO should set up within its Secretariat a special section to deal with copyright matters, in particular: (1) to assemble a universal documentation composed of the principal works and technical publications; (2) to centralize all activities in copyright matters and to publish in a bulletin from time to time, all documentation ... in support of the idea of a universal convention; (3) to organize and supervise the inquiries and studies; (4) to synthesize the results of the inquiries and studies, to prepare reports of the findings made as a result thereof; (5) to submit to the Director-General any useful suggestions'. It also proposed the creation of a Preparatory Committee of UNESCO to study copyright matters and prepare the draft text of a Universal Convention.

These recommendations were included in the Report of the Director-General on the Activities of the Organization in 1947 submitted to the second session of the General Conference at Mexico City (November 1947) during which proposals were adopted concerning: (1) UNESCO's field of action and the central role of copyright in relation to cultural dissemination; (2) the drafting of a Universal Copyright Convention; (3) the creation of a unit within UNESCO responsible for preparing this Convention and for convening a meeting of experts drawn from different countries.

In January 1948, François Hepp was appointed head of the Copyright Division. The first priority for that year was assigned to the Communication Programme of UNESCO which covered copyright, exchanges of persons and mass communication. That aspiration met with a broad international response and is also reflected in Article 27 of the Universal Declaration of Human Rights adopted by the General Assembly of the United Nations on 10 December 1948 which recognizes, in paragraph 1, the right freely to participate in cultural life and, in paragraph 2, authors' rights as basic human rights.

The first *Copyright Bulletin* was published in July 1948.

On 6 September 1952, after five years of preliminary work[5] the Universal Copyright Convention was adopted in Geneva under the auspices and administration of UNESCO. In 1971, the Diplomatic Conference convened for this purpose by UNESCO revised the Universal Convention with the main objective of introducing a preferential regime of compulsory licences for translation and reproduction in the developing countries.[6]

---

5. Cf. below, Chap. 12, Sect. 12.4.2.2., A, (f).
6. See below, Chap. 12, Sect. 12.4.2.2, F and G.

It was also under UNESCO's auspices that the following international conventions on copyright and neighbouring rights were adopted: the Rome Convention for the Protection of Performers, Producers of Phonograms and Broadcasting Organizations (1961) which it administers jointly with WIPO and ILO; the Convention for the Protection of Producers of Phonograms against Unauthorized Duplication of their Phonograms (Geneva, 1971); the Convention relating to the Distribution of Programme-Carrying Signals Transmitted by Satellite (Brussels, 1974) and the Multilateral Convention for the Avoidance of Double Taxation of Copyright Royalties (Madrid, 1979).

The International Copyright Joint Study Group meeting in Washington in September 1969,[7] held under the auspices of BIRPI and UNESCO, recommended that the latter should establish, as soon as possible, an International Copyright Information Centre designed to provide assistance to the developing countries which wished to gain access to protected works but encountered difficulties in doing so. As the outcome of this recommendation, the General Conference of UNESCO established, in 1970, the International Copyright Information Centre (ICIC) within whose framework concerted action has been taken by many Member States in order to overcome these difficulties.

Subsequently other priorities became the main focus of the Copyright Division's attention, particularly joint studies with WIPO relating to new technologies and their consequent uses (such as the distribution of programmes by cable, home taping, hire and rental and satellite broadcasting), which demanded a decade of joint meetings between governmental experts. Principles were defined and consolidated concerning the protection of authors, performers, producers of phonograms and broadcasting organizations in regard to programme distribution by cable, as were guiding principles for protection of the following major categories of works: audiovisual; architecture; visual arts; dramatic, choreographic and musical works; applied arts; printed and photographic works, and phonograms. The committees worked on

---

7. Cf. below Chap. 12, Sect. 12.4.2.1.

the basis of excellent reports prepared by the Secretariats of the two international organizations which recapitulated the various problems facing the owners of copyright and neighbouring rights and defined principles intended to guide governments in their approach to dealing with these problems. Although the principles lack binding force, they nevertheless reflect current thinking on the subject and seek as their ultimate objective, to propose solutions to safeguard the rights concerned and facilitate, for both creators and users, the utilization and performance, etc. of protected works.

The present 'Division of Books and Copyright' was set up by merging the Section for Book Promotion with the Copyright Division. The new title was adopted in 1990 (although it had been used previously until the two departments were separated). Mrs Milagros del Corral Beltrán is the head of this division.

UNESCO's copyright programme is currently centred on three main areas:
- promotion of accession to existing international conventions and encouragement of the Organization's Member States to adopt statutory provisions governing the rights of translators, the protection of folklore, the status of artists and the protection of works in the public domain;
- promotion of the development of education concerning author's rights by introducing such study into university courses in the developing countries (this activity includes seminars intended for authors, senior national officials and magistrates, journalists and librarians);
- provision of documentation for experts and for the general public through the publication of the quarterly *Copyright Bulletin*—referred to earlier—in English, French, Russian and Spanish.

Two editions of the *Repertorio Universal de Derecho de Autor*—well known as RUDA—have also been published in Spanish (the first between 1960 and 1978 and the second in 1990) and preparations are currently being made for the publication on a CD-ROM data carrier of a copyright legislation database (including a detailed analysis of national legislation and international conventions), together with case law and a relevant bibliography.

B. WIPO

The World Intellectual Property Organization (WIPO) was set up by the Stockholm Convention of 1967 (*Convention Establishing the World Intellectual Property Organization*) which came into force in 1970.

The origins of WIPO date back to the years 1883 and 1886 when the Paris Convention for the Protection of Industrial Property and the Berne Convention for the Protection of Literary and Artistic Works were adopted. Both these Conventions provided for the creation of a secretariat known as the 'International Office'.

Dr Arpad Bogsch, who has been Director General of WIPO since 1973, points out that a distinction must be drawn between three 'international bureaux' (a designation in vogue in the nineteenth century for the permanent secretariats of intergovernmental organizations) in the history of the Berne Convention: the International Bureau of the Berne Union, the United International Bureaux and the International Bureau of WIPO.

The International Bureau of the Berne Union was established by Article 16 of the original (1886) text of the Convention and 'placed under the high authority of the highest government authority of the Swiss Confederation'. When that text entered into force (1887), another International Bureau already existed in Berne. It was concerned with intellectual property and had been created at an earlier date. It, too, was placed under the authority of the Swiss Confederation. This was the Bureau set up by the Paris Convention for the Protection of Industrial Property (1883). Henri Morel, a member of the Swiss Federal Council was appointed Secretary-General of the United Bureaux whose existence was officially recognized by the Swiss Federal Council in a resolution adopted at the end of 1892 which fixed their organization.[8]

The United International Bureaux for the Protection of Intellectual Property were first established in Berne. In 1960 they

---

8. Arpad Bogsch, 'The First Hundred Years of the Berne Convention for the Protection of Literary Works' in the *Berne Convention Centenary Volume*, 1986, Geneva, WIPO, 1986, 241 pp., pp. 44–8.

moved to Geneva and have since been referred to by their French acronym BIRPI (Bureaux Internationaux Réunis pour la Protection de la Propriété Intellectuelle). No provision was made for the representation of the Member States of the two Unions (Paris and Berne) in these Bureaux. As a result, the idea was mooted of creating a system in which all the countries belonging to the Unions would be represented on a basis of parity. The aim was achieved at the diplomatic conference held in Stockholm in 1967 with the simultaneous reform of the administrative provisions of the Conventions of Paris and Berne and the adoption of the treaty establishing WIPO.

Article 24, Section (1)(a) of the Stockholm Act of the Berne Convention (confirmed by the Paris Act in 1971) stipulated that the International Bureau of WIPO was to take over from the BIRPI, i.e. from the United International Bureaux ('the International Bureau of the Berne union, united with the Bureau of the Paris Union'). The International Bureau of WIPO began to function in 1970 when the WIPO Convention entered into force, together with the administrative provisions of the Stockholm Acts of the Conventions of Paris and Berne. The old United Bureaux were to retain their formal existence until all the member countries of the Union had ratified the WIPO Convention. In practice, however, since 1970 the Government of the Swiss Confederation has ceased to exercise the functions assigned to it by the previous Acts.[9]

WIPO acquired the status of a Specialized Agency of the United Nations in 1974. The Director-General is the highest official of the Organization and represents it; he acts as the *depository* of most of the treaties administered by the organization.

The aims of WIPO are:
- to foster the worldwide protection of intellectual property through co-operation between the States, where necessary in collaboration with any other international organization; and
- to ensure administrative co-operation between the Unions.

---

9. Ibid.

In order to foster the protection of intellectual property throughout the world, WIPO encourages the conclusion of new international treaties and the modernization of national legislation; it provides technical assistance to the developing countries; acquires and disseminates information; maintains services which are intended to make it easier to obtain protection for inventions, marks and industrial designs when such protection is sought in more than one country; it also promotes administrative co-operation between the Member States. In regard to administrative co-operation between the Unions, WIPO centralizes the administration of the Unions in the International Bureau which is the Secretariat of WIPO and supervises that administration through its various bodies. It shares responsibility for administration of the International (Rome) Convention For the Protection of Performers, Producers of Phonograms and Broadcasting Organizations with UNESCO and ILO.

Today WIPO administers the following nine unions which all have separate budgets: Berne (for the protection of literary and artistic works); Paris (for the protection of industrial property); PCT—International Patent Co-operation Union (covering the filing, search and examination of international applications in respect of inventions for which protection is sought in more than one country); Madrid (for the international registration of marks); The Hague (for the international deposit of industrial designs); Lisbon (for the protection of appellations of origin and their international registration); IPC—International Patent Classification Union (which establishes a uniform worldwide patent classification): Nice (for the international classification of goods and services for the purposes of registration of marks) and Locarno (for the international classification of industrial designs).

As at 1 January 1995, WIPO was also responsible for administering the following treaties: the *Rome Convention* (for the protection of performers, producers of phonograms and broadcasting organizations); the *Phonograms Convention* (for the protection of producers of phonograms against unauthorized duplication of their phonograms); the *Satellite Convention* (relating to the distribution of programme-carrying signals transmitted by satellite); the *Treaty on the International Registration of Audio-*

Visual Works; the *Madrid Agreement* (for the repression of false or deceptive indications of source on goods); the *Vienna Union* (establishing an international classification of the figurative elements of marks); the *Budapest Union* (on the international recognition of the deposit of micro-organisms for the purposes of patent procedure) and the *Treaty of Nairobi* (on the protection of the Olympic symbol). Two treaties adopted in 1989 and another adopted in 1994 under the aegis of WIPO will also be administered by the organization when they enter into force. These are the *Washington Treaty* (on the protection of intellectual property in respect of integrated circuits), the *Madrid Protocol* (to promote the international registration of marks) and the Trademark Law Treaty (TLT) adopted in Geneva in 1994. WIPO also provides administrative and financial services for the *International Union for the Protection of New Varieties of Plants* (UPOV).

The International Bureau, headed by the Director-General, is the Secretariat of the various organs of WIPO and of the Unions listed above; as such it prepares the meetings of these bodies, essentially by providing reports and working documents. It is also responsible for the organization of the meetings themselves and arranges for the decisions taken at them to be communicated to all the interested parties. Under the supervision of the competent Governing Bodies of WIPO and of the Unions, it initiates new projects and implements those which already exist. It is supervised by the Member States meeting in the WIPO *General Assembly* and WIPO *Conference* and, in the case of the Berne and Paris Unions together with the other Unions, by the *Assembly* of each such Union. The Unions of Berne and Paris elect *Executive Committees* from among their members and the members of these two committees together constitute the WIPO Co-ordination Committee.

The International Bureau centralizes all types of information relating to the protection of intellectual property. Much of the information is prepared and published in two monthly reviews which appear in French (*Le Droit d'Auteur* and *La Propriété Industrielle*) and English (*Copyright* and *Industrial Property*); since 1989, two quarterly reviews have also been published, on a provisional basis, in Spanish (*Derecho de Autor* and *Propiedad*

Industrial). Information bulletins also appear regularly in Arabic, English, French, Portuguese, Russian, and Spanish. As from 1 January 1995, *La Propriété Industrielle* and *Le Droit d'Auteur* (and their English versions) have been merged to form a single monthly review (the Spanish review is a bi-monthly publication).

In addition, since April 1994 the International Bureau has produced a new CD-ROM—'IPLEX'—containing legislative texts concerning international treaties and regional and national legislation in its area of competence.

C. ILO

The International Labour Organization was the first intergovernmental organization to which performers turned, requesting it to study the question of their rights and to seek a solution concerning the alarming unemployment situation resulting from the rapid development of the gramophone and broadcasting from the early part of the twentieth century onwards which had completely transformed the performers' circumstances.

From the moment of this first appeal made in 1926 by the Congress of the International Union of Musicians up until 1961 when the Rome Convention became established, the ILO undertook the active defence of performers; during that action it maintained that the right of performers was based on labour law, for performances represented in the first place the product of the work of artists whose full economic value they were entitled to claim.

The activities of the ILO in respect of intellectual workers concern, on the one hand, the protection of the rights of salaried authors and inventors and, on the other, employment and working conditions and performers' rights regarding the secondary uses of their performances.

Concerning creative artists, and as indicated in the ILO study prepared for the Tripartite Meeting on Salaried Authors and Inventors, convened by the Governing Body of the ILO and held in Geneva from 24 November to 2 December 1987, systems of protection of inventions, through patent law, and of works, through copyright, do not fall within the jurisdiction of the ILO but within that of WIPO in the case of inventions and that of UNESCO and

WIPO in respect of works. Each organization plays a very important role in its particular sphere of competence in ensuring and promoting the protection of intellectual property. On the other hand, from the standpoint of labour law and social justice—the ILO's fields of competence—salaried authors and inventors encounter common problems arising from the same source: the existence of an employment relationship. Likewise, the protection of the rights attributed to these two categories of salaried workers in respect of the inventions or works they create within the context of such a relationship is based on similar principles. Unlike the case of the salaried inventor, it was only recently that the protection of salaried authors became the object of ILO's attention.[10]

As regards performers, a Tripartite Meeting on Conditions of Employment and Work of Performers was held from 5 to 13 May 1992 (also convened by the Governing body of ILO); an important report was prepared by the ILO for this meeting as a basis for the discussions. Its six chapters dealt with problems of employment and unemployment, labour relations and the fixing of employment conditions, working hours and remuneration, performers' rights in regard to the secondary uses of their performances, social security and problems associated with fluctuations in income, health, security and the working environment;[11] this summary of the report's themes illustrates the international scope of the ILO's action in regard to the category of owners of neighbouring rights.

9.2.2. National bodies established under public law. The supervisory function

This section deals with the public bodies (as opposed to agencies established under public law with responsibility for collective administration) which may have the role of defending certain aspects of author's rights and neighbouring rights. As a general rule these bodies are the National Copyright Offices (or National Directorates for Copyright on Intellectual Property, etc.). However, in

---

10. *The Protection of Salaried Authors and Inventors*, ILO, 1987.
11. See *Conditions of Employment and Work of Performers*, ILO, 1992.

some countries the supervisory functions involved may be entrusted to other institutions.

The *registration function* of these national copyright bodies or agencies will not be examined here. That particular aspect will be dealt with in the next chapter which is devoted to registration formalities. However, although the registration and supervisory functions are normally entrusted to the same body this need not necessarily be the case: for example, in Spain the Registro General de la Propiedad Intelectual (General Copyright Register) and the Sub dirección General de la Propiedad Intelectual (Subdirectorate-General for Intellectual Property) perform these tasks respectively.

The supervisory functions entrusted to the national public law agencies vary under each body of domestic legislation. The Mexican law makes particularly broad provision by attributing to the Copyright Directorate the task of registration together with those of arbitration, supervision of the users of works and the collective management bodies and the imposition of penalties in respect of infringements which do not constitute criminal offences.

A. ARBITRATION

The National Copyright Directorate often acts as mediator in disputes involving copyright and neighbouring rights, when the parties to the conflict request such action.

In Mexico, according to Articles 118(II) and 133, the National Copyright Directorate acts as an arbitrator in disputes arising in connection with the exercise of rights protected by the law:
- between authors;
- between societies of authors;
- between societies of authors and their members;
- between national authors' societies or their members and foreign authors' societies or their members, and
- between societies of authors or their members and the beneficiaries and users of the works.

Article 71 of the Bolivian Law, Articles 120.5 and 121 of the Honduran Law and Article 51.C of Decision 351 of the Cartagena Agreement provide for an administrative procedure for reconciliation and arbitration by joint agreement between the parties prior to taking judicial proceedings, under the authority of the National Directorates for Copyright and Neighbouring Rights, with a view to settling civil law disputes in the area covered by the law'; furthermore, provision is also made in the laws of Venezuela (Article 130(b)), El Salvador (Article 98(b)) and Panama (Article 109.6) for arbitration procedures of an optional kind.

B. Supervision of the users of works

In Mexico, the users of works must provide evidence to the Copyright Directorate (or the ancillary authorities stipulated in the Implementing Regulation) of the authorization by the right holders of performance or exhibition under the conditions laid down by the relevant regulation (Article 158).

C. Supervision of the collective administration agencies

Again in Mexico, the collective administration agencies are required to submit half-yearly reports to the Copyright Directorate on:
- the sums which their members have received through the action of the society;
- the sums which, through the action of the society, have been sent abroad in payment of the royalties of foreign authors, and
- the sums remaining in their custody, pending payment to Mexican authors or pending remission abroad to foreign authors (Article 102).

In *Colombia*, the recognition of the legal personality of associations of authors is granted by the National Copyright Directorate (Article 11 of law 44 of 1993, amending the Copyright Law. In addition, the Statutes that have been approved by the authors' associations in general assembly must be submitted to the National Copyright Directorate for verification of their legality and the exercise and accomplishment of the functions and responsibilities of these associations are subject to inspection and control by the same National Directorate (Arts. 24 and 26 to 29 of the Amending Law 44 of 1993 referred to above). Again, Article 5.1(f) of Decision 351 of the Cartagena Agreement provides that the National Directorates for Copyright and Related Rights should perform inspection and supervisory functions according to the terms of the national legislation of the member countries of the Agreement.

D. PUNISHMENT OF INFRINGEMENTS

Article 143 of the Mexican law stipulates that infringements of the copyright law and of its implementing regulations *which are not criminal in character* shall be dealt with by the Copyright Directorate which has the power to impose fines.

In *Peru*, the Director-General of Copyright holds jurisdiction and authority to apply the preventive measures and penalties of a civil character laid down in Articles 129 to 132 of the Copyright Law in the case of the following infringements:
- the performance, recitation, reading and in general, presentation or use in public of a work without the written authorization of its author or of the association which represents him;
- failure to submit the performance schedules within the time-limits indicated by the owners of the copyright or the association representing them;
- failure to name the author in the aforementioned cases when the latter appears on publications or recordings of the work which is presented.

All other infringements of copyright fall within the competence of the courts, with the further proviso that the terms of reference granted to the administrative authorities shall not prevent the authors from opting for referral to the courts whenever they consider that procedure to be appropriate for the more effective defence of their rights. The Director-General of Copyright may require the intervention of the relevant political authority and the assistance of the police force if he considers that necessary (Supreme Decrees Nos. 61-62-ED, 1962 and 0024-91-ED, 1991).

E. SUBSTANTIATION OF COMPLAINTS ALLEGING INFRINGEMENTS IN RESPECT OF WORKS IN THE PUBLIC DOMAIN

In Argentina, after the expiration of the periods of protection of the private domain, the National Copyright Directorate is responsible for substantiating complaints denouncing mutilations, additions or transpositions as well as inaccuracy of a translation, errors of judgement and deficiencies in the knowledge of the language of the original or of the version of works in the public domain (Article 83). In Uruguay this function is entrusted to the Consejo de los Derechos de Autor (National Copyright Board) (Article 43).

F. INFORMATION

The National Copyright Directorate provides the public authorities and individuals concerned with information on matters falling within its competence as well as on legislation, case law and theory—national and foreign—in regard to copyright and neighbouring rights.

G. STATISTICS

When the National Copyright Directorate also performs a registration function, it is usually made responsible for the preparation of statistics with respect to the number of works registered and their category, contracts covering copyrighted works and other administrative procedures of relevance in providing knowledge concerning intellectual production and activities linked with authors and their works.

H. RESEARCH AND DISSEMINATION CONCERNING COPYRIGHT AND NEIGHBOURING RIGHTS

The National Copyright Directorate has an important role to play in promoting and improving the legal protection afforded by copyright and neighbouring rights and in undertaking scientific research and disseminating findings concerning these subjects, through the establishment of a specialized public library service, a system of information exchange with counterparts in countries abroad, the publication of research studies, the organization of seminars and conferences, and so on.

Chapter 10

Formalities

Summary

10.1. Legal deposit
10.2. The National Copyright Registry
    10.2.1. Classification of registration. **10.2.2.** Survival of registers for constituent purposes and application of the international conventions ('reverse inequality'). **10.2.3.** Effects, subject of registration and procedures; entries in the register; publication of applications; opposition to registration
10.3 Registration of instruments and contracts

Protection is not dependent on compliance with any particular formalities since copyright originates in the act of creation itself. No administrative recognition is necessary for the right of the author in his work to be established.[1]

This criterion governing protection, which sets copyright clearly apart from industrial property rights (in particular patent and trade mark rights), is not invalidated by the provisions concerning the *legal deposit* and *registration of works and instruments and contracts* laid down by domestic legislation, *provided that these requirements are not a condition for the enjoyment or the exercise of the author's rights.*

A number of copyright laws draw express attention to this fact, sometimes in their opening provisions, e.g. Article 9 of the Colombian law of 1982 ('the protection granted to the author by this Law originates in the fact of intellectual creation, without any registration being necessary. The formalities specified herein are for the greater legal security of the owners of the rights protected'); Article 3 of the law of the Dominican Republic of 1986

---

1. See above Chapter 2, Section 2.1.4.

('Copyright is an inherent right that derives from the creation of a work. The provisions contained in this Law are destined to make better known and to give greater legal protection to owners of the rights protected therein'); Article 101 of the Costa Rican law of 1982 ('The protection provided for in this Law originates with the mere fact of creation, independently of any procedure or formality'); Article 12 of the Portuguese law of 1985 ('Copyright shall be recognized independently of registration, filing or any other formality'); Article 1 of the Guatemalan law of 1954 ('Copyright recognized by this Law is conferred by the mere creation of the work, without the need for deposit, registration or any other formality'); and the recent laws of Bolivia, which contain a wording similar to that of the Guatemalan Statute in its Article 2, of El Salvador (Article 96), Honduras (Article 3), Venezuela—according to the 1993 amendment—(Article 107) and Panama (Article 107).

The Berne Convention made an important contribution to the practically universal acceptance which can be seen today of the criterion of the absence of formalities as a condition for the protection of authors' rights through the inclusion in Article 4, second paragraph, of the 1908 Berlin Convention of a provision which has remained unchanged ever since: *the enjoyment and the exercise of these rights shall not be subject to the performance of any formality*.

This criterion has been gradually embodied in theory and legislation, thus superseding the former registers which established rights and had developed out of the old system of privileges that enabled writings to be censored by the government authorities. The requirement for works to be entered in public registers lapsed as a prerequisite for the recognition of rights since it corresponded to an obsolete concept: the idea of special protection designed to prevent a work, once disclosed, from falling into the public domain so that anyone might make use of it unless rights in the work were acquired by completing certain formalities laid down by law. That notion has been replaced, following French tradition, in continental Europe—and in the United Kingdom as well through the influence of the Berne Convention—by the modern view of copyright according to which authors' rights are vested in full in the creator as soon as the work is created.

However, legislation has continued to lay down—although their scope and objectives differ from those pursued previously—provisions relating to legal deposit and registration. These are two separate concepts which, as Larrea Richerand has pointed out, coexist in many countries, and produce different effects; they may become confused and it is important, then, to make a clear distinction between them.[2]

10.1. Legal deposit

Legal deposit is an obligation imposed by law on the publishers of printed works and, in general, on the producers of copies of works, to deposit one or more such copies at certain libraries or archives, with the primary aim of centralizing and preserving the embodiments of intellectual production in the country concerned and of supplying this material to certain specified libraries or main archives. The works may be delivered directly to these libraries and archives, via a legal deposit centre or else through the National Copyright Register or some other official agency.

Dietz points out that provisions on legal deposit exist in nearly all the Member States of the European Union. He cites the Belgian law of 8 April 1965 which establishes a legal obligation to deposit copies with the Royal Library of Belgium; the German law of 31 March 1969 on the German Library; the French law of 21 June 1943 amending the system of compulsory legal deposits; Section 15 of the British Copyright Act of 1911 which was still in force in 1976, date of publication of the work; Section 56 of the Irish Copyright Act and Articles 103–106 of the Italian Copyright Law. This author stresses the fact that the requirements relating to legal deposit are not in actual fact copyright provisions but statutory requirements pertaining to the sphere of cultural administration. Their inclusion in copyright legislation in fact tends to make the latter cumbersome and confused. He cites the regulatory

---

2. Gabriel Larrea Richerand, 'Funciones del registro en la legislación comparada', in *Proceedings of the V International Congress on the Protection of Intellectual Property,* Buenos Aires, 1990, p. 141.

provision contained in Article 106 of the Italian Law as an example of this.

Likewise, Dietz points out that the obligation to make a legal deposit of copies is not a condition, in any Member State of the European Union, for the establishment of copyright protection, even if compliance with the relevant provisions may be imposed by measures of administrative constraint or by the threat of penalties for failure to comply. That is apparent from Article 106 of the Italian Law which expressly states in paragraph 1 that failure to deposit shall not affect the acquisition or exercise of copyright in protected works. Dietz is of the opinion that this is made even clearer by paragraph 2 of this same article which stipulates that 'the omission of a deposit required in Part II of this Law shall prevent the acquisition or exercise of rights in respect of works specified in that part and to the extent specified therein'. (Part II sets out provisions regulating the acquisition and exercise of neighbouring rights.)[3]

The copyright law of the Dominican Republic also stipulates in its Article 155 that

fulfilment of the obligation of legal deposit in conformity with the provisions of this Law is a *sine qua non* requirement for the registration of the works to be deposited, which will be carried out following presentation of the relevant receipts. Failure to fulfil the obligation of legal deposit shall give rise to payment of an amount equivalent to ten times the commercial value of the copies not deposited. This amount shall be paid jointly by the persons responsible for the said deposit, but it shall not restrict exercise of the rights laid down in this Law.

The legal deposit does not have the effect of registration even though in some countries both obligations (that of legal deposit and that of registration) are laid down in a single statute with no distinction between the two, e.g. in Argentina and Nicaragua.

In Argentina, Article 57 of the Copyright Statute reads as follows: 'The publisher of works included in Article 1 must, within three months of publication, deposit at the National Copyright

---

3. Adolf Dietz, *Copyright Law in the European Community*. Sijthoff and Noordhoff, Alphen aan den Rijn—The Netherlands, 1978, pp. 24–5.

Registry, three complete copies of every published work. In the case of a *de luxe* edition or of an edition not exceeding one hundred copies, it shall be sufficient to deposit one copy.' Decree No. 41.233/34 (1934) implementing the Statute stipulates in its Article 17 that publishers shall effect the deposit by the submission of three complete copies of a printed work, one for the National Library, one for the Library of the National Congress and the third for the National Copyright Registry, accompanied by receipts attesting that the former two copies have been delivered and by the necessary application. A requirement was later added for one further copy to be delivered to the General National Archives (Decree 3079, 1957) together with a stipulation that all these copies were to be submitted to the National Copyright Registry. However, the purpose of these four copies differs: while three are intended to comply with the obligation of legal deposit, the fourth ensures compliance with the obligation of registration.

In Nicaragua, the Civil Code stipulates that 'the author shall present six copies of every printed book to the chief governmental authority of his locality' (Article 832). One of these copies 'shall be for the National Library and one other for the General Archives' (Article 835).

In Costa Rica both requirements are set out in the same statutory provision (Article 106, amended by Law 7.397 of 3 May 1994), but a distinction is drawn between the legal deposit which must be made by the person reproducing a work with each of the eight institutions designated as the recipients on the one hand and registration with the appropriate body on the other: the National Library, the Library of the University of Costa Rica, the Library of the National University, the Library of the Legislative Assembly and the Library of the Ministry of Justice, the General Archives, the Technological Institute of Costa Rica and the National Registry of Copyrights and Related Rights.

In other countries, the legal deposit and registration provisions are set out in different laws, e.g. in Venezuela, Bolivia and Mexico.

In Venezuela, Article 106, paragraph 2, stipulates that the Registry of Intellectual Products shall deliver one of the originals or copies deposited by the authors, performers, producers or disclosers of the works to the Autonomous National Library and Library Services Institute. Such delivery shall not affect the deposit obligation provided for in the Law which specifies the sending of works to the National Library and other similar institutions.

In Bolivia, the Supreme Decrees of 1979 and 1981 reorganized and regulated the legislation on legal deposit by stipulating that this term denotes 'the mechanism which, on the basis of a law, requires registration without payment and the delivery of a specified number of copies of every published, recorded or filmed work intended for circulation, to the depositary bodies designated for that purpose'. An obligation is laid down to deposit one copy of all audiovisual works with the Bolivian Cinematographic Library; three copies of sound recordings and published musical works with the Department of Ethnomusicology of the Bolivian Cultural Institute; two copies of works of a geodesic, cartographic and related nature with the Military Geographical Institute; five copies of publications in the public and/or mixed sector with the Office for Legal Deposit at the Ministry of Planning and Co-ordination; five copies of private sector publications with the Legal Deposit offices coming under the Bolivian Cultural Institute. These deposits are separate from the register established by the Copyright Statute (in Articles 8 to 10 of the previous law and in Article 63 of the 1992 law).

Use of the term 'register' in statutory provisions on legal deposit tends to cause confusion between these two concepts, even though the institution responsible for receiving the legal deposit must keep a register (an official list) of the items received by it.

In Mexico, a Presidential Decree of 1965 stipulated that all publishers in the country must forward to the National Library and the Congress of the Union Library two copies of each of the editions of the books, periodicals and reviews published by them for commercial purposes. The same obligation exists in respect of publications which are distributed free of charge when they are educational, instructional, technical or scientific works of general interest. The Directorate for Copyright is required, in conjunction with the libraries which receive the legal deposit, to see that this requirement is complied with by fixing fines which will be imposed in the event of non-compliance.

Larrea Richerand points out that many Mexican publishers confused the obligation to forward a number of copies for deposit with the National Library and the Congress of the Union Library with registration for copyright purposes. This confusion (as a result of which they ceased to register their works and contracts with the Public Copyright Register) was compounded, firstly, by the mistaken idea that the provisions on copyright gave them 'automatic' protection, whereas this automatic protection in fact applies to the authors and not to publishers, and, secondly, by a failure to realize that, pursuant to Article 114 of the Law, contracts took effect from the time of their entry in the Register. The result was a situation in which publishers were not effectively protected by copyright law in Mexico.[4]

Even though legal deposit, as distinct from the copyright register, lacks the effect of registration, it may nevertheless constitute evidence for certain legal purposes, e.g. to prove the fact of publication, or the year of such publication, or else the existence of a previously published work in actions on grounds of plagiarism. Then again it may constitute evidence of falsification in a 'pirated' edition by providing a means of comparison with the legitimate copy forwarded to the library or archives for the purpose of legal deposit.

10.2. The National Copyright Registry

The National Copyright Registry is the public agency responsible for registering works protected by copyright, the copies resulting from their exploitation and the indications relating thereto and also to authors, and the ownership of rights and other instruments and contracts[5] stipulated by domestic legislation for the purpose of *publicity* in order to satisfy the collective need for *legal certainty*.

Article 193 of the Colombian Law defines the purpose of

---

4. Gabriel Larrea Richerand, op cit., p. 142–3.
5. The registration of instruments and contracts in particular is discussed separately in Section 10.3.

registration of works and instruments subject to that formality as follows:

(a) to publicize the rights of the owners and the instruments and contracts that transfer or alter the ownership covered by the Law; and
(b) to give a guarantee of authenticity and security to the titles of intellectual property and to the instruments and documents referring thereto.

The Dominican Law adds in its Article 143: '(c) to publicize the constitution of societies of authors and performers'.

The primary purpose of the copyright register as a source of publicity reflects the modern understanding of this subject. In the now obsolete approach, the registration of a work had, in the first place, a 'constituent' effect since registration was a prerequisite for acquiring and upholding copyright. The same concept is also reflected in the registers established as a condition for the exercise of rights in legal proceedings or for the exclusive exploitation of a published work.

10.2.1. Classification of registration

Antequera Parilli points out that the nature of the register differs in national legislation according to the objective pursued. The following classification may be established:
- registration as a prerequisite for the constitution and existence of the right;
- registration as a requirement for the exercise of the right;
- registration with a declaratory function or serving to provide proof.[6]

A. REGISTRATION AS A PREREQUISITE FOR THE CONSTITUTION AND EXISTENCE OF A RIGHT

This is a derivative of the old registers established at the time when privileges existed, the governmental authority granting, at its own discretion, a monopoly of exploitation for a fixed period

---

6. Ricardo Antequera Parilli, *Consideraciones sobre el derecho de autor* (*con especial referencia a la legislación venezolana*), Buenos Aires, 1977, p. 283.

of time to printers and booksellers, provided that they had obtained the approval of the censors and had registered the published work.[7]

This concept of the register gained a firm foothold in Latin America under the influence of the Spanish Law of 1879 (now abrogated) which contained the following provision in its Article 36:

In order to enjoy the benefits of this Law, it shall be necessary for registration to be effected in the Copyright Register established in accordance with the provisions of the foregoing articles [...]. The time for effecting registration shall be one year, reckoned from the date of publication of work; however, the author shall enjoy the benefits of the Law from the date upon which publication began and he shall only lose such rights if he fails to fulfil the necessary requirements within the period of one year allowed for registration.

Failure to effect registration resulted in the provisional or definitive loss of rights (Article 38: 'Any work which is not entered in the Copyright Register may, during a period of ten years counted from the date upon which the right to apply for registration expired, be republished by the State, by scientific corporate bodies or by private individuals through reprinting', and Article 39: 'If a further period of one year elapses following the said period of ten years without the author or his successor in title having entered the work in the Register the work shall pass definitely and absolutely into the public domain').

That law was the precursor of all the domestic Latin American legislation which took over its principles with some changes:[8] Argentina (1933 Law, Articles 57 and 63); Bolivia (1909 Law, Articles 10 to 12); Colombia (1946 Law, Article 88); Costa Rica (1896 Law, Article 53); Cuba (which simply adopted the Spanish Law); Chile (Decree-Law of 1925 and Amending Act of 1949,

---

7. See above, Chapter 1, Section 1.2.
8. In Spain, the provisions of the Law of 10 January 1879 were only superseded as a result of the Law of 11 November 1987 in which the requirement of compulsory registration and the constituent purpose were rescinded, while the General Register of Intellectual Property was maintained.

Article 1); Ecuador (1927 Law, Article 25); El Salvador (1963 Law, Article 77); Nicaragua (Civil Code of 1904, Article 831); Panama (Administrative Code of 1916, Article 1912); Paraguay (Law of 1951, Article 58); Uruguay (1937 Law, Article 6), and so on.

In Nicaragua and Uruguay, the register is still a precondition for the constitution and existence of the right: in Nicaragua, Article 831 of the Civil Code stipulates that 'in order to acquire copyright, the author or his representative must apply to the Ministry of Development (Fomento) to secure the legal recognition of his right'; in Uruguay, Article 6 of the Law on Literary and Artistic Property provides that 'entry in the appropriate Register shall be required in order to secure the protection of this law'.[9]

B. REGISTRATION AS A REQUIREMENT FOR THE EXERCISE OF THE RIGHT

This type of registration shares the characteristics defined above. Although the author is the owner of the right, he must register his work in order to exercise that right.

a. In the United States of America, compliance with the registration requirement is a condition for the exercise of the right for all legal purposes.

The United States Act of 1976 stipulates in its Section 411 that

> no action for infringement of the copyright in any work shall be instituted until registration of the copyright claim has been made. However, where the deposit, application and fee required for registration have been delivered to the Copyright Office 'in proper form' and registration has been refused, the applicant is entitled to institute an action for infringement if notice thereof, with a copy of the complaint, is served on the Register of Copyrights. The Register may, at his or her option, become a party to the action with respect to the issue of registrability of the copyright claim by entering an appearance within 60 days after such service, but the Register's failure to become a party shall not deprive the court of jurisdiction to determine that issue.

---

9. See below, Section 10.2.2, A—interpretation of the effects of the Berne Convention on this provision of the Uruguayan law.

In conformity with the Berne Convention Implementation Act of 1988 by which the United States brought its legislation into line with the Berne Convention with effect from 1 March 1989, registration as a prerequisite to take action in the courts on grounds of infringement does not apply to works protected under the Berne Convention whose country of origin is other than the United States of America (Section 411(a)).

However, even in the case of works originating in the countries of the Berne Union, the United States Act continues to encourage registration (together with the mention of reserved rights—copyright notice)[10] although compliance is no longer compulsory. It does so through provisions whose compatibility with international law is highly dubious:
- in the case of all works, regardless of their country of origin, registration effected within five years of their publication confers upon them a *prima facie* presumption of originality and ownership;
- registration is a prerequisite for the award of 'statutory damages', i.e. the statutory compensation provided for in Section 504[11] and attorney's fees (Section 412);
- the registration of a document with the Copyright Office gives all persons formal notice of the facts stated in the recorded document, but only if the document has been registered (Section 205, para. (c)).[12]

b. Another variant of registration as a prerequisite for the exercise of copyright, is the provision which requires published works to be registered as a condition for the exclusive right to exploit them. Even though the author is the owner of his rights, should the publisher fail to comply with the registration requirement, the rights of exploitation will be deprived of their most important feature, namely exclusivity effective *erga omnes*.

Registration provisions of this kind apply in Argentina (Article 57: 'The publisher of works included in Article 1 must, within

---

10. See above, Chapter 1, Section 1.3.5.
11. See below, Chapter 11, Section 11.4. A.
12. See Leafer, *Understanding Copyright Law*, p. 190.

three months of publication, deposit at the National Copyright Registry three complete copies of every published work ...'; and Article 63:

> Failure to register shall result in the suspension of the rights of the author until such registration is accomplished. The rights of the author shall be recovered by the act of registration for the corresponding term and under corresponding conditions, without prejudice to the validity of the reproductions, editions, performances or any other publications made during the time the work was unregistered)

and in Paraguay (Article 50): 'To obtain the necessary registration, the publisher shall, within three months following the appearance of a work, deposit in the Registry two complete copies thereof ...', and Article 58 which is similar to Article 63 of the Argentine Law); in Paraguay, Article 2184 of the Civil Code enacted by Law 1.183 of 1985 has strengthened the registration obligation as a condition for copyright protection.

It will be noted once again that this registration relates solely to *published works* and that the obligation rests with the *publisher*. On the other hand, *the registration of unpublished works is optional* (Argentina, Article 62: '... In the case of unpublished works, the author or his successors in title *may* deposit a copy of the manuscript...'; and Paraguay, Article 57: 'In the case of an unpublished work, the author shall be *entitled* to register it ...').

C. REGISTRATION FOR DECLARATORY PURPOSES OR TO PROVIDE PROOF

This does not conflict with the legal foundation of author's rights, provided that it is not a condition for the enjoyment or exercise of copyright.

Article 151 of the Dominican Law embodies this principle in the following terms:

> Inclusion in the Register shall not guarantee the content nor does it constitute procedural admissibility for the exercise of the rights granted by this law. It only establishes the presumption of certainty concerning the facts and instruments recorded therein, in the absence of proof to the contrary. Registration excludes the rights of third parties.

Even when registration of this type is compulsory, *failure to register is not prejudicial to the copyright* (Article 106 of the Italian Law and Article 8 of the Mexican Law); it is generally punishable by a fine.

In Portugal registration is optional, *with the exception* of the title of a work which has not yet been published and the titles of newspapers and other periodical publications (Article 214), in which case *it is a condition for protection.*

In Colombia, the Supreme Court ruled, in Decision 9673 of 26 July 1984,[13] that a provision with similar effects set out in the second part of Article 209, was unconstitutional (the provision states that when the managers and directors of journals, reviews and, in general, all periodical publications, fail to comply on three consecutive occasions with the obligation to submit three copies of each of their publications, the registration of the title of the publication shall be cancelled by a decision accompanied by a statement of grounds).

The compatibility between registration with effects of presumption *juris tantum* of the veracity of the recorded declarations and the automatic protection established under the Berne Convention, has recently been highlighted with the creation of the International Registration of Audiovisual Works.[14]

10.2.2. Survival of registers for constituent purposes and application of the international conventions ('reverse inequality')

In the countries in which registers with constituent effects, or registers which affect the exercise of authors' rights still exist, the application of the multilateral international copyright conventions —the Berne Convention and the Universal Convention—produces 'reverse' inequality.

---

13. See CLTW, Item I, UNESCO/Bureau of National Affairs, Inc., Washington, D.C., 1984, p. 24.
14. See below, Chapter 12, Section 12.4.2.4 dealing with the WIPO Treaty on the International Registration of Audiovisual Works (Geneva, 20 April 1989).

A. THE BERNE CONVENTION

We have already pointed out that since the Berlin revision (1908), the Berne Convention establishes automatic protection ('the enjoyment and the exercise of these rights shall not be subject to the performance of any formality',[15] a principle which applies to all the works covered by the Union. It follows that in Argentina, Paraguay and Uruguay which belong to the Berne Union, protection of the author of a national published work is subject to compliance with a registration requirement, while authors of works belonging to the Berne Union are protected by the very act of creation without the need to perform any formality.

Since the Convention is not directly applicable in the country of origin of the work,[16] a situation of 'reverse inequality' exists, i.e. the authors of national works enjoy less effective protection than the authors of foreign works. The question arises as to whether this situation is admissible. In a previous study,[17] we drew attention to the fact that in some cases this circumstance has been held to affect the constitutional guarantee of equality before the law; on other occasions, emphasis has been placed on the paradoxical situation which results from the application of the principle of equal treatment for foreigners and nationals[18] if there is no equivalence in the other sense, in other words if a national does not enjoy rights as extensive as those granted to a foreigner.

Attention has been drawn to the fact that the principle of national treatment is founded on a still wider principle: that of the absence of discrimination between nationals and foreigners, bound up with the recognized nature of copyright as a basic hu-

---

15. Article 4, paragraph 1 of the Brussels Act (1948) and Article 5, paragraph 1 of the Paris Act (1971).
16. Article 4, paragraph 1, of the Brussels Act and Article 5, paragraph 3 of the Paris Act.
17. Delia Lipszyc, 'El plazo de protección post-mortem y la aplicación de los Convenios internacionales', in *Proceedings of the VII International Congress*, Santiago, Chile, 1992, pp. 344–5.
18. Article 4, paragraph 1 of the Brussels Act and Article 5, paragraph 1 of the Paris Act.

man right (Article 27, paragraph 2, of the Universal Declaration of Human Rights, Paris 1948, Article XIII of the American Declaration of the Rights and Duties of Man, Bogotá, 1948, and Article 15.1 of the International Covenant on Economic, Social and Cultural Rights, New York, 1966). In the countries whose political constitutions grant foreigners the same civil rights as nationals, the question arises as to whether the legal consequence of this principle of equality does not create an entitlement of the owners of national works to the exercise of the most favourable rights enjoyed by their counterparts who are authors of works within the Union.

The possibility that the owners of rights in national works may claim the higher level of protection enjoyed by the authors of works within the Union, and the reasons for doing so, will depend on the constitution of each State and on the effects which the accession to international treaties is recognized as having on domestic law.

In Uruguay, having regard to the contradiction between the formal requirement of registration as a condition for securing protection established in Article 6 of the Law, and the automatic protection adopted in the Berne Convention, Romeo Grompone, citing the opinion of Eduardo Jiménez de Aréchaga[19] on the supremacy of international law over domestic law maintains that Decree-law No. 14.910 of 19 July 1979 which approved the Paris Act eliminated 'the need for compliance with formalities on the basis of the overriding criterion that the international norm takes hierarchical precedence over domestic law'. He goes on to point out that in general

in the case of statutory provisions which, without falling within the scope of the previous paragraph (provisions which go beyond the minimum required by the Berne Convention) nevertheless create a contradiction between the precepts of domestic law and those of the Convention, the latter must hold sway.[20]

---

19. *Curso de Derecho Internacional Público*, Vol. I, p. 213.
20. *Uruguay y la Unión de Berna, Modificaciones a la ley del 17 de diciembre de 1937*; Montevideo, AGADU, 1979, pp. 10–11 and 14.

In a subsequent ruling of 13 May 1987, the Civil Appeal Court, third rota, held that 'In regard to the failure of the author to effect registration pursuant to the requirement set out in Article 6 of Law 9739, it will be noted that this provision has ceased to be valid following the ratification by Uruguay of the Berne Convention in respect of literary and artistic works by Decree-Law No. 14.910 of 19 July 1979 (Article 5).'[21]

B. THE UNIVERSAL COPYRIGHT CONVENTION

The Convention stipulates in its Article III, paragraph 1, that

> Any Contracting State which, under its domestic law, requires as a condition of copyright, compliance with formalities such as deposit, registration, notice, notarial certificates, payment of fees or manufacture or publication in that Contracting State, shall regard these requirements as satisfied with respect to all works protected in accordance with this Convention and first published outside its territory and the author of which is not one of its nationals, if from the time of the first publication, all the copies of the work published with the authority of the author or other copyright proprietor bear the symbol © accompanied by the name of the copyright proprietor and the year of first publication....

Nicaragua has acceded to the Universal Convention so that in the case of works by foreign authors it is sufficient to use the symbol © in the form stipulated in Article III of the Convention, while works published for the first time on the national territory of this country must be registered on pain of failure to acquire copyright or of being unable to exercise it.

10.2.3. Effects, subject of registration and procedures; entries in the register; publication of applications; opposition to registration[22]

A. EFFECTS

Registration of a work creates a presumption *juris tantum* of the existence of the work on a given date (this being of particular

---

21. Montevideo, LJU, Case 1130, pp. 126–7.
22. In general, we shall not deal here with the obligations relating to the registration of instruments and contracts; these are discussed in Section 10.3.

importance in the case of unpublished works), of its title and content, its author (and, where appropriate, translator and adapter), its publication, the form in which it exists (publication, sound recording, audiovisual fixation, etc.), its publisher or producer, and performers;[23] whoever has recourse to the register is freed from the obligation of providing proof for the *onus probandi* is reversed: anyone who contests the indications appearing in the register must prove that they are untrue.

As to the status of the author, the presumption may arise not only from the register but also from the indication of his name or pseudonym on the work in the accustomed manner in compliance with the provisions of Article 15, paragraph 1, of the Berne Convention which are reflected in certain domestic legislations, sometimes with a wider scope, e.g. the Venezuelan Law[24] and among others, the Mexican Law (Article 17).

The *evidence provided* by entries in the register plays a vital role for it makes it very much simpler to adduce appropriate proof when the authorship of a work is contested and when infringements consisting of unauthorized use, plagiarism and other offences against copyright and neighbouring rights are pursued in the courts.

B. SUBJECT OF REGISTRATION

All works protected by copyright, either unpublished or published, in the form of books, leaflets and other printed matter, may be

---

23. Article 80 of the Peruvian Law expressly states that 'registration produces the following effects: (1) all rights, acts, contracts and documents recorded shall be presumed to be true without prejudice to anything the Court of Justice may finally resolve [...]'.

24. In which Article 7 stipulates that '[...] it shall, in the absence of proof to the contrary, be presumed that the author of the work is the person whose name is indicated, as such, in the customary manner in the work or, where appropriate, the person who is announced as author in any performance of the work. For the purpose of the foregoing provision, the use of a pseudonym or any other indication which does not give rise to doubts as to the identity of the person presenting himself as author of the work may be assimilated with the indication of his name.'

registered together with cinematographic and other audiovisual works; drawings, paintings, sculptures, engravings, lithographs and works of architecture (plans, models, etc.); photographic works and works produced by similar techniques; two-dimensional artistic works applied to three-dimensional objects; maps and other geographical and topographical works, etc.; data carriers for computer programs and databases; phonograms (records and cassettes), etc.

Pseudonyms may also be registered (Costa Rica, Article 98; Mexico, Article 17). Such registration confers upon the author who avails himself of the pseudonym the right to make exclusive use thereof and to claim as his own works which are published in this form.[25] In addition, this pseudonym registration may have a decisive bearing on the period of protection of the work where the duration of protection of anonymous and pseudonymous works (when the pseudonym is equivalent to anonymity) is calculated from the date of publication (*post publicationem operis*) and not from the death of the author (*post mortem auctoris*).

C. REGISTRATION PROCEDURE

Formal registration is effected by presenting the work, or the elements representing the work, together with the material and documentation required for registration. The form in which copies of the works are to be presented for registration differs depending on whether they are unpublished or published and on their nature. The National Copyright Registers often have to lay down additional provisions to cover new forms of utilization of works.

In Argentina, unpublished works are submitted in a single copy in a sealed envelope. In the case of paintings, works of architecture, sculptures, etc. registration is made by submitting a sketch or photograph of the original, with additional indications permitting its identification. In the case of cinematographic works

---

25. See Hilda Retondo, 'Las funciones del registro en la legislación comparada. El tratado sobre el registro internacional de obras audiovisuales', in *Proceedings of the V International Congress*, Buenos Aires, 1990, p. 125.

and other audiovisual works, Article 57 of the Law stipulates that the deposit shall consist of an account of the plot, the dialogues and photographs and descriptions of the principal scenes, although today it has become normal for a video-cassette copy to be presented for registration.

The accumulation of works in the archives of the Registry generally poses problems of space which are hard to solve. One possible solution is the replacement of the copy of the work, for example, by a microfilm. In general, the methods involved are expensive and in some cases it is doubtful whether they can fully replace the original copy for the purpose of proof.

In the case of periodical publications, a special registration system has been introduced in Argentina (Article 30 of the Law) whereby registration is effected by submitting a copy of the last published issue; registration is renewed annually and the numeration and date of the copies published must be declared at monthly intervals to the Registry on the appropriate form. The owners of the registered periodical publications shall make a collection consisting of a copy of each publication, stamped with the words '*Ejemplar ley 11.723*' and shall be responsible for the authenticity thereof. The Registry may at any time require the submission of the copies in the collection and may verify compliance with the obligation. Failure to comply is punishable with a fine. If publication ceases definitively, the stamped collection must be sent to the National Library within six months from the expiration of the last registration; failure to comply with this obligation is punishable with a fine (submission of the collection to the National Library is a *legal deposit* requirement).

D. ENTRIES IN THE REGISTER

These are generally organized in separate sections, i.e.:
- indications relating to the works (including the instruments of acquisition, transfer and modification of rights in them, notes on precautionary measures, etc.);
- pseudonyms;
- publishers, cinematographic producers, phonogram producers, etc. and representatives of authors, including collective administration bodies;

- compulsory licences (for example, Article V of the Universal Copyright Convention).

This list is purely illustrative.

Use is made of a system of numbered sheets ('*folio real*') in entering references to the work as such.

Full details of the form in which the registration is habitually made will be found in the description set out in the 'Rules for Entries in the National Copyright Register of Peru' (Reglamento de inscripciones en el Registro Nacional de Derechos de Autor del Perú) adopted in 1989, which stipulate that the entries are to be made according to the '*folio real*' system, a separate sheet or card known as the 'Registration Record' being opened for each work, or, where appropriate, for each instrument, contract or judicial decision by virtue of which authors' rights are transferred, assigned, regulated, modified, encumbered or affected in cases where the work to which the latter measures relate has not been entered in the register. The 'Registration Record' will contain all the relevant entries (Article 38).

Each sheet or card known as the 'Registration Record' is numbered and contains a summary of the following information:
- the title of the work;
- the name of the author or authors, compiler, translator or co-ordinator and their pseudonyms where appropriate (if the work is anonymous or published under a pseudonym which is equivalent to anonymity, the entry shall be made by treating the publisher as the owner of copyright unless the author appears and proves his identity as such (Article 45);
- the name or legal style of the owner of the right if he is not the author;
- the key data concerning the work;
- the date of presentation;
- the number of the Registration Record;
- the date of the registration (Article 39).

The extension, modification or cancellation of any registered right shall require a new entry recording the circumstance concerned. These entries shall be made in the 'Registration Record' corresponding to the work or instrument, contract or legal decision concerned in a successive order without repeating the same number twice (Article 40).

For the purpose of entry in the register, any work whose content has undergone substantial modification shall be treated as a new work. Modifications confined to straightforward corrections, changes or additions shall be treated as a version of the existing work and an additional entry on the same sheet or card shall be used to identify them (Article 43).

In the case of unpublished works, the date of creation shall be deemed, for registration purposes, to be the date of presentation to the Registry, except where the application for an entry has been accompanied by a document showing a particular date, in which case that date shall appear in the register (Article 44). Once the registration has been made, the party concerned shall be given a certificate recording the basic information from the entry made in response to his application (Article 42).

E. PUBLICATION OF APPLICATIONS; OPPOSITION TO REGISTRATION

National laws habitually contain provisions (similar to those normally used in the area of industrial property) requiring publication in the Official Gazette of works presented for entry in the National Copyright Register, together with such other formalities as the Copyright Directorate considers necessary, with an indication of the title, author, publisher, category to which the work belongs and other data necessary for its identification, a time limit being set for lodging opposition to an entry. If opposition is made, substantiation and settlement of the matter shall rest with the Registry; the decision, which is habitually open to appeal through the hierarchical channels, is subject to the normal verification of the legality of administrative acts (Argentina, Articles 59 and 60; Mexico, Article 134).

10.3. Registration of instruments and contracts

The registration of instruments and contracts, which is also effected at the National Copyright Registry, generally covers:
- instruments and contracts which authorize the exploitation of protected works and transfer, modify or assign in any manner whatsoever, the economic rights of the author;

- instruments of foundation and statutes of the agencies responsible for the collective administration of authors' rights and neighbouring rights, together with amendments thereto;
- agreements on representation between collective administration bodies which operate in the country concerned and those which operate abroad;
- general powers of attorney to administer authors' rights and neighbouring rights.

The following are also entered in the Register:
- assignments of authors' rights *'mortis causa'*; and
- precautionary measures.

The register of instruments and contracts (which establishes certainty as to the date and content) is effective *erga omnes* by virtue of publicity given by registration to the instrument concerned. It will be noted that the term 'publicity' in this context does not signify advertising and circulation, but rather the possibility of taking cognizance of the information;[26] 'from the formal point of view of disclosure of the content of the register, the activity of the registration body is specific and confined solely to those persons who seek access to the registered information'.[27]

Legislation differs from country to country in respect of the scope of registration of instruments and contracts:
- in *Mexico*, 'any agreement which authors conclude which in any way modifies, transmits, encumbers or extinguishes the patrimonial rights conferred by this Law *shall take effect from the date of its registration in the Copyright Register*' (Article 114). Once the contract has been entered, registration shall create the presumption that the facts and acts therein stated are correct, unless the contrary is proved although 'all entries are without prejudice to the rights of third parties' (Article 122). However 'registered acts or contracts agreed upon or entered into by persons whom the Register shows to possess rights shall

---

26. J. L. Lacruz Berdejo and F. de A. Sancho Rebullida, *Derecho Inmobiliario Registral*, Barcelona, 1968, p. 11, cited by A. R. Coghlan, *Teoría general de derecho inmobiliario registral*, Buenos Aires, Abeledo-Perrot, 1991, p. 15.
27. Antonio R. Coghlan, op. cit., p. 14.

not become invalid to the prejudice of a third party acting in good faith, even though the original entry may subsequently be annulled' (Article 123);
- *Chile* (Articles 73 and 74) lays down a provision similar to Article 114 of the Mexican Law, although only in respect of the rights of the party who contracts with the author;
- *Colombian Law* stipulates that, to be effective against third parties, any instrument disposing of copyright, whether wholly or in part, shall only be valid if it is registered (Article 183);
- on the other hand, in *Venezuela* registration of instruments and contracts is optional (Article 105: 'May also be registered [...]');
- in *Argentina* (Article 53) registration is required simply as a condition for the validity of the total or partial assignment of economic rights 'otherwise such assignment shall not be valid'. Spota points out in this regard that the 'contract of assignment of intellectual property rights is completed by virtue of the sole consent of the assigning author and of the assignee who acquires the economic right. This contract is therefore consensual and the entry in the Register recognizes the completion of the contract but is not a precondition for the existence of the agreement as such. In consequence, when the law stipulates that the contract "shall be not valid" unless it is entered in the Register, this expression is inappropriate since the intention was to refer to the opposability of the assignment *vis-à-vis* third parties (*erga omnes*). But the contract is concluded even before the entry is made in the Register and either of the contracting parties acquires the optional right to require the other contracting party to participate in the registration of the assignment which has taken place. What is more, this entry may be requested by one of the contracting parties without the co-operation of the other, if the work concerned has already been published (Article 66, of the law already cited)'.[28]

---

28. Alberto G. Spota, *Instituciones de derecho civil. Contratos*, Buenos Aires, Ed. Depalma, 1981, Vol. VI, pp. 340–1.

Chapter 11

Infringements and other unlawful activities. Penalties

Summary

11.1. Classification of infringements
    11.1.1. Legal protection (penal sanctions). 11.1.2. Criteria for the application of penal sanctions. 11.1.3. Punitive measures. The 'open' approach to classification. 11.1.4. Categories of offences
11.2. Penal sanctions
11.3. Right to restrain the unlawful activity
11.4. Compensation for prejudice suffered
11.5. Procedural rules
11.6. Preventive measures

11.1. Classification of infringements

The classification of infringements depends on each body of legislation, although penalties are always stipulated in copyright legislation. Provision is generally also made for preventive measures.[1] Legislation which lacked sanctions to punish infringements of rights would serve no purpose.

In turn, preventive measures play a vital role in avoiding the occurrence of infringements. They may also ensure that copies, goods or litigious objects be seized for use as evidence and so prevent their disappearance or conversion, since uses that infringe copyright may be transient and it may also be relatively easy to dispose of the evidence. These measures may be sought before instituting proceedings and even before the infringement has occurred.

---

1. See Claude Colombet, *Major Principles of Copyright and Neighbouring Rights in the World,* Paris, UNESCO, 1987, p. 81.

11.1.1. Legal protection (penal sanctions)

In general, infringements of authors' rights are defined in the relevant specific law (as, for example, in Argentina, Bolivia, Colombia, Costa Rica, Chile, Dominican Republic, Italy, Mexico, Portugal, United Kingdom, Uruguay and Venezuela).

In some legal regimes, relevant provision for such infringements is made in the Penal Code (for example, Brazil, Articles 184 to 186; Spain, Article 534*bis*(a) to (c) and 534*ter*, and Peru, Articles 216 to 220, etc.). In France, the law of 1957 (Articles 70 to 74, now Intellectual Property Code, Articles L. 335-2 to L. 335-7) and then the law of 1985 (Articles 56 to 61, now Articles L. 335-4, L. 335-1 and L. 335-5 to 335-7) amended the wording of Articles 425 to 429 of the Penal Code which has traditionally governed the protection of literary and artistic property in that country and are regarded as the appropriate legal basis for this purpose (*le siège du sujet*).[2]

Penal codes often contain a stipulation to the effect that their general provisions concerning the infringement of authors' rights shall be applicable to all the infringements defined in special laws, save where otherwise provided in the latter (for example Argentine Penal Code, Article 4). The laws define certain infringements of the author's economic rights and moral rights and often also those of the performers and the economic rights of the producers of phonograms; on occasion, the economic rights of broadcasting organizations are defined.

In some countries whose legislation on this matter is relatively recent, a joint definition is given of infringements of copyright and neighbouring rights and the same penalties are imposed to punish such offences. These penalties are sometimes set out in the same provisions (for example, Bolivia, Article 68; Costa Rica, Article 117 *et seq.*; Colombia, Law 44 of 1993, Article 51 *et seq.*; Spain, Penal Code, Article 534*bis*(a) to (c), and 534*ter*) or in a joint sec-

---

2. André Françon, *Cours de propriété littéraire, artistique et industrielle*, Paris, Les Cours de Droit, 1985–86, p. 350.

tion (Portugal, Title IV, 'Infringement and Protection of Copyright and Related Rights').

In other countries, offences against neighbouring rights are dealt with separately, as, for example, in France where a special article was embodied in the Penal Code in 1985 (Article 426-1) and in Argentina where the 1989 Law added to the Law on Intellectual Property an Article 72*bis* which defines the unauthorized reproduction of phonograms (phonographic piracy); in both these cases, the penalties are the same as those stipulated to punish infringements of copyright. But in other instances, where separate statutory provisions exist, the penalties are different (for example in Ecuador, in Decree 2821 (1978), amended in 1992, and in the Congo, 1982 Law on Copyright and Neighbouring Rights).

11.1.2. Criteria for the application of penal sanctions

- The work must be protected by application of the general principles on the protection of works (see above Chap. 2, Sect. 2.1).
- The particular use must not fall within the scope of a limitation of copyright or of neighbouring rights.
- The period of protection must still be in force, i.e. the right must not have lapsed.
- The action of the infringer must correspond to a specific case of infringement, as defined.
- The infringer must have committed an intentional wrong (*dolus*).[3]

---

3. Among the *legal experts who subscribe to the principle of causality*, Sebastian Soler is of the opinion that 'fraudulent intent exists not only when a result has been sought, but also where the infringer was aware of the illicit nature of his own act but *nevertheless committed it*' (*Derecho penal argentino*, Buenos Aires, TEA, 1951, Vol. II, p. 115); among the legal experts who favour the doctrine of *finalism*, Eugenio R. Zaffaroni maintains that fraudulent intent is the 'deliberate intent of an objective nature, guided by a knowledge of the facts at issue in each concrete instance' (*Manual de derecho penal, Parte general*, Buenos Aires, Ediar, p. 339); Rodolfo A. Iribarne notes that 'infringements of authors' rights involve fraudulent intent. An involuntary error precludes fraudulent intent', 'El estado actual de la jurisprudencia en la represión penal', in *Proceedings of*

- The profit motive is not an indispensable feature of the specific cases of infringement of copyright and neighbouring rights, save where the statutory provision in which the infringement is defined expressly so stipulates (for example in Argentina, Article 72*bis*, paras. (a), (b) and (c), which deal with various kinds of phonographic piracy and in Chile, Article 80(b) concerning various forms of phonographic piracy, piracy of audiovisual works and computer programs).

11.1.3. Punitive measures. The 'open' approach to classification

In France (and in other countries which apply the French criterion, such as Algeria, Cameroon, Senegal, etc.) infringements of authors' rights are referred to under the generic name of '*contrefaçon*'. According to Article 425, paras. 1 and 2, of the French Penal Code:

> any publication of writings, musical composition, drawings, paintings or any other production, printed or engraved either wholly or partially, in violation of the laws and regulations relating to the rights of authors is a *contrefaçon*; every such *contrefaçon* is an offence.
>
> *Contrefaçon* in France of works published in France or abroad is punishable by a term of imprisonment ranging from three months to two years and a fine from 6,000 Francs to 120,000 Francs or either of these two penalties alone.

Paragraph 3 of Article 425 adds: 'The same penalties shall apply to the sale, export and import of such infringing works'; while according to Article 426: 'Reproduction, performances or circulation, by any means whatsoever, of a work of the mind in violation of the rights of the author, as defined and regulated by the law,[4] shall also constitute an offence of *contrefaçon*'.

According to Colombet, infringement or *contrefaçon*, whose applicability is likely to vary, may be almost universally defined as

---

the V International Congress, Buenos Aires, 1990, p. 252. He goes on to state that 'an error will generally be invoked in relation to the existence of an authorization' ('Los nuevos delitos fonográficos', in *Derechos Intelectuales*, Buenos Aires, Astrea, No. 5/1991, p. 198).
4. French Intellectual Property Code, Articles L. 335-2 and 335-3.

a breach of the rights of the author and in particular of his economic rights—with the exception of *'droit de suite'*, which generally gives rise only to an award for damages.[5]

In Portugal, the Code of Copyright and Related Rights deals in its Article 195, paragraph 1, with the offence of illegal exercise of rights and in its Article 196, paragraph 1, with the offence of infringement in the following terms:

Article 195(1): 'Any person who, without the authorization of the author or performer, the producer of the phonogram or videogram or the broadcasting organization, uses a work or performance for any of the uses provided for in this Code, shall be guilty of the offence of illegal exercise of rights'; Article 196(1): 'Any person who unlawfully represents as being his own creation or performance, a performance, a phonogram, videogram or broadcast programme which reproduces in whole or in part another person's work or performance, whether disclosed or not, or in such a way that it does not have its own specificity, shall be guilty of the offence of infringement.'

Commenting on these statutory provisions, Rebello points out that in a ruling handed down by a Lisbon court on 24 May 1941, the 'unauthorized and illicit appropriation of a work' was deemed to constitute an illegal exercise of rights, while 'the imitation or fraudulent alteration of a work' was held to constitute an offence of infringement'.[6]

The Latin American countries tend to adopt an 'open' classification (for example Argentina, Article 71,[7] Brazil, Penal Code, Article 184;[8] Chile, Article 78.[9] This has to do, no doubt, with the

---

5. See Claude Colombet, op. cit., p. 81.
6. Luiz Francisco Rebello, *Código do direito de autor e dos direitos conexos anotado, legislaçao complementar e convençoes internacionais*, Lisbon, Livraria Petrony, 1985, p. 248.
7. Argentina, Article 71: 'Any person who in any manner or in any form infringes the copyright recognized by this Law shall be liable to the penalty established by Article 172 of the Penal Code.'
8. Brazil, Penal Code, Article 184: 'Violation of copyright: Penalty— Detention for three months to one year or a fine of [...].'
9. Chile, Article 78: 'Violations of this Law shall be punished with fines from 5 to 50 monthly accounting units. The same sanction shall apply to violations of the Regulations.'

difficulty—due to the continuous progress of technology—of making advance provision for all possible infringements of copyright and neighbouring rights.[10]

However, both extremes—jeopardizing the guarantees afforded by criminal law or leaving the legal property unprotected —may lead to equally adverse situations. It is therefore preferable, whenever possible, for a detailed classification of infringements of copyright and neighbouring rights to be set out, having regard to their particular characteristics and to the rules which apply to the drafting of criminal law.[11]

In Spain the criminal law provisions adopted in 1987 simultaneously with the new protection of intellectual property, are

---

10. In Costa Rica, the Constitutional Division of the Supreme Court of Justice, in a ruling handed down on 9 October 1992, declared paragraph (c) of Article 117 of the Copyright Law (No. 6683, 1982) to be unconstitutional and, hence, null and void, inasmuch as the Article in question provided that: 'The following shall be punished by imprisonment for one to three months: [...] (c) the person who violates any provision of this Law, where such offence is not punished by another specific penalty.' The Constitutional Division considered that there was failure to provide 'the necessary details to enable the person interpreting the law easily to determine which acts characterized the specific penal case, for there would have to be consultation of the whole text of the provisions to determine which acts were punishable by a specific penal sanction and to establish, as regards the remainder, if such acts were punishable under the provisions of the rest of the penal law and, by a process of exclusion, to decide which other acts might also be punishable under the general provision under consideration. The formula used (the ruling stated) was a flagrant contravention of Article 39 of the Constitution for the acts which it sought to punish were not defined in terms of a penal category; their description was ambiguous and of a general nature, in violation of the guarantee which should be afforded by the characterization of acts, and, hence, contravened the legal principle set out in the aforesaid Article 39 of the Constitution.'
11. See Eugenio R. Zaffaroni, 'Reflexiones político-criminales sobre la tutela penal de los derechos de autor', in *Los ilícitos civiles y penales en derecho de autor*, Buenos Aires, ICI and Argentine Centre of ICI, 1981, pp. 86–7.

On this point, mention should be made of *Resolution No. 32* of the I Continental Conference of the Inter-American Copyright Institute (ICI), São Paulo, 1977, which states that: '[...] the definition of criminal offences should be perfectly established in the special law without the need for references to and analogies with the Penal Code'.

deemed to have brought about a substantial improvement of protection under criminal law by putting an end to the previous open-ended provision[12] contained in Article 46[13] of the Spanish Law on Intellectual Property of 1879. The latter provision also constituted the basis for Article 71 of the Argentine Law of 1933 (still in force) and Article 14 of the Bolivian Law of 1909[14] (from which a derogation was made and a new text substituted in 1992); in both these laws the terms 'fraud' and 'defrauder' are used generically.[15]

In Cuba, Puerto Rico and the Philippines, the Spanish Law of 1879 was also applied by the provisions of its Article 56. Subsequently, the Cuban Penal Code of 1936 took over this framework in its Article 392 by imposing a fine on anyone who, to the prejudice of the legitimate owner, commits any infringement of copyright registered in the name of such owner.

11.1.4. Categories of offences

For illustrative purposes, these offences can be divided into three groups:

---

12. See Antonio Delgado Porras, *Panorámica de la protección Civil y Penal en materia de Propiedad Intelectual*, Madrid, Civitas, 1988, p. 113.
13. Article 46 of the Spanish Law on Intellectual Property of 1879 reads as follows: 'In addition to the penalties stipulated in Article 552 and elsewhere in the currently valid Penal Code, persons who infringe intellectual property shall forfeit all the illegally published copies which shall be handed over to the proprietor whose rights have been infringed' (the Law of 1879 was replaced by Law 22 of 11 November 1987 on intellectual property and by Organic Law 6/1987 of the same date which amended the Penal Code in relation to the types of infringement and penalties applicable).
14. Bolivia, Article 14 of the Law of 1909, amended in 1919 and 1945, reads: 'Infringers of copyright shall forfeit ...'.
15. Argentine legal theory generally dissents from the use of the verb '*defraudar*' (to defraud). In this respect, Jorge E. Anzorreguy, Joaquín P. Da Rocha and Héctor H. Hernández Vieyra consider that since the infringing act is of the essence in arriving at a correct interpretation of the type of offence, it must be defined accurately to facilitate its understanding and proper application of the law; they are of the opinion that suitable terms to define these offences might be the verbs '*violar*' (to violate) or '*lesionar*' (to infringe). ('Delitos contra los derechos intelectuales', *Rev. de Jurisprudencia Argentina,* Doctrina, 1973, p. 549.)

- infringements of the moral right;
- infringements of economic rights;
- combined infringements of both the moral right and of the economic rights.[16]

A. INFRINGEMENTS OF THE MORAL RIGHT

The basic forms of infringement of the moral right—with no bearing on economic rights—are those in which the infringer, who is duly authorized to use the work by virtue of a contract or a non-voluntary licence or in general by reason of a statutory limitation, does so without respecting the rights of the author to the paternity and integrity of the work.

The infringement of the right of paternity occurs when the name of the author is omitted (if he does not specifically desire to remain anonymous) or changed (for example, if the author has chosen a pseudonym and the work is reproduced or disclosed to the public under the real name of the author, or if the latter wished to remain anonymous and his name or a pseudonym are given).

The right to respect for the work and its integrity is infringed when transformations are made (translations, adaptations, reductions, etc. and in general where changes or additions are made) without the necessary authorization, or when the limits of the authorized transformations are exceeded (e.g. if a translation of the work is authorized and it is also adapted or abridged and additions, etc. made; or if the adaptation which was strictly necessary to pass from one genre to another—from the theatre to television, for example—was authorized but a free version is made).

Several national laws categorize these infringements of the moral right without establishing any relationship with an infringement of the economic right, as in the example of the Ar-

---

16. See a similar classification in Vega Vega, 'Consideraciones de política criminal sobre el plagio como infraccíon de los derechos de autor', in: *International Review of Penal Law*, No. 1, 1978, quoted by Concepción Carmona Salgado, *La nueva ley de propiedad intelectual*, Madrid, Montecorvo, 1988, pp. 301–2.

gentina law, Article 72: '... (c) any person who publishes, sells or reproduces a work, omitting or changing the name of the author or the title of the work, or fraudulently altering its text'; (a similar provision is found in the Chilean law, Art. 79(c) *in fine*; see also Colombian law 44 of 1993, Article 51, paras. 2 and 3; the Peruvian Penal Code, Article 218, etc.).

Some laws (for example Portugal, Article 198) include in the same type of offence, infringements of the moral right of the author or of performing artists; sometimes other neighbouring rights are included (for example the Peruvian Penal Code of 1991, Article 217.2) which leads to confusion. It is therefore desirable to typify the various offences separately.

B. INFRINGEMENTS OF ECONOMIC RIGHTS

Statutory provisions on the protection of the economic rights of the author by means of penal sanctions classify as offences infringements of the right of reproduction, the right of communication to the public (performance, cinematographic showing, broadcasting, cable distribution, etc.) and the right of transformation of all or part of the literary, musical and artistic works concerned.

In addition to these acts which are universally classified as offences, certain legislations specify actions which constitute infringements of economic rights, for example:
- producing a larger number of copies than that stipulated in the contract (Argentina, Article 72, para. (d); Costa Rica, Article 119, para. (e));
- exceeding the limits of the authorization granted to use a work, the performance of an artist, a phonogram, a videogram or a broadcast, save in cases expressly provided for by the law (Portugal, Article 195, para. 2(c));
- making false declarations as to the number of copies actually sold (Chile, Article 80, para. (a));
- misrepresenting other circumstances on which the remuneration of the author is dependent: data relating to audiences, the type, price and number of tickets sold for a show or gathering or the number of tickets distributed free of charge (Colombia, Law 44 of 1993, Art. 525);

- making false declarations by omitting, substituting or wrongly inserting information in respect of the circulated works (Colombia, Law 44 of 1993, Art. 527);
- making a selection or compilation of published or unpublished works without the authorization of the author (Portugal, Article 195, para. 2(b), Mexico, Art. 136. III);
- making abusive use of the right of quotation (Costa Rica, Article 118, para. (a), Dominican Republic, Art. 165(a));
- causing a performance or public showing to be suspended without being the author, publisher, successor in title or representative of any of them or by falsely appropriating such identities (Argentina, Article 74; Colombia, Article 235; Costa Rica, Article 121; Uruguay, Article 49);
- usurping the name, pseudonym, professional designation or monogram of an author (Peru, Penal Code, Article 218). This action which is habitually designated as the 'false attribution of authorship' involves an infringement of the right to one's name to which all persons are entitled and not of copyright as such. As Delgado Porras points out, no prerogative of the author is infringed by attributing to him a work (or performance) which he has not created;[17]
- usurping the original protected title of a work or periodical of a third party (Costa Rica, Art. 118(b)). In Peru, Article 123, paragraph (j), describes as an offence 'unfair competition by usurping the title of the work'.

---

17. Antonio Delgado Porras, op. cit., p. 119: 'The treatment of this infringement is founded on the protection of the basic personal rights and, more specifically, on the statutory provisions which sanction the unauthorized use of the name of another person since, as established by Italian case-law (Milan Court Ruling of 19 June 1980), an infringement of the "right to a name" is not constituted solely by its use by a person who is not entitled to confuse his own name with that of the person legitimately entitled to its use, but also any use of the name which brings its owner into situations which misrepresent his person in relation to third parties, as will happen for example if a work (or artistic performance) is attributed to a person who is not its author (or performer).'

a. Piracy

'Piracy' of cultural works and products is a typical unlawful act infringing the exclusive right of reproduction. It consists in the manufacture, sale and commercial distribution in any form of illegal copies (books and printed matter in general, records, cassettes, etc.) of literary, artistic, audiovisual and musical works, or performances of such works, and of computer programs and data banks.

The term 'piracy' is also used to denote the performance, reprinting and any other unauthorized use of a work, broadcast, etc.

The draft WIPO Model Provisions for national laws state that the manufacturing or the preparation of copies shall constitute an act of counterfeiting, provided that such goods are manufactured on a commercial scale and without the authorization of the owner of the rights in the work, the performance, the phonogram or the broadcast which enjoy protection (hereinafter referred to as 'pirate copies'). A licensee may grant the authorization if, and to the extent that, he is entitled to do so pursuant to his licensing contract.

The term 'commercial scale' is defined as a notion 'which will have to be applied taking into consideration the circumstances accompanying the manufacture. The quantity of the goods manufactured, the way in which they were, are or are intended to be used and the will to make profit are among the factors which the courts will have to take into consideration.'[18]

In addition to the actions listed above, the following are also deemed to constitute acts of piracy: (i) the package or preparation of the package; (ii) exportation, importation and transit; (iii) the offer for sale, hire, loan or any other form of circulation; (iv) the sale, hire, loan or any other form of circulation; and (v) the possession, with intent to commit one or more of the acts listed in

---

18. For example, in Argentina the unauthorized reproduction of copies made for third parties against payment (Article 72*bis*, para. (c)) also constitutes piracy even where the reproduction is effected on an individual basis with one or more copies being made for each order.

points (i) to (iv) above, of pirate copies where the said act is committed on a commercial scale and without the authorization of the owner of the rights in the literary or artistic work, the performance, the phonogram or the broadcast. A licensee may grant authorization if he is entitled to do so by virtue of his contractual licence and to the extent provided for therein.[19]

Unlike existing multilateral treaties dealing with copyright and neighbouring rights which do not set out any obligation on the part of Contracting States to enact punitive measures,[20] the TRIPS Agreement of the WTO[21] lays down in its Article 61 an obligation for the parties to provide for criminal procedures and penalties to be applied at least in cases of wilful acts of infringement of trade marks or copyright piracy on a commercial scale:

Remedies available shall include imprisonment and/or monetary fines sufficient to provide a deterrent, consistently with the level and penalties applied for crimes of a corresponding gravity. In appropriate cases, remedies available shall also include seizure, forfeiture and destruction of the infringing goods and of any materials and implements the predominant use of which has been in the commission of the offence. Parties may provide for criminal procedures and penalties to be applied in other cases of infringement of intellectual property rights, in particular where they are committed wilfully and on a commercial scale.[22]

---

19. Cf. WIPO document C&P/CE/2 of 18 February 1988.
20. With the exception of the Caracas Agreement of 17 July 1911, Article 9 of which stipulates that '[...] The signatory States undertake to establish penalties in their legislation in respect of those who appropriate literary and artistic property illicitly.' In turn, the Phonogram Convention of 29 October 1971 includes, as an optional measure among those provided for in its Article 3 for the protection of producers of sound recordings against their unauthorized reproduction, protection by means of penal sanctions (see below, Chapter 12, Section 12.4.1.5 and 12.5.2, C, b, 1 respectively).
21. TRIPS: *Trade-Related Intellectual Property Rights*; WTO: World Trade Organization. The Treaty established by the WTO was signed in Marrakech on 15 April 1994 and came into force on 1 January 1995.
22. The main novelty in the TRIPS Agreement appears in Part III: 'Enforcement of Intellectual Property Rights' (Articles 41 to 61) and Part V: 'Dispute Prevention and Settlement' (Articles 63 and 64) (see Alberto Villalba Carlos, 'Los derechos de autor en el GATT', *DAT*, Buenos Aires, No. 45/1992, pp. 17–23).

The acts listed in the previous paragraphs are defined specifically in many domestic laws. In addition to the action of unauthorized reproduction, penalties are also imposed for the sale, exhibition for sale, importation, concealment or holding in deposit of copies of a work, a phonogram or a videogram produced in violation of copyright (for example Argentina, Article 72, para. (c) and 72*bis*(d); Brazil, Penal Code, Article 184, para. 2; Portugal, Article 199, para. 1, etc.).

Piracy is a common practice in respect of school textbooks, technical and scientific works and best-selling works of literature, recordings of musical works, audiovisual works, broadcasts, computer programs and data banks. It is prejudicial to both the author and publisher (in the case of piracy of protected literary and artistic works) and also to the owners of neighbouring rights (where the piracy involves fixations of protected performances, protected phonograms and protected broadcasts).

It is also prejudicial to workers in the cultural industries since it has an adverse impact on their output by replacing the sale of legitimate products; and it also affects the State, since pirates always pursue their activities, at least partially, on the margins of the established system. However, the pirates tend to defend their activities with the argument that, since their products are sold more cheaply, they are able to reach wider sections of the public which would otherwise have no access to them. But even where the pirated copies are sold at a lower price, this is not a result of their own efforts but of their parasitic activity: if works exist to pirate they do so despite the activities of the pirate and not because of his existence. Piracy adds nothing to national creativity; on the contrary, it destroys the very foundations of local industry and has an adverse influence on relations between the latter and foreign publishers and producers.

The illegal act exists regardless of the method by which the unauthorized copies are manufactured.

In the area of printed works, now that the means of offset reproduction has become widely available, the pirates reproduce an authorized edition by the facsimile technique. This permits the production on a large scale of pirate copies which are then marketed. Sometimes the copies are a slavish imitation of the original

edition (falsification of editions); sometimes the pirates use their own publishing imprint. In this way the pirate saves himself all the work and cost of translation, typesetting, etc. The commonest forms of production of pirated copies of printed works are the following:
- the recording on film of an authorized edition and reproducing it in series on copies which are a facsimile reproduction of the original;
- entering an authorized edition into a computer memory using a scanner and then duplicating the work in facsimile form;
- photocopying an authorized edition to produce a master copy which is then duplicated in series using small offset machines which permit rapid reproduction (rotaprint, multilite, etc.);
- direct photocopying of an authorized edition, generally in parts which are then sold in premises normally located in the immediate vicinity of study centres, etc.

In the case of phonographic piracy, according to Antequera Parilli the following techniques are those most widely used to produce illicit copies:
- the serial duplication in a rudimentary form of sound recordings from a master or copy of the phonogram, on cassettes whose external characteristics are readily distinguishable from a legitimate reproduction so that the fact that these are re-recordings can easily be detected by visual inspection;
- serial duplication in a sophisticated manner which imitates a legitimate production, but with a lithographic design which differs from that of the legitimate copies;
- serial duplication in a sophisticated manner imitating in a slavish, or near slavish, manner the authorized production so that the consumer will be unaware that he is buying a pirate copy (falsification);
- duplication in a manner similar to that described previously but deleting all reference to the name, designation, trade mark or monogram of the legitimate producer;
- small-scale 'copying' carried out to order for payment by an individual consumer;
- compilations made by disc jockeys or persons involved in the music trade.

In the case of video piracy (i.e. piracy of audiovisual works), the habitual forms of clandestine duplication are as follows:
- making use of a 35 mm copy of a cinematographic film temporarily removed from the custody of the distributor or from a cinema by a third party working in close association. This procedure is used to market the cinematographic work on video cassettes before the producer or his licensee does so;
- making use of an authorized copy of a videogram which is then duplicated on to blank cassettes;
- making use of a television broadcast which is recorded on to a blank cassette and then duplicated.[23]

In the case of piracy of computer programs the commonest practices, according to Millé, are as follows:
- the making of single copies of programs by persons who belonged to the production team or possess the source programs and technical documentation as authorized users and therefore have access to a program which is in limited circulation and extremely expensive or else to a 'customized' program; they then negotiate the sale of a copy to third parties who wish to use these programs without paying the full cost;
- by falsification of copies (i.e. by slavish reproduction in such a way that the purchaser is unable to determine whether or not the copy is authorized), which are sold at a price which is significantly lower than that of the original;
- illicit reproductions of authorized copies; these reproductions are made to order and sold without concealment of the fact that they are copies of this type (the data carriers are sold without the manufacturer's identification; the labels are handwritten or typewritten; the users' manuals and other documentation are photocopies, sometimes only part of the documentation being supplied);
- provision of 'free' copies by the retail suppliers of computer hardware who furnish the customer with the programs required

---

23. See Ricardo Antequera Parilli, 'La piratería de obras escritas, sonoras y audiovisuales (El problema y su importancia)', in *Proceedings of the II International Congress*, Bogotá, April 1987, pp. 115–17.

by him or with the commonest programs copied on to the internal memory (hard disc) of the computer or on to diskettes. In this case pirate copies are supplied with the aim of promoting hardware sales;
- user clubs which are set up for the loan or exchange of computer programs for the time necessary to enable the user to make his own copies;
- duplication of an authorized copy by companies for their own internal use;
- personal copying from authorized or pirate copies.[24]

b. Falsification of cultural products

The falsification of cultural products is one of the typical offences of piracy and consists in the reproduction of a published work, a phonogram, an audiovisual work, a computer program, and so on, with a false indication of the name, style or mark of the authorized publisher, producer or licensee. In these cases an offence of trade mark falsification is also generally committed.

Several national laws categorize the falsification of intellectual works separately from the offence of piracy; for example, Argentina, Article 72, paragraph (b); Chile (Article 79(c)) and the Dominican Republic, Article 164, paragraph (e), etc.

C. COMBINED INFRINGEMENTS (OF THE MORAL RIGHT AND OF ECONOMIC RIGHTS)

Here we shall discuss only those offences which *always* involve an infringement of both moral and economic interests; the unauthorized publication of an unpublished work, the unauthorized publication of a work in respect of which the author has exercised his right to reconsider or the right of withdrawal, and also plagiarism. We shall omit other cases in which infringements of the moral right and economic rights are both involved (for example

---

24. See Antonio Millé, 'Piratería de obras de software', in *La protección jurídica del software y de las bases de datos*, Instituto Venezolano del Software (Invesoft), 1990, pp. 67–9.

the unauthorized publication of a novel omitting the name of the author and/or altering the text) because, as we have seen, they need not necessarily be combined.

The occurrences of unauthorized publication of an unpublished work or other work in respect of which the author has exercised his right to reconsider or withdraw are self-explanatory (they infringe the moral rights of disclosure and reconsideration or withdrawal together with the economic right of reproduction or communication to the public). We shall therefore confine our attention here to plagiarism.

Plagiarism is the appropriation of all or some of the original features contained in the work of another author which are presented as those of the plagiarist himself. The infringement of the moral right of the plagiarized author always affects his right of authorship, since the plagiarist presents the work as his own. In a majority of cases, the right to respect for the work and its integrity is also infringed since the plagiarist usually attempts to disguise his plagiarism. The infringement of economic rights results from unauthorized transformation of the work and from its use (reproduction, communication to the public).

Legal theory draws a distinction between slavish plagiarism (which is less common) in which the work of a third party is appropriated in full, or nearly in full, and 'intelligent' plagiarism in which the plagiarist tries to dissimulate his act or appropriates certain substantial and original elements.

This is the form in which plagiarism habitually occurs. It therefore seems appropriate to assess plagiarism by the similarities between the offending work and the work which is plagiarized and not by the differences between them.

Unlike most laws which condemn the act of plagiarism without using the word itself, the Ecuadorian Law and the Spanish Penal Code do use the term 'plagiarism' as such.

In Ecuador, Article 128 of the Copyright Law stipulates that: '*Plagiarism* shall be punished by imprisonment for six months to two years and a fine of 5,000 to 20,000 sucres' (our italics).

In Spain, Article 534*bis*(a) of the Penal Code stipulates that: 'Any person who deliberately reproduces, *plagiarizes*, distributes or communicates to the public, in whole or in part, a literary, artistic or scientific work or its transformation or a performance or artistic interpretation fixed on any kind of support or communicated by any medium without the authorization of the owners of the corresponding rights of intellectual property or of their assignees shall be punishable [...] The same penalty shall be imposed upon any person who wilfully imports, exports or stores copies of such works or productions or performances without due authorization' (our italics).

The following article (534*bis*(b)) sets out a number of aggravating circumstances including paragraph (c) 'usurping authorship of a work or part thereof or the name of an artist in a performance'.

The study, in conjunction, of these two articles of the Spanish Penal Code—534*bis*(a) which defines the basic offence and 534*bis*(b) which sets out aggravating circumstances—reveals a number of important points:
- the offence of plagiarism always involves usurpation of the identity of the author so that it might be held that the distinction between the basic offence of plagiarism (Article 534*bis*(a)) and the aggravating circumstance (Article 534*bis*(b)) may be due to the influence of constant legal precedents in Spain which distinguish between plagiarism on the one hand and usurpation of the personality of the author on the other (Rulings of the Supreme Court, 2nd Chamber, of 14 February and 30 May 1984);[25]
- the act of plagiarism is characterized as an offence without its having been defined; and
- the provision includes the performances of artists or performers although there can be no plagiarism of such acts since performers do not benefit from the right of transformation.

On the other hand, when the infringement of the economic rights of the author or performer is accompanied by an infringement of

---

25. See Antonio Delgado Porras, op. cit., pp. 117–19 and José Manuel Gómez Benítez, and Gonzalo Quintero Olivares, *Protección penal de los derechos de autor y conexos*, Madrid, Civitas, 1988, pp. 158–61.

his moral right, it is fully justified and appropriate for the penalty to be more severe since in this case an attack is made on the personality of the author or performer himself. Article 122 of the Venezuelan law reflects the same interpretation. The Peruvian Penal Code (Article 217) also provides for a heavier penalty on the plagiarist.[26]

However, many national laws lay down a single penalty, regardless of whether the infringement of the economic rights is accompanied by a violation of the moral right.

11.2. Penal sanctions

The penalties are generally those provided for in the Penal Code of each country (prison sentence and/or fine). Sometimes the penalty is established by a direct reference to the Penal Code (for example in Argentina, Article 71: 'Shall be sanctioned by the penalty provided for in Article 172 of the Penal Code [...]'; in Chile, Article 79: '... shall be punished with the penalty of minor imprisonment (presidio menor) at its lowest level [...]'; and Article 80(a) '... shall be punished with the sanction specified in Article 467 of the Penal Code [...]').

For infringement of the rights of authors, their successors in title and the owners of neighbouring rights, the national laws habitually impose penal sanctions (prison sentences and/or fines) and accompanying penalties (destruction of illicit copies; of the material used for the production thereof; debarment from exercise of the profession connected with the committed offence; publication of the sentence, etc.).

The different national laws do not adopt uniform criteria in respect of the nature and severity of the sentences. For example, in Denmark and Spain the penalty imposed for the unauthorized reproduction of a work—an infringement which is recognized as

---

26. The preliminary draft law drawn up in Argentina between 1974 and 1976 by the Resolutions Committee No. 82 of 1974 (Ministry of Justice), contains a similar criterion in regard to the imposition of a more severe penalty when the author's moral right is infringed.

such by every national law—is a *fine* and a prison sentence only if there are aggravating circumstances (in Denmark there is a maximum prison sentence of three months, Article 55, and in Spain imprisonment plus a fine—Penal Code, 534*bis*(a) and 534*bis*(b)); in Costa Rica, a prison sentence of between 8 and 12 months may be imposed (Article 119, para. (b)); in Colombia, the prison sentence is for two to five years plus a fine (Law 44 of 1993, Article 51.1); while in Argentina it is the penalty imposed for fraud—a prison sentence ranging from one month to six years (Article 72, para. (a)).

In some countries the sentence varies depending on whether or not the infringement has been committed with commercial purposes in mind; for example in Peru detention for between one and three years (Arts. 216 and 217(a)) is stipulated by the Penal Code if there is no commercial purpose, while a prison sentence of between two and four years is imposed in other cases. In Spain the commercial purpose is treated as an aggravating circumstance of the same nature as infringement of the moral right (Penal Code, 534*bis*(b), para. 1).

Other acts which are also universally defined as offences include unauthorized public performance which is punishable under some laws by lighter penalties than unauthorized reproduction (in the Dominican Republic a fine, Article 165, para. (c)). The fines are, however, increased by up to three times the amount of the material prejudice occasioned when it has caused the victim serious difficulty in ensuring his livelihood (Art. 166); in Argentina, a prison sentence of between one month and one year *or* a fine (Article 73); in Costa Rica, a prison sentence of between one and three months (Article 117, para. (a)).

Some laws impose the same penalty on unauthorized reproduction as on public performance made without the permission of the owner of copyright or neighbouring rights (Peru, Spain, etc.).

The same disparity in respect of penalties can be observed in relation to the offences whose classification is less universal than those mentioned above, for example the fact of suspending a public performance without being the owner of the author's right in Argentina renders the offender liable for a prison sentence of between one month and one year *or* a fine (Article 74); in Costa

Rica, for a fine of between 10 and 30 daily units (Article 121); and in Colombia, for detention for a period from two to six months *and* a fine (Article 235).

The basis for calculating fines also tends to vary widely. In general, the amounts are stipulated in the currency of the country concerned but in some cases, to obviate the impact of inflation, reference is made to certain specific parameters; for example, Chile stipulates monthly accounting units in Articles 78 and 79 and basic annual salary rates scale (A) of the Department of Santiago in Article 81.

In the United States of America, Section 506, paragraph (a), stipulates that 'any person who infringes a copyright wilfully and for purposes of commercial advantage or private financial gain shall be punished in accordance with Section 2319, of Title 18 of the United States Code'. This Section—according to the amendments introduced by Law No. 102-561 of 28 October 1992—establishes in paragraph (b) that:

[Any person who commits an offence under subsection (a) ... —];
(1) shall be imprisoned not more than 5 years, or fined in the amount set forth in this title [not more than $250,000], or both, if the offence consists of the reproduction or distribution, during any 180-day period, of at least 10 copies or phonorecords, of one or more copyrighted works, with a retail value of more than $2,500;
(2) shall be imprisoned not more than 10 years, or fined in the amount set forth in this title, or both, if the offence is a second or subsequent offence under paragraph (1); and
(3) shall be imprisoned not more than 1 year, or fined in the amount set forth in this title, or both, in any other case.

Paragraph (b) of Section 506 goes on to stipulate that, in addition to the penalty therein prescribed, the court in its judgement of conviction, shall order the forfeiture and destruction or other disposition of all infringing copies or phonorecords and all implements, devices or equipment used in the manufacture of such infringing copies or phonorecords.

The nature and range of the penalties imposed on infringements of copyright and neighbouring rights must remain proportional to other penalties laid down in each penal code. The draft

Model Provisions of WIPO state that piracy is a theft and has to be punished as such.[27]

Criteria in regard to the range in the severity of the penalties tend to differ. Some seek a severe sanction in order to have a dissuasive effect; others draw attention to the disadvantages of imposing excessively severe penalties because persons who infringe copyright and neighbouring rights are 'white-collar' delinquents for whom the dissuasive effect is achieved by the mere fact that judges effectively apply the penalties in the cases laid before them. Judges will be less inclined to do so when the penalties are excessively high in relation to the value standards of the community in which they administer justice.

This opinion was expressed by the legal experts who participated in the first Continental Conference of ICI (São Paulo, 1977) whose Resolution No. 32 stated that '[...] the penal sentence must not be excessively severe in relation to the general attitude to copyright prevailing in the country concerned, since any such excess would encourage the benevolence of the judges and bring the statutory provision into abeyance or disrepute'.

11.3. Right to restrain the unlawful activity

The unlawful activity creates an entitlement to ask for its cessation. Some laws make express mention of the measures necessary to bring about the cessation of an unlawful activity, for example the United States of America, Section 503; Portugal, Article 201; and so on. In Article 124, paragraph 1, of the Spanish Law a highly instructive list will be found of the measures which may be taken to restrain unlawful activity:

(a) suspending the infringing exploitation;
(b) prohibiting the infringer from resuming it;
(c) withdrawing from the market and destroying unlawful copies;
(d) rendering useless any moulds, plates, matrices, negatives and other material intended solely for the reproduction of the unlawful copies, and where necessary destroying such materials;

---

27. See doc. cit., Observations concerning Article D, paras. 63–65.

(e) removing or placing seals on apparatus used for the unauthorized communication to the public.

Paragraph 2 of this article stipulates that the infringer may request that the destruction or rendering useless of the copies and materials mentioned, where they are susceptible of other uses, be effected to the extent necessary to prevent the unlawful exploitation; paragraph 3 provides that the owner of the right infringed may apply for the surrender to him of the copies and materials referred to at their cost price, with a corresponding reduction of his indemnification for damages; paragraph 4 states that the provisions of this Article 124 shall not apply to copies acquired in good faith for personal use.

The draft Model Provisions of WIPO also provide as a general rule for the destruction of the pirate copies and their packaging 'unless the injured party requests otherwise'. Another procedure may consist (according to the commentary) in the confiscation of the pirated copies and transfer of the property to the injured party or the sale (auction or otherwise) with the proceeds of the sale accruing to the injured party.

Where there is a risk that certain instruments may be used in future to continue to commit acts of piracy, the court shall order their destruction or surrender to the injured party. When there is a risk that the acts of piracy may continue, the court shall expressly order their cessation. Moreover the court shall fix the amount of the fine to be paid in the event of failure to comply with the order (see WIPO document C&P/CE/2).

11.4. Compensation for prejudice suffered

Sometimes the right to demand compensation for material and moral prejudice resulting from an unlawful activity which infringes copyright and neighbouring rights is stipulated in the relevant laws; for example, Colombia (Law 44 of 1993, Art. 57 and Penal Code, Art. 107); Finland, Article 57; Germany, Article 97; Spain, Articles 123 and 125; United States of America, Section 504, etc. Such provision often appears under the heading of penalties in civil law. In other cases, compensation has its origin in ordinary law (for example, in Argentina). Sometimes, the specific law makes reference to civil law provisions on liability (for example, Hungary, Article 52, para. 2).

A. Some copyright laws establish relatively specific rates of compensation for material or economic prejudice, e.g.

a. The United States Copyright Statute which is particularly precise: Section 504 provides for two systems of remedy which may not be combined: (1) the reparation of actual damages and profits; and (2) the determination of statutory damages.

In the first place, paragraph (a) of Section 504 lays down the general principle: except as otherwise provided in the law, an infringer of copyright is liable for damages in respect of such infringement. Two forms of remedy are then provided:

1. *Actual damages and profits* (Section 504, para. (b)): the copyright owner is entitled to recover the actual damages suffered by him or her as a result of the infringement and any profits of the infringer that are attributable to the infringement and are not taken into account in computing the actual damages. In establishing the infringer's profits, the copyright owner is required to present proof only of the infringer's gross revenue and the infringer is required to prove his or her deductible expenses and the elements of profits attributable to factors other than the copyrighted work (for example the fame of a performer).

2. *Statutory damages* (Section 504, para. (c)): instead of actual damages, the copyright owner may elect to recover an award of statutory damages as provided for in Section 504, paragraph (c). The court may fix the amount of such compensation between a minimum and maximum figure.

At any time before final judgement is rendered, the copyright owner may elect to recover, instead of actual damages and profits, a lump-sum award of statutory damages (which cannot be combined with actual damages). In this case the amount of the damages shall be fixed freely at the discretion of the court between a minimum of US$500 and a maximum of US$20,000. However, if the copyright holder who has suffered damage is able to prove that the infringement was committed wilfully, the court may, at its discretion, increase the fine to a maximum of US$100,000. If the infringer proves that he was not aware of the fact that his actions involved an infringement of copyright or can show that he had no reason to know that he was committing an infringement, the court may reduce the compensation to US$200.[28]

Section 504, paragraph (c)(2) provides for the possibility of the court remitting the statutory damages if the infringer believed that his or her use of a copyrighted work was a fair use in conformity with Section 107 of the law[29] and had reasonable grounds for so believing. This benefit may be granted only to certain specific persons:

(i) an employee or agent of a non-profit educational institution, library, or archives acting within the scope of his or her employement who, [or such institution, library or archives itself, which] infringed by reproducing the work in copies or phonorecords; or
(ii) a public broadcasting entity which, or a person who, as a regular part of the non-profit activities of a public broadcasting entity (as defined in sub-section (g) of Section 118), infringed by performing a published non-dramatic literary work or by reproducing a transmission programme embodying a performance of such a work.

b. Other laws also provide for the possibility of seeking additional compensation under certain circumstances, as, for example, in the Copyright Act of Finland (Art. 57, para. 2), where the infringement has been committed wilfully or by negligence.

c. In Spain (Art. 125), the criterion for establishing the amount of the compensation is different: the aggrieved party may choose, for his indemnification, between the profits that he would presumably have made had the unlawful use not occurred and the remuneration that he would have collected through having authorized exploitation. Moral prejudice shall afford entitlement to indemnification even where there is no evidence of economic prejudice. The amount of the indemnification shall be determined according to

---

28. Omission of the copyright reserved mention may result in what is known as an innocent infringement (see above, Chap. 1, Sect. 1.3.5 and Chapter 10, Sect. 10.2.1, B, (a)).
29. See above, Chap. 4, Sect. 4.3.1, A.

the circumstances of the infringement, the seriousness of the harm done and the extent of unlawful dissemination of the work.

B. In those countries whose laws do not establish scales of compensation, the judges experience difficulty in determining such compensation. In ordinary law, even in cases where an unlawful act has been committed, there may be no civil liability concerning compensation. On the other hand, in the area of copyright and neighbouring rights, the damage may be generated by the mere fact of the infringement; this is established very properly as a general principle in Section 504, paragraph (a) of the United States law.

In Argentina, where provision for compensation is based on ordinary law, Cifuentes has pointed out that it is *'jus receptum* in our Courts that the mere fact of infringement of the author's exclusive rights causes damage to which a pecuniary value can be set'.[30]

More recent procedural laws habitually entitle the courts to pass sentence on the basis of presumptions which are not set out in the substantive law, when they are supported by real and established facts and when their number, clear definition, gravity and concordance generate a conviction, according to the nature of the proceedings, in line with the rules of sound critical examination. They also establish an obligation for the court to fix the amount of the compensation or of the damages claimed in cases

---

30. Santos Cifuentes, cites the ruling of Chamber D of the National Appeal Court for civil cases of 30 April 1974 (*Rev. El Derecho*, Vol. 56, p. 344) in which the court ruled as follows: 'Hence a duty to make compensation arises since, as has been repeatedly maintained, the entitlement of the author to claim compensation for damage and prejudice suffered results from the very fact of the violation of the exclusive right which the law grants him to sell and distribute his work' ('Daños. Cómo evaluar el resarcimiento por la utilización no autorizada de las obras. Su incidencia en la jurisprudencia (desde la perspectiva del magistrado)'), in *Proceedings of the V International Congress*, Buenos Aires, April 1990, pp. 304–5).

where the existence of a prejudice is legally proven even if its amount is not evidenced.[31]

The draft Model Provisions of WIPO referred to above stipulate that the person who suffers prejudice as a result of an act of piracy (the draft refers solely to the counterfeiting of products in violation of industrial property rights and to piracy) shall be entitled to damages for the prejudice suffered as a consequence of that act and also to the payment of legal costs, including lawyers' fees; the amount of the damages shall be fixed taking account of the material and moral prejudice suffered by the injured party and of the profits earned as a result of the act of piracy (see WIPO document C&P/CE/2).

The TRIPS Agreement provides, in Article 45, for the right to damages:

(1) The judicial authorities shall have the authority to order the infringer to pay the right holder damages adequate to compensate for the injury the right holder has suffered because of an infringement of that person's intellectual property right by an infringer who knowingly, or with reasonable grounds to know, engaged in infringing activity.
(2) The judicial authorities shall also have the authority to order the infringer to pay the right holder expenses, which may include appropriate attorney's fees. In appropriate cases, Members may authorize the judicial authorities to order recovery of profits and/or payment of pre-established damages even where the infringer did not knowingly, or with reasonable grounds to know, engage in infringing activity.

C. To sum up, any unlawful action which infringes the author's rights or neighbouring rights causes *per se* prejudice which must be redressed. The particular features of immaterial rights require an assessment to be made of all the circumstances which have an impact on the amount of the compensation, without applying rigid formulas. The owners of the copyright or neighbouring right must be able to claim by way of compensation the profit which

---

31. See Argentina, *Código Procesal Civil y Comercial de la Nación*, Articles 163, paragraph 5, and 165, paragraph 3.

they would have obtained had there been no unlawful use, or the higher remuneration which they would have received by authorizing exploitation. This will ensure that it is not more profitable to infringe copyright and neighbouring rights than to respect them, since if the user arrives at a lower price in a legal process than in negotiations with the right holder, infringements will merely be encouraged.

11.5. Procedural rules

Some laws expressly stipulate the compatibility and independence of civil and criminal proceedings, for example Argentina, Article 77: 'Civil and criminal actions shall be independent of each other and the final judgements rendered in them shall not affect each other. The parties may, in defence of their rights, use the documentary evidence adduced in another suit, as well as admissions and the reports of experts, including the verdict of the jury, but not the judgements rendered by the respective judges.'

Similar provisions will be found in Costa Rica (Art. 128) and Colombia (Art. 238) where express provision is also made for a civil action for the redress of prejudice caused by infringement to be exercised within the criminal process or separately before the competent civil jurisdiction at the option of the injured party (that possibility also exists in Argentina, although the law on intellectual property does not provide for it).

In Spain, as Delgado Porras points out, full compatibility existed between civil and criminal proceedings until the 1987 reform which, as we have seen, put an end to the pre-existing system of a 'blank provision', full reference being made to the specific substantive law. According to Delgado Porras, in the classification of the cases liable for this kind of penalty a distinction was introduced between civil and criminal infringements which had previously been somewhat unclear. Delgado Porras goes on to maintain that there is now some doubt as to the compatibility between civil and criminal proceedings having regard to the fact that, by express provisions of the new law (Penal Code, Art. 534*ter*), the application of civil liability in respect of an offence is to be governed by the provisions of the intellectual property law relating to the cessation of the unlawful activity and to the compensation for damage and prejudice caused (Arts. 124 and 125). Once proceedings have been opened in the criminal courts, as a result of which this liability may be enforced, it would seem inappropriate to open other proceedings in the civil courts with the same end in view. The same consideration holds good in reverse, for if the infringement may be classified as a case for criminal proceedings and having regard to the fact that it is an offence which it is compulsory to prosecute, an action brought in the civil courts on grounds of infringement and seeking both cessation of the infringing activity and appropriate compensation, would still have to be placed before the judge or criminal court with which responsibility rests for an adjudication on the degree of liability determined by the civil court (Art. 362 LCE).[32]

Even though civil law has the aim of providing compensation and criminal law that of sentencing or punishing, it is admitted, in many countries, for reasons of juridical simplicity, that the claim for compensation (or the application of civil penalties, the heading under which, as we have seen, the means for obtaining redress often fall) may be settled through criminal proceedings. Of course, the same compensation cannot be claimed simultaneously in proceedings of both kinds; to do so might result in an objection on grounds of *lis alibi pendens* and the claim would then have to be substantiated at its primary source. If the claim for civil compensation were rejected, it would be hard to concede the possibility of taking further proceedings elsewhere, given that this sentence would have the effect of *res judicata* in the court to which the action was referred in the second instance.

In this respect, Colombia (Art. 238) expressly stipulates that 'the civil action for redress of damages or prejudice caused by violation of this Law may be exercised within the criminal process or separately, before the competent civil jurisdiction, at the option of the injured party'.

---

32. Antonio Delgado Porras, op. cit., Sect. 92, pp. 113–14.

11.6. Preventive measures

As Calamandrei has pointed out, the purpose of preventive measures is to 'prevent the sovereignty of the State in its supreme expression, namely Justice, from being reduced to a belated and pointless verbal expression, the vain workings of a cumbersome machinery destined, like the guards in a comic opera, always to arrive too late'.[33]

The preventive measures, which may be sought before an action has begun and even before the infringement has taken place, are vitally important to stop the infringement from occurring and also to secure proof and seizure of the litigious goods or the litigious object. There are very few actions against infringements of copyright and neighbouring rights that have not begun by seeking preventive (or precautionary or protective) measures. The immaterial nature of the work and its omnipresence mean that once it has been brought into circulation it escapes from the control of the author or his successors in title and is liable to be appropriated, used and transformed without his intervention.

The unlawful reproduction is commonly anonymous and the person who carries it out rarely leaves his name on the infringing copies. The right holder who is the victim of aggression accordingly lacks the means of identifying the infringer and proving the infringement. Moreover, it is relatively simple to arrange for the proof to disappear—since in general the objects concerned are easily transportable, e.g. books, plates, records, cassettes and other goods—so making it impossible to adduce any evidence of the unlawful action.

Proof that preventive measures are particularly important in the area of authors' rights is given by their inclusion in the Berne Convention since the original Act of 1886 (Art. XII) which provided for the possibility of ordering the seizure of any infringing

---

33. Piero Calamandrei, *Introducción al estudio sistemático de las providencias cautelares*, Buenos Aires, Ed. Bibliográfica Argentina, 1945, p. 140.

work, to be effected in conformity with the legislation of each country.

Similar provision is also made in the American Conventions of Buenos Aires, 1910 (Article 14: 'Every publication infringing a copyright may be confiscated [...]') and Washington, 1946 (Article 13):

> All infringing publications or reproductions shall be seized at the instance of the government, or upon petition by the owner of the copyright, by the competent authorities of the Contracting State in which the infringement occurs or into which the infringing works have been imported. Any infringing presentation or public performance of plays or musical compositions, shall, upon petition by the injured copyright owner, be enjoined by the competent authorities of the Contracting State in which the infringement occurs [...].

The Universal Copyright Convention contains no explicit provisions on preventive measures, but Articles I and II, paragraph 1, impose an obligation on each Contracting State to 'provide for the adequate and effective protection of the rights of authors' and to grant them national treatment. The effectiveness of the protection afforded by the Convention involves the application by the courts of effective measures to protect the rights in question; the principle of national treatment means that foreign works shall be treated in the same way as national works and that right holders in these works shall enjoy the same legal provisions and possibility of recourse in the courts as nationals.

In respect of infringements and other unlawful actions against authors' rights and neighbouring rights, preventive measures are one of the most important procedural problems which arise and they concern in equal measure authors, performing artists, producers and, in general, the authorized users of works and of cultural products.

Given the purpose of these preventive measures[34] they

---

34. See J. Ramiro Podetti, *Tratado de las medidas cautelares*, Buenos Aires, 1969, pp. 60 *et seq.*

involve, primarily, measures to secure property: (a) to prevent unlawful acts from being taken or continuing to be taken, (b) to ensure compulsory execution of a sentence, and (c) to maintain an existing situation or simply secure property; and, secondarily, measures necessary to ensure that elements of proof can be preserved.

A. In the event of the suspected or proven committal of acts of piracy, the application *inaudita parte* of preventive measures—against the infringer or third parties—may prove effective, such as:
- seizure or confiscation of the pirated copies and of the objects and instruments used to manufacture or package said copies;
- an inventory, description and confiscation of one of the infringing copies. If this measure is impossible because of the special characteristics of the object concerned, it may be replaced by photographs of that object taken from every angle necessary to identify it adequately, without prejudice to the presence of experts during the application of the measure;
- sealing of the premises in which the pirate copies are manufactured, packaged or stored;
- an order served on the person who holds these objects to declare:
  - the name and address of the persons who ordered, sold or delivered these objects and the dates on which those events occurred with production of the order, invoice or consignment note;
  - the number of units manufactured or sold and their price, the invoice or bill of sale to be produced;
  - the identity of the persons to whom these copies have been sold or delivered;
  - seizure or confiscation of the documents or accounting records relating to the pirate copies;
  - an injunction to desist from the performance of the acts which constitute the grounds of the proceedings, warning the infringer of the application of penalties; this does not exempt him from being charged in the event of non-compliance.

In cases of piracy, notarial affidavits taken before legal proceedings are opened, and separately therefrom, may well be very useful since the infringing copies are sometimes not exhibited and sold to the public in general but supplied solely to satisfy specific orders or requests. The courts must give their full attention to these notarial affidavits.

B. In cases of *communication to the public* in violation of copyright and neighbouring rights, the following preventive measures are effective:
- suspension of the performance, exhibition or broadcast;
- forfeiture of the earnings accruing from communication to the public;
- an injunction to produce written authorization from the author, his successors in title or representatives;
- a legal statement as to the use and recording or the communication to the public.

In some countries (for example, Argentina) statutory provisions have been laid down which, without introducing preventive measures in the strict sense of the term, do effectively help to prevent infringements in the areas of interest to us here, e.g. the requirement to produce the document in which authorization is given by the author as a prerequisite for a permit by the administrative authorities to arrange musical or theatrical performances, dance sessions, etc. or for the granting of loans, subsidies or benefits of any kind.

C. Without prejudice to the general measures which are embodied in the legal codes of each country, laws on copyright and neighbouring rights also contain more or less extensive lists of specific measures, such as Colombia (Arts. 244 and 245) and Costa Rica (Arts. 130 and 131) which provide for:
- preventive confiscation: (1) of all works, productions, editions or copies (Costa Rica adds 'and of the machinery and equipment used for the fraudulent act'); (2) of the proceeds of the sale or hire of such works, productions, editions or copies; (3) of the proceeds of theatrical, cinematographic, philharmonic or any other performances;

- the prohibition or suspension of the public performance, recital or showing of a theatrical, musical or cinematographic work (Costa Rica adds 'phonograms') or of any other similar work without due authorization from the owner of the copyright or neighbouring rights.

Similar measures are provided in many other countries. Some allow confiscation as in the cases already mentioned while others provide only for preventive seizure, i.e. without alienating ownership of the infringing objects (for example Argentina, Article 79; Dominican Republic, Article 173, which provides for the two possibilities).

D. Requirements for the admissibility of the preventive measures. The substantive requirements for the admissibility of preventive measures are the probability of the existence of the right and the risk inherent in any delay; the formal requirements are ownership of the right and the provision of a counter security or guarantee intended to ensure that the party against whom the measures are taken will be compensated should it transpire that the claim is unjustified.

The criterion for determining that all the substantive requirements are met and deciding on the adoption of measures has evolved—as Di Iorio points out—in a manner similar to the evolution of the criterion by which the general aims of procedural law are measured. Thus, when private interests prevailed—the primary aim being to obtain satisfaction of a legal claim by a ruling favourable to a private interest (involving an individualistic concept of legal proceedings)—it was held that measures to place goods in judicial custody, etc. must be interpreted restrictively because they immobilized or made it difficult to dispose freely of goods; such measures were therefore treated as exceptional.

However, as the public and social interests of procedural law began to gain ground, having regard to the importance to the State of upholding the rule of law and the interest of the community in the equitable settlement of disputes, interpretation moved towards a broad presumption of admissibility, with the imposition by corollary of a greater counterpart guarantee. This not only safeguards individual interests, but also ensures the effectiveness and certainty of the legal process by preventing private individuals from flouting the judicial authority.[35]

Account must also be taken of the fact that precautionary measures whose aim is the preventive or preliminary examination of a case to secure evidence, constitute means of identification which are in the interests not only of the party who requests them, but also of the party against whom they are directed, since they will enable the court to determine during the proceedings whether legitimate rights have been infringed with a specific purpose in mind.

The ease with which proof of infringements of authors' rights and neighbouring rights can be disposed of and the ephemeral nature of acts of public communication mean that, in principle, the risk inherent in delay must always be recognized and the probability of the existence of a right assessed broadly, having regard to the specific difficulties of producing detailed proof as to the identity of the author or right holder[36] and bearing in mind the fact that works, performances, phonograms and other cultural products are constantly used across national frontiers. For these reasons, and in order to simplify and speed up proceedings

---

35. Alfredo Jorge Di Iorio, 'Nociones sobre la teoría general de las medidas cautelares', Buenos Aires, *Rev. La Ley*, Vol. 1978-B, pp. 829 and 832.
36. The presumptions *juris tantum* must be seen in the context of these difficulties, i.e. in relation to the author, producer and legitimation established in Article 15, paragraphs 1 and 2 and 14*bis*, paragraph (2)(b) of the Berne Convention, and to the symbols © of the Universal Copyright Convention and ℗ of the Phonogram Convention incorporated into international legislation, together with the evidence resulting from the indications contained in the entries made in the National Copyright Registers (cf. above, Chapter 10, Sect. 10.2.3) and in the International Registration of Audiovisual Works (cf. below Chap. 12, Sect. 12.4.2.4, C, c).

What is more—as we have already noted—many laws class as an offence the fact of causing the suspension of public performance without being the author, publishers, successor in title or representative of any of them or by falsely claiming such a capacity (for example, Argentina, Article 74; Colombia, Article 235; Costa Rica, Article 121, etc.).

designed to impose preventive measures, it is usual to exempt the plaintiff from the requirement to prove the authorship or representation invoked by him (for example, Argentina, Article 79: [...] 'No formality shall be required to prove the rights of the author or his successors in title. In case of dispute, such rights shall be subject to the means of proof established by the laws in force'; Colombia, Article 249: 'The person who applies for the measures provided for in the foregoing Articles shall not be obliged to file, with his application, proof of legal capacity or of representation, which is referred to in his action').

In some countries an *ex lege* right of representation is granted to the organizations responsible for the collective administration of copyright and neighbouring rights, as, for example, in Costa Rica (Art. 132), and in Argentina (Decree 5146, 1969, Article 8 and Decree 461, 1973, Article 8, respectively).

In Costa Rica, Article 133, paragraph (ii) stipulates that when the action is brought on the initiative of a copyright or related rights collecting society as the agent of its members, the judge shall exempt it from the need to provide a sufficient guarantee to insure against possible prejudice that the defendant might be caused by its action; that obligation exists in all cases where the plaintiff is not a collective administration body. In Argentina, it is generally accepted that the organizations responsible for the collective management of authors' rights and neighbouring rights may provide a personal or legal guarantee in place of a material guarantee.

E. As a general rule, preventive measures may be applied for without opening the main proceedings, provided that the latter ensue within a relatively brief period, for example 8 days in Belgium, 15 days in Argentina and 30 days in France.

F. The authorities empowered to take preventive measures vary from country to country.

In Spain and Argentina, for example, the judges of the court of first instance within whose jurisdiction the infringement occurs have authority to reach decisions or (as indicated in the Spanish Law—Article 127, paragraph (i)) where the infringement may reasonably be expected to occur, or copies considered unlawful have been discovered, at the discretion of the party applying for the measures. Nevertheless, once the main claim has been filed, the court with which it had been filed shall have sole jurisdiction over everything relating to the measure adopted.

To avoid the risk of delay, provision exists in Argentina for the preventive measure to be imposed by a judge who does not hold jurisdiction although his jurisdiction shall not thereby be extended; immediately after the action has been taken, the files must be submitted to the competent court (Code of Civil and Commercial Procedure of the Nation, Article 196). In the case of the public performance of music without the necessary prior authorization or in the event of refusal to produce such authorization, Decree No. 8478 adopted by the National Executive Authority in 1965 stipulates that the authors or their societies or representatives may denounce to the judicial police of the city of Buenos Aires and of the national territory, in either verbal or written form, the organizer, manager of the premises, impresario, etc., without prejudice to the automatic action which will be taken when proof is adduced of any infringement of Law 11.723 on intellectual property. The judicial police shall prepare the relevant instrument by gathering the necessary items of proof and opening the pre-trial proceedings in conformity with the provisions of the Penal Procedures Code. The plaintiff may identify or indicate the works which are performed without authorization; he has no need to produce, for the purpose of the instrument, evidence of his ownership of copyright and acts under his own responsibility (similar provisions have been introduced in nearly all the provinces).

In France, Article L. 332-1, previously Art. 66, stipulates that 'the police commissioners and where there are no police commissioners, justices of the peace shall be required, upon the demand of any author of a work protected by this law, or his successors, to seize the copies constituting an unlawful reproduction of the work. If the seizure will have the effect of retarding or suspending public performances which are in progress or have already been announced, a special authorization shall be obtained from the President of the Court of Major Juridiction, by an order issued on demand'.

In Costa Rica provision is made for the action to be ordered 'as a mere preventive measure by the judicial police agency or the Commissioner of the Guardia de Asistencia Rural of the place in which the show is held, although the bodies concerned are not competent to hear the case. The files shall subsequently be transmitted to the corresponding judicial authority' (Art. 134).

Chapter 12

International law on copyright and neighbouring rights

Summary

12.1 Copyright relations between States. International protection systems
12.2 Protection in the absence of international treaties
   12.2.1. Protection of foreign works under domestic law. **12.2.2.** Applicable law. **12.2.3.** Reciprocity
12.3 Bilateral agreements on reciprocity
12.4 Multilateral copyright conventions (Berne Convention, Conventions of the Inter-American system, Universal Copyright Convention). General considerations
   12.4.1. Conventions of the Inter-American system. 12.4.1.1. The First Montevideo Treaty (11 January 1889). 12.4.1.2. The Mexico City Copyright Convention (27 January 1902). 12.4.1.3. The Rio de Janeiro Copyright Convention (23 August 1906) 12.4.1.4. The Buenos Aires Copyright Convention (11 August 1910). 12.4.1.5. The Caracas Copyright Agreement (17 July 1911). 12.4.1.6. The Havana Copyright Convention (18 February 1928). 12.4.1.7. The Second Montevideo Treaty (4 August 1939). 12.4.1.8. The Washington Copyright Convention (22 June 1946). **12.4.2.** World Copyright Conventions. 12.4.2.1. Berne Convention for the Protection of Literary and Artistic Works. Developments leading up to the current Paris Act (24 July 1971). 12.4.2.2. Universal Copyright Convention. Developments leading up to the revised version adopted in Paris (24 July 1971). 12.4.2.3. Multilateral Convention for the Avoidance of Double Taxation of Copyright Royalties (Madrid, 13 December 1979). 12.4.2.4. Treaty on the International Registration of Audiovisual Works (Geneva, 18 April 1989)
12.5 World Conventions on neighbouring rights
   12.5.1. International Convention for the Protection of Performers, Producers of Phonograms and Broadcasting Organizations (Rome, 26 October 1961). **12.5.2.** Convention for the Protection of Producers of Phonograms against Unauthorized Duplication of their Phonograms ('Phonograms' Convention, Geneva, 29 October 1971). **12.5.3.** Convention relating to the Distribution of Programme-carrying Signals Transmitted by Satellite ('Satellites' Convention, Brussels, 21 May 1974)
12.6 International recommendations approved by the General Conference of UNESCO.
   12.6.1. Recommendation on the legal protection of translators and translations and the practical means to improve the status of translators (Nairobi, 22 November 1976). **12.6.2.** Recommendation concerning the Status of the Artist (Belgrade, 27 October 1980). **12.6.3.** Recommendation for the Safeguarding and Preservation of Moving Images (Belgrade, 27 October 1980). **12.6.4.** Recommendation on the Safeguarding of Traditional Culture and Folklore (Paris, 15 November 1989)

12.1. Copyright relations between States. International protection systems

The universal nature of works of the mind and the ubiquity which characterizes them mean that protection of copyright within the confines of the country of origin would be insufficient to provide proper safeguards. Authors' rights must be recognized at an adequate level and effectively enforced in all the places where the works concerned may be used.

This view appears self-evident in regard to the countries which export works, despite the fact that the supply of foreign works always exceeds that of national works. However, the countries which are primarily importers of cultural works habitually take the view that the absence of protection of foreign works is preferable so as to permit their widespread use in the country concerned. But that criterion fails to recognize the fact that without copyright protection there can be no development of indigenous creativity: after all, without reward there can be no incentive and no local industry of cultural goods which is essential if a market is to exist for national works. For the investment to be attractive and viable it must be protected against piracy.

Consequently, for the protection of national works to be effective on their home territory, foreign works must also enjoy protection. We are therefore confronted with an apparent paradox: if national works are to be protected, so must foreign works.

Foreign works which do not enjoy protection can be used without the authorization of their authors and without payment. They therefore compete unfairly with protected national works and are liable to oust the latter because their use is less costly.[1]

In the early days, international protection of authors' rights

---

[1]. As long ago as 1889, the Argentine author, Calixto Oyuela, wrote: 'Why should our publishers pay for Argentine works even if they are good, when they can appropriate and exploit similar foreign works with impunity and at no cost? Is this not a conspiracy against the growth and progress of national artistic production? By a curious but undeniable process, the lack of protection of the foreign author means that his Argentine counterpart is also unprotected. It

was ensured by bilateral reciprocal agreements, concluded for the most part between European countries: these agreements, however, were of limited scope and lacked uniformity. Internationalization of the markets for books and music made it necessary to standardize the system of cross-border protection. Bilateral agreements proved insufficient. That is why copyright was one of the first areas in which codification of private international law was established between the European countries through a multilateral treaty: the Berne Convention for the Protection of Literary and Artistic Works adopted on 9 September 1886.

The Berne Convention and, subsequently, the Universal Copyright Convention replaced the reciprocal bilateral agreements which had become extremely numerous (before acceding to the Berne Convention in 1887, France was bound by 28 treaties with 25 countries).[2] A similar situation prevailed when the Universal Copyright Convention was adopted in 1952. At the time, copyright relations between the States were governed by a hundred or so bilateral treaties.[3]

Today, there are relatively few countries that have not acceded to one, or both, of the Conventions cited above: on 1 January 1995, 111 countries belonged to the Berne Convention and 96 to the Universal Convention. Allowing for the fact that some countries (such as Honduras) have acceded to the Berne Convention but not to the Universal Convention, while others (such as Algeria, Bangladesh, Cuba, Haiti, Nicaragua, Panama, among others) belong to the latter but not to the former, it is apparent that relations between the States in the area of copyright are particularly extensive.

---

deprives his works of all pecuniary value for the sole benefit of the cupidity of publishers. In the best of cases, the author will have to make a present of his work in order to see it in print' (*Estudios y artículos*, Buenos Aires, 1889, p. 500).
2. Valerio De Sanctis, 'The Development and the International Confirmation of Copyright', *RIDA* (Paris), January 1974, p. 222.
3. Arpad Bogsch, *El derecho de autor según la Convención Universal*, Buenos Aires, Ed. Ministerio de Justicia de la República Argentina, 1975, p. 124, paragraph 1.

12.2. Protection in the absence of international treaties

As Miaja de la Muela points out, the treaty is the specific source of international law, as regards both the public and the private context.[4] In the absence of international treaties, each country applies its own rules for the protection of foreign works: these are the rules of private international law contained in the relevant domestic law, generally in copyright legislation which sets out criteria for the protection of foreign works (i.e. the domestic provisions which determine whether a particular work is to be treated as national or foreign, the law applicable to foreign works and the conditions under which they are eligible for protection).

12.2.1. Protection of foreign works under domestic law

A. In principle, domestic rules protect national works alone. Exceptionally, the system of *equal treatment* of foreign and national works is adopted, e.g. in Belgium[5] and France.[6]

---

4. Adolfo Miaja de la Muela, *Derecho International Privado*, Madrid, Ed. Atlas, 1976, Vol. I, p. 59.
5. Since 1886 the Belgian law has placed foreign authors on the same footing as national authors; the law of 30 June 1994 extended this provision to holders of neighbouring rights. According to Article 79 of this law 'without prejudice to the provisions of the International Conventions, foreign authors and holders of neighbouring rights shall enjoy in Belgium the rights warranted by this law, whereby the term of such rights may not exceed the term laid down by Belgian law. However, should such rights expire at an earlier date in their own country, they shall cease at the same time to have effect in Belgium. Furthermore, where it is asserted that Belgian authors and Belgian holders of neighbouring rights enjoy less extensive protection in a foreign country, the nationals of such country may only enjoy the provisions of this law to that same extent. Notwithstanding the first paragraph, reciprocity shall apply to the right for remuneration for private copying, of publishers, performers and producers of phonograms or first fixations of films, without prejudice to the Treaty of the European Union.
6. The law of 11 March 1957 contains no provisions on international relations except for Art. 70 which adds two paragraphs to Art. 425 of the Penal Code: Article 58 of the law of 3 July 1985 (now Intellectual Property Code, Article L. 335-2) reformulates these paragraphs as follows: 'Infringement in France of works published in France or abroad shall be punished by imprisonment of be-

In general, the domestic rules indicate which works are to be treated as *national*, that status being attributed to works which have a point of attachment of some kind with the country by reason of the person *of the author*, for example, his nationality or habitual place of residence; *of the work*, for example, the place at which it was first published, or of both. The various *points of attachment* may thus be classified as *personal* (those which relate to individuals), *real* (those which relate to material aspects) or *mixed*.

Personal: In general, the laws provide for various types of personal links: that the author, or one of the co-authors, must be a national or domiciled[7] or resident in the country concerned either habitually or even temporarily.[8] Sometimes only the criterion of the nationality of the author is adopted (for example, Belgium, Art. 79).

Real: In the case of published works, regardless of the nationality, domicile or residence of the author, one or more material points of attachment are taken as the reference criteria:

---

tween three (3) months and two (2) years and a fine of between 6,000 francs and 120,000 francs or by one only of these penalties.' 'The sale, exportation or importation ... shall be subject to the same penalty.' As Desbois has pointed out, 'these provisions, which took over the substantive content of a Decree of 26–30 March 1852 and extended its scope, mean that works published on foreign territory are protected against *contrefaçon* carried out in France in the same way as those published in France (second para.) and that foreign works which are products of *contrefaçon* carried out abroad are subject to penal law when imported into France' (cf. Henri Desbois, *Le droit d'auteur en France*, Paris, Dalloz, p. 915, Sect. 784). As we shall see later, the Law of 8 July 1964 introduced a provision for retortion in respect of works disclosed for the first time in a State which does not grant sufficient and effective protection to works disclosed for the first time in France.

7. Chile, Art. 2: 'The present law protects the rights of all Chilean authors and of foreigners domiciled in Chile. (...)'; Costa Rica, Art. 2: 'This law shall protect the works of Costa Rican authors, whether or not they reside on the national territory, and those of foreign authors resident in the country.'

8. Mexico, Art. 29: 'Foreigners, permanently, temporarily or transitionally located in the Mexican Republic shall, in respect of their works, enjoy the same rights as national authors.'

- the work must have been published in the country for the first time;
- cinematographic works, works created by a process analogous to cinematography and also photographs must have been produced on the national territory;
- works of art must form a permanent part of a building situated on the national territory;
- works of architecture must be built on the national territory.

The domestic rule rarely makes provision for just one material point of attachment, for example the first publication of the work in the State (as in the case of Argentina, Art. 13 *Contrario sensu*).

Mixed: Domestic laws habitually provide alternative personal and real criteria for protection (e.g. Germany, Art. 120 and 121; Colombia, Art. 11, para. 3; Venezuela, Art. 125 to 128).

B. Works which have none of the points of attachment established in the domestic law are treated as *foreign works* and as such are protected by the international conventions to which the country concerned subscribes. In the absence of a treaty with the country of origin of the work, the protection for which provision is made in the internal rules of private international law is applied.

C. Some countries grant protection to foreign works *solely* on the basis of the provisions of treaties (*system of diplomatic reciprocity*), e.g., Chile, Art. 2,[9] Costa Rica, Art. 3;[10] in the absence of such treaties, works may be freely used or are deemed to belong to the common cultural heritage (e.g. Chile, Art. 11, d)).

---

9. Chile, Art. 2, first paragraph, *in fine*: '... The rights of foreign authors not domiciled within the country enjoy the protection to which they are entitled by virtue of the international conventions which Chile has subscribed to and ratified.'

10. Costa Rica, Art. 3: 'The works of foreign authors resident outside the country shall enjoy in Costa Rica the protection afforded them by international conventions to which the country is party. For these purposes, stateless persons shall be assimilated to nationals of the country of residence.'

D. However, even in cases where no rules are laid down in conventions, most legislations still protect foreign works, provided that the State which is deemed to be the country of origin of the works grants reciprocity.

12.2.2. Applicable law

National law may be held applicable to foreign works (*system of territoriality*) or else the law of the country of origin of the work may be deemed to apply (*lex loci originis*). The application of the law of the country of origin of the work is soundly based on legal doctrine. It ensures that the work will be governed by one single statute and will be accorded identical treatment in all countries.

On the other hand, application to foreign works of the law governing national works (*system of territoriality*) has a pragmatic foundation. The result is that the work will be protected by a whole mosaic of laws and have a separate status in each country. At the same time this provision helps to overcome the problems which arise from the international exploitation of works: it obviates the need for judges and interested third parties to have a detailed knowledge of all the relevant national legislations and avoids the delays and difficulties which result from the requirement to establish the right of the owner in conformity with the foreign law. The transient nature of most uses of works which constitute an infringement of authors' rights make the speed of recognition of the protection enjoyed by a foreign work in the country concerned essential for such protection to be effective.

Application to foreign works of the national legislation of the State in which protection is claimed (*system of territoriality*) has been adopted with few exceptions in domestic laws (and also in those international conventions—the Berne Convention and the Universal Convention—which embody the principle of *identical treatment* for foreign and national works, i.e. the principle of *national treatment*). However, the application to foreign works of the law of the country in which protection is claimed habitually excludes certain aspects such as the duration of the right where it is longer in the country of origin of the work (for example, Argentina, Art. 15. Also Berne Convention, Paris Act, 1971, Art. 7, para. 8, and Universal Convention, Art. IV.4).

12.2.3. Reciprocity

There are historical reasons for the inclusion of the principle of reciprocity in domestic legislation. The earliest laws on copyright were enacted in Europe at a time when recognition of the civil rights of foreigners was particularly limited.

The right of all people, irrespective of nationality, to the recognition of their civil rights was proclaimed for the first time by the Constituent Assembly of the French Revolution; subsequent laws continued to embody equal treatment for nationals and foreigners. However, the lack of any response from other countries led to the adoption in France of the system of *diplomatic reciprocity* governing the recognition of civil rights to foreigners, in Art. 11 of the Napoleonic Code.[11] One hundred and sixty years later, France adopted a similar position on recognition of the rights of the authors of foreign works through the law of 8 July 1964 (at present, Intellectual Property Code, Article L. 111-4) which enabled the benefit of protection to be withheld from works disclosed for the first time in a country which did not grant *adequate and effective* protection to works disclosed for the first time in France.

Vico points out that the theory of reciprocity stemmed from disenchantment. It was a retrograde step from the humanist and universalist concept by which the French Revolution proclaimed the Rights of Man and regulated them for the first time.[12] Reciprocity is a pragmatic principle. It consists in responding to good treatment by good and bad treatment by bad, with the twofold aim of compensating the inequality of treatment in foreign countries and of fostering in them higher levels of protection of authors' rights, in particular for foreign works. Such reciprocity may by legislative or diplomatic, effective or formal.

---

11. French Civil Code, Art. 11: 'A foreigner shall enjoy in France the same civil rights as are, or shall be, accorded to French nationals by the treaties of the nation to which that foreigner belongs.'
12. Carlos M. Vico, *Curso de Derecho Internacional Privado*, Buenos Aires, Biblioteca Jurídica Argentina, 1934; T.I., pp. 100–1.

Legislative reciprocity is laid down in law. *Diplomatic* reciprocity is stipulated in an international treaty.[13]

Effective reciprocity requires the foreign law to grant works originating in the country concerned protection which is *basically equivalent* to that accorded by the law of the latter country. The laws of Colombia,[14] Peru,[15] Venezuela,[16] Germany[17] and so on, stipulate effective reciprocity.

Formal reciprocity means that works originating in one State must receive in the foreign country the same protection as is granted to national works originating therein. There is no need for

---

13. The granting of rights to foreigners is said to be subject to the condition of diplomatic reciprocity when the law stipulates which rights arise, or shall arise, out of treaties (for example, Chile, Art. 2, second para.; Costa Rica, Art. 3, etc.). Therefore, the condition of diplomatic reciprocity is more restrictive than that of legislative reciprocity since the enjoyment by the foreigner of rights depends on the existence of a treaty with the State to which this foreign national belongs, while, under the system of legislative reciprocity, it depends, in principle, on recognition by the country to which the foreigner belongs of similar rights to nationals of the other State (for example, Argentina, Art. 13; Colombia, Art. 11, etc.).

14. Colombia, Art. 11, *in fine*: 'or the national laws of the country concerned assure Colombian nationals of effective reciprocity'.

15. Peru, Art. 6, second paragraph: '... shall receive *the same protection* as Peruvian authors receive in the respective countries of such foreign authors ...'.

16. Venezuela, Art. 126, second paragraph: 'provided that the State to which the author belongs grants equivalent protection to Venezuelan authors. It shall be the responsibility of the Court, *sua sponte*, to establish the existence of reciprocity; however, the interested party may establish it by means of an attestation by two lawyers practising in the country concerned. The said attestation shall be submitted, duly legalized, and shall not exclude other means of proof.'

As Antequera Parilli points out (*Consideraciones sobre el derecho de autor —con especial referencia a la legislación venezolana*—Buenos Aires, 1977, p. 68), the Venezuelan legislator resolves the problem of proving reciprocity by applying the provisions on evidence of the foreign law contained in Art. 408 and 409 of the Code of International Private Law (Bustamante Code).

17. Germany, Art. 121, fourth paragraph: 'In the absence of such treaties, such works will be protected by copyright if, according to a notice by the Federal Minister for Justice published in the *Bundesgesetzblatt*, German nationals enjoy, in the State of which the author is a national, a *protection corresponding* to that granted to their own works.'

the protection to be equivalent to that laid down in the State concerned (as in the case of effective reciprocity). It is sufficient for the foreign country to grant these works the same protection as it provides by law for its own national works regardless of the level of such protection (for example, Argentina, Art. 13).[18]

Even countries such as Belgium and France which adopt the *system of equal treatment* of foreign and international works, do not consider it reasonable to grant protection to works originating from countries in which Belgian or French works enjoy no such protection. In these cases, it seems logical to apply the mechanism of *retortion*[19] by analogy with the laws of the countries concerned.[20]

---

18. Argentina, Art. 13, *in fine*: 'provided they belong to countries which recognize copyright'. However, this law substantially restricted the protection of foreign works by laying down in its Art. 23 a requirement to register in the country the translation contract within a year of publication of the work; failing compliance with that requirement, anyone might publish a translation. That provision lapsed when Argentina acceded first to the Universal Convention and later to the Berne Convention.

19. 'In private international law, reciprocity and retortion are essentially a single provision; the difference between them resides in the fact that reciprocity is formulated in abstract terms, while retortion constitutes the practical implementation of reciprocity in a situation in which the foreign country does not recognize our own law. As that situation must be proved, the administrative authority is habitually involved in retortion' (Werner Goldschmidt, *Derecho Internacional Privado*, Buenos Aires, El Derecho, 1970, pp. 167–8, Sect. 151).

20. Belgium, Article 79(3): 'Furthermore, where it is asserted that Belgian authors and Belgian holders of neighbouring rights enjoy less extensive protection in a foreign country, the nationals of such country may only enjoy the provisions of this law to that same extent.'

France, Intellectual Property Code, Art. L. 111-4, previously Article 1 of the law of 8 July 1964: 'Without prejudice to the provisions of the international conventions to which France is a party, should it transpire, after consultation with the Ministry of Foreign Affairs, that a State does not grant works disclosed in any form whatever for the first time in France adequate and effective protection, works which are disclosed for the first time on the territory of that State shall not benefit from the copyright protection granted under French legislation. However, no encroachment on the integrity or paternity of such works shall be tolerated.'

At international level, the Berne Convention (Paris Act, 1971) does not permit the subordination of national treatment (or equal treatment of foreigners and nationals) to the condition of reciprocity, save in exceptional cases which are expressly provided: works of applied art when they are only protected in the country of origin by special legislation on industrial designs and models (Art. 2, (7)); when the legislation of the country in which protection is claimed lays down periods exceeding the minimum durations fixed by the Convention; save where otherwise provided by the legislation of the country concerned, the duration shall not exceed the period fixed in the country of origin of the work (Art. 7, (8)); in the case of the '*droit de suite*' (Art. 14*ter*, (2); in a developed country which is not a member of the Union and declares on accession to the Convention that it accepts the 'ten year' rule in the matter of exclusive translation rights (Art. 30, (2)(b) *in fine*); finally, with respect to certain works by nationals of some countries *which do not belong to the Union*, the Berne Convention expressly authorizes the application of *retortion* measures since Art. 6(1) provides for the possibility of limiting the protection of such works.

Today there is a welcome tendency to follow the French example which precludes the application of measures of retortion to the moral right (Article L. 111-4.2; previously Art. 1.2 of the law of 8 July 1964): 'Any derogation, however, of the integrity or the authorship of such works is forbidden.' This reflects a recognition of the author's right as an integral part of human rights in general. In the same spirit, the Spanish law of 1987 stipulates in its

---

In the case referred to in the first paragraph of this Article, the corresponding copyright royalties shall be paid to bodies or institutions in the public interest designated by decree. As regards software, Article L. 111-5, previously Art. 51 of the law of 3 July 1985, stipulates that: 'Subject to the international conventions, foreigners shall enjoy in France the rights afforded under this Title on condition that the law of the State of which they are nationals or on the territory of which they have their place of residence, their registered offices or an effective establishment affords its protection to software created by French nationals and by persons having in France their place of residence or an effective establishment.'

Art. 145, fourth paragraph: 'The moral rights of the author are hereby recognized, whatever his nationality.'

12.3. Bilateral agreements on reciprocity

The system of bilateral agreements on reciprocity for the international protection of authors' rights began with the agreements concluded between 1827 and 1829 by Prussia with 32 other German States. On the basis of formal reciprocity, i.e. of the application of local laws to works originating in the other States, the contracting parties granted equal protection to their nationals by way of reciprocity.

As Ricketson[21] points out, the years which followed brought a realization that, in a context of legislation which differed substantially, formal reciprocity was disadvantageous to the nationals of the country which granted greater protection (who suffered prejudice in the country which offered less or no protection, while the nationals of the latter country benefited in the former). Hence, the bilateral treaties that were signed after 1840 incorporated certain minimum rights: translation, public performance and showing and also included provisions on permitted limitations, protected works, the duration of protection, the reproduction of articles published in the press, etc. According to Ricketson, the first bilateral treaty to include provisions of this kind was concluded between Austria and Sardinia in 1840 and then extended to other Italian States by virtue of a special mechanism under which both contracting parties were able to invite these States, together with the Swiss canton of Ticino, to accede thereto (this invitation was taken up in the same year by Lucca, Modena, Parma, Rome and Tuscany). The system was followed in the Anglo-Prussian Convention of 1846 in relation to the other German States and in the agreements concluded between 1856 and 1857 by a number of Swiss cantons.

After 1847, the European countries concluded a large number

---

21. Cf. Sam Ricketson, *The Berne Convention for the Protection of Literary and Artistic Works: 1886–1986*, London, Queen Mary College, 1987, pp. 26 *et seq.*

of bilateral agreements, many of which formed part of wider commercial conventions or were signed concomitantly. This explains why most conventions on authors' rights included the most favoured nation clause by virtue of which national authors of a country who enjoyed protection under a pre-existing treaty were able to lay claim to the most favourable treatment agreed in a subsequent treaty for the benefit of nationals of another country. The effect was that clauses contained in a bilateral agreement might be replaced in full or in part by those of a subsequent treaty concluded by the contracting State with a third country. This made a system that was already complex still more obscure and cumbersome.

In 1886, when the Berne Convention was signed, a vast tangle of conventions, declarations and arrangements existed between the European and also between certain Latin American countries. The countries which had concluded the largest number of bilateral treaties were France (at the end of 1886 it had signed agreements with thirteen European countries) followed by Belgium, Italy, Spain, the United Kingdom and Germany. On the other hand, for various reasons, Russia and the Austro-Hungarian Empire had concluded very few reciprocal bilateral treaties, while Greece, Monaco, Serbia, Romania, Bulgaria and Montenegro had signed none at all.

The United States of America, for its part, remained in splendid isolation because of the pressure exerted by the North American publishers who wanted to retain their freedom to reproduce printed works, especially English books,[22] and by the printers and trade unions in the graphic arts sector which insisted

---

22. Jane C. Ginsburg and John M. Kernochan point out that the United States had no international copyright relations at the time when the Berne Convention was first concluded. 'At that time the United States had no international copyright relations. We were, and had long been, 'a pirate nation' for whom protection abroad offered fewer attractions than free copying at home of foreign, particularly British, works. There was no general provision protecting foreign works until the Chace Act of 1891. Over the intervening century the United States politics of intellectual property changed. From a user and importer of copyrighted works, the United States became a producer and leading exporter. The

on the manufacturing clause.[23] The consumer public for its part was interested in access to an extensive supply of books at low prices.[24]

Membership of multilateral treaties was now replacing the conclusion of bilateral agreements on reciprocity which were increasingly less common. However, they did not disappear altogether because they were still useful in some cases. This is shown by the agreements concluded by the former Soviet Union with Hungary, Bulgaria, Germany, former Czechoslovakia, Cuba and Poland,[25] Austria and Sweden; or by the United States of America with the Republic of Korea, Singapore and Indonesia[26] in

---

appeal of international protection became correspondingly manifest [...]' ('One Hundred and Two Years Later: the United States Joins the Berne Convention', *RIDA* (Paris), 141, p. 57).

23. According to the manufacturing clause, a special provision of the United States Federal Copyright Law, protection of foreign works required the copies of books, photographs, chromos and lithographs to be printed with characters composed in the United States or on plates obtained using characters so composed or by means of blocks or drawings on a stone surface manufactured in this country. A derogation from this provision was adopted on 1 July 1986 pursuant to the provisions of Section 601 (a) of Copyright Law (No. 94-553) first adopted in 1976 and amended by law No. 97-215 of 24 July 1982.

Ginsburg and Kernochan point out that this derogation was preceded by an action taken by various member countries of the European Economic Community which belonged to the Berne Convention; in 1986 they proposed an embargo worth many millions of dollars on United Stated products unless the manufacturing clause was deleted from the law on copyright (cf. *RIDA* (Paris), 141, p. 153, note 14).

24. Cf. Nicola Stolfi, *La Proprietà intellettuale*, Turin, Un. Tip., Ed. Torinese, 1917, T. II, pp. 633–5.

25. Cf. *Copyright Laws and Treaties of the World*, CLTW, Paris, UNESCO: USSR: II.1, II.2, II.3, II.4, II.5.

26. The former Soviet Union ratified the Universal Convention alone. Since 1994, the Russian Federation, Estonia and Lithuania have become parties to the Berne Convention. The Republic of Korea acceded to the Universal Convention in 1987, but not to the Berne Convention. Singapore and Indonesia did not join either the Universal Convention or the Berne Convention (Indonesia had been a member of the Berne Union between 1913 and 1960). (Situation as of 1 January 1995: see *Industrial Property and Copyright* (Geneva), WIPO, 1995.)

order to secure protection for its cultural products in the Asian Pacific area.

Stewart lays emphasis on the fact that reliance on bilateral agreements, even when supported by GATT procedures, instead of multilateral conventions means reverting to the situation one hundred years ago, i.e. to the situation of international copyright relations which prevailed prior to the Berne Convention. On the subject of the agreements referred to, Stewart points out that the recent tendency to conclude bilateral agreements (which had ceased to exist since the nineteenth century, i.e. when the first multilateral copyright convention was adopted) might be significant in that it is the superpowers which seem to be promoting arrangements of this kind by wielding their economic power. The disadvantage resides in the fact that, while the owners of copyright in the United States and the former Soviet Union are protected, copyright owners from the rest of the world enjoy no protection at all if the countries concerned do not belong to any of the multinational conventions.[27]

12.4. Multilateral copyright conventions (Berne Convention, Conventions of the Inter-American system, Universal Copyright Convention). General considerations

A. THE BERNE CONVENTION

This is the oldest multilateral treaty and the one which affords the highest level of protection. Its provisions have been developed in successive stages through regular revisions provided for in the Convention itself since the outset (Art. XVII of the original Act). These revisions take place at intervals of about 20 years.

In the words of De Sanctis, 'there is no doubt that the Berne Convention constitutes one of the most important international

---

27. Stephen M. Stewart, *International Copyright and Neighbouring Rights*, London, Butterworths, 2nd ed., 1989, pp. 344–5.

Acts of the nineteenth century'.[28] Since its adoption, it has played a decisive role in the harmonization of domestic legislation through the minimum provisions on protection, to such an extent that it has been the source of the relevant national laws in a great many countries long before they acceded to the convention itself (Argentina, Peru, Venezuela, for example).

However, even though the Original Act (1886) of the Convention claimed a universal vocation in that it was open to membership of all States (Art. XVIII) without discrimination on political or ideological grounds, it was nevertheless the result of a European initiative and at that time binding only on the European countries; for the time being at least, its extension to other continents was only possible through the 'colonial clause'.[29]

On other continents too it was viewed as a European treaty intended to protect European works. In America, that prejudice survived until relatively recently, to such an extent that in the first 80 years of its existence the only American countries to join the Convention were Haiti (between 1887 and 1943), Brazil and Canada which joined in 1922 and 1928 respectively.

B. THE CONVENTIONS OF THE INTER-AMERICAN SYSTEM

At the same time as the Berne Convention was approved, the Treaty on Literary and Artistic Property was signed in Montevideo as the outcome of the I South American Congress on Private International Law (1888–89). That treaty was of great value because it not only permitted protection of works originating in the countries of the Montevideo system (Argentina, Bolivia, Paraguay, Peru and Uruguay), but also extended this protection to others by the authority given in Art. 6 of the Additional Protocol.

The year 1889 was one which brought many developments of lasting importance in America: in the south, the proceedings of the Montevideo Congress ended and in the north, at the invitation

---

28. Valerio De Sanctis, op. cit., p. 230.
29. Ibid.

of the United States of America, the First Pan-American Conference was held in Washington. One of its subjects was the formation of a customs union between the Republics of the continent. Even though the aims formulated when the conference was convened were not achieved, it nevertheless marked the beginning of the Pan-American Union, later followed by the Organization of American States (OAS).[30]

This was the start of the work of the Pan-American agencies and a series of conferences dealing with many subjects relating to private international law ensued. A number of copyright conventions were concluded: in Mexico, 1902; Rio de Janeiro, 1906; Buenos Aires, 1910; Havana, 1928 and Washington, 1946, to which must be added the Caracas Agreement of 1911 and the Montevideo Treaty of 1939.

All this international activity was fraught with various obstacles, not least the difficulty of harmonizing the legal system of the Latin American countries with that of the United States, and the lack of interest both of the latter and of other countries on the continent in acceding to the Conventions even if they took part—sometimes actively—in their preparation, in the proceedings of the Conferences and in their adoption. Efforts to give the system a truly Pan-American dimension then followed, but none was successful.

The Buenos Aires Convention was the only one which managed to gain wide membership, including the United States, but it suffered from the absence of Argentina and Chile until the 1950s when its importance began to fade with the advent of the Universal Convention (Geneva, 1952)

The two major systems, i.e. that of the Berne Convention to which the European countries belonged together with their African and Asian colonies and the Commonwealth nations, and the Conventions of the Inter-American system, coexisted in their respective areas of influence.

---

30. Although the programme of the First Pan-American Conference did not include copyright protection, it is mentioned here because of its historical importance.

C. The Universal Convention

This simultaneous existence of the Berne Convention—which did not succeed in achieving universal validity—and the Inter-American Conventions, led to the idea of their unification, at least after 1928. The sixth resolution of the Berne Convention Revision Conference held at Rome in 1928 gave official expression to the desire to integrate these two systems.

However, the efforts made as a result of the resolution adopted at the Rome Conference did not bring positive results until 1947 when UNESCO took up the cause of unification and universality. This was a particularly propitious time since the Second World War was over and neither of the two remaining superpowers had ratified the Berne Convention or the Conventions of the Inter-American system. The United States of America had only joined the Mexico City Convention in 1908 and the Buenos Aires Convention in 1911. Furthermore, the liberation of the European colonies in Asia and Africa also reduced the scope of territorial validity of the Berne Convention, since the new States did not in principle consider themselves bound by the treaties in which they had been involved by virtue of the 'colonial clause'. The applicability of such treaties was made conditional on a subsequent act of confirmation or termination.

After seven years of preparation (during which meetings of experts were held in 1947, 1949, 1950 and 1951), the proceedings of the Intergovernmental Copyright Conference convened by UNESCO in Geneva culminated in the adoption of the Universal Convention on 6 September 1952.

During the Geneva Conference the idea prevailed of a third intermediate convention which would only embody certain principles shared by both systems (the European and Inter-American) and, after abandonment of the endeavour to achieve uniform legislation or a higher level of protection, the Universal Convention was able to attain the goal of harmonizing the various conventions, regulations and treaties in this area and to achieve *universal* international copyright protection.

The countries which still did not feel able to comply with the rights and guarantees accorded to authors by the Berne Convention were able to join the Universal Convention as a first step before accession to the Berne Convention. The intention was to leave no country outside the international system of copyright protection.

The Universal Convention did not have the effect of abrogating the Conventions of the Inter-American system. 'In the event of any difference either between the provisions of such existing conventions or arrangements and the provisions of this Conventions, or between the provisions of this Convention and those of any new convention or arrangement which may be formulated between two or more American Republics after this convention comes into force, the convention or arrangement most recently formulated shall prevail between the parties thereto' (Art. XVIII).

12.4.1. Conventions of the Inter-American system

12.4.1.1. *The First Montevideo Treaty (11 January 1889)*

The Montevideo Treaty on Literary and Artistic Property formed part of the proceedings of the I South American Congress on Private International Law which was held in the years 1888 and 1889[31] and attended by Argentina, Bolivia, Brazil, Chile, Paraguay, Peru and Uruguay.

---

31. During the I Montevideo Congress, eight treaties were concluded (under international civil, commercial, penal and procedural law, on literary and artistic property, patents, trade marks and registered designs and on the exercise of the professions), together with an Additional Protocol.

 This was the first implementation at international level of the ambitious project to codify private international law by means of formulas enabling legal conflicts in extra-national relations to be resolved; this demonstrated the early wish of the Latin American countries to achieve juridical integration.

 The Treaties of Montevideo of 1888–89 formed the basis for those subsequently adopted by the first Central American Juridical Congress (Guatemala, 1897) and later revised at the second Congress (El Salvador, 1901); these texts did not in fact enter into force.

The influence of the Original Act of the Berne Convention[32] is clearly apparent, although there were some major differences:
- protection is governed by the law of the country where the work was originally published (*lex loci publicationis* or *lex loci originis*, Art. 2); it follows that the protection granted in the contracting States to works published for the first time in one of them is that established by the law of the latter State. This law is therefore applicable instead of the law of the State in which protection is claimed (principle of *equal* or *national treatment* enshrined in the Berne Convention and in most multilateral and bilateral agreements). The adoption of the *lex loci publicationis* which was certainly attributable to the theoretical rigour of the international experts present in Montevideo was subject to an important limitation in Article 11 which stipulated that, in the area of *liability for copyright infringement*, the applicable jurisdiction and law were those of *the country in which the infringement had been committed*[33] (most claims for the protection of foreign works arise out of illicit use and, in regard to the criminal and procedural laws applicable in cases brought before the courts, the States, with few exceptions, reserve the right to apply their own domestic law);
- no provisions are made for unpublished works (which are expressly protected by the Berne Convention, Article II, first para.); since the law of the country in which the work is first published applies, it follows that unpublished works are not protected;
- the right of translation was given equal status with the other rights (right to dispose of the work, publish it and reproduce it

---

32. Some of the States which took part in the I Montevideo Congress (Argentina, Brazil and Paraguay) showed an interest in the preparations for the Berne Convention. In the end, they did not subscribe to it because they felt that its provisions were not appropriate for countries with only a small body of literary and artistic production.

33. Article 11: 'Responsibilities incurred by infringers of the rights in literary and artistic property shall be dealt with by the courts and shall be governed by the laws of the country in which the infringement was committed.'

in any form, Art. 3), while Article V of the original Berne Act granted protection only for ten years from the date of publication of the original work in one of the countries of the Union;
- the list of protected works mentions choreographic and photographic works (Art. 5), while Article I of the Final Protocol of the Berne Convention made protection of these works conditional on the provisions of national legislation;
- no reference is made to any formalities (Art. II, second para. of the Original Act of the Berne Convention, stipulates that the enjoyment of rights is conditional on compliance with the conditions and formalities prescribed by the law in the country of origin of the work).

Article 6 of the Additional Protocol to the Montevideo Treaty stipulated the possibility of extending protection to other States. At the time the Treaty was approved, the signatories were required to declare whether or not they agreed to such accessions.[34]

Ratifications: Argentina (1894), Bolivia (1904), Paraguay (1889), Peru (1889) and Uruguay (1892).

The accessions of France (1896), Spain (1899), Italy (1900) and Belgium (1903) *were accepted by Argentina and Paraguay*, while those of Austria (1923), Germany (1927) and Hungary (1931) *were accepted by Argentina, Bolivia and Paraguay*.

12.4.1.2. The Mexico City Copyright Convention (27 January 1902)

This convention was signed during the Second Pan-American Conference. The influence of the Berne Convention was greater on the Mexico City Convention than on the Montevideo Treaty because it stipulated that 'the signatory States constitute themselves into a Union for the purpose of recognizing and protecting the rights of literary and artistic property' (Article 1) and adopted the principle of *equal* or *national treatment* by providing that 'the authors who belong to one of the signatory countries or their assigns shall enjoy in the other countries the rights which their

---

34. Peru and Uruguay consented only to the accession of Latin American countries.

respective laws at present grant, or in the future may grant, to their own citizens' (Article 5).

To obtain recognition of the copyright of a work, the formal requirement was an application submitted to the official department designated by each signatory government accompanied by two copies of the work; if the author, or his assigns, should desire that his copyright be recognized in any other of the signatory countries, he shall attach to his petition a number of copies of his work equal to that of the countries he may therein designate. The said department shall distribute the copies mentioned among those countries, accompanied by a copy of the respective certificate, in order that the copyright of the author may be recognized by them'; however, omissions do not entitle those concerned to institute proceedings against the State (Article 4).

Ratifications: Costa Rica (1903), El Salvador (1902), United States (1908), Guatemala (1902), Honduras (1904), Nicaragua (1904) and Dominican Republic (1907).

12.4.1.3. The Rio de Janeiro Copyright Convention (23 August 1906)

This convention was concluded during the Third Pan-American Conference and made provision for the international protection both of copyright and of industrial property (literary and artistic property, patents, industrial designs and models and trade and commercial marks). It provided for adoption of the treaties on these subjects drawn up in Mexico City on 27 January 1902 (Article I), set up a Union of the Nations of America and created two Bureaux known as the Bureaux of the International American Union for the Protection of Intellectual and Industrial Property, one in Havana (for the countries of North America, Central America and the northern region of South America), and the other in Rio de Janeiro (for the other countries of South America), for the purpose of centralizing the registration of literary and artistic works, patents, trade marks, drawings, models, etc. which were to be registered in each one of the signatory nations according to the respective treaties and with a view to their validity and recognition by the others. This international registration was entirely optional for the persons interested, since they were free to apply, personally or through an attorney, for registration in each one of the States in which they sought protection (Article II). In fact, these Bureaux never became operational—hardly surprising since only nine countries ratified the convention.

This convention introduced innovations in respect of minimum periods of protection by providing that the period of international protection derived from the registration 'shall be that recognized by the laws of the country where the rights originated or have been recognized and if the said laws do not provide for such matters, or do not specify a fixed period, the respective periods shall be, for literary and artistic works, 25 years, counting from the death of the author thereof ...' (Article VII, second para.).

Ratifications: Brazil (1911), Costa Rica (1908), Chile (1910), Ecuador (1909), El Salvador (1910), Guatemala (1909), Honduras (1908), Nicaragua (1909), Panama (1911).

12.4.1.4. *The Buenos Aires Copyright Convention (11 August 1910)*

This convention was concluded during the Fourth Pan-American Conference and secured the largest number of accessions. The countries which had originally formed the Montevideo system joined, as did most of those that had ratified the previous American conventions, including the United States.

The Buenos Aires Convention took over the model of the Montevideo Treaty, although with some significant differences: it adopted the principle of equal treatment for foreigners and nationals (Article 6) and introduced the copyright notice obligation as a condition for maintaining copyright (Article 3) (the system of the 'mandatory notice' which remained in force in North American legislation until the adoption of the Berne Convention Implementation Act of 1988 by virtue of which the legislation of the United States was brought into line with the provisions of the Berne Convention.[35] The country of origin of the work is deemed

---

35. See above Chapter 1, Sect. 1.3.3.

to be that of its first publication in America and if it shall have appeared simultaneously in several of the signatory countries, that which fixes the shortest period of protection (Article 7). The text stipulates (in a manner analogous to the Berne Convention) that every publication which infringes copyright may be confiscated in the signatory countries in which the original work has the right to be legally protected (Article 14).

Ratifications: Argentina (1950); Bolivia (1914); Brazil (1915); Colombia (1936); Costa Rica (1916); Chile (1955); Dominican Republic (1912); Ecuador (1914); Guatemala (1912); Haiti (1919); Honduras (1914); Nicaragua (1913); Panama (1913); Paraguay (1917); Peru (1920); United States (1911); Uruguay (1919).

12.4.1.5. The Caracas Copyright Agreement (17 July 1911)

This Agreement was drawn up during the Bolívar Congress and was joined by Bolivia, Colombia, Ecuador, Peru and Venezuela. It followed the model of the Montevideo Treaty with a few exceptions: protection is granted *solely to citizens of the five signatory countries* (Article 1), while the Montevideo Treaty (Article 2) accorded protection *to all authors* in respect of works published for the first time in one of the contracting States. As to formalities, it stipulates that for the rights granted by the law of the State in which publication or production first occurred to be enjoyed in the signatory countries (the Montevideo system of *lex loci publicationis*), the interested party shall give the necessary notice, pay the fees established in each country and comply with the formalities of deposit of the work (Article 2).

The Agreement contained an unusual and particularly interesting provision: the signatory States undertook to maintain penalties, in their respective legislations, for infringers of literary and artistic property (Article 9).

Ratifications: Ecuador (1914), Peru (1915) and Venezuela (1914).

12.4.1.6. The Havana Copyright Convention (18 February 1928)

This was adopted in the framework of the Sixth Pan-American Conference which was the most fruitful in terms of the large number of conventions concluded during its proceedings, one of which was the Code of Private International Law known as the *Bustamente Code*.[36]

The Havana Copyright Convention was intended to replace the Buenos Aires Convention (1910); it was a revised version of the latter and took over most of its provisions, although with a number of significant changes:
- the list of specifically mentioned protected works was widened to include cinematographic works, reproductions by mechanical instruments designed for the reproduction of sounds, and works of the arts applied to any human activity whatever (Article 2);
- the list of authors' rights was widened to include the rights of reproduction, adaptation and public presentation by means of cinematography (Article 4*bis*) and of mechanical reproduction of literary and musical works, together with the performance of the latter by mechanical means (Article 5);
- the inalienable nature of the moral right of authors to the integrity of their works is recognized (Article 13*bis*) in line with the subjective approach. (In that same year, the Rome Conference incorporated in Article 6*bis* of the Berne Convention, the moral right to authorship and integrity of the work according to the objective concept, i.e. when deformation, mutilation or other modification of the work would be prejudicial to the honour or reputation of the author);
- the duration of protection granted by the Convention was fixed as the lifetime of the author and 50 years after his death (Article 6);
- the formalities were made more stringent by stipulating that the

---

36. This was drafted by the Cuban international law expert Antonio Sánchez de Bustamante y Sirvén and comprised 437 articles setting out general norms and provisions of international civil, commercial, penal and procedural law including extradition. It entered into force between Bolivia, Brazil, Costa Rica, Cuba, Chile, Ecuador, El Salvador, Guatemala, Haiti, Honduras, Nicaragua, Panama, Peru and Venezuela.

reservation of ownership must indicate the name of the person in whose favour registration is effected, the country of origin of the work (i.e. the country, or countries, in which simultaneous publication is made) and the year of first publication (Article 3).
Ratifications: Costa Rica (1933), Ecuador (1936), Guatemala (1932), Nicaragua (1934) and Panama (1929).

12.4.1.7. The Second Montevideo Treaty (4 August 1939)

This was concluded during the Second South American Congress on Private International Law held to commemorate the fiftieth anniversary of the 1888–89 Congress. The opening of the Congress coincided with the outbreak of the Second World War in 1939 and its proceedings took place in two sessions ending in 1940. The treaties signed during the Congress differed in many respects from those adopted in 1889.

In the Treaty on Intellectual Property, apart from the change of title (the previous version being known as the Treaty on Literary and Artistic Property), the most significant changes are as follows: adoption of the principle of equal or national treatment (Article 6); extension of the works expressly mentioned (Article 2) and of protected rights in order to cover the new forms of exploitation of works—cinematography, telephotography and 'any other technical means' (Article 3); recognition of the moral right of the author to the authorship and integrity of his work (Article 15) in conformity with the objective approach adopted in the Rome text (1928) of the Berne Convention; recognition of the international personality of societies of authors (Article 6 *in fine*); a provision permitting the confiscation of any illicit reproduction (Article 13) by analogy with the provisions of the Berne Convention (Article XII of the original Act and Article 16 of the subsequent versions).

Ratifications: Uruguay (1942) and Paraguay (1958).

12.4.1.8. The Washington Copyright Convention (22 June 1946)

The eighth Pan-American Conference held in Lima in 1938 decided to recommend to the Pan-American Union the preparation of the definitive draft of a Continental Convention based on the

Draft Protocol to the Buenos Aires Convention (1910) which had been drawn up by the North American National Committee of Intellectual Co-operation and took account of the observations made by the American countries. The Pan-American Union completed its work in January 1940 and submitted it to the governments; in conformity with the views expressed by a majority, the decision was taken to convene a special conference of experts, given the fact that the complexity and technical nature of the problems relating to the protection of copyright required a thorough study which would be difficult to perform at an Inter-American Conference.

Because of the Second World War, the meeting of experts was not convened immediately. Meanwhile the Pan-American Union prepared two successive new Draft Additional Protocols to the revised text of the Buenos Aires Convention which were submitted for consideration by the governments and incorporated the observations formulated by them. After the war, the Pan-American Union convened the Inter-American Conference of Experts on Copyright in Washington on 1 June 1946 for which a fourth draft dated September 1945 was prepared.[37]

The Washington Convention, modelled on the Buenos Aires Convention as revised in the Havana Convention which it was destined to replace, incorporated a number of significant improvements over its predecessors in regard to:
- the terminology used (the term *copyright* replaces *literary and artistic property*, etc.);
- the list of protected economic rights (Article 2);
- protection of unpublished works (Article 4.1.);
- protection of articles published in newspapers and magazines, since unsigned articles are also included (Article 6.2 makes no distinction between signed and unsigned articles);

---

37. See Carlos Mouchet and Sigfrido A. Radaelli, *Los derechos del escritor y del artista*, Buenos Aires, Ed. Sudamericana, 1957, pp. 263–5.

- abolition of the copyright notice requirement (Article 9); although use of the expression 'copyright reserved', or its abbreviation 'Copr' or the letter 'c', is recommended, this 'is not to be interpreted as a condition of protection of the work under the provisions of the present Convention' (Article 10); and
- protection of the title of a copyrighted work which has become internationally famous (Article 14).

No definition of the country of origin of the work is indicated (we may infer from the provisions of Articles 8, 9 and 10 that the place of first publication of the work in any of the contracting countries is to be considered as the place of origin).

This text made less extensive provision in the area of:
- the period of protection in that (Article 8) the Havana provisions are deleted (the author's life and 50 years after his death); and
- the authorization of the assignment or waiver of the moral right to the integrity of the work (in the Havana Convention the moral right is defined as *inalienable*).

These retrograde steps are attributable to the intention, which was not in the event achieved, of enabling the United States to join, so creating an effective Pan-American system of copyright protection.

Ratifications: Argentina (1953), Bolivia (1947), Brazil (1949), Costa Rica (1950), Cuba (1955), Chile (1955), Dominican Republican (1947), Ecuador (1947), Guatemala (1952), Haiti (1953), Honduras (1947), Mexico (1947), Nicaragua (1950), Paraguay (1949).

The importance of the conventions of the Inter-American system today

The importance of the conventions of the Inter-American system today resides in their historic value. Although many of them continue to be formally valid, their application to the countries of the continent (and between some of these and the European countries which acceded to the Montevideo Treaty of 1889) has been superseded by accession to the Berne Convention and the Universal Convention.

12.4.2. World Copyright Conventions

12.4.2.1. Berne Convention for the Protection of Literary and Artistic Works. Developments leading up to the current Paris Act (24 July 1971)

A. GENESIS

a. ALAI

In 1878, at the initiative of the *Société des Gens de Lettres*, an international literary congress chaired by Victor Hugo was held in Paris. In the course of that congress, the *International Literary Association* was set up. In 1884 its membership was extended to artists and the word *artistic* added to its title. Since then this association has been known as *ALAI*.[38]

In the area of international copyright protection, the 1878 Congress approved two resolutions favouring the application to foreign works of the principle of *national treatment* without the need for accomplishing any formalities other than those required in the country of origin of the work. These resolutions were similar to those which had been adopted 20 years earlier by the Congress on Literary and Artistic Property held in Brussels in 1858.[39]

---

38. See above, Chapter 9, Sect. 9.1.1.2.
39. Cf. Sam Ricketson, op. cit., pp. 46–7. This author points out that the Brussels Congress was attended by some 300 persons including delegates from scientific societies, economists, men of letters, artists, journalists, lawyers, publishers and printers in addition to officials, politicians, judges and the like. Some States such as Saxony, Denmark, the Netherlands, Sardinia, Parma and Portugal sent official delegates and there were unofficial representatives from each major European country. The 1858 Congress reached a general consensus on the need for international copyright protection, but one of the chief points of difference arose in relation to the question of the length of protection. A strong body of opinion favoured perpetuity, but this was ultimately rejected in favour of a definite time limit, although the period preferred was longer than that then accorded under most national laws. In the area of international copyright protection, the 1858 Congress advocated its recognition in the legislation of all the civilized peoples, even in the absence of reciprocity, and the absolute and complete identity of treatment for foreign and national authors without the need for the accomplishment of formalities other than those required by the law of the

However, although the 1858 Congress was an isolated event with no follow-up, the work of ALAI had a decisive impact on the genesis of international copyright protection. From its inception, it advocated the conclusion of a treaty which was originally to be known as the Universal Convention on the Protection of Literary Property. The underlying idea of the programme developed by ALAI was that 'all the authors of works published or performed in a contracting country, regardless of their nationality, shall be treated in the other countries in the same way as the national authors of these countries, without being required to complete any formality whatever'.[40] That concept was gradually to be embodied in the Berne Convention through three of its basic principles: *national treatment* (or *equal* treatment of works of the countries of the Union and national works), *automatic protection* (without the requirement for any particular formalities) and the *independence of protection*.

b. *The Congress of the ALAI in Rome (1882) and the Berne Conference (1883)*

During the ALAI Congress in Rome, three of its members (Lermina, the first Secretary-General of the Association, Schmidt from the German Association of Publishers and Baetzmann, the Norwegian representative) proposed the creation of a *Union for Copyright Protection* similar to the Universal Postal Union (the participation of Dr Paul Schmidt in this initiative underlines the interest taken by the industrial sector in international protection). This proposal was immediately adopted unanimously, since it

---

country of origin of the work concerned. As Ricketson rightly points out, these resolutions constituted a rudimentary outline of a programme for a universal copyright law (ibid., pp. 41–3).

40. '[...] *tous les auteurs des œuvres publiées ou représentées dans un pays contractant, à quelque nationalité qu'ils appartiennent, seront assimilés dans les autres pays aux auteurs nationaux de ces pays sans être astreintes à la moindre formalité*' (cf. Henri Desbois, André Françon and André Kerever, *Les conventions internationales du droit d'auteur et des droits voisins*, Paris, Dalloz, 1976, p. 10).

reflected the interests of authors and composers and also those of the publishers of books and musical works.

However, this Union was not put into effect in France (the home of ALAI) or in Italy (where the idea was born), but in Switzerland where the next ALAI Congress was held. Switzerland was thought to be the appropriate country for the discussion and creation of the foundations of a copyright protection union as it was the venue for important international meetings and was already the seat of various international organizations, such as the Postal and Telegraphy Unions and the International Red Cross. The Swiss Government supported the initiative in response to representations by Numa Droz, a member of the Federal Council of the Swiss Confederation who was particularly interested in all matters pertaining to the defence of the rights of creators and, following the ALAI Congress in Rome, had published an article advocating an international convention in this area in the *Revue Universelle de Lausanne*.

The preparatory ALAI congress held in Berne in September 1883 was chaired by Droz (as were the three diplomatic conferences which followed in Berne in 1884, 1885 and 1886). During this conference, a preliminary draft international convention containing ten articles was adopted.

c. The 1884 Diplomatic Conference

In December 1883, at the request of ALAI, the Swiss Federal Council addressed a circular letter to all the 'civilized countries' in which it called their attention to the idea of a diplomatic conference for the formation of the Union proposed by ALAI. Favourable replies were soon forthcoming, and the Swiss Government convened a diplomatic conference in Berne in September 1884 with a view to preparing at governmental level the first formal draft of a multilateral international copyright convention.

The ALAI draft was the basis of a document with 18 articles, a transitional provision and a final protocol put forward by the Swiss Government as the programme for the conference which was attended by representatives of Austria-Hungary, Belgium, France, Germany, Haiti, Italy, Netherlands, Norway, Sweden, Switzerland and the United Kingdom.

At the opening of the proceedings, Germany proposed that a universal codification should be attempted (a uniform legal convention on copyright which would replace national laws and so create legislative uniformity), but this proposal was rejected by several countries which stressed the many differences between national legislation in this area. The idea was felt to be premature ('Time must be allowed to take its course' was the feeling, as De Sanctis recalls),[41] but it was used as the basis of a proposal from Switzerland for one of the two committees to prepare a list of general principles.

The proceedings of the conference ended with the adoption of five documents: a draft convention for the constitution of a General Union for copyright protection with 21 articles, an additional article, a final protocol, a series of principles seeking *further unification* and the final minutes of the conference.

d. The 1885 Diplomatic Conference

The results of the first Diplomatic Conference were favourably received by the governments and the Swiss Federal Council went on to convene a second Diplomatic Conference in Berne in September 1885 to draw up a definitive draft. It was attended by representatives of Argentina, Belgium, France, Germany, Haiti, Honduras, Italy, the Netherlands, Norway, Paraguay, Spain, Sweden, Switzerland, Tunisia, the United Kingdom and the United States.

This conference confined itself to making a number of amendments to the 1884 draft, without any substantive change to the criteria set out previously (the most important changes were made in the final Protocol). That is how the final draft of the Original Act of the Berne Convention was prepared.

B. Historical development

Starting out from the Original Act of 1886, the Berne Convention has undergone successive phases—with five revisions (in 1908,

---

41. Cf. Valerio De Sanctis, op. cit., p. 230.

1928, 1948, 1967 and 1971) and three supplements (1896, 1914 and 1979)—to improve the juridical system established between the Member States constituting the Union. A number of reforms have also been introduced to protect new forms of creation (photographic and cinematographic works), widen the specific rights granted to authors—as new techniques of use and circulation of works were invented and developed (mechanical reproduction, broadcasting)—impose more stringent minimum criteria for protection (abolition of formalities, duration of protection), introduce uniform regulatory provisions under the Convention, carry out organizational and structural reform and establish specific provisions for the developing countries.

To follow the evolution of the Convention and the purpose of the successive amendments, its basic structure, and each of its phases, will be outlined below and a succinct description given of the main provisions of the Original Act, the most significant changes, and the content of the 1971 Act.

C. STRUCTURE OF THE CONVENTION

As Masouyé has pointed out, the provisions of the Convention fell into two classes from the beginning: those of substance, governing what is known as the material law and those administrative and final clauses which cover matters of administration and structure. The first class is often subdivided into rules of the convention proper and rules for referring matters back.[42]

a. The substantive provisions

1. *Rules of the Convention*: since the differences between national legislations were, and still are, substantial, it was felt that effective protection could not depend solely on the internal law of each country of the Union. Provision was therefore made for a set of uniformly applicable rules giving minimum protection. Where the national legislation of a member country of the Union did not attain the minimum protection stipulated in the Convention, the

---

42. Claude Masouyé, op. cit., p. 5.

latter made good the omission through common regulatory provisions. In the case of works belonging to the Union, the minimum rights laid down in the Convention were therefore added to the domestic law applicable to national works.

2. *Rules for referring matters back*: these rules, as Masouyé points out, do not provide solutions but seek to overcome conflicts between different legal provisions by referring the matter back to the legal order of the country in which protection is claimed.

b. Administrative provisions and final clauses

These establish the organs of the Berne Union and contain provisions of a purely administrative nature. In terms of public international law, they define the rights and obligations of the member countries of the Union.[43]

D. THE BERNE ACT OF 1886

On 6 September 1886, the third Diplomatic Conference convened in November 1885 by the Swiss Federal Council met in Berne. Delegates from Belgium, France, Germany, Haiti, Italy, Liberia, Spain, Switzerland, the United Kingdom and Tunisia attended, together with observers from the United States and Japan. After four days' work, during which some minor amendments were made to the draft prepared by the Conference held in the previous year, the *Berne Convention for the Protection of Literary and Artistic Works* was adopted on 9 September. It consisted of 21 articles and a number of annexes: the Additional Article and the Final Protocol which in turn contains seven articles. The Berne Act was signed by the ten countries which were represented by delegates.

The original text sets out the basic structure of the Convention. It is preceded by a *Preamble* which defines the purpose of the Convention: 'to protect, in as effective and uniform a manner as possible, the rights of authors in their literary and artistic works'.

---

43. Ibid., p. 125, Section 22.1.

As Masouyé points out, this sentence reflects three criteria for the protection which is to be provided: effectiveness (reflecting the desire of those who drafted the Convention to ensure a high level of protection), uniformity (stressing the wish to establish as far as possible identical provisions for all the beneficiaries of this protection) and its subject matter (i.e. to protect copyright).[44]

Its main provisions may be summarized as follows:

a. Constitution of a Union

The countries to which the Convention applies constitute a Union for the protection of the rights of authors in their literary and artistic works (Article I).

b. Area of application of the Convention: criteria for protection and points of attachment

The Convention is applicable both to *works which have already been published* and to *unpublished works*. In the case of unpublished works, the Convention is applicable only to those whose author belongs to a member country of the Union (*personal criterion*); in the case of published works, applicability of the Convention is guided by the place of first publication (*real criterion*) (Article II, para. 1 and Article III).

c. Principle of national treatment (or of equal treatment of foreigners and nationals)

Authors belonging to a member country of the Union, or their lawful representatives, shall enjoy in the other countries for their works, whether published in one of these countries or unpublished, the rights which the respective laws do now may hereafter grant to natives (Article II, para. 1).

d. National treatment

Therefore means that works produced in the Union shall be treated in the same way as national works, i.e. equated with the

---

44. Ibid., p. 7.

latter. In other words, the applicable law will be the national law of the member country of the Union in which protection is sought.

However, the application of the principle of *national treatment* in the original Act of the Convention is fragmentary and restricted, as we shall see.

e. Protection is dependent on that provided in the country of origin of the work (subordination of the principle of national treatment to compliance with the conditions and formalities established by the 'lex originis')

Enjoyment of the rights which the law of the country in which protection is claimed grants to its nationals, is subject to compliance with the conditions and formalities prescribed by the legislation of the country of origin of the work; similarly, the duration of protection granted in the country of origin may not be exceeded in the others (Article II, para. 2).

In consequence, the system adopted in 1886 incorporated features of both the system of territoriality and the system of nationality, but was closer to the latter. (The Berlin revision of 1908 reverted to application of territorial law: on the one hand, any requirement for compliance with formalities was deleted and the principle of *independence of protection* was consolidated since it was stipulated that the enjoyment and exercise of the rights recognized by territorial law do not depend on the existence of protection in the country of origin of the work, save in respect to duration.)

f. Definition of the country of origin

The country of origin of the work is considered to be that in which the work is first published; if publication is made simultaneously in more than one country of the Union, it is considered to be the country whose legislation accords the shortest protection. In the case of unpublished works, the country of the author is to be treated as the country of origin of the work (Article II, paras. 3 and 4).

g. Protected works

'Literary and artistic works' are protected and examples are given: books, pamphlets and other writings; dramatic or dramatico-musical works; musical compositions with or without words; works of drawing, painting, sculpture and engraving; lithographs, illustrations, geographical charts; plans, sketches and plastic works relative to geography, topography, architecture or science in general. The non-exhaustive nature of this list is indicated in the last part of Article IV which goes on to include 'every production whatsoever in the literary, scientific or artistic domain which can be published by any mode of impression or reproduction'.

The Final Protocol sets out special provisions for photographic and choreographic works in its Articles 1 and 2 respectively.

h. Minimum protection. Right of translation: duration

Articles V to X grant the author certain *minimum rights* in his work, in particular the rights of translation, representation and public performance. These rights, which are applicable *jure conventionis* in all the countries of the Union, are nevertheless subject to many limitations. The right of translation is only protected for ten years counting from the publication of the original work in one of the member countries of the Union (the 'ten-year' system).

i. Free mechanical reproduction of musical works

Article 3 of the Final Protocol stipulates that 'the manufacture and sale of instruments for the mechanical reproduction of musical airs in which copyright subsists, shall not be considered as constituting an infringement of musical copyright'.[45]

---

45. This provision was a concession to the Swiss industry of mechanical musical instruments, as Erich Schulze points out (*Protection of Mechanical Recording Rights and Legal Evolution*, BIEM, 1979; see above Chap. 7, Effects of the fixation and mechanical reproduction of musical works on copyright).

j. Freedom to reproduce press articles

Articles from newspapers or periodicals published in any of the countries of the Union may be reproduced in the others, unless the authors or publishers have expressly forbidden this. However, such prohibition shall not apply to articles of political discussion or to the reproduction of news of the day or miscellaneous information (Article VII).

k. Presumption of authorship (Article XI)

The Convention does not define the term 'author', despite the fact that it is frequently used in the substantive text and that it is the author who enjoys protection. The explanation for this notable fact must lie in the differences between the two principal legal concepts of authors' rights (namely the continental European or Roman law notion of *'droit d'auteur'* and the Anglo-American concept of *copyright*) in respect of the persons to whom the capacity of author is attributed, together with ownership of the rights in literary and artistic works.[46] To facilitate acceptance by countries which subscribe to one or other of these legal traditions, the Convention confines itself to stipulating a presumption of authorship in favour of the person whose name is cited as the author of the work when it is circulated. Domestic legislation is left with the latitude to attribute ownership of copyright in each particular case.

The Convention accordingly determines which persons are authorized to lay claim to protected rights since the indication of the name or pseudonym of the author on the work in the habitual manner is sufficient—save where proved otherwise (presumption *juris tantum*)—for him to be considered as such and permitted to pursue actions against infringers in the courts of the countries of the Union.

In the case of anonymous or pseudonymous works (where the pseudonym is equivalent to anonymity), the publisher whose

---

46. See above, Chapter 1, Section 1.3.2.

name is indicated on the work is authorized to defend the rights pertaining to the author and is to be treated save where otherwise proved, as the lawful representative of the author of the anonymous or pseudonymous work; however, this is without prejudice to the possibility of the courts requiring a certificate issued by the competent authority to prove that the formalities established by the legislation of the country in which the work originated have been complied with. This latter condition was deleted in the Berlin revision when all the conditions concerning the compliance with formalities were abolished.

l. Preventive measures in respect of illicit reproductions

Any work which is reproduced without authorization may be seized on importation into the countries of the Union in which the original work is entitled to legal protection. This seizure will take place in accordance with the *lex fori* (Article XII).

m. Regulatory control

The countries of the Union retain their authority to verify and prohibit by measures of domestic legislation or the police, the circulation, representation or exhibition of any work or publication (Article XIII). This rule is laid down essentially in connection with the censorship.

n. Rule of retroactivity

The Convention is applicable to all works which, at the moment of its coming into force, have not yet fallen into the public domain in the country of origin by reason of the expiry of the periods of protection (Article XIV). Thus the rights acquired by third parties are preserved from the time at which the work ceases to be protected.

o. Special arrangements (restricted Unions)

The countries of the Union may enter into particular agreements among themselves, provided that such arrangements confer rights which are more extensive or embody other stipulations which are not contrary to the Convention (Article XV).

p. The International Office

The Office of the International Union for the Protection of Literary and Artistic Works is set up and placed under the high authority and direction of the Superior Administration of the Swiss Confederation (Article XVI).[47]

q. Revision of the Convention

Provision is made for periodic revisions of the Convention with the unanimous consent of the member countries of the Union (Article XVII).

r. Universal vocation of the Convention

The 'open-ended' nature of the Convention and its universal vocation are reflected in Article XVIII which stipulates that the countries which have not already become parties and which grant legal protection of the rights forming the purpose of the Convention may accede to it at their request.

s. Colonial clause

The countries which accede to the Convention are entitled to extend its application to their colonies or foreign possessions (Article XIX).

---

47. The Office of the Berne Union was established in 1887 in the city of the same name. In 1883, the Paris Convention for the Protection of Industrial Property had adopted the same system: for reasons of economy, the two bureaux were grouped together in 1893 under the title *United International Bureaux for the Protection of Intellectual Property* and widely referred to as the 'Berne Bureaux'. In the early 1960s, the seat of these Bureaux was transferred to Geneva after which they came to be known by their French acronym BIRPI (*Bureaux Internationaux Réunis pour la Protection de la Propriété Intellectuelle*). The Stockholm revision (1967) set up the World Intellectual Property Organization, known as WIPO, and stipulated that it was to take over the role of the BIRPI.

t. The Additional Article

Provides for the maintenance of existing Conventions which grant more extensive rights than those secured by the Union or contain other stipulations that are not contrary to the Berne Convention.

u. Final Protocol

This contains provisions relating to certain works (see above), to the non-application of the Convention to works in the public domain and other administrative measures.

v. Ratifications and accessions[48]

The Berne Convention entered into force on 5 December 1887 when it was ratified by nine of the ten countries which had signed: Belgium, France, Germany, Haiti, Italy, Spain, Switzerland, Tunisia and the United Kingdom; Liberia went on to join in 1908 The ratification by the United Kingdom also extended to South Africa, Australia, Canada, India and New Zealand.

The following countries also acceded: Monaco (1889), Montenegro (1893), Denmark (1903), Japan (1889), Luxembourg (1888), Norway (1896) and Sweden (1904).

Haiti, Liberia and Montenegro later left the Convention which was applicable in Haiti between 1887 and 1943, in Liberia between 1908 and 1930 and in Montenegro between 1893 and 1900.

The extension by Belgium, France, Germany, Spain and the United Kingdom to their colonial possessions considerably widened the geographical coverage of the Convention. But many European countries were absent from the Union, e.g. the Austro-Hungarian Empire, Portugal, the Netherlands and Russia (which joined only recently, the Russian Federation becoming a member of the Convention on 13 March 1995).

---

48. Acceptance of the Acts of the Convention is possible by either ratification or accession. The countries of the Union which subscribed to the Act signified their acceptance by *ratification*; those which did not sign it accepted its provisions by *accession* (see Article 28, para. 1(a) of the Paris Act, 1971).

E. THE PARIS ADDITIONAL ACT AND
INTERPRETATIVE DECLARATION (1896)

The Final Protocol of the 1886 Act stipulated that the first revision Conference was to be held in Paris within four to six years of the entry into force of the Convention (Art. 6). The brevity of this period is explained by the fact that some delegations (especially those of France and Switzerland) felt that frequent revisions were essential to preserve the dynamic character of the Convention; that criterion was not shared by the delegates of the United Kingdom who wished to avoid the need for repeated changes to their domestic legislation in order to bring it into line with subsequent amendments to the Convention. The Diplomatic Conference of Paris was finally convened on 15 April 1896, some years later than anticipated and was attended by 12 of the 13 member countries of the Union (Belgium, France, Germany, Italy, Luxembourg, Monaco, Montenegro, Norway, Spain, Switzerland, Tunisia and the United Kingdom—Haiti was absent). Observers attended from 14 non-member countries.[49]

Two leading French legal experts who had already attended the previous conferences were present: the eminent specialist in authors' rights Eugéne Pouillet, who had been the Chairman of ALAI since 1890, and the international law expert Louis Renault, who was responsible for drafting the final report. On 4 May, a text of limited scope was adopted. It took the form of an Additional Act and Interpretative Declaration and did not change the structure of the original Act but simply amended Articles II, III, V, VII, XII and XX of the Convention and 1 and 4 of the Final Protocol.

With reference to Article II, a clarification was added: it stipulated that for the purposes of protection, the term 'published' meant 'published for the first time' in a country of the Union. A new paragraph was added to include posthumous works among those to be protected (Article I.1 of the Additional Act).

---

49. Argentina, Bolivia, Brazil, Bulgaria, Colombia, Denmark, Greece, Guatemala, Mexico, Peru, Portugal, Romania, Sweden and the United States of America.

An anomaly in Article III was corrected. In the old text, only the publishers of works appearing in one of the countries of the Union were protected when the author belonged to a country which was not a member of that union. This was replaced by the following provision (2): 'Authors not being subjects or citizens of one of the countries of the Union who first publish or cause to be first published, their literary or artistic works in one of those countries shall enjoy, in respect of such works, the protection granted by the Berne Convention and by the present Additional Act (Article I.2 of the latter).'

An important modification related to Article V concerning the right of translation ('*the international question par excellence*' as Renault described it in the report of the Conference[50]); the duration of this right was extended to the general period of protection of the original work *on condition*, however, that the author availed himself of this right within ten years of the date of the first publication of the original work by publishing in one of the countries of the union a translation in the language of the country for which protection was sought (Article I.3 of the Additional Act).

Traditionally, the right of translation has been a point of contention between the exporting and importing countries of works whose interests in this area diverge; the condition set out in Article V was the outcome of a compromise proposed by Belgium between the proponents (such as France) of the idea that translation is simply another method of reproduction of the work and therefore proposed its complete assimilation, and those countries (such as Norway) which were opposed to this concept.

Norway had recently amended its domestic legislation to bring it into line with the 1886 Act and, together with Sweden, did not ratify the Additional Act (but only the Interpretative Declaration) with the result that, in regard to the disputed Article V, these countries were bound solely by the 1886 Act. This paved the way for the system of restricted Unions (the United Kingdom for

---

50. Cf. *Berne Convention Centenary*, WIPO, 1986, Sect. 168.

its part ratified the Additional Act but not the Interpretative Declaration.)

In regard to Article VII, it was stipulated that the reproduction authorized therein did not include serial stories or short stories published in newspapers or periodicals (Article I.4 of the Additional Act).

Attention should be drawn to the amendment of Article 1 of the Final Protocol of the 1886 Act to extend the benefit of the Convention to works of architecture in those countries which granted protection not only to architectural plans but also to the architectural works themselves (Article II, 1, A of the Additional Act).

Mention must also be made of the provision in the Interpretative Declaration (para. 2) to the effect that the term *published works* denotes works of which copies have been *issued* to the public in one of the countries of the Union. Consequently, representation of a dramatic or dramatico-musical work and the performance of a musical work or the exhibition of a work of art do not constitute *publication*.

Ratifications and accessions: the Additional Act and the Interpretative Declaration came into force on 9 December 1897 after their ratification by Australia, Belgium, Canada, France, Germany, India, Italy, Luxembourg, Monaco, New Zealand, Norway Spain, Switzerland, Tunisia and the United Kingdom.

Haiti (1898), Japan (1899), Liberia (1908), Denmark (1903), and Sweden (1904) also ratified.

It should be noted that the United Kingdom ratified the Additional Act alone and declared that it also applied to Australia, Canada, India, New Zealand and South Africa; Norway and Sweden acceded to the Interpretative Declaration alone; and Haiti and Liberia later terminated their membership of the Convention (see above).

F. THE BERLIN REVISION (1908)

The Berlin Diplomatic Conference was convened on 14 October 1908 and attended by delegations from 15 of the 16 countries of the Union (Belgium, Denmark, France, Germany, Italy, Japan, Luxembourg, Monaco, Montenegro, Norway, Spain, Sweden,

Switzerland, Tunisia and the United Kingdom; Haiti was absent) with observers from 21 non-member countries.[51] Once again Louis Renault was appointed Rapporteur-General.

The Conference worked on the basis of the documentation prepared by the Berne Office and the German Government, envisaging a far-reaching revision of the Convention to comply with the requests made by a number of non-governmental organizations, in particular ALAI (which, at all its Congresses, had proposed a series of reforms for consideration at the Berlin Conference; this was to result in a draft new text of the Convention).[52]

After one month, on 13 November, the work of the Berlin Conference ended with the adoption of an Act in which, in the first place, the texts of Berne and Paris were consolidated in accordance with the recommendation of the previous Conference (1896). A text was then adopted incorporating such far-reaching changes that the basic provisions were substantially modified;

a. Absence of formalities as a condition for protection

All conditions requiring compliance with formalities were eliminated: 'The enjoyment and the exercise of these rights shall not be subject to the performance of any formality' (Article 4, second para.).

b. The principle of the independence of protection (with the exception of its duration)

The principle of independence of protection was strengthened by the stipulation that the enjoyment and exercise of the rights established by the legislation of the country in which protection was claimed were not dependent on the existence of protection in the country of origin of the work. Without prejudice to the

---

51. Argentina, Colombia, Chile, China, Ecuador, Greece, Guatemala, Liberia, Mexico, Netherlands, Nicaragua, Paraguay, Persia, Peru, Portugal, Romania, Russia, Siam, United States of America, Uruguay and Venezuela.
52. In 1900, ALAI had begun work on a draft model law for the unification of national laws on this subject.

provisions uniformly applicable in all the countries of the Berne Union, the extension of protection and the means of redress available to the author of a work to safeguard his rights within the Union 'shall be governed exclusively by the laws of the country where protection is claimed' (Article 4, second para.).

c. Protected works

The list of protected works was widened and clarified (Art. 2) to include choreographic works and entertainments in dumb show, the acting form of which is fixed in writing or otherwise, and also works of architecture. More detailed reference was made to the fact that translations, adaptations, arrangements of music and other reproductions in an altered form of a literary or artistic work as well as collections of different works were to be protected as original works without prejudice to the rights of the author of the original work. A final paragraph stipulated that works of art applied to industrial purposes shall be protected so far as the domestic legislation of each country allows.

d. Photographic works

Protection of photographic works was dealt with in a separate provision (Article 3) which stipulated that the Convention shall apply to such works and to works produced by a process analogous to photography. However, their assimilation to the other categories of works was restricted in Article 7, third paragraph, which provided for the possibility of granting protection for a shorter period than that generally allowed.

e. Cinematographic works

In 1908, cinematography had already begun to develop the features which were to make it one of the most important industries in the world of the performing arts. During the Conference, France (the birthplace of the brothers Louis and Auguste Lumière who developed and patented the invention of cinematography) proposed that the protection granted by the Convention should be extended to cinematographic productions. The French proposal was approved and protection provided for cinematographic works 'if, by the arrangement of the acting form or the combinations of the incidents represented, the author has given the work a personal and original character' (Article 14, second para.). The authors of literary, scientific or artistic works were granted the exclusive right of authorizing the reproduction and public representation of their works by cinematography (Article 14, first para.).

f. Right of translation

Finally, the right of translation was in principle recognized with the same status as the other exclusive rights of the author, without any conditions and for the same duration as the rights in the original work (Article 8). However, opinions differed: on the one hand observers representing the Netherlands and Russia expressed their anxiety over this proposed assimilation, while the delegation of Japan made the following proposal: 'The translation into Japanese of a work written in a European language and vice versa shall be completely free.' Among the reasons cited was this: 'if to the difficulties of translation resulting from natural differences in idioms and customs you also add the restrictions of the Convention on literary property, translators, disheartened, will give up the struggle'.[53] The proposal was rejected; nevertheless Italy, Ireland, Japan, the Netherlands, Thailand and Yugoslavia ratified the Berlin Act subject to the following limitation: 'Article 8 of the Convention is replaced by Article V of the Berne Convention of 1886, as modified by Article 1.3, of the Paris Additional Act, 1896, in respect of the exclusive right of authors to make or to authorize the translation of their works.' *Mutatis mutandis*, the Japanese objection of 1908 evokes the licences provided for, first in Article V, para. 2 of the Universal Convention (Geneva, 1952), later in the Protocol regarding Developing Countries of the Berne Convention, Stockholm Act (1967) and, finally, in the revisions of Paris (1971) of the Universal Convention (Article V*bis*, 5*ter* and

---

53. See Final Report of the Rapporteur-General, Louis Renault, in *Centenary* ..., Sects. 247 and 248.

5*quater*) and of the Berne Convention (Appendix) to which we shall be returning later.

g. *Duration of protection*

The general rule of protection of copyright during the life of the author and for 50 years after his death (*p.m.a.*) was adopted (Article 7, first para.) but without imposing this as a minimum requirement. If the national law provided for a shorter period, that would apply: 'Consequently, the contracting countries shall only be bound to apply the provisions of the preceding paragraph in so far as such provisions are consistent with their domestic laws' (Article 7, second para. *in fine*).

Under the Berlin Act, if the term of 50 years *p.m.a.* was not uniformly adopted by all the countries of the Union, the duration was to be regulated 'by the law of the country where protection is claimed and must not exceed the term fixed in the country of origin of the work' (Article 7, second para.). This 50-year term was therefore only applicable to the countries which had adopted it. In the others, the method of comparison of the different terms was to be applied: the term applicable in the country of origin was to apply if it was shorter than that stipulated in the country where protection was claimed.[54]

No minimum term of protection had been provided previously (in the preliminary drafts, the Original Act of 1886 and the Additional Act of 1896). To avoid the inequalities which would have resulted from disparity between the terms, Article II, second para. *in fine* of the Act of 1886 had stipulated that the term of protection granted in the said country of origin shall not be exceeded in the others. It follows that by virtue of the method of comparison of terms, in the area of the duration of the applicable right the *principle of national treatment* applied solely to the extent that the two legislations coincided (that of the country in which protection was claimed and that of the country of origin of the work).

---

54. See above, Chapter 5, Sect. 5.1.3, G.

During the Berlin Conference, the proposal by the French Delegation seeking to establish a compulsory minimum duration of 50 years *p.m.a.* gained extensive support.[55] But the delegates of the United Kingdom expressed reservations and although, even at this time, 9 of the 15 countries belonging to the Union had already adopted either this term or an even longer period (Belgium, Denmark, France, Luxembourg, Monaco, Norway, Spain, Sweden and Tunisia), the 1908 Act only provided for this term as an option. This is confirmed by Article 30; this required the States which introduced the 50-year term into their legislation to give notice thereof to the Government of the Swiss Confederation 'who shall communicate it at once to all the other States of the Union'.

h. Right of mechanical reproduction. Limitations

A derogation was made from Article 3 of the Final Protocol to the 1886 Act ('the manufacture and sale of instruments for the mechanical reproduction of musical airs [...] shall not be considered as constituting an infringement of musical copyright') by the express recognition in Article 13 that 'the authors of musical works shall have the exclusive right of authorizing: (1) the adaptation of those works to instruments which can reproduce them mechanically; (2) the public performance of the said works by means of these instruments'.

But the countries of the Union were not obliged to adopt this protection. Reservations and conditions were permitted, although with effects strictly limited to the country which formulated them. The main reason for which non-voluntary licences were permitted in national legislation was the desire to preserve the sound recording industry from possible abuses which might occur in the music publishing industry and in the area of the exercise of

---

55. During the previous decade, a strong current of opinion led by ALAI had arisen in favour of the term of 50 years *post mortem auctoris*.

exclusive rights by the societies of authors and music publishers if no provision were made for limiting the latter.

i. Extension of the system of reservations

The States which joined the Union via the Berne Act were allowed the possibility of substituting for one or more provisions of the Berlin Act those of the Original Act of 1886, whether modified or not by the Additional Act of 1896 (Article 25). The same possibility was also laid open to the countries which already belonged to the Union (Article 27). These provisions sought as much to encourage the accession of new countries, as to arrive at the necessary unanimity of voting and prevent the defection of existing members which might consider that the level of their national legislation prevented them from becoming bound by the new text of the Convention. The wider provision for reservations also strengthened the system of restricted Unions established in Paris.

j. Applicability of the Berlin Act and of the previous Acts

At the time of the Berlin revision the need arose to regulate relations between the countries of the Union which were bound by different texts of the Convention. This matter was dealt with in Article 27 whose first paragraph provides that the revised Convention shall replace the previous texts (the Original Act of 1886 supplemented by the Additional Act and the Interpretative Declaration of 1896).

But the new text could only produce its full impact on relations between those countries which accepted it in its entirety; as some countries might postpone their acceptance or prefer to continue to be bound by previous texts, it was appropriate to provide for this eventuality in the Convention. That was the purpose of the second paragraph of Article 27 which stipulated that the previous texts would remain binding on relations between those countries which did not ratify the Berlin Act. That provision was later maintained in the Rome revision (1928) and in the Brussels revision (1948), even though the situation was becoming increasingly complex; each of the resulting texts constituted an *Act of the*

Convention and as such might be treated as a Convention in its own right, despite the fact that only one Union existed.[56]

k. *Ratifications and accessions*

The Berlin revision entered into force on 9 September 1910 after ratification by Belgium, France[a] Germany, Haiti[b], Japan[a], Liberia[b], Luxembourg, Monaco, Norway[a] and Spain.

The following countries also joined: Australia (1928[a-c]), Austria (1920), Brazil (1922), Bulgaria (1921), Canada (1928[c]), Czechoslovakia (1921), Denmark (1912[a]), Estonia (1927[d]), Finland (1928[a]), Greece (1920[a-c]), Hungary (1922), India (1928[a-c]), Ireland (1927[a]), Italy (1914[a-c]), Lebanon (1924), Liechtenstein (1931), Morocco (French Protectorate, 1917) the Netherlands (1912[a]), New Zealand (1928[a-c]), Poland (1920), Portugal (1911), Romania (1927[a]), Syria (1924[b]), Sweden (1920[a]), Switzerland (1920), Thailand (1931[a]), Tunisia (1930[a]), Union of South Africa (1928[a-c]), United Kingdom (1912[a]), and Yugoslavia (1930[a]).

Notes
a. Acceptance subject to certain reservations (relating for the most part to the right of translation, the reproduction of articles published in the press, the protection of works of art applied to industry and the rule of retroactivity).
b. Subsequently withdrew from the Convention; it applied to Syria between 1924 and 1962 (see above, in regard to Haiti and Liberia).
c. The year in which it joined the Berlin Act as an independent country. Previously this Act was applicable by virtue of the extension made by the United Kingdom.

---

56. With the adoption of the successive Acts, the main difficulty resided in determining which particular Act was applicable to relations between the countries which joined the Union by acceding to a later Act and those countries which had joined previously but had not ratified this subsequent Act (for example, relations between Argentina and Canada, since Argentina joined the Union in 1967 by ratifying the Brussels Act—the only one to which accession was then possible—while the last text ratified by Canada was the Rome Convention). This problem was solved for the future by the Stockholm Act (1967) and will be dealt with in our analysis of that revision.

d. The Convention was applicable to Estonia between 1927 and 1940, the year in which that country became a Republic of the Soviet Union. Independent again since 20 August 1991, Estonia rejoined the Convention on 26 October 1994 through accession to the Paris Act of 1971.

e. Greece waived its reservations in 1956; Italy did so in 1931.

The basic provisions of the Berlin Act continued to be applicable to Thailand[57] since its accession to a later Act (Paris 1971) excluded the material right (Articles 1 to 21 and the Appendix) and was confined to the administrative provisions and final clauses (Articles 22 to 38).

G. THE BERNE ADDITIONAL PROTOCOL (1914)

The Additional Protocol to the Berlin Act was signed on 20 March 1914 in Berne without a revision Conference and on the eve of the First World War. It was drawn up at the request of the United Kingdom by reason of the situation created by Art. I.2 of the Additional Act of 1896 (which replaced Article III of the Original Act) by virtue of which the benefit of the Convention was extended to authors belonging to countries that were not members of the Union in respect of works published for the first time in a contracting country.

For authors and publishers in North America the first publication in Canada, a member country of the Union, became a means of access to protection under the Berne Convention, while the authors of works belonging to the Union in general, and particularly of works in the English language, had great difficulty in securing protection in the United States of America because of the restrictions contained in its copyright legislation. Even after the adoption of the 1909 law which granted protection to foreign works, the manufacturing clause still applied to works written in English.

Since Article 6 of the Berlin Act adopted a text analogous to the provision whereby the Paris Additional Act of 1896 had remedied the anomaly contained in Article III of the Original Act, the

---

57. Situation as at 1 January 1995.

United Kingdom government raised the matter with the International Office and proposed the adoption of a Protocol which would enable restrictive measures to be taken in respect of the protection of works of authors who were nationals of a non-member country of the Union.

The International Office prepared an Additional Protocol to the Berlin Act which was termed the 'Reciprocity Protocol'; pursuant to this text, if a country which was not a member of the Union did not adequately protect the works of authors belonging to a member country of the Union, the latter was authorized in turn to restrict the protection of the works of authors who, at the time of the first publication of their works, were subjects or citizens of that foreign country and not effectively domiciled in one of the member countries of the Union. The countries which restricted protection in conformity with the provisions of the Protocol were required to notify this fact to the Government of the Swiss Confederation by means of a written declaration naming the countries in respect of which protection was so restricted. The Swiss Government would then notify this fact to all the other Member States of the Union.

Ratifications and accessions: The Berne Protocol entered into force on 20 April 1915. It was ratified by all the countries which had acceded to the Berlin Act apart from Haiti, India, Ireland, Liechtenstein and Portugal. Only Canada made the declaration provided for in the Protocol stipulating that it would restrict protection in respect of the United States of America.

H. THE REVISION OF ROME (1928)

Forty-five years after the famous ALAI Congress had first mooted the idea of the creation of a Union of Literary Property, the Conference responsible for the revision of the Convention embodying this Union was held in Rome. A decision on the venue had been taken at the closing session of the Berlin Conference which had expressed the view that the next revision should take place after six to ten years. However, the convening of the Conference was seriously delayed by the events of the decade which followed, and in particular the First World War which involved a number of the countries belonging to the Berne Union at the time

(Belgium, France, Germany, Italy, Japan and the United Kingdom) and put an end to the Austro-Hungarian Empire out of which were born new independent states. The political map of Europe was in effect redrawn.

Meanwhile a number of countries had amended their laws to bring them into line with the Berlin text, e.g. the United Kingdom in 1911 and Italy in 1925 by means of a decree which became law in the following year. This law involved a far-reaching review of the previous legislation and was to have a substantial influence on the revision of the Berne Convention adopted in Rome, in particular by recognizing the moral right of authors.

In 1928, 37 countries belonged to the Berne Union: most European countries (with the notable exception of the former Soviet Union), Australia, Canada, India, Ireland and New Zealand as independent countries, two Latin American countries (Brazil and Haiti), together with Japan, Lebanon, Liberia, Morocco, Syria, Tunisia and the Union of South Africa.

The Rome Diplomatic Conference was convened on 7 May 1928 and attended by 35 Member Countries of the Union (Haiti and Liberia being absent) and 21 non-member (12 Latin American countries, 4 European countries, the United States of America, Egypt, Persia, Siam—later known as Thailand—and Turkey). Two eminent specialists in authors' rights, Edoardo Piola Caselli and Georges Maillard who had presided over ALAI since 1905 (and was to held that office until 1942) were appointed Rapporteur-General and Chairman of the Drafting Committee respectively.

The programme prepared by the Italian government and the International Office, together with the proposals submitted by a number of member countries of the Union, formed the working documents of the Conference which ended on 2 June with the adoption of a new text of the Convention and a number of recommendations. The most notable innovations embodied in the Rome Act concerned the specific rights of authors: the moral right and the broadcasting right were both now recognized. In addition, the list of works was extended to include oral works and the right to formulate reservations for countries joining the Union for the first time was restricted.

a. Inclusion of oral works

The list of protected works now included 'lectures, addresses, sermons and other works of the same nature' (Article 2.1). Some countries objected to the inclusion of oral works; that is the reason why the list was limited to the wording given here and a new Article 2*bis* added stipulating that 'it shall be a matter for legislation in the countries of the Union to exclude, wholly or in part, from the protection provided by the preceding Article [Article 2] political speeches and speeches delivered in the course of legal proceedings' and 'to determine the conditions under which lectures, addresses and other works of the same nature [...] may be reproduced by the press [...]'.

b. The moral right

Protection of the moral right of the author had already begun to be embodied to a varying extent in certain national laws[58] and was advocated by several delegations (Italy, France, Belgium, Poland, Czechoslovakia and Romania) which put forward a number of drafts.

At the first working session of the Conference, Piola Caselli was a fervent advocate of protection of the moral right in the international order. He stressed the fact that the principle of the existence of personal rights of the author in his work, in particular the right to claim authorship and to oppose any modification of the work that might be prejudicial to his moral interests, had already been recognized by the case law and theory of a number of countries. Additionally, the reasons for the proposal had been set out in a memorandum presented to the Conference: the vast circulation of works of the mind, and the widespread use of new means of communication and expression due to modern inventions were resulting in a proliferation of infringements of the integrity of works and of the most profound personal interests of the author, while increasing inroads were being made on their

---

58. Bulgaria (1922), Switzerland (1922), Romania (1923), Italy (1925), Poland (1926), Czechoslovakia (1926), Finland (1927).

exclusive economic privilege for reasons of a political, cultural and social order. All this made it necessary to grant independent protection to the personal interests of the author.[59]

Countries with a common law tradition lodged a number of objections because the rights of the author of a personal kind were not directly protected in them by copyright, but indirectly by other means. This led to a compromise solution embodied in Art. 6*bis* which reads: 'Independently of the author's copyright, and even after transfer of the said copyright, the author shall have the right to claim authorship of the work, as well as the right to object to any distortion, mutilation or other modification of the said work which would be prejudicial to his honour or reputation.'

The Convention therefore adopted an impartial attitude to the legal nature of the moral right; only its two aspects of authorship and integrity were protected *jure conventionis* and this was done by applying the objective concept[60] without making any reference to duration. However, since paragraph 2 left the national legislator the possibility of regulating not only the procedural means for the defence of these rights, but also the conditions for their exercise in their application, they might be reduced to their lowest possible expression.[61]

c. Broadcasting right. Authorization of non-voluntary licences

Article 11*bis* was introduced to satisfy the requirements arising out of technological progress. It recognized the exclusive right of authors to authorize the communication of their works to the public by radio broadcasting. However, the broadcasting organizations stressed their need for access to works for broadcasting and maintained that if no limits were imposed on the exclusive right of authors they might find themselves without any form of protection against potential abuses by societies of authors as the holders of a monopoly. As a compromise solution between these

---

59. See Valerio De Sanctis, op. cit., pp. 252–4.
60. See above, Chapter 4, Sect. 4.2.3.
61. Henri Desbois, André Kerever and André Françon, op. cit., p. 41, Section 53.

different points of view, the second paragraph allowed the national legislations of the countries of the Union to regulate the conditions under which the new right was exercised in their respective territories; that meant authorizing the countries of the Union to establish *non-voluntary licences*. It was further stipulated that such licences would be strictly limited in their effect to the country which granted them and must in no case prove prejudicial to the moral right of the author or to the author's right to obtain equitable remuneration fixed by the competent authority, failing amicable agreement.

d. Limitation of the possibility of entering reservations

Because of the wide scope of the system of reservations permitted in the previous texts, these had proliferated to such an extent that the state of relations between the Member Countries of the Union had ceased to be clear—a fact which militated against the aim of unification embodied in the preamble since the 1886 Convention ('to protect, in as effective and uniform a manner as possible, the right of authors in their literary and artistic works'). As a compromise solution, the system of reservations was limited, the intention being to achieve their ultimate disappearance. For countries which joined the Convention for the first time, Article 25 stipulated that the right to enter reservations was to be confined to translations into the language or languages of the country. In the case of countries that already belonged to the Union, Article 27 allowed them to retain the benefit of reservations formulated previously on condition that a declaration to that effect was made at the time of the deposit of their ratification.

e. Recommendations of the Conference

The Conference made a number of recommendations on certain matters on which no agreement had yet been reached at international level but which paved the way for the subsequent evolution of the rules embodied in conventions and domestic internal legislation: protection of the moral right after the death of the author, recognition of the rights of performing artists, the '*droit de suite*' and a closer relationship between the Berne Convention and the Conventions of the Inter-American System; this was to result in the conclusion of the Universal Copyright Convention in Geneva in 1952.

f. Ratifications and accessions

The Rome Revision entered into force on 1 August 1931 when it was ratified by Bulgaria, Canada, Finland, Hungary, India, Italy, Japan[a], Liechtenstein, the Netherlands, Norway, Sweden, Switzerland, the United Kingdom and Yugoslavia[a].

The following countries also acceded: Australia (1935), Austria (1936), Belgium (1934), Brazil (1933), Czechoslovakia (1936), Denmark (1933), France (1933[a]), Germany (1933), Greece (1932[a-c]), the Holy See (1935), Iceland (1947[a]), Indonesia (1949[b]), Ireland (1935[a]), Israel (1950), Latvia (1937[d]), Lebanon (1933), Luxembourg (1932), Monaco (1933), Morocco (French Protectorate, 1934), New Zealand (1947), Pakistan (1948), Poland (1935), Portugal (1937), Romania (1936), Spain (1933), Syria (1933), Tunisia (1933[a]), the Union of South Africa (1935).

Notes
a. Acceptance subject to certain reservations.
b. Year in which it joined the Rome Act in its own right. Previously the Convention had been applicable to the Dutch East Indies as a result of the notification forwarded by the government of the Netherlands. The Convention was later denounced; it was applicable to Indonesia between 1931 and 1960.
c. Greece lifted its reservations in 1956.
d. The Convention was applicable to Latvia between 1937 and 1940, the year in which it became a Republic of the former Soviet Union.

The substantive provisions of the Rome Act continue to be applicable to Canada, Iceland, Lebanon, Malta, New Zealand, Pakistan, Romania, Sri Lanka and Zimbabwe, since the accession of these countries to the Stockholm or Paris Acts excluded the material right (Articles 1 to 21 and the Appendix) and was confined to the administrative provisions and the final clauses (Articles 22 to 38).[62]

---

62. Situation as at 1 January 1995.

I. THE REVISION OF BRUSSELS (1948)

The third revision of the Berne Convention was due to take place in Brussels in 1935 pursuant to a resolution adopted by the Rome Conference at its session of 1 June 1928.

The Belgian Government and the International Office had begun preparations in 1932, but at that time various countries which played an important role in the Convention had not yet ratified its latest text. It was therefore felt opportune to postpone the preparatory work. On 20 July 1935, the first preliminary documentation was sent out with a view to the convening of a conference at the latest in 1936. But the preparatory work was once again interrupted following a decision taken by the General Assembly of the League of Nations on 18 November 1935 by virtue of which two of its bodies, the International Institute of Intellectual Co-operation (Paris) and the International Institute for the Unification of Private Law (Rome), were given the task of preparing, with a view to bringing the Conventions of Berne and Havana more closely into line with one another, a general agreement designed to ensure effective protection of intellectual works on both continents.[63] Subsequently, the two institutes appointed a Committee of Experts which unanimously proposed to the Belgian Government that the revision of the Berne Convention be held over until it was possible to convene in Brussels a 'universal' Conference with a view to the conclusion of the General Agreement advocated by the League of Nations. That suggestion was accepted. However, the Second World War led to the postponement *sine die* of the preparatory work which was resumed in 1946.

Between the revisions of 1928 and 1948, two countries left the Convention (Haiti and Liberia), two ceased to exist as independent states (Estonia and Latvia) and several others joined the Union: in 1928 the Union of South Africa in its own right, in 1930 Yugoslavia, in 1931 Liechtenstein and Siam (now Thailand), in

---

63. Cf. *Documents de la Conférence réunie à Bruxelles du 5 au 26 juin 1948*, Berne, Bureau de l'Union Internationale pour la Protection des Œuvres Littéraires et Artistiques, 1951, p. 13.

1935 the Holy See, in 1947 Iceland and Lebanon and in 1948 Pakistan. When the Diplomatic Conference was convened in Brussels, the Union had 40 members, 35 of which were represented by delegates (Japan, Romania and Siam being absent, while Germany—represented by a British delegate from the Allied Control Commission—and Bulgaria were recognized as observers only). Eighteen countries which did not belong to the Union sent observers (11 from Latin America, together with the United States, China, Egypt, Iraq, Iran, Liberia and Turkey), as did UNESCO. A number of non-governmental organizations such as CISAC and representatives of the industrial sector, in particular broadcasting organizations, were not recognized as observers because it was felt that this was a strictly intergovernmental conference. However, the representatives of the societies of authors and composers, performing artists and broadcasters did take part in the Conference since many of them were included in the delegations as experts and consultants.

The Brussels Conference met between 5 and 26 June 1948. Its efforts concentrated on consolidating and further developing the rights already recognized in the revisions of 1908 and 1928; to a greater extent than ever before the need was felt to prevent these rights from being nullified by the impact of technological advances, as is apparent from the words of Marcel Plaisant, General Rapporteur of the Conference, at the end of his report.[64]

For 20 years we have been witnessing such a prodigious development in inventions and the means of communicating thought that we are continually dismayed by the revolutionary achievements of science, and the unforeseeable forms that it is capable of imposing on intellectual exchanges. At the same time, our world, and most especially Europe, has undergone such profound political and social transformations as a result of this long war and its aftermath that we are powerless to imagine its configuration at any one time in a society caught up in a spate of development. Our task was to ensure the protection of copyright at a time when books have been left far behind by electrical and mechanical means of exploitation and will be by still others that are germinating in future in-

---

64. *Conference in Brussels, 1948—General Report (Marcel Plaisant), Centenary of the Berne Convention*, Section 109.

ventions. This Conference has been above all the Conference of broadcasting, discs, cinema and artificial or natural screens. Your great work is to have reconciled copyright, a spiritual concept, to these at once so powerful and so changeable material realities.

a. Protected works

The list of protected works set out in Article 2 now included 'cinematographic works and works produced by a process analogous to cinematography' and 'photographic works and works produced by a process analogous to photography'. Article 3 of the Rome text by which the countries of the Union undertook to ensure protection of the latter was accordingly deleted.

Although the protection of 'works of applied art' (previously referred to as 'works of art applied to industry') was consolidated by their inclusion in the list set out in Article 2, this protection was diminished by paragraph 5 of the same Article which stated that 'it shall be a matter for legislation in the countries of the Union to determine the extent of the application of their laws to works of applied art and industrial designs and models, as well as the conditions under which such works, designs and models shall be protected.'

b. Definition of simultaneous publication

The previous Acts of the Convention provided for its application in cases where a work was published simultaneously in a country which was not a member of the Union and in a member country of the Union, but did not define the meaning of such simultaneous publication. That omission was made good in the Brussels Revision which stipulated that simultaneous publication meant publication in two or more countries, within 30 days of the first publication (Article 4, 3, last para.)

c. Moral right

The duration of the moral right was not dealt with at the Rome Conference. This question was covered by Article 6*bis* of the Brussels Act which affirmed the author's personal rights; Article 6*bis* 1 stipulates that the author shall retain these rights 'during his lifetime'.

In regard to the protection of the moral right after the death of the author, a new paragraph 2 was added stipulating that 'in so far as the legislation of the countries of the Union permits, the rights granted to the author in accordance with the preceding paragraph shall, after his death, be maintained, at least until the expiry of the copyright, and shall be exercisable by the persons or institutions authorized by the said legislations. The determination of the conditions under which the rights mentioned in this paragraph shall be exercised shall be governed by the legislation of the countries of the Union'.

It follows that protection of the moral right of the author after his death remains a possibility to the extent permitted by domestic legislation.

d. Duration of protection

The previous revision (Rome, 1928) made no changes to the duration of protection, despite the fact that most countries belonging to the Union at the time had adopted a period of 50 years after the death of the author or a still longer period.[65] During the proceedings of the Conference, emphasis had been laid on the fact that Article 7, paragraph 2, of the Berlin Act constituted an exception to the fundamental principles of *national treatment* and *independence of protection* expressly recognized in Article 4, and that material reciprocity was still required between the Member States in respect of the duration of protection. Despite the fact that these points of view were the subject of intense debate, it proved impossible to arrive at a consensus on the matter or to reach agreement on the proposals for complete unification of the term of protection.

---

65. The countries of the Berne Union which in 1928, at the time of the Rome Conference, had already stipulated a period of 50 years or longer after the death of the author were: *50 years*: Australia, Belgium, Canada, Czechoslovakia, Denmark, Estonia, Finland, France, Greece, Hungary, India, Ireland, Italy, Luxembourg, Morocco, Monaco, Norway, New Zealand, the Netherlands, Poland, United Kingdom, Syria, Lebanon, South Africa and Tunisia; *60 years*: Brazil; *80 years*: Spain; *in perpetuity*: Portugal.

In 1948, adoption of the period of 50 years after the death of the author had become still more general between the member countries of the Union and the Brussels Conference introduced it as an obligatory provision of the Convention: 'The term of protection granted by this Convention shall be the life of the author and 50 years after his death' (Article 7, para. 1). Comparison of different durations was now reserved for cases in which the terms were longer than that indicated, i.e. where the country in which protection is claimed establishes a longer term than the minimum stipulated in the Convention: 'However, where one or more countries of the Union grant a term of protection in excess of that provided by paragraph 1, the term shall be governed by the law of the country where protection is claimed, but shall not exceed the term fixed in the country of origin of the work' (Article 7, para. 2).

In consequence, the applicable law was that of the country in which protection was claimed (principle of *national treatment* or of *equal treatment* for foreign and national works), but the countries of the Union were required to respect the minimum term of 50 years after the death of the author (*jus conventionis*) counting from 1 January of the year after his death (Article 7, (6)).

There was nothing to prevent members of the Union from adopting terms longer than the minimum stipulated in the Convention, but in such cases they were not obliged to grant works originating in countries of the Union protection for a term longer than that established by the country of origin of the work. On the other hand, if the *lex loci publicationis* established a term longer than that of the country in which protection was claimed, the latter was under no obligation to protect the work beyond the term stipulated in its own law.

The same Article 7 includes a series of provisions on the duration of rights in certain types of work:
- in the case of *cinematographic and photographic works and of works of applied art*, the term of protection shall be governed by the law of the country where protection is claimed, but shall not exceed the term fixed in the country of origin of the work (para. 3);
- in the case of *anonymous and pseudonymous works* the term of protection shall be fixed at 50 years *post publicationem operis*

(*p.p.o.*). However, when the pseudonym adopted by the author leaves no doubt as to his identity, the term of protection shall be 50 years after the death of the author. If the author of an anonymous or pseudonymous work discloses his identity during the 50-year period *p.p.o.*, the term of protection shall be 50 years after the death of the author (para. 4);
- in the case of *posthumous works* which do not fall within the categories included in paragraphs 3 and 4, the term of protection shall be 50 years after the death of the author (para. 5).

e. Right of public presentation and public performance

The right of presentation and public performance was strengthened with the widening of the scope of Article 11 and clarification of its wording; it was now divided into two parts: (1) the exclusive right of authors to authorize the public presentation and public performance of the works was recognized; and (2) authors were given the exclusive right of authorizing the public transmission by any means of the presentation and performance of their works (without prejudice to the reservations allowed in Articles 11*bis* and 13).

f. Broadcasting right

The 1928 Act had recognized the right of broadcasting in general; subsequent developments now made it necessary to widen the text to include the many and complex forms of exploitation of means of broadcasting. Consequently, Article 11*bis* was reworded in Brussels to stipulate that the broadcasting right expressly included sound broadcasting, uncoded television (wireless or hertzian waves) and cable, the retransmission of such broadcasts and the communication thereof to the public by loudspeaker or any other similar instrument transmitting the broadcasting of the work by signs, sounds or images.

g. Right of public recitation

An Article 11*ter* was added granting the authors of literary works the exclusive right of authorizing the public recitation of their works.

h. Cinematographic works

A paragraph 2 was added to Article 14 stipulating that a cinematographic work shall be protected as an original work.

i. Other amendments

The wording of various provisions was improved, e.g. Articles 12, 13, paragraph 2, and 14 (as we have seen, para. 2 of this article is new).

j. 'Droit de suite'

In conformity with one of the recommendations made by the Rome Conference, the Convention recognized the inalienable right of authors and composers (although transmissible to their heirs) to an interest in any sale of original works of art and manuscripts subsequent to the first disposal of the work by the author (Article 14*bis*, para. 1).

However, resistance to the idea of the '*droit de suite*'[66] is reflected in the recognition of its optional applicability to the member countries of the Union subject to material reciprocity (Article 14*bis*, para. 2), unlike the other rights *jure conventionis* which the countries are required to grant without any condition of reciprocity and regardless of the consideration as to whether identical rights exist in the country of origin of the work (Article 4, paras. 1 and 2, of the Brussels Act).

k. International jurisdiction clause

An Article 27*bis* was added, stipulating that the International Court of Justice shall be competent to settle disputes arising *between the countries of the Union* in respect of the interpretation or application of the Convention.

---

66. See above, Chapter 4, Section 4.2.4.

l. Languages of the convention

A new Article 31 stipulated that the official Acts of the Conference shall be established in French, that an equivalent text shall be established in English and that in case of dispute as to the interpretation of the Acts, the French text shall always prevail. Authoritative texts may also be drawn up in other languages at the request of any member country of the Union.

m. Resolution and recommendations ('vœux')

The Brussels Conference adopted one resolution and made nine recommendations.

The resolution set up a Consultative Committee consisting of 12 Members of the Union, three of whom were to be renewed at three-yearly intervals, in order to assist the International Bureau in the areas of responsibility entrusted to it by Article 24, paragraph 2; the main task of this Committee was to prepare the next revision conference.

The recommendations concerned a wide range of matters (some of which had already been the subject of recommendations adopted at the Rome Conference); the more complete and general recognition of the rights of intellectual workers; universal copyright protection; protection of literary and artistic works with a view to preventing their destruction; the fee-paying public domain and the provident and welfare funds set up for the benefit of authors; double taxation of the income of authors; protection of phonogram manufacturers; protection of radio broadcasts; neighbouring rights, in particular the protection of performing artists, and finally the statute of the Berne Office.

n. Ratifications and accessions

The Brussels revision entered into force on 1 August 1951 after ratification by Belgium, France, the Holy See, Israel, Liechtenstein, Luxembourg, Monaco, the Philippines, Portugal, Spain, the Union of South Africa and Yugoslavia[a].

The following countries also ratified or acceded: Argentina (1967), Austria (1953), Bahamas (1973), Brazil (1952), Cameroon (1964), Chad (1971), Chile (1970), Congo (Brazzaville, now the

Congo), (1962), Congo (Kinshasa, now Zaire), (1963), Côte d'Ivoire (1962), Cyprus (1964), Dahomey (now Benin), (1961), Denmark (1962), Fiji (1971), Finland (1963), Gabon (1962), Federal Republic of Germany, now Germany (1966), Greece (1957), India (1958), Ireland (1959), Italy (1953), Madagascar (1966), Mali (1962), Mexico (1967[a]), Morocco (1952), Niger (1962), Norway (1963), Republic of the Upper Volta (now Burkina Faso) (1963[c]), Senegal (1962), Sweden (1961), Switzerland (1956), Tunisia (1952), Turkey (1952[a]), the United Kingdom (1957[b]) and Uruguay (1967).

Notes
a. Acceptance subject to declaration.
b. Acceptance subject to reservations.
c. The Republic of Upper Volta (which changed its name to Burkina Faso in 1984) left the Convention in 1969 which applied to it initially for the period between 1963 and 1970. It subsequently acceded to the Paris Act with effect from 24 January 1976.

The substantive provisions of the Brussels Act continue to be applicable to Argentina, Bahamas, Belgium, Chad, Fiji, Ireland, Israel, Liechtenstein, Madagascar, Norway, the Philippines, South Africa, Switzerland and Turkey since the accession of those countries to the Acts of Stockholm or Paris excluded the material right (Articles 1 to 21 and the Appendix) and was confined to the administrative provisions and final clauses (Articles 22 to 38).[67]

J. THE STOCKHOLM REVISION (1967)

On 12 June 1967 when the Fifth Revision Conference was convened in Stockholm, the Berne Union comprised 60 members, i.e. 20 more than at the time when the previous conference had been held in Brussels. The Latin American countries had begun to overcome their old prejudices over the restricted European nature

---

67. Situation as at 1 January 1995.

of the Convention:[68] Argentina, Mexico and Uruguay were brand-new members. In Africa and Asia, the movement for the liberation of the European colonies which had begun immediately after the Second World War spread, giving rise to the creation of many new States which, in particular from the late 1950s, began to join the Convention as independent countries. In 1959 Ceylon (subsequently known as Sri Lanka); in 1961 Dahomey (sub-

---

68. These prejudices may have been influenced by the following arguments: (a) the resistance to any upsurge of the hegemonistic policy of Europe at a time when the independence movement which had begun in 1810 and the system of national organization had not yet achieved their aims—hence the need for regional integration (e.g. the Montevideo Congresses, 1888–89, the Central American Congresses, Guatemala, 1897 and El Salvador, 1901, the Pan-American Conferences, etc.); (b) the conviction that it was not appropriate for countries which imported cultural works to subscribe to treaties that limited the right to make free use of foreign works in the belief that they were pursuing a policy of cultural development; however, by so doing, they overlooked the fact that this approach permitted the illegitimate use of works incompatible with any educational programme; in addition, the lack of protection for foreign creations led to unfair competition with protected national works; (c) the idea that legal obstacles existed because of the lack of concordance between national legislation and the protection sought by the Convention; this disregarded the fact that the domestic laws of various Latin American countries had already been reformed following, to a large extent,—either directly or indirectly—the model of the Convention or else leaving differences which were not impossible to overcome, while the high level of protection afforded by the Convention was an incentive further to improve the protection of national works with a consequent encouragement of local creativity which would automatically obtain international protection—in conformity with the provisions of the Convention—in all the Member Countries of the Union.

In his discussion of the factors which led to a change of view on the part of the Latin American countries in the mid-1960s, Carlos Mouchet draws attention to the following: a greater conviction of the need to protect intellectual creators; the realization that 'intellectual ressources' were a source not only of spiritual, but also of material wealth and a 'professionalization' of creative activity in those countries where the scheme of protection of authors' rights had in any case been improved. Mouchet points out that in regard to the accession to the Berne Convention '... the societies of authors played a decisive role and will continue to do so, as is apparent from the Inter-American Congresses on Copyright organized by the Pan-American Council of CISAC' (*América latina y el derecho de author*, Buenos Aires, Consejo Panamericano de la CISAC, 1973, p. 41.

sequently known as Benin); in 1962 Congo, Côte d'Ivoire, Gabon, Mali, Niger and Senegal; in 1963 Zaire; in 1964 Cameroon and in 1966 Madagascar. Following the Brussels revision, the Union had also been joined by the Philippines in 1951, Turkey in 1952 and Cyprus and Malta in 1964.

The 20 years that had elapsed since the Brussels Conference had witnessed a number of events which were to influence the Stockholm revision to varying degrees:

- in 1952, the Universal Copyright Convention was adopted in Geneva. It was joined by most member countries of the Union and many non-member countries;
- in 1961, the International Convention for the Protection of Performers, Producers of Phonograms and Broadcasting Organizations was signed in Rome; it recognized neighbouring rights and granted international protection for them outside the framework of the Berne Convention which was reserved for the protection of creative works[69] even though the influence of industrial interests on authors' rights was growing, particularly on the part of phonogram producers;
- in August 1963, during the African Symposium on Copyright convened jointly by BIRPI and UNESCO in Brazzaville, the idea was mooted of introducing special provisions into the Berne Convention in favour of the young nations that had recently gained their independence, having regard to the fact that these countries were confronted with the vast problem of ensuring the education of broad sectors of their population. For this purpose they needed teaching personnel and materials and the use of both formal and informal methods. Until national teaching materials could be produced (which would inevitably require a great deal of time) foreign works would have to be used originating, for the most part, in the developed countries. They therefore needed to have easy and rapid access to the rights of translation, reproduction and broadcasting of such works. However, the economic conditions prevailing in some of these

---

69. See below: Future revision of the Berne Convention: (c) Producers of sound recordings (phonograms) and continuation of preparatory work.

countries, as in those which were to achieve their independence soon afterwards, made it practically impossible for them to grant foreign works the level of protection established by the Berne Convention, and in particular by the Brussels Act.

The Brazzaville Recommendation (August 1963) which dealt simply with the term of protection and bilateral agreements evolved rapidly. In November of the same year, it was forwarded to the Swedish Government BIRPI study Group and in the following month it was the subject of a resolution in New Delhi which highlighted the need to permit the granting of compulsory licences for teaching and translation purposes. In July 1964, this resulted in the drafting of a new Article—25*bis*—which was the first version of the Protocol subsequently discussed by the Stockholm Conference, *as a result of which the Fourth Revision of the Convention never took full effect.* As we have seen, once the idea had been launched it gained immediate support backed by most countries of Africa and Asia, for which India acted as spokesperson. It was also defended by a leading international organization: the European Broadcasting Union.[70]

The co-ordinators of the Stockholm Conference certainly considered it preferable for these countries to be able to organize copyright protection within the context of the Berne Union, even if this made it necessary to incorporate in the Convention certain provisions which would be applicable for a certain period of time until the economic and social situation of the countries concerned improved, allowing the latter to limit protection when the works were used for educational purposes. These provisions would also ensure that the countries which had been parties to the Union via the 'colonial clause' would not leave it after achieving their independence.

The Stockholm Conference was scheduled by the Swedish Government for 1967 (the venue but not the time by which the next revision was to take place had already been fixed in Brussels—1948). It dealt not only with the revision of the Berne Con-

---

70. Cf. 'The Protocol Regarding Developing Countries', *RIDA*, Paris, October 1967/January 1968, pp. 393–7.

vention but also, at a number of separate conferences, with the revision of the Paris Convention for the Protection of Industrial Property and the adoption of the Convention setting up WIPO. This event was attended by representatives from 52 member countries of the Union (Ceylon, Cyprus, Dahomey, Lebanon, Mali, New Zealand, Pakistan and the Republic of Upper Volta being absent) with observers from 23 other countries and various intergovernmental organizations (including the United Nations, UNESCO, the EEC and COMECON) as also from many nongovernmental organizations (ALAI, CISAC, IFPI, EBU, etc.). The Conference worked on the basis of the programme drawn up by the Swedish Government/BIRPI (drafting had begun in 1963 and was the subject of a series of consultations). The eminent German specialist in authors' rights, Eugen Ulmer, Professor at Munich University and Director of the Max Planck Institute, was appointed Chairman of the main Commission. The General Rapporteur was Svante Bergström, the representative of Sweden, who had been a member of the Swedish Government/BIRPI study group.

The main changes introduced by the Stockholm revision were: extension of the *personal criterion* to published works and the addition of new points of attachment with the Convention; express recognition of the right of reproduction; identical term of protection of the moral right and the economic right; adoption of minimum terms of protection for certain works; abolition of the possibility of making the right of public performance by mechanical means conditional on the system of non-voluntary licences; the statute of cinematographic works; reform of the administrative provisions, final clauses and preferential provisions for the developing countries. Other changes were also made, intended for the most part to improve the drafting and structure of the Convention.

a. Area of application of the Convention: criteria or points of attachment; concept of the 'country of origin' and of 'publication'

The Stockholm revision introduced a fundamental change which was influenced by the Universal Convention: the personal criterion—in previous texts this had applied only to unpublished works—was now also extended to published works. The scope of application of the Convention was thus widened.

In consequence, pursuant to the new Article 3 in respect of published works, the personal criteria (nationality and habitual place of residence of the author) were added to the material link (the place of first publication of the work) and the Convention was made applicable both to works whose author was a national or had his habitual place of residence in a country of the Union and to those published for the first time in a member country of the Union or in a *non-Union* country, provided, in the latter instance, that the author was a national of a member country or had his habitual place of residence in such a country. The notion of 'country of origin of the work' was also changed in the case of published works: if the work was first published in a country outside the Union, the country of origin of the work was deemed to be the country of the Union of which the author was a national (Article 5, para. 4, (c)).

At the same time a new subsidiary point of attachment was introduced for cinematographic works: pursuant to Article 4(a), even if the conditions of Article 3 were not fulfilled (that is to say if none of the co-authors was a national of a member country of the Union or had his habitual residence there and if the first publication was made in a country outside the Union) the cinematographic work was still protected under the Convention if the author was a corporate body which had its headquarters in a country of the Union or a natural person with a habitual residence in such a country.

Again in the case of cinematographic works the notion of 'published works' was also made more flexible. The Brussels Act required a sufficient number of copies of the work to be made available to the public (Article 4, para. 4). The Stockholm text required the availability of copies to be such as to 'satisfy the reasonable requirements of the public having regard to the nature of the work' (Article 3, para. 3, which added the requirement of consent by the author to prevent publication from being the result of illicit reproduction).

b. Right of reproduction; exceptions

Despite the fact that the right of reproduction is an authors' right par excellence, and recognized as such by all domestic legislations, sufficient provision was not made for it in the previous Acts of the Convention although it was implicit in various provisions, for example those which recognized rights of translation and adaptation (Articles 8 and 12) and those which established limitations e.g. for quotations and illustrations (Article 10) and other exceptions to the right of reproduction (Article 10*bis*), which are necessarily based thereon.

The Stockholm text embodies the right of reproduction in Article 9, paragraph 1: 'Authors of literary and artistic works protected by this Convention shall enjoy the exclusive right of authorizing the reproduction of these works, in any manner or form.' Notwithstanding the broad scope of this provision, paragraph 3 stipulates that any sound or visual recording shall be considered as a reproduction for the purposes of the Convention. That provision might appear superfluous. However, having regard to the fact that the previous Acts included the right of mechanical reproduction expressly in paragraph 1 of Article 13 and this recognition in the Berne Convention was not easy to secure, the clarification given in paragraph 3 of the new Article 9, even if superfluous, is still justified since it tends to prevent any misinterpretation which might result from the elimination of paragraph 1 of Article 13.

The latter also recognized the right of public performance by mechanical means, but its deletion had no effect since Article 11, paragraph 1, recognized the right of public performance in general. On the other hand, the remaining paragraphs of Article 13 were maintained in substance except for paragraph 1 (formerly para. 2) as we shall see in the context of the abolition of the possibility of making the right of public performance by mechanical means conditional on the system of non-voluntary licences.

Paragraph 2 of Article 9 enables exceptions from the exclusive right of reproduction to be included in the legislation of member countries of the Union 'in certain special cases' subject to two concurrent conditions: the reproduction must not conflict with the normal exploitation of the work nor may it cause unreasonable prejudice to the legitimate interests of the author. The scope of this exception concerning reprographic reproduction and the photocopying of printed works for personal use and the private or domestic copying of sound and audiovisual recordings, together with the scope and conditions of the further exceptions set out in Articles 10 and 10*bis*, have been analysed earlier (see above Chap. 4, Sects. 4.3.1. and 4.3.2.).

c. Protected works

In regard to choreographic works and entertainments in dumb show, the first paragraph of Article 2 of the Stockholm Act deleted the sentence by virtue of which these works could only be protected if their acting form was fixed 'in writing or otherwise'. In regard to cinematographic works and works *produced* by a process analogous to cinematography, together with photographic works and works *produced* by a process analogous to photography, the verb *produced* was replaced in Stockholm by the verb *expressed*; it was felt that the term *produced* implied prior fixation while *expression* signified that the effects were analogous to those which, in the case of audiovisual works, result from the projection of cinematographic works by virtue of which the rule would include live television broadcasts, i.e. broadcasts without prior fixation.

However, the widening of protection resulting from the changes described in relation to choreographic works and entertainments in dumb show, together with audiovisual works, was not binding on national legislation since the new numbered paragraph 2 of Article 2 provided for the possibility of requiring fixation: 'It shall, however, be a matter for legislation in the countries of the Union to prescribe that works in general or any specified categories of work shall not be protected unless they have been fixed in some material form.' Given the general scope of this provision, it also covers oral works; this is of particular interest to the countries of the Anglo-American system in which the requirement of fixation continues to be decisive for the work to enjoy protection under copyright law (see above Chap. 1, Sect. 1.3.1.).

In regard to protected works, Articles 2 and 2*bis* also introduced other changes to the wording and structure of the Convention.

d. The moral right after the death of the author

In the Brussels text (Article 6*bis*, para. 2) protection of the moral right after the death of the author was possible 'in so far as the legislation of the countries of the Union permits'. This last phrase was deleted in Stockholm, despite strong opposition from the countries whose legal tradition was based on common law. An obligation on member countries of the Union to protect the moral right at least until the cessation of the economic right was thus introduced into the Convention. Nevertheless, the Conference did take into consideration the special situation of the countries referred to earlier: the United Kingdom delegation explained that in its country the right to claim authorship of a work fell within the scope of copyright legislation, while the right to oppose any deformation, mutilation or other modification of the work or any encroachment on it which caused prejudice to the honour or reputation of the author was a matter for ordinary law, and more particularly, for the law on libel and slander; that law did not permit legal action to be pursued after the death of the person who had been libelled or slandered.[71] As a compromise solution, an exception was allowed from the obligation to protect the moral right at least until the economic rights lapsed; the countries whose legislation in force at the time of ratification or accession to the Stockholm Act did not contain provisions relating to protection of all the moral rights after the death of the author 'may provide that some of these rights may, after his death, cease to be maintained' (last part of Article 6*bis*, para. 2).

---

71. The UK *Copyright, Designs and Patents Act* of 1988 was adjusted to the criterion embodied in the Berne Convention by including the right to be identified as the author or director (Sect. 77) and the right to oppose any derogatory treatment of the work (Sect. 80). The Act stipulated that these rights may be exercised as long as the work enjoys protection (Sect. 86, para. (1)).

e. Adoption of minimum periods of protection for certain works

Article 7 underwent substantial changes relating to cinematographic and photographic works and works of applied art. The Brussels text had allowed the countries of the Union to fix terms for the protection of such works by applying the provisions of the law of the country in which protection was claimed, but without exceeding the duration stipulated in the country of origin of the work (method of comparison of terms).

In Stockholm, this criterion was amended and minimum terms were laid down in respect of the works referred to above, although Article 7, paragraph 8, retained, in general, the principle of material reciprocity if the country in which protection was claimed stipulated a term longer than the minimum period provided in the Convention: 'unless the legislation of that country provides otherwise, the term shall not exceed the term fixed in the country of origin of the work'.

In regard to *cinematographic works*, the second paragraph of Article 7 of the Stockholm Act maintained the validity of a minimum period of 50 years after the death of the author. However, as some legislations treat the producer as the author, and as the producer tends to be a corporate body whose duration is not the same as the life of a natural person, the countries of the Union have the option to stipulate that the term of protection shall expire 50 years after the date on which the cinematographic work was made available to the public with the consent of the author. Masouyé points out that the notion of availability to the public is more restrictive than the notion of publication (to which reference is made in para. 3 of Article 3) since it not only requires the cinematographic works to be made available through the distributors, but also for them to be shown for viewing by the public in general either in cinemas or on television.[72] Finally, this rule provides that where national legislation does not stipulate a link between the period of protection of the cinematographic work and the life of its author but with the time at which it is made available to the

---

72. Claude Masouyé, op. cit., p. 47, Section 7.6.

public, the latter event must occur during the 50 years following the making of the work in question. Should that not be the case, protection lapses 50 years after the making of the work (Article 7, para. 2 *in fine*).

In regard to photographic works and works of applied art, Article 7, paragraph 4, stipulates that the term of protection 'shall last at least until the end of a period of 25 years from the making of such a work'. Article 7, paragraph 7, introduced an exception in favour of the countries of the Union which were bound by the Rome Act and grant less extensive periods of protection than those provided in Article 11 in their national legislation in force at the time of their accession to the Stockholm Act: these countries may maintain their existing provisions when ratifying or acceding to the Stockholm Act. This is a right of reservation similar to those authorized in the Berlin Act consequently leading to a breach of the unity of the Convention which, as we saw earlier, the Rome Conference sought to uphold.

f. Abolition of the possibility of making the right of public performance by mechanical means conditional on the system of compulsory licences

The new paragraph 1 of Article 13 contained two important changes: firstly the non-voluntary licence to make a recording of a musical work was extended to the words thereof; secondly, the possibility of non-voluntary licences being stipulated in national legislation for public performance by mechanical means was abolished. In other words, the exclusive right of public performance could not be subjected to the same regime as the right of sound recording (or right of mechanical reproduction) as authorized by paragraph 2 of Article 13 of the Brussels Act.

g. Cinematographic works

The Stockholm Conference laid down a new system for cinematographic works which, having regard to the differences between domestic laws in the matter of authorship and ownership of such works, attracted special attention at the preparatory stage and was the subject of a number of studies and lengthy discussions.

The statute for cinematographic works adopted in Stockholm

contained a series of provisions: Article 2, paragraph 1, included these works in the list of protected works; Article 4(a) established subsidiary criteria or points of attachment for such works with the Convention; Article 5, paragraph 4(c) (i), defined the country of origin of a cinematographic work; Article 7, 2, fixed a minimum term for the right in such works; Article 14 established the cinematographic rights of the authors of existing works; Article 14*bis* regulated the rights of the authors of the cinematographic work, and Article 15, 2 specified the person who shall be presumed to be the maker of the cinematographic work for the purpose of the exercise of the relevant rights. Some of these provisions were taken over from the Brussels Act (Article 2, para. 1 and Article 14 which was redrafted in Stockholm), but most were new and we have discussed some of them (Article 4; Article 5, para. 4(c); Article 7, para. 2).

The new Article 14bis, governing the rights of authors in the cinematographic work as an independent work and also covering the exploitation of those rights, was the outcome of lengthy discussion and complex negotiation to harmonize widely varying legislative solutions with a view to facilitating the task of the producer and the international exploitation of films. Paragraph 1 reiterates a concept which was already embodied in paragraph 2 of Article 14 of the Brussels Act: 'A cinematographic work shall be protected as an original work.' Consequently the owner of copyright enjoys therein all the rights pertaining to an author.

However, the countries of the Union use different systems for the definition of the original owner of copyright in cinematographic works, since in the Anglo-American legal tradition the system of film copyright of the producer prevails (the capacity of author and original ownership of rights in the cinematographic work being granted to the producer), while in the continental European or Roman legal tradition only natural persons who took part in the creation of the cinematographic work may be classified as authors and, hence, the original owners of copyright.[73] The Convention left this problem open, except for the

---

73. See above, Chapter 3, Section 3.4.

stipulation in paragraph 2(a) *that ownership of the copyright should be a matter for legislation in the country in which protection is claimed.*

Paragraph 2(b) goes on to establish, in favour of the maker, a *presumption of legitimation* which dispenses him from the need to prove the title by virtue of which he exercises the rights of exploitation expressly mentioned in the text.[74] This provision, intended for the countries of the Union which subscribe to the Roman law tradition, established that the authors of the contributions to the making of the cinematographic work to whom national legislation accords the capacity of authors thereof, 'if they have undertaken to bring such contributions, may not, in the absence of any contrary or special stipulation, object to the reproduction, distribution, public performance, communication to the public by wire, broadcasting or any other communication to the public, or to the subtitling or dubbing of texts of the work'.

In principle, the scope of the presumption appears to be considerably more extensive than in many national legislations,[75] but paragraph 3 of the same Article 14*bis* introduced a substantial limitation in the Convention: unless national legislation provided to the contrary, the presumption would not be applicable to authors of scenarios, dialogues, and musical works created for the making of the cinematographic work, nor to the principal director thereof. In relation to the latter, para. 3 stipulated that the countries of the Union whose legislation did not provide for application of the presumption of legitimation contained in para. 2(b) to the principal director shall notify the Director-General of WIPO accordingly.

The scope *jure conventionis* of the presumption established in paragraph 2(b) of Article 14*bis* is limited, then, to certain persons

---

74. See above Chapter 3, Section 3.1.2.
75. For example, Argentina, Article 21, first paragraph, grants the producer the right to *show* the cinematographic work; France, Article L. 132-24.1, previously, Article 63-1, first paragraph, provides for the assignment to the producer of the exclusive rights to *exploit* the audiovisual work.

who are exceptionally mentioned in national legislation among the co-authors of cinematographic works (such as the director of photography, second directors, assistant directors, cameramen, the scenographer, the wardrobe manager and the actors).

Article 15, paragraph 2 stipulates that 'the person or body corporate whose name appears on a cinematographic work in the usual manner shall, in the absence of proof to the contrary, be presumed to be the maker of the said work'. This rule assumes particular importance for the exercise of the rights conferred upon the producer, in particular where those rights are infringed.

h. Other changes

Article 11ter: the content of the right of public recitation was widened and harmonized with Article 11 in relation to the right of public performance and presentation. *Article 15, paragraph 3*: this paragraph refers to works of national folklore although they were not specifically mentioned (see above, Chap. 2, Sect. 2.2.1.7— *international protection of works of folklore*).

i. The Protocol Regarding Developing Countries

It was initially proposed that the provisions relating to the developing countries should be included in the body of the Convention in the form of a new Article 25*bis*. That gave rise to objections because it would have involved a return to the system of reservations which the Rome Conference had tried to end. It was suggested that the preferential provisions might be set out in an additional protocol which would leave the Convention intact. However, an independent text to which countries could accede at their own discretion separately from the Act, did not satisfy the aspirations of the developing countries since if these reservations were not incorporated into the Convention they would lose their *raison d'être*.

The Stockholm Conference finally decided in favour of an annexed Protocol forming an integral part of the Convention and consisting of six articles establishing preferential provisions in favour of all the States classified as developing countries—in conformity with the practice laid down by the General Assembly of the United Nations[76]—which ratified or cceded to the Stockholm Act and, having regard to their economic situation and social or cultural needs, considered that they were unable immediately to make the arrangements necessary to ensure protection of all the rights as provided for in the Convention.

In conformity with the Protocol, these countries were able to declare, at the time of their accession, that for the stipulated term (the first ten years, with the possibility of extension) they proposed to make use of all or some of the reservations laid out in the Protocol. This gave them the following possibilities:
- to replace the minimum terms of protection by other much shorter periods, analogous to those set out in the Universal Convention (Article 1, para. (a));
- to grant non-exclusive licences subject to specific conditions for: (a) translation and publication of a translation in any of the national, official or regional languages in which the work has not been published (Article 1, para. (b), (ii)); and (b) reproduction and publication for educational or cultural purposes of a work which has not been published in the country concerned in the original form in which it was created, or if all previous editions of such work in its said original form in that country are out of print (Article 1, para. (c) (i));
- to establish conditions for the exercise of the broadcasting right (Article 1, para. (d) (ii)); and
- to restrict the protection of works—subject to certain specific conditions—exclusively for teaching, study and research purposes in all areas of education (Article 1(e)).

---

76. The Stockholm Conference considered that a formal criterion must be adopted and believed that this could be the practice laid down by the General Assembly of the United Nations, i.e. the list drawn up by the Economic and Social Council of that institution and adopted by a Resolution of the General Assembly of the United Nations. That list comprised all the countries of Asia (with the exception of Japan, Israel and the Republics of the former Soviet Union), Africa, Central America, South America, Panama and the Caribbean. Argentina, Mexico and Uruguay, declared that they could not, in their opinion, be classified as 'developing countries'. A similar declaration was made by the Moroccan Delegation in Stockholm.

This Protocol was the reason why the Stockholm Act did not enter into force in full. The developed nations considered that the derogations from the general principles of the Convention permitted by the Protocol went too far, in particular Article 1, paragraph (e), since the reference to 'teaching, study and research purposes in all areas of education' was an excessively broad definition which enabled the developing countries to restrict protection of works inordinately. Moreover, both the procedures for imposing the restrictions and the amount of the remuneration and the method for its payment, were left entirely to the discretion of each of these countries.

j. Reform of the administrative provisions and final clauses

The BIRPI were placed under the authority of the Government of the Swiss Confederation but no provision was made for the representation of member countries of both Unions (the Paris Union for the Protection of Industrial Property and the Berne Union for the Protection of Literary and Artistic Works.) This lack of autonomy led to an initiative to develop a system by virtue of which the countries of the Union would be represented on an equal basis. The Permanent Consultative Committee created by the resolution of the Brussels Conference was the first step towards a far-reaching transformation of the Organization[77] which led, in Stockholm, to the simultaneous reform of the administrative provisions of both Conventions (Paris and Berne), and to the adoption of the Convention setting up the World Intellectual Property Organization. Each Union has its own organs with responsibility in the areas pertaining to them, and the WIPO Convention to which States may belong without subscribing to any of the Unions (e.g. Andorra, Angola, Bhutan, Brunei Darussalam, Guatemala, Laos, Nicaragua, Panama, Qatar, Saudi Arabia, Sierra Leone, Somalia, United Arab Emirates and Yemen[78]), provides the resources nec-

---

77. Cf. Valerio De Sanctis, op. cit., p. 290.
78. Situation as at 1 January 1995, *Industrial Property and Copyright* (Geneva), WIPO, January 1995.

essary to ensure administrative co-operation between the Unions (the Union of Paris, the particular Unions and specific agreements, the Berne Union and any other agreement designed to develop protection of intellectual property and whose administration is entrusted to WIPO).

A list of the countries which are parties to the WIPO Convention will be found at the end of this section (12.4.2.1).

In the Stockholm revision, the administrative provisions were set out in Articles 22 to 26 and the final clauses in Articles. 27 to 38. Article 22 established the Assembly of the Union consisting of all the member countries. It is assisted by an Executive Committee to which a number of countries of the Union equivalent to one-fourth of the total number of members of the Assembly belong (Article 23); administrative tasks are the responsibility of the International Bureau of WIPO (Article 24)—this is a continuation of the International Bureau of the Berne Union which, together with its counterpart for the Paris Union, form the BIRPI (Bureaux Internationaux Réunis pour la Protection de la Propriété Intellectuelle); Article 25 deals with the budget of the Union, while Article 26 amends the administrative provisions.

The text went on to make provision for the revision of the Convention, the different procedures for adoption and entry into force in relation to the members of the Union and non-member countries, the applicability of the Convention and of the separate Acts, the international jurisdiction clause, the duration and option of withdrawing from the Convention and the requirement for the member countries of the Union to be in a position under their domestic law to give effect to the provisions of the Convention.

Article 30 listed four cases in which derogations were possible (in the Brussels Act, these were included in Article 25, para. 3 and Article 27, para. 2) including (para. 2(b)) the 'ten year rule' (Article V of the Original Act and Article 1, para. 3 of the Additional Act of 1896) by virtue of which the exclusive right of translation shall lapse if, within a period of ten years from the date of the first publication of the original work, the author has not published or caused to be published in one of the member countries of the Union a translation into the language for which protection is claimed.

Article 32 provided a solution applicable in *future* to the problem arising in relations between the member countries of the Union by reason of the simultaneous existence of different Acts of the Convention.

k. The possibility for member countries of the Union to accede solely to the administrative provisions and final clauses

Article 28, para. 1(b) granted the member countries of the Union the option to exclude from their ratification or accession the substantive provisions (Articles 1 to 21 and the Protocol regarding Developing Countries which forms an integral part of the Act) and to accept only the administrative provisions and the final clauses (Articles 22 to 38). It follows that the new administrative regime, which the countries were perfectly willing to accept as became apparent at the drafting stage, was now separated from the revision of the substantive clauses. The countries which had excluded the substantive clauses from their ratification or accession were authorized to review their decision at any time by depositing a declaration to this effect with the Director-General of WIPO.

l. Recommendations

The Stockholm Conference adopted three recommendations on copyright, in particular one relating to the extension of the term of protection.[79]

m. Ratifications and accessions

The Act was accepted in full by: Chad (1971), German Democratic Republic (1968 and 1970), Mauritania (1972 and 1973) Pakistan (1969 and 1970), Romania (1969 and 1970) and Senegal (1967, 1968 and 1970).

The administrative provisions and final clauses only were accepted by: Australia (1972), Austria (1973), Belgium (1975), Canada (1970), Denmark (1970), Fiji (1972), Finland (1970),

---

79. See above: Chapter 5, Section 5.1.3, G.

Federal Republic of Germany (1970), Ireland (1970), Israel (1970), Liechtenstein (1972), Morocco (1971), Spain (1970), Sweden (1970), Switzerland (1970) and the United Kingdom (1970).

In consequence, *Articles 22 to 38 entered into force on 26 April 1970* with the ratification or accession of Denmark, German Democratic Republic, Ireland, Israel, Romania, Senegal, Spain, Sweden, Switzerland and the United Kingdom.

K. THE PARIS REVISION (1971)

Preparations for the Paris Revision began shortly after the end of the Stockholm Conference. During the meeting of the Permanent Committee of the Berne Union which was held in Geneva in December 1967, it became clear that the Stockholm Act would in all probability not be ratified in its entirety because of the inclusion of the Protocol Regarding Developing Countries. The developed countries felt that this Protocol went beyond the reasonable level of sacrifice that might be asked of the owners of rights in works originating in them (the United Kingdom did not sign the Act). The developing countries for their part were not interested in subscribing to a text that was not ratified by the developed countries or with which they disagreed (Argentina, Brazil and Uruguay did not sign the Act either).

One of the first ideas to be mooted was that of suspending, for the benefit of the developing countries,the safeguard clause of the Berne Convention set out in the Universal Copyright Convention (Article XVII and the Appendix Declaration), but for that to be possible it would first be necessary to revise the Universal Convention. These countries therefore began to insist on such a revision.

In September 1969, under the auspices of BIRPI and UNESCO, a study group was convened in Washington (with representatives drawn from 26 member countries of both Conventions). It recommended, as a matter of priority, that the Universal Convention and the Berne Convention should both be revised at conferences held simultaneously and in the same place. In regard to the Universal Convention, one of the recommendations concerned, precisely, the suspension of the safeguard clause for the benefit of the developing countries.

However, to allow these countries to transfer from the Berne Convention to another Convention offering them arrangements which suited them better, was not a plausible solution either. The Washington Study Group therefore advocated the revision of the Universal Convention and the Berne Convention at conferences held simultaneously and in the same place in order to achieve the following objectives:
- *in the Universal Convention*: (1) the suspension, for the benefit of the developing countries, of Article XVII and of the Appendix Declaration relating thereto; (2) the inclusion of the fundamental authors' rights of reproduction, broadcasting and public presentation and performance; (3) the inclusion of provisions enabling these rights to be relaxed in the same way as the right of translation, for the benefit of the developing countries, without material reciprocity.
- *in the Berne Convention*: (1) the revision of Article 21 of the Stockholm Act in order to separate from the Act the Protocol Regarding Developing Countries; (2) the inclusion of a provision to the effect that the revision of Article 21 would only become effective after ratification of the revised text of the Universal Convention by France, Spain, the United States and the United Kingdom; (3) the inclusion of a provision allowing the developing countries which belonged to the Berne Union to apply the revised text of the Universal Convention in their relations with the other member countries of the Union, and (4) suspension of the obligation to pay contributions to the Berne Union by the developing countries which had indicated their wish to belong to classes VI or VII (Article 25, 4(a)).

A joint meeting of the Intergovernmental Copyright Committee of the Universal Convention and the Permanent Committee of the Berne Union was held in December 1969. Thereafter, both decided to convene *ad hoc* preparatory committees in May 1970 to draw up draft programmes for approval at the extraordinary sessions scheduled for September of the same year. UNESCO and WIPO went on to convene the Diplomatic Conferences for revision of the two Conventions which were held simultaneously and in the same place on the basis of the programmes established by the Intergovernmental Copyright Committee and the Permanent

Committee of the Berne Union. These programmes provided for the introduction into both Conventions of substantially identical provisions in favour of the developing countries, reflecting the outcomes of the negotiations that had taken place between the countries in the light of the experience acquired with the Protocol to the Stockholm Act, with a view to the attainment of a 'delicate balance' between the demands made by one side and the provisions which the other was willing to accept. This was a 'package deal' arrived at after considerable difficulty by the Committees of Experts and the Committees of both Conventions at a series of preparatory meetings, particularly those held in Washington (1969) and Geneva (May and September 1970).

The revision Conference of the Berne Convention was convened by the administering organization (without the participation of the government of a member country of the Union). The number of the members of the Berne Union was the same as on the occasion of the Stockholm conference, since Chile had joined (in 1970) while the Republic of Upper Volta had withdrawn from the Convention with effect from 1970 (although it subsequently rejoined with effect from 24 January 1976). The fifth revision conference of the Berne Convention was attended by delegates from 48 countries of the Union (Bulgaria, Dahomey, Iceland, Madagascar, Mali, Malta, New Zealand, Philippines, Poland, Romania, Thailand and Zaire being absent), with observers from 27 countries, four intergovernmental organizations (ILO, UNESCO, Council of Europe and the African and Malagasy Industrial Property Office (OAMPI)) and numerous non-governmental organizations (International Literary and Artistic Association (ALAI), International Bureau of the Societies Administering the Rights of Mechanical Recording and Reproduction (BIEM), International Confederation of Societies of Authors and Composers (CISAC), International Federation of the Phonograph Industry (IFPI), International Federation of Actors (FIA), International Federation of Film Producers' Associations (FIAPF), International Federation of Musicians (FIM), International Law Association, Internationale Gesellschaft für Urberrecht (INTERGU), European Broadcasting Union (EBU), International Publishers Association (IPA) and others).

The Berne Convention Revision Conference opened in the afternoon of 5 July. (The Revision Conference for the Universal Copyright Convention had opened on the morning of the same day.) Once again (as in Stockholm) Professor Eugen Ulmer was elected Chairman of the Main Commission. The Rapporteur-General was Mr Ousmane Goudiam, head of the Delegation of Senegal. The working sessions began one week later on 12 July (after the working sessions of the Main Commission at the Conference for Revision of the Universal Copyright Convention had been completed) and ended in the third week. The Conference closed on 24 July (after the ending on the same day of the Conference for the Revision of the Universal Convention) with the adoption of the Paris Act in which the substantive provisions (Articles 1 to 20) of the Stockholm Act of 1967 were confirmed as they stood, together with the administrative provisions (Articles 22 to 26). The amendments listed below were made:

Preamble. For the first time in the history of the Convention, the Preamble was amended by adding two paragraphs to link the Paris Act to the previous Stockholm revision in order to recognize the importance of the latter and put on record the fact that Articles 1 to 20 and 22 to 26 of that Act remained unchanged.

Article 29bis. This article was introduced to deal with a specific situation relating to the application of the 1967 Convention establishing WIPO.

The Appendix. This was the only substantive amendment embodied in the Paris Act by comparison with the previous text. The Appendix replaced the Protocol Regarding Developing Countries contained in the Stockholm Act and, apart from formal matters, its provisions are substantially identical to those set out in Articles 5*bis*, 5*ter* and 5*quater* of the revised text of the Universal Copyright Convention. Their content is discussed below.

Ratifications and accessions. Following the 1971 Revision, the number of countries which were party to the Berne Convention increased considerably: when the Paris Conference was convened, the Berne Union had 60 members. This total had risen to 111 by 1 January 1995 (the complete list will be found at the end of this Section 12.4.2.1 preceding the list of Member States of the WIPO Convention).

L. THE ACT WHICH REMAINS IN FORCE TODAY (PARIS, 24 JULY 1971)

Following our survey of the historical evolution of the Convention from the Original Act of 1886 to the Paris Act of 1971, a brief description of the latter is given below in order to provide an overview of the Act which is currently in force.

a. Constitution of a Union

Article 1 dates back to the Original Act and stipulates that the countries to which the Convention applies constitute a Union for the protection of the rights of authors in their literary and artistic works.

b. Owners of copyright

The Convention does not define the term author. Article 15 merely stipulates the persons who are entitled to claim protected rights.

Paragraph 1 establishes a presumption *juris tantum* of authorship in favour of the person whose name (or pseudonym, which is sufficiently well known to leave no doubt as to the identity of its user—a transparent pseudonym) is indicated in the usual manner on the work. Consequently, in the absence of proof to the contrary, this person shall be regarded as the author of the work and entitled 'to institute infringement proceedings in the countries of the Union'. If the author remains anonymous, or uses a pseudonym which is equivalent to anonymity, the Convention appoints as his representative the publisher 'whose name appears on the work' who, without the need for further proof 'shall be entitled to protect and enforce the author's rights'. This provision ceases to apply when the author has revealed his identity and established his claim to authorship of the work (para. 3).

In the case of cinematographic works, the maker shall be presumed *juris tantum* to be the person or body corporate whose name appears on that work in the usual manner (para. 2).

In regard to works of national folklore (which are not specifically mentioned), paragraph 4(a) states that it is a matter for the legislation of the country of which the author is presumed to be a national to appoint the competent authority to represent him and 'protect and enforce his rights in the countries of the Union'. The designation shall be notified to the Director-General of WIPO who shall communicate this declaration to all other countries of the Union (para. 4(b)).

c. Criteria for protection: points of attachment to the Convention

1. *Main criteria* (*Article 3, paras. 1 and 2*). Nationality or habitual place of residence of the author (personal points of attachment). The Convention protects the published and unpublished works of authors who are nationals of a country of the Union or have their habitual residence in any such country.
Place of first publication of the work (*material point of attachment*). Protection is also granted to authors who are not nationals of a member country of the Union and do not have their habitual place of residence in such a country in respect of works published by them for the first time in any one of these countries or, simultaneously, in a country that does not belong to the Union and in a member country of the Union.

2. *Subsidiary criteria* (*Article 4*). These are applied subsidiarily to certain works ('even if the conditions of Article 3 are not fulfilled'). The subsidiary points of attachment are as follows:
- *in the case of cinematographic works*: when the headquarters or habitual residence of the maker are situated in any of the countries of the Union. It follows that even if a cinematographic work has not been published in any of the countries of the Union and none of its authors are nationals of such countries or have their habitual residence in one of them, the work shall likewise be protected by the Convention if its maker is a corporate body which has its registered office in a country of the Union or a natural person whose habitual place of residence is also in any such country. In the case of co-productions, it is sufficient for one of the makers to have his registered office or habitual residence in a member country of the Union;
- *in the case of architectural works*: construction in a member country of the Union;
- *in the case of works of the graphic and plastic arts*: incorporation in a building located in a member country of the Union.

3. *The concept of publication* (*Article 3, para. 3*). The expression 'published works' means works published with the consent of their authors, whatever may be the means of manufacture of the copies, provided that the availability of such copies has been such as to satisfy the reasonable requirements of the public, having regard to the nature of the work. The performance of a dramatic, dramatico-musical, cinematographic or musical work, the public recitation of a literary work, the communication by wire or the broadcasting of literary or artistic works, the exhibition of a work of art and the construction of a work of architecture shall not constitute publication.

The requirement for the consent of the author of the work is intended to prevent publication being a consequence of unauthorized reproduction; illicit conduct must not be allowed to generate the effects which derive from the act of publication and, in particular, from determination of the country of origin of the work.

The condition relating to the method of manufacture of the copies is flexible: the only requirement is that the quantity of copies made available to the public must satisfy its reasonable requirements, having regard to the nature of the work. Consequently the concept of publication comprises cinematographic works, even if the copies thereof are not placed on sale but communicated to the public by projection, showing or television broadcasting, certain musical works (symphonies, concertos) and dramatico-musical works (operas, operettas, *zarzuelas*, etc.) whose scores are published in a few copies which the publishers do not sell but hire out to impresarios or performers.

4. *Concept of simultaneous publication* (*Article 3, paragraph 4*). A work shall be considered as having been published simultaneously in several countries if it has been published in two or more countries within 30 days of its first publication.

5. *Concept of the country of origin of the work* (*Article 5, para. 4*). In the case of *published works*, the country of first publication; in the case of works published simultaneously in several countries of

the Union which grant different terms of protection, the country whose legislation grants the shortest term of protection;

In the case of *works published simultaneously* in a country which does not belong to the Union and in a country of the Union, the latter;

In the case of *unpublished works* or *works first published in a country outside the Union* (without simultaneous publication in a country of the Union) the country of the Union of which the author is a national will be the country of origin. *Cinematographic works are excepted* if their maker has his headquarters or habitual residence in a country of the Union, in which case that country shall be the country of origin. *In the case of architectural works* erected in a country of the Union and *works of the graphic and plastic arts* incorporated in a building located in a country of the Union, that country shall be the country of origin.

d. Basic principles of protection. Protection under the Convention

The protection provided by the Convention is based on the fundamental principles of national treatment (Article 5, para. 1), independence of protection (Art. 5, para. 2), the absence of formalities—automatic protection—(Art. 5, para. 2) and minimum protection (Art. 5, para. 1, *in fine*).

1. *National treatment* (identical treatment for foreign and national works). The law applicable to protected works by virtue of the Convention is the law of the country of the Union in which protection is claimed; consequently, works of the Union shall receive the same treatment as national works without any requirement of reciprocity (Article 5, para. 1): 'Authors shall enjoy, in respect of works for which they are protected under this Convention [...] the rights which their respective laws do now or may hereafter grant to their nationals [...].')

The possibility of making national treatment *conditional on reciprocity* is excluded from the Convention, save in certain exceptional instances:
- in the case of works of the applied arts where the work is protected solely as a design or industrial model in a country and does not enjoy copyright protection, only the special protection

stipulated for industrial designs and models may be claimed for it (Article 2, para. 7) in the other countries of the Union;
- where the legislation of the country in which protection is claimed establishes periods longer than the minimum terms laid down in the Convention, and unless the legislation of that country stipulates otherwise, the duration shall not exceed the term fixed in the country of origin of the work (Article 7, para. 8);
- in the case of the *'droit de suite'* (Article 14*ter*, para. 2);
- where a developed country which is not a member of the Union but accedes to the Convention, adopts the 'ten-year' rule for translations into a language that is generally used in the said country, all the other countries shall be entitled to offer protection equivalent to that granted in the latter country (Article 30, para. 2(b) *in fine*) and
- in regard to specific works of nationals of some countries outside the Union, the Convention explicitly authorizes restriction of protection of works whose authors are, at the date of the first publication of such works, nationals of the other country and are not habitually resident in one of the countries of the Union (Article 6.1).

This latter rule, which was the subject of the Berne Additional Protocol (1914) and figured in the text of the Convention with effect from the Rome Act (1928), explicitly authorizes measures of retortion against a country which does not belong to the Union and does not sufficiently protect works by authors of the Union. It will be recalled that the Berne Additional Protocol (1914) originated from a desire to ensure that nationals of countries outside the Union (in particular the United States) did not benefit from the *jus conventionis* through the application of rules of the Convention on national treatment and simultaneous publication of works (in this case in Canada) where the protection granted by the legislation of the country concerned did not provide equal protection for works of the Union (in this particular case works by English authors).

Article 6 stipulates that if the country of first publication avails itself of this right, the other countries of the Union shall not be required to grant to works thus subjected to special treatment a wider protection than that accorded to them in the country of first publication (para. 1); the restriction shall not have retroactive effect on rights acquired before it was put into force (para. 2); and the countries which decide to apply these rules shall notify the Director-General of WIPO by a written declaration specifying the countries in regard to which protection is restricted, and the restrictions to which rights of authors who are nationals of those countries are subjected (para. 3).[80]

2. *The independence of protection.* The scope of protection is that granted by the country in which protection is claimed, regardless of the extent of the protection granted under the law of the country of origin of the work (Article 5, para. 2: 'The enjoyment and exercise of these rights [...] shall be independent of the existence of protection in the country of origin of the work. Consequently, apart from the provisions of this Convention, the extent of protection, as well as the means of redress afforded to the author to protect his rights, shall be governed exclusively by the laws of the country where protection is claimed').

3. *Absence of formalities* (*automatic protection*). Protection shall be granted without requiring compliance with formalities established in national legislation as a condition for the existence or exercise of the right (Article 5.2)): 'The enjoyment and the exercise of these rights shall not be subject to any formality [...].'

4. *Minimum protection*: by virtue of the principle of national treatment, the law applicable is that of the country in which protection is claimed. However, since substantial differences exist between national laws, the Convention establishes certain minimum rights with a view to mitigating these differences and ensuring the effectiveness of protection (as stated in the Preamble, the

---

80. Masouyé points out that Article 6 has not yet been applied. Governments always hesitate before putting in place measures to this effect and diplomatic considerations take precedence over all others. 'Nevertheless this "legal weapon" remains available to member countries' (op. cit., Sect. 6.8, p. 40).

purpose of the Convention is 'to protect, in as effective and uniform a manner as possible, the rights of authors in their literary and artistic works'). Where the domestic law of a country of the Union does not achieve the minimum standards prescribed in the Convention, the latter shall make good the omission through joint regulatory provisions and a set of uniformly applicable rules, i.e. the *jus conventionis*. In the case of works of the Union, it follows that the minimum standards laid down in the Convention shall be added to the domestic law applicable to national works. Expressed differently, where the provisions of domestic law do not reach the minimum rights guaranteed *jure conventionis* they shall be supplemented by the latter (Article 5, para. 1: 'Authors shall enjoy [...] in countries of the Union [...] the rights which their respective law do now or may hereafter grant to their nationals, as well as the rights specially granted by this Convention.')

5. *Non-applicability of the Convention in the country of origin of the work.* The Convention expressly rules out application in the country of origin of the work (Article 5, para. 3, first sentence: 'Protection in the country of origin is governed by domestic law.')

The provisions ensuring minimum protection are those concerning *protected works* (Article 2); the rights recognized: *the moral right* (Article 6*bis*), *the economic rights*—of reproduction including the right to record musical works (Article 9), of translation (Article 8), adaptation, arrangements and other alterations of their works (Article 12), presentation and public performance (Article 11), public recitation (Article 11*ter*), broadcasting (Article 11*bis*), rights in cinematographic works (Articles 14 and 14*bis*) and the *'droit de suite'* (Article 14*ter*)—and the *duration of the rights* (Article 6*bis*, para. 2, Article 7). The Convention also sets out the permitted *limitations* (Article 2, para. 8, Article 2*bis*; Article 9, para. 2; Articles 10 and 10*bis*; Article 11*bis*, paras. 2 and 3; Article 13, para. 1; Article 16 and Article 30, para. 2(b)).

i) Protected works
Article 2, paragraph 1, stipulates that: 'The expression "literary and artistic works" shall include every production in the literary, scientific and artistic domain, whatever may be the mode or form

of its expression, such as books, pamphlets and other writings; lectures, addresses, sermons and other works of the same nature; dramatic or dramatico-musical works; choreographic works and entertainments in dumb show; musical compositions with or without words; cinematographic works to which are assimilated works expressed by a process analogous to cinematography; works of drawing, painting, architecture, sculpture, engraving and lithography; photographic works to which are assimilated works expressed by a process analogous to photography; works of applied art; illustrations, maps, plans, sketches and three-dimensional works relative to geography, topography, architecture or science.'

The list set out in Article 2, paragraph 1, *is not exhaustive* (it uses the expression 'such as ...'). Protection is provided solely for formal creations and not for ideas.

Protection is extended to all creative works, both original (paras. 1 and 7) and derived (translations, adaptations, musical arrangements and other transformations of a literary or artistic work), together with collections of literary or artistic works such as encyclopaedias and anthologies which, by reason of the selection and arrangement of their contents, constitute intellectual creations (paras. 3 and 5).

By virtue of these provisions, the works of member countries of the Union shall be protected by the contracting States and 'this protection shall operate for the benefit of the author and his successors in title' (para. 6).

Works of applied art are included in the list of works protected *jure conventionis*, but the Convention leaves the countries of the Union free to determine the nature of the protection accorded to them. If a work is protected in one country solely as an industrial design or model, i.e. if it does not enjoy copyright protection, only the special protection established for industrial designs and models may be claimed in the other countries of the Union, that is to say, the condition of material reciprocity applies. However, since some countries do not have a specific legal system governing industrial designs and models and protect them simply as works of art, the Convention also takes account of such situations and stipulates that works of the applied arts must be protected in their capacity as artistic works, i.e. they must enjoy copyright protection (Article 2, para. 7 *in fine*: 'however, if no such special protection is granted in that country, such works shall be protected as artistic works').

Where the works of applied art are protected as artistic works, i.e. by the law on copyright, the term of protection shall not be less than 25 years, counting from the date on which the works were made (Article 2, para. 7 which refers back to Article 7, para. (4)).

The Convention (Article 2, para. 2) takes into account those legislations which, in general or in regard to certain works in particular, make protection conditional on the existence of a fixation of the work. This is the case, firstly, of legislation in the Anglo-American legal tradition under which protection of copyright is generally conditional on the work being fixed in writing or in some other material form; and secondly in countries such as Brazil, France, Italy and the Netherlands in regard to choreographic works and entertainments in dumb show.

With that end in view, Article 2, paragraph 2, provides that legislation may make protection conditional on fixation in some material form ('it shall, however, be a matter for legislation in the countries of the Union to prescribe that works in general or any specified categories of works shall not be protected unless they have been fixed in some material form'). That provision must be interpreted, in particular, as being applicable to certain works mentioned in the list set out in the first paragraph of the same Article 2 such as 'lectures, addresses, sermons and other works of the same nature' (oral works) and other works which may or may not be fixed such as 'choreographic works and entertainments in dumb show' and 'works expressed by a process analogous to cinematography' (for example, television works which may be broadcast either live or from a fixation).

ii) The moral right
Article 6*bis* defines the content of the moral right in its paragraph 1. Protection is given under the Convention in respect of two basic aspects alone; the author's right to claim authorship of the work and to oppose any distortion, mutilation or other modification of,

or other derogatory action in relation to, the said work which would be prejudicial to his honour or reputation (Article 6*bis*, para. 1). Paragraph 2 goes on to stipulate the duration of the moral right after the death of the author: 'at least until the expiry of the economic rights'. However, the countries whose legislation in force at the time of ratification or accession to the Paris Act does not contain provisions on protection of the moral right after the death of the author, are entitled to stipulate that some of these rights may cease to be maintained after his death.

iii) Economic rights
The Convention recognizes the following specific and exclusive economic rights of the author: reproduction (Article 9), translation (Article 8), adaptation, arrangements and other transformations (Article 12), communication to the public and public performance (Article 11), broadcasting (Article 11*bis*), public recitation (Article 11*ter*). It also recognizes rights in cinematographic works and the right of participation or '*droit de suite*' (Article 14*ter*) which, unlike the other rights, is not compulsory for the countries of the Union and is subject to the condition of material reciprocity.

The right of reproduction: Article 9, paragraph 1, grants the authors of literary and artistic works protected by the Convention the exclusive right to authorize the reproduction of these works, in any manner or form.

This rule has been drafted in sufficiently broad terms to cover all the procedures of reproduction including mechanical and magnetic reproduction (records, tapes, films, microfilms, etc.); however, paragraph 3 of the same article stipulates that 'any sound or visual recording shall be considered as a reproduction'.

The right of translation: Article 8 grants authors the exclusive right of making or authorizing the translation of their works throughout the term of protection of their rights in the original works.

The right of adaptation, arrangement and other alterations: Article 12 recognizes the exclusive right of authors of authorizing adaptations, arrangements and other alterations of their works.

The right of communication to the public and public performance: Article 11, paragraph 1, grants the authors of dramatic works, dramatico-musical and musical works the exclusive right of authorizing: '(i) the public performance of their works, including such public performance by any means or process; (ii) any communication to the public of the performance of their works'. The first part refers: (1) to live public presentation or performance; and (2) to communication to the public and performance by mechanical means; thus the public use of sound recordings and visual and audiovisual fixations is expressly assimilated with direct public presentation or performance. The second part does not refer, as might seem at first sight, to the broadcasting of a public presentation or performance since the broadcasting right is expressly covered by Article 11*bis*, but to other forms of communication, such as the transmission of a performance by a telephone network.

The second paragraph of Article 11 grants the same rights in respect of the translations of dramatic and dramatico-musical works. This provision is a necessary consequence of the recognition of the right of translation (Article 8) since the author enjoys both this right and the exclusive right of authorizing the performance of his translated work, inasmuch as these are two independent rights and two different forms of exploitation.

The right of public recitation: this right granted by Article 11*ter*, paragraph 1, to authors of literary works is equivalent to the right of communication to the public and of public performance set out in Article 11 for the authors of dramatic and dramatico-musical works.

The first subparagraph of Article 11*ter*, paragraph 1, of the Convention grants authors the exclusive right of authorizing the public recitation of their works (this is not the same as a performance), regardless of whether this recitation is live or recorded ('public recitation by any means or process'); the second subparagraph of paragraph 1 relates to the exclusive right of the author to authorize any communication to the public of the recitation of his works (as distinct from broadcasting, to which express reference is made in Article 11*bis*).

The second paragraph of Article 11*ter* recognizes the exclusive right of the author to authorize the public recitation of a translation of his work.

The broadcasting right: the first paragraph of Article 11*bis* of the Convention recognizes that the exclusive right of authors in respect of broadcasts of their works shall apply in an independent and cumulative manner to: (i) the purely sound or television broadcasting of their works (broadcasting of their works or the communication thereof to the public by any other means of wireless diffusion of signs, sounds or images); (ii) any communication to the public by wire or wireless means of broadcasts, when this communication is made by an organization other than the original one (retransmission of the broadcast by cable or by open broadcasting, when made by an organization other than the original one; on the other hand, the author's consent is not required if the retransmission—simultaneous and integral—is made by a broadcasting organization which was given the original authorization); and (iii) the public communication by loudspeaker or television screen (public showing and performance of the broadcast work).

The Convention therefore protects the author's right to authorize both broadcasting and subsequent use of the original broadcast, either by a cable distribution system or else by wireless (open broadcasting) provided that the rebroadcast is made by a different organization than that of the first broadcast. Similarly, the exclusive right to authorize public reception of the broadcast by loudspeaker or any analogous instrument for the transmission of signs, sounds and images of the broadcast work (a television screen) is protected.

In all cases the communication must be public.

Rights pertaining to cinematographic works: these are the rights set out: (1) in Article 14 concerning the authors of pre-existing works; and (2) in Article 14*bis* concerning the authors of cinematographic works.

The rights of authors of pre-existing works: (literary works—novels, short stories, poems, etc.—dramatic works, dramatico-musical, musical and artistic works, etc.). These authors have the exclusive right to authorize the 'cinematographic adaptation and reproduction' of their works, 'the distribution of the works thus adapted or reproduced' and communication to the public of the works thus adapted or reproduced by means of the 'public per-

formance and communication to the public by wire' (Article 14, para. 1). It follows that the authors of pre-existing works enjoy a series of rights:
- of adaptation (for example of a novel in the form of a film scenario);
- of reproduction (synchronization of musical works);
- of translation of the adapted work (by subtitling or dubbing);
- of distribution of the cinematographic work for projection in a cinema;
- the projection (showing) of the film in cinemas;
- communication to the public by wire (for example by cable systems).[81]

They also have the right of adaptation 'into any other artistic form, of a cinematographic production derived from literary or artistic works' (Article 14, para. 2). This means that if a novel has been made into a film and a dramatist in his turn wishes to make an adaptation for the theatre, he must secure the authorization both of the author of the cinematographic adaptation and of the author of the original novel on which the film was based.

The rights of authors of cinematographic works are governed by Article 14*bis*.

Paragraph 1 stipulates that the 'cinematographic work shall be protected as an original work' and that the owner of copyright therein shall enjoy the same rights as the author of an original work, including the rights referred to in Article 14. As to the person who is to be regarded as the owner of copyright in the cinematographic work, having regard to the diversity of the criteria set out in the various national laws, the Convention makes no specific stipulations and refers back to the provisions of legislation of the country in which protection is claimed (para. 2(a)).

---

81. Article 14, para. 1, does not mention the right of broadcasting; this omission has cast some doubt on the obligation of the member countries of the Union to grant this right to authors of pre-existing works in respect of the cinematographic reproductions or adaptations thereof. However, these authors are held to enjoy the broadcasting right since it is generally conferred by Article 11*bis* even though it may be the subject of the compulsory licences which are permitted in the second paragraph thereof (see Ricketson, op. cit., p. 569).

Paragraph 2(b) goes on to establish a presumption of legitimation in favour of the producer for the exploitation, in the broadest sense, of the cinematographic work ('reproduction, distribution, public performance, communication to the public by wire, broadcasting or any other communication to the public, subtitling and dubbing of texts'). This presumption *jure conventionis* is intended for those countries in which the systems of film copyright do not apply (the common law countries) and in which there is no *cessio legis* in favour of the maker of the film (Austria, Italy). However, despite the conclusion that might be reached at first sight, its scope is considerably restricted since it does not apply to the authors of the pre-existing works (whose rights are governed by Article 14) and, 'unless the national legislation provides to the contrary' (Article 14*bis*, para. 3), it does not apply to the authors of scenarios, dialogues and musical works created for the making of the cinematographic work or to the principal director thereof.[82]

This presumption of legitimation applies except in the case of 'contrary or special stipulation', once the authors of the contributions to the making of the cinematographic work 'have undertaken to bring such contributions' (para. 2(b)). The form of the agreement is governed by the legislation of the member country of the Union in which the maker has his headquarters or habitual residence; but 'it is a matter for the legislation of the country of the Union where protection is claimed to provide that the said undertaking shall be in a written agreement or a written act of the same effect'. The countries which make use of this possibility shall notify that fact to the Director-General of WIPO by a written declaration which the latter shall communicate to all the other countries of the Union (para. 2(c)). The term 'contrary or special stipulation' must be understood to denote any restrictive condition which is relevant to the aforesaid undertaking (para. 2(d)).

The 'droit de suite': Article 14*ter* (Article 14*bis* of the Brussels Act) recognizes that the author has the right to obtain a share of

---

82. See above, Stockholm revision (1967).

the proceeds of the sales of the original works of arts and manuscripts which take place after the first transfer by the author (para. 1). This right shall be deemed to be inalienable, although transmissible after death, but, pursuant to paragraph 2, its recognition is not compulsory in countries of the Union and is subject to material reciprocity: the *'droit de suite'* may be claimed 'only if legislation in the country to which the author belongs so permits and to the extent permitted by the country where this protection is claimed'.

The determination of the procedures for collection and the amounts is a matter for national legislation (para. 3).

iv) Duration of the rights
In the case of the *moral right*, Article 6*bis*, paragraphs 1 and 2, stipulates that it is enjoyed by the author in his lifetime; after his death the countries of the Union are obliged to maintain the moral right 'at least until the expiry of the economic rights'. However, the countries whose legislation in force at the time of ratification or accession to the Paris Act does not contain provisions relating to protection of moral rights after the death of the author have the possibility of stipulating that some of these rights may not be maintained after the death of the author.

In regard to *economic rights* the Convention stipulates as a general rule that protection shall be granted in the lifetime of the author and for 50 years after his death (Article 7, para. 1). The countries of the Union are obliged to respect this term which is a minimum under the Convention.

The possibility of *shorter terms* is confined to the situation stipulated in paragraph 7. With a view to facilitating the acceptance of the new Article 7 by the countries of the Union attached to the Convention by the Rome Act, which, at the time of signing the Paris Act (24 July 1971), granted in their national legislation terms shorter than those stipulated in Article 7, those terms may be maintained on accession to this new Act.

On the other hand, the countries of the Union may grant longer terms (para. 6) which shall apply to works of the Union (principle of national treatment) but, unless the national legislation of the country which establishes the longer term provides otherwise, the method of comparison of the terms (the comparison rule) shall be applied in such a way that the term shall not exceed that fixed in the country of origin of the work (para. 8).

In consequence, if a country establishes a term of more than 50 years after the death of the author—for example Brazil (60 years)—it must apply that term to the works whose country of origin is, for example, Colombia (80 years), but not to works originating in Argentina, Costa Rica, Ecuador, Peru or Paraguay (50 years); the latter works shall only be protected in Brazil for 50 years after the death of the author, a period which shall also apply to works originating in Uruguay (40 years),[83] 50 years after the death of the author being the minimum term under the Convention.

In their turn, in the countries of the Union whose national legislation continues to provide terms which do not correspond to the minimum stipulated in the Convention, works of the Union are to be protected for 50 years after the death of the author because the member countries of the Union are obliged to respect this term in the case of works to which the Convention applies. On the other hand, the nationals of these countries to which the Convention is not applicable (Article 5, para. 3: 'Protection in the country of origin is governed by domestic law'), only enjoy the term established in domestic law. Their works therefore benefit from less protection than works of the Union. This applies not only to the term of protection after the death of the author as in the case of Uruguay, but also in regard to other terms, for example in Peru which joined the Berne Union through the Paris Act but maintained in Articles 22 to 30 of its law on author's rights (1961) a number of periods which are shorter than those stipulated in Article 7 of the Convention (these terms were extended following adoption of decision 351 of 17 December 1993 under the Cartagena Agreement—Articles 18 and 59).

For certain types of works, Article 7 establishes particular rules. This is the case of:

---

83. Situation as of 30 March 1992.

- *cinematographic works* in respect of which the countries of the Union may provide that the term of protection shall expire 50 years after the work has been made available to the public with the consent of the author or, failing such a event within 50 years from the making of such a work, 50 years after the making (para. 2);
- *photographic works and works of applied art* which shall be protected 'at least until the end of a period of 25 years from the making of such a work' (Article 7, para. 4). In the case of photographic works, this provision takes account of the fact that some countries refuse to treat photographs in the same way as other works of art and impose special conditions on them.[84] In regard to works of the applied arts, Article 7, paragraph 4, must be read in conjunction with Article 2, paragraph 7, which leaves the countries of the Union free to determine the legal arrangements applicable to works of this kind and the conditions under which protection shall be granted, but limits that freedom in regard to the duration of the right by establishing that when works of applied art are protected by copyright in one of these countries the term of protection may not be shorter than that indicated (25 years counting from the making of such works);
- *anonymous and pseudonymous works* for which the minimum term of protection is 50 years from the date on which the work was lawfully made available to the public, save where the pseudonym adopted by the author leaves no doubt as to his identity, in which case the general rule applies (para. 3).

Article 7, paragraph 5, of the Convention stipulates how the terms of protection are to be calculated: both the term of protection after the death of the author and the other terms stipulated in Article 7 begin to run from the date of death or of the event referred to in paragraphs 2, 3 and 4, but the duration shall be calculated from 1 January of the year which follows the death or the said event.

---

84. See above, Chapter 2, Section 2.2.1.4, E.

In regard to *works of joint authorship*, Article 7*bis* stipulates that the term measured from the death of the author 'shall be calculated from the death of the last surviving author'.

v) Limitations

Some of the limitations on economic rights are laid down *jure conventionis*. Others—the majority—are left to the discretion of the countries of the Union:[85] the Convention accepts these derogations but the member countries are at liberty to decide whether to introduce them; to invoke them in a country of the Union in respect of a work of the Union to which the Convention is applicable, the country must make express provision to that effect.

■ Limitations *jure conventionis*: these are the limitations applicable to news of the day (Article 2, para. 8) and to quotations (Article 10, para. 1).

News of the day: pursuant to Article 2, paragraph 8, the protection of this Convention 'shall not apply to news of the day or to miscellaneous facts having the character of mere items or press information'. News or miscellaneous facts are not protected as such nor is the simple telling of them since these items lack originality.[86]

According to Masouyé 'it is worth noting, however, that those items, even if not protected by copyright, are not simply thrown to the wolves of theft and piracy. Other means of defence may be brought into play against parasites; for example the laws of unfair competition allow for action against newspapers which steal their news from competitors rather than subscribe to news agencies'.[87]

Quotations: the Convention establishes the permissibility of quotations from all types of work (the Brussels Act, Article 10, para. 1, limited them to literary works) but imposes three conditions:

---

85. Cf. Henri Desbois, André Françon and André Kerever, op. cit., p. 185.
86. Cf. above Chapter 2, Section 2.2.1.1 (unprotected literary works).
87. Claude Masouyé, *Guide to the Berne Convention*, p. 23.

- they must be taken 'from a work which has already been lawfully made available to the public', i.e. quotations may not be taken from unpublished works, but may be from works of national folklore since the Convention uses in Article 10, paragraph 1, the expression 'which has [...] been lawfully made available to the public' that is also employed in Article 7, paragraph 3, referring to anonymous and pseudonymous works;
- the use of the quotation must be 'compatible with fair practice', an expression which is somewhat imprecise and leaves a broad margin of freedom to appreciate the permissibility of a quotation (the Brussels Act referred to 'short quotations'); however, the reference is clearly to current practice in this matter;
- the extent of the quotation must 'not exceed that justified by the purpose'; this wording is intended to limit the length of the quotation according to the type of work in which it is used (a newspaper article, literary manual, etc.).

The quotations must mention 'the source and [...] the name of the author if it appears thereon' (Article 10, para. 3) with a view to ensuring compliance with the obligation to respect the moral right.

■ Limitations reserved for national legislation

* Limitations for information purposes

Official texts (Article 2, para. 4). The Convention authorizes complete or partial exclusion from protection, by virtue of national statutory provisions, for official texts of a legislative, administrative or judicial nature, together with official translations of those texts.

The Stockholm Conference held that the reference to administrative texts did not leave countries free to deny protection to all publications of the government, for example, school textbooks.

Certain *speeches* (Article 2*bis*, para. 1). The Convention also reserves the possibility for the legislation of the countries of the Union to exclude, wholly or in part, political speeches and speeches delivered in the course of legal proceedings from protection. That provision limits protection of the oral works mentioned in this Article. On the other hand, the authors retain the exclusive right to make a collection of these works (Article 2*bis*, para. 3), that is to say to compile or authorize the compilation of political speeches and of speeches made in legal proceedings (accusations, statements in defence, pleas, etc.).

Some uses of lectures and addresses (Article 2*bis*, para. 2). The Convention states that it is a matter for legislation in the countries of the Union to determine the conditions under which lectures, addresses and other works of the same nature which are delivered in public may be reproduced by the press, or broadcast, where such use is justified by the informatory purpose that is pursued.

As in the case of political speeches and speeches delivered in legal proceedings (Article 2*bis*, para. 1), the authors of lectures, addresses and other works of the same nature delivered in public (Article 2*bis*, para. 2) retain the exclusive right to make compilations thereof (Article 2*bis*, para. 3).

Articles on current topics (Article 10*bis*, para. 1). The Convention grants national legislation the right 'to permit the reproduction' by the press and by radio or television broadcasting of certain articles published in newspapers or periodicals and of broadcast works, provided that all the following conditions are satisfied:
- that national legislation expressly so authorizes;
- that the articles relate to current affairs;
- that they concern current economic, political or religious topics;
- that they have been previously published in the press or broadcast, i.e. the new publication is a reproduction;
- that their use has not been expressly prohibited by the owner of the right.[88]

The source must always be clearly indicated (as in all cases where the author's rights are limited, the moral right must be fully re-

---

88. The Brussels Act, on the other hand, in its Article 9, paragraph 2, authorized the free reproduction *jure conventionis* of articles on current affairs dealing with economic, political or religious topics if the reproduction was not expressly reserved by the owner of the rights, but this limitation referred solely to reproduction in the written press.

spected). The legislation of the country in which protection is claimed will stipulate the penalty for failure to comply with this requirement.

Reports on current events (Article 10*bis*, para. 2). The Convention allows national legislation to establish the conditions under which, for the purpose of reporting current events by means of photography, cinematography, broadcasting or communication to the public by wire, literary or artistic works seen or heard in the course of the event may be reproduced and made available to the public to the extent justified by the informatory purpose.[89]

This concerns the reproduction of works involved in public reporting not initially provided for but rendered inevitable in the course of the provision of news. As Masouyé points out, the Convention seeks to avoid abuse and does so by stipulating firstly that the works involved must be those which can be seen and heard during the current affairs report such as the unveiling of a statue or pictures which are being shown at the opening of an exhibition or a musical composition which accompanies a public event; on the other hand if a particular piece of music is subsequently synchronized with a news film, the use of that music may not be treated as an integral part of the report. The other limitation imposed by the Convention is that the use must occur to the extent justified by the informatory purpose which may not result, for example, in the totality of the musical works performed during the ceremony or at a concert being reproduced or made available to the public.[90]

---

89. Stewart considers the fact that the Convention reserves here (as in Article 2*bis*, para. 2) the right for national legislation 'to determine the conditions' to imply that provision is made not only for the possibility of free use being authorized (as in the case of Article 10*bis*, para. 1, where the Convention speaks of the right 'to permit the reproduction') but also for national legislation to establish compulsory licences creating an obligation to pay for the use made (*International Copyright and Neighbouring Rights*, 1989 edition, p. 137, Sects. 5.59 and 5.61).

90. Claude Masouyé, op. cit., pp. 62–3.

* Limitations for educational purposes: illustrations (Article 10, para. 2)

The Convention provides that it shall be a matter for national legislation in the countries of the Union and for special agreements existing or to be concluded between them, to permit lawful use of literary or artistic works 'by way of illustration in publications, broadcasts or sound or visual recordings for teaching'.

This exception to the author's economic rights is justified by the needs of teaching, it being understood that the term 'illustration' for teaching purposes presupposes the more extensive use of literary works than quotations or even the use in full of relatively short works. Article 10, paragraph 2, makes the lawfulness of illustrations subject to the same conditions as quotations (Article 10, para. 1), i.e. they may be made 'to the extent justified by the purpose' and this use must be 'compatible with fair practice'. Similarly 'mention shall be made of the source and of the name of the author if it appears thereon' (Article 10, para. 3).

* The possibility of limiting the right of reproduction

Article 9, paragraph 2, stipulates that it is a matter for national legislation to permit the reproduction of literary and artistic works 'in certain special cases', provided that this reproduction 'does not conflict with a normal exploitation of the work and does not unreasonably prejudice the legitimate interests of the author'.[91]

Unlike the limitations examined previously which concern specific situations, this provision on the right of reproduction in general establishes two conditions that must be satisfied simultaneously: the reproduction must not be prejudicial to the normal exploitation of the work, neither may it unreasonably prejudice the legitimate interests of the author. As a result, the development of photocopying and similar techniques and of the home taping of sound recordings and audiovisual works has meant that such procedures have become habitual methods of making copies of

---

91. See above, Chapter 4, Section 4.3.1, A.

protected works having regard to the vast quantity made by the public directly. Whereas in 1967, when the Stockholm Conference was held, it was possible—in the light of technological development at the time—to consider these reproductions as special cases which did not conflict with the normal exploitation of the work or unreasonably prejudice the legitimate interests of the author, today this is no longer the case.[92]

Ephemeral recordings: Article 11*bis*, paragraph 3, applies the principle of the independence of economic rights,[93] leaving the author the exclusive right to permit the recording (*reproduction*) of the work whose broadcast (*communication to the public*) has been authorized by him. Nevertheless it shall be a matter for legislation in the countries of the Union to lay down rules for ephemeral recordings made by a broadcasting organization by means of its own facilities and used for its own broadcasts. Domestic legislation may authorize the preservation of such recordings in official archives because of their exceptional documentary character.

* Compulsory licences

These are permitted by the Convention both for broadcasting (Article 11*bis*, para. 2) and for sound recordings (Article 13, para. 1).

In regard to broadcasting. Article 11*bis*, paragraph 2, allows national legislation to replace the exclusive right of broadcasting which is recognized as being vested in the author by a system of compulsory licences.

The possibility of issuing compulsory licences covers the three aspects referred to in paragraph 1 of the same Article 11*bis* (broadcasting, communication to the public by wire—cable distribution—or wireless means—public broadcasting or broadcasting by hertzian waves—of the broadcast work when this is done by an organization other than the original one, and public communication of the work either by loudspeaker or by television

---

92. See above, Chapter 4, Section 4.3.2.
93. See above, Chapter 4, Section 4.2.

screen). The Convention leaves it to the countries of the Union to make suitable provisions for compulsory licences but such licences:
- must have an effect which is strictly confined to the country that issued them;
- shall in no case encroach upon the moral rights of the author (the works concerned must be those in respect of which the author has already exercised the right of disclosure), his right to respect for his name and for the work must also be observed; and
- must not encroach upon the author's right to secure equitable remuneration which shall be fixed by the competent authority failing an amicable agreement.

In regard to mechanical reproduction. Article 13, paragraph 1, allows national legislation to lay down a similar scheme of compulsory licences in regard to the 'exclusive right granted to the author of a musical work and to the author of any words, the recording of which together with the musical work has already been authorized by the latter, to authorize the sound recording of that musical work, together with such words if any'.

* The 'ten-year rule'

In relation to the exclusive right of translation, Article 30, paragraph 2(b), offers any country outside the Union which decides to accede to the Convention the possibility of replacing, at least temporarily, Article 8 by Article V of the Original Act of 1886 as amended by the Additional Act of 1896. By virtue of this procedure, which only affects the exclusive right of translation into a language that is generally used in the country concerned, this right shall expire if the author does not make use of it within ten years counting from the date of first publication of the original work, by publishing or causing to be published in one of the countries of the Union, a translation into the language for which protection is claimed.

The possibility of invoking the 'ten-year rule' is open to all countries which join the Union but except in the case of a developing country, the other member countries shall be entitled to apply equivalent protection (material reciprocity provided for in Article 30, para. 2(b) *in fine*).

Countries which have made use of this right may at any time withdraw such reservations by addressing notification to the Director-General of WIPO (Article 30, para. 2(c)).

* Regulatory control

The contracting States reserve the right to adopt such legislative or regulatory measures as they consider appropriate to 'permit, to control, or to prohibit, by legislation or regulation, the circulation, presentation or exhibition of any work or production in regard to which the competent authority may find it necessary to exercise that right' (Article 17).

During the Stockholm Conference it was pointed out that this article referred essentially to censorship, i.e. the authority to verify a work which is to be made available to the public with the consent of its author and, in the light of such verification to 'permit' or 'prohibit' the circulation of the work concerned. However, in conformity with the fundamental principles of the Berne Union, the countries of the Union are prohibited from introducing any kind of compulsory licence on the basis of Article 17. Under the rules of the Convention the authorization of the author is needed for a work to be circulated. It is therefore impossible for countries to permit such circulation without the consent of the author.[94]

* Preventive measures

Paragraph 1 of Article 16 stipulates that 'infringing copies of a work shall be liable to seizure in any country of the Union where the work enjoys legal protection'. Paragraph 2 stipulates that this provision shall also apply to 'reproductions coming from a country where the work is not protected, or has ceased to be protected' (a work of a German author published for the first time in Germany which has fallen into the public domain in the country where the copies are made—e.g. Argentina, 50 years after the death of the author—but which remains in the private domain in the country of origin—70 years after the death of the author—

---

94. Cf. *Records*, Vol. II, p. 1174, para. 262.

and also in the country to which the copies are imported—e.g. Brazil, 60 years after the death of the author). The seizure shall take place in accordance with the legislation of each country (para. 3).

Article XII of the 1886 Act provided for the right of seizure solely at the time of importation of infringing reproductions, i.e. seizure by the customs authorities, but the Additional Act of 1896 deleted any reference to importation[95] and the 1908 revision adopted the present wording and numbering. Article 16 of the Convention therefore covers both customs seizure (in the case of imported copies) and seizure on the territory of the country to which the infringing copies are taken or in which they were manufactured: procedures shall be governed by the provisions of domestic law.

e. The effects of the Convention

1. Retroactive effects of the Convention (Article 18)

In conformity with paragraph 1, once a work has passed into the public domain in its country of origin as a result of expiry of the term of protection it must not be protected in other countries. This rule involves the application of the method of comparison of terms: if the term of protection established in the country of origin is shorter than that adopted in the country in which protection is claimed, the term applicable in the latter shall be the shorter of the two.

But what happens in the opposite situation, i.e. if at the time when a country accepts the currently valid Act, a particular work of the Union has fallen into the public domain as a result of the expiry of the term of protection granted previously? In that case,

---

95. *1886 Act, Article XII*: '(1) Pirated works may be seized on importation into those countries of the Union where the original work enjoys legal protection. (2) The seizure shall take place in accordance with the domestic legislation of each country.' *Additional Act of 1896, Article 1, 5; Article 12*: '(1) Pirated works may be seized by the competent authorities of any country of the Union where the original work enjoys legal protection....'

although the work is protected in its country of origin but is not so protected in the country in which protection is claimed, it shall not revert to the private domain even though if the minimum term established in the currently valid Act in respect of this work were applied it would be so protected (para. 2). As Masouyé points out, the Convention does not accept the possibility of a work reverting to the sphere of private rights and enjoying protection anew: that would be prejudicial to the rights acquired by third parties in the period during which the work had ceased to be protected.[96]

Application of the general principle embodied in paragraph 1, and of its corollary set out in paragraph 2, will ensure conformity with the stipulations contained in the existing or future bilateral Conventions between the countries of the Union, and failing such arrangements the countries shall be free to regulate 'each in so far as it is concerned, the conditions of application of this principle' (para. 3) but the effect shall be confined to its own territory. The above provisions are also applicable in certain special cases: new accessions to the Union, application of protection as a consequence of changes brought about by Article 7 in comparison with the Brussels text or through the abandonment of reservations formulated previously (para. 4).

2. Effects of the Convention in relation to national legislation

The provisions of the Convention shall not preclude the making of a claim to the benefit of any greater protection which may be granted by legislation in a country of the Union (Article 19). This rule confirms the pre-eminence of the principle of national treatment; the *jus conventionis* grants a minimum—not maximum— protection which applies as a supplementary measure if local legislation does not attain this specified minimum. However, this does not preclude a claim to application of more favourable dispositions (save in the few cases where the Convention allows assimilation to be disregarded and material reciprocity to be requested: Article 2,

---

96. Claude Masouyé, op. cit., Section 18.3, p. 100.

para. 7 *in fine*; Article 6; Article 7, para. 8; Article 14*ter*, para. 2 and Article 30, par. 2(b) *in fine*).

3. Effects of the Convention in relation to particular agreements
Pursuant to Article 20 'the Governments of the countries of the Union reserve the right to enter into special agreements among themselves, in so far as such agreements grant to authors more extensive rights than those granted by the Convention or contain other provisions not contrary to this Convention. The provisions of existing agreements which satisfy these conditions shall remain applicable'.

The Convention was, in fact, created to secure international protection for literary and artistic works in an effective and uniform manner by putting an end to the uncertainty and confusion which derived from a mass of bilateral treaties and from the application of the 'most favoured nation' clause since these treaties often had as their main objective the regulation of commercial relations; however, it did not propose to terminate those provisions and still less to prohibit the States concerned from concluding particular agreements (restricted Unions). From the days of the Original Act (Article XV), the Convention has always included provision for particular agreements, including a second paragraph incorporated in the Berlin Act (Article 20) stipulating that the provisions of existing agreements which satisfy these 'conditions shall remain applicable'.

Article 20 makes special Agreements conditional on the two following alternative conditions: either they must grant authors more extensive rights than those granted by the Convention or they must embody other stipulations which are not contrary to the Convention.

f. Preferential arrangements for the developing countries

These are set out in the six articles of the Appendix which forms an integral part of the Convention (Article 21). The special provisions relating to the developing countries are intended to enable some countries of the Union, under certain conditions, for a specified period of time and in particular cases, to derogate from the minimum standards of protection laid down in the Convention in regard to the right of translation and reproduction[97] without this implying any reciprocity for the developed countries (Article I, para. 6(b) of the Appendix).

1. *Countries which may use these arrangements.* To determine the countries which may apply the preferential provisions stipulated in the Appendix, two criteria are used, as was already the case in the Protocol to the 1967 Act, i.e. an objective criterion and a subjective criterion:[98] any country which is regarded as a developing country in conformity with the established practice of the General Assembly of the United Nations (*objective criterion*) which ratifies or accedes to the Paris Act, and which, having regard to its economic situation and its social or cultural needs (*subjective criterion*), does not consider itself immediately in a position to make provision for the protection of all the rights as provided for in this Act may, by a notification deposited with the Director-General of WIPO at the time of depositing its instrument of ratification or accession, declare that it will avail itself of the faculties provided in regard to the right of translation and the right of reproduction or both (Article I, para. 1).

A developed country may also make this declaration in regard to its dependent territories for whose external relations it is responsible and whose situation may be treated as analogous to that of the developing countries (Article I, para. 5). (This declaration contains provisions parallel to those set out in Article 31, para. 1.)

The developing countries which have availed themselves of any of the faculties provided for in the Appendix may also apply them to their relations with any country of the *Union which is not bound by the substantive provisions of the Paris Act* (Articles 1 to 21 and the Appendix) *provided that* the latter country has agreed to the application of the provisions of the Appendix (Article 32, para. 3).

---

97. See Claude Masouyé, op. cit., p. 146.
98. Cf. Claude Colombet, *Major Principles of Copyright and Neighbouring Rights in the World. A Comparative Law Approach*, op. cit., p. 117.

2. *Validity of notification.* The notification referred to above shall remain valid for a period of ten years. It may be wholly or partially renewed for further successive periods of ten years, a new notification being deposited on each occasion with the Director-General of WIPO within a period of not more than 15 months and not less than three months prior to the expiry of the current ten-year period (Article I, para. 2) so that the renewal may be brought in advance to the attention of the countries of the Union which are affected by the consequences of the application of the provisions of the Appendix to the works of their own nationals. If a country of the Union ceases to be regarded as a developing country, it will no longer be authorized to renew its declaration. It will also lose the possibility of restricting the rights of translation and/or reproduction three years after it has ceased to be a developing country or else at the end of the current ten-year period if the latter terminates before these three years have elapsed (Article I, para. 3). However, if copies produced pursuant to the licence granted by virtue of the provisions of the Appendix still exist at the time when the declaration ceases to be effective these copies may continue to be distributed until the stock is exhausted (Article I, para. 4).

3. *Beneficiaries.* To benefit from the system of compulsory licences for translation and publication of the translation of a work and/or to publish a reproduction of a particular edition of a work, the beneficiary must be a national of the developing country which has invoked the possibilities held out by the Convention. The expression 'national of such countries' (Article II, para. 2(a) and Article III, para. 2(a) of the Appendix) covers not only natural persons but also legal entities, including the State as such, its national or local authorities and corporations owned by the State or by such authorities; this expression has been used to prevent foreign companies from benefiting from the system of compulsory licences.[99]

---

99. Cf. Claude Masouyé, op. cit., para. A.II.5, p. 155 and para. A.III.3, p. 162.

4. *Features of the compulsory licences.* The special arrangements for the developing countries include a system of compulsory licences whose features are those shared by all non-voluntary licences:
- they are *non-exclusive* and *non-transferable* (Articles II, para. 1 and III, para. 1);
- *they must respect the moral right of the author*: in this particular case, an indication of his name and, for translations, the original title of the work, must appear on all the copies (Article IV, para. 3); due provision shall be made by national legislation to ensure a correct translation of the work or an accurate reproduction of the particular edition, as the case may be (Article IV, para. 6(b)); and authorization shall not be granted if the author has withdrawn all the copies of his work from circulation (Article II, para. 8);
- *the effects of the licence shall be confined to the country which has granted it*. Article IV, paragraphs 4 and 5, imposes an absolute ban on the export of all copies produced under the compulsory licence and stipulates that the latter must contain a notice in the corresponding language stating that this copy is brought into circulation solely in the country, or on the territory to which the said licence applies.

However, in regard to licences for translation where the translation is into a language other than English, French or Spanish (world languages), the Convention permits certain exceptions concerning nationals of the developing countries who are permanently or temporarily resident abroad: if a governmental or public organization of a country which has granted a licence for translation sends copies of the translation published under licence to another country, 'such sending of copies shall not [...] be considered to constitute export if all of the following conditions are met: (i) the recipients are individuals who are nationals of the country whose competent authority has granted the licence, or organizations grouping such individuals [...]; (ii) the copies are to be used only for the purpose of teaching, scholarship or research; (iii) the sending of the copies and their subsequent distribution to recipients is without any commercial purpose; and (iv) the country to which the copies

have been sent has agreed with the country whose competent authority has granted the licence to allow the receipt, or distribution, or both, and the Director-General has been notified of the agreement by the government of the country in which the licence has been granted'.
On the other hand, the Convention allows no derogations from the ban on exports in the case of licences for reproduction;
- *Payment shall be made.* Article IV, paragraph 6, stipulates that due provision shall be made at national level to ensure that the licence provides for just compensation that is consistent with standards of royalties normally operating on licences freely negotiated between persons in the two countries concerned and that payment and transmittal of the compensation are made: should national currency regulations intervene, the competent authority shall make all efforts, by use of international machinery, to ensure transmittal in internationally convertible currency or its equivalent (Article IV, para. 6(a)). This wording is certainly well intentioned but does not stipulate what will happen if the authorities fail to take the necessary steps for the owner of the copyright to receive the remuneration in internationally convertible currency or its equivalent.

5. *Compulsory licences for translation* (Article II of the Appendix). Licences for translation may be granted only 'for the purpose of teaching, scholarship or research' (para. 5). The phrase 'teaching and scholarship' must be understood as denoting not only teaching activities at all levels in tutorial establishments, primary and secondary schools, colleges and universities, but also any organized educational activities intended for the participation of persons in all age groups in the study of any subject. The word 'research' cannot be construed as permitting the translation of works that are protected by copyright by institutions of industrial research or private companies engaged in research for commercial purposes.[100]

---

100. Cf. Section 73 of the Report of the General Rapporteur of the Revision Conference for the Universal Copyright Convention held in Paris from 5 to

These licences may be granted in respect of all types of works published with the consent of their authors, but, pursuant to paragraph 1, only when the works have been 'published in printed or analogous forms of reproduction' (rotaprint, offset, photocopying, etc.) which, as Kaminstein points out, excludes 'musical, dramatic and cinematographic works, together with works of painting, engraving and sculpture'.[101]

In the case of works composed mainly of illustrations, pursuant to paragraph 7, a licence may only be granted to make and publish a translation of the text and reproduce and publish the illustrations if the conditions set out in Article II in respect of translation licences are respected, together with those contained in Article III in respect of licences for reproduction (both rights being involved in the case of illustrated works).

6. *Compulsory licences of translation for broadcasting* (Article II, paragraph 9, of the Appendix). These licences did not form part of the 'package deal' proposed in the programmes for the Paris revisions and when the suggestion to include them was put to the Revision Conference for the Universal Convention by the Kenyan Delegation whose adviser was Dr Georges Straschnow, legal adviser to the European Broadcasting Union (EBU), it was the subject of lengthy debate. In support of this proposal, it was

---

24 July 1971 simultaneously with the Revision Conference for the Berne Convention (*Records of the Revision Conference for the Universal Copyright Convention*, UNESCO, Paris, 1973, p. 75). Following the procedure used at both of these conferences, the preferential provisions for the developing countries were examined first at the Revision Conference for the Universal Convention and then at the Revision Conference for the Berne Convention. It follows that declarations made during the discussions at the Universal Convention Revision Conference are applicable, where appropriate, to the interpretation of the similar provisions of the Appendix to the Paris Act of the Berne Convention (see Report by Goudiam, *Records* ..., WIPO, Sect. 24, p. 175; see also the Report by Kaminstein and the commentaries by Masouyé in his *Guide to the Berne Convention*).
101. Ibid., Section 87, 1, p. 79.

argued that broadcasting was destined to play an increasingly important role in the educational programmes of the developing countries which suffered from the scarcity of books and teaching staff, and that a translation licence for broadcasting was at least equally important for these countries as a licence to publish.[102] Finally, translation licences for broadcasting were approved, as set out in the revised Text of the Universal Convention in Article V*ter*, paragraph 8, and in the Appendix to the Paris Act of the Berne Convention in Article II, paragraph 9.

This paragraph 9 permits the granting of a licence to make a translation for broadcasting purposes to a broadcasting organization having its headquarters in a country belonging to the Berne Union, provided that all of the following conditions are complied with: the translation must be made 'of a work which has been published in printed or analogous forms of reproduction'; 'from a copy made and acquired in accordance with the laws of the said country' and may be used 'only in broadcasts intended exclusively for teaching or for the dissemination of the results of specialized technical or scientific research to experts in a particular profession' (this somewhat lengthy and detailed formulation is explained by the fact that a number of delegates were unable to agree to a simple reference to 'research';[103] the word 'exclusively' indicates that the broadcast must be special); 'all uses made of the translation are without any commercial purpose': this also implies that none of the uses of the translation, including the broadcast as such and the exchange of recordings, may have such purposes. According to the report by Kaminstein, the Revision Conference for the Universal Copyright Convention, agreed that the exclusion of a 'commercial purpose' in the context of broadcasting meant that the broadcasting organization concerned must not be a profit-making private corporation and that the programme which in-

---

102. Cf. Report by the General Rapporteur of the Revision Conference for the Universal Convention, op. cit., para. 82, p. 77.
103. Ibid., para. 84, 2, p. 78.

cluded the translation must not be interrupted by any commercial advertisements. Nevertheless, its intention was not to preclude the broadcasting organization from broadcasting commercial advertisements at other times, nor was it intended to exclude the frequent practice of making the owners of receivers pay a tax or licence fee.[104]

Article II, para. (9)(a)(iii) of the Appendix authorizes broadcasting organizations to broadcast 'sound or visual recordings lawfully and exclusively made for the purpose of such broadcasts'. Kaminstein points out that this means that the translation may be fixed and not necessarily broadcast live; it is immaterial whether the broadcast is made by radio or television, by land relay stations or by satellite and the terms 'sound or visual recordings' include all types of audiovisual fixations such as films, phonograms and videotapes in their various forms.[105] With the consent of the broadcasting organization which obtained the licence and produced the recordings, these may also be used by another broadcasting organization for the purposes and under the conditions indicated above on condition that it has its headquarters in the country of the Union which granted the licence (para. (9)(b)).

Later, in Article II, paragraph (9)(c), the Convention goes further than the general limitation set out in paragraph (1) of the same article since it permits the granting of a licence 'to translate any text incorporated in an audiovisual fixation where such fixation was itself prepared and published for the sole purpose of being used in connection with systematic instructional activities'. It follows that the licence may be granted in respect of works which were not intended for *publication* in the strict sense of the term (Kaminstein points out that except where the text is incorporated in books on art and in the audiovisual fixations to which particular reference is made in the Universal Convention—by analogy

---

104. Ibid., Sect. 84, 6, p. 78.
105. Ibid., Sect. 84, 4, p. 78.

with this paragraph 9(c) of Article II of the Appendix—this provision shall apply solely to the texts of non-dramatic works).[106]

7. Requirements governing compulsory licences for translation

Period: where the translation is made into a language which is generally used in one or more developed countries (English, French, Spanish, etc.), licences to translate and publish the translations may be granted if, after a term of three years from the date of first publication of the work, a translation into this language has not yet been published (Article II, para. (2)(a)); if the language is not one that is in general use (Arabic, Hindi, Guarani, etc.) the period is reduced to one year (para. (3)(a)).

Paragraph (3)(b) goes on to set out an exception to this rule (explained basically by the requirements of Brazil in regard to the Portuguese language): 'any country referred to in paragraph (1) may, with the unanimous agreement of the developed countries which are members of the Union and in which the same language is in general use, substitute, in the case of translations into that language, for the period of three years referred to in paragraph (2)(a) a shorter period as determined by such agreement but not less than one year. However, the provisions of the foregoing sentence shall not apply where the language in question is English, French or Spanish. The Director-General shall be notified of any such agreement by the governments which have concluded it.'

Procedure: the possibility of obtaining a compulsory licence arises as soon as the likelihood of a direct contract being concluded between the parties has ceased to exist. Article IV, paragraph (1), requires the applicant to justify that he has sought authorization from the owner of the translation rights and, after taking the necessary steps, has been unable to trace the owner or obtain his authorization. In presenting his application for a licence to the competent national authority, the applicant must simultaneously forward by registered air mail copies of his application to

---

106. Ibid., Sect. 87, 1, p. 79.

the publisher whose name appears on the work and to any national or international information centre which may have been designated for this purpose (para. (2)).

The licence may not be granted before the expiry of a further period of six months if it is obtainable after three years, or of nine months if it is obtainable after one year (Article II, para. (4)(a)). If, during one of these periods, the owner of the right publishes a translation or concludes a contract with a third party, the licence shall not be granted (para. (4)(b)). Otherwise the competent authority may grant the licence once the supplementary periods referred to have expired. The determination of the competent authority and of the procedures to be followed shall rest with the national legislation and shall be subject to the compulsory rules set out in the Convention and more particularly in the Appendix thereto.

8. *Termination of the licence* (Article II, para. (6) of the Appendix). The owner of the translation right shall be entitled to terminate the compulsory licence by publishing the work, or entering into a contract for its publication, at a price comparable to that normally charged in the country for works of a similar nature. But the publication must be 'in the same language and with substantially the same content as the translation published under the licence'.

The possibility of termination of the licence being brought about by the owner of the translation right may cause serious prejudice to the beneficiary of the licence. However, this beneficiary may continue to distribute copies made before the licence ended until stocks have been used up. This provision is consistent with the temporary and substitutive nature of the compulsory licence. Otherwise, a definitive derogation would be made from the exclusive right granted by Article 8 of the Convention.

9. *The 'ten-year' rule.* The developing countries which are able to avail themselves of the preferential provisions set out in the Appendix may, instead of the prerogative stipulated in Article II of the latter, *opt for* the 'ten-year' rule in the area of

translations—Article V(1)(a), which refers to Article 30(2)(a) but is not cumulative therewith. In other words, it is not possible to claim the benefit of both arrangements (that set out in Article II and the 'ten-year' principle).

As we have already seen, the 'ten-year system' is open to all the countries (developed and developing) which do not belong to the Union but do accede to the Convention. However, the effects are different in the two cases: in regard to the developed countries, the other countries may apply material reciprocity pursuant to Article 30, para. (2)(b) *in fine*; on the other hand, that is not possible in respect of developing countries having regard to the provisions of Article I, paragraph (6)(b) of the Appendix.

10. *Compulsory licences for reproduction* (Article III of the Appendix). These licences are intended to facilitate the publication of works in their original language, given that English, French and Spanish are either official languages or widely used unofficial languages in many of the developing countries. The licences for reproduction are generally similar to those for translation, but have certain specific features: first of all, no translation is required. Secondly, they may only be granted 'for use in connection with systematic instructional activities' (para. (2)(a), *in fine*), thereby excluding research; the cost of a reproduction is less than the cost of publishing a translation which involves the work and remuneration of the translator.

Licences for reproduction are applied 'solely to works published in printed or analogous forms of reproduction' (para. (7)(a)), thus including musical and artistic works but excluding sound and audiovisual recordings.

11. *Compulsory licences for the reproduction of audiovisual fixations* (Article III, para. 7(b) of the Appendix). Despite the general limitation set out above, the Convention takes account of the role played by educational audiovisual works in teaching and authorizes the granting of licences for 'lawfully made audiovisual fixations including any protected works incorporated therein and [...] the translation of any incorporated text into a language in general use in the country in which the licence is applied for,

always provided that the audiovisual fixations in question were prepared and published for the sole purpose of being used in connection with systematic instructional activities'. The text therefore excluded audiovisual works created for entertainment purposes.

The reference to 'the translation of any incorporated text into a language in general use in the country in which the licence is applied for' is not superfluous because Article II, paragraph (9) refers to translation of the text *solely for broadcasting purposes*, while paragraph (7)(b) of Article III permits the owner of the reproduction licence, when reproducing the audiovisual fixation and as a part of that process, to arrange for a translation to be made of the sound-track and for the translation to be reproduced 'aurally or visually along with his reproduction of the visual images'.[107]

12. *Requirements relating to compulsory licences for reproduction*: *Period*: in principle these licences may only be granted after a period of five years—calculated from the date of first publication of a particular edition of a work—has expired (para. (2)(a) and (3)), but this is reduced to three years 'for works of the natural and physical sciences, including mathematics, and of technology', para. (3)(i) and increased to seven years 'for works of fiction, poetry, drama and music and for art books'. These provisions differ from those relating to licences for translation because the periods are not defined as a function of the language but of the nature and subject matter of the work itself.

The Convention also provides for the possibility that, when copies of the edition published with the consent of the owner of copyright have been placed on sale, once the corresponding waiting period has expired (three, five or seven years) sales of the said copies may have ceased. In that case, once an additional period of six months has elapsed without any copy of the said edition being

---

107. Cf. Report by Kaminstein on Article V*quater*, paragraph (3)(b) of the revised text of the Universal Convention, op. cit., para. 111, 1 and 2, p. 85.

placed on sale at a price comparable to that charged in the said country for similar works (para. (2)(b)), the licence may be granted.

Conditions:
- during the waiting period, the publisher authorized by the author shall not have placed on sale in the country concerned copies which are sold at a price comparable to that charged in the said country for similar works (para. (2)(a) last part); this supposition differs from that set out in paragraph (2)(b) since, in the first instance the publisher authorized by the author never placed copies on sale in the country in question while in the second case he did so, but the copies have since ceased to be sold;
- the edition which is the subject of the licence must be sold at the same price or at a lower price (para. (2)(b)).

Procedure: this is similar to the procedure laid down for compulsory translation licences with the following differences: the additional periods (which are not termed 'supplementary' as in Article II) are:
- six months if the basic waiting time is three years (para. (4)(a)), but the point of departure varies depending on whether the owner of the reproduction right has been traced or not;
- three months when the basic waiting time is five or seven years (para. (4)(b)), but this must be respected only if the owner of the reproduction right has not been traced.

13. *Developing countries which have availed themselves of the preferential arrangements established for them in the Berne Convention* as at 1 January 1992 were China, Egypt, India, Jamaica, Lesotho, Liberia, Malaysia, Mauritius, Mexico and the United Republic of Tanzania; their declarations were valid until 10 October 1994 (see *Industrial Property and Copyright* (Geneva), January 1995).

g. Administrative provisions (Articles 22 to 26) and final clauses (Articles 27 to 38)

These date from the Stockholm revision with the exception of Article 29*bis* and certain amendments made by the Assembly of the Berne Union in conformity with the provisions of Article 26.[108]

1. *Assembly and Executive Committee of the Union* (Articles 22 and 23). Article 22 establishes the Assembly of the Union consisting of all those countries of the Union bound by Articles 22 to 26; the government of each country shall be represented by one delegate and shall have one vote. The Assembly shall determine the programme, adopt the budget of the Union[109] and approve its final accounts. The Assembly shall also elect the Members of the Executive Committee which assists it and is made up of a number of countries of the Union equivalent to one-fourth of the members of the Assembly (Article 23, para. (3)). The Executive Committee meets annually in ordinary session (para. (7)(a)) and also in extraordinary session (para. (7)(b)), generally once every two years.

2. International Bureau of WIPO (Article 24). The administrative tasks are performed by the International Bureau of WIPO which is a continuation of the Bureau of the Berne Union united with the Bureau of the Paris Union to form BIRPI. The International Bureau is responsible, in particular, for providing the secretariat of the various organs of the Union: it participates in all the meetings of the Assembly, the Executive Committee and any other Committee of Experts or Working Party; acting on the instructions of the Assembly, and in co-operation with the Executive Committee, it makes preparations for the conferences of revision of the provisions of the Convention. The Director-General of WIPO is the Chief Executive of the Union which he represents.

---

108. For example, the amendments adopted on 2 October 1979; cf. *Copyright*, Geneva, WIPO, January 1980, pp. 5–9.
109. Pursuant to the amendment adopted on 2 October 1979 by the Governing Bodies of WIPO and the Unions administered by the latter, the system of triennial and annual programmes and budgets was replaced by a *biennial* system applicable both to WIPO and to the nine Unions which have their own independent budgets.

3. *Annual contributions* (Article 25). The Union has a budget which is financed in the first instance by contributions paid by the member countries. These contributions are based on a system of classes (of which there are fourteen; I to IX including IV*bis*, VI*bis* and S, S*bis* and S*ter*; classes VIII, IX and S to S*ter* were established by the Assembly of the Berne Union, each of them being applicable to a country only if certain conditions are met).

Each country is free to choose the class to which it wishes to belong and, unless it has already done so, must do this at the time it deposits its instrument of ratification or accession. The amount of the contribution varies according to the class, being 25 units for class I and 20, 15, 10, 7.5, 5, 3, 2, 1, 1/2, 1/4, 1/8, 1/16 and 1/32 for the subsequent classes (in 1995, 1 unit was equivalent to 56,385 Swiss francs). Class VII is the highest class available to member countries of WIPO which do not belong to any Union. Classes S are applicable to developing countries which have low percentages on the contribution scale of the United Nations (between 0.02 per cent and 0.10 per cent for class S and 0.10 per cent for class S*bis*, while class S*ter* is applicable to all the 'least-developed' countries). Classes VIII, IX or S*bis* and S*ter*, are automatically applied unless the State concerned asks to be included in a higher class. The rights of each State are the same regardless of the contribution class chosen by it.

4. *Amendment of the administrative provisions* (Article 26). Proposals for the amendment of Articles 22 to 26 may be presented by any country member of the Assembly, by the Executive Committee or by the Director-General of WIPO. The amendments are adopted by the Assembly and must receive three-quarters of the votes cast, except for amendments to Article 22 and the second paragraph of Article 26, which require four-fifths.

5. *Revision of the Convention* (Article 27). Paragraph (1) contains a provision which dates from the Original Act of the Convention: the possibility of submitting the Convention for revision with a view to the introduction of amendments designed to improve the system of the Union. Any revision of the Convention, including its Appendix, requires unanimity of the votes cast (except for

amendments to Articles 22 to 26 which, as specified in the latter, are adopted by the Assembly).

6. *Different procedures for accession to the Paris Act and entry into force in respect of the members of the Union and countries not belonging to it* (Articles 28 and 29). Article 28, paragraph (1) offers the countries of the Union the possibility of acceding solely to the administrative provisions and final clauses (Articles 22 to 38). For this purpose, the country concerned must declare in its respective instrument that its ratification or accession does not apply to Articles 1 to 21 or to the Appendix. A country which has excluded application of the substantive or material provisions may at any later date declare that it extends the effects of its ratification or accession to those provisions.

In regard to the countries that do not belong to the Union but do accede to the Convention, the latter shall take effect three months after the date on which the Director-General of WIPO has notified the deposit of its instrument of accession, unless a subsequent date has been indicated in the instrument deposited.

7. *Reservations* (Article 30). The Convention allows reservations in only four instances:
- Article 28, paragraph (1)(b): this permits exclusion of the substantive provisions (Articles 1 to 21 and the Appendix) from the ratification or accession;
- Article 30, paragraph (2)(a): this extends to the countries of the Union the possibility of retaining the benefit of the reservations formulated during the period of validity of previous Acts on condition that they declare their intention of doing so when their instrument of ratification or accession is deposited;
- Article 30, paragraph (2)(b): this grants any country outside the Union, and which accedes to the Convention, the possibility of replacing Article 8 concerning the right of translation by the provisions of Article V of the Original Act of 1886 as amended by the additional Act of 1896, so that if within a period of ten years counting from the date of first publication of the work, the author does not publish or cause to be published in a country of the Union a translation of his work in a language

which is generally used in the country that avails itself of the reservation, the right of translation into that language *shall lapse* in that country and there will be no need to request authorization for translation and publication of that version of the work (Article 30, (2)(b); and
- Article 33, paragraph (2): this allows any country at the time of signing, ratifying or acceding to the Act, to declare that it does not consider itself bound by the provisions of paragraph (1) of that article which stipulates the international jurisdiction of the International Court of Justice at The Hague over the interpretation or application of the Convention in cases where a negotiated settlement cannot be reached.

8. *Relations between the countries of the Union: applicability of the different Acts* (*Article 32*). The existence of different Acts of the Convention raises the following question: which Act is applicable to relations between a country that continues to be bound by a previous Act and another which has joined the Union through a later Act, for example between countries such as Canada or Iceland, which continue to be bound by the Rome Act and Argentina, Bahamas, etc., which acceded to the Union by the Brussels Act and have not yet ratified the Paris Act?[110] Although these countries, regardless of the latest Act to which they have acceded, have all joined the Berne Union for the protection of literary and artistic works which automatically presupposes a link between them, and although the successive Acts contain more or less similar provisions, the fact is that the level of protection afforded by them differs.

This problem has arisen since the Berlin Act and although the provisions of its Article 27 were intended to replace the earlier texts (the Act of 1886 supplemented in 1896), the fact is that it was applicable only to relations between countries which accepted the new Act. Other countries continued to be bound by the previous text which was the only one that they had joined or ratified.

---

110. These examples relate to the situation as at 1 January 1995.

As new Acts were adopted, the situation became still more complex. However, a solution was recently found for the future in Article 32 of the Stockholm Act, confirmed by the Paris Act.

Article 32 is divided into three paragraphs.

Paragraph (1) regulates relations between the countries which are already members of the Union and does so in a form similar to Article 27 of the previous Acts (Berlin, Rome, Brussels): the latest revised text replaces all the previous documents, but the latter continue to be applicable until all the countries have accepted the new text; this means that, in relations between the countries which have accepted the Paris Act in full, the latter is applicable to the exclusion of all the previous Acts accepted by these countries (for example in relations between Brazil and Uruguay). In regard to relations between a country which has accepted the Paris Act in its entirety (for example Uruguay) and a country which has accepted only the administrative provisions (for example, Argentina), as far as the substantive provisions are concerned both countries continue to apply the previous Act ratified by them (relations between Uruguay and Argentina are governed by the substantive provisions of the Brussels Act and also by Articles 22 to 38 of the Paris Act).

Paragraph (2) deals with a point which had not been covered previously: relations between countries which join the Union and those which were already members. This question was settled as follows:

- the countries outside the Union which become parties thereto through the Paris Act—for example, Paraguay—shall apply it in their relations *with all the countries of the Union,* that is to say with those which have not acceded to it—for example, New Zealand—or have not accepted the substantive provisions thereof—for example, Argentina;
- in their turn, countries which joined the Union via the Paris Act (for example, Ecuador and Paraguay) agree that the countries which already belonged to the Union but are not bound by the Paris Act (for example, New Zealand) or have not accepted the substantive provisions thereof (for example, Argentina) shall apply, in their mutual relations, the provisions of the latest Act which is binding on them (Rome, in the case of New Zealand,

Brussels in that of Argentina); alternatively, they shall waive this option and adopt the level of protection fixed by the Paris Act, despite the fact that they have not acceded to it.

As Masouyé points out, those responsible for drafting the Stockholm Text, confirmed by the Paris Act, thought it 'reasonable and legally correct' not to oblige existing member countries to apply an Act in their respective territories which they had no wish to accept; on the other hand, they did not wish to impose on the countries which joined the Union the application, on their territory, of an earlier Act whose provisions no longer corresponded in those countries to the level of protection that they intended to grant.[111]

Paragraph 3 refers to the application of the provisions of the Appendix to countries which did not accept the substantive provisions of the Paris Act. The developing countries may only apply these provisions if the country which does not accept the Paris Act (for example, New Zealand) or the substantive provisions thereof including the Appendix (for example, Belgium), nevertheless agrees to the application of the provisions set out in the Appendix.

9. *International jurisdiction clause between Member Countries of the Union* (Article 33). This provision dates from the Brussels revision (Article 27*bis*) and stipulates that the International Court of Justice at The Hague shall hold jurisdiction for the interpretation or application of the Convention if disputes arise between countries belonging to the Union (but not between citizens or between citizens and a State) which it has not been possible to settle by negotiation. In that case, the International Bureau of WIPO shall be informed of the dispute placed before the Court by the applicant country and the Bureau shall inform the other countries of the Union.

The Brussels text imposed an *obligation* to submit the dispute to the International Court of Justice, but the Stockholm revision

---

111. Claude Masouyé, op. cit., Sect. 32.10, p. 135.

replaced this obligation by an *option* to allow for the position of some countries which were unable to accept the compulsory jurisdiction of the Court at The Hague. Any member country of the Union was accordingly able to refuse this jurisdiction by declaring, when it signed the Act or deposited the instrument of ratification or accession, that it did not consider itself bound by the International Jurisdiction Clause (para. (2)).[112] However, that declaration could be withdrawn at any time (para. (3)).

10. *Closure of previous Acts* (Article 34). Following the entry into force of Articles 1 to 21 and of the Appendix, no country may ratify or accede to previous Acts (para. (1)).

The Paris Act entered into force on 10 October 1974.

11. *Application of the Convention by the countries party thereto* (Article 36). This provision, which dates from the Stockholm revision, stipulates that 'any country party to this Convention undertakes to adopt, in accordance with its constitution, the measures necessary to ensure the application of this Convention' (para. (1)); the aim is to ensure that the immediate application of the self-executing provisions of the Convention is not impeded by the need for special national legislation subsequent to that which approves and promulgates the Convention and the deposit, at international level, of the relevant instrument of ratification or accession.

An equivalent, although not identical, provision, will be found in Article 25, para. 1, of the Brussels Act which, referring to the accession of new countries to the Union, states that they must ensure legal protection of the rights which are the subject of the Convention (a more distant antecedent will be found in the first paragraph of Article XVIII of the Original Act of 1886 which stipulated that the 'countries which have not become parties to the present Convention and which make provision [...] for the

---

112. On 1 January 1992 this declaration had been made by the following countries: Bahamas, Bulgaria, Egypt, India, Lesotho, Liberia, Libya, Malta, Mauritius, Romania, South Africa, Thailand, Tunisia and Venezuela.

protection of the rights forming the object of the present Convention shall be admitted to accede thereto on request to that effect').

12. *Languages* (Article 37). The Paris Act was signed in a single copy in the French and English languages (para. (1)(a)[113] and deposited with the Director-General of WIPO who shall establish 'official texts [...] after consultation with the interested governments, in the Arabic, German, Italian, Portuguese and Spanish languages and in such other languages as the Assembly may designate' (para. (1), (b)).

In case of differences of opinion on the interpretation of the various texts, the French text shall prevail (para. (1), (c)).

M. THE FUTURE REVISION OF THE BERNE CONVENTION

In November 1991, February 1992, June 1993 and December 1994, the first four meetings of a Committee of Experts were held in Geneva to draft a possible Protocol to the Berne Convention. At these meetings consideration was given to the Memorandums prepared by the International Bureau of WIPO. According to the provisions of the WIPO programme for the 1990–1991 biennium:

> [...] the protocol would be mainly destined to clarify the existing, or establish new, international norms where, under the present text of the Berne Convention, doubts may exist as to the extent to which that Convention applies.
>
> The need for such an exercise lies in the fact that there are certain questions in respect of which professional circles have no uniform views and, what is of particular concern in international relations, even governments which legislated or plan to legislate on such questions seem to interpret their obligations under the Berne Convention differently. Such discrepancies in views have already surfaced, or are likely to surface in the near future, in respect of certain subject-matters of protection (e.g., computer programs, phonograms, computer-generated works), certain rights (e.g., right of rental, public lending right, right of distribution of copies of any kind of works, right of display), the applicability

---

113. Previously the official Acts of the conferences were drawn up in French alone. Article 31, paragraph 2 of the Brussels Act provided for an equivalent text to be established in English.

of the minima criteria (no formalities, term of protection, etc.) and the obligation of granting national treatment (without reciprocity) to foreigners. In this connection, it will also be examined whether countries whose national law protects subject-matters as works under their copyright law, or recognize the protection of certain rights in their copyright law, may refuse the application of the minima criteria or the granting of national treatment to foreigners or make the protection of foreign works or the application of certain rights to foreigners dependent on reciprocity.[114]

The form proposed—i.e. a Protocol or a supplementary Treaty to the Berne Convention on the terms stipulated in its Article 20 (by virtue of which the governments of the countries of the Union reserve the right to enter into special agreements among themselves, in so far as such agreements grant to authors more extensive rights than those granted by the Convention, or contain other provisions not contrary to the Convention) was subject to the provision set out in Article 27, paragraph 3, of the Convention requiring 'the unanimity of the votes cast' for its revision. There were doubts as to whether this could be achieved in respect of the programme of proposed changes.

The first session of the Committee of Experts on a Possible Protocol to the Berne Convention for the Protection of Literary and Artistic Works (Geneva, WIPO Headquarters, 4–8 November 1991) was attended by delegations consisting of experts from 45 countries of the Union and the Commission of the European Communities. Also taking part as observers were experts from 11 States not members of the Union, four intergovernmental organizations (GATT (General Agreement on Tariffs and Trade), UNCTAD (United Nations Conference on Trade and Development), UN and UNESCO) and 39 non-governmental organizations. During the session the Committee examined the items set out in the first part of the Memorandum prepared by the

---

114. Document WIPO BCP/CE/I/2 of 18 July 1991 (*Copyright* (Geneva), WIPO, Feb. 1992). In October 1991 and in October 1993, the Governing Bodies decided that the project should be continued in the programme for the 1992–93 and 1994–95 biennia, respectively, with the same terms of reference as had been decided for the 1990–91 biennium.

International Bureau of WIPO[115] dealing with the subject matters of protection—computer programs, databases, expert systems and other systems of artificial intelligence, computer-produced works—as well as the question of the rights of producers of sound recordings (phonograms).

a. Computer programs. Databases

There was agreement within the Committee of Experts[116] that computer programs and databases should be protected by copyright, but in the light of the widely diverging views expressed, discussion as to whether the proposed Protocol should or should not cover these categories of works was deferred. If the decision proved to be in the affirmative, which seemed the most likely outcome, the form of such protection would have to be settled. That being so, it was felt that there was no reason why the International Bureau should not continue its work and submit to a subsequent session of the Committee a revised working document on computer programs and databases, including a study of the possibility of protecting databases which contained large quantities of data or elements of information, but did not satisfy the criterion of originality, e.g. sales catalogues.

b. Expert systems and other systems of artificial intelligence. Computer-produced works

The Committee agreed that the proposed Protocol should not deal with systems of artificial intelligence; it was thought premature to adopt any provisions applicable to artificial intelligence and 'computer-produced works'.

c. Producers of sound recordings (phonograms)

In regard to the protection of producers of sound recordings, the document prepared by the International Bureau proposed that the

---

115. Ibid.
116. See Report adopted by the Committee, WIPO document BCP/CE/1/4 of 8 November 1991 (*Copyright* (Geneva), WIPO, February 1992, pp. 30–53).

countries which became parties to the Protocol—regardless of whether they recognized sound recordings as a category of literary and artistic works (i.e. countries belonging to the *copyright* areas or those subscribing to the *authors' rights* system)—should be obliged to grant the producers of sound recordings, by way of minimum rights, not only those of reproduction, distribution and importation (already recognized in Article 10 of the Rome Convention—1961—and in Article 2 of the Phonograms Convention—Geneva, 1971), but also the rights of radio broadcasting stipulated in Article 11*bis*(1) of the Berne Convention, i.e. the rights of public performance and communication to the public by wire. These rights would be subject to the same limitations as laid down in Article 9(2), Article 10, Article 10*bis*(2) and Article 11*bis*(3) of the Berne Convention and, in the event of their acceptance, would also be subject to the restrictions on the right of distribution proposed in the second document. Domestic legislation would have the possibility of establishing compulsory fee-paying licences in respect of the proposed rights of broadcasting, public performance and communication to the public by wire for the benefit of the producers of sound recordings.

As to the term of protection of these rights, the memorandum proposed a period of not less than 50 years from the date of the first publication of the sound recording made with the consent of its producer or, in the case of an unpublished recording, from the date of production (fixation) of the sound recording. The same document provided for the possibility of examining whether it was appropriate to allow the countries party to the Protocol to grant phonogram producers rights of radio broadcasting, public performance and communication to the public by wire, this being subject to the condition of material reciprocity.

Some delegations and observers from non-governmental organizations supported the idea that the proposed Protocol should deal with the issue of the protection of producers of sound recordings, while others signified their willingness to accept different solutions for the updating of international rules applicable to the protection of phonogram producers. However, the great majority were opposed to the extension of the scope of the Protocol to protect these rights and insisted that the protection of producers of sound recordings must be modernized in the context of the Rome Convention and of other appropriate instruments, either through a revision or by adopting a special arrangement by virtue of Article 22 of that Convention. It followed that sound recordings should not be covered by the possible Protocol since they were not works within the meaning of the Berne Convention. The delegations and observers from non-governmental organizations who expressed the majority opinion maintained that this was the only solution which could guarantee the preservation of an appropriate balance between the three categories of beneficiaries of the Rome Convention without endangering the rights of authors by granting an unduly high level of protection involving certain conflicting rights which might be an obstacle to the proper enjoyment and exercise of the exclusive rights of authors.

A consensus was reached within the Committee to the effect that protection of the rights of producers of phonograms must be consolidated and that this goal might be pursued in various ways. The International Bureau would have to consider the nature of a possible new instrument and, in particular, determine whether it should be confined to authors' rights or also include neighbouring rights. It must also be recognized that the outcome of the GATT negotiations would have an impact on the efforts of the Committee. In its work, the International Bureau would need to take account of the interests of the three categories of neighbouring rights and of all the questions that had arisen during the discussions.

The *second session* of the Committee of Experts (held in Geneva at WIPO Headquarters from 10 to 17 February 1992) was attended by delegations consisting of experts from 38 countries of the Union and from the Commission of the European Communities. Experts from eight non-member countries of the Union, six intergovernmental organizations (UN, UNCTAD, UNESCO, GATT, the Islamic Educational Scientific and Cultural Organization (ISESCO) and the Organization of African Unity (OAU)) and 38 non-governmental organizations also attended as observers. During this session, the second part of the Memorandum prepared by the International Bureau of WIPO was examined. It contained proposals on (1) rights protected, (2) the term of protection and (3) the collective administration of rights.[117]

1. The provisions relating to *rights protected* may be divided into four categories: (A) *interpretative* provisions concerning certain rights recognized by the Berne Convention; (B) provisions relating to certain *new* rights; (C) provisions relating to the *abolition of non-voluntary licences* currently permitted under the Berne Convention; and (D) the definition of the *public* aspect of certain acts.[118]

i) The interpretative provisions
These relate in particular to the right of reproduction, and also to the application of the broadcasting right in the particular case of transmission by satellite.

Proposals concerning the *right of reproduction* were as follows:
- express recognition in regard to the fact that the storage of a work in a computer system constitutes reproduction. In the Committee of Experts[119] a number of delegations considered a provision on the storage of works in computer systems to be unnecessary. However, some were flexible since they indicated that they would accept this provision if it were drafted such that it showed clearly that it was no more than an interpretation.

---

117. Document WIPO BCP/CE/I/3 of 18 October 1991 (*Copyright* (Geneva), March 1992, pp. 66–82). The references which follow are to this second part of the memorandum.
118. Cf. Carlos Fernández Ballesteros. 'El propuesto Protocolo al Convenio de Berna'. In *Libro-memoria del VII Congreso Internacional sobre la protección de los derechos intelectuales*, Santiago, Chile, April 1992, pp. 458–62, which sets out a particularly clear and instructive analysis of the proposals contained in the second document of the International Bureau of WIPO, where the author himself is Assistant Director-General.
119. Report approved by the Committee, document WIPO BCP/CE/II/1 of 19 February 1992. The references to the proceedings of the second session of the Committee will be found in that document.

Differences of opinion arose on the alternative texts proposed in paragraph 75 of the Memorandum, but it was felt that draft provisions on this subject should be contained in a future document on the possible Protocol;
- detailed provisions firstly on *public* reprographic reproduction (including *internal* reproduction) by libraries, archives and educational establishments and, secondly, on private reproduction for personal use by means of equipment designed for this purpose (machines and other optical, mechanical, electric or electronic devices), that is to say private copying (home taping) of sound recordings and similar instances of private reproduction.

In regard to *reprographic reproduction* by libraries, archives and educational establishments, the majority of delegations did not appear to support the proposals put forward in the Memorandum. On a proposal by the Director-General of WIPO, the discussion on the subject of reprographic reproduction was closed and the matter deleted from the agenda, although the search for new solutions was to continue.

In regard to *private reproduction* for personal use, by means of equipment designed for this purpose (home-taping), the Memorandum clearly indicated that this reproduction should not be permitted if it conflicted with the normal exploitation of the works concerned, e.g. through the increasingly widespread use of the technique of digital and optical reproduction by means of which works, other than musical works, contained in sound recordings can be easily and perfectly reproduced (CD-ROM databases, videodiscs, 'interactive' CDs on which various categories of works can be stored using digital and optical techniques). Such reproduction should also be prohibited if it causes unjustified prejudice to the legitimate interests of the authors, save where the prejudice is reduced to a reasonable level by introducing an obligation to make payment in respect of the equipment and/or material used for reproduction.

The proposal not to permit, without the authorization of the author of the work or the producer of the phonogram, the private reproduction of books (in their entirety), computer programs, electronic databases or sheet music by mechanical or electronic devices and the serial digital reproduction for private purposes of any works or sound recordings, even where such reproduction is effected for personal purposes (para. 102(a)), did not receive sufficient support from the Committee of Experts, *except in the case of computer programs*. A considerable number of participants favoured—except for reprographic reproduction—the recognition of a right to remuneration payable by the manufacturers of the equipment or material (except where the latter was intended for export) or by the importers of such equipment or material into the country (except in cases where a private individual imported it for his own personal use) (para. 102(b) and (c)). However, some delegations felt that the question of private home copying should be solved by means of arrangements for protection or collective management of copies and by means of new techniques for granting licences. Some aspects of the proposed right to remuneration, the exceptions and their application required more detailed analysis.

In regard to the *application of the broadcasting right to direct broadcasting by satellite*, the Memorandum points out that there can be no doubt that direct broadcasting by satellite (DBS) is covered by Article 11*bis* (1), of the Berne Convention (an act of communication of works to the public by any wireless means). However, since this act of communication to the public habitually has its origin in one country (or in international waters, that is to say in a zone which is not subject to national jurisdiction) (upleg phase) and is completed in another (downleg phase), in accordance with the theory of communication known as the '*Bogsch theory*', if the owner of the rights is not the same person in the country from which the broadcast is made and in the country where the work is receivable, it will not be sufficient to take account of the rights of the right-holder in the country from which the broadcast is made. On the contrary at least identical allowance must be made for the rights of the right-holder in the country of the satellite footprint where the work is effectively communicated to the public. The possibility may therefore arise of applying the laws of more than one country (the law of the country from which the programme-carrying signals originate or the *broadcasting country*, and the law of each one of the countries falling within the satellite footprint, or the *receiving countries*).[120]

Given the conflicting opinions in regard to the applicable law and to the exercise of the rights of the various owners of authors' rights in the country from which the broadcast is made and in the country in which the signals are normally received, the second part of the Memorandum of the International Bureau of WIPO proposed, with a view to overcoming these differences, that a possible future Protocol should stipulate that, as a general rule, *the law of the broadcasting country would be applied*. However, if the work was not protected in the broadcasting country (or if the programme was broadcast from a place other than the territory of a particular country, for example from international waters) or if non-voluntary licences applied to broadcasting while, in the country of reception, the work was protected or non-voluntary licences did not apply, the *law of the country of reception* should be applicable. Moreover, if in the country, or countries, of reception the copyright owner was not the same person as in the broadcasting country, the rights of the other copyright owner must also be respected.

The Committee of Experts reached general agreement on the need for the possible Protocol to clarify the fact that satellite broadcasting constituted broadcasting within the meaning of the Berne Convention in cases where programmes were received directly. Relatively general agreement was also reached on the fact that in such cases only one body of law should apply, and the majority view was that it should be that of the country in which the programme originated. However, some participants felt that further study should be made of the additional application of the law of the country in which the programme was received. Consideration should also be given to the proposal by certain delegations to the effect that the future Protocol should not deal with the issue of the applicable law at all.

---

120. See above Chapter 4, Section 4.3.2.4.

ii) Provisions applicable to certain new rights
These are:
- the *right of public presentation or display* which covers both the direct exhibition and the indirect showing of a work, e.g. on a screen. The Committee of Experts reached a general consensus in favour of a further study of this right in the context of the future Protocol. Differences were noted between the direct exhibition or display of a work, particularly that of a work of the graphic or plastic arts in a gallery or museum, and the indirect showing or display of a work, particularly the showing or display of a text on a computer screen. It was felt appropriate to establish more specific exceptions to the rights of public presentation or display, and also to take account of the rights of the owners of physical objects incorporating such works;
- the *right of rental* and the *right of public loan* as the exclusive right of the author to permit the hire or public lending of copies of certain works: audiovisual works, those embodied in sound recordings, computer programs, databases and sheet music, regardless of who is the owner of the copies of the works involved and irrespective of whether the rights of ownership of these copies have been transferred (para. 129). The Committee agreed that the possible Protocol should make provision for a right of rental. On the other hand, the proposal for a right of public loan to be recognized did not gain sufficient support. The experts were of the opinion that the scope of the right of rental and the definition of the term 'rental' should be given further clarification and that specific exceptions should be made in respect of computer programs included in products;
- the *right of importation*. 'It is proposed that in the possible Protocol, it should be provided that, except where the importation is by a private person for his personal use, it is the exclusive right of the author to authorize the importation of copies of his work, even where such copies were made with his authorization, into a country party to the Protocol or into the territory of a group of countries party to the Protocol that constitute an economic community or a single market' (para. 134). In this case, it was felt (para. 135) that national treatment should apply, together with the provisions on duration

laid down in the Convention and those on the presumption of authorship and on seizure (Art. 16).

This proposal was widely discussed. The Committee felt that matters pertaining to the right of importation should be kept on the agenda for further discussion, and in particular that a detailed analysis should be made of the circumstances under which this right would be justified.

iii) In regard to the provisions on the abolition of non-voluntary broadcasting licences currently permitted by the Berne Convention in Article 11*bis*(2), and as pointed out in the Memorandum of the International Bureau, events since the Rome revision (1928)—when these provisions were introduced into the text of the Convention, together with the broadcasting right—had shown that the risk of not being able to gain ready access to works for broadcasting had been exaggerated. In cases where problems of this kind had arisen, they had been solved by establishing suitable systems of collective administration and the arguments relating to possible abuse by authors' societies had proved unfounded. The Memorandum proposed that the countries parties to the Protocol which did not provide for non-voluntary licences pursuant to Article 11*bis*(2) of the Berne Convention would continue this practice, while those which did make such provision under domestic legislation would undertake to eliminate them within a specified period (e.g. five years).

A great many delegations and observers from non-governmental organizations were in favour of the abolition of non-voluntary licences for direct broadcasting, at least in regard to satellite broadcasting. Some delegations wished to confine abolition to cases in which the system of collective management existed. The abolition of non-voluntary licences for rebroadcasting did not gain sufficient support, even though it was felt that further consideration might be given to this matter.

iv) In regard to the notion of the *public* element applicable to rights of *public performance* and *communication to the public* protected by the Convention and the *new* proposed right of *public display or exhibition*, it was felt appropriate to include in the possible Protocol definitions which might put an end to differences of opinion, since the principle that every use should be considered 'public', and not 'private', if it went beyond the circle of family members and close social acquaintances of a family or an individual person was increasingly being recognized—the question as to whether members of the public were present in the same place being irrelevant.

The Memorandum points out that 'communication to the public' is still regarded as such even where, in fact, the communication—although receivable—is not received by anyone or is received only by one person or very few persons, or, again is received by such persons in different places. For example, where each room of a hotel contains a television set into which certain programmes are fed through wires controlled by the management of the hotel, the communication constitutes 'communication to the public', but where each room of the hotel contains a television set with its own antenna and the transmitted programme is picked up by each receiving set, the communication constitutes 'broadcasting' as a specific variant of the communication to the public (because it is by wireless means).

The Committee reached broad agreement to the effect that a possible Protocol should clarify the concept of certain public acts, although some delegations were in favour of leaving the whole matter to national laws. It was felt that in future work, the various proposals concerning detailed aspects and the wording of the definitions should be taken into account; the possibility that a simpler definition concentrating on the notion of 'public' might be more appropriate should also be considered.

2. *The provisions on the period of protection.* These refer to a minimum of 50 years and to the *term of protection* of photographic works. In regard to the general term of protection, the Memorandum points out that at the Stockholm Conference (1967), a resolution was adopted which required negotiations to be continued between the countries concerned for the conclusion of a special agreement on the question. The main reason for envisaging a possible extension of the term of protection was that the 50-year *post mortem auctoris* term of protection (the minimum

provided for in the Berne Convention) had originally been adopted to make reasonably certain that at least the first generation of the authors' heirs should normally be able to enjoy the benefits of protected rights; because of the continuous increase in life expectancy, such certainty no longer existed. No such negotiations have taken place and no special agreement has been concluded so far. Nevertheless, a number of national laws, adopted since 1967, have provided for terms of protection longer than 50 years, so that consideration should be given to the inclusion in a possible Protocol of a provision to the effect that the reference to 50 years in the Berne Convention would be replaced by 70 years (under this wording the general term *post mortem auctoris* and that applicable to anonymous or pseudonymous works covered by paragraphs 1 and 3 of Article 7 would be extended to 70 years, as would the term laid down in paragraph 2 for *cinematographic works*).

Regardless of whether the extension of the general term was adopted or not, it was proposed that the term of protection for photographic works should be the same as that allowed for other categories of works; it should begin to run from the death of the author or from the date on which the photographic work was produced.

No general consensus was reached in the Committee on the proposal for a general extension of the minimum term of protection, even though some delegations were in favour. On the other hand, they all supported the extension of the minimum term of protection for photographic works. It was felt that a possible Protocol should include provisions on the minimum term of protection. However, since some delegations thought that it was not appropriate to base the extension of the duration of protection on the continued increase in life expectancy, it was held that any revised working document should contain other justifications of an economic and social nature for a possible increase in this minimum term.

3. *The collective administration of rights.* Finally, the last chapter of the Memorandum covers the collective administration of rights and proposes the following rules to ensure compatibility between

collective administration and the Berne Convention:
- that governmental intervention in the determination of fees and conditions for the use of works imposed by a collective administration organization should only be allowed if, and to the extent that, such intervention was indispensable to prevent or eliminate *actual* abuse by a collective administration organization (in particular, abuse of a *de facto* monopoly position);
- that the fees collected by a collective administration organization should be distributed to the copyright owners concerned in a proportion that was as close as possible to the actual use of their works (after deducting the effective costs of administration);
- that the use of fees collected by collective administration organizations on behalf of copyright owners for any purpose other than the distribution of fees to the right-holders and payment of the actual costs of collective administration of the rights concerned should be prohibited in the absence of authorization by the copyright owners concerned, or by persons or bodies representing them;
- that foreign copyright owners should enjoy exactly the same treatment as national owners whose rights are administered by the same organization;
- that, while the establishment of collective administration is a right rather than an obligation of authors, national legislation may only prescribe in an obligatory manner the collective administration of those rights for which the Berne Convention allows non-voluntary licences (Article 9(2)); Article 11*bis*(2); Article 13(1) and Article 14*ter*), that is to say when the rights may amount to nothing more than a straightforward entitlement to remuneration. For lack of time, the Committee agreed that the matter of collective administration (paras. 164–8) would be examined at its next session.

Continuation of work on the preparation of a possible Protocol to the Berne Convention; preparation of a possible new instrument on the protection of the rights of performers and producers of phonograms:[121] the Assembly of the Berne Union (Geneva, 21 to 29

---

121. See document WIPO B/A/XIII/2 Prov., 29 September 1992.

September 1992) responded to the views of the majority expressed at the two sessions of the Committee of Experts in deciding on the continuation of its work and the establishment of a Committee of Experts on a possible new instrument on the protection of the rights of performers and producers of phonograms (independently of the Rome Convention, 1961). In the Committee of Experts on a Possible Protocol to the Berne Convention, the States party to the Berne Convention and the Commission of the European Communities would have the status of members, whereas the other members states of WIPO would have the status of observers. In turn, in the Committee of Experts on a Possible Instrument on the Protection of the Rights of Performers and Producers of Phonograms, the Member States of WIPO and the Commission of the European Communities would have the status of members.

The Committee of Experts on a Possible Protocol to the Berne Convention would examine the following ten issues: (1) computer programs; (2) databases; (3) rental right; (4) non-voluntary licences for the sound recording of musical works; (5) non-voluntary licences for primary broadcasting and satellite communication; (6) distribution rights, including importation right; (7) duration of the protection of photographic works; (8) communication to the public by satellite broadcasting; (9) enforcement of rights; and (10) national treatment.

In the preparatory documents for this Committee, the International Bureau would deal with items (6), (9) and (10) (the 'new items') in a manner similar to that which was followed in the documents prepared for the first two sessions, whereas, in respect of the questions already examined by the Committee—items (1) to (5), (7) and (8)—, the preparatory document would contain what was set out in the preparatory documents mentioned above which were drawn up for the first two sessions of that Committee (BCP/CE/I/2 and 3) and the relevant passages of the reports of those sessions (BCP/CE/I/4 and BCP/CE/II/1). These documents would be ready by the end of March 1993 and the Committee of Experts would meet, in principle, from 21 to 25 June 1993.

Immediately afterwards (in principle from 28 June to 2 July 1993) the Committee of Experts on a Possible Instrument for the Protection of the Rights of Performers and Producers of Phonograms would meet. In the preparatory documents, the International Bureau would deal with all questions in the way it would deal with the new items referred to above.

The Assembly of the Berne Union decided also to establish a 'Committee of Experts on a WIPO Model Law on the Protection of the Rights of Performers and Producers of Sound Recordings'.

Continuation of work by the Committee on a possible Protocol to the Berne Convention: The Committee's third session was held from 21 to 25 June 1993. Discussions were based on the Memorandum prepared by the International Bureau of WIPO (documents BCP/CE/III/2; BCP/CE/III/2-I, II and III) of 5 May 1993 and centred on the three 'new items', i.e. distribution rights, including importation right, enforcement of rights (where, in accordance with the views of the Committee, the provisions of Part III—Articles 41 to 61—of the TRIPS Agreement, were to be incorporated: see Chapter 11, note 22 above), and national treatment (the report appears in document BCP/CE/III/3 of 25 June 1993). The Committee's fourth session took place from 5 to 9 December 1994; the basis for its discussions was the Memorandum of the International Bureau of WIPO (document BCP/CE/IV/2 of 5 October 1994), the following questions representing the focus of the Committee's attention: computer programs; databases; distribution rights, including importation right (distribution right; rental right; importation right); non-voluntary licences for the sound recording of musical works; non-voluntary licences for 'primary' broadcasting and satellite communication; duration of the protection of photographic works; communication to the public by satellite broadcasting; and enforcement of rights (the report will be found in document BCP/CE/IV/3 of 9 December 1994).

The Committee's fifth session was held from 4 to 8 September 1995; its discussions were based on the Memorandum prepared by the International Bureau of WIPO (documents BCP/CE/V/2 to 5) and dealt with computer programs, databases, non-voluntary licences for phonograms and primary broadcasting; including satellite communication; duration of the protection of photographic works; communication to the public by way of satellite broadcasting (the report will be found in document BCP/CE/V/2 to 5 of 12 September).

The sixth session of the Committee took place from 1 to 5 February 1996, discussions being based on the memorandum drawn up by the International Bureau of WIPO (documents BCP/CE/VI/12).

The Committee's seventh session was held from 21 to 24 May 1996. Discussions focused on the form and content of the provisions to be introduced in the future Protocol to the Berne Convention concerning the right of reproduction, the right of communication to the public in the digital environment and the technical protection system. The Committee also examined the proposal of the United States concerning the protection *sui generis* of non-original databases. These questions were also discussed at regional meetings (Africa, Latin America, Asia and the Pacific, and Europe) designed to finalize the provisions of the definitive text of the Protocol for submission to the Diplomatic Conference in December 1996.

Berne Convention
for the Protection of Literary and Artistic Works* Berne Convention (1886),
completed at Paris (1896), revised at Berlin (1908),
completed at Berne (1914), revised at Rome (1928), at Brussels (1948),
at Stockholm (1967) and at Paris (1971) and amended in 1979
(Berne Union)

State	Date on which State became party to the Convention	Latest Act[1] of the Convention to which the State is a party and date on which it became party to that Act
Albania	6 March 1994	Paris: 6 March 1994
Argentina	10 June 1967	Brussels: 10 June 1967
		Paris, Art. 22–38: 8 October 1980
Australia	14 April 1928	Paris: 1 March 1978
Austria	1 October 1920	Paris: 21 August 1982
Bahamas	10 July 1973	Brussels: 10 July 1973
		Paris, Art. 22–38: 8 January 1977[2]
Barbados	30 July 1983	Paris: 30 July 1983
Belgium	5 December 1887	Brussels: 1 August 1951
		Stockholm, Art. 22–38: 12 Feb. 1975
Benin	3 January 1961[3]	Paris: 12 March 1975
Bolivia	4 November 1993	Paris: 4 November 1993
Bosnia and Herzegovina	6 March 1992	Paris: 6 March 1992[4]
Brazil	9 February 1992	Paris: 20 April 1975
Bulgaria	5 December 1921	Paris: 4 December 1974
Burkina Faso	19 August 1963[5]	Paris: 24 January 1976
Cameroon	21 September 1964[3]	Paris, Art. 1–21: 10 October 1974
		Paris, Art. 22–38: 10 November 1973
Canada	10 April 1928	Rome: 1 August 1931
		Stockholm, Art. 22–38: 7 July 1970
Central African Republic	3 September 1977	Paris: 3 September 1977
Chad	25 November 1971	Brussels: 25 November 1971[6,7]
		Stockholm, Art. 22–38: 25 Nov. 1971
Chile	5 June 1970	Paris: 10 July 1975
China	15 October 1992	Paris, 15 October 1992[8]
Colombia	7 March 1988	Paris: 7 March 1988
Congo	8 May 1962[3]	Paris: 5 December 1975
Costa Rica	10 June 1978	Paris: 10 June 1978
Côte d'Ivoire	1 January 1962	Paris, Art. 1–21: 10 October 1974
		Paris, Art. 22–38: 4 May 1974
Croatia	8 October 1991	Paris: 8 October 1991[4]
Cyprus	24 February 1964[3]	Paris: 27 July 1983[4]
Czech Republic	1 January 1993	Paris: 1 January 1993

State	Date on which State became party to the Convention	Latest Act[1] of the Convention to which the State is a party and date on which it became party to that Act
Denmark	1 July 1903	Paris: 30 June 1979
Ecuador	9 October 1991	Paris: 9 October 1991
Egypt	7 June 1977	Paris: 7 June 1977[2,8]
El Salvador	19 February 1994	Paris: 19 February 1994
Estonia	26 October 1994[9]	Paris, 26 October 1994
Fiji	1 December 1971[3]	Brussels: 1 December 1971 Stockholm, Art. 22–38: 15 March 1972
Finland	1 April 1928	Paris: 1 November 1986
France	5 December 1887	Paris, Art. 1–21: 10 October 1974 Paris, Art. 22–38: 15 December 1972
Gabon	26 March 1962	Paris: 10 June 1975
Gambia	7 March 1993	Paris: 7 March 1993
Germany	5 December 1887	Paris, Art. 1–21: 10 October 1974[10] Paris, Art. 22–38: 22 January 1974
Ghana	11 October 1991	Paris: 11 October 1991
Greece	9 November 1920	Paris: 8 March 1976
Guinea	20 November 1980	Paris: 20 November 1980
Guinea-Bissau	22 July 1991	Paris: 22 July 1991
Guyana	25 October 1994	Paris, 25 October 1994
Holy See	12 September 1935	Paris: 24 April 1975
Honduras	25 January 1990	Paris: 25 January 1990
Hungary	14 February 1922	Paris, Art. 1–21: 10 October 1974 Paris, Art. 22–38: 15 December 1972
Iceland	7 September 1947	Rome: 7 September 1947[4] Paris, Art. 22–38: 28 December 1984
India	1 April 1928	Paris, Art. 1–21: 6 May 1984[8,11,12] Paris, Art. 22–38: 10 January 1975[2]
Ireland	5 October 1927	Brussels: 5 July 1959 Stockholm, Art. 22–38: 21 December 1970
Israel	24 March 1950	Brussels: 1 August 1951 Stockholm, Art. 22–38: 29 January or 26 February 1970[13]
Italy	5 December 1887	Paris: 14 November 1979
Jamaica	1 January 1994	Paris: 1 January 1994[8]
Japan	15 July 1899	Paris: 24 April 1975
Kenya	11 June 1993	Paris: 11 June 1993
Latvia	11 August 1995	Paris: 11 August 1995
Lebanon	30 September 1947	Rome: 30 September 1947
Lesotho	28 September 1989	Paris: 28 September 1989[2,8]
Liberia	8 March 1989	Paris: 8 March 1989[2,8]

State	Date on which State became party to the Convention	Latest Act[1] of the Convention to which the State is a party and date on which it became party to that Act
Libya	28 September 1976	Paris: 28 September 1976[2]
Liechtenstein	30 July 1931	Brussels: 1 August 1951
		Stockholm, Art. 22–38: 25 May 1972
Lithuania	14 December 1994	Paris: 14 December 1994[2]
Luxembourg	20 June 1888	Paris: 20 April 1975
Madagascar	1 January 1966	Brussels: 1 January 1966
Malawi	12 October 1991	Paris: 12 October 1991
Malaysia	1 October 1990	Paris: 1 October 1990[8]
Mali	19 March 1962[3]	Paris: 5 December 1977
Malta	21 September 1964	Rome: 21 September 1964
		Paris; Art. 22–38: 12 December 1977[2]
Mauritania	6 February 1973	Paris: 21 September 1976
Mauritius	10 May 1989	Paris: 10 May 1989[2,8]
Mexico	11 June 1967	Paris: 17 December 1974[4]
Monaco	30 May 1889	Paris: 23 November 1974
Morocco	16 June 1917	Paris: 17 May 1987
Netherlands	1 November 1912	Paris, Art. 1–21: 30 January 1986[14]
		Paris, Art. 22–38: 10 January 1975[15]
New Zealand	24 April 1928	Rome: 4 December 1947
Niger	2 May 1962[3]	Paris: 21 May 1975
Nigeria	14 September 1993	Paris: 14 September 1993
Norway	13 April 1896	Paris, Art. 1–2: 11 October 1995
		Paris, Art. 22–38: 13 June 1974
Pakistan	5 July 1948	Rome: 5 July 1948[6]
		Stockholm, Art. 22–38: 29 January or 26 February 1970[13]
Paraguay	2 January 1992	Paris: 2 January 1992
Peru	20 August 1988	Paris: 20 August 1988
Philippines	1 August 1951	Brussels: 1 August 1951
		Paris, Art. 22–38: 16 July 1980
Poland	28 January 1920	Paris, Art. 1–21: 22 October 1994
		Paris, Art. 22–38: 4 August 1990
Portugal	29 March 1911	Paris: 12 January 1979[15]
Romania	1 January 1927	Rome: 6 August 1936[6]
		Stockholm, Art. 22–38: 29 January or 26 February 1970[2–13]
Russian Federation	13 March 1995	Paris: 13 March 1995
Rwanda	1 March 1984	Paris: 1 March 1984
Saint Kitts and Nevis	9 April 1995	Paris: 9 April 1995

State	Date on which State became party to the Convention	Latest Act[1] of the Convention to which the State is a party and date on which it became party to that Act
Saint Lucia	24 August 1993	Paris: 24 August 1993[2]
Senegal	25 August 1962	Paris: 12 August 1975
Slovakia	1 January 1993	Paris: 1 January 1993
Slovenia	25 June 1991	Paris: 25 June 1991[4]
South Africa	3 October 1928	Brussels: 1 August 1951
		Paris, Art. 22–38: 24 March 1975[2]
Spain	5 December 1887	Paris, Art. 1–21: 10 October 1974
		Paris, Art. 22–38: 19 February 1974
Sri Lanka	20 July 1959[3]	Rome: 20 July 1959
		Paris, Art. 22–38: 23 September 1978
Suriname	23 February 1977	Paris: 23 February 1977
Sweden	1 August 1904	Paris, Art. 1–21: 10 October 1974
		Paris, Art. 22–38: 20 September 1973
Switzerland	5 December 1887	Paris: 25 September 1993
Thailand	17 July 1931	Paris, Art. 1–21: 2 September 1995
		Paris, Art. 22–38: 29 December 1980[2]
The former Yugoslav Republic of Macedonia	8 September 1991	Paris: 8 September 1991[4]
Togo	30 April 1975	Paris: 30 April 1975
Trinidad and Tobago	16 August 1988	Paris: 16 August 1988
Tunisia	5 December 1887	Paris: 16 August 1975[2]
Turkey	1 January 1952	Paris: 1 January 1996
United Kingdom	5 December 1887	Paris: 2 January 1990[10]
United Republic of Tanzania	25 July 1994	Paris: 25 July 1994[2,8]
United States of America	1 March 1989	Paris: 1 March 1989
Uruguay	10 July 1967	Paris: 28 December 1979
Venezuela	30 December 1982	Paris: 30 December 1982[2]
Yugoslavia	17 June 1930	Paris: 2 September 1975[4]
Zaire	8 October 1963[3]	Paris: 31 January 1975
Zambia	2 January 1992	Paris: 2 January 1992
Zimbabwe	18 April 1980	Rome:18 April 1980
		Paris, Art. 22–38: 30 December 1981

(Total: 111 States)

* Situation as of 1 January 1995, see *Industrial Property and Copyright* (Geneva), WIPO, January 1995, pp. 14–16.

1. 'Paris' means the Berne Convention for the Protection of Literary and Artistic Works as revised at Paris on 24 July 1971 (Paris Act); 'Stockholm' means the said Convention as revised at Stockholm on 14 July 1967 (Stockholm Act); 'Brussels' means the said Convention as revised at Brussels on 26 June 1948 (Brussels Act); 'Rome' means the said Convention as revised at Rome on 2 June 1928 (Rome Act); 'Berlin' means the said Convention as revised at Berlin on 13 November 1908 (Berlin Act).

2. With the declaration provided for in Article 33(2) relating to the International Court of Justice.

3. Date on which the declaration of continued adherence was sent, after the accession of the State to independence.

4. Subject to the reservation concerning the right of translation.

5. Burkina Faso, which had acceded to the Berne Convention (Brussels Act) as from 19 August 1963, denounced the said Convention as from 20 September 1970. Later on, Burkina Faso acceded again to the Berne Convention (Paris Act); this accession took effect on 24 January 1976.

6. This State deposited its instrument of ratification of (or of accession to) the Stockholm Act in its entirety; however, Articles 1 to 21 (substantive clauses) of the said Act have not entered into force.

7. In accordance with the provision of Article 29 of the Stockholm Act applicable to the State outside the Union which accede to the said Act, this State is bound by Articles 1 to 20 of the Brussels Act.

8. Estonia acceded to the Berne Convention (Berlin Act, 1908) with effect from 9 June 1927. It lost its independence on 6 August 1940 and regained it on 20 August 1991.

9. This State has declared that it admits the application of the Appendix of the Paris Act to works of which it is the State of origin by States which have made a declaration under Article VI(1)(i) of the Appendix or a notification under Article 1 of the Appendix. The declarations took effect on 18 October 1973 for Germany, on 8 March 1974 for Norway and on 27 September 1971 for the United Kingdom.

10. This State declared that is ratification shall not apply to the provisions of Article 14*bis*(2)(b) of the Paris Act (presumption of legitimation for some authors who have brought contributions to the making of the cinematographic work.)

11. This State notified the designation of the competent authority provided by Article 15(4) of the Paris Act.

12. These are the alternative dates of entry into force which the Director-General of WIPO communicated to the States concerned.

13. Ratification for the Kingdom in Europe.

14. Ratification for the Kingdom in Europe, Articles 22–38 of the Paris Act apply also to the Netherlands Antilles and Aruba.

15. Pursuant to the provisions of Article 14*bis*(2)(c) of the Paris Act, this State has made a declaration to the effect that the undertaking by authors to bring contributions to the making of a cinematographic work must be in a written agreement. This declaration was received on 5 November 1986.

Convention establishing the World Intellectual Property Organization*
(WIPO Convention, Stockholm, 14 July 1967, amended in 1979)

State	Date on which State became Member of WIPO	Member of Paris Union (P) and/or Berne Union (B)[1]	
Albania	30 June 1992	–	B
Algeria	16 April 1975	P	–
Andorra	28 October 1994	–	–
Angola	15 April 1985	–	–
Argentina	8 October 1980	P	B
Armenia	22 April 1993	P	–
Australia	10 August 1972	P	B
Austria	11 August 1973	P	B
Azerbaijan	25 December 1995	P	–
Bahamas	4 January 1977	P	B
Bahrain	22 June 1995	–	–
Bangladesh	11 May 1985	P	–
Barbados	5 October 1979	P	B
Belarus	26 April 1970	P	–
Belgium	31 January 1975	P	B
Benin	9 March 1975	P	B
Bhutan	16 March 1994	–	–
Bolivia	6 July 1993	P	B
Bosnia and Herzegovina	6 March 1992	P	B
Brazil	20 March 1975	P	B
Brunei Darussalam	21 April 1994	–	–
Bulgaria	19 May 1970	P	B
Burkina Faso	23 August 1975	P	B
Burundi	30 March 1977	P	–
Cambodia	25 July 1995	–	–
Cameroon	3 November 1973	P	B
Canada	26 June 1970	P	B
Central African Republic	23 August 1978	P	B
Chad	26 September 1970	P	B
Chile	25 June 1975	P	B
China	3 June 1980	P	B
Colombia	4 May 1980	–	B
Congo	2 December 1975	P	B
Costa Rica	10 June 1981	–	B
Côte d'Ivoire	1 May 1974	P	B
Croatia	8 October 1991	P	B
Cuba	27 March 1975	P	–

State	Date on which State became Member of WIPO	Member of Paris Union (P) and/or Berne Union (B)[1]	
Cyprus	26 October 1984	P	B
Czech Republic	1 January 1993	P	B
Democratic People's Republic of Korea	17 August 1974	P	–
Denmark	26 April 1970	P	B
Ecuador	22 May 1988	–	B
Egypt	21 April 1975	P	B
El Salvador	18 September 1979	P	B
Estonia	5 February 1994	P	B
Fiji	11 March 1972	–	B
Finland	8 September 1970	P	B
France	18 October 1974	P	B
Gabon	6 June 1975	P	B
Gambia	10 December 1980	P	B
Georgia	25 December 1991	P	–
Germany	19 September 1970	P	B
Ghana	12 June 1976	P	B
Greece	4 March 1976	P	B
Guatemala	30 April 1983	–	–
Guinea	13 November 1980	P	B
Guinea-Bissau	28 June 1988	P	B
Guyana	25 October 1994	P	B
Haiti	2 November 1983	P	–
Holy See	20 April 1975	P	B
Honduras	15 November 1983	P	B
Hungary	26 April 1970	P	B
Iceland	13 September 1986	P	B
India	1 May 1975	–	B
Indonesia	18 December 1979	P	–
Iraq	21 January 1976	P	–
Ireland	26 April 1970	P	B
Israel	26 April 1970	P	B
Italy	20 April 1977	P	B
Jamaica	25 December 1978	–	B
Japan	20 April 1975	P	B
Jordan	12 July 1972	P	–
Kazakhstan	25 December 1991	P	–
Kenya	5 October 1971	P	B
Kyrgyzstan	25 December 1991	P	–
Laos	17 January 1995	–	–

State	Date on which State became Member of WIPO	Member of Paris Union (P) and/or Berne Union (B)[1]	
Latvia	21 January 1993	P	–
Lebanon	30 December 1986	P	B
Lesotho	18 November 1986	P	B
Liberia	8 March 1989	P	B
Libya	28 September 1976	P	B
Liechtenstein	21 May 1972	P	B
Lithuania	30 April 1992	P	B
Luxembourg	19 March 1975	P	B
Madagascar	22 December 1989	P	B
Malawi	11 June 1970	P	B
Malaysia	1 January 1989	P	B
Mali	14 August 1982	P	B
Malta	7 December 1977	P	B
Mauritania	17 September 1976	P	B
Mauritius	21 September 1976	P	B
Mexico	14 June 1975	P	B
Monaco	3 March 1975	P	B
Mongolia	28 February 1979	P	–
Morocco	27 July 1971	P	B
Namibia	23 December 1991	–	B
Netherlands	9 January 1975	P	B
New Zealand	20 June 1984	P	B
Nicaragua	5 May 1985	–	–
Niger	18 May 1975	P	B
Nigeria	9 April 1995	P	B
Norway	8 June 1974	P	B
Pakistan	6 January 1977	–	B
Panama	17 September 1983	–	–
Paraguay	20 June 1987	P	B
Peru	4 September 1980	P	B
Philippines	14 July 1980	P	B
Poland	23 March 1975	P	B
Portugal	27 April 1975	P	B
Qatar	3 September 1976	–	–
Republic of Korea	1 March 1979	P	–
Republic of Moldova	25 December 1991	P	–
Romania	26 April 1970	P	B
Russian Federation	26 April 1970[2]	P	B
Rwanda	3 February 1984	P	B
Saint Christopher and Nevis	16 November 1995	P	B

State	Date on which State became Member of WIPO	Member of Paris Union (P) and/or Berne Union (B)[1]	
Saint Lucia	21 August 1993	–	B
Saint Vincent and the Grenadines	29 August 1995	P	B
San Marino	26 June 1991	P	–
Saudi Arabia	22 May 1982	–	–
Senegal	26 April 1970	P	B
Sierra Leone	18 May 1986	–	–
Singapore	10 December 1990	P	–
Slovakia	1 January 1993	P	B
Slovenia	25 June 1991	P	B
Somalia	18 November 1982	–	–
South Africa	23 March 1975	P	B
Spain	26 April 1970	P	B
Sri Lanka	20 September 1978	P	B
Sudan	15 February 1974	P	–
Suriname	25 November 1975	P	B
Swaziland	18 August 1988	P	–
Sweden	26 April 1970	P	B
Switzerland	26 April 1970	P	B
Tajikistan	25 December 1991	P	–
Thailand	25 December 1989	–	B
The former Yugoslav Republic of Macedonia	8 September 1991	P	B
Togo	28 April 1975	P	B
Trinidad and Tobago	16 August 1988	P	B
Tunisia	28 November 1975	P	B
Turkmenistan	25 December 1991	P	–
Turkey	12 May 1976	P	B
Uganda	18 October 1973	P	–
Ukraine	26 April 1970	P	–
United Arab Emirates	24 September 1974	–	–
United Kingdom	26 April 1970	P	B
United Republic of Tanzania	30 December 1983	P	B
United States of America	25 August 1970	P	B
Uruguay	21 December 1979	P	B
Uzbekistan	25 December 1991	P	–
Venezuela	23 November 1984	–	B
Viet Nam	2 July 1976	P	–
Yemen	29 March 1979	–	–

State	Date on which State became Member of WIPO	Member of Paris Union (P) and/or Berne Union (B)[1]	
Yugoslavia	11 October 1973	P	B
Zaire	28 January 1975	P	B
Zambia	14 May 1977	P	B
Zimbabwe	29 December 1981	P	B

(Total: 157 States)

* Situation as of 1 January 1995; see *Industrial Property and Copyright* (Geneva), WIPO, pp. 6–90.
1. 'P' means that the State is also a member of the International Union for the Protection of Industrial Property (Paris Union), founded by the Paris Convention for the Protection of Industrial Property.
 'B' means that the State is also a member of the International Union for the Protection of Literary and Artistic Works (Berne Union), founded by the Berne Convention for the Protection of Literary and Artistic Works.
2. Date of ratification of the Soviet Union, continued by the Russian Federation as from 25 December 1991.

12.4.2.2. Universal Copyright Convention. Developments leading up to the revised version adopted in Paris (24 July 1971)

A. GENESIS

In this chapter, attention has been drawn more than once to the fact that the origin of the Universal Copyright Convention can be traced back to the endeavour to unify—or at least to reconcile—and extend the protection provided by the Berne Convention and by the inter-American Conventions in the European countries and their colonies on the one hand and the Republics of the American continent on the other.

The Berne Convention was regarded as an essentially European treaty designed to protect European works and, with a few exceptions such as Haiti, Brazil and Canada, its extension to the American continent was not achieved; the Conventions of the inter-American system (with the exception, to a certain extent, of the Montevideo Treaty) were, on the one hand, not open to the accession of countries from other continents and, on the other, did not manage to gain the support of all the American countries either (until the 1950s, both Argentina and Chile, which are countries with a large publishing industry, had not ratified the Buenos Aires Copyright Convention signed in 1910).

a. The recommendation of the Rome Conference (1928)

The first official expression of the idea of a Universal Convention for the protection of literary and artistic works is to be found in one of the recommendations made by the Berne Convention Revision Conference held at Rome in 1928: this is Recommendation VI concerning the unification of the Conventions of the Berne Union and of Buenos Aires, revised at Havana, formulated on a proposal by the Brazilian and French delegations as follows:

The Conference,
In view of the identity of the general guiding principles of, and the ends aimed at by, the Convention of Berne, as revised in Berlin and later in Rome, and the Convention signed by the American States in Buenos Aires in 1910 and later revised in Havana in February of 1928; and in view of the manifest agreement between the majority of provisions of the two Conventions;
Expresses the wish, in conformity with the proposals made by the delegations of Brazil and France, that, on the one hand, the American Republics which are signatories of a Convention to which non-American States cannot adhere, shall adhere, in accordance with the example set by Brazil, to the Convention of Berne, as revised in Rome, and on the other hand, all the interested governments shall co-operate with a view to preparing a general agreement which shall have as its basis the similar rules of the two conventions and as its object the worldwide unification of the laws protecting the creation of the spirit.

As Bogsch points out, this recommendation was 'extremely vague' in proposing solutions to the dilemma created by the existence of two parallel multilateral conventions on copyright.[122] On the one hand, it seemed to propose that the American Republics should

---

122. Arpad Bogsch, 'Co-existence of the Universal Copyright Convention with the Berne Conventions', in T. R. Kupferman and M. Foner (eds.), *Universal Copyright Convention Analysed* (1955), 141, 143, cited by Ricketson, op. cit. p. 843.

subscribe to the Act of Rome, while on the other envisaging the creation of a new multilateral convention which would be genuinely universal in scope.[123]

However, despite its imprecision, a few months later the recommendation made by the Rome Conference was taken up again by the General Assembly of the League of Nations.

b. The recommendation ('vœu') of the Ninth Ordinary Session of the Assembly of the League of Nations (1928)

On 24 September 1928, the Ninth Ordinary Session of the Assembly of the League of Nations made a recommendation which was very similar to that of the Rome Conference. After noting the 'general identity of principles between the Convention of Berne, as revised first in Berlin and then in Rome, and the Copyright Convention signed in 1910 at Buenos Aires by the American States, and revised in Havana in 1928', the Assembly requested the Council of the League of Nations to 'have its competent organs make all the necessary investigations and consultations regarding the desirability of a general agreement having for its object the unification, on an international basis, and in full conformity with the wish expressed at the Rome Conference for the revision of the Berne Copyright Convention, of all laws and measures for the protection of intellectual property'. In conformity with that recommendation, the Council instructed the Committee on Intellectual Co-operation to perform the requested studies. That Committee in turn sought the co-operation of the International Institute for the Unification of Private Law at Rome and the International Institute of Intellectual Co-operation in Paris which made comparative studies of the Rome revision and the Havana Convention.

c. The Paris Draft (1936)

Subsequently, the League of Nations adopted two further resolutions in support of the proposal to bring the two international

---

123. Ricketson, ibid.

copyright protection systems into a closer relationship; the second of these, adopted on 18 September 1935 by the Sixteenth Ordinary Session of the Assembly (to which reference has already been made in our examination of the Brussels revision of the Berne Convention which was postponed *sine die*), entrusted the institutes of Paris and Rome with the task of 'pursuing their studies and efforts to promote, by bringing into harmony the Berne and Havana Conventions, the conclusion of a general agreement affording effective protection to intellectual works in the countries of both continents'.

The two institutes appointed a Committee of specialists (in which a number of American experts also took part, together with International Literary and Artistic Association (ALAI), International Federation of Societies of Authors and Composers (CISAC) and the International Federation of Journalists).

The methods proposed to bring the principles of the two international systems for copyright protection into line with one another were basically as follows:
- a simple amendment to Article 25 of the Rome Act of the Berne Convention in such a way as to favour the accession of the American Republics;
- a new Convention which would completely replace the Berne Convention and the Havana Convention (*a single universal statute*);
- a '*bridging convention*' between the European system and the American system proposed in 1935 by Fritz Ostertag, at the time Director of the International Bureau of the Berne Union (he held that post between 1926 and 1938) published in *Le droit d'auteur*[124] set out from the assumption that any proposal to unify the two systems was merely utopian. According to the proposal of the International Bureau, the two conventions—of Berne and Havana—were to continue and relations between the States governed by either of them would not be affected by the new Convention which would be open to the accession of

---

124. 'Le rapprochement de Berne et de la Havane', *Le droit d'auteur* (Geneva), WIPO, 1935, pp. 100 *et seq.*

members both of the Berne Union and of the Havana Convention. The countries belonging to either of the two groups would undertake to grant national treatment to works published for the first time in one of the countries of the other group (one of the drawbacks of the 'bridging Convention' was that of excluding countries which were members neither of the Berne Union nor of the Havana Convention; another resided in the disparity in the degree of protection afforded by the two systems: while that given in the member countries of the Union to works originating in the countries of the inter-American system would be the protection accorded by the Berne Convention, works of the Union would not enjoy equivalent protection on the American continent);

- A *third intermediate Convention* which would simply contain some principles common to the two systems and might establish a consensus between the countries of the two groups. The Berne Convention and the Havana Convention would both remain in force.

This last was the criterion adopted by the Committee of Experts which, in April 1936, tabled a report and a draft convention known as the 'Paris Draft'. Article 19 stipulated that: 'This Convention shall in no way affect the continued validity of the conventions which at present exist between the contracting countries, if those conventions confer on authors, or on their successors-in-title, rights which are more extensive than those granted by the present convention or contain other stipulations which are not contrary to this same convention'.

The Paris Draft which was to be considered by an International Diplomatic Conference in Brussels immediately prior to the diplomatic conference for the revision of the Berne Convention, included proposals made by the American Institute of International Law, ALAI and the VII Pan-American Conference held in Montevideo in 1933: it consisted of 23 articles, was based on the principle of national treatment and embodied a minimum degree of protection based on recognition of the fundamental rights of authors: the moral right and economic rights of reproduction, translation, adaptation, mechanical reproduction, broadcasting and cinematographic showing. As to formalities, it provided for an international system of registration of works to be effected within a specified time-limit at the International Bureau in Berne: a draft regulation governing the register was added. The new convention was to be open to accession by all countries and not only the States party to the Berne Convention and to the conventions of the inter-American system.[125]

d. The Montevideo Project (1937)

Some years previously, the VII Pan-American Conference held in Montevideo in December 1933, acting on the basis of various reports tabled by the American Institute of International Law and by the delegation of the Oriental Republic of Uruguay, had set up a special commission consisting of members designated by Argentina, Brazil, Cuba, Mexico and Uruguay, to undertake the drafting of a Convention which was to bring the principles of American law into line with those of the Berne Convention, having regard to the domestic legislation of the member countries. In 1937, that Commission submitted a report and a draft universal convention known as the 'Montevideo Project' in which the North American National Committee of Intellectual Co-operation also took part. This document was based on the 12 points laid down by the Pan-American Conference.

In 1938, the VIII Pan-American Conference, meeting at Lima, confirmed the interest of the countries of the continent in the diplomatic conference for the conclusion of a universal convention which was due to be convened by the Belgian Government in Brussels, immediately before the conference called to revise the Rome Text of the Berne Convention.

e. The Brussels meeting (1938) of the Committee of Experts

As a consequence of the recommendation made on 18 September 1935 by the General Assembly of the League of Nations, the revision conference of the Berne Convention which was due to be

---

125. Cf. Valerio De Sanctis, *La convenzione universale del diritto di autore*, Rome, SIAE, 1953, pp. 10–11.

convened in Brussels in September 1936 was postponed and the Belgian Government, in co-operation with the Institutes of Paris and Rome, began preparations for a world conference to be held in 1939. In 1938 the Belgian Government convened a preparatory meeting of the Committee of Experts which was held in Brussels in October of that year and attended, as on the first occasion, by a number of American experts and this time also by delegations from Japan, which was concerned by the subject of translation rights, and the United States of America, which took a particular interest in the aspects of formalities, moral rights and retroactivity. The Committee of Experts maintained the Paris draft, although with some amendments, particularly in respect of formalities, as a consequence of the opposition expressed by a number of countries to any international system involving such formalities.[126]

The conference was then due to be held in September or October 1939, but the outbreak of the Second World War led to its indefinite postponement

f. The activities of UNESCO

Once the Second World War had ended, the Belgian Government set up a Committee to gather official proposals which would constitute the basis of the proceedings of the conference on the Universal Convention. However, this activity proved sterile for various reasons—in particular, the conclusion of the inter-American Convention in Washington on 22 June 1946 (on the rights of authors of literary, scientific and artistic works). On 5 June 1948, the postponed Berne Convention revision conference was convened in Brussels but was not preceded, as had been anticipated in the prewar years, by a conference on the Universal Convention.

After 1947, UNESCO, which had recently been set up, took the initiative of encouraging the conclusion of the Universal Convention by virtue of the link which existed between the international protection of copyright and the Universal Declaration of Human Rights (Paris, 1948). Article 27(2) of the Declaration recognized that everyone has the right to the protection of the

---

126. Ibid.

moral and material interests resulting from any scientific, literary or artistic production of which he is the author. This work, which was pursued in a methodical and efficient manner, together with the two surveys addressed to the governments of the countries concerned and the detailed answers received, made it possible to bring together the information necessary to ensure a realistic harmonization of the various tendencies and interests at stake.

Between 1947 and 1951, UNESCO held a number of meetings of experts: two in Paris (1947 and 1949), one in Washington (1950) and the last again in Paris (1951). The second meeting of the Committee of Experts (Paris, 1949) produced a series of recommendations with a view to the preparation of a draft universal convention open to all countries of the world without prejudice to the existing conventions.

UNESCO went on to transmit its first 'request for views' to the States.

However, two major obstacles stood in the way of the preparation of a possible Universal Convention: firstly, the fear that many countries would desert the Berne Convention in favour of the new—and less demanding—instrument and, secondly, the insistence, particularly by the United States of America—the country which was giving decisive political support to the project—for certain fundamental principles of its own legislation to be maintained, such as those relating to the accomplishment of formalities and the duration of the right based on publication of the work.

It was at the third meeting of the Committee of Experts (Washington, October–November 1950) that mechanisms capable of overcoming these two major obstacles became apparent: firstly, the 'safeguarding clause of the Berne Convention' and secondly the symbol ©. The latter was proposed by the United States experts and was a development of the earlier copyright notice stipulated in Section 19 of Title 17 of the United States code. At this meeting (which had at its disposal the replies by 44 countries to the first UNESCO survey), the idea of a 'bridging convention' was definitively abandoned and many of the basic principles of the future convention were outlined.

Thereafter, at the suggestion of the experts, a new survey ('a further request for views') was sent to a number of governments;

it made reference to a number of specific aspects such as the minimum level of protection, the categories of works to be protected, the definition of the term 'publication' etc. With the answers received, the Committee of Experts, meeting again in Paris in June 1951, drew up the final version of the draft convention which was to be the working document of the Diplomatic Conference that adopted the Universal Convention in the following year.

B. THE INTER-GOVERNMENTAL CONFERENCE IN GENEVA (1952)

On a proposal from the Swiss Government, Geneva was the venue chosen by UNESCO for the Inter-governmental Conference to which its Member States were invited, together with those of the United Nations and the non-Member Countries set out in a list approved by the Executive Board. The Conference was held in the Electoral Palace at Geneva from 18 August to 6 September 1952 and was attended by delegations from 50 countries, together with observers from nine inter-governmental organizations (UN, ILO, OAS (Organization of American States), ICAO (International Civil Aviation Organization), ITU (International Telecommunication Union), the Universal Postal Union, Office of the United Nations High Commission for Refugees (UNHCR), International Bureau of the Berne Union, International Institute for the Unification of Private Law) and six non-governmental international organizations including the International Law Association, ALAI (International Literary and Artistic Association), CISAC (International Confederation of Societies of Authors and Composers), IFPI (International Federation of the Phonographic Industry)). Plinio Bolla (Switzerland) was elected President and John Blake (United Kingdom) Rapporteur. François Hepp, the Head of UNESCO's Division of Copyright acted as Secretary-General of the Conference and Arpad Bogsch, who was then working in the same division (and was to become Director-General of WIPO in 1973) was appointed Secretary.

The Universal Copyright Convention, adopted on 6 September 1952 in Geneva, was not intended to replace the Berne Convention or the other multilateral or bilateral conventions, as is expressly pointed out in its Article XVII: 'This Convention shall not in any way affect the provisions of the Berne Convention' and also in Article XVIII: 'This Convention shall not abrogate multilateral or bilateral copyright conventions or arrangements that are, or may be, in effect exclusively between two or more American Republics' and XIX: 'This Convention shall not abrogate multilateral or bilateral conventions or arrangements in effect between two or more Contracting States.' Neither was there any intention of competing with the Berne Convention, but simply of making sure that no countries were left outside the international system of copyright protection. The idea was that countries which were reluctant to join the Berne Union could accede in a first phase to a convention which was less demanding in terms of the level of protection ensured by it for authors' rights, and more consonant with their legal traditions; they would still have the option of accession to the Berne Convention at a later stage. In regard to the member countries of the Berne Union, the Universal Convention may be regarded as a special agreement under the provisions of Article 20 of the Berne Convention, although it is not applicable between member countries of the latter, but only in their relationships with countries which belong to the Universal Convention but not to the Union (Appendix Declaration relating to Article XVII, para. (b)).

It has been pointed out that the new Convention 'differs appreciably, in content and intention, from the previous conventions. These had aimed at the immediate establishment of an International Copyright Code. This Universal Copyright Convention, on the other hand, is designed to provide a basis for and method of conciliation between countries differing widely in civilization, culture, legislation and administrative practice, and sometimes having conflicting interests.'[127]

---

127. 'Report on the Results of the Inter-Governmental Copyright Conference' presented by the Director-General of UNESCO to the General Conference of UNESCO (Seventh Session, 1952). *Copyright Bulletin* (Paris), UNESCO, Vol. V, No. 3–4/1952, p. 189.

As Villalba points out, 'the Universal Convention pursued the aim of harmonizing existing legislation, regardless of its level. It accordingly abandoned any underlying claim to create a uniform body of legislation and any programme designed to attain higher levels of protection. It fulfilled its purpose of harmonizing the separate conventions, arrangements or treaties on the subject. On that basis, it implemented one of the historical principles, namely that of a universal system'.[128]

C. THE 1952 TEXT

The Universal Convention followed the same model as the Berne Convention. It adopted the principles of national treatment and of minimum protection, although the latter is markedly less developed than in the Berne Convention. That is because the intention was to attract the largest possible number of members[129] and facilitate acceptance by the countries which considered the level of protection granted by the Berne Convention as being too high. Protection under the Universal Convention rests on national treatment to a much greater extent than in the case of the Berne Convention.

The text is preceded by a *preamble* which, as is generally the case in international treaties, contains no statutory provisions or dispositions having legal effect, but simply explains the purpose of the convention which is 'to assure in all countries copyright protection of literary, scientific and artistic works' by a system 'appropriate to all nations of the world', 'additional to, and without impairing international systems already in force', with a view to encouraging 'respect for the rights of the individual'. (That

---

128. Carlos Alberto Villalba, 'Introduccion a los tratados internacionales en materia de derecho de autor', Buenos Aires, *Rev. La Propiedad Industrial* (Buenos Aires), Ed. Depalma, 1980, pp. 331–49.
129. Cf. Henri Desbois, André Françon and André Kerever, op. cit., p. 75, Section 79.

expression reflects the wish of some delegations to make reference to 'human rights' and of others to avoid any reference to the 'moral right'). The system must 'encourage the development of literature, the sciences and the arts' and 'the wider dissemination of works of the human mind'.

a. Proprietors of copyright

Article I of the Convention stipulates that protection is to be granted to 'the rights of authors and other copyright proprietors'. That wording takes account of the two main legal concepts of copyright and overcomes the differences presented by them as regards who is or may be considered to be the author and to whom original ownership may be attributed in certain cases.

b. Criteria of protection: points of attachment to the Convention

Article II stipulates that the Universal Convention is to be applicable by virtue of the nationality of the author—regardless of whether his works are published or not—and of the place of first publication. Comparison with the Berne Convention in force in 1952 shows the field of application of the Universal Convention to be much wider since, until the adoption of the Stockholm Act, the Berne document was applicable only to works published by nationals of a Member Country of the Union in cases where first publication had taken place in a country of the Union (in the case of published works, the first publication in a country of the Union—*real* point of attachment—was the factor which determined whether or not the Convention was applicable).

The innovation introduced—at the request of the United States of America—by the Universal Convention considerably broadened the number of works included in its field of application, since it granted protection to all works published by all authors who were nationals of all the contracting countries (in addition to the unpublished works of nationals of the contracting countries and those published for the first time in one of these countries, criteria which coincided with that incorporated into the Berne Convention until the Brussels Act of 1948).

The points of attachment to the Berne Convention were

broadened after the Act (1967) referred to, by analogy with the Universal Convention.

1. *Nationality or domicile of the author (personal points of attachment)*

Nationality of the author: the Universal Convention protects works of the nationals of any Contracting State (Article II(1)—both *published* (para. 1) and *unpublished* (para. 2).

The Convention—like the Berne Convention—does not stipulate which nationality takes precedence in the case of successive nationalities, i.e. whether it is the nationality of the author at the time of creation of the work, or of its first publication or at the time of seeking protection or indeed at any other time. According to Bogsch, it would appear that the relevant nationality is as follows:

- in the case of unpublished works, the nationality of the author at the time of creation of the work;
- in the case of published works (only covering works published for the first time in a non-contracting country), the nationality which the author had when he made the first publication.[130]

No reference is made either to works of co-authorship when one author is a national of a Contracting State and the other not, although it is held that protection must be granted by virtue of the principle *in dubiis benigniora praeferenda sunt*.[131]

Protection for the works of stateless persons and refugees with habitual residence in a Contracting State is covered by Protocol 1, additional to the Convention; these persons are to be treated in the same way as nationals of the State concerned.

Domicile of the author: in regard to persons who are not nationals of a Contracting State but are domiciled in one, paragraph 3 of Article II, proposed by the United States of America, stipulates that:

---

130. Arpad Bogsch, op. cit., p. 17, para. 19.
131. Ibid., p. 19, paragraph 21.

'For the purpose of this Convention, any Contracting State may, by domestic legislation, assimilate to its nationals, any person domiciled in that State.'

The effects of this provision are confined to the country which assimilates persons domiciled in it to its own nationals, since the Convention does not make this assimilation obligatory. In other words a country may assimilate persons domiciled on its territory to its own nationals (for example the United States of America, Argentina, etc.), but the other contracting countries are not obliged to do likewise, that is to say, they are not obliged to treat persons domiciled on their territory as if they were their own nationals.

This provision also influenced the evolution of the Berne Convention since, with effect from the 1967 Act, the habitual place of residence of the author in a Member Country of the Union was taken as a point of attachment equivalent to nationality.

2. *Place of first publication of the work (real point of attachment)*. Works published for the first time on the territory of a Contracting State are also protected (Article II, para. 1). Given that published works are covered by both criteria of attachment (in an alternative but not cumulative form), it is apparent that there are two categories of protected published works: works published (regardless of the place of publication) by authors who are nationals of a contracting country and works published for the first time in a contracting country (regardless of the author's nationality).

Concept of publication (Article VI): Since the points of attachment to the Convention differ depending on whether the works are *published*, to which both provisions apply (personal and real) or *unpublished*, in which case only one criterion (personal) is applied, the Convention clearly had to define the meaning of the term 'publication' for the purpose of its implementation. It did so in Article VI which defines publication as: 'the reproduction in tangible form and the general distribution to the public of copies of a work from which it can be read or otherwise visually perceived'.

That wording takes in cinematographic works and video works, but, as Bogsch points out, it excludes phonograms since sound recordings are copies of the recording and not copies of the musical (or any other) works whose performance has been fixed.[132]

A very important difference in comparison with the Berne Convention can also be seen here, for the latter provides that the fixation of a work in a sound recording can be regarded as 'publication', provided that copies of the said sound recording are made available to the public in a sufficient quantity to satisfy its reasonable requirements, having regard to the nature of the work (Art. 3(3)).

c. The principles of protection

In the Universal Convention, as in the Berne Convention, the principle of national treatment (or of placing foreign works on the same footing as national works) is one of the principles underlying protection, for it means that foreign works will be accorded exactly the same treatment as national works and the protection will not have to be reciprocal. In other words, the protection of foreign works will be governed by the same provisions as that of national works, save for specific aspects such as the duration of the right (Article IV(4)) for which purpose the method of comparison of periods is to be used.

The principle of national treatment is established in Article II (jointly with the points of attachment to the Convention). It implies that each Contracting State must grant:
- published works the same protection as is accorded to works first published by its nationals on its own territory (para. 1);
- unpublished works the same protection as is granted to the unpublished works of its own nationals (para. 2).

Article I stipulates that 'each Contracting State undertakes to provide for the adequate and effective protection of the rights of authors and other copyright proprietors'.

As Desbois, Françon and Kerever point out, this provision lays down the two conditions which are to govern the protection granted by the Contracting States to authors' rights: it must be

---

132. Ibid., p. 77, paragraphs 6 and 7.

both *adequate* and *effective*. The first term relates to the rule of law and the second to the effective application of that law. It follows that the Contracting State will not have complied with Article I by the mere fact of having adopted regulatory provisions that are, in theory, extremely favourable to authors in this area. Provision must also be made for legal penalties.[133]

d. Minimum protection

The provisions embodied in the 1952 text which ensure minimum protection relate to *protected works* (Article I), *formalities* (Article III), the *length of protection* (Article IV), the *right of translation*, and the compulsory licence for translation (Article V).

1. *Protected works.* Article I contains a non-exhaustive list of protected works; the fact that the list merely cites examples is shown by the use of the word 'including'. Comparison with Article 2(1) of the Berne Convention shows the same method to have been used: literary, scientific and artistic works are protected, but the list of works cited is shorter. It refers only to writings, musical, dramatic and cinematographic works and painting, engravings and sculpture.

This is partly due to the fact that some delegations considered it dangerous to include a more extensive list which might then have been regarded as exhaustive, while the mention of particular works might have placed difficulties in the way of the accession of certain countries. For example, the Constitution of the United States of America would not permit the protection of works of architecture, while in other countries works of the applied arts are covered by a type of protection which differs from that accorded to authors' rights. Canada suggested that works should not be enumerated, but that the article should refer solely to literary and artistic works of all kinds, the word 'scientific' being unnecessary. However, it was explained that this term was necessary to cover

---

133. Henri Desbois, André Françon and André Kerever, op. cit., pp. 73–4, Section II.

clearly certain works such as logarithm tables and treaties on nuclear physics.[134]

2. *Formalities*. The principal difference between the countries belonging to the Berne system and those of the inter-American system lay, as we have seen, in the type of formalities required, particularly in the United States of America where compliance with them was an indispensable condition for protection ('a condition of copyright').

The way of overcoming this problem was to simplify the formalities: under Article III 'any Contracting State which, under its domestic law, requires as a condition of copyright, compliance with formalities such as deposit, registration, notice, notarial certificates, payment of fees or manufacture[135] or publication in that Contracting State' undertakes to regard those requirements as having been satisfied in the case of any work protected by the Convention if, from the date of first publication of the work 'all the copies of the work published with the authority of the author or other copyright proprietor bear the symbol © accompanied by the name of the copyright proprietor and the year of first publication' (para. 1).

This provision does not preclude the Contracting States from requiring the performance of formalities in respect of 'works first published in its territory or works of its nationals wherever published' (para. 2). No formality is required, however, in respect of unpublished works falling within the sphere of the Convention (para. 4).

---

134. Cf. 'Report by the Rapporteur General', p. 85.
135. As Desbois points out, the manufacturing clause which is specific to United States legislation is not a formality, but pursues a different objective: it is protectionist in nature, being intended to safeguard a branch of industry and trade against foreign competition. However, in relations with the United States of America, the *neutralization* of this clause was regarded as fundamental by the United Kingdom, Canada and the other Commonwealth countries. 'The Evolution of Copyright in International Relations since the Brussels Conference (1948)', *RIDA*, January 1974, p. 306.

The simplification of formalities involved a sacrifice by both groups of countries: for the American Republics, it signified a breach with systems of formalities that were deeply rooted and widely maintained (for the United States, in particular, it involved laying aside the strict requirements of the copyright notice, registration, deposit and manufacturing clause); for the Member Countries of the Berne Union, acceptance of the symbol © was also a major concession, in view of the fact that the absence of formalities (or the principle of automatic protection) has been an important feature of the system established by the Berne Convention since the Berlin Revision of 1908.[136]

3. *The duration of protection*
Basic national rule. Article IV(1) stipulates the application of the principle of national treatment also in regard to the duration of protection: the length of protection is the period established by the law of the Contracting State in which protection is sought.

Minimum periods. Article IV(2) goes on to stipulate the *minimum terms* under the Convention which fall into four categories: the first three apply to works of all kinds apart from photographs and works of the applied arts which are covered by the minimum stipulated in the fourth and last instance. The differences between the first three categories of minimum duration are explained by the fact that these were fixed having regard not only to the legislations which lay down the general duration by reference to the life of the author, but also to the laws which do so from the time of publication or prior registration of the work (in the case of unpublished works).

As *a general principle*, the first subparagraph of Article IV(2) establishes that the term of protection shall not be less than the life of the author and twenty-five years after his death. This provision follows the model of the Berne Convention, but is considerably less protective (the figure in the Berne Convention is 50 years after the death of the author). The period indicated here was

---

136. Cf. S. Ricketson, op. cit., pp. 851–2, Section 15.23.

adopted to enable the Convention to be ratified by the many Member Countries which, in 1952, fixed general durations of 25 years after the death of the author or shorter terms (Haiti, where the term was the lifetime of the widow, twenty years for the children and ten years in the absence of children, Liberia and Poland which stipulated a term of 20 years and the former Soviet Union which provided for 15 years).[137]

Exceptions. The Convention provided for certain *exceptions to the basic rule* indicated above, with a view to facilitating acceptance of the Universal Convention firstly by the countries which did not use a single procedure for the calculation of terms but made use of a mixed system, i.e. in the case of one category of works the term is calculated from the date of first publication; and secondly by other countries, especially the United States of America, where legislation does not recognize the system based on the lifetime of the author so that this provision is not applicable to any category of works (the other country with a similar law being the Philippines). These *exceptions*, which are valid only in the States where the above criteria apply, are as follows:

- any Contracting State which, on the effective date of this Convention in that State, has limited the term of protection for certain classes of works to a period computed from the first publication of the work, shall be entitled to maintain these exceptions and to extend them to other classes of works. However, the term of protection shall not be less than twenty-five years from the date of first publication (Article IV(2), second subpara.). Bogsch points out that this option applied not only in relation to the classes of works for which the term of protection is calculated—on the effective date of entry into force of this Convention in that State—from the date of first publication but also to any other category of works to which the country may subsequently wish to extend the principle of computation of the period from first publication;
- the Convention goes on to stipulate (Article IV(2), 3rd sub-

---

137. Cf. Arpad Bogsch, op. cit., p. 48, paragraph 5.

para.) that any Contracting State which, on the effective date of this Convention in that State does not compute the term of protection on the basis of the life of the author, shall be entitled to compute the term of protection from the date of the first publication of the work or from its registration prior to publication (in the case of unpublished works), with the proviso that the term of protection shall not be less than twenty-five years from the date of the first publication or from registration prior to publication. The fourth paragraph goes on to add that 'if the legislation of a Contracting State grants two or more successive terms of protection, the duration of the first term shall not be less than one of the minimum periods specified above'.

The provisions of subparagraphs 3 and 4 of Article IV(2) must, as we have seen, be interpreted in the context of the legislation applicable in the United States (until it was replaced by the 1976 Act) which granted protection to published works from the date of publication for a term of twenty-eight years renewable for another of the same length. In regard to unpublished works, referring to the legislation applicable at the time, Bogsch points out that the applications for copyright protection in those works must be registered, although there is no explicit provision on the date of commencement or on the duration of protection of unpublished works in respect of which an application for copyright has been filed at the Copyright Office;[138]

- finally, Article IV(3) of the Convention makes provision for the duration of rights in *photographic works* and *works of the applied arts* by stipulating that the provisions of paragraph 2 shall not apply to them. However 'the term of protection in those Contracting States which protect photographic works, or works of applied art in so far as they are protected as artistic works, shall be not less than ten years for each of said classes of works'.

Method of comparison of the terms. Rule of the shortest duration. Following the Berne model, the Universal Convention stipulates a method of comparison of terms in Article IV(4) to (6):

---

138. Ibid., p. 53, paragraph 17.

- *duration in the country of origin of the work:* paragraph 4 establishes that no Contracting State shall be obliged to grant protection to a work for a period longer than that fixed in its country of origin; in the case of unpublished works, that is the State of which the author is a national and in the case of a published work, the State in which the work was first published (the Convention does not use the term 'country of origin', although this expression is habitually used for greater brevity). In the case of a work published for the first time in a non-contracting State, but whose author is a national of a member country of the Convention, the work shall be regarded as having been published for the first time in the latter (para. 5); and
- *simultaneous publication*: Article IV(6), also influenced by the Berne Convention, makes provision for *simultaneous publication*, by stipulating that when the work has appeared in two or more countries within 30 days of its first publication, it shall be regarded as having been published for the first time in the country which grants the shorter period of protection.

4. *Right of translation: compulsory licence (Article V).* Unlike the Berne Convention which recognizes and guarantees the basic and exclusive rights of the author, the only right applicable *jure conventionis* in the 1952 text of the Universal Convention on an exclusive basis is that of translation. This is explained by the importance of translations both in multilingual countries (for example India, the former Soviet Union, etc.) and in the Latin American Republics in which Spanish and Portuguese are spoken. Translations were and continue to be essential to facilitate the circulation and dissemination of works among countries where different languages are spoken.

The subject of translations therefore remained the 'international issue *par excellence*'[139] and assumed even greater prom-

---

139. This qualification, to which reference was made earlier, comes from the report by Louis Renault to the 1896 Conference on the Paris Additional Act and Interpretative Declaration (see above).

inence given the fact that some national legislations contained provisions which were highly prejudicial to foreign authors.[140] On the other hand, it was normal for the rights of reproduction and public communication to be generally recognized to varying degrees in national legislation with the result that, by application of the principle of assimilation (or national treatment), authors of works protected by the Convention benefited from the same degree of protection as authors of national works.

During the Geneva Conference, the text of Article V was the subject of lenghthy discussion. As the Rapporteur-General pointed out, the countries which wished to limit the right of translation considered it vital for the works of foreign authors to be readily available in their own national language. Some of these countries already belonged to the Berne Convention and had formulated reservations on the exclusive right of the author to permit the translation of a work into their languages; they stipulated that if the author failed to publish a translation within ten years of the first publication of the work (this was known as the 'ten-year rule') his right would lapse. They added that they could not be expected to subscribe to a Convention which granted authors a more extensive right of translation, while pointing out that other countries had been unable to accede to the Berne Convention because they felt that, even with their reservation, it did not give them sufficient guarantees that translations of foreign works could

---

140. Argentina provides a good illustration. Article 23 of the Law on Intellectual Property (1933) made it obligatory to register the translation contract with the National Copyright Registry within 12 months of the publication of the work. If this requirement is not met, anyone may publish a translation. The reasons for this provision reside in a strong current of Argentine opinion in favour of permitting the free translation into Spanish of foreign works or at least of imposing the manufacturing clause by analogy with the provisions which existed in the United States of America for works published in English. Ratification of the Universal Convention had highly beneficial effects in the case of works originating in the Contracting States by suspending application of this Article 23 to them since the authors enjoyed the exclusive right of translation *jure conventionis*.

be placed at the disposal of their citizens within a sufficiently short space of time. Many countries pointed out that scientific works became rapidly out of date and that a shorter period of exclusive protection was more essential in this particular case than for the translation of other works (three to five years).[141]

In the end, the Conference approved a text in which paragraph 1 recognized the exclusive right of the author to *make, publish* and *authorize the making and publication* of translations of protected works.

Compulsory translation licence. Paragraph 2 of Article V goes on to grant the Contracting States the possibility of restricting the exclusive right of translation by incorporating into their legislation a *compulsory licence* which must be subject to the following basic requirements set out at length in the relevant provisions:
- the compulsory translation licence may be established only in respect of written works;
- it may only be granted in respect of works whose translation into the national language or into one of the national languages of a Contracting State has not been published during a *period of seven years counting from the date of first publication of the work*; if it has been so published, the editions of the relevant translations must be out of print at the end of the stipulated term;
- the applicant must be a national of this Contracting State, and the licence will be for the translation and publication of the work in the national language in which it has not previously been published;
- the applicant must show that he has applied to the proprietor of the translation right for permission to make and publish the translation and that, after taking all the appropriate steps, he has been unable to trace the proprietor and obtain authorization from him;
- if the proprietor of the translation right has not been traced by

---

141. *Report*, op. cit., p. 90.

the applicant, the latter must transmit copies of his request to the publisher whose name appears on the copies of the work and to the diplomatic or consular representative of the State of which the former is a national, if his nationality is known, or to the agency designated by the government of that State;
- the licence may not be granted before a period of two months has elapsed from the date on which a copy of the application was forwarded.

Features of the compulsory translation licence. These features are shared by all non-voluntary licences:
- the licence is non-exclusive and non-assignable;
- it must guarantee respect for the moral right of the author (even without any mention thereof): that is to say, national legislation must guarantee a correct translation of the work, the title and name of the author of the original work must be printed on all copies of the published translation and the licence may not be granted if the author has withdrawn copies of the work from circulation;
- its effects are limited to the country which has granted the licence, but the importation and sale of copies in other Contracting States will be possible if that State has as its national language the language into which the work has been translated, if its national legislation permits a licence and if no legislative provisions prevent importation and sale;
- it shall earn remuneration: the national legislation of the State which establishes the compulsory licence must grant the owner of the translation right equitable remuneration in conformity with international practice, together with the payment and effective remittance of such remuneration.

The provision contained in Article V(2) is not self-implementing (capable of immediate application): it simply grants the Contracting States the possibility of adopting an internal provision (law, decree, regulation, etc.) establishing a compulsory translation licence. If one of these States decides to make use of this option, the national provision which is then adopted must be modelled on the rules which are laid out in the Convention in great detail.

e. Effects of the Convention

1. *Retroactive effect of the Convention (Article VII).* The Convention shall not apply to works or to rights in works which, on the date of its entry into force in the Contracting State in which protection is claimed, definitively fell within the public domain in that State (Article VII). This provision embodies a rule analogous to that set out in Article 18(2) of the Berne Convention.

The date to be taken into account is that of the entry into force of the Convention in the Contracting State in which protection is claimed. The reason for which the work is in the public domain is irrelevant. The obvious reason for the cessation of protection of works (in respect of economic rights) is the expiry of the term of protection of the right, although this is not the sole possibility.

2. *Effects of the Universal Convention in relation to other multilateral or bilateral conventions or agreements. Relations with the Berne Convention: safeguard clause (Article XVII and Appendix Declaration thereon).* Faced with the danger of massive desertion by the countries that had ratified the Berne Convention to join the Universal Convention which is less restrictive, the latter incorporates a clause to safeguard the former.

Article XVII stipulates that the Universal Convention shall not in any way affect the provisions of the Berne Convention or membership in the Union created by that Convention. With this aim in view, the Convention established two mechanisms intended to prevent desertion which are set out in the Appendix Declaration relating to Article XVII:
- The Universal Convention shall not apply to the relations between countries which are bound by the Berne Convention in regard to the protection of works which, in conformity with the latter, have, as their country of origin, one of the countries of the Berne Union (para. (b)); and
- works which, according to the Berne Convention, have as their country of origin a country which has withdrawn since 1 January 1951 from the International Union created by the said Convention, shall not be protected by the Universal Copyright Convention in the countries of the Berne Union (para. (a)).

Hence the general principle which is that the Berne Convention shall not be affected by the Universal Convention gives rise to two consequences: the priority of the Berne Convention in relations between the States which belong to both Conventions and the non-application of both to works originating in countries which have withdrawn from the Berne Union subsequent to a specific date.

Relations with the Conventions of the inter-American system (Art. XVIII). The Universal Convention also regulates its relations with the multilateral or bilateral conventions or agreements concluded between the American Republics by laying down three basic rules in Art. XVIII:
- the Universal Convention shall not abrogate conventions or agreements of the inter-American system;
- in the event of a divergence between the Universal Convention and the conventions or agreements of the inter-American system, the most recent texts shall prevail; and
- the Universal Convention shall not affect rights acquired in any Contracting State by virtue of conventions and agreements existing prior to the date on which the former came into force in the country concerned.

Relations with other conventions (Article XIX). The Universal Convention also regulates its relations with multilateral or bilateral conventions or agreements on authors' rights applicable between two or more Contracting States *which are not American Republics*, by establishing three basic rules in its Article XIX:
- the Universal Convention shall not abrogate the existing conventions and agreements;
- in the event of any difference between the provisions of such conventions or agreements and the Universal Convention, the provisions of the latter shall prevail;
- the Universal Convention shall not affect the rights acquired in a work by virtue of conventions or agreements in force in one of the Contracting States prior to the date of entry into force of the Convention in that State.

Article XIX stipulates in its final paragraph that it shall only be applied to relations between the Universal Convention and multilateral or bilateral conventions other than the Berne Convention (regulated by Article XVII and the Appendix Declaration thereon) or conventions of the inter-American system (which are governed by Article XVIII).

f. Provisions relating to the validity of the Convention

1. *Accession.* The *open* nature of the Universal Convention is clearly revealed by Article VIII(2) which states that 'any State which has not signed this Convention may accede thereto'.

In paragraph 3 of the same article, the Convention states that the States may become parties to the Convention by *ratification, acceptance* or *accession* which shall be done by depositing an instrument to that effect with the Director-General of UNESCO.

2. *Entry into force.* The Convention established in Article IX that the initial entry into force shall be three months after the deposit of 12 instruments of ratification or accession, among which there shall be those of four States which are not members of the Union (para. 1); subsequently the Convention shall come into force in respect of each State three months after that State has deposited its instrument of ratification or accession (para. 2).

3. *Reservations.* Article XX stipulates that 'reservations to this Convention shall not be permitted'. In other words, unlike the Berne Convention which did permit certain reservations, the Universal Convention may only be accepted in its entirety.

4. *Application by the Contracting States.* By virtue of paragraphs 1 and 2 of Article X, the Contracting States undertake that, at the time of deposit of their instruments of ratification, acceptance or accession, their national legislation will be such as to permit the application of the Convention. Each State will therefore take 'in accordance with its constitution' such measures as are necessary to ensure the application of this Convention.

A similar text was adopted in Article 36 of the Stockholm/Paris Act of the Berne Convention with a view to preventing the validity of self-executing or immediately applicable measures from being impeded in a Contracting State by failure to enact the provisions of domestic law necessary pursuant to the Constitution of the country concerned, for the application of these rules.

5. *Dependent territories.* The Convention provides in Article XIII for the possibility of its application to all dependent territories of a Contracting State ('for the international relations of which it is responsible'). A specific declaration must be made to that effect at the time when the instrument of ratification or accession is deposited, or subsequently, by notification to the Director-General of UNESCO with an indication of the countries or territories in which the Convention is to apply. The extension will take effect on the day following the expiration of three months from the date of deposit of the instrument of ratification or accession or, where appropriate, of notification.

6. *Denunciation of the Convention.* The only way in which a contracting country may terminate its membership of the Convention is by denunciation. Article XIV lays down the procedure: the denunciation shall be made by notification addressed to the Director-General of UNESCO and shall operate only in respect of the State or of the country or territory on whose behalf it was made and shall not take effect until 12 months after the date of the receipt of the notification.

7. *Revision.* The Convention provides for the possibility of its revision but, unlike the Berne Convention (Article 27(3)), unanimity of the votes cast is not required. The conditions for convening a revision conference set out in Article XII are as follows:
- a decision by the Intergovernmental Committee 'whenever it deems necessary'; or
- a decision by a specified number of Contracting States, not fewer than 10 or a majority if the number of Contracting States is fewer than 20.

The revision is a new Convention, even if it contains unrevised sections. Once the revised Convention has entered into force, accession to its predecessor will be impossible, but the countries which do not ratify the new text shall continue to be bound by the previous version.

g. The Intergovernmental Committee (Article XI and annexed resolution)

Article XI establishes an Intergovernmental Committee whose tasks are defined in paragraph 1 and membership in paragraph 2 and also in the resolution on the same article, adopted by the Geneva Conference on the same date as the Convention.

Paragraph 1 stipulates that the Committee shall be responsible for: (a) studying problems relating to the application and operation of the Convention; (b) preparing periodic revisions of the Convention, (c) studying any other problems concerning the international protection of copyright in co-operation with the various interested international bodies such as UNESCO, the Berne Union and the Organization of American States (this list is not exhaustive); and (d) informing the Contracting States as to its activities.

Bogsch points out that it emerges from the list set out in Article XI(1) that the Committee has no judicial authority, cannot settle controversies and cannot give interpretations of the Convention which are binding on contracting countries (although at its own initiative or at the request of a State or intergovernmental organization it may deliver opinions and produce advice on the meaning of the various provisions of the Convention and on whether the copyright law in a given country or proposed domestic legislation in this area satisfies the requirements of the Convention. However, these opinions are binding on no one, not even on the Committee itself, which may freely revise them). Neither has the Committee any legislative authority (it cannot amend the Convention) or administrative functions save in regard to the preparation (Article XI(1)(b) and convening (Article XII) of the revision conferences).[142]

The Committee shall consist of the representatives of 12 Contracting States to be selected with due consideration to fair

---

142. Arpad Bogsch, op. cit., p. 107.

geographical representation (Article XI(2)).[143] Each Member State of the Committee appoints a representative and an alternate who may be assisted by advisers. Members are eligible for re-election on an indefinite basis. Their term of office lasts for six years but one-third of the members are renewed every two years. Membership of the Committee lapses if the State concerned denounces the Convention or if its representative is unjustifiably absent from two successive ordinary sessions. The new members are elected by a simple majority of votes cast.

Pursuant to the decision reached by the Conference in the last but one paragraph of the resolution concerning Article XI, UNESCO provides the secretariat of the Committee. The communications of the Committee are therefore addressed to the Contracting States via the Director-General of UNESCO.

h. Functions of UNESCO

The Convention and the three Protocols contain various other references to the administrative functions of UNESCO. Some provisions assign specific tasks to the Director-General: he is the depository of the single original copy of the Convention (Article VIII), the instruments of ratification, acceptance and accession (Article VIII), the instruments relating to the application of the Convention to dependent countries or territories (Article XIII) and the instruments of denunciation (Article XIV).

The Director-General may attend—or appoint a representative to attend—meetings of the Intergovernmental Committee in an advisory capacity (Article XI); he will be responsible for arranging the preparation, at the request of any Contracting State or group of States, of texts of the Convention in languages other than the official languages (Article XVI); he shall forward duly certified copies of the Convention (Article XXI); he shall inform

---

143. In the resolution concerning Article XI the Geneva Conference designated the first 12 members of the Committee: Argentina, Brazil, France, Germany, India, Italy, Japan, Mexico, Spain, Switzerland, United Kingdom and the United States.

all the States concerned of the deposit of instruments of ratification, and accession, of the date of entry into force of the Convention, of the notification stipulated in Article XIII and all denunciations (Article XXI).

i. Other final clauses

1. *Languages.* The Convention was signed in English, French and Spanish and the three texts are equally authoritative. Official texts were also drawn up in German, Italian and Portuguese without prejudice to the possibility stipulated in Article XVI(2), second subparagraph, that one or more Contracting States may have other texts established by the Director-General of UNESCO, and by arrangement with him, in the languages of their choice.

2. *International jurisdiction clause.* Article XV stipulates that a dispute 'between two or more Contracting States concerning the interpretation or application of this Convention, not settled by negotiation, shall, unless the States concerned agree on some other method of settlement, be brought before the International Court of Justice for determination by it'.

This provision, which is modelled on the first paragraph of Article 27*bis* added to the Berne Convention by the Brussels revision (1948), relates only to the settlement of disputes between States and not between private individuals who are not allowed to appear as plaintiffs or defendants before the Court.

Bogsch reminds us that Article XV must be read in conjunction with the Statute of the International Court of Justice of the Hague which states in its Article 36 that 'the jurisdiction of the Court comprises [...] all matters specially provided for [...] in treaties or conventions in force', the Universal Convention being one such treaty or convention. The dispute may, for instance, refer to a matter of a legal nature (see Statute of the Court, Article 36(2)). Questions of 'interpretation' are those which concern the exact meaning of the provisions of the Convention; they are also known as structural questions. Typical disputes over the 'application' of the Convention relate to the existence of a particular fact which, once it has been established, constitutes a breach of an obligation set out in it (see Statute of the Court, Article 36(1)(c) or controversies concerning the nature and extent of the reparation to be made for the breach of an obligation resulting from the Universal Convention (see Statute of the Court, Article 36(1)(d).[144]

D. THE PROTOCOLS ATTACHED TO THE CONVENTION

The Conference approved three protocols attached to the Universal Convention.

Protocol 1, concerning the application of the Convention to the works of stateless persons and refugees, stipulates that such persons who 'have their habitual residence in a State party to this Protocol shall, for the purposes of the 1971 Convention, be assimilated to the nationals of that State'.

Protocol 2 provides for the Convention to be applicable to works published for the first time by certain international organizations: the United Nations (UN), the Specialized Agencies in relationship therewith (e.g. ILO, FAO, UNESCO, ICAO, WIPO, etc.) or the Organization of American States (OAS).

Both Protocols are in effect 'additional' because they do not form part of the Convention. Each must be accepted individually and the methods by which a country may become a party to the Protocols are similar to those required to belong to the Convention. They enter into force in each State on the date on which the State deposits its instrument of ratification, acceptance or accession to the Protocol, on condition that the State is already party to the Convention.

Protocol 3 on conditional accession to the Convention, authorizes any State which is party to it, on depositing its instrument of ratification, acceptance or accession to the Convention, to declare that this deposit shall not take effect for the purpose of Article IX (entry into force of the Convention) until another State ('any other State') named in such notification shall have deposited its instrument of ratification, acceptance or accession.

If a country makes its accession to the Convention conditional on that of another country which is expressly designated,

---

144. Arpad Bogsch, op. cit., p. 117.

the deposit of its instrument of ratification or accession shall not take effect until the same step is taken by the other country designated in the instrument of deposit of the Protocol (Bogsch[145] points out that the countries that have acceded to this Protocol have not designated another State on whose accession their own would be conditional).

E. RECOMMENDATIONS

The Geneva Conference made recommendations on the following questions: the activities of UNESCO in the area of copyright, pending the creation of the Intergovernmental Committee referred to in Article XI; the desirability of continuation in the Member States, the United Nations and UNESCO, of studies on methods of preventing double taxation; the restrictions on the transfer of currency representing the payment of copyright royalties; the possibility of creating a *fee-paying public domain* to obtain a modest payment in respect of the exploitation for gainful purposes of works falling within the public domain with a view to helping voluntary organizations or funds designed to aid authors (this recommendation resembled the wish already expressed on the same subject by the Berne Convention Revision Conference in Brussels in 1948). A recommendation was also made requiring the countries represented in the Tangiers Control Commission to examine without delay the application of the Universal Convention in that territory.

Ratifications and accessions: the Universal Convention came into force on 16 September 1955 three months after the twelfth instrument of ratification had been deposited pursuant to Article IX(1) including, in conformity with the stipulated minimum requirement, four countries not belonging to the Berne Union (these were Andorra, Cambodia, Costa Rica, Chile, United States, Haiti and Laos: the other five, all members of the Berne Union, were Germany, Spain, Israel, Monaco and Pakistan). Ratifications of and accessions to the Universal Convention went ahead rapidly.

---

145. Ibid., p. 170.

When the Revision Conference was held (Paris, July 1971) the Convention had 61 Contracting States.

The 1952 text continues to be applicable to the following countries (which did not ratify the 1971 revision):[146] Andorra, Argentina, Belarus, Belgium, Belize, Cambodia, Canada, Chile, Cuba, Fiji, Ghana, Greece, Guatemala, Haiti, Iceland, Ireland, Israel, Kazakstan, Laos, Lebanon, Liberia, Liechtenstein, Luxembourg, Malawi, Malta, Mauritius, Nicaragua, Nigeria, New Zealand, Pakistan, Paraguay, Philippines, Tajikistan, Ukraine, Venezuela and Zambia.

F. THE PARIS REVISION (1971)

The 1971 revision of the Universal Copyright Convention was preceded by a great many preparatory meetings dating back to 1966 at which it became apparent that the basic objective of the Paris Conference, in the words of the General Rapporteur, could not consist in a complete revision of the Convention but must be designed to satisfy the practical requirements of the developing countries by facilitating their access to educational, scientific and technical works, without weakening the structure and scope of copyright protection offered by developed countries under both the Universal Convention and of the Berne Convention.[147]

The programme for the Conference was based on a text proposed by the Intergovernmental Committee at the second Extraordinary Meeting held in Paris in September 1970 and arising from the recommendations of the Joint Study Group which had been convened in Washington in September 1969 under the auspices of BIRPI and UNESCO.[148] It was stipulated as a precondition that both conventions must be revised at the same time and place, while the priority objective in regard to the Universal Convention was to obtain the suspension for the benefit of the

---

146. Situation as at 1 January 1995. The list of Contracting States will be found at the end of the discussion of the 1971 text.
147. *Report* by the General Rapporteur of the Conference, p. 58.
148. See above; preparations for the Paris revision of the Berne Convention.

developing countries of the safeguard clause set out in the 1952 text of the Berne Convention (Article XVII and Appendix Declaration thereon) together with the inclusion, firstly, of provisions intended to facilitate translation and reproduction for these countries at least for teaching and research purposes and without material reciprocity, and secondly (perhaps by way of compensation), recognition of the 'basic rights constituting the author's economic right'. Specific mention was made of the rights of reproduction, broadcasting and public performance while leaving States free to establish their own limitations.

The Conference for revision of the Universal Copyright Convention was held in accordance with the Recommendations of the Washington Group approved by the Intergovernmental Committee 'on the same date and at the same place' as the Conference for revision of the Stockholm Act of the Berne Convention (by invitation of UNESCO at its Headquarters in Paris from 5 to 24 July 1971). However, the meetings of the two conferences were never simultaneous.

The Conference for revision of the Universal Convention opened in plenary session on the morning of 5 July and was attended by delegations from 45 Contracting States, observers from another 30 States, three intergovernmental organizations (ILO, WIPO and Council of Europe) and 16 non-governmental international organizations. Ambassador Pierre Charpentier (France) was elected President of the Conference, Abraham L. Kaminstein (United States), at the time Register of Copyrights, General Rapporteur, with the assistance, for health reasons, of Barbara Ringer (Assistant Register of Copyrights and, subsequently, Register of copyrights). Rafik Saïd (Tunisia) was appointed Chairman of the Main Commission and William Wallace (United Kingdom), Chairman of the Drafting Committee.

G. THE CURRENT TEXT (24 JULY 1971).
DIFFERENCES FROM THE 1952 CONVENTION

The recommendations of the Washington Study Group reflect the three principal differences between the 1971 and 1952 texts:
- the new Article IV*bis* which, while recognizing the existence of 'the basic rights ensuring the protection of the author's eco-

nomic interests' (para. 1) allows national legislation to impose limits on these rights (para. 2);
- Articles V*bis*, *ter* and *quater* lay down provisions in favour of the developing countries with a content which is deliberately similar to that of the Appendix adopted at the same time by the Berne Convention Revision Conference (both amendments correspond to the Washington Recommendations I(2) and (3): inclusion of the author's basic rights of reproduction, broadcasting, public performance and showing, and inclusion of rules in favour of the developing countries to allow them to restrict the economic rights pertaining exclusively to the author, together with the scope of the translation right; and
- the temporary suspension, for the benefit of the developing countries, of the safeguard clause of the Berne Convention throughout the period for which a developing State is able, in conformity with the provisions of the new Article V*bis*, to lay claim to the exceptions provided in the 1971 Convention for these countries (new para. (b) of the Appendix Declaration relating to Article XVII which corresponds to the Washington Recommendation I(1)—suspension of Article XVII and of the Appendix Declaration for the benefit of the developing countries).

a. Recognition of economic rights; possibility of imposing limitations (Article IVbis)

The new Article IV*bis* is divided into two parts: the first recognizes the basic rights ensuring the author's economic interests, while the second grants the Contracting States the possibility of imposing limitations on these rights, provided that they 'do not conflict with the spirit and provisions of this Convention'.

The wording of paragraph 1 of Article IV*bis* shows it to be an addition to Article I[149] (which imposes on the States the obligation to 'provide for the adequate and effective protection of the

---

149. Cf. Henri Desbois, André Françon and André Kerever, op. cit., p. 238, Section 203.

rights of authors and other copyright proprietors') by stipulating that: 'The rights referred to in Article I shall include the basic rights ensuring the author's economic interests, including the exclusive right to authorize reproduction by any means, public performance and broadcasting.'

Furthermore, the last part of Article IV*bis*(1) recognizes the right of adaptation by stipulating that 'the provisions of this article shall extend to works protected under this Convention either in their original form or in any form recognizably derived from the original'.

It follows that the exclusive right of translation embodied (*jure conventionis*) in the 1952 text (Article V) is supplemented in the 1971 revision by the rights—again exclusive—granted by Article IV*bis*.

Paragraph 2 enables the exclusive rights embodied in the previous paragraph to be considerably reduced by authorizing any Contracting State: 'by its domestic legislation, to make exceptions that do not conflict with the spirit and provisions of this Convention, to the rights mentioned in paragraph 1 of this Article. Any State whose legislation so provides, shall nevertheless accord a reasonable degree of effective protection to each of the rights to which exception has been made'.

This wording, which is not altogether precise, warrants careful analysis and prudent interpretation. It sets out the conditions which Article IV*bis* imposes on the right of the States to introduce limitations on the economic rights recognized in the Convention:

1. *The exceptions must not conflict with the spirit and provisions of the 1971 Convention.* In his report, the General Rapporteur drew attention[150] to the view of the Conference that over and above the requirement of 'adequate and effective protection' stipulated in Article I, the 'spirit' of the Convention also included the principles set out in paragraphs 1 and 2 of Article 27 of the Universal Declaration of Human Rights: everyone 'has the right freely to participate in the cultural life of the Community' and everyone is

---

150. *Report* of the General Rapporteur, para. 46, p. 67.

likewise entitled to the 'protection of the moral and material interests resulting from any scientific, literary or artistic production of which he is the author'.

The General Rapporteur points out that paragraph 83 of the Report of the Intergovernmental Copyright Committee which accompanied the programme for the Conference (IGCP text, September 1970) drew attention to the Committee's view that the 'inclusion in the Convention of special provisions permitting the developing countries to publish certain works and translations by virtue of compulsory licences meant, *a contrario*, that except as provided in Article V, there could be no question of the developed countries instituting a general system of compulsory licensing for the publication of literary, scientific and artistic works'. The Conference approved this principle on the understanding that a 'general system' referred either to a system applying to a specific type of work with respect to all forms of uses or to a system applying to all types of works with respect to a particular form of use.[151]

As a corollary to the *a contrario* principle, the Conference held that the reference to the 'provisions' of the revised Convention concerned Articles V*ter* and *quater*. This meant that a country that was not regarded as a developing country under Article V*bis* was not entitled to establish licensing systems similar to those provided in Article V*ter* and *quater*.[152]

2. *The State must grant a 'reasonable degree of effective protection' to each of the designated rights.* The General Rapporteur points out that by virtue of the second sentence of Article IV*bis*(2), no State would be entitled to withhold entirely all rights relating to reproduction, public performance and showing and broadcasting and that such exceptions as might be made must have a logical basis and not be applied arbitrarily; moreover, protection must be effectively enforced by the laws of the Contracting State.[153]

---

151. Ibid.
152. Ibid.
153. Ibid.

Desbois, Françon and Kerever rightly believe that the words *'a reasonable degree of effective protection'* lead on to the compulsory licence which involves payment of equitable remuneration in return for free use. The protection which continues even after cessation of the exclusive right would seem to refer to this remuneration. The compensation must be calculated at a reasonable rate and be effectively paid.[154]

b. Licences for translation and reproduction which may be established by the developing countries (Article Vbis, ter and quater)

The system of compulsory licences for translation and reproduction that may be adopted by the developing countries figures in Article V*bis, ter* and *quater* of the 1971 Convention which correspond to Articles I to IV of the Appendix to the Paris Act of the Berne Convention.

The discussion of the system of compulsory licences authorized in the developing countries and substantially similar in both Conventions, took place primarily at the Conference on the Universal Convention. As the General Rapporteur points out, the discussions on the procedures to be applied for the granting of translation and reproduction licences which were held during the meetings of the Main Commissions of the Berne Convention and the Universal Convention, together with the debates in plenary session on the Universal Convention, were among the 'thorniest and most time-consuming that the delegates had to endure'.[155]

In the text of the Universal Convention, the special provisions relating to the developing countries were inserted in the existing

---

154. '*"Un niveau raisonnable de protection effective" doit être respecté par ce régime des licences. Cette formule oriente l'esprit vers la licence obligatoire, qui comporte en contrepartie de la libre exploitation, le versement d'une rémunération équitable. C'est à cette rémunération que paraît se référer la protection qui servit à l'ablation du droit exclusif. L'indemnité doit être calculée à un taux raisonnable et donner lieu à un paiment effectif*' (Henri Desbois, André Françon and André Kerever, op. cit., p. 243, para. (b)).
155. *Report*, para. 50, p. 68.

numbering (instead of appearing in an Appendix as in the case of the Berne Convention). Their main characteristics are as follows.

Article Vbis (corresponding to Article I of the Berne Appendix) defines the Contracting States which may avail themselves of the system concerned as developing countries 'in conformity with the established practice of the General Assembly of the United Nations'; the procedure to be followed for this purpose and the period of validity of exceptions; the disposal of copies in existence after the expiry of this period and the extension of the system to dependent territories.

During the discussion of Article V*bis*, the question arose as to whether, as the General Rapporteur points out, since the draft text of the revised Berne Convention contained a provision by virtue of which material reciprocity shall not apply to those States which use special translation and reproduction licences,[156] it was appropriate or not to include a similar clause in the revised text of the Convention. There was no disagreement whatever on the content of this question: *the Conference unanimously decided that material reciprocity could not apply in this situation*. It had already agreed in the same debate that if a provision of this kind were to be included in the text of the Universal Convention it should not appear in Article V*bis* but in a general clause later in the Convention. A decision had to be taken as to whether this declaration opposing material reciprocity should be contained in the text of the Convention itself or be included in the General Report. The latter option was finally chosen. In consequence, the report included the relevant text in which note was taken of the general agreement by the Conference on the following points:

1. With regard to material reciprocity, no discrimination should be made between the exceptions in Articles V*ter* and V*quater* and those in Article IV*bis*.
2. The fact of a State availing itself of any exception should in no case permit other Contracting States to reduce the level of protection granted by them to works originating in the State in question.

---

156. This provision figures in Article I, para. 6(b) of the Appendix to the Paris Act of the Berne Convention.

3. The principle of the absence of material reciprocity already exists in the 1952 Convention. It derives from the principle of the assimilation of foreign authors and works to national authors and works.

The fact that this reciprocity applies only on one specific point, namely the duration of protection, emphasizes that this is the sole exception to a general principle; if the text is silent, that silence can only be interpreted in the light of the principle of non-reciprocity.[157]

Article Vter deals with all aspects relating to the translation licence (reflected in Articles II and IV of the Berne Appendix) while *Article Vquater* (corresponding to Article II and IV of the Berne Appendix) follows the same procedure in respect of the reproduction licence. The method used in the Universal Convention, as compared to that followed in the Appendix to the Berne Convention, has the advantage of facilitating knowledge of all the provisions concerning each compulsory licence without the need to read all the articles. But it does involve repetitions in Article V*ter* and V*quater* which were avoided by the method used in the Appendix to the Berne Convention.[158]

Article V*ter* stipulates that licences for translation and publication of a translation are non-exclusive and non-transferable and may be granted solely for teaching, scholarship or research purposes in respect of works published in the printed form or by an analogous method of reproduction if, on the expiry of a period of three years from the date of first publication of the work, the latter has not been translated into a language in general use in one or more developed countries. This term is reduced to one year in the case of a translation into a language which is not in general use in one or more developed countries.

The applicant, who must be a national of the Contracting State which grants the licence, must prove that he has sought authorization from the proprietor of the translation right and could

---

157. *Report*, para. 59, p. 71.
158. Henri Desbois, André Françon and André Kerever, op. cit., Section 256, p. 308.

not trace him or obtain the necessary authorization. The licence cannot be granted before an additional period of six months has expired when it is obtainable after a period of three years. The additional period is of nine months when the licence is obtainable on the expiry of a period of one year. During these additional periods, the proprietor of the translation right has the opportunity to publish a translation or to enter into a contract with a third party, in which case the licence shall not be granted; the licence will not be valid for export; it must stipulate equitable remuneration, that payment will be made and the remuneration duly remitted. The licence lapses if the proprietor of the translation right publishes, or enters into a contract for publication of the work at a price comparable to that normally charged in the country in question. Provided that certain conditions are respected, the Convention authorizes the granting of a licence to make a translation for broadcasting purposes.

Article V*quater* (corresponding to Articles III and IV of the Berne Appendix) deals with all aspects of licences for the reproduction of works in their original language which may be granted only to satisfy the requirements of the general public and of school and university users at a price similar to that normally charged for equivalent works in the State in which the licence is applied for.

The licences for reproduction are non-exclusive and non-transferable. They apply solely to literary, scientific or artistic works published in printed form or by any other analogous means of reproduction. However, they also apply to the reproduction in audiovisual form of authorized audiovisual fixations and to the translation of any text accompanying them into a language generally used in the State which grants the licence, provided that these works have been produced and published for the sole purpose of school or university use.

They may only be granted to a national of the State in which the application is made when a period of five years has expired from the date of the first publication of a particular edition. That period shall be reduced to three years for works of the natural and physical sciences and of technology, but increased to seven years for works of the imagination such as fiction, poetry, drama and music and for art books. The Convention provides additional terms of three or six months to attempt to obtain a reply from the proprietor of the reproduction right.

Reproduction made under licence must faithfully respect the work and show the name of the author and the title in printed form on every copy. The licence will not be valid for export but only for publication on the territory of the State which grants it. It involves the effective payment of an equitable remuneration and the remittance of that remuneration. It will lapse if copies of an edition of a published work are put on sale by the proprietor of the reproduction right or with his authorization.

The licence for reproduction may not be granted if the author has withdrawn all copies of the edition from circulation.

Developing countries which have availed themselves of the preferential system created for them in the Universal Convention as at 1 March 1993: Algeria, Bangladesh, Bolivia, Mexico, Republic of Korea and Tunisia (see *Copyright Bulletin* (Paris), UNESCO, No. 1/1993, pp. 14–18).

c. Temporary suspension of the safeguard clause in the Berne Convention in favour of the developing countries (new para. (b) of the Appendix Declaration relating to Article XVII)

In accordance with the Washington Recommendations (I,1) approved by the Intergovernmental Committee, a new paragraph (b) was inserted in the Appendix Declaration relating to Article XVII (the previous para. (b) in the 1952 text has become (c) in the 1971 text). Under this new paragraph (b), a country which is regarded as a developing country in conformity with the established practice of the General Assembly of the United Nations, may avoid the consequences established in the safeguard clause if, at the time of its withdrawal from the Berne Union, it deposits with the Director-General of UNESCO a notification to the effect that it regards itself as a developing country. This means that despite its withdrawal from the Berne Convention after the date established in the safeguard clause (1 January 1951), this developing country will be governed by the Universal Convention in its relations with the member countries of the Berne Union for the whole period during which the State in question may avail itself, pursuant to the provisions of Art. V*bis*, of the exceptions set out in the 1971 Convention. In consequence, the safeguard clause continues to exist and no derogation in regard to the developed countries is permitted (*Declaration* ..., para. a)), although it is in the case of the developing countries.

d. Other differences from the 1952 Convention

1. *Relations between Member States of the Universal Convention: applicability of the texts of 1952 and 1971.* Relations between the two texts are governed by paragraphs 3 and 4 of Article IX of the 1971 Convention.

Paragraph 3 stipulates that if a State is not a party to the 1952 Convention but does accede to the 1971 Convention, it will automatically belong to the 1952 Convention and once the 1971 Convention has entered into force, it will be impossible for it to subscribe solely to the 1952 Convention. This provision ensures the existence of a common text between two States which are members of the Convention of 1952 or 1971 by establishing a legal basis for their mutual obligations in the area of copyright; however, it also enables the 1971 text to supersede the 1952 text as it attracts more and more ratifications and accessions.[159]

This provision drew on the experience gathered within the Berne Union in connection with the problem of relations between member countries of the Union caused by the existence of different Acts of the Convention. The problem of their applicability was not settled until the Stockholm Revision (Article 32).

The first part of paragraph 4 stipulates that relations between the States which are parties to the 1971 Convention and those that have acceded only to the 1952 Convention, shall be governed by the latter.

Nevertheless the second part of paragraph 4 lays down that any State which is a party only to the 1952 Convention may, by a notification deposited with the Director-General of UNESCO,

---

159. *Report*, para. 120, p. 87.

declare that it agrees to the application of the 1971 text to works of its nationals or those published for the first time in its territory (i.e. works originating in its territory).

This latter possibility reflected the need of the developing countries which wanted special measures in their own favour, to obtain the greatest possible certainty that the developed countries belonging to the Universal Convention would allow the provisions of Article V*bis*, *ter* and *quater* to be applied to their works, even if they did not ratify the 1971 Convention.

2. *Amendments to Articles II, X, XI, XIII and XVI*. Article II: in this article, which lays down the basic principle of national treatment for both published and unpublished works, an additional reference is made to 'the protection specially granted by this Convention'. That phrase, which is similar to the wording of Article 5, paragraph 1, last part, of the Berne Convention emphasizes the fact that the rules of minimum protection are uniformly applicable to works falling within the sphere of applicability of the Universal Convention.

Article X: under the 1952 text each Contracting State was required to be in a position to give effect to the provisions of the Convention at the time of depositing its instrument of ratification or accession. The 1971 text grants an additional period of three months, by stipulating that the State must be able to apply the provisions on the date on which the Convention enters into force.

Article XI: the number of members of the Intergovernmental Committee which was fixed at 12 in the 1952 text, is increased to '18 States party to this Convention or only to the 1952 Convention'. The latter reference makes it perfectly clear that, although there are two Conventions, the Intergovernmental Committee is the same for both; this is logical, given the number of identical provisions contained in the different texts and the relationship between them (for example Article IX, paras. 3 and 4, commented on above).

Article XIII: a new paragraph is added to stipulate that the decision of a Contracting State which declares that the Convention is applicable to a country or territory for whose external relations it is responsible must not be 'understood as implying the recognition or tacit acceptance' of a political situation by any other contracting State.

Article XVI: Arabic is added to the second paragraph as one of the languages in which the official texts of the Convention are to be established.

3. *Ratifications and accessions*: the 1971 Convention entered into force on 10 July 1974, three months after the deposit of the twelfth instrument of ratification pursuant to Article IX, paragraph 1 (in which there was no longer any reference to the requirement of four countries not belonging to the Berne Union that had been included in the equivalent provision of the 1952 text).

The following list shows that these countries were Algeria, Cameroon, France, Germany, Hungary, Kenya, Senegal, Spain, Switzerland, United Kingdom, United States and former Yugoslavia.

*Treaties in the Field of Copyright and Neighbouring Rights
not Administered by WIPO*[1]
*Universal Copyright Convention
Adopted at Geneva (1952), Revised at Paris (1971)*

State	Date on which the State became a party to the Convention	
	1952 text	1971 text
Algeria[2]	28 August 1973	28 August 1973
Andorra[a)(b)]	–	–
Argentina	13 February 1958	–
Australia	1 May 1969	28 February 1978
Austria	2 July 1957	14 August 1982
Bahamas	13 October 1976	27 December 1976
Bangladesh[2]	5 August 1975	5 August 1975
Barbados	18 June 1983	18 June 1983
Belarus	27 May 1973	–
Belgium	31 August 1960	–
Belize	1 March 1983	–
Bolivia	22 March 1990	22 March 1990
Bosnia and Herzegovina	11 May 1966	3 October 1973
Brazil	13 January 1960	11 December 1975
Bulgaria	7 June 1975	7 June 1975
Cambodia	3 November 1953	–
Cameroon	1 May 1973	1 May 1973
Canada	10 August 1962	–
Chile	18 April 1955	–
China[2]	30 October 1992	30 October 1992
Colombia	18 June 1976	18 June 1976
Costa Rica	7 March 1955	7 March 1980
Croatia	11 May 1966	3 October 1973
Cuba	18 June 1957	–
Cyprus	19 December 1990	19 December 1990
Czech Republic	6 January 1960	17 April 1980
Denmark	9 February 1962	11 July 1979
Dominican Republic	8 May 1983	8 May 1983
Ecuador	5 June 1957	6 September 1991
El Salvador	29 March 1979	29 March 1979
Fiji	13 March 1972	–
Finland	16 April 1963	1 November 1986
France	14 January 1956	11 December 1972
Germany	3 September 1955	18 January 1974

State	Date on which the State became a party to the Convention	
	1952 text	1971 text
Ghana	22 August 1962	–
Greece	24 August 1963	–
Guatemala	28 October 1964	–
Guinea	13 November 1981	13 November 1981
Haiti	1 December 1954	–
Holy See	5 October 1955	6 May 1980
Hungary	23 January 1971	15 December 1972
Iceland	18 December 1956	–
India	21 January 1958	7 April 1988
Ireland	20 January 1959	–
Israel	6 July 1955	–
Italy	24 January 1957	25 January 1980
Japan	28 April 1956	21 October 1977
Kazakstan	27 May 1973	–
Kenya	7 September 1966	4 April 1974
Laos	19 November 1954	–
Lebanon	17 October 1959	–
Liberia	27 July 1956	–
Liechtenstein	22 January 1959	–
Luxembourg	15 October 1955	–
Malawi	26 October 1965	–
Malta	19 November 1968	–
Mauritius	20 November 1970	–
Mexico[2]	12 May 1957	31 October 1975
Monaco	16 September 1955	13 December 1974
Morocco	8 May 1972	28 January 1976
Netherlands	22 June 1967	30 November 1985
New Zealand	11 September 1964	–
Nicaragua	16 August 1961	–
Niger	15 May 1989	15 May 1989
Nigeria	14 February 1962	–
Norway	23 January 1963	7 August 1974
Pakistan	25 July 1954	–
Panama	17 October 1962	3 September 1980
Paraguay	11 March 1962	–
Peru	16 October 1963	22 July 1985
Philippines	19 November 1955	–
Poland	9 March 1977	9 March 1977
Portugal	25 December 1956	30 July 1981

State	Date on which the State became a party to the Convention	
	1952 text	1971 text
Republic of Korea[2]	1 October 1987	1 October 1987
Russian Federation	27 May 1973	9 March 1995
Rwanda	10 November 1989	10 November 1989
Saint Vincent and the Grenadines	22 April 1985	22 April 1985
Saudi Arabia	13 July 1994	13 July 1994
Senegal	9 July 1974	9 July 1974
Slovakia	6 January 1960	17 April 1980
Slovenia	11 May 1966	3 October 1973
Spain	27 January 1955	10 July 1974
Sri Lanka	25 January 1984	25 January 1984
Sweden	1 July 1961	27 September 1973
Switzerland	30 March 1956	21 September 1993
Tajikistan	27 May 1973	–
Trinidad and Tobago	19 August 1988	19 August 1988
Tunisia[2]	19 June 1969	10 June 1975
Ukraine	27 May 1973	–
United Kingdom	27 September 1957	19 August 1972
United States of America	6 March 1955	18 December 1972
Uruguay	12 April 1993	12 April 1993
Venezuela	30 September 1966	–
Yugoslavia	11 May 1966	3 October 1973
Zambia	1 June 1965	–

(Total: 95 States)

1. According to the information received by the International Bureau.
2. Pursuant to Article V*bis* of the Convention as revised in 1971, this State has availed itself of the exception provided for in Articles V*ter* and V*quater* in favour of developing countries
(a) 31 March 1953—Communication from the President of the French Republic, co-Prince of Andorra.
(b) 22 March 1953—Communication from the Bishop of Urgel, co-Prince of Andorra.

Editor's Note
The three Protocols annexed to the Convention were ratified, accepted or acceded to separately: they concern: (1) the application of the Convention to the works of stateless persons and refugees, (2) the application of the Convention to the works of certain international organizations, and (3) the effective date of instruments of ratification or acceptance of or accession to the Convention. For detailed information in this respect, and as to notifications made by governments of certain Contracting States concerning the territorial application of the Convention and the Protocols, see *Copyright Bulletin*, quarterly review published by UNESCO.

12.4.2.3. Multilateral Convention for the Avoidance of Double Taxation of Copyright Royalties (Madrid, 13 December 1979)

A. ORIGIN OF THE CONVENTION

The problem of the double taxation of copyright royalties arises for all natural and legal persons who engage in international activities of any kind. A traditional example is that of the author who has authorized the translation and performance of his work abroad. Taxes are withheld on the royalties accruing to him in the country in which these uses are made (*taxation at source*), to which must be added a further tax in the country in which the author habitually resides (*taxation based on residence*). Because of this double taxation and the costs of collection and transfer, the author receives only a negligible proportion of the royalties that were originally due to him. This situation affects the legitimate interests of the author and is an obstacle to the exchange of cultural works and goods. The need to find a remedy is self-evident.

Solutions may take the form of bilateral reciprocal conventions between States or of general agreements for which models have been developed by the Organization for Economic Co-operation and Development (OECD) and the United Nations. It will be noted that as far back as 1952, the Geneva Conference which adopted the Universal Convention also adopted the following recommendation on double taxation of copyright royalties: 'The Conference expresses the wish that the various States, the United Nations and UNESCO continue to study the ways and means by which the double taxation of copyright fees (royalties) could be avoided.'

In 1975, 1976 and 1978, three Committees of Governmental Experts met in Paris at the joint invitation of UNESCO and WIPO. Their work led to the diplomatic conference that was held in Madrid in 1979.

Although some would have preferred the procedure of general agreements referred to above with models drawn up by the OECD and the United Nations, the three Committees chose the system of specific agreements for the following fundamental reasons:
- it is easier to reach agreement on the taxation of copyright royalties alone, since the financial implications of this for the States are exceptionally low;
- owing to the irregularity of returns, their legal peculiarities, intellectual origin and the place they occupy in the development of culture and education, these royalties cannot be assimilated to other forms of income but require special protection.

Once the method of specific agreements had been adopted, the choice between measures involving a multilateral instrument or bilateral agreements remained open.[160]

The second Committee of Experts (1976), after noting that tax and copyright laws differed so widely that it was impossible to draw up a detailed multilateral convention, instructed the Secretariats of UNESCO and WIPO to establish a draft multilateral convention restricted to general principles, and accompanied by a model bilateral agreement, drawn up in several alternative versions for submission to States by way of illustration. This compromise solution was approved by the Third Committee (1978) which prepared the drafts that were used as a basis for the work of the Conference.[161]

B. MADRID DIPLOMATIC CONFERENCE (1979)

The International Conference of States on the Double Taxation of Copyright Royalties remitted from one country to another, con-

---

160. See 'Final Act of the International Conference'. *Copyright Bulletin* (Paris), UNESCO, No. 1-2/1980, p. 44.
161. Ibid.

vened jointly by the Directors-General of UNESCO and WIPO, was held in Madrid at the invitation of the Spanish Government from 26 November to 13 December 1979. The Conference approved the text of the multilateral Convention which contains 17 Articles to which is attached an optional Model Bilateral Agreement for the avoidance of double taxation of copyright royalties, and an Additional Protocol.

C. THE TEXT OF THE CONVENTION

The Madrid Convention is a treaty under public international law. It does not establish individual rights but is an agreement between States.

a. The purpose of the Convention

The fundamental provision is set out in Article 8 (1) whereby each Contracting State undertakes to make every possible effort, in accordance with its constitution and the guiding principles set out in the Convention, to avoid double taxation of copyright royalties, where possible and, should it subsist, to eliminate it or to reduce its effect.

This provision fixes the scope of the agreement entered into by the States in that it defines the basic obligation incumbent upon them by virtue of the Convention as being to '*make every possible effort* [...] *to avoid* ...'.

b. Means of implementing action to avoid the double taxation of copyright royalties

Article 8(1) concludes by stipulating that the action 'shall be carried out by means of bilateral agreements or by way of domestic measures'.

According to the interpretation given by the French delegation during the Conference, this Article 8.1 lays down an obligation of methods but not an obligation as to results.[162] The

---

162. Ibid., p. 50.

bilateral agreements referred to in this first paragraph of Article 8 may be general agreements on double taxation or specific agreements on the double taxation of copyright royalties.

c. Annexed Model Bilateral Agreement

A model agreement is attached to the Convention by way of illustration, but does not form an integral part thereof.

d. The guiding principles for action

Articles 5–7 set out guiding principles for action against double taxation of copyright royalties.

Article 5 defines the conditions under which this action is to be taken and puts forward three substantive ideas:
- the action shall be taken in accordance with the provisions of Article 8 which establishes the content of the agreement entered into by the States by virtue of the Convention;
- it must respect the fiscal sovereignty of the State of some of the royalties and the State of residence; and (c) must have due respect for the equality of the right of both the States to tax these royalties.

Article 6 stipulates that the measures taken against double taxation shall not produce fiscal discrimination of any kind based on nationality, race, sex, language or religion. This text embodies one of the oldest principles of international tax law and is simply a corollary to the general principle of tax equality founded on the criterion of fiscal justice. The enumeration of cases of discrimination given in Article 6 is merely indicative.[163]

e. Definitions

Articles 1 to 4 set out definitions of (1) copyright royalties; (2) the beneficiary of copyright royalties; (3) the State of residence of the beneficiary and (4) the State of source of the royalties.

---

163. Ibid., p. 49.

f. Fiscal privileges of members of diplomatic or consular missions

Article 9 stipulates that the Convention does not affect the fiscal privileges of members of diplomatic or consular missions of the Contracting State as well as of their families, either under the general rules of international law or under the provisions of special conventions. During the Conference, it was agreed that the broadening of the guarantee to the 'families' of members of diplomatic or consular missions extended only to members of the family living under the same roof.

g. Reservations

Since some delegations pointed out that the practices existing in their countries did not permit this extension of fiscal privileges to the 'families' of members of diplomatic or consular missions, it was decided that this provision might be the subject of reservations pursuant to Article 12 of the Convention.[164] This latter article also provides for the possibility of entering reservations over the conditions of application of the provisions contained in Articles 1–4 (definitions) and 17 (international jurisdiction clause).

h. Entry into force

Pursuant to Article 13, the Convention is to enter into force three months after the deposit of the tenth instrument of ratification, acceptance or accession. Despite the considerable time that has elapsed since its adoption, entry into force has not yet become effective. As of 1 March 1993 only five countries had acceded to the Madrid Convention.[165]

However, many double taxation agreements have been concluded between the industrialized countries belonging to the

---

164. Ibid.
165. Ricketson is of the opinion that the reason why so few countries have acceded to the Madrid Convention may reside in the fact that its requirements are exhortatory rather than mandatory. (op. cit., p. 885).

OECD and, although fewer, some also with developing countries. Some national legislations lay down additional rules which help to avoid double taxation. On the other hand, few agreements of this kind have been reached between developing countries, despite the fact that cultural exchanges between them are frequent.[166] In this regard, the *preamble* to the Madrid Convention places particular emphasis on the need to find solutions which will enable the developing countries to gain the widest possible access to works of the mind. Attention is also drawn to the encouraging results achieved by bilateral agreements and domestic measures against double taxation. The conclusion of a multilateral convention specific to copyright royalties could be expected to improve these results. However, the Convention has so far failed to achieve this.

---

166. Reinhold Kreile points out that agreements concluded between developing countries and industrialized countries also provide for the remuneration paid in respect of the authorization to use literary, artistic and scientific works to be protected against double taxation in the same way as payments made for industrial and commercial licences. This principle is set out in Article 12 of the United Nations model agreement. However, the model drawn up by the member countries of the Cartagena Agreement or the Andean Pact for the conclusion of agreements with the industrialized countries constitutes an exception in this regard since its Article 9 is confined to industrial property rights ('Taxation of Authors under International Fiscal Law and the Madrid Convention for the Avoidance of Double Taxation of Copyright Royalties', *Copyright* (Geneva), WIPO, September 1984, p. 319.

*Multilateral Convention for the Avoidance of Double Taxation of Copyright Royalties and Additional Protocol*ª adopted in Madrid, 13 December 1979

State	Date of deposit of the instrument		Reservations
	Convention	Protocol	
Czech Republic	28 May 1993	28 May 1993	
Ecuador	26 October 1994		
Egypt	11 February 1982		
India	31 January 1983		
Iraq	15 July 1981		
Peru	15 April 1988		
Slovakia	30 September 1993	30 September 1993	*

(Total: 7 States)

a. Situation as at 1 February 1995; see *Copyright Bulletin* (Paris), UNESCO, No. 1, 1996.
(* Reservations): India does not consider itself bound by Articles 1 to 4 and 17 of the Convention.

12.4.2.4. Treaty on the International Registration of Audiovisual Works (Geneva, 18 April 1989)

The creation of an international register of audiovisual works responded to the need to increase legal security in transactions relating to such works and to facilitate the control of piracy[167] by defining the identity of the beneficiaries of each of the rights (reproduction, distribution, public communication etc.) on each

---

167. The term '*Piracy*' denotes the manufacture, sale, etc. of copies effected on a commercial scale in contravention of rights protected by copyright. (See *Model Provisions of WIPO for National Laws*, memorandum by the International Bureau, doc. C&P/CE/2 dated 18 February 1988, p. 2).

territory, having regard to the international extent and economic scale reached by the exploitation of cinematographic works and television films.

A. ORIGIN OF THE TREATY[168]

In March 1981, during the 'WIPO Worldwide Forum on the Piracy of Sound and Audiovisual Recordings' held in Geneva, the possibility of establishing this international register was first mooted. The idea was discussed between 1981 and 1984 under the auspices of WIPO and with the involvement of representatives of the cinematographic industry. The debates revealed a desire for the introduction of international registration of audiovisual works for the purposes indicated above. WIPO—in co-operation with the International Federation of Film Producers' Associations (FIAPF)—convened a group of consultants to look into the advisability of setting up an international register of audiovisual works. The group met at WIPO Headquarters in July 1984.

This group—consisting of nine experts acting in a personal capacity and six representatives of FIAPF—unanimously agreed on the need to set up an international register of audiovisual works as a matter of great priority and urgency. It also expressed its views on the desirable content of such a register and pointed out that it must be established and administered by WIPO and be financially self-supporting, in other words wholly financed from the fees paid by applicants for registration and persons seeking information, without depending on government contributions.

Subsequently, with a view to ascertaining in more detail the degree of interest that prospective user associations might have in an international register and their readiness, if any, to advance the funds necessary to cover the initial investment required for setting

---

168. Cf. commentary on the 1989 Diplomatic Conference for the conclusion of a Treaty on the International Registration of Audiovisual works prepared by the International Bureau of WIPO, published in *Copyright* (Geneva), June 1989, pp. 165–7.

up such a register, the Director-General of WIPO held several discussions with representatives of such associations who expressed interest, but failed to confirm this in writing and made no proposals for the initial financing. Nevertheless, at their meetings in September 1987, the governing bodies of WIPO invited the Director-General to make a fresh attempt and to convene a diplomatic conference with a view to the adoption of a treaty creating an international register of audiovisual works.

Two preparatory meetings were held at WIPO Headquarters in 1988. The first (March 1988) was attended by 36 States and 9 non-governmental organizations; although no concrete proposals were made, the Austrian delegation expressed the view during the proceedings that its government might be ready to advance the funds needed to cover the costs of the initial investment on condition that the International Register was established in Vienna. The second meeting (November–December 1988) was attended by 31 countries, one intergovernmental organization and 9 non-governmental organizations. On this occasion, consideration was given to new drafts of the Treaty and Regulations prepared by the Director-General of WIPO on the basis of the debates of the Committee of Experts held in March of the same year. On that same basis, the draft agenda and rules of procedure of the diplomatic conference were drawn up. That conference was to be held in the following year. In regard to the seat and initial financing of the International Register, the Director-General of WIPO maintained contacts with representatives of the Austrian Government which resulted in a draft agreement.

B. THE GENEVA DIPLOMATIC CONFERENCE (1989)

The Conference was convened on 10 April 1989. All the member countries of WIPO were invited, pursuant to the provisions of Rule 2 of the Rules of Procedure drawn up previously (membership of the organization was maintained as a condition in Article 11(1) of the Treaty). Delegations from 59 States and observers from 2 intergovernmental organizations (UNESCO and the EEC) and 9 non-governmental organizations attended. On 18 April, the Conference adopted the Treaty and annexed Regulations, together with the Final Act.

C. The text of the Treaty

a. Purpose of the Treaty

The *preamble* points out that the International Register has three main purposes:
- to increase legal security in transactions relating to audiovisual works;
- to enhance the creation of audiovisual works and the international flow of such works and
- to contribute to the fight against piracy of audiovisual works.

b. Constitution of a Union. Definition of an 'audiovisual work'

By virtue of Article 1, the States party to the Treaty constitute a Union for the international registration of audiovisual works (all WIPO Treaties begin with a similar provision).

Article 2 defines an 'audiovisual work' by establishing that, for the purposes of the Treaty, the term means any work that consists of a series of fixed related images, with or without accompanying sound, susceptible of being made visible and, where accompanied by sound, susceptible of being made audible.

This formula includes silent films; images fixed on a series of slides may also be regarded as included, but not straightforward sound recordings, in other words those which are not accompanied by images.[169]

c. Purpose of the Treaty

The purpose of the Treaty is to establish the International Register of Audiovisual Works. The legal effect of the Register is the creation of a presumption *juris tantum* of the accuracy of the registered statements. This provision does not conflict with the Berne Convention because the latter prohibits registration and other formalities only when they are a condition for the enjoyment or

---

169. See: *Records of the Diplomatic Conference for the conclusion of a Treaty on the International Registration of Audio-visual Works*, Geneva, WIPO, 1990, pp. 142–6.

exercise of authors' rights, but not registration resulting in a rebuttable presumption (or *prima-facie* evidence).

1. The International Register. Article 3(1) provides for the creation of an International Register of Audiovisual Works 'for the purpose of the registration of statements concerning audio-visual works and rights in such works, including, in particular, rights relating to their exploitation'.

The commentary on the 1989 Conference prepared by the International Bureau of WIPO stresses the fact that the International Register was created primarily for recording, before or after the creation or release of any audiovisual work, statements about the identity of the work and about the initial owner or owners of the various rights therein; for reflecting any changes in the ownership of those rights and for containing information as regards the licensing of such rights. Another important purpose of the Register is to record any limitation that the owner of the rights may be subject to as a consequence of, for example, a bank loan or tax lien.[170]

2. The International Registry. Article 3(2) provides for the setting up of an International Registry of Audiovisual Works responsible for keeping the International Register. The International Registry is an administrative unit of the International Bureau of WIPO.

Location. Pursuant to Article 3(3), the International Registry shall be located in Austria as long as a Treaty to that effect between the Republic of Austria and WIPO is in force (otherwise it shall be located in Geneva). The Assembly of the Union created by the Treaty decided that this Registry would commence operations on 1 September 1991 in Austria (at Klosterneuburg near Vienna), pursuant to the treaty between Austria and WIPO.

Applications for registration. Article 3(4) provides that the registration of any statement in the International Register shall be based on an application filed to this effect and shall be conditional

---

170. See note 168, ibid., pp. 168–9.

on payment of a fee. The form and content of the application are defined in Rule 2 of the regulations accompanying the Treaty and the rates are prescribed in Rule 8 of these Regulations.

Applications for registration may make reference to an *initial registration* of an audiovisual work or to a *registration that has already been effected*. This subsequent application may be filed with a view to the inclusion of new indications in the Register or to the incorporation of changes relating to the same work.

Persons entitled to file an application. Article 3(5) establishes different criteria for attachment to the Treaty depending on whether
- the application is for first or subsequent registration, and
- the applicant is a natural person or a legal entity.

i) When the application refers to an *initial registration*, Article 3(5)(a) stipulates that it may be filed by a natural person or by a legal entity provided that the following non-cumulative conditions are satisfied:
- *A natural person*: who is (a) a national of a Contracting State or (b) domiciled in a Contracting States or (c) has his habitual residence in a Contracting State or (d) has a real and effective industrial or commercial establishment in a Contracting State. The criteria for attachment to the Treaty referred to in points (a) and (c) are also found in the Berne Convention (Articles 3(1) and (2)). Those cited in points (b) and (d) will be found in the Paris Convention (Article 3).
- *Legal entity*: (a) this must be organized under the laws of a Contracting State or (b) have a real and effective industrial or commercial establishment in a Contracting State (this latter criterion is also laid down in Article 3 of the Paris Convention).

If the first registration could be made by anyone without any conditions there would be no incentive for States to adhere to the Treaty nor would the legal effect defined in its Article 4(1) be achieved.

ii) When the application refers to a *subsequent registration*, that is to say to a registration already effected, Article 3(5)(b) provides that it may be presented by any person, natural or legal, who may or may not satisfy the conditions set out in paragraph (a).

The commentary by the International Bureau already referred to points out that the reason for permitting anyone at all to present subsequent applications reflects the intention that the International Register should be as complete and as transparent as possible. Moreover if the assignment, licence, etc. were made or granted for the benefit of a person who is not a national, resident, etc. of a Contracting State, that person would not be able to submit an application to the International Register. In that case—unless the initial applicant took care of registration of the assignment or licence—the register would no longer reflect the true legal situation since it would continue to show the assignor and the granter of a licence as the full owner of rights which they no longer possess.[171]

Applications relating to a work and those relating to a person. Rule 1 of the Treaty Regulations establishes a number of definitions, including those relating to the two types of application for which provision is made:
- *work-related application* (para. (v))—which will certainly be the most frequent—identifies an existing or future work at least by its title or titles; and
- *person-related application* (para. (vi))—which is the application seeking registration in the International Register of statements in respect of the interest of the applicant or of another person identified in the application in one or more existing or future works, described but not identified by their title or titles; in this case, the work must be identified differently, at least by naming the natural or legal person who has produced or is expected to produce it. Statements in person-related applications may, for example, refer to the rights and obligations of the applicant or of another person resulting from safeguard measures, pledges, bankruptcy etc.

Information. Rule 6 of the Treaty Regulations stipulates that the International Registry shall publish a gazette in which it shall indicate the prescribed elements in respect of all registrations.

---

171. Ibid., p. 170.

Pursuant to Rule 7, against payment of the prescribed fee, the Registry shall
- provide information on any registration together with certified copies of any registration, certificate or document relating to this registration;
- provide a certificate answering questions about the existence in the International Register of statements concerning specific matters included in the Register or in any document or material added to the application;
- allow the inspection of any application and of any document or material annexed thereto;
- provide written information on all registrations made in respect of specific works or persons during a specific period.

The utility of the Register. As Ficsor points out, the International Register serves the interests of producers and other proprietors of copyright and also those of the distributors and assignors of rights, licence holders and users of works. The single centralized Registry data bank enables the sources from which rights may be obtained to be traced and also permits verification as to whether persons offering licences, sub-licences or copies are legally authorized to do so (or are pirates or other copyright infringers).[172]

d. The basic undertaking by the Contracting States

Under Article 4(1) 'each Contracting State undertakes to recognize that a statement recorded in the International Register shall be considered as true until the contrary is proved [...]'.

This provision creates a presumption *juris tantum* of the accuracy of the recorded information. States which ratify or accede to the Treaty undertake to recognize that the registered statements are to be treated as true until the contrary is proved (save in two cases defined in the same provision). By virtue of this provision of the Treaty, the Courts and administrative authorities of the Con-

---

172. See Mihály Ficsor, 'El nuevo Tratado de la OMPI sobre el registro internacional de obras audiovisuales, in '*Libro-memoria, I Congreso Iberoamericano de Propiedad Intelectual*, Madrid, 1991, Vol. II, p. 768.

tracting States must accept such declarations as *prima facie* evidence. The probative value of statements recorded in a Register constitutes a well-known legal effect in many countries.[173] However, as Ficsor points out, the procedure for registration has as its effect the creation of a rebuttable presumption but does not establish, extend, restrict or otherwise eliminate any right.[174]

e. Exceptions to the probative effect of the International Register

As we have seen, the probative effect of the International Register is subject to two exceptions set out in Article 41(1):

The first exception (para. (i)) is that the probative effect of the statements recorded in the Register does not apply 'where the statement cannot be valid under the copyright law, or any other law concerning intellectual property rights in audiovisual works' of a particular State.

The following typical examples of situations covered by this exception may be cited:

- the case in which the statement recorded in the International Register says that the applicant is the original owner of copyright in a particular country but the applicant is in fact a person who, under the law of that country, cannot be the owner of copyright, for example because he is the producer of the audiovisual work and not its author and under the law of the State concerned, producers cannot be original proprietors of copyright—this can be vested only in the authors;
- if the statement entered in the International Register affirms that the applicant who is an actor in the audiovisual work owns the right of reproduction, but the law of the Contracting State does not recognize that right to actors so that the statement would not have the legal effect provided for in Article 4(1).[175]

---

173. Cf. *Records* ..., note 168, p. 171.
174. Mihály Ficsor, op. cit., p. 764.
175. Cf. *Records* ..., note 168, p. 171.

The second exception (para. (ii)) is that the statement entered in the Register does not produce legal effect if it is 'contradicted by another statement recorded in the International Register'. To avoid such contradictions, the Treaty Regulations lay down special measures relating to the application phase and also to examination of the application by the Registry Office with a view to making sure that only true statements are included in the Register. *Rule 2* establishes that the application shall contain a statement of veracity relating to its content and to any accompanying document (para. 10) and must be signed by the applicant or his official representative (para. 11). In addition to the indication of the applicant's interest in the work (para. 7), he must also indicate the source of his rights in the work (para. 8). The applicant may likewise present documents in support of the declarations made in the application and material enabling the audiovisual work to be identified (para. 9). *Rule 3* goes on to stipulate that

- if the International Registry finds in the application what it considers to be an involuntary omission, an incompatibility between two or more statements, a mistake of transcription or other manifest error, it shall invite the applicant to correct his application; and (2)
- when the Registry considers that a statement appearing in an application contradicts any previous entry in the International Register, it must inform the applicant and any other interested party and give them the possibility of remedying that contradiction.

f. Effects of the Treaty

Pursuant to Article 4(2) no provision of the Treaty shall be interpreted as affecting the copyright law, or any other law concerning intellectual property rights in audiovisual works, of any Contracting State or, if that State is party to the Berne Convention or any other Treaty concerning intellectual property rights in audiovisual works, the rights and obligations of the said State under the said Convention or treaty. It follows that no registered statement will be regarded as true if it cannot be valid pursuant to the laws of the State concerned and in particular pursuant to provisions deriving from a different legal system (for example, if it indicates the producer as the original proprietor of the rights when, by virtue of the legislation of the State concerned, authors are the original proprietors).[176]

g. Administrative and final provisions

1. *Administrative provisions* (Articles 5–8). The Treaty provides for the membership, tasks and operation of the Assembly (Article 5); the tasks of the International Bureau (Article 6); provisions on finance based on the self-supporting financing of the International Registry (Article 7) and the adoption of the Regulations at the same time as the Treaty to which they are annexed. In the event of any conflict between the provisions of the Treaty and those of the Regulations, the former shall prevail (Article 8).

2. *Provisions on the revision and amendment of the Treaty* (Articles 9 and 10). The Treaty provides for its revision and the procedure to be followed for that purpose (Article 9), together with the possibility of the modification of some of its provisions by the Assembly (Articles 9(3) and 10).

3. *Final provisions* (Articles 11–17). These regulate the procedure for accession to the Treaty (the country concerned must be a Member State of WIPO; this is a 'closed' convention) and the deposit of the relevant instrument with the Director-General of WIPO (Article 11), the initial entry into force of the Treaty (three months after the date of deposit of the fifth instrument of ratification or accession) and subsequent implementation on the territory of each of the Contracting States (three months after the date of deposit of the relevant instrument) (Article 12); the principle of the non-admissibility of reservations, save for the notification to be made at the time of accession to the Treaty that the provisions of Article 4(1) in respect of statements which do not concern the exploitation of intellectual property rights in audiovisual works shall not apply; that declaration may be subsequently withdrawn

---

176. Mihály Ficsor, op. cit., p. 764.

(Article 13). They also regulate denunciation of the Treaty (not prior to five years from the date of entry into force of the Treaty on the territory of the State concerned) which shall take effect one year after the notification of denunciation (Article 14); signature and languages of the Treaty (Article 15); duties of the depositary of the Treaty (Article 16); and notifications to be made to the Contracting States concerning: amendments to the regulations, provisions of the Treaty adopted by the Assembly and their entry into force, and accessions, reservations and denunciations of the Treaty (Article 17).

Ratifications and accessions. The Treaty entered into force on 27 February 1991 with the ratifications of Austria, Burkina Faso, France and Mexico and the accession of former Czechoslovakia.

Ficsor points out that the future of the Treaty will depend on the film industry which advocated its adoption. It is dependent in the first instance on the governments being persuaded to ratify and subsequently make active use of the Registry. However, following the adoption of the Treaty, the Motion Pictures Association of America (MPAA) in the United States of America changed its initial attitude and began to oppose the Treaty, although the American Film Marketing Association (AFMA) takes a different view.[177] Because of the campaign launched by some members of MPAA against the Treaty, the future of the International Register is now uncertain.

---

177. Ficsor points out that the MPAA is the Association of the major producers and AFMA that of the 'independents'; this does not mean that they are necessarily small since they are the producers of films such as *Amadeus, The Last Emperor, Hannah and her Sisters, Platoon, Driving Miss Daisy* etc. and, according to many reports, the main reason for MPAA opposition would seem to reside in the fact that the distribution techniques of the 'major' producers differ from those used by the 'independents': the former use methods of distribution which are relatively direct and have an established world network to control the use of their works while the 'independents' have no such network and, partly as a result of that fact, are obliged to use techniques which involve the granting of more complex licences. AFMA therefore recognizes the fact that for its members the International Register of audiovisual works is an essential means of obtaining effective protection of their rights in foreign countries and of combating piracy (op. cit., pp. 764–7).

Treaty on the International Registration of Audiovisual Works*
Film Register Treaty (Geneva, 1989)
(FRT Union)

State	Date on which State became party to the Treaty	State	Date on which State became party to the Treaty
Argentina	29 July 1992	Czech Republic	1 January 1993
Austria	27 February 1991	France	27 February 1991
Brazil	26 June 1993	Mexico	27 February 1991
Burkina Faso	27 February 1991	Peru	27 July 1994
Chile	29 December 1993	Senegal	3 April 1994
Colombia	9 May 1994	Slovakia	1 January 1993

(Total: 12 States)

* Situation as of 1 January 1995; *see Industrial Property and Copyright* (Geneva), WIPO, January 1995.

12.5. World Conventions on neighbouring rights

12.5.1. International Convention for the Protection of Performers, Producers of Phonograms and Broadcasting Organizations (Rome, 26 October 1961)

A. GENESIS

The appearance of the phonograph and of radio broadcasting in the early twentieth century and their enormous development in subsequent decades, completely transformed the circumstances of performing artists. Initially, new employment opportunities became available, but this situation was soon reversed. Performances had now been separated from the person of the performer. They could be stored and circulated independently of the performers, depriving them of opportunities for employment. This situation, coupled with the economic crisis which followed the First World War, profoundly affected the professional activity of artists who were faced with inevitable unemployment that, to begin with, assumed alarming proportions and later became catastrophic.

The representative organizations of performing artists advocated a number of provisions tending to create new employment opportunities and regulate contracts in the profession, and so forth. Measures designed to restore the economic situation and grant these artists a statute which would take account of the far-reaching changes brought about by the appearance of the new techniques included the creation for their benefit of certain rights in the broadcasting sector and the mechanical reproduction of sounds.[178]

The claims put forward by the organizations of performing artists through their professional groupings and general organizations of intellectual workers at national and international meetings coincided with a different movement which began with lawyers specializing in copyright who had also taken an interest in the legal problems arising from the new techniques for the conservation and circulation of artistic performances. The need to find solutions was felt at both national and international levels.[179]

a. The beginnings

As far back as the early years of the century, ALAI examined the rights of soloists at its Congress in Weimar (1903); the topic had first been raised at the Congress in Vevey (1901) and was later dealt with at those in Copenhagen (1909) and Luxembourg (1910).

In its turn, at the Berlin Conference (1908) convened for the revision of the Berne Convention, the United Kingdom Government proposed the international protection of phonographic producers. The Conference was of the opinion that the subject was

---

178. See above, Chapter 7, 7.1, B.
179. See *Rights of Performers in Broadcasting, Television and the Mechanical Reproduction of Sounds*, ILO, Geneva, 1939.

'on the borderline between industrial property and copyright and might conceivably be held to belong more properly to the former category'.[180]

b. The work of the ILO and the International Bureau of the Berne Convention. Proposals for inclusion in the Berne Convention

The *International Labour Organization* was the first intergovernmental organization to which musicians turned in seeking support for the adoption of regulations covering the rights claimed by them. The II Congress of the International Union of Musicians held in Paris in 1926 declared that 'the question should be transmitted to the International Labour Office for examination and for preparation of a course of action to be recommended to all governments'.

From then on, the idea that the ILO would act in this matter remained ever-present and expectations grew until the Rome Convention was signed in 1961. However, ILO activities were held up for some time by the attempt that was made to adopt regulations governing the rights of performing artists within the framework of the Berne Convention.

The recommendation of Rome Conference (1928). The Italian Government, which was entrusted with the task of preparing the programme of the Second Berne Convention Revision Conference, and the International Bureau of the Berne Union put forward a proposal which sought the introduction into the Convention of two clauses on the rights of performing artists. One of them was designed to ensure that 'artists who execute literary or artistic works enjoy the exclusive right to authorize the diffusion of their performances by means of telegraphy with or without wire, or any other process analogous thereto and used to transmit sounds or images'. The other concerning instruments for the mechanical reproduction of music, provided that 'when a musical work is adapted to mechanical instruments with the aid of

---

180. See Stephen Stewart, op. cit., pp. 202–3.

interpretative artists, the latter shall also benefit from the protection which the adaptation enjoys'.[181]

The proposal met with strong opposition at the Conference, not so much because the principle of protection of the performing artist was objected to, but because it was felt that this protection could not be adequately covered by a convention which was intended solely to protect the rights of authors. During the debate, attention was drawn to the different theories on the legal nature of these rights. It was finally agreed that the solution must lie in the drafting of a new international Convention, although the time did not yet seem ripe for that. In this connection, the Italian delegation expressed the following wish concerning the protection of the rights of performing artists: 'that the governments which have participated in the work of the Conference should consider the possibility of action with a view to safeguarding the rights of performers'.

The criterion which prevailed at the Rome Conference (1928) was endorsed by CISAC and also by ALAI. The VIII CISAC Congress held at Copenhagen in 1933 expressed the unanimous view that the question of performers' rights did not fall within the ambit of the Berne Convention. It felt that CISAC should keep in touch with the ILO to which study of the problem of protecting performing artists had been entrusted. CISAC maintained that position at the X Congress held in Seville in 1935.

ALAI, for its part, during a general meeting held at Montreux in 1935 to examine the programme of the future Berne Convention Revision Conference, unanimously rejected the idea of any recognition of the rights of performers in that Convention.

In February 1937, the Governing Body of the International Labour Office set up a Committee of Experts to make a preliminary review in preparation for a study of the rights of performing artists which would enable the International Labour Conference to deal with this matter more easily.

---

181. Cf. *The Rights of Performers* ..., op. cit., ILO, p. 28.

In February 1939, the Governing Body, having been apprised of the results of the work of the Committee of Experts, placed the question of the performers' rights on the agenda of the twenty-sixth session of the International Labour Conference convened in 1940.

Again in 1939, Fritz Ostertag, in his capacity as Director of the International Bureau of the Berne Union, prepared a draft International Convention 'connected to' the Berne Convention. In that same year, the International Bureau of the Berne Union and the International Institute for the Unification of Private Law convened a meeting of experts which was held at Samedan (Switzerland) and gave support to the 'Ostertag draft'. It also drafted four proposed treaties in 'connection' with the Berne Convention and intended to be annexed thereto:
- on the rights of performers and producers of phonograms and similar instruments;
- on the rights of broadcasting organizations;
- on rights in press news; and
- establishing a *droit de suite* on the resale price of works of art.

All these activities were halted by the Second World War.

The recommendations of the Brussels Conference (1948). The question was again raised during the Berne Convention Revision Conference held in Brussels in 1948. On this occasion, there was renewed opposition to the protection of the rights of performing artists, phonogram producers and broadcasting organizations by copyright and to their inclusion in the Berne Convention. However, three recommendations were made which marked a new approach to the question since work was now directed towards the adoption of an independent Convention to regulate the three categories of rights concerned.

The Conference called upon the governments of the Member Countries of the Union to look into ways and means of ensuring the protection of the manufacturers of instruments for the mechanical reproduction of musical works (recommendation VI) and of broadcasts made by broadcasting organizations so as to prevent any use not authorized by them (recommendation VII), but *without prejudice to authors' rights*.

In relation to performing artists (recommendation VIII), the

Conference based protection on the artistic nature of the performances and used the term '*droits voisins du droit d'auteur*' ('rights neighbouring on copyright'). It adopted a recommendation calling for the active pursuit of studies of this matter.

During the Brussels Conference an Executive Sub-Committee of the Permanent Committee of the Berne Union was set up. It went on to convene a Joint Committee of Experts for the international protection of the three categories of rights, bringing together representatives of the ILO, the International Federation of the Phonographic Industry (IFPI) and the European Broadcasting Union (EBU). This meeting was held in Rome in 1951. Following laborious discussions, the Joint Committee approved a preliminary draft International Convention regarding the protection of performers, manufacturers of phonographic records and broadcasting organizations. The draft text which was submitted to the States for their consideration, elicited numerous criticisms and reservations, especially from performing artists and authors. It was then shelved.

c. Work from 1956 onwards. The involvement of UNESCO

In 1956 a meeting of a Committee of Experts was convened in Geneva by the Governing Body of the International Labour Office. It approved a 'draft International Convention for the protection of interpretative or performing artists, record manufacturers and broadcasting organizations', known as the *ILO Draft*.

Still in 1956, on the occasion of a meeting convened by the International Bureau of the Berne Union and attended by a number of prominent figures, a draft known as the *Inter-authors' Draft* was prepared. The conclusions reached were examined during the next few days by a joint ALAI–CISAC Committee which reserved its opinion on some of the provisions.

In 1957, UNESCO and the International Bureau of the Berne Union convened a Committee of Governmental Experts which met in Monaco and—on the basis of the text prepared jointly by the two international organizations—drew up a draft international regulation on the three categories of related rights which came to be known as the *Monaco Draft*.

Since the Universal Copyright Convention had been concluded in Geneva in 1952 and its administration entrusted to UNESCO, and having regard to the fact that any international convention on neighbouring rights, being closely bound up with copyright, might affect that Convention, it was felt that it was not appropriate for UNESCO to be represented as a mere observer but that it should be called upon to be the third participant (with the ILO and the Berne Union) in the preparation of the future international instrument.[182]

In 1960, at the invitation of the Netherlands Government, a Committee of Experts was convened at The Hague jointly by the ILO, the International Bureau of the Berne Union and UNESCO. On the basis of the two drafts prepared by the international agencies that convened the meeting, namely the ILO and Monaco Drafts, the Committee prepared and unanimously approved a new text which came to be known as *The Hague Draft*. This was the working document used by the Diplomatic Conference convened in Rome in the following year.

B. THE DIPLOMATIC CONFERENCE IN ROME (1961)

The Directors-General of the ILO and UNESCO and the Director of the International Bureau of the Berne Union jointly convened a Diplomatic Conference which, at the invitation of the Italian Government, met in Rome on 10 October 1961. The Conference was attended by delegations from 44 countries and observers from two others and also from the United Nations, the Council of Europe and the International Institute for the Unification of Private Law. Observers were present from 15 non-governmental international organizations. Abraham L. Kaminstein (United States of America) was appointed Rapporteur-General of the Conference.

The proceedings ended on 26 October with the adoption of the International Convention for the Protection of Performers,

---

182. See Claude Masouyé, *Guide to the Rome Convention and to the Phonograms Convention*, op. cit., p. 9.

Producers of Phonograms and Broadcasting Organizations which is habitually referred to as the *Rome Convention*.

C. THE TEXT OF THE CONVENTION

Masouyé points out that the Rome Convention is characterized by its flexibility. 'The Rome Convention, as will be seen, allows a lot of latitude to Member States in the way they apply it. As well as the basic *table d'hôte* menu—the conventional minima—there exist *à la carte* provisions which allow each country a choice of the obligations which it must undertake. Besides, this Convention of 1961 was a landmark in the evolution, during the last few decades, in the nature and role of conventions regulating international intellectual property relationships. The conventions concluded at the end of the nineteenth century were the result of a common denominator between national legislations and attempt to make clear the reciprocal obligations of Member States, whereas those drawn up more recently tend to define the rights and obligations which each State should incorporate into its domestic law.' These instruments are therefore the precursors of domestic legislation and that is particularly true of the Rome Convention which, since its adoption, has served as the basis for the drafting of many domestic laws.[183]

Like other international instruments, the Rome Convention has a *preamble*—very brief in this instance—which lacks legal effect and simply sets out the purpose of the Convention.

a. Definitions

Article 3 sets out definitions of the main terms used in the Convention in relation to (1) performers; (2) producers of phonograms; and (3) broadcasting organizations.

---

183. Masouyé also points out that the strong impulse given by the Rome Convention to national legislation was enhanced by the preparation of a model law known as the 'Model law concerning the protection of performers, producers of phonograms and broadcasting organizations' with the accompanying commentary; these texts were approved in 1974 by the Intergovernmental Committee set up under Article 32 of the Convention itself (op. cit. p. 12).

1. In relation to performers. Article 3(a) defines performers as 'actors, singers, musicians, dancers, and other persons who act, sing, deliver, declaim, play in, or otherwise perform literary or artistic works'.

During the Conference[184] it was agreed that:
- the meaning of the expression 'literary and artistic works' used in the foregoing definition, and in other provisions of the Convention, would be the same as that adopted for this expression in the Berne Convention and Universal Copyright Convention and that it specifically included musical, dramatic and dramatico-musical works (although the Convention does not require them to be protected works, i.e. works that do not fall within the public domain);
- the conductors of orchestras or singers were also regarded as being included in the definition of 'performers';
- whenever the Convention uses the term 'performance'—or '*exécution*' in the French text—this is regarded as a generic term which includes both recitation (*récitation*) and presentation (*représentation*);
- the term 'performance' is to comprise the activity of the artist reflected in a particular performance or recitation (so resolving the question of a difference between the definition of an interpretative and performing artist).

The Convention omitted to include in its scope of protection variety artists (acrobats, clowns etc.) because they do not perform 'works'. However, States are not obliged to confine protection to artists who perform literary or artistic works since Article 9 stipulates that 'any Contracting State may, by its domestic laws and regulations, extend the protection provided for in this Convention to artists who do not perform literary or artistic works'.

2. In relation to producers of phonograms. Article 3(b) defines the '*phonogram*' as meaning 'any exclusively aural fixation of sounds

---

184. Cf. *Records of the Rome Conference*, ILO–UNESCO–BIRPI, 1961, *Report* of the Rapporteur-General; pp. 39–40.

of a performance or of other sounds'. This notion is particularly wide because it comprises both sounds which have their origin in a performance and those of different origin. During the Conference it was pointed out that birdsong and other sounds of nature are examples of sounds which do not have their origin in a performance.[185]

Article 3(c) states that a *producer of phonograms* means 'the person who, or the legal entity which, first fixes the sounds of a performance or other sounds'.

During the Conference, it was noted that when an employee of a legal entity fixes sounds in the course of his employment, the legal entity which is the employer and not the employee is to be considered as the producer.[186]

Article 3(d) states that *'publication'* means the 'offering of a phonogram to the public in reasonable quantity'.

Article 3(e) defines *'reproduction'* as 'the making of a copy or copies of a fixation'.

During the Conference, it was pointed out that the expressions 'phonogram' and 'fixation' were used in the Convention with different meanings: phonograms are exclusively aural fixations while the term 'fixation' also includes visual or audiovisual fixations.[187]

In this regard, it must be remembered that *fixations of images or of images and sounds are excluded from the Convention* which does not apply to all fixations but only to phonograms.

3. In relation to broadcasting organizations. Article 3(f) defines *'broadcasting'* as 'the transmission by wireless means for public reception of sounds or of images and sounds'. This definition shows that, in the terms of the Convention, broadcasts are those of sound radio and also of television ('of sounds or of images and sounds') and that only transmission by Hertzian waves or by other wireless means should constitute broadcasting.

---

185. Ibid., p. 40.
186. Ibid.
187. Ibid.

During the Conference, it was explained that the words 'for public reception' used in the definition were designed to make it clear that broadcasts intended for one person or a well-defined group of persons (as in the case of ship or aircraft voyages, taxis in a town etc.) are not regarded as broadcasts.[188]

It follows that the distribution of programmes by cable networks, despite the importance which this has acquired today, is not covered by the Rome Convention.

Article 3(g) indicates that *'rebroadcasting'* means 'the simultaneous broadcasting by one broadcasting organization of the broadcast of another broadcasting organization'.

During the Conference, a proposal made by Austria to the effect that the term 'rebroadcasting' should also cover deferred broadcasts was rejected because the latter necessarily used a fixation of the previous broadcast. The exclusion of deferred broadcasts clearly arises from the expression 'simultaneous broadcast' used in the definition.

Although a proposal by the United States for the inclusion of a definition of the expression 'broadcasting organization' was finally withdrawn, discussion of this proposal did enable a number of questions referred to previously to be clarified.[189]

b. *The principle of national treatment*

On a proposal from the United States, the Conference decided to deal separately with matters relating to (a) the persons who enjoy protection by the Convention and in which particular cases (Articles 4, 5, 6), and (b) the nature and content of that protection (Article 2).

The basic protection accorded by the Convention consists in ensuring that foreigners enjoy the same treatment as nationals.

Article 2 defines what is meant by national treatment in relation to each of the three categories of beneficiaries of the Convention. It stipulates that 'for the purposes of this Convention,

---

188. Ibid.
189. See above, Chapter 7, Section 7.3.2: holders of rights.

national treatment shall mean the treatment accorded by the domestic law of the Contracting State in which protection is claimed: (a) to performers who are its nationals as regards performances taking place, broadcast, or first fixed, on its territory; (b) to producers of phonograms who are its nationals, as regards phonograms first fixed or first published on its territory; (c) to broadcasting organizations which have their headquarters on its territory, as regards broadcasts transmitted from transmitters situated on its territory'.

The above definition is completed by the second paragraph of the same Article 2 which stipulates that *'national treatment* shall be subject to the protection specifically guaranteed, and the limitations specifically provided for, in this Convention'.

This is a reference to the *minimum protection which the States undertake to grant*—with the exception of certain permitted reservations and limitations—*even when they are not granted to national performances, phonograms or broadcasts*. This minimum protection is specifically provided for in Articles 7 (in respect of performers), 10 (in respect of producers of phonograms), 12 (in respect of performers and producers of phonograms) and 13 (in respect of broadcasting organizations).

In his report, the Rapporteur-General gives the following example: pursuant to Article 16, a Contracting State may deny or limit rights of secondary use (Article 12) in respect of phonograms regardless of whether its domestic legislation grants such protection. He points out that in the course of the debate, several delegations expressed the view that the second paragraph of Article 2 was unnecessary as a matter of strict legal logic. However, the majority felt that this provision would make the Convention easier to understand and favoured a clear statement to the effect that the obligation imposed on the States by the Convention did not coincide precisely with 'national treatment' since the protection might be greater or less than that represented by equal treatment with nationals.[190]

---

190. See *Records of the Rome Conference*, p. 39.

Masouyé points out that the Rome Convention applies the principle of national treatment to a lesser extent than the Berne Convention or the Universal Convention since it has a different approach. 'This provision, whereby foreigners are assimilated to nationals in all States party to the Convention, is to be found in the multilateral copyright conventions, though in the Rome Convention its impact is less because the approach is different. Although it refers to performances, phonograms and broadcasts to define national treatment and the various points of attachment, the object of protection is not the thing but specified beneficiaries. The copyright conventions on the other hand protect the work itself. Again, many national laws are not, at least up to now, familiar with the concept of a 'neighbouring' right. The result is, for these, a rather different pattern of international protection.'[191]

c. Criteria of protection: points of attachment to the Convention

In respect of the persons protected by the Convention and the instances in which it gives protection (i.e. the beneficiaries of the national treatment defined in Article 2), the Convention adopts *different points of attachment* for the different categories of beneficiaries: performers (Article 4), producers of phonograms (Article 5) and broadcasting organizations (Article 6). It also permits the States to refrain from applying certain specific criteria.

In regard to the three articles mentioned (4, 5 and 6), the problem arose as to whether the Convention was to apply exclusively to international situations or also to those of a national nature: in other words, whether a Contracting State must apply the Convention solely to foreign performances, phonograms and broadcasts or must also do so in respect of its domestic performances. The conclusion reached was that the Convention referred

---

191. Claude Masouyé, *Guide*, p. 20. In 1995, national legislative systems in the situation indicated in the commentary cited here were far fewer than when the commentary was published (1982) and fewer still than at the time when the Convention was adopted (1961).

solely to international situations[192] (as in the case of the Berne and the Universal Conventions).

1. *Protected performances.* Article 4 defines the *points of attachment to the Convention in the case of performers.* It provides that the Contracting States shall grant them protection when: (a) the performance takes place in another Contracting State; (b) the performance is incorporated into a phonogram which is protected under Article 5 of this Convention; or (c) the performance, not being fixed on a phonogram, is carried by a broadcast which is protected by Article 6 of this Convention.

In consequence, in the case of performers, the Convention adopts only *real* points of attachment. The criterion of the nationality of the performer (*a personal point of attachment*) is eliminated because of the complications which might arise in the case of collective performances (by orchestras, choirs, etc.).

2. *Protected phonograms*
Criteria for the protection of producers of phonograms: Article 5(1) of the Convention stipulates that each Contracting State shall grant national treatment to producers of phonograms when: (a) the producer of the phonogram is a national of another Contracting State; (b) the first fixation of the sound was made in another Contracting State; or (c) the phonogram was first published in another Contracting State.

Simultaneous publication. Article 5(2) of the Convention widens the scope of protected phonograms by adopting the criterion of simultaneous publication (taken from the Berne and Universal Conventions): where a phonogram has been published for the first time in a non-contracting State, but has also been so published *within 30 subsequent days in a Contracting State*, it shall be regarded as having been 'first published' in the Contracting State. This other 'publication' made in a Contracting State must correspond to the definition in Article 3(d) of the Convention ('offering copies of a phonogram to the public in reasonable quantity').

---

192. Cf. *Records*, p. 41.

Option for the Contracting States to preclude the application of certain specific criteria. Article 5(3) permits each State to enter a reservation by declaring that it will not apply the criterion of publication or that of fixation.

This provision is attributable to the fact that a number of delegations declared that their States could not grant protection on the basis of the criterion of *fixation*. Others indicated that their States could not accept the criterion of *first publication*. Others, again, declared that they wished to accept no criterion other than that of fixation and rejected that of *nationality*.

The third paragraph was adopted as a compromise solution which allows a Contracting State to exclude the criterion of fixation, or that of first publication, but does not allow simultaneous exclusion of the application of both criteria. Similarly it may not exclude application of the criterion of nationality, save in the case of a country whose legislation in force on 26 October 1961 (the date on which the Convention was concluded) granted protection to producers of phonograms on the sole basis of the criterion of fixation. On that assumption, Article 17 permits a country to declare under these conditions when it deposits the instrument of ratification or accession that it will apply the criterion of fixation alone. That reservation takes account of the particular situation of certain countries (Denmark, Finland, Iceland, Norway and Sweden) which, shortly before the Rome Conference, had promulgated laws that recognized only the criterion of fixation.[193]

3. *Protected broadcasts. Criteria of protection for broadcasting organizations*: Article 6(1) lays down two conditions of which one at least must be satisfied for the Contracting States to grant national treatment to broadcasting organizations: (a) the headquarters of the broadcasting organization is situated in another Contracting State; (b) the broadcast is transmitted from a transmitter situated in another Contracting State.

During the Conference, it was agreed that the State on whose

---

193. Ibid.

territory the headquarters of a broadcasting organization is situated is the State whose legislation governs that organization. It was also decided that, in the French text, *'siège social'* should be understood as the equivalent of *'siège statutaire'*; and that the legal entity in question might be what is known in some European countries as *'offene Handelsgesellschaft'* or *'Kommandit-gesellschaft'*.[194]

Right of the Contracting States to require the simultaneous existence of both points of attachment: Article 6(2) stipulates that any Contracting State may reserve for itself, at any time, the right to protect broadcasts solely if they satisfy *both conditions laid down in Article 6(1)*, that is to say the broadcasting organization must have its headquarters on the territory of a Contracting State and the transmitter must also be situated on the territory of such a State.

4. *Form and occasion for the exercise of the options provided for in Article 5(3) and in Article 6(2)*. By notification deposited with the Secretary-General of the United Nations at the time of ratification or accession or at any other time; in the latter case, the declaration will not take effect until six months after the date on which notification was deposited.

d. Content of the Law of the Convention

In addition to national treatment, the States undertake to grant certain minimum rights which must be applied in their mutual relations without reference to the provisions of their domestic legislation. *These minimum rights may be the subject of reservations and limitations.*

Content of the Convention in regard to performers. Article 7 stipulates the minimum protection granted to performers in respect of *economic rights* (Article 12 sets out the right concerning *secondary uses* of sound recordings in respect of the performers and producers of phonograms and will be dealt with separately).

---

194. Ibid. p. 43. Masouyé points out that the companies designated by these German terms are the equivalent of limited or general partnerships. (*Guide* ..., p. 32).

Article 7(1) of the Convention *does not grant performers an exclusive right to authorize or prohibit* certain uses of their performances, but stipulates that the protection granted to performers 'shall include the possibility of preventing' certain acts to which they have not given their consent.

During the Conference, some delegations objected to this expression and former Czechoslovakia proposed its replacement by the term 'shall have the right to authorize or prohibit' which is that used at the beginning of the provisions listing the minimum rights of producers of phonograms (Article 10) and broadcasting organizations (Article 13). None the less, the Conference decided to keep this expression, while declaring that it was used to enable certain countries, such as the United Kingdom, to continue to grant protection to performers under the provisions of criminal law.[195]

The more complex expression 'shall include the possibility of preventing' means, according to Masouyé, 'that contrary to the provisions stipulated for the two other categories of beneficiaries of the Convention, the minimum does not grant performers an exclusive right of authorization or prohibition. This may seem paradoxical and is felt by some observers to be unfair, but it is so. But it is of course only a minimum and national laws can go further'.[196]

Françon points out that

> the Convention is far from giving *performers* the lion's share [...]. Commentators of the Convention have drawn attention to the fact that performers have not been granted an exclusive right. This solution is even more surprising in that producers of phonograms and broadcasting organizations are, on the contrary, accorded an exclusive right [...]. It appears paradoxical that performers, whose work bears the mark of their personality more than that of producers of phonograms and broadcasting organizations, have not been treated as well as the latter.[197]

---

195. Cf. *Records of the Rome Conference*, p. 43.
196. Claude Masouyé, op. cit., p. 34.
197. André Françon, 'International Protection of Neighbouring Rights', *RIDA*, Paris, January 1974, p. 426.

As Masouyé points out 'the reason for the wording in this paragraph is to leave complete freedom of choice as to the means used to implement the Convention, and to choose those which member countries think most appropriate and best. They may be based on any one or more of a number of legal theories: law of employment; of personality, of unfair competition or unjust enrichment etc.—and of course, if they wish, an exclusive right.'[198]

Pursuant to Article 7(1)(a), performers have the possibility of preventing the *broadcasting* and the *communication to the public* of their performance without their consent. This provision protects the performer in cases where a *direct*[199] performance (a theatrical performance, concert etc.) might, *without his consent*, be communicated to the public by means of broadcasting, loudspeakers, cable networks etc., so that the performance reaches a wider public than the one for which it was originally intended.

The same paragraph (a) goes on to establish the cases in which the *consent of the performer is not necessary for broadcasting and communication to the public*: when the performance used in the broadcast or the public communication is itself already a broadcast performance or is made from a fixation.

This means that the performer *may not invoke the Convention to oppose*:
- rebroadcasting when the original broadcast was made with his consent;
- broadcasting using a fixation made with his consent;
- public communication of a broadcast made with his consent (for example, by means of radio or television sets installed in public places); and
- the public communication of fixations made with his consent.

---

198. Claude Masouyé, *Guide to the Rome Convention and to the Phonograms Convention,* p. 34.
199. The performance or public showing is *direct* when the artist is in direct contact with the audience without a fixation or a broadcasting agency (a radio station, cable distributor) or both. When the public communication is direct, it is necessarily 'live'.

(The secondary use of sound recordings is governed by Article 12 of the Convention.)

Article 7(1)(b) permits performers to prevent the *fixation*, without their consent, of their unfixed performance.

Finally, Article 7(1)(c) establishes the cases in which performers may prevent the *reproduction, without their consent, of a fixation of their performance*:

- if the original fixation itself was made without their consent. That would be the case with a first fixation made in an illicit manner, for example, if the sound engineer made an unauthorized recording of a concert and handed that fixation over to a phonographic producer who used it to make records;
- if the reproduction is made for purposes different from those for which the performers gave their consent, e.g. if a performance given to produce a phonogram is used as the sound track of an audiovisual work; and
- if the original fixation was made in accordance with the provisions of Article 15, and the reproduction is made for purposes different from those referred to in those provisions. Article 15 permits the Contracting States to provide for exceptions, in their domestic laws and regulations, to the protection guaranteed by the Convention, e.g. if a fixation is made within those limitations, for example, an ephemeral fixation made by a broadcasting organization by means of its own facilities and for its own broadcasts (Article 15(1)(c)), is then sold on records or video cassettes.

Relations between performers and broadcasting organizations: Article 7(2) of the Convention enables the Contracting States to regulate, through their domestic legislation, certain matters concerning relations between performers and broadcasting organizations in such a way that the provisions benefiting the former are restricted in favour of the latter.

These matters touch on *rebroadcasting, fixation* for broadcasting and *reproduction of that fixation* with the same objective.

Subparagraphs (1) and (2) of Article 7(2) lay down that: 'if broadcasting was consented to by the performers' or in the event of 'the use by broadcasting organizations of fixations made for broadcasting purposes', the Contracting States may determine whether the artists are entitled to oppose, and if so to what extent, the retransmission and fixation for broadcasting and the reproduction of that fixation with a view to broadcasting.

However, paragraph (3) of the same Article 7(2) stipulates that the domestic law referred to in paragraphs (1) and (2) 'shall not operate to deprive performers of the ability to control, by contract, their relations with broadcasting organizations'. In his report, the Rapporteur-General points out that *this provision recognizes the pre-eminence of freely negotiated contractual agreements.* During the discussion it was agreed that, in this context, the term 'contract' denoted both collective contracts and the decisions of an arbitration board if this was the method habitually applicable between performers and broadcasting organizations.[200]

Group performances. Article 8 allows the Contracting States to specify the manner in which performers will be represented in connection with the exercise of their rights, if several of them participate in the same performance. The discussions that took place during the Conference highlighted the importance of this provision since more than one artist is involved in practically all performances. It was made clear during the discussions that Article 8 did not allow domestic laws to fix all the conditions for the exercise of these rights; they should be limited to the question of how members of a group were *represented* when they exercised their rights.[201]

In countries in which performing artists have joined together in musicians' and actors' unions, or in other professional organizations, these are habitually responsible for representing their members in the exercise of their rights in respect of group performances.

The non-applicability of Article 7 when the performer has agreed to the inclusion of his performance in a visual or audiovisual fixation. Pursuant to Article 19 of the Convention, once a performer has consented to the incorporation of his performance in a

---

200. See *Records of the Rome Conference*, p. 45.
201. Ibid. p. 46.

visual or audiovisual fixation, protection under the Convention will cease to be applicable to him.

This deprivation of protection under the Convention in respect of visual or audiovisual fixations made with the consent of the performer is far-reaching and significant on account of the importance of participation in audiovisual works for the professional activity of performers and because, as Masouyé points out, by virtue of this Article 19 once the performers have consented to the fixation of the images and of the accompanying sound, they are deprived of all means of controlling the uses that might be made of this fixation (and, hence, any possibility of receiving payment under this heading).[202]

Masouyé points out that this provision defines the position of the Convention on cinematographic works and on other visual and audiovisual fixations and that, in order to understand the reasons for its adoption, it is important to remember 'that the Rome discussions took place at a time when changes in copyright protection enjoyed by the cinematographic works were also under active debate. (A few years later (1967) the revision in Stockholm of the Berne Convention produced new Articles 14 and 14*bis*.) Film producers feared damage to their interests if performers and broadcasting organizations were to enjoy rights in their films. It was on copyright rather than on neighbouring rights that they had set their sights, and it was to the Berne revision in Stockholm, rather than to Rome, that they now looked. Their preoccupation in Rome was simply to steer clear of the Convention.'[203]

1. *Omission of the moral right.* Finally it will be noted that the Convention makes no reference to the *moral right* of performers (basically the right to be named and the right to respect of the performance when it is reproduced); this does not mean that laws must not recognize the moral right of performers. The omission in the Convention has to be seen in the context of the traditional

---

202. Claude Masouyé, op. cit., p. 67.
203. Ibid., pp. 65–6.

resistance of the countries forming part of the Anglo-American legal system to give express recognition to the moral right, even in relation to authors. In consequence, so as not to jeopardize the success of the Convention, the Conference preferred to remain silent on this matter.[204]

2. *Content of the Convention relating to producers of phonograms.* Article 10 grants producers of phonograms the exclusive right to authorize or prohibit the direct or indirect reproduction of their phonograms.

During the Conference, it was agreed that 'direct or indirect reproduction' included, among other forms, reproduction by means of: (a) moulding and pressing; (b) recording the sounds produced by an existing phonogram, (c) recording off the air a broadcast of the sounds produced in the radio studio using a disc or a tape.[205] Consequently, the wording used in Article 10 must be considered to cover both direct reproduction from the master copy and indirect reproduction from a disc or tape reproduced by means of a suitable appliance or taken from a broadcast, a wire or cable transmission etc.

Both complete and partial reproduction of the phonogram are included, i.e. reproduction of one or more of the works whose performances are recorded thereon (a proposal by Belgium that an express declaration be included to this effect was considered superfluous, since the right of reproduction is not qualified and is to be understood as including rights against partial reproduction of the phonogram). The same interpretation, it was agreed, should apply to the reproduction of other fixations and should cover performers and broadcasters as well as producers of phonograms.[206]

However, the Convention does not contain provisions expressly establishing protection against the unauthorized importation and distribution to the public of phonograms, unlike the Phonograms Convention signed ten years later in Geneva.

---

204. Cf. Henri Desbois, André Françon and André Kerever, op. cit., p. 331.
205. *Records of the Rome Conference*, pp. 46–7.
206. Ibid.

3. *Content of the Convention in regard to broadcasting organizations.* Article 13 grants broadcasting organizations the exclusive right to authorize or prohibit certain actions relating to their broadcasts.

Article 13(a) stipulates the right to authorize or prohibit '*the rebroadcasting of their broadcasts*'. The definition of 'rebroadcasting' will be found in Article 3(g) which indicates that the repetition must be made simultaneously. Paragraph (a) does not include deferred repetition but this is no obstacle to its protection by national laws. However, as a further operation is generally required, i.e. fixation, the latter is covered by paragraph (b) of Article 13. Neither does the protection afforded by the Convention cover rebroadcasting by wire or cable nor, in general, rebroadcasting by closed circuit systems.

Pursuant to Article 13(b), broadcasting organizations enjoy the right to authorize or prohibit '*the fixation of their broadcasts*'. During the Conference it was proposed (by Austria and Switzerland) that a provision be included to the effect that the prohibition of the fixation of a television broadcast implied a ban on the making of still pictures of the telecast. The Conference agreed that the prohibition against fixing the broadcast extended to fixing parts of the broadcast. However, no indication was given as to whether a still picture of a telecast constituted part of that telecast; this question was simply left to the discretion of the Contracting States.[207]

Article 13(c) grants broadcasting organizations the right to authorize or prohibit: (a) *the reproduction* of fixations, made without their consent, of their broadcasts; and: (b) *the reproduction* of fixations, made in accordance with the provisions of Article 15, of their broadcasts, if the reproduction is made for purposes different from those referred to in these provisions (para. (c) of Article 13 is the equivalent for broadcasting organizations of para. (c) of Article 7(1) applicable to performers).

Finally, Article 13(d) grants broadcasting organizations a television exhibition right, that is to say a right to prohibit the

---

207. Ibid., p. 50.

communication to the public of television broadcasts if such communication is made in places accessible to the public and if an entrance fee is charged. In the course of the discussion of Article 13, proposals were made to the effect that this minimum right should be deleted, but the Conference did not accept them (however, Article 16 does enable reservations to be entered on this provision).[208]

In the last part of Article 13(d), the Convention states that it shall be a matter for the domestic law of the State where protection of this right is claimed to determine the conditions under which it may be exercised. Attention has been drawn to the vagueness of this wording since the question arises as to whether it simply authorizes the Contracting States to determine the meaning of 'places accessible to the public' and 'entrance fee' or whether it authorizes them to replace this exclusive right by the right to fair remuneration.[209]

4. *Provisions relating to different categories of beneficiaries.* These concern: (1) *'secondary uses'* of phonograms (Article 12); (2) the possibility of entering *reservations* against the right laid down in Article 12 for the benefit of performers and producers of phonograms and in Article 13(d) for the benefit of broadcasting organizations (Article 16); (3) the *formalities* relating to phonograms (Article 11); (4) the *minimum duration* of protection (Article 14); and (5) other permitted *limitations* (Article 15).

i) Secondary uses of phonograms
The Rapporteur-General points out that the term 'secondary uses' is widely employed but not included in the Convention; however, it is used in the Report to designate the use of phonograms in broadcasting and communication to the public[210] (pursuant to Article 12 of the text of the Convention).

---

208. Ibid., p. 50.
209. Poulain, *La protection des émissions de radiodiffusion*, p. 224 (quoted by Henri Desbois, André Françon and André Kerever, op. cit., p. 333).
210. Cf. *Records of the Rome Conference*, p. 48.

In this regard, Article 12 stipulates that if a phonogram published for commercial purposes 'or a reproduction of such phonogram' is used directly for broadcasting or for any communication to the public, a single equitable remuneration shall be paid by the user to the performers, or to the producers of the phonograms, or to both. By virtue of that provision, the persons designated in this article do not have a right to prevent (Article 7) or to authorize or prohibit (Article 10) the 'secondary uses' of phonograms; *they only have a right to receive an equitable remuneration for such uses.* The permissibility of use does not depend, therefore, on the authorization by the performers or producers or both since the Convention has laid down a non-voluntary licence for secondary uses giving rise to an entitlement to straightforward remuneration.

During the Conference, it was repeatedly pointed out—as is apparent from the text of Article 12—that the obligation to make payment for 'secondary uses' did not apply to *all types* of phonograms, but was subject to two conditions:
- that the phonograms concerned must already have been published (the notion of publication being defined in para. (d) of Article 3) and only in cases where publication has been made for commercial purposes;
- that the use is direct, so that the use through rebroadcasting would not be a direct use. On the other hand, it would be so if a broadcasting organization first reproduced a commercial disc on a tape and then made a broadcast from that tape.[211]

Each Contracting State has the possibility of choosing any one of the three following solutions: (a) to grant the entitlement to equitable remuneration solely to the performer; (b) solely to the producer of the phonogram; (c) to grant this right both to performers and to producers of phonograms. Failing any agreement between them, in the latter case it will be necessary to determine the conditions under which this remuneration is to be allocated (second part of Article 12).

---

211. Cf. *Records of the Rome Conference*, p. 49.

This provision which is regarded as the most important of the Convention and its focal point[212] was the subject, during the preparatory work and the Conference itself, of wide-ranging debate as regards both its scope and practical application and the opposition to which it gave rise. The Rapporteur-General pointed out in his Report that the problem of the provision on 'secondary uses' of phonograms was beyond doubt the most difficult which the Conference had been called upon to resolve.[213]

Payment for secondary uses of phonograms has always made authors fear the effects that it might have on them for the following reasons among others: it is a well-known fact that users are prepared to earmark only a part of their resources for the payment of remuneration (whether destined for the authors and composers, the holders of neighbouring rights or for any other category of beneficiary). The sharing of this amount between an increasingly large number of beneficiaries creates the possibility that the share accruing to the creators might be reduced (this is the 'cake slice' theory) and the excessive burden of pressure by an increasingly large number of claimants might set off a widespread reluctance by users to make payments. The rights of authors built on solid foundations after two centuries, would then finally give way in face of the many demands put forward on a similar basis by other claimants.

The broadcasting organizations (one of the three categories of beneficiaries of the Rome Convention) also opposed the obligation to make payment under Article 12 as users of phonograms, pointing out that it represented a distortion of reality; their broadcasts were not only the main method of promoting record sales, as was proved by the fact that when producers launch their new records on the market they send them free of charge for broadcasting, but in many countries they even pay broadcasting organizations and disc jockeys to include their records in certain programmes.

---

212. Cf. Claude Masouyé, op. cit., p. 46.
213. See *Records of the Rome Conference*, p. 48.

The arguments put forward by performers in favour of the payment of remuneration centre on the 'secondary uses' of phonograms which create a substantial reduction in their possibilities of employment so that compensation must be provided. For their part the producers of phonograms have defended their right to a share in this remuneration on the grounds that the use of their phonograms for broadcasting purposes may have adverse consequences on the record market, both because the unlimited increase in the size of the audience results in a reduction in the number of persons wishing to buy the records and also because the public becomes fed up with the constant plugging of hits on the radio and loses the desire to purchase the records in shops. They also point out that phonograms occupy the bulk of radio time to such an extent that broadcasters could not function without using them. The original intention of the phonogram published for commercial purposes has therefore been broadened and altered; the phonographic producers claim that they should, at the very least, share in the profits made by broadcasters.[214]

In consequence, the question of the 'secondary uses' of phonograms was resolved in the Rome Convention by introducing in Article 12 a non-voluntary licence which gives entitlement to equitable remuneration. This provision of the Convention must be subsequently regulated by the domestic legislation of the Contracting State in regard both to beneficiaries, and in the event of disagreement between them, to the means of distributing the remuneration.

However, as is pointed out in the Report by the Rapporteur-General, Article 12 must be read in conjunction with Article 16 which deals with reservations to the Convention.[215] Article 12 is rendered more flexible by the inclusion in Article 16(1)(a) of the possibility of formulating at any time the reservations which are discussed below.

---

214. Cf. Claude Masouyé, op. cit., pp. 50–1.
215. See *Records of the Rome Conference*, p. 49.

ii) Reservations

Reservations are provided for in Article 16 and allowed in the context of Articles 12 and 13(d);[216] the Contracting States may make these reservations at the time of deposit of their instrument of ratification or accession or at any other time, but in that case the reservations will only take effect six months after the date on which notification is deposited.

Reservations permitted in respect of Article 12. These are specified in Article 16(1)(a) as follows:
- the Contracting State will not apply any of the provisions of Article 12. This is a total reservation and hence the most important;
- the Contracting State will not apply the provisions of Article 12 in respect of certain uses. The Conference agreed that, by virtue of this provision, a country might decide that it would make no payment for certain broadcasting uses or communication to the public, or for certain kinds of broadcasting or communication to the public;[217]
- the Contracting State will not apply the provisions of Article 12 when the producer of phonograms is not a national of another Contracting State. This provision means that the application of Article 12 may be refused even if the phonogram was fixed or published for the first time in a Contracting State, as long as it was not first fixed by a producer who is a national of a Contracting State;
- a Contracting State may restrict protection of the rights of secondary use granted pursuant to the terms of its own domestic legislation, even if the phonogram has been fixed by a producer who is a national of another Contracting State, to the extent that the latter grants equivalent protection in respect of phonograms fixed for the first time by a national of the State making the declaration. This clause admits *material reciprocity* by

---

216. The Conference rejected a proposal by Poland which would have allowed the Contracting States to make reservations on any provision of the Convention (Ibid., p. 52).
217. Ibid., pp. 52–8.

virtue of which the State which formulates the reservation may cut back the protection granted by it to the same level as the protection which it receives. This means that, in regard to the secondary uses of phonograms, the Contracting States may replace the principle of national treatment by the condition of material reciprocity.

Pursuant to Article 16(1)(a)(iv), the possibility of comparison and cutting back shall also apply to the term of protection. None the less, the comparison may not be applied in respect of beneficiaries. A State which grants protection to performers and producers cannot cut back protection vis-à-vis a State which grants such protection only to performers or only to producers. Similarly, a State which grants protection only to the producer may not refuse protection to a State which grants it only to performers and vice versa. The Conference reached that decision after a lengthy debate, based on a document prepared by a working party. The latter put before the Conference the necessity for deciding whether the principle of material reciprocity also extended to beneficiaries.[218]

Reservation permitted in regard to Article 13, paragraph (d). The other reservation permitted under Article 16 is set out in its paragraph (b) and refers to the right of broadcasting organizations to communicate to the public their television broadcasts pursuant to Article 13(d). This is the only reservation permitted by the Convention in regard to the rights of this category of beneficiaries. If a Contracting State makes this reservation, the other Contracting States shall not be obliged to grant the right in question to broadcasting organizations whose headquarters are situated in that State (*clause of material reciprocity*).

iii) Formalities relating to phonograms

Article 11 contains a provision which is directly inspired by Article III(1) of the Universal Copyright Convention (Geneva 1952): by virtue of this provision, the formalities required by the domestic legislation of a Contracting State as a condition for protection

---

218. Ibid., p. 52.

of the rights of producers of phonograms, or of performers, or both, in relation to phonograms, shall be regarded as having been satisfied if all the copies in commerce of the published phonogram or their containers bear a notice consisting of the symbol ℗, accompanied by the year date of the first publication, placed in such a manner as to give reasonable notice of claim of protection.

If the copies or their containers do not identify the producer or the licensee of the producer (by carrying his name, trade mark or other appropriate designation), the notice shall also include the name of the owner of the rights of the producer. And, furthermore, if the copies or their containers do not identify the principal performers, the notice shall also include the name of the person who, in the country in which the fixation was effected, owns the rights of such performers.

iv) *Minimum term of protection*

The Convention specifies the minimum duration of the rights granted by it: Article 14 provides that this term shall not be less than 20 years. The term is identical for the three categories of beneficiaries of the Convention and is counted from the end of the year, but the point of departure differs for each category:
- from the date of fixation in the case of phonograms and for performances incorporated therein;
- from the date on which the performance took place in the case of performances not incorporated in the phonograms; and
- from the date of the broadcast in the case of broadcasts.

The Rapporteur-General points out in his Report that the Hague Draft (1960)—which served as the working document for the Conference—apart from establishing minimum terms of protection, specified in the article on duration that this would be determined by the law of the country in which protection was claimed and would contain a provision on the 'comparison of terms' under which no country would be obliged to grant protection for a period longer than that fixed by the country of origin.

However, these provisions do not appear in the Rome Convention because the Conference considered them to be superfluous. It held that there was no need to indicate the fact that the term was stipulated by the law of the country in which protection was claimed, as this was implicit in the provision on national treatment. In regard to the comparison of terms, the Conference pointed out that this might be important only in the case of secondary use rights. However, it noted that this point was adequately covered by Article 16(1)(a)(iv) which expressly permitted material reciprocity in respect of duration. Comparison of terms was not considered essential in regard to the right of reproduction of fixations especially as, in the majority of countries, unauthorized reproduction is an act of unfair competition without any well-defined time limits.[219]

v) Other authorized exceptions
By analogy with the copyright Conventions, Article 15 of the Rome Convention permits the Contracting States to provide in their national legislations for certain exceptions to the protection granted by the Convention. The permitted exceptions are identical in respect of the three categories of beneficiaries of the Convention.

Article 15(1) sets out four instances that are generally encountered in copyright conventions. They concern:
- private use;
- use of short excerpts in connection with the reporting of current events;
- ephemeral fixation by a broadcasting organization by means of its own facilities; and
- use solely for the purpose of teaching or scientific research.

The first part of Article 15(2) stipulates that, irrespective of paragraph 1, any Contracting State may, in its domestic laws and regulations, provide for the same or parallel kind of limitations with regard to the protection of performers, producers of phonograms and broadcasting organizations, as it provides for, in its domestic laws and regulations, in connection with the protection of copyright in literary and artistic works.

The purpose of this *parallel with copyright* is to make sure that the rights protected by the Rome Convention are not given

---

219. Ibid., pp. 51–2.

preferential treatment, as compared to those granted to authors. This provision seeks to create a uniform legal system and ensure that the proprietors of neighbouring rights do not receive privileged treatment by comparison with authors in regard to the limitations imposed on the rights of the latter.

The Convention does not require the States to respect a *strict parallel* between national legislation on neighbouring rights and their legal provisions on copyright. However, this provision does contain a clear indication of the need for the States to legislate in such a way that the limitations which are imposed on the protection of neighbouring rights are compatible with those admitted in connection with copyright.[220]

The last sentence of Article 15(2) states that 'compulsory licences may be provided for only to the extent to which they are compatible with this Convention'. As examples of compulsory licences which would be incompatible with the Convention, mention may be made of the following: in regard to performers, a system of compulsory licences in regard to the rights set out in Article 7(1) would not be compatible, i.e. in respect of the possibility of preventing the fixation, without their consent, of an unfixed performance etc. On the other hand a system of compulsory licences might be permitted in the instance covered by Article 7(2), i.e. in a case where the performer has authorized the broadcasting of his performance.[221]

e. Effects of the Convention

1. *Relations between the Rome Convention and copyright.* The authors and their national or international representatives watched the drafting of the Rome Convention with apprehension as they were aware of the adverse effect that the recognition of exclusive rights for the benefit of the proprietors of neighbouring rights might have on the rights enjoyed by the proprietors of the creative

---

220. Cf. Claude Masouyé, op. cit., pp. 58–9.
221. Henri Desbois, André Françon and André Kerever, op. cit., pp. 337–8.

works themselves. A number of provisions were adopted to allay those fears.

i) Article 1 states that the protection granted under the Convention 'shall leave intact and shall in no way affect the protection of copyright in literary and artistic works'. Consequently 'no provision of this Convention may be interpreted as prejudicing such protection'. That statement leads to the conclusion that in cases in which the exercise of exclusive rights of authors in the work that is performed, fixed or broadcast would be impaired by the provisions of the Rome Convention, the protection of copyright shall take precedence (Colombia, Art. 257; Ecuador, Art. 138; Mexico, Art. 6).

ii) Article 23 stipulates that States wishing to sign the Rome Convention must satisfy two conditions: they must have been invited to attend the Conference, although their actual presence is not a condition; and they must belong to the Universal Copyright Convention or be a member of the Berne Union. In regard to the first of these conditions the invitations to attend the Conference were sent out to the Member States of UNESCO, of the ILO and the Berne Union and also to the States party to the Universal Copyright Convention. In regard to the second condition, the Rapporteur-General pointed out in his Report that there were two opposing schools of thought at the Conference.

Some delegations considered that there was no point in permitting countries which did not belong to one or both the Conventions on copyright to sign and accede to the Convention on neighbouring rights as that accession would produce no effects. They therefore proposed that a country should be required to be a party to at least one of the two Conventions on copyright before being authorized to sign or accede to the Convention. France and Italy in particular argued that the use of literary and artistic works was habitually implicit in the work of performers, producers of phonograms and broadcasting organizations. It was therefore logical to establish a relationship between the copyright Conventions and the Convention on neighbouring rights; they felt that it would not be equitable for performers, producers of phonograms and broadcasters in a particular country to enjoy international protection if the literary and artistic works that they used did not enjoy protection in that country because it was not a member of at least one of the copyright Conventions.

The contrary position was defended by Poland and former Czechoslovakia. The latter country also suggested that the Convention should be open to all nations. It was felt that there was no logical reason for establishing the relationship with copyright, particularly since the Convention would also protect the performance of literary and artistic works which had fallen into the public domain, together with phonograms and broadcasts that made no use of such works.

The majority of the Conference participants voted for the establishment of a link with copyright by adopting Article 23.[222]

iii) Article 24(2) stipulates that the Convention shall be open for accession by any State member of the United Nations provided that such State is a party to one of the two copyright Conventions.

iv) Articles 27(1) and 28(4) and (5) contain provisions consonant with the criteria mentioned above:
- Article 27(1) refers to the procedure to be employed to extend application of the Convention to dependent territories by stipulating that such extension may be made on condition that the Universal Copyright Convention or the Berne Convention is applicable in the same territories.

Pursuant to paragraphs 4 and 5 of Article 28, the Convention shall cease to apply in any country or dependent territory when that country or territory ceases to belong to at least one of the two copyright Conventions.

2. *Non-retroactive effect of the Convention.* Article 20 provides for non-retroactivity in two regards: (1) the Convention shall not prejudice rights acquired in any Contracting State before the date

---

222. See *Records of the Rome Conference*, pp. 54–5.

of entry into force of this Convention in that State; and (2) no Contracting State shall be bound to apply the provisions of the Convention to performances or broadcasts which took place, or to phonograms which were fixed, before the date of coming into force of the Convention for that State. The provision is optional so that a country may decide to grant retroactive protection.[223]

3. *Effects of the Convention in relation to other protective provisions.* Article 21 states that the protection provided for in the Convention shall not prejudice any protection otherwise secured to performers, producers of phonograms and broadcasting organizations. This provision highlights the fact that the protection granted by the Convention does not prevent the application of any other—present or future—national or international legislation providing a greater degree of protection that may be accorded to the beneficiaries of the Convention.

4. *Special agreements.* Article 22 stipulates that the Contracting States reserve the right to enter into special agreements among themselves in so far as such agreements grant more extensive rights than those granted by the Convention itself, or contain other provisions not contrary to the Convention. This provision is directly inspired by Article 20 of the Berne Convention.

f. Administrative and final provisions

1. *Application, denunciation and revision (Articles 23–29)*
Application. We have already referred to Articles 23, 24(2), 27(1) and 28(4) and (5) in regard to the condition that a State may become a party to the Rome Convention only if it is also a member of the Universal Copyright Convention or of the Berne Union or of both.

Articles 23 and 24 also establish the other conditions to which ratification or accession to the Convention is subject.

Article 25 stipulates the date of initial entry into force of the

---

223. See Henri Desbois, André Françon and André Kerever, op. cit., p. 341.

Convention (three months after the date of deposit of the sixth instrument of ratification or accession) and subsequent dates in regard to each of the Contracting States (three months after the date of deposit of its instrument of ratification or accession).

Article 26(1) points out that each Contracting State undertakes to adopt, in accordance with its constitution, the measures necessary to guarantee application of this Convention. Paragraph 2 stipulates that at the time of deposit of its instrument of accession, the State must be in a position under its domestic law to give effect to the terms of this Convention (this provision is analogous to Article X of the Universal Convention).

Article 27 refers to the procedure to be used to extend application of the Convention to dependent territories (the '*colonial clause*').

Denunciation. Pursuant to Article 28(1), (2) and (3), the Convention shall cease to apply in a particular State or dependent territory when the Contracting State denounces it. The denunciation shall take effect 12 months after the relevant notification has been received by the Secretary-General of the United Nations. The right of denunciation may be exercised by a State only after it has been a member of the Convention for five years.

Revision. Article 29 establishes the procedure for convening revision conferences. Paragraph 1 describes the procedure to be followed to convene such conferences; paragraph 2 specifies the procedure for the approval of amendments to the Convention, while paragraph 3 determines the way in which the 1961 text and any other text of the revised Convention shall coexist, depending on the particular case.

2. *Limits to the possibility of formulating reservations.* Article 31 stipulates that reservations may be formulated only with respect to those provisions of the Convention where the Convention specifically establishes the possibility of reservations. Only Articles 5(3), 6(2), 16(1) and 17 permit such reservations. Those provisions have been examined above and it only needs to be added here that Article 18 allows any Contracting State that has formulated reservations to limit their scope or to withdraw the corresponding declaration at any time.

3. *Settlement of disputes between Contracting States.* Pursuant to Article 30 any dispute which may arise between two or more Contracting States concerning the interpretation or application of the Convention and which is not settled by negotiation shall, at the request of any one of the parties to the dispute, be referred to the International Court of Justice at The Hague for a decision (that provision is directly based on Article 27*bis* of the Brussels Act (1948) of the Berne Convention and Article XV of the Universal Convention).

4. *Languages of the Convention.* Pursuant to Article 33, the Convention is drawn up in English, French and Spanish, the three texts being equally authentic. The Convention was signed in all three languages.

The same article stipulates that official texts shall be drawn up in German, Italian and Portuguese. As the Rapporteur-General points out in his report,[224] it was understood that these official texts, which would not be authentic, were to be drawn up by the governments concerned and published by the Secretariats of the ILO, UNESCO and the Berne Union (later WIPO).

5. *The Intergovernmental Committee.* Article 32 established an Intergovernmental Committee (similar to the Committee set up under Article XI of the Universal Copyright Convention): it is responsible for examining questions concerning the application and operation of the Convention, collecting proposals and preparing documentation for possible revision conferences. The members of the Committee are chosen with due regard to equitable geographical distribution and are appointed by the governments of the Contracting States. The Committee was to have between 6 and 12 members, depending on the number of Contracting States, and to meet whenever the majority of its members consider that necessary. The other working procedures of the Committee are also described in this article.

---

224. See *Records*, p. 59.

The same article provides that the Secretariat of the Committee shall be made up of officials drawn from the Secretariats of ILO, UNESCO and the Berne Union (later WIPO). These officials are designated by the Directors-General of the three organizations concerned.

The model law on neighbouring rights.[225] In 1971, the Intergovernmental Committee approved the idea put forward by some delegations concerning the drafting of a model law to facilitate the application of the Rome Convention or its acceptance. It was decided that its Secretariat would prepare a text in consultation with various experts and that this document would be forwarded to the Contracting States for their comments, and also to the non-governmental international organizations concerned. The Committee was thereafter to examine the text and comments. The Secretariat convened a Non-Governmental Study Group to examine the draft model law, and it met in Geneva in 1973. A second Non-Governmental Study Group convened by the Secretariat met in Geneva in January 1974.

Finally, the Intergovernmental Committee adopted the model law (which consists of 13 sections and the accompanying commentary) during an Extraordinary Session which was held from 6 to 10 May 1974 at the Palais d'Egmont in Brussels where the Diplomatic Conference was simultaneously in progress with a view to the conclusion of an International Convention intended to settle the problem of piracy of signals in response to requests made by the broadcasting organizations. The General Rapporteur of the Brussels Conference[226] pointed out that, as was clear from the report of this meeting of the Intergovernmental Committee and from various statements by participants in the Brussels Conference, the results of the two meetings were closely related to each other.[227]

---

225. See *Model Law on Neighbouring Rights*, ILO–UNESCO–WIPO publication, 1974.
226. See below, Section 12.5.3, B.
227. Cf. Report of the General Rapporteur of the Brussels Conference, *Records*, Ed. UNESCO–WIPO, 1977, p. 38, paragraph 23.

Ratifications and accessions. The Rome Convention entered into force on 18 May 1964 with the ratification or accession of Congo, Ecuador, Mexico, Niger, United Kingdom and Sweden.

Subsequent accessions were slow. At the end of 1971, ten years after its adoption, only 12 States belonged to the Convention. Countries were reluctant to ratify it, largely because of the objections to the Convention put forward by authors and by the broadcasting organizations. By 1 January 1995, the number of members had risen to 47, in accordance with the list set out below.

The Rome Convention has still not been revised, despite the fact that it reflects the state of technology in 1961. Progress since then in the technological sphere has brought about far-reaching changes in the forms of exploitation of artistic performances and of cultural products and services; that is why repeated calls have been made of late for the revision of the Convention.

*International Convention for the Protection of Performers, Producers of
Phonograms and Broadcasting Organizations*[a]
(Rome Convention, 26 October 1961)

State	Date on which it became party to the Convention	Reservations
Argentina	2 March 1992	
Australia	30 September 1992	Art. 5(3) (concerning Art 5(1)(c), 6(2), 16(1)(a)(i) and 16(1)(b))
Austria	9 June 1973	Art. 16(1)(a) (iii) and (iv) and 16(1)(b)
Barbados	18 September 1983	
Bolivia	24 November 1993	
Brazil	29 September 1965	
Bulgaria	31 August 1995	Art. 16(1)(a)(iii) and (iv)
Burkina Faso	14 January 1988	
Chile	5 September 1974	
Colombia	17 September 1976	
Congo	18 May 1964	Art. 5(3) (concerning Art. 5(1)(c) and 16(1)(a)(i))
Costa Rica	9 September 1971	
Czech Republic	1 January 1993	Art. 16(1)(a)(iii) and (iv)
Denmark	23 September 1965	Art. 6(2), 16(1)(a)(ii) and (iv) and 17
Dominican Republic	27 January 1987	
Ecuador	18 May 1964	
El Salvador	29 June 1979	
Fiji	11 April 1972	Art. 5(3) (concerning Art. 5(1)(b)); Art. 6(2) and 16(1)(a)(i)
Finland	21 October 1983	Art. 6(2), 16(1)(a)(i), and (iv), 16(1)(b) and 17
France	3 July 1987	Art. 5(3) (concerning Art. 5(1)(c)) and Art. 16(1)(a), (iii) and (iv)
Germany	21 October 1966	Art. 5(3) (concerning Art. 5(1)(b)) and 16(1)(a)(iv)
Greece	6 January 1993	
Guatemala	14 January 1977	
Honduras	16 February 1990	
Hungary	10 February 1995	

State	Date on which it became party to the Convention	Reservations
Iceland	15 June 1994	Art. 5(3) (concerning Art. 5(1)(b)), 6(2) and 16(1)(a)(i), (ii), (iii) and (iv)
Ireland	19 September 1979	Art. 5(3) (concerning Art. 5(1)(b)); 6(2) and 16(1)(a)(ii)
Italy	8 April 1975	Art. 6(2); 16.1(a)(ii) and (iv); 16(1)(b) and 17
Jamaica	27 January 1994	
Japan	26 October 1989	Art. 5(3) (concerning Art. 5(1)(c)), 16(1)(a)(ii) and (iv)
Lesotho	26 January 1990	Art. 16(1)(a)(ii) and 16(1)(b)
Luxembourg	25 February 1976	Art. 5(3) (concerning Art. 5(1)(c)), 16(1)(a)(i) and 16(1)(b)
Mexico	18 May 1964	
Monaco	6 December 1985	Art. 5(3) (concerning Art. 5(1)(c)); 16(1)(a)(i) and 16(1)(b)
Netherlands	7 October 1993	Art. 16(1)(a)(iii) and (iv), 6(2) and 16(1)(a)
Niger	18 May 1964	Art. 5(3) (concerning Art. 5(1)(c)) and 16(1)(a)(i)
Nigeria	29 October 1993	Art. 5(3) (concerning Art. 5(1)(c)), 6(2) and 16(1)(a)(ii), (iii) and (iv)
Norway	10 July 1978	Art. 6(2) and 16(1)(a)(ii), (iii) and (iv)
Panama	2 September 1983	
Paraguay	26 February 1970	
Peru	7 August 1985	
Philippines	25 September 1984	
Republic of Moldova	5 December 1995	Art. 5(3) (concerning Art. 5(1)(b)), 6(2), 16(1)(a)(ii), (iii) and (iv)
Slovakia	1 January 1993	Art. 16(1)(a)(iii) and (iv)
Spain	14 November 1991	Art. 5(3) (concerning Art. 5(1)(c)), 6(2) and 16(1)(a)(iii) and (iv)
Sweden	13 October 1962	Art. 16(1)(b)
Switzerland	24 September 1993	Art. 5(3) (concerning Art. 5(1)(b)) and 16(1)(a)(iii) and (iv)

State	Date on which it became party to the Convention	Reservations
United Kingdom	30 January 1964	Art. 5(3) (concerning Art. 5(1)(b)); 6(2) and 16(1)(a)(ii), (iii) and (iv); the same declarations were made for Gibraltar and Bermuda
Uruguay	4 July 1977	

(Total: 49 countries)

a. Situation as of 1 January 1995, see *Industrial Property and Copyright* (Geneva), WIPO, January 1995.

12.5.2. Convention for the Protection of Producers of Phonograms against Unauthorized Duplication of their Phonograms ('Phonograms' Convention, Geneva, 29 October 1971)

A. ORIGIN OF THE CONVENTION

In the 1960s, the progress of techniques for the fixation and reproduction of sounds resulted in an extraordinary expansion of the market for recorded music; it also led to a substantial increase in the phenomenon of phonographic piracy, not only in the developing countries but also in the main centres of production. Accessions to the Rome Convention were making little progress and many of the more important phonogram-producing countries did not belong to it and had no immediate intention of joining (the United States is still not a member). Although the Rome Convention granted the producers of phonograms the exclusive right to authorize or prohibit the direct or indirect reproduction of their phonograms (Article 10), it did not stipulate measures to prevent the importation of unauthorized copies. In turn, the national legislations did not recognize rights for producers which would have enabled them to defend their products on their own account. The right of reproduction was recognized only in favour of the authors of the works fixed on the phonograms.

In the United States of America the lack of specific protection, and a highly fluid and uncertain body of case law, greatly alarmed the phonographic industry which saw unauthorized reproductions increasing on a scale never experienced hitherto.[228] It was estimated that at least 18,000 illicit tape recordings were manufactured in that country daily, so depriving the North American phonographic industry and its performing artists of a sum estimated at 100 million dollars from the annual sales of phonograms.[229]

In May 1970, during the meeting of the Ad Hoc Preparatory Committee convened to prepare a preliminary draft text of the proposals for revision of the Universal Copyright Convention (which was to be held in the following year simultaneously with the fifth revision of the Berne Convention), the representatives of the phonographic industry asked the Committee to look into the possibility of including in the text of the new version of the Universal Convention provisions banning the manufacture and importation of illicit recordings. The prevailing general opinion was that, however important this issue might be, it nevertheless formed part of the protection of neighbouring rights and did not fall within the ambit of the international conventions for the protection of literary, artistic and scientific works.[230]

---

228. Cf. Valerio De Sanctis, *Rev. Il Diritto di Autore*, No. 2/1972, p. 247.
229. Report by Senator McClellan, quoted by Walter J. Derenberg, in *Copyright* (Geneva), 1971, p. 129, where he points out that to avoid the consequences of action on grounds of unfair competition, the 'pirates', as was found to be the case in the *Spies* proceedings, habitually sold their illicit records with the following disclaimer: 'No relationship of any kind exists between (the pirate) and the original recording company nor between this recording and the original recording artists. This tape is not produced under a licence of any kind from the original recording company nor the recording artist(s) and neither the original recording company nor artist(s) receives a fee or royalty of any kind (from the pirate). Permission to produce this tape has not been sought nor obtained from any party whatsoever.'
230. Cf. *Copyright*, WIPO, 1970, p. 167.

However, the urgent need to establish international protection for producers of phonograms which would enable them to combat phonographic piracy had been recognized, and the request was accepted by the competent bodies of UNESCO and WIPO under whose joint initiative a Committee of Experts was convened. It met in Paris in March 1971. The Committee prepared a draft Convention which was to constitute the working document for the Diplomatic Conference which opened in Geneva on 18 October of the same year.

On 15 October 1971, just before the Geneva Conference met, the United States of America enacted Law 92-140 amending Title 17 of the US Code by establishing limited copyright in sound recordings with a view to protecting them against unauthorized reproduction and counterfeiting, etc. The law was to be applicable to recordings made and published with legal reservation of copyright with effect from 15 February 1972 and was to remain in force until 31 December 1974 since it was believed that the general copyright law including protection of sound recordings would be adopted by 1 June 1975.

The adoption of that law was necessary not only to permit the ratification by the United States of the new international instrument covering phonograms but also to provide some copyright protection for sound recordings which did not enjoy protection under the 1909 law and for which, following certain rulings of the Supreme Court (*Sears* and *Compco* cases),[231] only limited means of redress remained, i.e. on grounds of unfair competition within the ambit of Federal or State legislation.[232]

---

231. *Sears, Roebuck & Co.* vs *Stiffel Co.*, 376 US 225 (1964) and *Compco Corp.* vs *Day-Brite Lighting Inc.*, 376 US 234 (1964) in which the Supreme Court held in 1964 that prohibition of copying of an article which was not patented or copyrighted would be contrary to the principles of Federal Law and of the Constitution which provided for the protection of authors and inventors in respect of their writings and inventions for a limited period of time.

232. Cf. Walter J. Derenberg, op. and loc. cit.

B. The Diplomatic Conference of Geneva (1971)

The Diplomatic Conference was convened by the Directors-General of UNESCO and WIPO and met in Geneva on 18 October 1971. On 29 October, i.e. after less than two weeks, it concluded an international instrument of 13 articles usually known as the *Phonograms Convention*. The Conference was attended by delegations from 50 States and territories and observers from another five States, two intergovernmental organizations (ILO and the League of Arab States) and 13 non-governmental international organizations. The head of the Swiss delegation, Mr Pierre Cavin, was elected President of the Conference and the head of the Cameroon delegation, Mr Joseph Ekedi Samnik, General Rapporteur.

C. The text of the Convention

By comparison with the Rome Convention (1961), the Phonograms Convention presents the following specific features:
- it refers solely to the protection of producers of phonograms against the reproduction, importation and distribution of unauthorized copies of their phonograms;
- it does not provide for national treatment;
- it does not grant exclusive rights in favour of producers of phonograms; its basis is an outline provision (Article 2) which establishes a commitment to reciprocal obligations between the Contracting States;[233]
- no reservations are permitted (except in Article 7(4));
- the Convention makes no provision for subsequent revision.

The report by the General Rapporteur shows that the Conference decided to follow the criterion of the delegations which declared that the new treaty must be as simple as possible and also open to membership of all countries in order to permit its wide acceptance at an early date. In the opinion of these delegations, these concepts of simplicity and universality should be reflected in a

---

233. Cf. Claude Masouyé, *Guide to the Rome Convention and the Phonograms Convention*, p. 102.

convention consisting of a relatively small number of articles which should be limited to determining the obligations of the Contracting States, leaving them to choose the legal means of ensuring protection; and the same concepts should also be reflected in the conditions to be provided for accession or ratification.[234]

Like the Rome Convention, the Phonograms Convention is preceded by a preamble (a feature shared by all the world Conventions on copyright) and by a preliminary provision (Article 1) which sets out definitions of four key expressions for the purpose of the Convention: *phonogram, producer of phonograms* (both identical to the definitions given in Article 1 of the Rome Convention), *duplicate* and *distribution to the public*. We shall return to the latter in our brief outline of the Convention.

a. The basic undertaking by the States. Criterion and purpose of protection under the Convention

Article 2 stipulates that 'Each Contracting State shall protect producers of phonograms who are nationals of other Contracting States against the making of duplicates without the consent of the producer and against the importation of such duplicates, provided that any such making or importation is for the purpose of distribution to the public, and against the distribution of such duplicates to the public'.

The Convention does not establish exclusive rights in favour of its beneficiaries. It simply lays down a commitment by the States to recognize reciprocal obligations. Articles 2 and 3—the substantive dispositions of the Convention—are outline provisions which require the Contracting States to adopt their own complementary domestic measures to give them operational effect.

As the Phonograms Convention does not make provision for national treatment, the Contracting States may establish different provisions for their own nationals.

---

234. *Records* of the International Conference of States on the Protection of Phonograms, Geneva, 1971, published by WIPO–UNESCO, 1975, pp. 37–46, paragraph 25.

Desbois, Françon and Kerever point out that Article 2 and the definitions contained in Article 1 of the terms used in the Convention circumscribe the subject of protection from three points of view: the product which is to be protected; the beneficiaries of such protection and, lastly, the operations in respect of which protection is to be given.[235]

1. *The products covered by protection are the phonograms* defined in Article 1(a) (as in the Rome Convention) as meaning 'any exclusively aural fixation of sounds of a performance or of other sounds'. Two widespread forms of piracy are thus excluded: bootlegging[236] and piracy of videograms since in neither of those instances is a phonogram reproduced while, in the case of audiovisual works, protection is provided by the Copyright Conventions (Berne and Universal).

In regard to the soundtracks of audiovisual works, the General Rapporteur pointed out in his Report that since the definition of the phonogram refers to an exclusively aural fixation, two different interpretations of the Convention would be examined in regard to the situation of records produced from the soundtrack of cinema films or of other audiovisual works.

According to a first body of opinion, the soundtrack is the raw material for the recording in such a way that when an exclusively aural fixation of sounds is made from that track, the resulting recording constitutes a phonogram within the meaning of the Convention. That point of view seems to be strengthened by the fact that the soundtrack is nearly always the subject of alterations or arrangements when the recording is manufactured; a new exclusively sound version may be created in this way.

According to the other interpretation, the sounds embodied in the recordings produced from a soundtrack which was fixed

---

235. Henri Desbois, André Françon and André Kerever, op. cit., p. 356.
236. *Bootlegging* denotes the unauthorized recording, generally on a contraband basis, of musical works performed at concerts, recitals, theatre performances, etc. or when they are broadcast (but not from a phonogram) for subsequent duplication and sale.

for the first time in the form of an audiovisual work, do not have any independent character corresponding to an exclusively aural fixation; it follows that the recording cannot be regarded as a phonogram within the meaning of the Convention, but rather as a part of the original audiovisual work. It was pointed out that, even under this second view, the Convention does not establish anything other than minimal standards of protection, leaving each Contracting State responsibility for protecting soundtracks as phonograms in conformity with its domestic legislation, if it so wishes.

The Conference held that, at all events, the beneficiary of the protection should be the person who fixed the phonogram as such for the first time. It also held that any exclusively aural fixation of sounds should be regarded as a phonogram, even if it is an ephemeral fixation by a broadcasting organization.[237]

2. In regard to the *beneficiaries of protection* (Art. 2), these are the *producers of phonograms* (individuals or legal entities who fix for the first time the sounds of a performance and other sounds (Art. 1(b)) and *are nationals of other Contracting States.*

The Convention adopts then, in principle, only one criterion of personal attachment, *the nationality of the producer*; this is applicable both when the producer is a natural person, or as generally happens, a legal entity. The adoption of the criterion of nationality, in principle, as the sole point of attachment to the Convention may create difficulties even when the producer is a natural person. But in the case of legal entities, the situation is particularly complex since the criteria for the attribution of nationality are many and none of them has been successfully protected against the fraud to which they all lend themselves, especially with the growth of the phenomenon of multinational companies and corporations. In the countries which refuse to attribute nationality to legal entities (for example, Argentina), the adoption of the criterion of nationality in the Phonograms Con-

---

237. Cf. *Records*, op. cit., paras. 35–7.

vention creates even greater problems (the question did not arise with the Rome Convention which also permitted the application of the criterion of the place of first fixation or first publication—Art. 5).

Desbois, Françon and Kerever are of the opinion that in the case of legal entities, it must be concluded that the country of which the producer is a national is in general the country in which the company is domiciled (*le siège de la société*).[238] In consequence, when the producer is a legal entity, account must be taken of the commercial domicile of the company. However, the acceptance of this criterion does not solve the problem, since the 'commercial domicile' (or 'domicile of the company'), is not an unambiguous notion. To lend substance to this notion, each Contracting State will apply the concept adopted by it in its own law: the registered office, the place at which the management or main administration works, the place at which the main place of business or the main operating centres are located.

Article 2 must, however, be read in conjunction with Article 7(4) which states that 'any Contracting State which, on 29 October 1971, affords protection to producers of phonograms solely on the basis of the place of first fixation may, by a notification deposited with the Director-General of the World Intellectual Property Organization, declare that it will apply this criterion instead of the criterion of the nationality of the producer'. However, the effects of this reservation are strictly limited (see above remarks on Art. 5(3) of the Rome Convention which allows certain Contracting States to exclude the criterion of nationality—Sect. 12.5.1, C, c, 2.

3. In regard to the *operations in respect of which protection is provided*, Article 2 stipulates the three following actions: (1) the making of duplicates without the consent of the producer; (2) the importation of such duplicates, provided that any such making or importation is for the purpose of distribution to the public; and (3) the distribution of such duplicates to the public.

---

238. Henri Desbois, André Françon and André Kerever, op. cit., p. 358.

The definition of the term *'duplicate'* is given in Article 1(c), which states that it is 'an article which contains sounds taken directly or indirectly from a phonogram and which embodies all or a substantial part of the sounds fixed in that phonogram'. The term 'article' covers records, tapes, cassettes, etc.; indirect taking refers to successive duplicates made from an authorized or unauthorized copy of a broadcast of a phonogram. As the General Rapporteur points out, the adjective 'substantial' is to be understood as a qualitative as well as a quantitative concept. In the latter sense, the inclusion of even a small part of a phonogram may be regarded as substantial.[239]

Distribution to the public is defined in Article 1(d) as meaning 'any act by which duplicates of a phonogram are offered, directly or indirectly, to the general public or any section thereof'. The Conference Report highlighted the fact that this definition made no express reference to 'commercial purposes' so as not to restrict the field of application of the Convention unnecessarily. It was held that the commercial purpose was implicit in the very terms of the definition of 'distribution to the public'.

The Conference looked at various examples of the meaning of the word 'act' by which duplicates of a phonogram are offered, directly or indirectly, to the public. It held, accordingly, that the term 'act' should, in particular, include the supply of duplicates to a wholesaler with a view to direct or indirect sale to the public.[240]

Pursuant to Article 7(3), the commitment entered into in the Convention refers to phonograms fixed after the entry into force of the provisions of the Convention in each Contracting State.

b. Legal means of protection

1. *Means for application of the Convention.* Article 3 provides for four legal systems of protection: the grant of copyright; the grant of another specific right; protection by the law on unfair competition; and protection by means of penal sanctions. The choice of

---

239. Cf. *Records*, op. cit., paragraph 41.
240. Ibid., paragraph 43.

one or more of these legal means for application of the Convention is left to the domestic legislation of the Contracting States which may choose the system (or systems) which is (are) most consonant with their own legal tradition.

i) The granting of copyright to the producer of phonograms is characteristic of the countries in which the Anglo-American legal system prevails (the United States of America, United Kingdom, Commonwealth countries, Ireland, Israel, etc.). On the other hand, the concept of copyright is not found in the legislation of countries which subscribe to the continental European legal system.

ii) The granting of another specific right refers to protection of the producer by the recognition of a neighbouring right (for example Austria, Germany, Italy, Japan, Norway, Portugal, Sweden, etc.) similar to that granted by Article 10 of the Rome Convention, but extended to the other two operations in respect of which Article 2 of the Phonograms Convention makes provision for protection.

iii) Protection by the law relating to unfair competition comes into play when no specific right exists either in the form of copyright or in that of a neighbouring right (for example Netherlands). Masouyé points out that in the context of international relations, unfair competition is defined as 'any act of competition contrary to honest practices in industrial or commercial matters' (Paris Convention for the Protection of Industrial Property, Art. 10*bis*, para. 2).[241] Desbois, Françon and Kerever point out that the provisions on unfair competition do not protect producers of phonograms as effectively as the granting of an exclusive right. The victim of the competition will have to demonstrate that he has suffered prejudice which is imputable to the sale of copies made without his consent.[242]

---

241. Cf. Claude Masouyé, op. cit., p. 101.
242. Henri Desbois, André Françon and André Kerever, op. cit., p. 364.

iv) The system of protection for producers of phonograms against the operations listed in Article 2 by penal sanctions is completely adequate. Many legislations have adopted this either as the sole system of protection (for example, Argentina) or more generally in conjunction with the grant of a specific right—copyright or a neighbouring right (Brazil, Colombia, Costa Rica, Chile, Dominican Republic, Japan, Portugal, Spain, United Kingdom, United States of America, etc.).

2. *Minimum term of protection.* Article 4 establishes that the duration of the protection given shall be a matter for the domestic law of each Contracting State. However, it provides for a term of not less than 20 years from the end either of the year in which the sounds embodied in the phonogram were first fixed or of the year in which the phonogram was first published.

By comparison with Article 14 of the Rome Convention, the system embodied in the Phonograms Convention is more liberal because it allows the Contracting States to choose between the year of first publication and the year of fixation, while the Rome Convention allows only the latter (choice of the year of publication may provide longer protection; moreover, it is habitually easier to prove than the date of fixation, particularly having regard to Article 5 of the Convention which provides for an identifying symbol containing the year of first publication).

The Report of the Conference indicates that it took account of the impossibility of determining a minimum duration of protection in cases where this is fixed by the national law on unfair competition. However, it was assumed that in such cases protection should not, in principle, end before 20 years counted by the method set out in Article 4 with a view to ensuring a balance between the different systems.[243]

Article 4 also differs from the Rome Convention (and from the international copyright conventions) in that it does not provide for *material reciprocity* in regard to the term of protection.

---

243. See *Report*, paragraph 51.

3. *Formalities.* Article 5 stipulates that in cases where, as a condition of protecting the producers of phonograms, a Contracting State, under its domestic law, requires compliance with formalities, these shall be regarded as fulfilled if all the authorized duplicates of the phonogram distributed to the public or their containers bear a notice consisting of the symbol ℗, accompanied by the year date of first publication (this notice is similar to the provision set out in Article 11 of the Rome Convention). If these duplicates or their containers do not enable the producer, his successor-in-title or the exclusive licensee to be identified (by carrying his name, trade mark or other appropriate designation), the notice shall also include the name of the producer, his successor-in-title or the exclusive licensee.

The draft examined by the Conference also referred to the year of fixation, but in order to avoid possible complications only the year of first publication was finally adopted.[244]

The Conference felt that should there be no proprietor of an exclusive licence, it would be sufficient to enter the name of the producer without the need to mention whether this was the name of the licensee, his successor-in-title or the producer. The possibility of indicating a name other than that of the producer has no effect on the criterion of protection which remains that of the nationality of the producer.[245]

4. *Limits on protection.* Article 6 establishes the limitations which the Contracting States may provide in their domestic law with regard to the protection of producers of phonograms. The permitted limitations are of the same kind as those provided in connection with the protection of the authors of literary and artistic works.

However, pursuant to this provision, *compulsory licences* shall only be permitted if all three of the following conditions are met:

---

244. Ibid., paragraphs 52 and 54.
245. Ibid., paragraph 55.

- the duplication is for use *solely for the purpose of teaching or scientific research*;
- the exportation of copies produced by virtue of the licence is prohibited; and
- the original producer receives equitable remuneration fixed by the competent authority granting the licence, taking account, *inter alia*, of the number of duplicates made.

Article 6 begins by stating that 'any Contracting State which affords protection by means of copyright or other specific right, or protection by means of penal sanctions' may provide these limitations. That is to say, these limitations are permitted only when the protection is given through the granting of exclusive rights. The omission of any reference to the instance in which protection is applied through the legislation on unfair competition is due, as Desbois, Françon and Kerever point out, to the fact that, by reason of the legal nature of the procedural action involved, exceptions analogous to those which limit the exclusive right are not conceivable since this action tends only to permit redress for the benefit of the protected party in respect of a pecuniary prejudice and damage caused by an unfair competitor. The assessment of the prejudice, of the unfair action and the other circumstances which constitute unfair competition must be the subject of a circumstantiated appraisal and, that being so, it is impossible to determine in advance the cases in which an unauthorized copy will not give rise to any form of compensation.[246]

c. The effects of the Convention

1. *Relations between the Phonograms Convention and copyright and neighbouring rights. Effects of the Convention in relation to other protective rules.* Both the preamble and Article 7(1) and (2) of the Convention reflect concern to safeguard the copyright which is embodied in the Berne and Universal Conventions, together with the rights granted by the Rome Convention.

The preamble places on record the conviction that the pro-

---

246. See Henri Desbois, André Françon and André Kerever, op. cit., pp. 367–8.

tection of producers of phonograms against the unauthorized duplication of their phonograms will also benefit performers and authors whose performances and works are recorded on the phonograms (second para.), and the desire not to impair in any way international agreements already in force and, in particular, in no way to prejudice wider acceptance of the Rome Convention (fourth para.).

Article 7(1) makes the same points by stating that 'this Convention shall in no way be interpreted to limit or prejudice the protection otherwise secured to authors, to performers, to producers of phonograms or to broadcasting organizations under any domestic law or international agreement'.

The international agreements referred to are the Berne Convention and the Universal Copyright Convention, the Rome Convention on Neighbouring Rights and the Paris Convention for the Protection of Industrial Property (in particular para. 2 of Art. 10*bis* in regard to any system based on the notion of unfair competition).[247]

Article 7(1) is based on Articles 1 and 21 of the Rome Convention and the commentary on those provisions applies again here (see above, Section 12.5.1, C, (e), 1 and 3).

However, it has been most aptly pointed out[248] that, in some respects, the Phonograms Convention is more prejudicial to authors than the Rome Convention since it permits the possible protection of the producers of phonograms even in those countries which do not recognize copyright. Pursuant to Article 9 of the Phonograms Convention, ratification or accession are open to any member of the United Nations, of any of its Specialized Agencies, of the International Atomic Energy Organization or any party to the Statute of the International Court of Justice. Membership of a copyright convention is therefore unnecessary since the condition set out in Articles 23 and 24 of the Rome Convention is not included. Françon sees this as a serious blow to

---

247. Cf. Claude Masouyé, op. cit., p. 107.
248. Cf. André Françon, 'International Protection of Neighbouring Rights', *RIDA* (Paris), January 1974, pp. 462–4, and the authors cited in note 33.

the pre-eminence of copyright over the rights of the auxiliaries of literary and artistic creation.

In regard to a possible 'superimposition' of the texts of both Conventions (Rome and Phonograms), Masouyé points out that the countries which are parties to both must apply the one which grants the higher level of protection.[249]

Article 7(2) stipulates that it shall be a matter for the domestic law of each Contracting State to determine the extent, if any, to which performers whose performances are fixed in a phonogram are entitled to enjoy protection and the conditions for enjoying any such protection.

This provision might appear superfluous since it indicates to the Contracting States that they have a self-evident prerogative but, since the Convention applies only to the protection of the producers of phonograms, the Conference wished to remind those States that the sale of unauthorized copies of phonograms also violated the rights of performing artists.[250]

Similarly, it should be noted that on considering Article 7(2), the Conference rejected the proposal by the Netherlands which sought to impose on the Contracting States an obligation to protect performers in such a way as to avoid a situation in which, should the producer of phonograms refrain from taking action against the infringer, the performers whose performances were recorded would be without any remedy. The Conference held that the obligation of the producer to take action against the infringer in cases where the performer shares the receipts must normally be stipulated in the contract between the producer and the performer. Nevertheless, the Conference agreed that if the producer failed to exercise the rights vested in him by virtue of the Convention, it would be appropriate for the contracts to be drafted in such a way as to permit performers to take action directly against the infringer.[251]

---

249. Cf. Claude Masouyé, op. cit., pp. 107–8.
250. See Henri Desbois, André Françon and André Kerever, op. cit., p. 370.
251. Cf. *Records*, op. cit., paragraph 65.

2. *Non-retroactive nature of the Convention.* Article 7(3) establishes a provision similar to that set out in Article 20(2) of the Rome Convention by stipulating that no Contracting State shall be required to apply the provisions of this Convention to any phonogram fixed before this Convention entered into force with respect to that State.

As was the case in the previous Convention, this is an optional provision enabling States in which no constitutional obstacles exist, to prohibit, after the entry into force of the Convention, any further reproductions of phonograms made illegally beforehand.

d. Administrative and final provisions

These are set out in Articles 8 to 13; they are similar to those contained in the Conventions already studied and we shall merely list them at this point:
- WIPO is entrusted with the administration of the Convention and with some of the functions that are habitually the responsibility of the depository of an international treaty. WIPO is to perform these tasks in co-operation with UNESCO and ILO in matters falling within their respective terms of reference (Article 8). The Phonograms Convention makes no provision for an Intergovernmental Committee;
- questions relating to the signature of the Convention and its deposit with the Secretary-General of the United Nations are dealt with, the procedures for joining the Convention (ratification or acceptance and accession) are enumerated, and the need to bring domestic law into line with the provisions of the Convention is stipulated (Article 9);
- no reservations are permitted to the Convention (this provision is identical to that set out in Article 16 of the Convention establishing WIPO—Stockholm, 1967), save, of course, that embodied in Article 7(4) (Article 10);
- conditions for the initial entry into force of the Convention are laid down (three months after deposit of the fifth instrument of ratification, or accession) with subsequent conditions for each Contracting State; the 'colonial clause' and the declaration that

this must in no way be interpreted as recognition or tacit acceptance of the factual situation of such territories (a similar declaration appeared for the first time in the Patent Co-operation Treaty (PCT) adopted in Washington in 1970)[252] (Article 11);
- formalities are laid down for denunciation of the Convention, which would take effect 12 months after receipt of the relevant notification (Article 12);
- the languages in which the Convention was drafted (English, French, Russian and Spanish) are listed and provision made for official texts in other languages (Arabic, Dutch, German, Italian and Portuguese); the arrangements for notification are also specified (Article 13).

Ratifications and accessions. The Phonograms Convention entered into force on 18 April 1973 with the accession of Fiji and ratification by Finland, France, Sweden and the United Kingdom.

Other countries joined rapidly. At the end of 1976, five years after its adoption, the Convention had 20 Contracting States, including some of the leading producers and consumers of phonograms. By 1 January 1995, the number of Member Countries had risen to 52, as shown in the following list:

---

252. See Claude Masouyé, op. cit., p. 115.

*Convention for the Protection of Producers of Phonograms against
Unauthorized Duplication of their Phonograms*[a]
(Phonograms Convention, Geneva, 29 October 1971)

State	Date of membership of the Convention
Argentina	30 June 1973
Australia	22 June 1974
Austria	21 August 1982
Barbados	29 July 1983
Brazil	28 November 1975
Bulgaria	6 September 1995
Burkina Faso	30 January 1988
Chile	24 March 1977
China	30 April 1993
Colombia	16 May 1994
Costa Rica	17 June 1982
Cyprus	30 September 1993
Czech Republic	1 January 1993
Denmark	24 March 1977
Ecuador	14 September 1974
Egypt	23 April 1978
El Salvador	9 February 1979
Fiji	18 April 1973
Finland*	18 April 1973
France	18 April 1973
Germany	18 May 1974
Greece	9 February 1994
Guatemala	1 February 1977
Holy See	18 July 1977
Honduras	6 March 1990
Hungary	28 May 1975
India	12 February 1975
Israel	1 May 1978
Italy*	24 March 1977
Jamaica	11 January 1994
Japan	14 October 1978
Kenya	21 April 1976
Luxembourg	8 March 1976
Mexico	21 December 1973
Monaco	2 December 1974
Netherlands**	12 October 1993
New Zealand	13 August 1976

State	Date of membership of the Convention
Norway	1 August 1978
Panama	29 June 1974
Paraguay	13 February 1979
Peru	24 August 1985
Republic of Korea	10 October 1987
Russian Federation	13 March 1995
Slovakia	1 January 1993
Spain	24 August 1974
Sweden	18 April 1973
Switzerland	30 September 1993
Trinidad and Tobago	1 October 1988
United Kingdom	18 April 1973
United States of America	10 March 1974
Uruguay	18 January 1983
Venezuela	18 November 1982
Zaïre	29 November 1977

(Total: 53 countries)

a. Situation as of 1 January 1996; see *Industrial Property and Copyright* (Geneva), WIPO, January 1996.
* This State has declared, in accordance with Article 7(4) of the Convention, that it will apply the criterion according to which it affords protection to producers of phonograms solely on the basis of the place of first fixation instead of the criterion of the nationality of the producer.
** Accession for the Kingdom in Europe.

12.5.3. Convention relating to the Distribution of Programme-carrying Signals Transmitted by Satellite ('Satellites' Convention), Brussels, 21 May 1974

A. ORIGIN OF THE CONVENTION

Because of the increasing development and use of orbiting or geo-stationary satellites in international telecommunications[253] since 1965, the broadcasting organizations expressed the need for adequate protection against the 'piracy of signals' when their television programmes were transmitted by space satellites. They maintained that these programmes were not protected by copyright since many of them broadcast sporting events of major international economic significance (such as the Olympic Games, the World Football Cup, boxing matches, etc.) or public events of general interest (coronations, processions, etc.).

The Rome Convention had left a measure of uncertainty as to whether Article 13 granted protection to broadcasts by broadcasting organizations in cases where the means of transmission was a satellite, that is to say when the broadcasts were transmitted through a satellite, as this Convention covered only wireless transmission.

A preliminary examination of the legal problems arising from intercontinental broadcasts of television programmes by satellite was made at a number of international meetings in 1968 and 1969, following which UNESCO and BIRPI decided to convene jointly a Committee of Governmental Experts to examine the problems arising in the sphere of copyright and protection of performers, producers of phonograms and broadcasting organizations by reason of broadcasts made via space satellites.

The Committee of Governmental Experts held three meetings: in Lausanne (1971), Paris (1972) and Nairobi (1973), preparing the way for the Diplomatic Conference in Brussels (1974).

In the Report of the Diplomatic Conference in Brussels (1974), the General Rapporteur pointed out that the three Committees of Governmental Experts, recognizing the urgency of the problem, had examined several possible solutions:
- the revision of the International Telecommunication Convention or of the annexed Radio Regulations;
- the revision of the Rome Convention (1961);
- the adoption of a new multilateral Convention; or

---

253. See above, Chap. 4, Sect. 4.3.2.4.

- some other formula, such as the confirmation of the existing international agreements or the adoption of a straightforward resolution condemning the piracy of signals.

As the preparatory work progressed, a consensus emerged in favour of the third solution; even though some countries considered that the Rome Convention granted broadcasters protection against unauthorized rebroadcasting of their signals transmitted by satellites, it was still clear that, because of the few accessions to that Convention, it did not immediately lend itself to a solution of this problem at world level. The International Telecommunication Convention was also felt to be inadequate because of its technical specialization, even though Switzerland, for example, felt it to be the appropriate framework for a solution to the problem of signal piracy—an opinion which it reiterated at the opening of the 1974 Conference.[254]

At the meetings of the three Committees of Experts, discussions focused mainly on a number of drafts of a new multilateral convention designed to prevent the rebroadcasting of signals transmitted via satellites by distributors for whom they were not intended; but it proved particularly difficult to arrive at a general consensus on the content and terms of this Convention.[255]

The Report referred to above highlighted the fact that the main difficulty arose at the meeting of the *First Committee* of Governmental Experts (Lausanne, 1971) and took up a great deal of the proceedings of all three preparatory meetings. The problem was to know whether, if exclusive rights were granted to the originating broadcasting organizations in the sphere of private law and within a new international Convention, that facility would be compensated by the granting of correlative rights to the 'contributors' to the programmes. The Lausanne Report drew attention to the fact that 'several delegations said that they could accept an independent treaty only if it contained provisions safe-

---

254. Cf. *Records of the Conference of States on the Distribution of Programme-carrying Signals Transmitted by Satellite*, ed. UNESCO–WIPO, 1977, para. 39.
255. Ibid., para. 9.

guarding the interests of authors, performers and producers of phonograms, and did not prejudice the future of the Rome Convention'. A draft Convention was prepared and the pursuit of the preparatory work recommended.[256]

The *Second Committee* (Paris, 1972) did not manage to solve the problem of the recognition of correlative rights for 'contributors' to programmes. The way forward was found by the *Third Committee* of Governmental Experts (Nairobi, 1973) which changed both the general concept and the legal structure of the draft Convention as a consequence of a proposal submitted by the delegations of Morocco, Brazil, India and Mexico. The Report of the 1974 Conference points out that the Nairobi draft proposed that the Convention should pass from the field of private international law into that of public international law, by eliminating any reference to private rights and leaving the States free to decide for themselves the most suitable means of eliminating piracy on their respective territories. Instead of requiring the States to ensure respect for individual property rights by recognizing an exclusive right of authorization, the Nairobi text called upon them to adopt all appropriate measures to prevent the distribution on their territories of signals broadcast from satellites by distributors for whom those signals were not intended.

Since the Convention itself did not grant new rights to broadcasters, the majority of the delegations and almost all the observers present in Nairobi therefore felt that there was no longer any need to create additional new rights in parallel within the ambit of the Convention to protect the interests of 'contributors' to the programmes. The Nairobi draft was accordingly approved by the Third Committee which considered that it could be generally accepted and recommended the convening, in 1974, of a diplomatic conference to draw up an International Convention in this area.[257]

---

256. Ibid.
257. Ibid., paras. 12–13.

B. The Diplomatic Conference in Brussels (1974)

The Directors-General of UNESCO and WIPO jointly convened the Diplomatic Conference which, at the invitation of the Belgian Government, met in Brussels on 6 May 1974. The Conference was attended by delegations from 47 States and observers from a further 10 States, 5 intergovernmental organizations (United Nations, ILO, Council of Europe, Organization of Arab States for Education, Culture and Science (ALECSO) and the International Telecommunications Satellite Organization (INTELSAT)) together with 17 non-governmental international organizations. Gérard de San (one of the leaders of the Belgian delegation) was elected Chairman of the Conference and Miss Barbara Ringer (United States) was appointed General Rapporteur.

The Report of the Conference pointed out that, in the course of the general introductory debate, several delegations emphasized very strongly that the Rome Convention and the new Convention must be complementary and not competitive. The existence of the new Convention must on no account be permitted to undermine the growth of the Rome Convention.[258] In their turn, a number of speakers referred to the interrelationship between developments leading to the Brussels Conference on the one hand and the preparation of a model law for the application of the Rome Convention on the other. The delegate of the United Kingdom stated that, unless the broadcasters and their representatives were to show a substantial change of attitude to the Rome Convention and until such time as that change occurred, his Government would be unlikely to consider signing or acceding to the new Treaty on Satellites. The imperious need for a change in attitude on the part of the broadcasting organizations in regard to the Rome Convention was also stressed in the observations made by the delegates of Brazil, Mexico, Denmark, Austria, Australia and the then Federal Republic of Germany, which expressed the hope that the Brussels Conference would be a decisive

---

258. See above, Sect. 12.5.1, C, f, 5.

turning point in achieving peaceful, symbiotic relations between broadcasters and the other beneficiaries of the Rome Convention and a major step forward in the history of that Convention.[259]

The proceedings of the Conference ended on 21 May 1974 with the adoption of the Convention on the Distribution of Programme-carrying Signals Transmitted by Satellite—commonly referred to as the *Satellites Convention*.

C. THE TEXT OF THE CONVENTION

The Convention preserves the general concept and legal structure of the Nairobi draft (1973); it refers only to protection of the programme-carrying signals transmitted by satellite by broadcasting organizations. It does not create exclusive rights for those organizations since it is a treaty in public international law which leaves the States free to choose the most appropriate means of putting an end to piracy of signals on their respective territories.

By analogy with the other Conventions on neighbouring rights that we have already dealt with, it contains a *preamble* reflecting the concepts underlying the Nairobi draft and the Phonograms Convention, while *Article 1* sets out definitions lending technical precision to some of the terms used in the text of the Convention and facilitating its understanding. We shall return to them in due course.

a. The purpose of the Convention

The fundamental provision of the Convention is to be found in Article 2(1): 'Each Contracting State undertakes to take adequate measures to prevent the distribution on or from its territory of any programme-carrying signal by any distributor for whom the signal emitted to or passing through the satellite is not intended.

---

259. See *Records*, op. cit., para. 38. It should be noted that the resistance by the broadcasting organizations to the Rome Convention stemmed from Art. 12 which granted performers or producers of phonograms or both a right to remuneration in respect of the 'secondary uses' of phonograms in broadcasting.

This obligation shall apply where the originating organization is a national of another Contracting State and where the signal distributed is a derived signal.'

This provision also points to the sphere of application of the Convention and the scope of the obligations contained in it.

1. *The scope of application of the Convention.* This is defined by Article 2(1) in conjunction with Article 3 which reads: 'This Convention shall not apply where the signals emitted by or on behalf of the originating organization are intended for direct reception from the satellite by the general public.'

In consequence, the Convention does not apply to the distribution of signals taken from direct broadcasting satellites (DBS). It emerges from the Report of the Conference that this exclusion might have been made in Article 2, but the matter was felt to be important enough to warrant a separate article.[260]

In the case which is excluded from the Convention, there is only one distributing organization, that of origin, since the signals broadcast or rebroadcast by space stations are intended for *direct* reception by the general public.

The Convention concerns itself only, then, with cases of *indirect* broadcasting which have the following features:
- the originating organization must be a national of a Contracting State;
- a signal must have passed through a satellite;
- a chain of distributors must take that signal over after it has passed through the satellite;
- a distributor for whom the signal was not intended must intercept it at a point in the distribution chain; and
- distribution must be effected on or from the territory of a Contracting State.[261]

Desbois, Françon and Kerever maintain that an originating organization which is a national of a Contracting State may address

---

260. Ibid., para. 84.
261. Ibid., para. 99.

itself to the competent authorities in another Contracting State to ask them to prevent a distributor who has not been authorized by the former from distributing a particular programme 'in or from' its territory. For the obligation under the Convention to arise, both the State of which the originating organization is a national and the State in or from which the distribution is made, must be Contracting States. Nationality therefore constitutes the criterion of attachment to the Convention.[262] Since the originating organization is necessarily a public organization or a legal entity, it is the place of the domicile of the company in a Contracting State which determines the attachment to the field of application of the Convention (Article 8(2), as we shall see later on, permits certain States to formulate a reservation in regard to the criterion of nationality).

The Convention also excludes from its field of application the supposition referred to in Article 2(3) which states that 'the obligation provided for in paragraph 1 shall not apply to the distribution of derived signals taken from signals which have already been distributed by a distributor for whom the emitted signals were intended'. The Report of the Conference points out that the fundamental concept underlying Article 2(3) is that the Convention has as its main object space communications so that its applicability must not extend to situations that are essentially terrestrial. If the signals were intended for at least one of the distributors situated at prior stages of the chain, the fact that the signals have been emitted through a satellite would not render the Convention applicable. This is a case of rebroadcasting which falls entirely within the sphere of application of the Rome Convention.[263]

2. *Definitions*. Some of the terms used in the Convention are defined in Article 1. They are taken directly from the ITU Radio Regulations.

---

262. See Henri Desbois, André Françon and André Kerever, op. cit., pp. 380–1.
263. See *Records of the Conference of States on the Distribution of Programme-carrying Signals Transmitted by Satellite*, para. 100.

In the first place, the protected object is the signal which carries the programme and not the programme itself. During the Conference, attention was often drawn to the fact that the Convention relates to the container (the signal) and not the content (the programme).[264] Pursuant to Article 1 the *signal* is an electronically generated carrier capable of transmitting programmes, and a *programme* is a body of live or recorded material consisting of images, sounds or both, embodied in signals emitted for the purpose of ultimate distribution (the Convention is therefore not confined to television signals, but also covers sound broadcasting). The signal to which the Convention refers is one which has passed through a satellite and is ultimately intended for distribution. A *satellite* is any device in extra-terrestrial space capable of transmitting signals, and *distribution* is the operation by which a distributor transmits derived signals to the general public or any section thereof.

As the Conference report[265] points out, the concept of *distribution* is the most important in the Convention since it constitutes the act which the Contracting States undertake to prevent in certain circumstances. The key element in the concept of *distribution* is that the programme-carrying signals must be transmitted 'to the general public or any section thereof', and that the *distributor* is defined as the person or legal entity which decides that the transmission of the derived signals to the general public or any section thereof should take place.

b. Scope of the obligations under the Convention

Pursuant to Article 2(1), each of the Contracting States 'undertakes to take adequate measures to prevent' the distribution on or from its territory of any programme-carrying signals by any distributor for whom the signal emitted to or passing through the satellite is not intended. That is the basic obligation entered into by the States under the Satellites Convention.

---

264. Ibid., para. 64.
265. Ibid., para. 74.

1. *Adequate measures.* Unlike Article 13 of the Rome Convention which establishes that the States shall enjoy the right of authorizing or prohibiting the rebroadcasting of their broadcasts and the fixing and reproduction thereof, the Satellites Convention does not grant an exclusive right to broadcasting organizations, but stipulates that the States will take 'adequate measures'. Unlike Article 3 of the Phonograms Convention which limits the legal means for its application to four, the Satellites Convention does not define the 'adequate measures' that the Contracting States undertake to put in place.

According to the Report of the Conference, it became clear that the Contracting States were left with complete freedom to satisfy this fundamental requirement in whatever manner they felt appropriate. While the obligation of the Convention might well be performed within the legal framework of intellectual property laws granting protection to signals pursuant to the theories of copyright or neighbouring rights, a Contracting State could just as rightly adopt administrative measures, penal sanctions or telecommunications laws or regulations on the subject. As stated in paragraph 62 of the Report of the Nairobi Committee 'the good faith of the States in providing effective measures against piracy could and should be assumed'.[266]

2. *The duration of adequate measures.* Article 2(2) reads as follows:

In any Contracting State in which the application of the measures referred to in paragraph (1) is limited in time, the duration thereof shall be fixed by its domestic law. The Secretary-General of the United Nations shall be notified in writing of such duration at the time of ratification, acceptance or accession, or if the domestic law comes into force or is changed thereafter, within six months of the coming into force of that law or of its modification.

This provision settled the dispute between two opposing trends: one in favour and the other against the fixing of a minimum term.

---

266. Ibid., para. 79.

(1) The body of opinion in favour of fixing a minimum term maintained that it would otherwise be possible to interpret the text as an attempt to impose a permanent obligation in respect of recorded signals, or else the opposite risk—that the States might consider their obligation to take all 'adequate measures' to have been fulfilled shortly after the satellite broadcast was made. Concern was also expressed as to whether the States party to the Rome Convention could accede to a Convention which did not require a minimum term of 20 years for broadcasts. (2) The other body of opinion maintained that a provision establishing a minimum term would be incompatible with a treaty carrying no obligation to protect private property rights and leaving States free to decide for themselves on the most effective ways of preventing the distribution of signals broadcast by satellite by distributors for whom they were not intended. It was also argued that although a specified minimum term might be relevant when it came to the programme content of a signal, it became difficult to apply logically if one was speaking only of the signal as such. According to the Conference Report, some delegates were also worried by a legal situation in which new terms would start for particular signals upon each new emission, even though the programme contained in the signal might be old or even in the public domain.

After a lengthy discussion, Article 2(2) was adopted by the Conference on the understanding that the Report would contain an account of the events leading up to that approval and conclude with the following interpretative paragraph which was also adopted by the Conference without objection: 'With respect to the duration of the measures referred to in Article 2(1), it was generally considered that a period of 20 years could constitute a reasonable period.'[267]

3. *Limitations on the obligation to take adequate measures.* Article 4 does not require any Contracting State to apply 'adequate measures' when it may be considered that the programme-

---

267. Ibid., paras. 86–98.

carrying signal distributed on its territory by an unauthorized distributor falls within the limitations on copyright because it: (i) includes short excerpts of reports of current events; or (ii) includes quotations from the programme carried by the emitted signal; or (iii) where the said territory is that of a Contracting State regarded as a developing country in conformity with the established practice of the General Assembly of the United Nations (this is a repetition of the criterion embodied in Article I(1) of the Appendix to the Paris Text of the Berne Convention and also in Article V*bis*(1) of the Paris Revision of the Universal Copyright Convention), distribution is solely for the purpose of teaching, including teaching in the framework of adult education, or scientific research.

During the Conference it became clear that if a State had contracted obligations by virtue of other treaties such as the Copyright Convention, the Rome Convention or the ITU Convention, these would not be superseded by the exceptions referred to in Article 4. Similarly, it was pointed out that the Satellites Convention would apply solely at international level and that none of its provisions could have limitative effects of any kind in respect of legislation regulating purely national situations in any Contracting State.[268]

c. The effects of the Convention

1. *Relations with copyright and neighbouring rights.* Article 6 stipulates that the Convention shall in no way be interpreted as limiting or prejudicing the protection secured to authors, performers, producers of phonograms or broadcasting organizations, under any domestic law or international agreement.

As to the meaning of the word 'secured' used in the wording of Article 6, the Conference agreed that the Report should clarify the fact that this term meant 'the right existing at the time when distribution was made' and not 'rights secured in the past'.[269]

---

268. Ibid., para. 111.
269. Ibid., para. 118.

2. *Effects of the Convention in relation to national rules to prevent abuses of monopoly.* Article 7 stipulates that the Convention shall in no way be interpreted as limiting the right of any Contracting State to apply its domestic law in order to prevent abuses of monopoly.

The 1974 Report points out that the purpose of this article is fully to preserve the application of domestic laws against abuses of monopoly and other dominant positions. In the area of the Satellites Convention, the application of these laws means that if the conditions required for the enforcement of the law exist, a distributor not designated by the originating organization may be authorized by the competent national authorities to distribute programme-carrying signals. However, such a measure may not be applied when the originating organization does not possess the rights in the programme carried by the signals for the country concerned. The Report points out that a measure under Article 7 would not be justified either by the mere fact that the originating organization asks a price that is considered too high for the signal, if it has not been established that this price is not justified by the costs of production and transmission. The Conference adopted the article in question, on the clear understanding that the Contracting States would apply it in good faith and only in cases where its application was felt by them to be fully legitimate.[270]

3. *Non-retroactive nature of the Convention.* Pursuant to Article 5, no Contracting State shall be required to apply the Convention with respect to any signal emitted before the Convention entered into force for that State. This provision is based directly on Article 20(2) of the Rome Convention and Article 7(3) of the Phonograms Convention.

d. Reservations

Article 8(1) does not permit reservations except in the two cases defined in paragraphs (2) and (3) of that article.

---

270. Ibid., pp. 122–3.

Article 8, para. 2 deals with the case of Contracting States whose legislation in force on the date of approval of the Convention (21 May 1974) is based on the criterion of the place from which the signals are emitted and permits a declaration by them that they will apply the latter instead of the criterion of nationality of the originating organization adopted by the Convention as a general rule in its Article 2(1).

Article 8(3) refers to Contracting States whose legislation in force on the above-mentioned date considers that retransmissions by cable distribution systems intended for subscribers are not covered by copyright. Those States may declare that, as long as their domestic legislation limits or denies protection, they will not apply the Convention to such distribution.

As indicated in the Report, the Conference recognized the need for a clause to permit reservations in this respect in order to secure broad ratification of the Convention. However, having regard to the provisions of the ITU Convention and the aims of the Satellites Convention, it was agreed that a cable system should not, relying on a reservation made by virtue of Article 8(3), pick up and distribute signals from a satellite before those signals have been distributed terrestrially in the area where the cable system can receive the terrestrial broadcast.[271]

The second part of Article 8(3) establishes the obligation on the Contracting States that have deposited a notification within the meaning of the first subparagraph, to notify the Secretary-General of the United Nations in writing, within six months of their coming into force, of any changes in their domestic law whereby the reservation under that subparagraph becomes inapplicable or more limited in scope.

e. Administrative and final provisions

The provisions set out in Articles 9 to 12 are very similar, *mutatis mutandis*, to those contained in the Conventions already dealt with, and, in particular, in the Phonograms Convention:

---

271. Ibid., paras. 125–9.

- they deal with matters relating to the signature of the Convention and to its deposit with the Secretary-General of the United Nations. Procedures for access to the Convention are listed (ratification or acceptance and accession) and the harmonization of national law with the conditions of the Convention is stipulated (Article 9);
- conditions are laid down for the initial entry into force of the Convention (three months after the deposit of the fifth instrument of ratification or accession) and for subsequent entry into force in each Contracting State (Article 10);
- formalities are laid down for denunciation of the Convention which will take effect 12 months after the receipt of the written notification (Article 11);
- the languages in which the Convention was drafted are listed (English, French, Russian and Spanish); provision is made for official texts in other languages (Arabic, Dutch, German, Italian and Portuguese) and the procedure for notifications by the Secretary-General of the United Nations is defined (Article 12).

Ratifications and accessions: The Satellites Convention entered into force on 25 August 1979 with ratification by Germany, Kenya, Mexico and Yugoslavia and the accession of Nicaragua.

On 1 March 1995, there were 19 Contracting States, as listed below.

*Convention Relating to the Distribution of Programme-carrying Signals
Transmitted by Satellite*[a]
(Satellites Convention, Brussels, 1974)

State	Date on which it became party to the Convention
Armenia	13 December 1993
Australia	26 October 1990
Austria	6 August 1982
Bosnia and Herzegovina	6 March 1992
Croatia	8 October 1991
Germany*	25 August 1979
Greece	22 October 1991
Italy*	7 July 1981
Kenya	25 August 1979
Mexico	25 August 1979
Morocco	30 June 1983
Nicaragua	25 August 1979
Panama	25 September 1985
Peru	7 August 1985
Russian Federation**	20 January 1989
Slovenia	25 June 1991
Switzerland	24 September 1993
United States of America	7 March 1985
Yugoslavia	25 August 1979

(Total: 19 States)

a. Situation as of 1 January 1995; see *Industrial Property and Copyright* (Geneva), WIPO, January 1995.
* With a declaration, pursuant to Article 2(2) of the Convention, that the protection accorded under Article 2(1) is restricted in its territory to a period of 25 years after the expiry of the calendar year in which the transmission by satellite has occurred.
** Date of accession by the Soviet Union, continued by the Russian Federation as from 25 December 1991.

12.6. International recommendations approved by the General Conference of UNESCO

The international recommendations approved by the General Conference of UNESCO which will be considered below contain provisions on a variety of subjects. Some concern copyright and neighbouring rights in the true sense of the term; others touch upon matters which fall within these rights in a broad interpretation. Some of them on the other hand include concepts which are of a completely different legal nature and fall within the ambit of the right to culture.

The recommendations in question encourage policies which must have a bearing on copyright and neighbouring rights, both because they are linked by virtue of the subject matter and purposes involved and because they refer to the needs of the community in the area of access to culture. It is important to bear in mind that the various interests involved do not come into conflict but are complementary. The protection of translations as derived works, for example, comes within the context of copyright in the strict sense of the term, while the protection of artistic performances is covered by the right of performing artists. Within these areas and taken in a broader sense are other matters as well which are essential for the exercise of recognized rights, such as the regulation of contracts and professional collective administration organizations.

Other matters dealt with in the recommendations refer to the right to culture and to cultural legislation, such as the protection and preservation of moving images.

12.6.1. Recommendation on the legal protection of translators and translations and the practical means to improve the status of translators (Nairobi, 22 November 1976)

At its nineteenth session, the General Conference of UNESCO approved the Recommendation on the legal protection of translators and translations and the practical means to improve the status of translators (Nairobi, 22 November 1976).

The provisions of the Recommendation were to be applied by the Member States through the adoption of national legislative or other necessary measures in conformity with the constitutional practices and principles of each State.

The Recommendation applies to all translators regardless of (a) their legal status (independent or salaried translators); (b) the discipline to which the translated work belongs and (c) the nature of their activity (full-time or part-time).

In relation to the *general legal situation of translators,* the Member States are required to grant them, in respect of their translations, the protection which they grant to authors in conformity with the provisions of the international copyright Conventions to which they are parties or with their national legislation, or both, and without prejudice to the rights of the authors of the original works.

In regard to *the measures to ensure the application of protection afforded translators under international conventions and in national laws relating to copyright,* it is considered desirable for the translator and the user of the translation to conclude a written agreement. As a general rule, both this contract and any other legal instrument governing relations between the translator and the user, together with the other conditions set out in the Recommendation, must:
- accord an equitable remuneration to the translator, whatever his or her legal status;
- at least when the translator is not working as a salaried translator, remunerate him or her in proportion to the proceeds of the sale or use of the translation with payment of an advance, the said advance being retained by the translator; or by the payment of a sum calculated in conformity with another system of remuneration independent of sales where it is provided for or permitted by national legislation; or by the payment of an equitable lump sum which could be made where payment on a proportional basis proves insufficient or inapplicable;
- make provision, when appropriate, for a supplementary payment should the use made of the translation go beyond the limitations specified in the contract;
- specify that the authorizations granted by the translator are limited to the rights expressly mentioned, this provision applying to possible new editions;

- stipulate that in the event that the translator has not obtained any necessary authorization, it is the user who is responsible for obtaining such authorization;
- stipulate that the translator guarantees the user uncontested enjoyment of all the rights granted and undertakes to refrain from any action likely to compromise the legitimate interests of the user and, when appropriate, to observe the rule of professional secrecy, etc.

With a view to facilitating the application of the measures recommended and without prejudice to the translator's freedom to enter into an individual contract, the Member States should encourage the parties concerned, in particular the professional organizations of translators and other representative bodies on the one hand and the representatives of users on the other, to adopt model contracts or to conclude collective agreements, taking account of the content of the Recommendation and all situations that may occur in regard to the person of the translator and the nature of the translation.

The Member States are asked to promote the organization and development of professional associations of translators responsible for defining the rules and obligations which should govern the exercise of the profession, for defending the moral and material interests of translators and facilitating linguistic, cultural, scientific and technical exchanges. To this end, such organizations might undertake, to the extent that national law so allows, activities such as the following:

- promotion of the adoption of standards governing the translation profession. Such standards should stipulate, in particular, that the translator has a duty to provide a translation of high quality from the linguistic and stylistic points of view and to guarantee that it will be a faithful rendering of the original;
- study of the bases for remuneration acceptable to translators and users;
- establishment of procedures to assist in the settlement of disputes arising in connection with the quality of translations;
- provision of advice to translators, and so on.

In regard to the *social and fiscal situation of translators*, those who work on an independent basis should benefit from all the social security systems and from the tax arrangements adopted in favour of the authors of literary or scientific works in general, including technical works. Salaried translators should be treated on the same basis as other salaried professional staff and enjoy the same social schemes.

In regard to the *training and working conditions of translators*, Member States should recognize in principle that translation is an independent discipline requiring an education distinct from exclusively language teaching and that this discipline requires a special training. Member States should consider organizing terminology centres which might undertake the following activities: to communicate to translators current information concerning terminology required by them in the general course of their work; and to collaborate closely with terminology centres throughout the world with a view to standardizing and developing the internationalization of scientific and technical terminology.

With a view to improving the quality of translations: translators should be given a reasonable period of time to accomplish their work; any documents and information necessary for the understanding of the texts should be made available to them; as a general rule, a translation should be made from the original work; and the translator should, as far as possible, translate into his own mother tongue or into a language of which he has a mastery equal to that of his mother tongue.

12.6.2. Recommendation concerning the Status of the Artist (Belgrade, 27 October 1980)[272]

At its twenty-first session, the General Conference of UNESCO adopted the Recommendation concerning the Status of the Artist (Belgrade, 27 October 1980). This Recommendation applies to all creative artists and authors within the meaning of the Universal Copyright Convention and the Berne Convention and also to performing artists within the meaning of the Rome Convention.

Member States, recognizing the essential role of art in the life

---

272. Cf. *Copyright Bulletin* (Paris), UNESCO, No. 4/1980, pp. 7–17.

and development of the individual and of society, have a duty to protect, defend and assist artists and their freedom of creation. For this purpose, they should acknowledge their right to enjoy the fruits of their work. They should endeavour to increase the participation of artists in decisions affecting the quality of life. They should demonstrate and confirm by all possible means that artistic activities have a part to play in the nations' global development effort.

Similarly, they should ensure that artists have the freedom and the right to establish trade unions and professional organizations of their own choosing and to become members of such organizations if they so wish. Without prejudice to the rights that should be accorded to them under copyright legislation, including resale rights (*droit de suite*) when this is not part of copyright, and under neighbouring rights legislation, artists should enjoy equitable conditions and their profession should be given the public consideration that it merits. Since freedom of expression and communication is the prerequisite for all artistic activities, Member States should ensure that artists are unequivocally accorded the protection provided for in this respect by international and national legislation concerning human rights.

In regard to the *vocation and training of artists*, the Member States should, among other things, recognize the importance in arts and craft training of the traditional ways of transmitting knowledge and in particular of the initiation practices of various communities, and take all appropriate measures to protect and encourage them. They should promote the free international movement of artists and not hinder the freedom to practise their art in the country of their choice.

As far as possible, and without prejudice to the freedom and independence that artists and educators must enjoy, Member States should take or support initiatives designed to give artists in the course of their training a more authentic awareness of the cultural identity of their community, including traditional culture and folklore.

As to the *social status* of artists, Member States should ensure the conditions necessary for respect and development of the work of artists and the economic safeguards to which they are entitled as cultural workers. Measures must accordingly be taken to ensure that artists enjoy the rights and protection provided for in international and national legislation on human rights. An endeavour must be made to take suitable measures to enable artists to enjoy the rights conferred on a comparable group of the active population in the area of employment, living and working conditions, and to ensure that the self-employed artist enjoys, within reasonable limits, protection as regards income and social security. They must also recognize the importance of international protection of artists by virtue of the Berne, Universal and Rome Conventions.

Concerning *employment, working and living conditions of the artist, professional and trade union organizations*, and having regard to the importance of artists in the life of the community, Member States should give them support in respect of conditions of employment and working and living conditions in general.

Having regard to the role played by professional and trade union organizations in the defence of employment and working conditions, Member States are invited to take appropriate steps to observe and secure observance of the standards relating to freedom of association, the right of organization and collective bargaining, set forth in international employment conventions.

Recognizing in general that national and international legislation on the status of artists is lagging behind the general advances in technology, the development of the mass communication media, the mechanical reproduction of works of art and of performances, the education of the public and the decisive part played by the cultural industries, Member States are invited to adopt appropriate measures to ensure that artists are remunerated for the distribution and commercial exploitation of their work and provide for artists to maintain control of their work against unauthorized exploitation, modification or distribution. As far as possible, provision should be made for a system guaranteeing their exclusive moral and material rights. Artists, and their organizations, should be helped to remedy the adverse effects of the new technologies on their employment or work possibilities.

Having regard to the manifestly unstable nature of artists' incomes and their sudden fluctuations, the special features of artistic activity and the fact that many artistic callings can be exercised only for a relatively short period of life, Member States are invited to make provision for pension rights for certain categories of artists according to the length of their careers and not the attainment of a certain age and to ensure that their tax system takes account of the particular conditions of their activities.

Having regard to the growing importance of international exchanges of works of art and contacts between artists and the need to encourage them, Member States are invited to assist greater freedom of movement for these works—more especially by flexible custom arrangements and exemptions from customs duties, particularly in respect of temporary importation. Similarly, measures should be taken to promote international travel and exchanges by artists, giving due attention to national artists on tour.

In regard to *cultural policies and participation by artists*, Member States are invited to take the necessary measures to enable artists and their organizations to take part in discussions and decision-making processes and in the subsequent application of measures designed in particular to enhance the status of artists in society, to promote culture and art within the community and encourage international cultural co-operation.

12.6.3. Recommendation for the Safeguarding and Preservation of Moving Images (Belgrade, 27 October 1980)[273]

Again on the occasion of its twenty-first session, the General Conference of UNESCO approved the Recommendation for the Safeguarding and Preservation of Moving Images (Belgrade, 27 October 1980). This recommendation relates to movable cultural property which is covered by a number of international instruments already approved by the General Conference of UNESCO.

Moving images are an expression of the cultural identity of peoples but because of the nature of their material embodiment

---

273. Cf. *Copyright Bulletin* (Paris), UNESCO, No. 4/1980, p. 21–9.

and the various methods of their fixation, they are extremely vulnerable and should be maintained under specific technical conditions; each State should therefore take appropriate complementary measures to ensure the safeguarding and preservation for posterity of this particularly fragile part of its cultural heritage, just as other forms of cultural property are safeguarded and preserved as a source of enrichment for present and future generations.

For the purpose of the recommendation, the term 'moving images' is taken to include cinematographic productions, television productions made by or for broadcasting organizations and videographic productions other than those already mentioned.

Among the *general principles* adopted in the recommendation, the following warrant particular attention:

- All the moving images produced nationally should be regarded by Member States as an integral part of their 'moving image heritage'. Moving images of foreign production may also form part of the cultural heritage of a country when they are of particular national importance from the point of view of the culture or history of the country concerned. Should it not be possible for this heritage to be handed down in its entirety to future generations, for technical or financial reasons, the largest possible proportion should be safeguarded and preserved.
- Since poor storage conditions accelerate the deterioration process to which material supports are continuously subject and may even lead to their total destruction, moving images should be preserved in officially recognized film and television archives and processed according to the highest archival standards.
- Access should be made available as far as possible to the works and information sources represented by moving images which are acquired, safeguarded and preserved by public and private non-profit-making institutions. Their utilization should not prejudice either the legitimate rights or the interests of those involved in the making and exploitation thereof pursuant to the provisions of the Universal, Berne and Rome Conventions.

In regard to the *recommended legal and administrative measures*, the Member States are invited to take measures whereby officially recognized archives can acquire, for safeguarding and preservation, any part or all of their country's national production.

Should legal deposit systems be adopted, they should stipulate that, subject to the provisions of international conventions and of national legislation governing copyright and the protection of performing artists, producers of phonograms and broadcasting organizations, the officially recognized archives should be authorized:
- to take all the necessary measures to safeguard and preserve the moving image heritage and, wherever possible, to enhance their technical quality; where the reproduction of moving images is involved, due account should be taken of all the rights applicable to the images concerned;
- to permit the viewing on their premises of a projection copy on a non-profit-making basis by a limited number of viewers for purposes of teaching, scholarship or research, provided that such use does not conflict with the normal exploitation of the work and on condition that no deterioration of, or damage to, the material deposited is thereby caused.

Should it not be possible to safeguard and preserve all moving images produced within a country, Member States are invited to establish the principles for determining which images should be recorded and/or deposited for posterity, including 'ephemeral recordings' having an exceptional documentary interest. Provision should be made for the selection to be based on the broadest possible consensus of informed opinion, bearing in mind the appraisal criteria established by archivists.

Technical and supplementary measures are also recommended. Member States are invited, *inter alia*, to encourage the competent authorities and other bodies concerned with the safeguarding and preservation of moving images, to pursue public information activities designed to promote appreciation of the lasting value of these images and to highlight their educational, cultural, artistic, scientific and historic importance.

In regard to *international co-operation*, Member States are invited to associate their efforts in order to promote the safeguarding and preservation of moving images and to co-operate to ensure that any State has access to these works, in so far as they are related to the history or culture of the country and of which it has no pre-print material or projection copies.

12.6.4. Recommendation on the Safeguarding of Traditional Culture and Folklore (Paris, 15 November 1989)[274]

At its twenty-fifth session, the General Conference of UNESCO approved the Recommendation on the Safeguarding of Traditional Culture and Folklore (Paris, 15 November 1989). This recommendation was summarized in our examination of the protection of works of national folklore to which we would refer the reader (see above, Chapter 2, Section 2.2.1.7).

---

274. *See Copyright Bulletin* (Paris), UNESCO, No. 1/1990, p. 8–12.

BIBLIOGRAPHY

I. GENERAL WORKS

ANTEQUERA PARILLI, Ricardo. *Consideraciones sobre el derecho de autor (con especial referencia a la legislación venezolana)*. Buenos Aires, 1977.

ASCARELLI, Tullio. *Teoría de la concurrencia y de los bienes inmateriales*. Barcelona, Ed. Bosch, 1970. Translated by E. Verdera and L. Suáez-Llanos.

ASCENSÃO, José de Oliveira. *Direito Autoral*. Rio de Janeiro, Forense, 1980.

BAYLOS CORROZA, Hermenegildo. *Tratado de derecho industrial. Propiedad industrial, propiedad intelectual, derecho de la competencia económica, disciplina de la competencia desleal*. Madrid, Ed. Civitas, 1978.

BOGSCH, Arpad. *El derecho de autor según la Convención Universal*, Vol. I, *Análisis y comentario de la Convención*. Buenos Aires, Ministerio de Justicia, 1975.

CHAVES, Antonio. *Direito de Autor*. Vol. I, Rio de Janeiro, Forense, 1987.

COLOMBET, Claude. *Propriété littéraire et artistique et droits voisins*. Paris, Dalloz, 1986.[1]

———. *Major Principles of Copyright and Neighbouring Rights in the World. A Comparative Approach*. Paris, UNESCO, 1987, 138 pp.

CORNISH, William Randolph. *Intellectual Property: Patents, Copyright, Trade Marks and Allied Rights*. London, Sweet and Maxwell, 1989.

DELGADO PORRAS, Antonio. *Panorámica de la protección civil y penal en materia de propiedad intelectual*. Madrid, Civitas, 1988.

DELLA COSTA, Héctor. *El derecho de autor y su novedad*. Buenos Aires, Cathedra, 1971.

---

[1] Editor's note: This work is now in its seventh edition (1994). 464 pp. 192 FF.

DESBOIS, Henri. *Le droit d'auteur en France.* Paris, Dalloz, 1978.

DIETZ, Adolf. *Copyright Law in the European Community.* Sijthoff & Noordhoff, The Netherlands, 1978, 312 pp.

DUMAS, Roland. *La propriété littéraire et artistique.* Paris, Presses Universitaires de France, 1987.

FRANÇON, André. *Cours de propriété littéraire, artistique et industrielle.* Paris, Les cours de droit, 1985–86.

GRECO, Paolo; VERCELLONE, Paolo. *I diritti sulle opere dell'ingenio.* Turin, Unione Tipográfico-Editrice Torinese, 1974.

JESSEN, Henry. *Derechos intelectuales.* Santiago de Chile, Ed. Jurídica de Chile, 1970. (Translated by Luis Grez Zuloaga.)

LEAFFER, Marshall A. *Understanding Copyright Law.* New York, Matthew Bender, 1989.

MASOUYÉ, Claude. *Guide to the Berne Convention.* Geneva, WIPO, 1978.

MOUCHET, Carlos; RADAELLI, Sigfrido A. *Los derechos del escritor y del artista.* Buenos Aires, Editorial Sudamericana, 1957.

PIOLA CASELLI, Edoardo. *Trattato del diritto di autore.* Naples, E. Marghieri; Turin, Unione Tip.-Ed. Torinese, 1927.

———. *Codice del diritto di autore.* Turin, Unione Tip.-Ed. Torinese, 1943.

PLAISANT, Robert. *Propriété littéraire et artistique (Droit interne et conventions internationales).* Extrait du Juris-Classeur Civil, Paris, Librairies Techniques, 1954.

———. *Propriété littéraire et artistique.* Paris, Delmas, 1985.

PLAZAS, Arcadio. *Estudios sobre derecho de autor. Reforma legal colombiana.* Bogotá, Themis Librería, 1984.

SATANOWSKY, Isidro. *Derecho intelectual.* Buenos Aires, TEA, 1954.

STEWART, Stephen M. *International Copyright and Neighbouring Rights.* London, Butterworths, 1983 and (2nd edition), 1989.

UNESCO. *Copyright Laws and Treaties of the World* (CLTW). Paris, UNESCO, 1987.

———. *The ABC of Copyright.* Paris, UNESCO, 1981, 73 p.

WIPO. *Background Reading on Intellectual Property.* Geneva, WIPO, 1988.

———. *Glossary of Terms of the Law of Copyright and Neighbouring Rights.* Geneva, WIPO, 1980, 281 pp.

II. DOCUMENTS

Annotated Principles of Protection of Authors, Performers, Producers of Phonograms and Broadcasting Organizations in Connection with

Distribution of Programs by Cable. ILO/UNESCO/WIPO, *Copyright* (Geneva), April 1984.

Draft WIPO *Model Provisions for Legislation in the Field of Copyright and Comments*. Documents: WIPO, CE/MPC/I/2/I, II and III; CE/MPC/II/2, 1989 and CE/MPC/III/2, 1990, C&P/CE/2, 1990.

Principles on the Protection of Copyright and Neighbouring Rights in Respect of Various Categories of Works. Doc. UNESCO/WIPO/CGE/SYN 3-1; I Add., II, III, UNESCO/WIPO/CGE/SYN/4, 1988.

Questions Concerning the Protection of Copyright in Respect of the Printed Word. UNESCO/WIPO/CGE/PW/3-I, II and 4, 1987.

III. WORKS

Chapter 1

ABRAHAMS, Robert J. *Copyright in the United Kingdom.* (document).

BOYTHA, György. 'The Justification of the Protection of Author's Rights as Reflected in Their Historical Development'. *RIDA* (Paris), No. 151, pp. 53–101.

CIFUENTES, Santos. *Los derechos personalísimos.* Buenos Aires, Ed. Lerner, 1974.

CLARK, Charles. 'The New United Kingdom Copyright Legislation; a Publishing Perspective'. *Rights* (Geneva), Fall 1988.

COHEN JEHORAM, Herman. 'Critical Reflections on the Economic Importance of Copyright'. *Rights* (Geneva), Winter 1988–89 and Spring 1989.

———. 'Relationship between Copyright and Neighbouring Rights'. *RIDA* (Paris), No. 144, April 1990, pp. 81–133.

CORRAL BELTRAN, Milagros, DEL. 'Historia y naturaleza del derecho de autor', *Noticias sobre El Libro* (Bogotá), CERLALC, No. 51, July-September 1986.

———. 'Data Bases and Intellectual Property'. *Copyright Bulletin* (Paris), UNESCO, 1983, No. 4. pp. 8–15.

DE FREITAS, Denis. 'Letter from the United Kingdom'. *Copyright* (Geneva), WIPO, January 1990, pp. 32–49.

DE SANCTIS, Valerio. 'The Development and the International Confirmation of Copyright'. *RIDA* (Paris), No. LXXIX, January 1974, pp. 206–90.

DOCK, Marie-Claude. 'The Origin and Development of the Literary Property Concept'. *RIDA* (Paris), No. LXXIX, January 1974, pp. 126–204.

ESCARRA, Jean; RAULT, Jean; HEPP, François. *La doctrine française du droit d'auteur.* Paris, Bernard Grasset, 1937.

GINSBURG, Jane C.; KERNOCHAN, John M. 'One Hundred and Two Years Later: the United States Joins the Berne Convention'. *RIDA* (Paris), No. 141, July 1989, pp. 57–197.

MICHAÉLIDÈS-NOUAROS, Georges. *Le droit moral de l'auteur.* Paris, A. Rousseau, 1935.

MILLÉ, Antonio. 'Las nuevas tecnologías y su impacto sobre los derechos intelectuales'. *Derecho de la alta tecnología* (Buenos Aires), October 1989.

NABHAN, Victor. 'A Glance over the Amendments to Canada's Copyright Law'. *RIDA* (Paris), No. 142, October 1989, pp. 174–220.

OLSSON, Henry. 'La Importancia Económica del derecho de autor'. *Derecho de la alta tecnología (*Buenos Aires), October 1988.

OMAN, Ralph. 'Letter from the United States of America'. *Copyright* (Geneva), WIPO, May 1991, pp. 117–20.

PHILIPPS, Jeremy. 'The Concept of "Author" in Copyright Law—Some Reflections on the Basis of Copyright Law in the United Kingdom'. *Copyright* (Geneva), WIPO, January 1990, pp. 26–30.

PICARD, Edmond. *Le droit pur.* Paris, Flammarion, 1908.

Chapter 2

Banques de données et droit d'auteur. Paris, Librairies Techniques, 1987.

BERTRAND, André R. 'Legal Protection of Computer Software: Domestic and International'. *Rights* (Geneva), Vol. 2, No. 3, Fall 1988.

———. *Protection juridique du logiciel. Progiciels, vidéo jeux, logiciels spécifiques, firmware.* Paris, Ed. des Parques, 1984.

DELGADO, Antonio. 'El derecho de autor y las modernas tecnologías'. In: Libro-memoria, *IV International Congress on the Protection of Intellectual Rights,* Guatemala, 1989, pp. 131–62.

DELLA COSTA, Héctor. 'Las obras del folklore'. In: *Temas de Derecho de autor, afines y conexos.* Buenos Aires, Ed. IIDA y Centro Argentino del IIDA, 1983, pp. 19–22.

LARREA RICHERAND, Gabriel. 'El folklore. Los derechos humanos y los derechos de la cultura. Derechos de autor'. In: Libro-memoria, *IV International Congress on the Protection of Intellectual Rights,* Guatemala, 1989, pp. 177–85.

LIPSZYC, Delia. 'Legal Protection of Titles of Literary and Artistic Works and Publications: Copyright and Trademark Law.' *Copyright* (Geneva), WIPO, September 1982, pp. 268–72.

MILLE, Antonio. 'El *software* y los bancos de datos a la luz de la jurisprudencia'. In: Libro-memoria, *V International Congress on the Protection of Intellectual Rights*, Buenos Aires, 1990, pp. 151–75.
MOUCHET, Carlos; LIPSZYC, Delia; VILLALBA, Carlos Alberto. 'Legal Protection of Ideas (Copyright Law and Industrial Property Law)'. *Copyright* (Geneva), WIPO, July–August 1978, pp. 179–91.
PURI, Kanwal. 'Copyright Protection of Folklore: a New Zealand Perspective'. *Copyright Bulletin* (Paris), UNESCO, No. 3, 1988, pp. 18–27.
SCHIRO, Heriberto. 'La protección de las expresiones del folklore por la propiedad intelectual'. *Noticias sobre El Libro* (Bogotá), CERLALC, No. 51, July–September 1986.
UCHTENHAGEN, Ulrich. 'La protección de las obras musicales'. In: Libro Memoria, *IV International Congress on the Protection of Intellectual Rights*, Guatemala, 1989, pp. 97–106.
VILLALBA, Carlos Alberto. 'La protección de los programas de computación y de los bancos de datos'. In Libro-memoria, *III International Congress on the Protection of Intellectual Rights*, Lima, 1988, pp. 57–90.

Chapter 3

ANTEQUERA PARILLI, Ricardo. '*El término autor*'. Study presented at the VII International WIPO–SUISA course (training in copyright and neighbouring rights), Guatemala, 17–26 April 1989 (document).
ILO. *The Protection of Salaried Authors and Inventors*. Geneva, ILO, 1987.
PLAISANT, Robert. 'The Employee-Author and Literary and Artistic Property'. *Copyright* (Geneva), WIPO, October 1977, pp. 274–80.

Chapter 4

ANTEQUERA PARILLI, Ricardo. 'El conflicto entre el autor y el propietario del ejemplar de la obra'. Study presented at the VII International WIPO–SUISA course (training in copyright and neighbouring rights), Guatemala, 17–26 April 1989 (document).
———. 'Intellectual Rights, Satellite Television and Cable Television'. Study presented at the WIPO Regional Forum on the Impact of Emerging Technologies on the Law of Intellectual Property for Latin American and Caribbean Countries, Montevideo, 13–15 December 1989 (document).

CIFUENTES, Santos. *Los derechos personalísimos*. Buenos Aires, Ed. Lerner, 1974.

CORRALES, Carlos. 'New Reproduction and Communication Techniques: Satellites and Cable Transmission'. WIPO Worldwide Forum on the Impact of Emerging Technologies on the Law of Intellectual Property, Geneva, September 1988, pp. 151–8.

DELGADO PORRAS, Antonio. 'La propiedad intelectual y la explotación videográfica de las obras del ingenio'. *Revista de derecho privado*, Madrid, December 1983, pp. 117–35.

———. 'Utilización de obras audiovisuales por satélite y cable. La intervención de las sociedades de autores'. In: Libro-memoria, *V International Congress on the Protection of Intellectual Rights*, Buenos Aires, 1990, pp. 213–44.

———. 'Private Copying in Spain'. *RIDA* (Paris), No. 145, pp. 2–124.

DUCHEMIN, Wladimir. 'The Droit de Suite', *RIDA* (Paris), April 1974, pp. 4–50.

ESPIN CANOVAS, Diego. *Las facultades del derecho moral de los autores y artistas*. Madrid, Civitas, 1991.

FABIANI, Mario. 'Broadcast Transmissions via Satellite or Cable and Copyright'. WIPO Worldwide Forum on the Impact of Emerging Technologies on the Law of Intellectual Property, Geneva, September 1988, pp. 159–63.

FERNANDEZ BALLESTEROS, Carlos. 'La noción de radiodifusión y la ley aplicable en el caso de la radiodifusión directa por satélite. In: Libro-memoria *of the VI International Congress on the Protection of Intellectual Rights*, Mexico City, February 1991, pp. 225–35.

FICSOR, Mihály. 'Direct Broadcasting by Satellite and the "Bogsch Theory"'. Study presented at the Section of Business Law Conference (Committee of Intellectual Property, Establishment and Communications) of the International Bar Association, Strasbourg, 2–6 October 1989 (document).

HÖKBORG, Karin. 'La televisión bajo la aurora boreal'. WIPO Regional Forum, Montevideo, 13–15 December 1989 (document).

ILO–UNESCO–WIPO. 'Annotated Principles of Protection of Authors, Performers, Producers of Phonograms and Broadcasting Organizations in Connection with Distribution of Programs by Cable'. *Copyright* (Geneva), April 1984, p. 131–218.

LIPSZYC, Delia. 'La piratería de obras escritas y la reprografía'. In: Libro-memoria, *III International Congress on the Protection of Intellectual Property*, Lima, 1988, pp. 111–41.

MICHAELIDES-NOUAROS, Georges. *Le droit moral de l'auteur*. Paris, Lib. Arthur Rousseau, 1935.

ROGEL VIDE, Carlos. 'From Copyright Limitations to Copyright Infringement in Spain'. *Copyright* (Geneva), WIPO, January 1989, pp. 18–26.

SCHUSTER VERGARA, Santiago. 'La ejecución pública de música: su protección por el derecho de autor'. In: Libro-memoria, *VI International Congress on the Protection of Intellectual Rights*, Mexico City, 1991, pp. 65–78.

UNESCO. 'Droit de suite', *Copyright Bulletin* (Paris), UNESCO, Vol. XVII, No. 3, 1983, pp. 38–54.

———. 'Study of Comparative Copyright Law: Moral Rights'. *Copyright Bulletin* (Paris), No. 4, 1978, pp. 36–52.

VILLALBA, Carlos Alberto; LIPSZYC, Delia. 'The Need to Regulate Private Copying of Musical and Audiovisual Works'. *Copyright World* (London), No. 5, July 1989, pp. 16–23.

VILLALBA, Carlos Alberto. 'El denominado contrato de edición musical. Los contratos en la ley sobre propiedad intelectual'. *Rev. La Ley*, Buenos Aires, Vol. 1990-A, pp. 551–69.

———. 'Fundamentación de la copia privada como límite al derecho de autor. Justificación de la remuneración por copia privada (en general)' In: Libro-memoria, *I Ibero-American Congress on Intellectual Property*, Madrid, 1991, Vol. II, pp. 581–97.

ZAPATA LÓPEZ, Fernando. 'El arrendamiento y préstamo público de obras y producciones protegidas'. In: Libro-memoria, *VII International Congress on the Protection of Intellectual Property*, Santiago, Chile, 1992, pp. 91–104.

Chapter 5

CIAMPI, Antonio. *La durata del diritto d'autore nel quadro dell'integrazione europea*. Milan, Vallardi, 1974.

LIPSZYC, Delia. 'El dominio público sobre obras intelectuales'. *Revista del Derecho Industrial* (Buenos Aires), No. 8, March–August 1981, pp. 385–95.

———. 'El plazo de protección post mortem y la aplicación de los convenios internacionales'. In: Libro-memoria, *VII International Congress on the Protection of Intellectual Rights*, Chile, 1992, pp. 331–48.

MOUCHET, Carlos. *El dominio público pagante*. Buenos Aires, Ed. Fondo Nacional de las Artes, 1970.

RICKETSON, Sam. 'Duration of Term of Protection under the Berne Convention'. *Copyright* (Geneva), WIPO, April 1991, pp. 84–93.

VILBOIS, Jean. *Le domaine public payant.* Paris, Sircy, 1929.

Chapter 6

ANTEQUERA PARILLI, Ricardo. 'La ejecución pública de obras grabadas'. In: Libro-memoria, *V International Congress on the Protection of Intellectual Property*, Buenos Aires, 1990, pp. 177–211.

BOYTHA, György. 'Disposiciones sobre contratos de autores en las leyes de derecho de autor socialistas'. *Derecho de la alta tecnología* (Buenos Aires), June 1989.

CHAVES, Antonio. 'El contrato de edición de obras escritas y musicales'. In: Libro-memoria, *II International Congress on the Protection of Intellectual Rights*, Bogotá, 1987, pp. 25–44.

CLARK, Charles. 'Summary of the Symposium'. (International copyright symposium organized by the International Publishers Association (IPA) in Heidelberg, April 1986), Munich, Ed. J. Schweitzer, 1986. §5—*Publishers' Rights*—p. 236.

DE SANCTIS, Valerio. *Contratto di edizione. Contratti di rappresentazione e di esecuzione.* Milan, Ed. Giuffré, 1965.

FICSOR, Mihály. *Collective Administration of Copyright and Neighbouring Rights.* Geneva, WIPO, 1991.

JESSEN, Henry. 'Relaciones de los autores y de las empresas de grabación con las sociedades de autores y de artistas intérpretes'. Study presented at the V International WIPO–SUISA course (training in copyright and neighbouring rights). Bogotá, March 1987 (document).

LIPSZYC, Delia. 'El contrato de representación de obras dramáticas'. In: Libro-memoria, *II International Congress on the Protection of Intellectual Rights*, Bogotá, 1987, pp. 45–58.

REZZONICO, Juan Carlos. 'Contrato, concepto y tipo'. *Rev. La Ley* (Buenos Aires), Vol. 1985-B, pp. 927–37.

SCHULZE, Erich. 'Protection of Mechanical Recording Rights and Legal Evolution'. In *BIEM 1929–1979.* (Commemorative publication), Paris, pp. 7–11.

SPOTA, Alberto G. *Instituciones del derecho civil. Contratos.* Buenos Aires, Ed. Depalma, 1981, pp. 298–325 and 350–70.

UCHTENHAGEN, Ulrich. 'El contrato de edición en el ámbito musical.' In: Libro-memoria, *V International Congress on the Protection of Intellectual Rights*, Buenos Aires, 1990, pp. 15–33.

VILLALBA, Carlos Alberto. 'Los contratos en derecho de autor'. *Revista*

Mexicana de la Propiedad Industrial y Artística, No. 29–30, México 1977, pp. 251–65.

———. 'El denominado contrato de edición musical. Los contratos en la ley sobre propiedad intelectual'. *Rev. La Ley* (Buenos Aires), Vol. 1990-A, pp. 551–69;

———. 'Los derechos del autor sobre la obra a raíz de los derechos de grabación y radiodifusión'. *Rev. La Ley* (Buenos Aires), Vol. 1985, pp. 805–17.

VILLALBA, Carlos Alberto and LIPSZYC, Delia. 'El contrato de fijación fonográfica. Administración de derechos del autor y del intérprete'. *Rev. El Derecho* (Buenos Aires), Vol. 121, pp. 119–31.

———. 'Una sentencia indispensable (Sobre el derecho de ejecución de música grabada'. *Rev. La Ley* (Buenos Aires), Vol. 1988-C, pp. 163–8.

ZEA FERNANDEZ, Guillermo. 'La ejecución pública de obras musicales y fonogramas'. In: Libro-memoria, *II International Congress on the Protection of Intellectual Rights*, Bogotá, 1987, pp. 59–66.

Chapter 7

BRUCH Walter. *Del registro musical al fonograma.* In: *BIEM 1929–1979 Commemorative Publication*, pp. 14–50.

DE SANCTIS, Valerio. 'La convenzione internazionale per la protezione degli artisti interpreti o esecutori, dei produttori di fonogrammi e degli organismi di radiodiffusione'. *Il diritto di autore*, 1962, Nos. 1 to 4.

ILO. *Rights of Performers in Broadcasting, Television and the Mechanical Reproduction of Sounds.* Geneva, ILO, 1939.

ILO-UNESCO-BIRPI. *Records of the Diplomatic Conference on the International Protection of Performers, Producers of Phonograms and Broadcasting Organizations.* Rome, 10 to 26 October 1961, 1968.

ILO-UNESCO-WIPO. 'Annotated Principles of Protection of Authors, Performers, Producers of Phonograms and Broadcasting Organizations in Connection with Distribution of Programs by Cable'. *Copyright* (Geneva), WIPO, April 1984, pp. 131–83.

JESSEN, Henry. 'Los derechos conexos de artistas intérpretes y ejecutantes, productores de fonogramas y organismos de radiodifusión'. In: Libro-memoria, *I International Congress on the Protection of Intellectual Rights*, Caracas, 1986, pp. 163–86.

LIPSZYC, Delia. 'El derecho moral de intérprete. Los modelos de fotografías', *Rev. La Ley* (Buenos Aires), Vol. 1981-C, pp. 554–62.

MASOUYÉ, Claude. *Guide to the Rome Convention and to the Phonograms Convention.* Geneva, WIPO, 1981.

MORAES, Walter. *Artistas intérpretes e executantes.* São Paulo, Ed. Revista dos Tribunais, 1976.

MOUCHET, Carlos. 'Los derechos de los artistas ejecutantes en la ley 11, 723'. *Rev. Gaceta del Foro* (Buenos Aires), 22 November 1940.

OBON LEON, J. Ramón. *Derecho de los artistas intérpretes. Actores, cantantes y músicos ejecutantes.* Mexico City, Ed. Trillas, 1986.

PIOLA CASELLI, Edoardo. 'Sul regolamento dei conflitti fra il diritto di autore e taluni diritti vicini o similari', *Il Diritto di Autore* (Milan), 1937, pp. 155–62 and 307–31 and 1939, pp. 9–21.

TOURNIER, Alphonse. 'The Author and the Performer'. *RIDA* (Paris), July 1960.

UNESCO-WIPO. *Records of the International Conference of States on the Protection of Phonograms* (Geneva, 1971), 1975.

VILLALBA, Carlos Alberto and LIPSZYC, Delia. *Derechos de los artistas intérpretes o ejecutantes, productores de fonogramas y organismos de radiodifusión. Relaciones con el derecho de autor.* Buenos Aires, Víctor P. de Zavalía Editor, 1976.

———. 'Reflexiones para un homenaje'. *Il Diritto di Autore* (Milan), Ed. Giuffré, 1979, pp. 518–28. (Commemorative issue marking the 50th anniversary of the review. Tribute to Valerio de Sanctis.)

Chapter 8

ABADA, Salah. 'Collective Administration of Authors' Rights in the Developing Countries'. *Copyright* (Geneva), WIPO, Sept. 1985, pp. 277–85.

ALLAIN, Annie. 'Droit Social'. In: Robert Plaisant (ed.), *Propriété Littéraire et Artistique*, Paris, Delmas, 1985, pp. 211–36.

ALPI, Jean Bernard. 'La Societá francese degli autori, compositori e editori di musica'. Rev. *Il diritto di autore* (Milan), pp. 479–83.

ANTEQUERA PARILLI, Ricardo. 'Naturaleza jurídica de las entidades autorales y del contrato con sus autores o artistas miembros o asociados'. Document presented at the VIII WIPO–SUISA course, Buenos Aires, 1990.

———. 'Sociedad única o pluralidad de sociedades'. Document presented at the IX WIPO–SUISA course, Puebla, México, 1991.

———. 'La fijación de tarifas por las entidades autorales y el contencioso administrativo'. Barquisimeto, Venezuela, Instituto de Estudios Jurídicos del Estado Lara, Diario de Tribunales, 1986.

BONCOMPAIN, Jacques. 'Le droit d'être auteur'. In: *La Révolution des Auteurs*, Paris, SACD, 1984, pp. 7–31.
BORDA, Guillermo A. *Tratado de derecho civil. Parte general.* Vol. I, Buenos Aires, Ed. Perrot, 7a. ed. 1980.
CARMET, Olivier. Statutes of SACEM. *RIDA* (Paris), No. 140, April 1989, pp. 19–73.
CISAC. *Décisions, délibérations et vœux adoptés par les Congrès et Assemblées.*
———. *Documentation and Distribution Guide for Non-theatrical Music (Small Rights).* Technical Commission CISAC/BIEM, Cracow, 25–26 October 1988 (Document CT/88/880).
COSTA NETTO, José Carlos. *A Reorganização do Conselho Nacional de Direito Autoral.* Brasilia, Ministério da Educação e Cultura–Conselho Nacional de Direito Autoral, 3a. ed. 1983, pp. 11–39.
DAVIES, Gillian. 'El interés público en la administración colectiva de los derechos de autor'. *Derecho de la alta tecnología* (Buenos Aires), November 1989, pp. 1–11.
DESURMONT, Thierry. 'The SACEM and Competition Law.' *RIDA* (Paris), No. 140, April 1989, pp. 116–79.
Federación de Gremios de Editores de España. *Libro blanco sobre reprografía ilegal.* 1986.
FICSOR, Mihály. *Collective Administration of Copyright and Neighbouring Rights.* Geneva. WIPO, 1991.
———. 'Development and Objectives of Collective Administration of Authors' Rights'. *Copyright* (Geneva), WIPO, Oct. 1985, pp. 341–53.
GASTALDI, José M. *'Representación, poder y mandato'.* In: *Enciclopedia Jurídica OMEBA*, Buenos Aires, 1967, Vol. XXIV, pp. 716–40.
IFPI. *Private Copying Legislation and Implementation with Guidelines for New Legislation* (document).
IFRRO. *Minutes* of the Constitutional General Meeting of the International Federation of Reproduction Rights Organizations, 1988 and 1994 (brochures).
———. *Statistics and Information.* Economic Co-operation Group of the Reprographic Rights Organizations, March 1991 (document).
KARNELL, Gunnar. 'The Relations between Authors and Organizations Administering Their Rights'. *Copyright* (Geneva), WIPO, February 1986, pp. 45–66.
KERNOCHAN, John, M. 'Music Performing Rights Organizations in the United States of America: Special Characteristics, Constraints, and

Public Attitudes'. *Copyright* (Geneva), WIPO, November 1985, pp. 389–410.

LIPSZYC, Delia. 'La piratería de obras escritas y la reprografía' (Chap. VII, Sistemas legales y administrativos vigentes en materia de derechos reprograficos). In: Libro-memoria, *III International Congress on the Protection of Intellectual Rights*, Lima, 1988, pp. 131–40.

——. 'La protección social de los autores y de los artistas intérpretes'. Document presented at the IX WIPO–SUISA course, Puebla, México, 14–22 February 1991.

LIPSZYC, Delia; DELLA COSTA, Héctor. 'Sistemas de administración de derechos de autor'. *Rev. La propiedad intelectual* (Geneva), WIPO, No. 3, 1978, p. 131–47.

MALAPLATE, Léon. 'The Role of Societies or Associations of Authors and of CISAC'. Symposium on practical aspects of copyright, Geneva, 1968, pp. 20–7.

MARIZCURRENA ORONOZ, Martín. 'Las entidades de gestión colectiva de los artistas intérpretes o ejecutantes en América Latina—Experiencias concretas'. In: Libro-memoria, *I Ibero-American Congress on Intellectual Property*, Madrid, 1991, Vol. II, pp. 1043–46.

MATTHYSSENS, Jean and MATTHYSSENS, Isabelle. 'Gestion collective et exclusivité'. *Il diritto di autore* (Milan), April–September 1979, pp. 536–43.

MILLE, Antonio. 'La protección de los artistas intérpretes o ejecutantes en el derecho de los paises latinoamericanos'. In: Libro-memoria, *I Ibero-American Congress on Intellectual Property*, Madrid, 1991, pp. 1029–38.

PERROTTI, Máximo. *Creación y derechos (La creación de obras musicales, derechos que genera y su administración)*. México, Consejo Panamericano de la CISAC, 1978.

SACD. *La Révolution des auteurs (1777–1793)*. Paris, 1984, 36 pp. (brochure).

SANTIAGO, Vanisa. 'Las entidades de gestión colectiva de los artistas intérpretes o ejecutantes en América Latina—Experiencias concretas'. In: Libro-memoria, *I. Ibero-American Congress on Intellectual Property*, Madrid, 1991, pp. 1039–42.

SIAE. *What is SIAE?* (brochure).

SUISA, *Droit et Musique* (brochure).

TOURNIER, Jean-Loup. 'Collection and Distribution of Public Performance Fees for Musical Works'; Symposium on practical aspects of copyright. BIRPI, Geneva, 1968, pp. 30–7.

———. 'The SACEM/Discotheque Conflict: an Unprecedented Legal War'. *RIDA* (Paris), No. 140, April 1989, pp. 2–16.
TOURNIER, Jean-Loup; JOUBERT, Claude. 'Collective Administration and Competition Law'. *Copyright* (Geneva), WIPO, March 1986, pp. 96–103.
UCHTENHAGEN, Ulrich. 'Licence Agreements made with Users'. Symposium on practical aspects of copyright, BIRPI, Geneva, 1968, pp. 76–9.
———. 'Technical Problems of Collective Administration of Authors' Rights'. *Copyright* (Geneva), WIPO, January 1986, pp. 26–34.
———. 'The Setting-up of New Copyright Societies; Experience and Reflections'. *Copyright* (Geneva), WIPO, Geneva, June 1991, pp. 125–39.
UNESCO. 'Committee of Experts to Draft Model Statutes for Institutions Administering Authors' Rights in Developing Countries'. Report, *Copyright Bulletin* (Paris), No. 3, 1980, pp. 4–17.

Chapter 9

BOGSCH, Arpad. 'The First Hundred Years of the Berne Convention for the Protection of Literary and Artistic Works'. In: *Berne Convention Centenary (1886–1986)*, Geneva, WIPO, 1986.
CHEDIAK, Natalio. 'O Instituto Interamericano de Direito de Autor'. *Revista Inter-americana de Derecho intelectual (RIDI)*, São Paulo, IIDA, No. 2/1978, pp. 54–65.
DE SANCTIS, Valerio. *La convenzione universale del Diritto de Autore*. Rome, SIAE, 1953.
IFPI. *Information Brochure*. London, 1992, IFPI.
ILO. *The Protection of Salaried Authors and Inventors*. Geneva, ILO, 1987.
———. *Conditions of Employment and Work of Performers*. Geneva, ILO, 1992.
SCHULTZE, Erich. 'Protection of Mechanical Recording Rights and Legal Evolution'. In: *BIEM 1929–1979* (Commemorative publication), Paris, BIEM, 1980, pp. 7–13.
WIPO. *General Information*. Geneva, WIPO, 1995.
ZIEGLER, Jean-Alexis. 'Sociedades de Autores. La cooperación internacional'. In: Libro-memoria, *V International Congress on the Protection of Intellectual Rights*, Buenos Aires, 1990, pp. 101–8.

Chapter 10

COGHLAN, Antonio R. *Teoría general de derecho immobiliario registral.* Buenos Aires, Abeledo-Perrot, 1991.

GROMPONE, Romeo. *Uruguay y la Unión de Berna (Modificaciones a la ley del 17 de diciembre de 1937).* Montevideo, AGADU, 1979.

LARREA RICHERAND, Gabriel. 'Funciones del registro en la legislación comparada'. In: Libro-memoria, *V International Congress on the Protection of Intellectual Rights,* Buenos Aires, 1990, pp. 141–50.

RETONDO, Hilda. 'Las funciones del registro en la legislación comparada. El tratado sobre el registro internacional de obras audiovisuales'. In: Libro-memoria, *V International Congress on the Protection of Intellectual Rights,* Buenos Aires, 1990, pp. 119–27.

TISCORNIA, Ricardo. 'Sentido de los registros de obras intelectuales'. *Revista Interamericana de derecho intelectual (RIDI),* São Paulo, IIDA, No. 2/1978, pp. 17–27.

Chapter 11

ALSINA, Hugo. *Derecho procesal.* Buenos Aires, Ediar, 1962.

ANTEQUERA PARILLI, Ricardo. 'La piratería de obras escritas, sonoras y audiovisuales (El problema y su importancia)'. In: Libro-memoria, *II International Congress on the Protection of Intellectual Rights,* Bogotá, 1987, pp. 111–25.

ANZORREGUY, Jorge E.; DA ROCHA, Joaquín P.; HERNANDEZ VIEYRAS, Héctor H. 'Delitos contra los derechos intelectuales'. *Rev. Jurisprudencia Argentina.* Buenos Aires, Doctrina 1973, pp. 543–54.

BRACAMONTE ORTIZ, Guillermo. 'La piratería'. In: Libro-Memoria, *VI International Congress on the Protection of Intellectual Rights,* Mexico City, 1991, pp. 355–67.

CALAMANDREI, Piero. *Introducción al estudio sistemático de las providencias cautelares.* Buenos Aires, Ed. Bibliográfica Argentina, 1945.

CARMONA SALGADO, Concepción. *La nueva ley de propiedad intelectual.* Madrid, Ed. Montecorvo, 1988.

CIFUENTES, Santos. 'Daños. Como evaluar el resarcimiento por la utilización no autorizada de las obras. Su incidencia en la jurisprudencia (desde la perspectiva del magistrado)'. In: Libro-memoria, *V International Congress on the Protection of Intellectual Rights,* Buenos Aires, 1990, pp. 303–11.

DI IORIO, Alfredo Jorge. 'Nociones sobre la teoría general de las medidas cautelares'. *Rev. La Ley* (Buenos Aires), Vol. 1978-B, p. 829.

EMERY, Miguel Angel. 'La piratería fonográfica'. In: Libro Memoria, *VI International Congress on the Protection of Intellectual Property*, Mexico City, 1991, pp. 325–40.

GARZON, ALVARO. 'Piracy: Contribution to an Analysis of the Phenomenon'. *Copyright Bulletin* (Paris), UNESCO, No. 2, 1983, pp. 10–20.

GOMEZ BENITEZ, José Manuel; QUINTERO OLIVARES, Gonzalo. *Protección penal de los derechos de autor y conexos*. Madrid, Civitas, 1988.

IRIBARNE, Rodolfo A. 'Los nuevos delitos fonográficos. Artículo 72bis, ley 11.723'. *Rev. Derechos Intelectuales*, Buenos Aires, No. 5, ed. Astrea, 1991, pp. 183–214.

———. 'El estado actual de la jurisprudencia en la represión penal'. In: Libro-memoria, *V International Congress on the Protection of Intellectual Rights*, Buenos Aires, 1990, pp. 245–54.

IRIBARNE, RODOLFO A.; RETONDO, Hilda. 'Plagio de obras intelectuales'. In: *Los ilícitos civiles y penales en derecho de autor*. Buenos Aires, ICI and Centro Argentino del ICI, 1981, pp. 109–20.

LEDESMA, Julio C. 'Derecho penal intelectual. Obras y producciones literarias, artísticas y científicas'. Buenos Aires, Ed. Universidad, 1992.

LIPSZYC, Delia. 'Las medidas precautorias'. In: *Los ilícitos civiles y penales en derecho de autor*. Buenos Aires, ICI and Centro Argentino del ICI, 1981, pp. 68–74.

———. 'La piratería de obras escritas y la reprografía'. In: Libro-memoria, *III International Congress on the Protection of Intellectual Rights*, Lima, 1988, pp. 111–41.

———. 'Sanciones y procedimientos'. Study presented at the X WIPO–SUISA course, Viña del Mar, Chile, 1992 (document).

MILLE, Antonio. *Piratería de obras de software*. Instituto Venezolano del Software (Invesoft), 1990, pp. 67–74.

PODETTI, J. Ramiro. *Tratado de las medidas cautelares*. Buenos Aires, 1969.

RADAELLI, Sigfrido A. and MOUCHET, Carlos. *La nueva ley de 'propiedad intelectual'. Naturaleza de los delitos contra los delitos contra los derechos intelectuales*. Buenos Aires, Ed. Claridad, 1934.

SOLER, Sebastián. *Derecho penal argentino*. Buenos Aires, TEA, 1951.

VILLALBA, Carlos Alberto. 'Daños. Cómo evaluar el resarcimiento por la utilización no autorizada de las obras. Su incidencia en la jurisprudencia (desde la perspectiva del abogado)'. In: Libro-memoria, *V International Congress on the Protection of Intellectual Rights*, Buenos Aires, 1990, pp. 313–28.

———. 'La jurisprudencia penal en materia de propiedad intelectual. Evolución y estado actual'. *Rev. El Derecho* (Buenos Aires), 1992.
ZAFFARONI, Eugenio Raúl. *Manual de derecho penal, Parte general.* Buenos Aires, Ediar.
———. 'Reflexiones político-criminales sobre la tutela penal de los derechos de autor'. In: *Los ilícitos civiles y penales en derecho de autor*, Buenos Aires, ICI and Centro Argentino del ICI, 1981, pp. 86–92.
ZANNONI, Eduardo A. *El daño en la responsabilidad civil.* Buenos Aires, Ed. Astrea, 1982.

Chapter 12

BOSCH, ARPAD. *El derecho de autor según la Convención universal.* Translated by Ricardo Tiscornia. Buenos Aires, Ministerio de Justicia de la República Argentina, 1975.
DARRAS, Alcide. *Du droit des auteurs et des artistes dans les rapports internationaux.* Paris, Libr. Arthur Rousseau, 1887.
DE SANCTIS, Valerio. *La Convenzione Universale del Diritto di Autore.* Roma, SIAE, 1953.
———. 'Some Reflections'. *RIDA* (Paris), October 1967/January 1968, pp. 53–85.
———. 'The Development and the International Confirmation of Copyright'. *RIDA* (Paris), No. LXXIX, January 1974, pp. 206–90.
DESBOIS, Henri. 'The Evolution of Copyright and International Relations since the Brussels Conference (1948)'. *RIDA* (Paris), January 1974, pp. 292–404.
DESBOIS, Henri; FRANÇON, André; KEREVER, André. *Les conventions internationales du droit d'auteur et des droits voisins.* Paris, Dalloz, 1976.
Documents de la Conférence réunie à Bruxelles du 5 au 25 juin 1948. Berne, Bureau de l'Union de Berne, 1951.
FERNANDEZ BALLESTEROS, Carlos. 'El propuesto Protocolo al Convenio de Berna'. In Libro-memoria, *VII International Congress on the Protection of Intellectual Rights*, Santiago, Chile, April 1992, pp. 451–62.
FICSOR, Mihály. 'El nuevo Tratado de la OMPI sobre el Registro Internacional de Obras Audiovisuales'. In: Libro-memoria, *I Ibero-American Congress on Intellectual Property*, Madrid, 1991, Vol. II, pp. 761–8.
'Final Act of the International Conference of States on the Double Taxation of Copyright Royalties Remitted from One Country to

Another'. *Copyright Bulletin* (Paris), UNESCO, No. 1–2/1980, pp. 40–67.

FRANÇON, André. 'International Protection of Neighbouring Rights'. *RIDA* (Paris), January 1974, pp. 406–76.

'Geneva Conference, 1952'. *Copyright Bulletin* (Paris), UNESCO, Vol. V, No. 3–4, 1952.

KOUMANTOS, Georges. 'Sur le droit international privé du droit d'auteur'. *II Diritto di autore* (Milan), 50th anniversary issue, 1979, pp. 456–77.

———. 'Private International Law and the Berne Convention'. *Copyright* (Geneva), WIPO, October 1988, pp. 425–8.

KREILE, Reinhold. 'The Taxation of the Author in International Tax Law and the Madrid Convention for the Avoidance of Double Taxation of Copyright Royalties'. *Copyright* (Geneva), WIPO, September 1984, pp. 343–51.

LIPSZYC, Delia. *Conferencias de Revisión de las Convenciones de Berna y Universal (Paris-Julio de 1971). Enfoque argentino.* Buenos Aires, Consejo Panamericano de la CISAC, 1975.

———. 'La protección de la obra extranjera y los convenios internacionales'. In: Libro-memoria, *I International Congress on the Protection of Intellectual Rights*, Caracas, 1986, pp. 49–84.

———. 'La proteccion internacional en la jurisprudencia'. In: Libro-memoria, *V International Congress on the Protection of Intellectual Rights*, Buenos Aires, 1990, pp. 329–60.

———. 'La protección internacional del derecho de autor en los países latinoamericanos'. In: Libro-memoria, *I Ibero-American Congress on Intellectual Property*, Madrid, 1991, pp. 923–38.

———. 'El plazo de protección post-mortem y la aplicación de los convenios internacionales'. In: Libro-memoria, *VII International Congress on the Protection of Intellectual Rights*, Santiago, Chile, 1992, pp. 331–48.

MASOUYÉ, Claude. *Guide to the Rome Convention and to the Phonograms Convention.* Geneva, WIPO, 1981.

———. 'Stockholm: a Landmark'. *RIDA* (Paris), October 1967/January 1968, pp. 9–23.

MOUCHET, Carlos. *América latina y el derecho de autor.* Buenos Aires, Consejo Panamericano de la CISAC, 1973.

PEIRETTI, Graciela. 'El sistema internacional de protección del derecho de autor: el Convenio de Berna'. In Libro-memoria, *VII International Congress on the Protection of Intellectual Property*, Santiago, Chile, April 1992, pp. 433–49.

Records of the Conference for Revision of the Universal Copyright Convention. (UNESCO, 5–24 July 1971), Paris, UNESCO, 1973.

Records of the Diplomatic Conference for the Revision of the Berne Convention. (Paris, 5–24 July 1971). WIPO, 1974.

Records of the Conference on the International Protection of Performers, Producers of Phonograms and Broadcasting Organizations. (Rome, 10–26 October 1961), ILO–UNESCO–BIRPI, 1967.

Records of the Intellectual Property Conference of Stockholm. (11 June-14 July 1967), WIPO, 1968.

Records of the International Conference of States on the Distribution of Programme-carrying Signals Transmitted by Satellite. (Brussels, 6–21 May 1974), UNESCO–WIPO, 1977.

Records of the International Conference of States on the Protection of Phonograms. (Geneva, 18–29 October 1971), WIPO–UNESCO, 1975.

RICKETSON, Sam. *The Berne Convention for the Protection of Literary and Artistic Works: 1886–1986*. London, Queen Mary College, 1987.

———. 'Duration of Term of Protection under the Berne Convention'. *Copyright* (Geneva), WIPO, April 1991, pp. 84–93.

STOLFI, Nicola. *La Proprietà Intellettuale.* Turin, Unione Tipografico-Editrice Torinese, Vol. II, 1917.

'The Protocol Regarding Developing Countries'. *RIDA* (Paris), October 1967/January 1968, pp. 393–425.

ULMER, Eugen. 'Retrospect'. *RIDA* (Paris), October 1967/January 1968, pp. 25–41.

VAN NUS, J. 'The Preparatory Work'. *RIDA* (Paris), October 1967/January 1968, pp. 121–97.

VILLALBA, Carlos Alberto. 'Introduccion a los tratados internacionales en materia de derecho de autor'. In *Revista del Derecho Industrial* (Buenos Aires), Depalma, 1980, pp. 331–49.

WIPO. *Berne Convention Centenary 1886–1986*. Geneva, 1986.

———. 'Diplomatic Conference for the Conclusion of a Treaty on the Registration of Audiovisual Works'. *Copyright* (Geneva), WIPO, June 1989, pp. 165–90.